CRIMINAL JUSTICE IN THE UNITED STATES

DEAN J. CHAMPION
University of Tennessee

MERRILL PUBLISHING COMPANY
Columbus ■ Toronto ■ London ■ Melbourne

To Mitzi, Jamie, and Macho,
my three closest friends,
who love, accept, and understand unconditionally

Cover Photos: James Colburn/Photoreporters *(left)*; Bob Daemmrich/The Image Works *(right)*

Published by Merrill Publishing Company
Columbus, Ohio 43216

This book was set in Century Oldstyle.

Administrative Editor: Stephen Helba
Developmental Editor: Monica Ohlinger
Production Editor: Carol Sykes
Cover Designer: Russ Maselli
Photo research: Anne Vega

Library of Congress Catalog Card Number: 89–63840
International Standard Book Number: 0–675–20672–3
Printed in the United States of America
1 2 3 4 5 6 7 8 9—94 93 92 91 90

PREFACE

Programs in criminal justice are included in the curricula of departments of sociology, psychology, public administration, and political science. Many schools also offer specific criminal justice programs. These programs are of interest to law enforcement officers, pre-law students, persons preparing for careers in corrections (such as probation and parole), those engaged in private security work, and, of course, those who merely wish to learn more about how our criminal justice system works.

Criminal Justice in the United States is written to serve as an introductory text for all of the above programs and students. The objectives of the text are

- To acquaint students with all aspects of our criminal justice system.

- To help students understand those components.
- To prepare students for subsequent courses in criminal justice programs.

This textbook is about the criminal justice system in the United States, a vast network of agencies and persons who react to and deal with crime and handle punishment and rehabilitation of criminal offenders. The chapters describe each component of the criminal justice system, including the courts, the police, and correctional institutions. Students can follow the entire criminal justice process from beginning to end and acquire a better understanding of how criminals are processed.

The legalistic perspective throughout the text uses case law as the basis for discussion of

Supreme Court decisions or other judgments that have influenced the present state of criminal justice in the United States. Almost all landmark cases have been included, together with brief commentaries about their application and interpretation.

Criminal Justice in the United States also covers the topic of crime prevention. The popularity of television shows that reenact crimes, ask viewers to phone in crime tips for rewards, and film cops on their beats mirrors the public's interest in both the rise in crime and ways to prevent it; therefore, the text examines the issues and describes the increasing cooperation between communities and law enforcement agencies.

In addition, the text includes a chapter on the criminal justice systems of Canada, Great Britain, and the Soviet Union, which highlights similarities with and differences from that of the United States. The comparative perspective enables students to learn how criminals in other countries are processed and thereby to appreciate fully the strengths and weaknesses of our own system.

The text is divided into five parts, which follow the pattern of the criminal justice system:

■ The History and Theories of Crime in Society
■ Constitutional Criminal Law and Procedure
■ The Courts
■ Corrections
■ Juvenile Justice, Comparative Justice, and Crime Prevention

Because the overriding goal of this book is to promote student understanding of our criminal justice system, a number of features have been incorporated throughout the text to interest, challenge, and aid students in their studies.

Part Openers. Each part opens with a discussion of a recent, trendsetting case that will interest and motivate students:

■ The trial of Oliver North
■ The release of Randall Adams
■ The Supreme Court's decision on *Webster v. Reproductive Services*

■ The Court's ruling on *Mistretta v. United States*
■ The arrest, conviction, and release by the Soviet Union of Matthias Rust

Highlight Boxes. Two types of highlight boxes focus on key concepts that are important for beginning criminal justice students to understand:

■ "A Day in Court" features landmark cases, many of which have changed the course of criminal law in the United States.
■ "Crime Beat" describes current events and the drama transpiring daily throughout the criminal justice system.

Research Tools. An extensive bibliography (over 1300 references), a glossary (more than 300 entries), and three indexes (by case, name, and subject) will help students with research for this course and for subsequent ones.

Pedagogical Aids. A consistent chapter format will help students grasp and retain the important concepts:

■ Chapter outline
■ Chapter summary
■ List of key terms
■ Review questions
■ Suggested readings

The text is also accompanied by a complete ancillary package that will benefit instructors and students:

The *Instructor's Manual* includes chapter highlights and 2000 test questions (true/false, multiple choice, and short essay). The questions are designed so that professors can adjust tests to fit semester or quarter courses.

The *Computerized Test Bank* is in an IBM format and allows professors to select randomly from the 2000 questions as well as to add their own questions to the bank.

The *Study Guide* includes questions and exercises to enhance the beginning student's understanding of the text material. Special projects give students direct, hands-on exposure to the real world of criminal justice. Readings are listed so that students can do their own research. Each part opens with an interview with a criminal justice professional.

Acknowledgments

All books rely upon the evaluations of others for their ultimate configuration. This book is no exception. Acknowledgments is extended to the following persons who gave their valuable time and assistance in evaluating selected portions of the manuscript:

Vincent P. Accardi, Attorney-at-Law; Stephen Brodt, Ball State University; Dennis C. Brown, Kearney State College; Frances S. Coles, California State University–San Bernadino; Daryl L. Cullison, Columbus State Community College; Pamela Hart, Iowa Western Community College; Leonard Larsen, Eastfield College; G. Larry Mays, New Mexico State University; Donald B. Olsen, Kansas Wesleyan University; Ken Peak, University of Nevada–Reno; Roger L. Pennell, Central Missouri State University; Richard T. Shigley, Stephen F. Austin University; Glenn C. Ware, North Harris County College; Stanley W. Wisnioski, Jr., Broward Community College; and Gennaro F. Vito, University of Louisville.

CONTENTS

CRIMINAL JUSTICE
IN THE
UNITED STATES

In July 1989, Colonel Oliver North, an ex-Marine, was sentenced to 3 years' probation, obligated to pay a $150,000 fine, and ordered to perform 1,200 hours of public service pertaining to juveniles and drug avoidance. This culminated a lengthy investigation of several key government officials believed to have negotiated arms deals with foreign powers without congressional or presidential approval. Later known as the Iran-Contra scandal, the affair involved arms sales to Iran and diversion of the monies from these sales to Contra rebels in Nicaragua. Allegedly, these machinations involved the CIA and other agencies, and most of this activity was conducted in a clandestine manner.

North testified before a congressional committee appointed to investigate the Iran-Contra affair. Subsequently, it was disclosed that he had lied to the

THE HISTORY AND THEORIES OF CRIME IN SOCIETY

committee regarding some of the details of the arms transactions and other matters. He admitted shredding important documents and withholding information from investigatory agencies such as the FBI. Because North was considered by many to be the fall guy and a little fish, his sentence was not particularly popular with the public. A U.S. News and World Report survey conducted in January 1989 disclosed that about a third of those surveyed believed that North should be imprisoned, while half believed President George Bush should pardon him if he were eventually convicted.

Crime is pervasive in our society; therefore, Part I examines the criminal justice system in its historical context and looks at various explana-

tions of criminal conduct. The criminal justice system is made up of laws that have been established to protect citizens from criminals and an elaborate system to investigate and process criminals whenever criminal activity is reported.

Chapter 1 examines the origins of United States laws and identifies the functions of these laws. Many of our laws are rooted in early English common law, although branches of government have enacted specific laws. This chapter distinguishes different kinds of crimes and presents various measures of crime. It describes crime patterns, criminals, and victims, as well as current crime trends.

Chapter 2 investigates theories of criminal behavior, presenting several theories of criminal and deviant conduct. It discusses biological, sociological, and psychological theories that criminologists use to explain deviance and criminal conduct.

Chapter 3 is an overview of the criminal justice system. It distinguishes civil and criminal laws and identifies jurisdictions. The various components of the criminal justice system include the police, prosecution, courts, and corrections. The chapter presents the goals of these system components and describes their interrelatedness.

The Origins of Our Justice System: Society and Law

CHAPTER 1

■ THE STUDY OF CRIMINAL JUSTICE

Criminal justice encompasses several disciplines, including but not limited to law, sociology, psychology, political science, public administration, history, and economics. In fact, many of these departments at universities and colleges offer courses in criminal justice as part of their regular curricula. A former Berkeley, California, chief of police, August Vollmer, established the first school of criminology at the University of California-Berkeley in 1916. Although his interest was police officer training and professionalism, other schools eventually established similar curricula and the formal study of criminal justice emerged. Since then, more than 1,200 criminal justice programs have been developed, eventually serving the needs and interests of over 1 million students.

What Criminal Justice Studies

This book is about criminal justice, an interdisciplinary field that studies the nature and operations of organizations providing justice services to society. The **criminal justice system** consists of lawmaking bodies, such as state legislatures and Congress, as well as local, state, and federal agencies that try to enforce laws and punish law violators. These agencies and organizations include the police, the courts, and corrections. The police detect crime and attempt to prevent or control it. The courts deal with the issue of a defendant's guilt and sentence those found guilty of crimes. Corrections officers supervise offenders in jails or prisons, as well as through probation and parole programs.

Students in criminal justice courses learn about the criminal justice system, its components, and the ways it deals with crime and processes criminals. Students study various aspects of the process, such as police work. They examine correctional institutions, including jails and prisons. They also learn about programs for offenders who either are not incarcerated or are released after serving a period of time. Thus, study of corrections includes prison and jail culture, management, and administration; prisoners' rights; and probation and parole services.

An important dimension of the criminal justice system is a parallel system for juveniles. While not the same as the justice process for adult offenders, the juvenile justice system apprehends, classifies, and rehabilitates juvenile offenders. The term *offense* is often used interchangeably with *crime,* but offenses do not carry adult penalties. Therefore, juveniles commit offenses, and depending upon the evidence presented, a judge determines juveniles to be delinquent or nondelinquent. Judges of juveniles prescribe appropriate juvenile punishments, such as warnings, foster home placement, fines, compensation to victims, or detention in secure facilities.

Some authors say that criminal justice is applied criminology (Hagan, 1986:2–3). **Criminology** is the study of crime. It is a discipline that scientifically examines crime and criminal behavior, including the forms of criminal behavior, the causes of crime, and the societal reaction to crime (Hagan, 1986:2). Criminology involves extensive use of theory in the explanation of crime and the etiology of criminals, while criminal justice focuses upon the processing of criminals. *Applied* has the connotation of action or utility. Thus, those in criminal justice do something about crime and criminals, whereas criminologists primarily speculate about crime and its causes through their theories. Although an exaggeration, of course, this distinction highlights the extremes of both disciplines.

Criminal justice is not synonymous with *criminology,* but there is considerable overlap between the two disciplines. Members of criminal justice societies also belong to criminology organizations, and they do research on similar subjects (Hagan, 1986:2–3). Chapter 2 looks at theories of criminal behavior in an effort to show some of the explanations of crime upon which crime control and correctional policies are based.

The Purpose of This Chapter

This chapter presents the origin of our present laws and discusses how those laws affect us. It discusses different kinds of crime as well as crime patterns. It features some crime victims, especially the very old or very young. The criminal justice system has become increasingly formalized and bureaucratic in order to cope more effectively with growing amounts of crime and changing crime trends.

■ THE SOURCES OF LAW

The legal system of the United States is derived from the English system of common law. It is based on decisions by judges who settled complaints on the basis of custom or precedent. Thus, instead of legislative lawmakers, judges defined crimes such as murder and theft. Over the years, most state legislatures have gradually incorporated common law into their legal codes and statutes to reflect social changes and evolving threats to society. However, there is a distinction between common law and statutory law.

Common and Statutory Law

Common law is authority based upon court decrees and judgments that recognize, affirm, or enforce certain usages and customs of the people *(People v. Rehman).* **Statutory law** is an enactment of a legislature. The Oklahoma legislature, for instance, enacts, eliminates, or changes statutory laws in every session.

A DAY IN COURT

In the following cases, no specific statutes could be applied to determine whether or not crimes were being committed. In each case, the court had to rely on either custom or the morality of the conduct in question. Often, the courts asked whether a reasonable person would engage in such conduct, but if a custom were followed by persons in the town or province, this custom determined how cases were settled.

☐ In the 1881 case of *Ghen v. Rich*, Ghen, a whaler in Massachusetts Bay, used a bomb lance to shoot and kill a finback whale. The whale sank almost immediately, but several days later, it surfaced and washed ashore in Brewster township, some 17 miles from where it had initially sunk.

Someone else found the dead whale and sold it to another party, Rich, who stripped the blubber from the whale, made oil from the blubber, and sold the oil. Neither the finder nor Rich knew who had killed the whale initially, *but it was customary in the Cape Cod vicinity at that time that the hunter continued to have possession of the whale after killing it in spite of the fact that it sank and drifted several miles away.*

Therefore, when Ghen determined that Rich had profited from a whale that Ghen had hunted and killed, he sued Rich in court for damages, which were the market value of the oil obtained from the whale. Since no statutes applied in this case, the judge upheld the custom of Cape Cod whale hunters by ruling in favor of Ghen and awarding him damages. The judge declared, "I hold the usage [custom of whale hunting by Cape Cod whale hunters] to be *valid,* and that the property [interest in] the whale was in the libellant [Ghen]."

☐ Another example of the use of common law in the absence of statutes is the case of *State v. Bradbury* (1939). Bradbury lived in a two-story building with his sister, who was in failing health. One evening she fell and injured herself so severely that she died during the night. Bradbury took his sister's body to the cellar furnace and burned it. The disagreeable odor and dark smoke attracted the attention of police, who asked to see his sister. Bradbury took them to the basement, shoveled some ashes from the furnace, and said, "There she is."

The case was reviewed by the Maine Supreme Court, which noted that the subsequent charges against Bradbury made no reference to violations of any existing statutes. Technically, Bradbury had violated no statute defining the proper disposal of a human body. Rather, the question for the court to determine was whether this was a crime under the common law.

The court held that Bradbury's offense was, indeed, a crime under common law. The indictment charged that Bradbury "with force of arms, unlawfully and indecently did take the human body of one Harriet P. Bradbury, and then and there indecently and unlawfully put and placed said body in a certain furnace, and then and there did dispose of and destroy said body of the said Harriet P. Bradbury by burning the same in said furnace, to the great indecency of Christian burial, in evil example to all others in like case offending, against the peace of said State and contrary to the laws of the same." In convicting Bradbury of disposing of a human body in an indecent manner, the court said, "We have no doubt that the common law casts on someone the duty of carrying to the grave, decently covered, the dead body of any person dying in such a state of indigence as to leave no funds for that purpose. . . . [w]e are satisfied that the indictment charges an offense at common law." Bradbury's conviction for the common law offense was upheld.

Common laws are divided into two classes. One class regulates acts of violence, such as murder and assault, while the other class regulates property rights. In early English communities, property was important, and citizens derived social status from their land holdings. Property trespass was a very serious offense. Deceit and misrepresentation about property sales or exchanges were equally offensive.

Some statutory laws have been derived from common laws, but other statutory laws have been passed because of technological changes in society. For instance, early English communities did not have automobiles or computers. Thus, legislatures have passed laws regulating vehicular traffic and the misuse of computers. Where statutory law fails to include a particular offense, however, courts often rely on common law for deciding specific cases.

Every United States Supreme Court decision has the potential for setting a legal policy, or precedent. In 1972, for example, the United States Supreme Court held in *Furman v. Georgia* that the death penalty, as it was then applied, constituted cruel and unusual punishment. It said that the death penalty was racially discriminatory, in part, because disproportionate numbers of blacks were on death row. Persons who opposed the death penalty claimed a victory and interpreted the *Furman* decision as a ban against capital punishment for any crime.

For several years following the *Furman v. Georgia* decision, the death penalty was suspended in all states. In 1976, however, the United States Supreme Court ruled in *Gregg v. Georgia* that the death penalty is *not* a form of punishment that may *never* be imposed regardless of the circumstances of the offense, but opponents of the death penalty continued to lodge appeals with the United States Supreme Court on behalf of their clients. For example, in 1987, the Supreme Court heard the case of Warren McCleskey, a 41-year-old black who had been sentenced to die by electrocution for the 1978 murder of a white police officer in Georgia. McCleskey alleged that because he was black, the death penalty in his case was discriminatory. In a narrow, 5–4 decision, the United States Supreme Court rejected his argument and upheld the original sentence of death (*McCleskey v. Kemp,* 107 S.Ct. 1756, 1987). Speaking for the majority, Justice Lewis Powell said, "there is . . . some risk of racial prejudice influencing a jury's decision . . . but apparent disparities in sentencing are an inevitable part of our criminal justice system."

The Civil Rights Acts of 1957, 1960, and 1964 established several statutes giving the federal government power to force state and local governments to grant all citizens their civil rights under the United States Constitution. Discrimination because of race, religion, color, or age was prohibited by some of these statutes. As a result, judges at local, state, and federal levels were obligated to decide cases involving certain violations of the Civil Rights Acts. In subsequent years, a number of cases have reached the United States Supreme Court. The rights of several minorities, including women, have been the subjects of recent rulings under Title 42, Section 1983 of the United States Code. While these cases are primarily civil, many criminal cases have also been heard by the United States Supreme Court.

Our laws are made by our legislatures, influenced by the executive branch, and interpreted by the judiciary. The criminal justice system is the process of enforcing these laws. However, we often rely on the United States Supreme Court to interpret these laws and apply them in criminal cases. Presidents of the United States approve or veto laws submitted by Congress, which is the primary lawmaking body of the United

States. Each session, Congress recommends new laws, abolishes old laws, and changes other laws significantly. The United States Supreme Court also affects laws through its interpretation of the constitutional amendments.

Substantive and Procedural Law

Laws are divided into two general classifications: (1) substantive and (2) procedural. **Substantive laws** govern behaviors that are required or prohibited. **Procedural laws** specify how statutes should be applied against law violators. Trials are held according to certain established procedural laws and rules of criminal or civil procedure. Persons accused of crimes are brought to trial, and the state must follow previously established rules when introducing evidence against the alleged offenders. These rules are found in published state or federal regulations and dictate whether certain kinds of evidence are admissible.

■ THE MEANING OF LAW

Law is more than the mere expression of the will of the people or state. **Law** is a body of rules of specific conduct, prescribed by existing, legitimate authority in a particular jurisdiction at a particular point in time.

Rules of Specific Conduct

Criminal laws apply to specific behaviors and not mere thoughts. Whether a statute pertains to concealing faulty construction in a building project or assaulting another person, it defines the behaviors of criminal conduct. Thinking about committing a crime is not a crime.

Legitimate Authority and Jurisdiction

In the United States, the Congress, the president, and Supreme Court constitute legitimate authority. These parties function to represent the interests of the people of the society and to maintain existing social organization. In different ways, they administer the rules created by statute or common law. Each level of authority in local, state, or federal government oversees a particular jurisdiction. Lower or municipal courts, for instance, make decisions about lesser offenses, such as traffic violations or minor infractions. Thus, defendants accused of murder are not within the jurisdiction (or power) of a municipal court. By the same token, federal district court judges never conduct jury trials involving trivial city traffic tickets. Minor matters are not within the range of serious offenses handled by United States district court judges (one exception is that United States magistrates frequently hear cases involving traffic citations issued in United States parks and recreational areas). Each of these courts has a specific **jurisdiction,** or sphere of authority, governing the kinds of cases heard.

Particular Point in Time

The particular-point-in-time restriction means that current laws apply in specific criminal cases, and former laws are not applicable. Prohibition was the law during the

1920s, for example. However, because most laws are subject to change and dependent upon the will of the people, Prohibition was eventually repealed.

State laws may vary at a particular point in time. In one state, the drinking age may be 21. In an adjacent state, drinking may be permitted for 18-year-olds. Nineteen-year-olds may enter the adjacent state on weekends to drink, where such behavior is lawful.

■ THE FUNCTIONS OF LAW

The functions of law are to:

1. Legitimize the existing social structure.
2. Regulate social conduct.
3. Regulate freedom.
4. Resolve disputes.

Legitimizing the Existing Social Structure

A body of laws requires all of us to follow certain standards of conduct. By conforming to these standards, we help to perpetuate existing social arrangements. In addition, laws provide a degree of predictability. We expect others to follow the laws and we act in accordance with these expectations. A simple example is a traffic ordinance. When a traffic light at an intersection is red, the traffic moving in the direction of green light relies on the other motorists to obey the red light. If a motorist chooses to disregard the red light and proceed through the intersection, drivers and passengers may be seriously injured or killed in an automobile collision. Thus we rely on others to comply with particular standards of conduct.

Standards of conduct are not limited to traffic ordinances. They include criminal and civil laws embodied in local, state, and federal statutes. Regulatory agencies such as the Federal Communications Commission issue rules and regulations as well.

Regulating Social Conduct

Local police forces, state militia (particularly under conditions of mass rioting or natural disasters), state police, and the Federal Bureau of Investigation (FBI), and many other agencies maintain order through the regulation of social conduct. People who violate laws of social conduct are often apprehended by these law enforcement agencies and processed through the criminal justice system.

Regulating Freedom

The United States Constitution, the nation's highest law, provides several individual freedoms, or rights, including free speech, a speedy trial, assembly, and freedom to worship any religion. No state may infringe upon these freedoms. The Constitution also ensures all citizens the right to due process, or fair procedures if they are ever charged with crimes. Due process protects citizens against unwarranted government seizures of property or interference with other freedoms provided in the United States Constitution. All citizens accused of crimes have the right to have their case aired in court, regardless of the seriousness of the offense.

Resolving Disputes

It citizens cannot resolve disputes about property or other matters themselves, they can seek assistance from the courts. Our courts interpret law based on precedent or statute. If someone steals your car while it is parked in a public parking lot, who is responsible for the loss? You? The parking lot attendant? Your insurance company? If the responsibility for the loss is unclear, the court decides who should pay.

■ THE DEFINITION OF CRIME

The criminal justice system includes the entire process of enforcing laws (Black, 1979). Before examining the basic components of the criminal justice system, we must distinguish between civil and criminal actions.

Civil and Criminal Actions

The criminal justice system deals exclusively with criminal laws and those who violate these laws. However, courts generally deal with both criminal and civil matters. With the exception of special criminal courts in various jurisdictions, much action at law in courts is civil. In federal district courts, for instance, about 85 percent of all cases are civil, while only about 15 percent involve alleged criminal acts (Cook, 1973; Cramer, 1981; Farr, 1984). Civil court actions may include resolving child custody disputes between divorcing parents, settling conflicting land claims, fulfilling the terms of wills, and deciding whether one's civil rights have been violated by others. Other civil actions involve claims for damages arising from someone's negligence or intentional misconduct. These civil actions involve tort claims.

A **tort** is a civil wrong involving one's duty to someone else, a breach of that duty, and injuries arising from that breach (Black, 1979). Civil wrongs include suits to recover damages for injuries arising from automobile accidents. One person may sue another for printing false statements in public documents such as newspapers. If retail store owners are negligent and permit slippery substances to accumulate on their store floors, for instance, customers may slip and fall, suffering injuries. Tort actions may follow such incidents, but store owners will not be charged with or found guilty of committing criminal acts. Criminal laws do not apply in such cases. A **crime** is a violation of a criminal law by a person held accountable by that law.

A useful distinction between crimes and torts is that tort actions seek damages, usually monetary compensation, for injuries sustained. In contrast, criminal actions are conducted to punish offenders of criminal laws. In all actions at law, one party opposes another party for a wrong allegedly committed, for the protection of a right, or for the prevention of a wrong. Criminal actions are called prosecutions. In civil actions, the proceedings are called litigations.

Crime is defined by seven specific criteria, or elements (Cole, 1975:79–81; Hall, 1947:18). These elements are:

1. *Legality*, where a specific behavior must be described by statute or constitutional provision.
2. ***Actus reus,*** or an overt act that is prohibited by statute or other provision.

3. **Mens rea,** or the intent to do harm. This is known as evil intent and is crucial in determining whether someone premeditated a crime or thought about committing it.
4. *Consensus,* or the combination of *mens rea* and *actus reus.* A prohibited act must be accompanied by the thought or evil intent to commit it.
5. *Harm,* where damage to people or property results from the act, although victimless crimes may be perpetrated where no one is actually harmed or injured directly.
6. *Causation,* where a cause-effect relation must be established between the perpetrator of the act and the harm inflicted. If a truck driver negligently fails to set truck brakes on a steep hill and the truck goes out of control and kills or injures a pedestrian, the truck driver's negligence is the cause of the death, even if the *mens rea,* or intent to commit a criminal act, is not proved.
7. *Punishment,* where a specific punishment accompanies criminal conduct. Punishments may include fines, imprisonment or both.

Laws and Jurisdictions

The criminal justice system refers to (1) a set of agencies and organizations, and (2) a series of interrelated stages by which alleged criminal offenders are processed. Clearly, this process is prefaced by established criminal laws, which have been created by the legislatures or executives, interpreted by the courts, and made explicit through local, state, and federal statutes and ordinances.

An important distinction is made between different levels of the criminal justice system. While the criminal justice system is procedurally uniform, it may be analyzed according to several different levels. Thus, violations of federal laws locate alleged offenders within the jurisdiction of the federal criminal justice system. Violations of state laws place alleged criminals within the jurisdiction of the state criminal justice system.

If the laws of one state conflict with the laws of other states, for instance, the United States Supreme Court has the jurisdiction, or power, to hear such disputes and resolve them. No state may dictate to another state the laws and policies that it must follow. If a burglary is committed at a branch of a United States Post Office, the law violation occurs within the jurisdiction of a United States district court. At the same time, the United States Post Office branch is located in a given state and community, and the burglary violates the law in each of these jurisdictions as well. Therefore, **concurrent jurisdiction** may exist. There may be several separate prosecutions for the same offense if a federal law was violated, and simultaneously, state and local laws were violated. Federal charges may be filed, and state and local charges may also be filed.

For example, a man living in New York City conspired with several burglars to steal motion picture films from a New York City film company warehouse. The warehouse was burglarized and the films were stolen, transported, and sold to another person in Ohio. Later, the identity of the man in New York became known to the local police, and state charges of burglary and larceny were filed against him. The New York City film company alerted the FBI, which conducted its own independent investigation of the matter.

The United States Department of Justice later brought criminal charges against the New York man for committing several federal crimes, including criminal copyright infringement, conspiracy, and interstate transportation of stolen property with a value in excess of $5,000. The man in New York was subsequently prosecuted for the federal crimes in a United States district court in that state. Later, a criminal court in New York

City conducted state criminal proceedings against the same man. In this illustration, *both* federal and state crimes were alleged.

Criminal laws vary among states. Some states have more (or fewer) criminal laws than do other states. Also, states vary in their procedures for punishing persons who commit the same types of crimes. In Morton Grove, Illinois, it is against the law to possess a gun. In Kennesaw, Georgia, however, it is against the law *not* to have a gun on one's premises.

In 1962, the American Law Institute developed a Model Penal Code, which unified diverse state and federal laws. The institute's efforts led to a uniform set of laws, with consistent punishments as guidelines for the states and the federal government. While no state or the federal government is obligated to follow or adopt any part of the Model Penal Code, the code nevertheless provides a consistent definition of criminal conduct. Several jurisdictions have adopted portions of the Model Penal Code in their own codifications of statutes and penalties. The code precisely defines such terms as *knowingly, purposely,* and *recklessly,* as well as such terms as *entrapment* and *deadly force.* An objective of the Model Penal Code is to introduce consistent application of the law, as well as uniformity of punishment for similar offenses, among the states.

Crime Distinguished from Deviance

Throughout the United States, most people follow certain social customs, ranging from regular bathing to respecting the rights and property of others. Those who do not follow these accepted codes of conduct are labeled deviant. **Deviance** is any departure from the accepted code of conduct.

There are many degrees and types of deviance. When streaking was a fad in the 1970s, for instance, many college students ran nude across their campuses. These were violations of public decency and exhibitionism laws, but authorities were lenient in dealing with streakers. Even though some streakers were apprehended, most were given stern warnings and released by school authorities without any further punishment. Punk hairstyles and strange clothing may be regarded as deviant, but such deviance is not criminal, because there are more serious kinds of deviant conduct. Some persons rob others or steal their property, physically assault others, or commit homicide or murder.

Criminal behavior is the violation of codified criminal laws by persons who are held responsible by those laws. Responsibility is determined by one's capacity to understand the laws and the consequences for violating the law. Those defined as insane, mentally retarded, or senile, for example, are often treated as incapable of understanding the law. Ordinarily, they are not held accountable for the consequences of their actions. These people are not necessarily immune from punishment, but allowances are usually made for their limited abilities or diminished mental capacity. Primarily because they are incapable of formulating the requisite criminal intent to qualify their behavior as intentionally criminal, medical or psychological treatment or hospitalization is prescribed for them rather than punishment by confinement in a jail or prison.

When John Hinckley attempted to assassinate President Ronald Reagan, he was arrested and brought to trial. His attorney used the insanity defense and sought to show that Hinckley was not responsible for his actions at the time. The defense was successful, and Hinckley was acquitted. Nevertheless, he was hospitalized under strict supervision. Public outrage over Hinckley's use of the insanity defense caused many lawmakers to revise their insanity statutes in order to limit the frequency with which such a defense can be used in the future. Many states either eliminated or redefined their concept of insanity, and several jurisdictions created a guilty but mentally ill plea instead of the standard not guilty by reason of insanity. Chapter 4 discusses several defenses used by criminal defendants besides insanity, including mistake, duress, and intoxication.

We can say that probably most crime is deviance, but only some deviance is crime. Some deviance is classified as residual rule breaking because it does not fit easily into any identifiable crime category (Scheff, 1966). The national media have exposed the private lives of some political and religious leaders, labeling them as womanizers or perverts. While not all forms of sexual misconduct are illegal, some sexual misconduct, if brought to the public's attention, results in moral condemnation (Smith and Pollack, 1975).

■ CRIMINAL RESPONSIBILITY AND LEGAL DEFINITIONS

Certain law violations are labeled **victimless crimes** because the "victims" are willing participants in the illegal activity. Thus, no one is actually harmed (Schur, 1965). Some observers consider prostitution and gambling to be victimless crimes. Those seeking sexual gratification solicit it from others for a fee. This is a normally violation of the law, although the prostitute and client mutually consent to the conditions of the activity.

In localities where gambling is outlawed, covert gambling operations are often conducted. Those who want to gamble seek out such gambling establishments. Thus, gamblers and gambling house operators mutually consent to participating in these illegal activities. As each sees it, no one is harmed as the result of these activities. It is helpful to contrast such crimes with certain violent crimes, where persons are injured, or with property crimes, where things of value are taken, where victims can easily be identified.

In recent years, however, the public has been confronted with the spread of AIDS (Acquired Immune Deficiency Syndrome), which is a deadly virus often spread through sexual contact. Prostitution is one means of spreading this virus; therefore, experts question whether prostitution is really a victimless crime. In addition, some authorities say that gambling, another victimless crime, causes the financial ruin of families or those dependent upon gamblers. Organized crime realizes substantial profits from gambling and prostitution, and these profits support other illegal activities. Therefore, it is sometimes claimed that there is no such thing as a victimless crime, because someone is inevitably hurt as a result of the conduct.

■ CLASSIFYING CRIMES

Law enforcement officials have designated major or more serious crimes as felonies and minor or less serious crimes as misdemeanors. These categories are ordinarily distinguished by the severity of punishment prescribed. A **felony** is a crime punishable by imprisonment in a state or federal prison for 1 year or longer. A **misdemeanor** is a crime punishable by a fine or imprisonment in a city or county jail for less than 1 year. There are exceptions to these definitions among jurisdictions, however.

There are exceptions to the standard definition of crime. In Morgan Hill, California, a 2½-year-old toddler, James Soto, was killed by a pit bull terrier in November 1987. The owner of the terrier, Michael Patrick Berry, 37, was charged with murder. While Berry didn't kill or contemplate killing Soto, he possessed dog-fighting magazines and attack-training equipment, knew his dog was extremely dangerous, and yet kept his dog in a neighborhood area accessible to children.

Felonies include murder, rape, robbery, aggravated assault, arson, vehicular theft, larceny, and the selling or distributing of such a controlled substance as marijuana or cocaine. Misdemeanors include simple possession of marijuana (not for resale), driving while intoxicated, and simple trespass. In felony cases, the penalties are usually severe, while in misdemeanor cases misdemeanants (those who commit misdemeanors) are usually fined or receive suspended sentences.

Crimes can also be classified according to *mala in se* or *mala prohibita*. **Mala in se** refers to crimes that are intrinsically evil or wrong, such as murder, rape, and arson. In contrast, **mala prohibita** are offenses defined by legislatures who pass criminal laws. Such offenses include selling liquor on Sunday and vagrancy. Most *mala in se* offenses are statutorily prohibited anyway.

■ THE MEASUREMENT OF CRIME

The Uniform Crime Reports (UCR)

The **Uniform Crime Reports (UCR)** is the major sourcebook of crime statistics in the United States. It is published annually by the Federal Bureau of Investigation (FBI).

This publication includes statistics about crimes reported in the United States annually by over 15,000 law enforcement agencies. The UCR is compiled on twenty-nine types of crime from participating law enforcement agencies. Crime information is requested from all rural and urban law enforcement agencies. However, not all agencies report their crime information consistently (for example, New Mexico authorities may report an offense to the FBI differently from California authorities). Further complicating the problem, some agencies do not report their crime information on a regular basis, and others do not report at all.

Many jurisdictions use the UCR to evaluate the effectiveness of their law enforcement agencies in controlling crime. Higher numbers of reported crimes may mean less efficient police work, while lower numbers of crime reports may signify better police work. Of course, higher numbers of reported crimes may also mean better police-community relations or any of several other explanations unrelated to crime per se. During mayoral campaigns in various cities, incumbent candidates widely quote UCR statistics to show the effectiveness of their administrations. Opposition candidates use the same information to draw different conclusions, however. Depending upon the particular crime and the time period covered, many contradictory interpretations can be made about crime trends in any city.

The FBI has established a crime classification index. **Index offenses** include eight serious types of crime used by the FBI to measure crime trends. The FBI also compiles information about twenty-one less serious offenses, ranging from forgery and counterfeiting to curfew violations and runaways. Index offense information is presented in the UCR for each state, city, county, and township that has submitted crime information during the most recent year. The eight index offenses and their definitions according to the Uniform Crime Reporting Program follow.

1. *Murder and nonnegligent manslaughter:* the willful (nonnegligent) killing of one human being by another.
2. *Forcible rape:* the carnal knowledge of a female forcibly and against her will; assaults or attempts to commit rape by force or threat of force are also included.
3. *Robbery:* the taking or attempting to take anything of value from the care, custody, or control of a person or persons by force or threat of force or violence and/or by putting the victim in fear.
4. *Aggravated assault:* an unlawful attack by one person upon another for the purpose of inflicting severe or aggravated bodily injury.
5. *Burglary:* the unlawful entry of a structure to commit a felony or theft.
6. *Larceny-theft:* the unlawful taking, carrying, leading, or riding away of property from the possession or constructive possession of another, including shoplifting, pocket picking, purse snatching, thefts from motor vehicles, and thefts of motor vehicle parts or accessories.
7. *Motor vehicle theft:* theft or attempted theft of a motor vehicle, including automobiles, trucks, buses, motorcycles, motorscooters, and snowmobiles.
8. *Arson:* any willful or malicious burning or attempt to burn, with or without intent to defraud, a dwelling house, public building, motor vehicle or aircraft, and the personal property of another.

Table 1.1 shows official trends for these index offenses for the years 1986–1987.

TABLE 1.1 FBI Index Offenses and Trends, 1986–1987

Index Offense	Year	Number of Offenses	Rate per 100,000 Inhabitants
1. *Murder and nonnegligent*	1986	20,613	8.6
manslaughter	1987	20,096	8.3
Percent change		− 2.5	− 3.5
2. *Forcible rape*	1986	91,459	37.9
	1987	91,111	37.4
Percent change		− 0.4	− 1.3
3. *Robbery*	1986	542,775	225.1
	1987	517,704	212.7
Percent change		− 4.6	− 5.5
4. *Aggravated assault*	1986	834,322	346.1
	1987	855,088	351.3
Percent change		+ 2.5	+ 1.5
5. *Burglary*	1986	3,241,410	1,344.6
	1987	3,236,184	1,329.6
Percent change		− 0.2	− 1.1
6. *Larceny-theft*	1986	7,257,153	3,010.3
	1987	7,499,851	3,081.3
Percent change		+ 3.3	+ 2.4
7. *Motor vehicle theft*	1986	1,224,137	507.8
	1987	1,288,674	529.4
Percent change		+ 5.3	+ 4.3
8. *Arson*	1986	86,455	8.8
	1987	102,410	9.4
Percent change		+ 18.5	+ 6.8

Source: United States Department of Justice, *Crime in the United States* (Washington: D.C.: U.S. Government Printing Office, 1988), pp. 7–39.

Violent and Property Crimes. Index crimes reported by the UCR are distinguished also according to crimes against the person and crimes against property. **Crimes against the person,** or **violent crimes,** are those committed directly against someone else in their presence. Aggravated assault (possibly involving a personal attack with a dangerous weapon), rape, homicide, and robbery are crimes against persons. **Crimes against property,** or **property crimes,** are considered nonviolent, or passive. No physical harm is inflicted upon the crime victims because the victims are ordinarily absent when these crimes are committed. Examples include vehicular theft, burglary (breaking and entering unoccupied premises), and larceny (theft).

For the index offenses of murder, forcible rape, robbery, aggravated assault, burglary, larceny-theft, and motor vehicle theft, crime clocks provide information about how often violent and property crimes are committed. Figure 1.1 shows a crime clock for these index offenses. For instance, a violent crime is committed every 21 seconds somewhere in the United States, while a property crime occurs every 3 seconds. And one forcible rape occurs every 6 minutes *somewhere* in the United States.

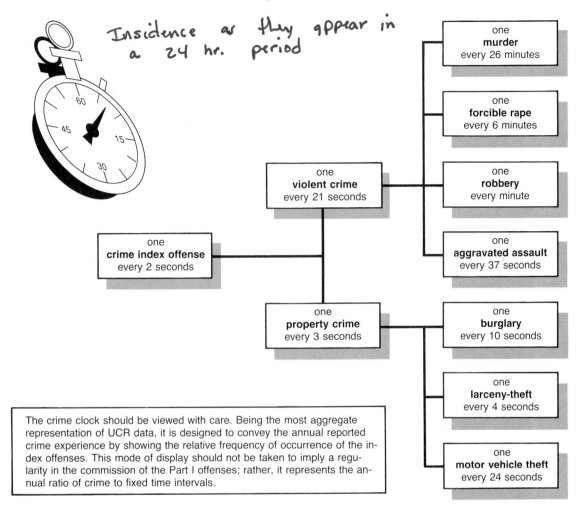

Insidence as they appear in a 24 hr. period

The crime clock should be viewed with care. Being the most aggregate representation of UCR data, it is designed to convey the annual reported crime experience by showing the relative frequency of occurrence of the index offenses. This mode of display should not be taken to imply a regularity in the commission of the Part I offenses; rather, it represents the annual ratio of crime to fixed time intervals.

FIGURE 1.1 Crime Clock, 1987

Source: United States Department of Justice, *Crime in the United States* (Washington: D.C.: U.S. Government Printing Office, 1988), p. 6.

The frequency of occurrence of these offenses does not mean there is a rape every 6 minutes in Philadelphia, or New York City, or Los Angeles. Nor does it mean that because a larceny-theft occurs every 4 seconds, there is a larceny-theft occurring every 4 seconds in Detroit or Miami. These are aggregate statistics, which reflect nationwide figures for the entire year, where the annual total number of specific crimes reported is divided by some unit of measurement, such as seconds or minutes. For example, if 240 rapes occur in a 24-hour period, 240/24 = 10 rapes per hour (or one rape every 6 minutes), but many rapes occur during evening hours. Thus, crime clock figures are somewhat misleading. Crimes also fluctuate from one month to the next and vary in frequency among cities and towns. However, crime clocks do provide general information about the frequency of certain crimes compared with the frequency of others.

Criticisms of the UCR. Even though the UCR publishes the most current crime figures from reporting law enforcement agencies, many experts believe that crime clocks are inaccurate in several respects (Gove, Hughes, and Geerken, 1985; Green, 1985; Sherman and Glick, 1984). First, UCR figures fail to take into account population increases. Thus, the UCR does not provide an accurate per capita measure of crime frequency.

Second, questioning criminals about other crimes they have committed, police find discrepancies between the self-report information and the UCR figures. In short, criminals escape police detection or capture for many crimes they commit because some crimes are never reported to the police. For instance, someone who is beaten and robbed by the associates of a prostitute is unlikely to report the incident to the police, because soliciting prostitutes for sexual activity is unlawful. Thus, it is generally accepted that more crime is committed each year than official estimates, such as the UCR, disclose.

Third, when crimes are reported to the UCR, only the most serious offenses are often reported. For example a burglary suspect arrested at a crime scene may possess burglary tools (a law violation), stolen goods (another violation), and a concealed weapon (still another law violation). However, law enforcement officials may report a single crime, burglary. Thus, reporting the most serious offense where more than one offense has been committed also causes some experts to charge that the UCR underestimates the actual amount of crime in the United States.

Fourth, not all law enforcement agencies report crimes in a uniform manner. Many jurisdictions define crimes differently (Sherman and Glick, 1984). In addition, clerks in local police departments make errors in tabulating arrest statistics (for example, a clerk may classify a robbery as a burglary). Sloppy record keeping also contributes to faulty reporting. Some critics say that the UCR is more a reflection of police arrest practices than a true measure of the amount of crime that really occurs (Green, 1985).

Fifth, in some jurisdictions, police crackdowns lead to numerous arrests but few convictions. The implication is that arrest statistics are more a measure of police activity than of criminal activity (Greenberg, 1981). In these instances, there is often an underlying political motive, such as a mayor's election. A police department's making numerous arrests gives voters the impression that the incumbent mayor is really doing something about crime. However, such arrests often mean that many of the cases never result in prosecution and are dismissed outright. A continuing hazard of police work is that citizens may file lawsuits alleging false arrest. The weaker the provocation for an arrest, the greater the likelihood that such a suit will be filed.

Nevertheless, high arrest rates have apparent political advantages. In an investigation of Florida sheriff elections in different counties, arrest rates fluctuated significantly during the election periods. According to the 1976 Florida county sheriff election data, arrest figures fairly accurately predicted the winner and losers of the sheriff's election (Surette, 1985). More aggressive arrest strategies may cause crime rate statistics to increase even though there is no real increase in the frequency of crime committed in the community. However, in the view of the public, better police work means more arrests, demonstrating that law enforcement agencies are doing something to combat crime.

Some investigators feel that the UCR is a valid indicator of the incidence of serious crimes (Gove, Hughes, and Geerken, 1985). This belief is supported by the fact that serious crimes, involving death, serious bodily injury, and thefts of valuable property, are more likely to be reported to the police and insurance companies. In contrast, lesser offenses, or petty crimes leaving the victim uninjured, may not be reported.

Other experts believe that the UCR should improve the quality of information reported and ensure greater comparability with other crime data bases. For instance, a study of arrest record keeping by 3,411 law enforcement agencies in 1982–1983 showed that arrest data were frequently hand tabulated and laden with errors (Poggio, et al., 1985).

How well do law enforcement agencies respond to various crimes? The UCR maintains records indicating the proportion of crimes cleared by arrest each year. Cleared by arrest means that a law enforcement agency has identified possible offenders, has sufficient evidence to charge them, and actually takes them into custody. Crimes may also be cleared in exceptional ways, such as when an offender dies, offers a deathbed confession, or commits suicide. Also, crime victims may decide not to prosecute, simply because the time consumed is not worth the loss sustained from the crime committed. In these instances, law enforcement officers know the identity of offenders, have sufficient evidence to support their arrest, and know the offenders' whereabouts. Thus, crimes cleared by arrest do not reflect these exceptional cases. Figure 1.2 shows crimes cleared by arrests for 1987.

It is important to understand that the phrase "crimes cleared by arrest" does not mean that those crimes have been solved. It means simply that someone has been arrested and charged. Overzealous law enforcement may lead to many arrests, but more than half of all arrests do not result in convictions. Therefore, the information in Figure 1.2 is somewhat misleading. However, despite the poor relation between the number of crimes cleared by arrest and the resulting convictions, these figures are indicative to some degree of crime control, although we don't know how indicative.

The National Crime Survey (NCS)

The limitations of the UCR and other official documents measuring the amount of crime have led some experts to draw comparisons between the UCR and the National Crime Survey (NCS), which is conducted annually in cooperation with the United States Bureau of the Census. The **National Crime Survey (NCS)** is a random survey of approximately 60,000 dwellings, about 127,000 persons age 12 and over, and approximately 50,000 businesses. Smaller samples of persons from these original figures form the data base from which the crime figures are compiled. Carefully worded questions lead people to report incidents that can be classified as crimes. This material is statistically manipulated to make it comparable with UCR statistics. This material is usually referred to as victimization data. The NCS distinguishes between victimizations and incidents. A victimization is the basic measure of the occurrence of a crime and is a specific criminal act that affects a single victim. An incident is a specific criminal act

FIGURE 1.2 Crimes Cleared by Arrest, 1987

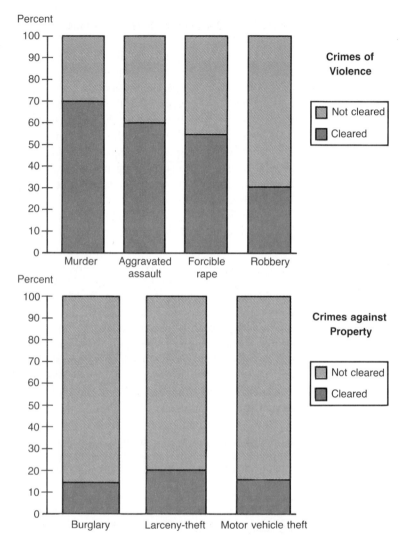

Source: United States Department of Justice, *Crime in the United States* (Washington: D.C.: U.S. Government Printing Office, 1988), p. 154.

involving one or more victims. Using NCS victimization data, Table 1.2 gives some indication of crime in the United States.

The result of comparing NCS (victimization) information with UCR (officially reported) data is that the amount of crime reported by the NCS is from two to three times greater than the amount of crime reported by the UCR. Independent researchers studying similar phenomena have reached almost identical conclusions. One investigator studied crime rates for six offenses in twenty-six cities in 1972 and 1973 (Decker, 1977). The average number of specific offenses per 100,000 persons was compared with the same types of offenses listed in the UCR. It was found that the overall rate of crime reported by victims was 19,478 per 100,000, whereas the overall rate of crime reported by police in the UCR was only 6,868 per 100,000 for the same time period.

TABLE 1.2 Victimization Rates by Type of Crime, 1987

Type of Crime	Rate
1. *Violent crimes* (rate per 1,000 population age 12 and over)	
Crimes of Violence...	28.6
Completed violent crimes...	10.5
Attempted violent crimes	18.1
Rape...	.7
Completed rape...	1.3
Attempted rape	.5
Robbery...	5.2
Completed robbery	3.4
Attempted robbery	1.8
Assault...	22.7
2. *Property crimes* (rate per 1,000 households)	
All household crimes...	171.4
Completed household crimes....................................	144.5
Attempted household crimes	26.8
Burglary..	61.3
Larceny	94.0
Motor Vehicle Theft..	16.1
Crimes of Theft	67.5

Source: U.S. Department of Justice, Bureau of Justice Statistics, *Criminal victimization in the United States, 1987.* Washington, D.C.: U.S. Government Printing Office (October 1988), p. 2.

Despite its safeguards, the NCS has certain persistent problems. Some crime victims cannot remember when or where an offense occurred. Other victims are reluctant to report a rape, particularly if they know the rapist, such as a family member or friend. Nonreporting is also related to victim apathy, perceived powerlessness of police, and fear of the authorities themselves (Kidd and Chayet, 1984). The poor are especially reluctant to report crime because they fear reprisals from the criminals, whom they often know. Also, some victims may fear that police will detect evidence of the victims' own crimes or statutory violations, such as health code infractions, illegal alien status, or overcrowded apartment dwellings, in their investigations.

Additionally, both the UCR and NCS overemphasize street crimes and de-emphasize corporate crimes. It is often difficult to know, for instance, who has been a direct victim of corporate crime, such as the theft of a company's secrets by a current or former employee. Sometimes, embezzlement of a corporation's funds is handled without police intervention.

■ CRIME PATTERNS AND OFFENDER CHARACTERISTICS

About two thirds of all single-offender violent crimes are committed by whites. Although handguns are frequently blamed for much violent crime, deadly weapons are not used

Handguns are blamed for much of the violent crime that occurs in the United States. Organizations such as the National Rifle Association and Handgun Control, Inc., make conflicting claims about the seriousness of gun ownership and the true relation between guns and crime.

IN 1985, HANDGUNS KILLED
46 PEOPLE IN JAPAN
8 IN GREAT BRITAIN
31 IN SWITZERLAND
5 IN CANADA
18 IN ISRAEL
5 IN AUSTRALIA
AND 8,092 IN THE UNITED STATES.

GOD BLESS AMERICA.

The pen is mightier than the gun.
Write Handgun Control, Inc. Now.
1225 Eye Street, NW, Washington, D.C. 20005
Or call (202) 898-0792

STOP HANDGUNS BEFORE THEY STOP YOU.

in 80 percent of all violent crime cases. About 71 percent of all violent crimes (primarily rapes and assaults) are committed by offenders acting alone, while over half of the robberies are committed by two or more offenders. Currently, the experts say the relationship between gun availability, gun laws, and gun usage in crimes is inconclusive (Wright and Rossi, 1986:10–11).

Most violent crimes occur between 6:00 P.M. and midnight. Streets are common sites for personal crimes of violence, and most of these crimes involve contact with strangers. Nonstranger violent crimes, including rape and assault, typically occur in the victim's home or somewhere on the victim's property.

In 1985, 50 percent of all crimes were committed by persons under age 25. Involvement in criminal activity declines with age, although recent data suggest that crime committed by the elderly is on the increase (Champion, 1988a; Hirshi and Gottfredson, 1985; Wilbanks and Kim, 1984). Also, attempts to account for variations in crime because of age ignore important variables, such as personality and socioeconomic characteristics (Greenberg, 1985). Considering the unreliability of the UCR and NCS in accounting for the true amount of crime in the United States, it is unlikely that we will ever know the true relation between age and crime.

■ THE VICTIMS OF CRIME AND VICTIMS' RIGHTS

There have always been crime victims. However, media attention has typically focused upon criminals and how they are processed by the criminal justice system (Karmen,

1984). Some United States Supreme Court decisions in the 1960s and 1970s seemed to show more concern for protecting the rights of criminals than those of crime victims (Karmen, 1984:12–22). Many citizens believed that legal technicalities were loopholes used by criminals to beat the system. Many believed that United States Supreme Court decisions handcuffed the police in the process. Civil liberties groups frequently labeled these Supreme Court decisions as antivictim (Karmen, 1984:21–22).

In 1947, researcher Benjamin Mendelsohn coined the term *victimology* (Galaway and Hudson, 1981). **Victimology** is the scientific study of victims. There is disagreement about how victims should be defined, however. Some people wish to restrict definitions of victims to those affected by crime, while others wish to expand the category to include *all* persons injured or affected by accidents, discrimination, war, genocide, or political repression. In any case, the victim was rediscovered (Karmen, 1984:1, 23). Table 1.3 highlights the history of victimology.

TABLE 1.3 Highlights of the Brief History of Victimology*

1941	Hans Von Hentig writes an article about the victim–criminal interaction.
1947	Benjamin Mendelsohn coins the term *victimology* in an article.
1957	The British criminal justice reformer Margery Fry stimulates discussion and debate about how to reimburse victims.
1958	Marvin Wolfgang sheds light on victim-precipitated homicide.
1964	Congress rejects victim compensation legislation but studies the victim's plight for the first time.
1965	California enacts victim compensation legislation and begins keeping records of financial hardships imposed by crime.
1966	The first nationwide victimization survey is carried out.
1968	Stephen Schafer writes the first textbook about victims.
1973	The First International Symposium on Victimology is held in Jerusalem.
1975	The International Study Institute on Victimology is held in Bellagio, Italy. The National Organization for Victim Assistance is founded.
1976	The Second International Symposium on Victimology is held in Boston. *Victimology: An International Journal* begins publication.
1979	The Third International Symposium on Victimology is held in Münster, West Germany. The World Society of Victimology is founded.
1980	The First World Congress on Victimology is held in Washington, D.C.
1981	President Ronald Reagan proclaims April 8–14 Victims Rights Week.
1982	The Second International Study Institute on Victimology is held in Bellagio, Italy. The Fourth International Symposium on Victimology is held in Tokyo.
1983	The President's Task Force on Victims of Crime studies problems and recommends changes in the Constitution and in federal and state laws to guarantee victims' rights.

*From Galaway and Hudson, 1981; Schneider, 1982.

Source: Reprinted with permission from Andrew Karmen, *Crime Victims: An Introduction to Victimology* (Monterey, Cal.: Brooks/Cole, 1984), p. 26.

Characteristics of Crime Victims

While there is much variation in the amount of crime reported in the UCR and the NCS, there is some agreement between these official sources. For instance, males are twice as likely as females to be victims of violent crimes. Less violent crimes, such as theft and burglary, reflect similar victimization patterns. There is a negative relationship between age and incidence of violent crimes. For example, young persons, in the age range of 12–24, have the highest victimization rates, but the incidence of victimization decreases as one grows older. Blacks are victimized more frequently than whites are, although victimization rates for whites and other ethnic and racial categories excluding blacks are similar to each other. Victims of crimes are more likely to be single, divorced, or separated than married.

In 1983, employed persons had much lower victimization rates than unemployed persons, regardless of whether they were male, female, black, or white. Unemployed persons were victimized at the rate of 75 per thousand, while employed persons were victimized at the rate of only 37 per thousand (U.S. Department of Justice, 1985:28). One explanation is that unemployed persons were exposed to criminals a greater portion of the time than were employed persons. Also, unemployed persons may live in low-rent, high-crime areas, while employed persons may live in affluent neighborhoods, where greater police protection exists.

About a third of all robbery and assault victims suffered physical injury, and about 75 percent of all violent crime victims took self-protective measures, such as attempting to reason with the offender, fleeing from the offender, screaming or yelling for help, hitting, kicking, or scratching (U.S. Department of Justice, 1985:6–7).

Official Reactions to Victimization

After a crime has been committed against a victim, what recourse does the victim have? What is the response of law enforcement agencies to the victimization? Evidence from the 1983 NCS shows that over 95 percent of the victimizations resulted in economic loss through theft of or damage to property. In 83 percent of the cases, no recovery or restitution occurred.

The victim must report a crime in order for police to do something about it. Surprisingly, however, only half of all violent crime victimizations were reported to police in 1983. Many rape victims didn't report to police either, because they were afraid of reprisals, they were too embarrassed, or they were afraid of having to testify in open court later about the incident. The most frequent reason victims gave for not reporting crimes was that the offense was "not important enough to warrant police attention" (U.S. Department of Justice, 1985:98–99). Another reason was that victims believed that police couldn't do anything about it anyway. When a crime *is* reported, it is not automatically investigated in many jurisdictions. In fact, the National District Attorneys Association Commission on Victim Witness Assistance has consistently found that victims of crime and witnesses to crime are themselves "victims of an inadequate, indifferent criminal justice system" (Lynch, 1976).

The National District Attorneys Commission published a survey in 1975 about the settlement (that is, restitution or compensation) of victims' cases. Some of their findings from the Alameda County, California, field office showed:

1. Almost 12 percent of those surveyed were never notified that an arrest had been made in their cases.
2. Almost 73 percent of all victims suffering physical injuries received no compensation.
3. Almost 30 percent of all victims never got their property back even though the property had been recovered and had been used in court as evidence.
4. Almost 78 percent of all those surveyed lost pay from their employment because of their required court appearances.
5. About 42 percent of those surveyed were never notified of the outcome of the case in which they were involved (Lynch, 1976:172–173).

In their New Orleans field office, the commission reported that 30 percent of the respondents had no idea what action had been taken in their cases. And in 70 percent of the reported victimizations, the District Attorney's Screening Division had refused to pursue those cases in court, giving little or no explanation to the victims.

The Development of the Victim's Bill of Rights

In the late 1970s, the New York State Compensation Board established a bill of rights for victims of serious crimes. Among its other provisions, the **Victim's Bill of Rights** includes protection from further criminal violence. Furthermore, victims must be kept informed by law enforcement agencies of the status of the defendant(s) in custody and if and when the defendant(s) are released. They should be notified of a plea bargain arrangement or any other discretionary disposition of their case. They should know the release date of the defendants if they were incarcerated. Victims should also be informed of financial and social service assistance available to them, and they should receive information about how to apply for such assistance (Hudson, 1980).

Programs designed to compensate victims of criminal acts are not new. New Zealand and Great Britain were among the first countries to enact common law programs to reimburse victims for their lost income and medical, hospital, or burial expenses. However, these government-sponsored programs failed to provide for return of or

CRIME BEAT

By 1987, Son of Sam laws had been enacted by Congress and forty-one states. These laws prohibit criminals from profiting from their crimes through book and movie royalties involving stories based on their experiences. The laws are named after David Burkowitz, who murdered six young people during the late 1970s. The New York State Legislature granted the New York State Victims Board authority to prevent Burkowitz and others from profiting from their crimes through sales of stories to the media. Burkowitz had purportedly bragged to others that he would make millions from the sale of his story about the murders.

Others convicted of crimes who have written about their experiences for profit include Sydney Biddle Barrows (the Mayflower Madam), Jean Harris (the convicted killer of Dr. Herman Tarnower, a diet specialist), and John Wojtowicz (a bank robber). Wojtowicz's story was made into a movie, *Dog Day Afternoon*, starring Al Pacino. In 1987, royalties from the movie profits amounted to $84,397, but because of the Son of Sam laws, these monies have been distributed to Wojtowicz's victims rather than Wojtowicz.
Source: *Newsweek* (August 24, 1987), p. 48.

compensation for stolen or damaged property. Furthermore, the governments set relatively low limits on their liability in situations where victims suffered substantial economic losses (Lamborn, 1979; van Dijk, 1985).

In the United States, many **victim compensation programs** have been established (Coates, 1985). Among the first states to introduce such programs were California (1966), New York (1966), and Hawaii (1967). Other states have followed suit, including Rhode Island (1972), Louisiana (1976), and Tennessee (1976). Most of these programs have been created by statute. In Tennessee, the Criminal Injuries Compensation Act of 1976 identifies four classes of eligible persons for compensation:

1. A victim of a crime is eligible for compensation.
2. The victim's dependent is eligible if the victim was killed.
3. Legal representatives of the estate may be compensated for unreimbursed or unreimbursable funeral or burial expenses if the victim was killed.
4. Any person responsible for the victim may be compensated for expenses incurred as a result of the crime if the victim suffered personal injury.

Upper limits of awards to victims of crimes range from $1,500 in Colorado to no limit in New York, although the most common figures are $10,000–15,000 (Karmen, 1984:208). Table 1.4 shows state-by-state variations in victim compensation figures. Victims are seldom given the maximum compensation allowable by statute, because first, the victim must apply for damages. The application process itself is costly. Victims must spend time away from work and pay legal fees. Second, a circuit court judge must determine the extent of injury and a reasonable compensation figure. Currently, no guidelines regulate these compensation programs and the amounts to be awarded victims. Victim-witness assistance programs are similarly flawed. Few provisions exist for protecting and compensating victims who must appear later in court as witnesses against the defendants who injured them (DeGraw and Hunter, 1987).

In 1982, the President's Task Force on Victims of Crime issued several proposals for legislators to consider about the protection and treatment of crime victims (Walker, 1985:137–139). Some of these proposals involved changing laws that favor the rights of criminals. One suggestion was that states abolish the exclusionary rule, which prohibits the introduction of illegally seized evidence in a criminal trial. Another proposal was to deny bail to and detain criminal defendants considered likely to present a clear and present danger to the community or who might flee the jurisdiction. In 1987, for example, two alleged Mafia figures awaiting trial on organized crime charges challenged the legality of pretrial detention, but their arguments were rejected when the United States Supreme Court upheld the constitutionality of preventive detention.

■ EMERGING ISSUES IN CRIMINAL JUSTICE

Elderly Victims

In 1980, the United States Bureau of the Census reported that there were 25.5 million Americans age 65 or over, representing 11 percent of our total population. By the year 2,000, this figure is projected to be 32 million. Every day, at least 5,000 persons turn 65. Also, about 3,400 persons age 65 or over die annually (Harris and Cole, 1980).

TABLE 1.4 Variations in State Compensation Programs*

State†	Year started	Reporting deadline (Days)	Filing deadline (Years)	Minimum loss	Maximum award allowed	Source of funding	Repay from profits?	Must show hardship?	Grants emergency loans?	Pays attorney fees?	Pays out-of-state residents?
Alaska	'72	5	2	$ 0	$25,000	Tax	Yes	No	Yes	Yes	Yes
California	'65	None	1	100	25,000	Pen.	No	No	Yes	Yes	No
Colorado	'82	3	1½	25	1,500	Pen.	No	No	Yes	—	No
Connecticut	'79	5	2	100	10,000	Pen.	No	No	Yes	Yes	Yes
Delaware	'75	None	1	25	10,000	Pen.	No	No	No	Yes	Yes
Florida	'78	3	1	0	10,000	Pen.	No	Yes	Yes	Yes	No
Hawaii	'67	None	1½	0	10,000	Tax	No	No	Yes	Yes	Yes
Illinois	'73	3	1	200	15,000	Tax	Yes	No	No	Yes	Yes
Indiana	'78	2	3 mos.	100	10,000	Both	No	No	Yes	Yes	No
Kansas	'78	3	1	100	10,000	Tax	No	Yes	No	Yes	Yes
Kentucky	'76	2	1	100	15,000	Both	Yes	Yes	Yes	No	Yes
Maryland	'68	2	6 mos.	100	45,000	Both	No	Yes	Yes	Yes	Yes
Massachusetts	'69	2	1	100	10,000	Tax	Yes	No	No	Yes	No
Michigan	'77	2	1 mo.	100	15,000	Tax	No	Yes	Yes	Yes	No
Minnesota	'74	5	1	100	10,000	Both	Yes	No	Yes	No	Yes
Missouri	'82	2	1	200	25,000	Pen.	No	No	Yes	—	No
Montana	'78	3	1	0	25,000	Pen.	Yes	No	No	Yes	Yes
Nebraska	'79	3	2	0	10,000	Tax	Yes	No	Yes	No	Yes
Nevada	'75	5	1	100	5,000	Pen.	Yes	Yes	No	Yes	No
New Jersey	'71	90	1	100	25,000	Both	No	No	Yes	Yes	Yes
New Mexico	'81	30	1	0	12,500	Tax	No	No	Yes	—	No
New York	'66	7	1	0	No limit	Tax	Yes	Yes	Yes	Yes	Yes
North Dakota	'75	3	1	100	25,000	Tax	No	No	Yes	Yes	Yes
Ohio	'76	3	1	0	25,000	Pen.	No	No	Yes	Yes	Yes
Oklahoma	'81	3	1	0	10,000	Both	Yes	No	Yes	—	Yes
Oregon	'78	3	6 mos.	250	23,000	Tax	No	No	Yes	No	Yes
Pennsylvania	'77	3	1	100	25,000	Pen.	No	No	Yes	Yes	Yes
Tennessee	'76	2	1	100	50,000	Pen.	No	No	Yes	Yes	Yes
Texas	'80	3	6 mos.	0	50,000	Pen.	Yes	Yes	Yes	Yes	No
Virginia	'76	2	6 mos.	100	10,000	Pen.	No	Yes	Yes	Yes	Yes
Washington	'75	3	6 mos.	0	15,000	Both	No	No	No	Yes	—
West Virginia	'81	3	2	0	20,000	Pen.	No	No	No	—	Yes
Wisconsin	'77	5	2	0	12,000	Tax	No	No	Yes	Yes	Yes

Key to terms and symbols:
 Year Started: when the program began to consider claims
 Reporting Deadline: the number of days a victim can wait before telling the police about the crime
 Filing Deadline: the time limit, in years, after which applications will not be considered.
 Minimum Loss: costs must exceed this amount
 Maximum Award Allowed: upper limit for all money granted to reimburse victims or their dependents for all kinds of expenses
 Source of Funding: whether the money comes from general tax revenues or from penalties imposed on convicted offenders, or from both sources
 Repay from Profits?: whether convicted offenders have to repay victims from profits derived from the publicity surrounding the crime
 Must Show Hardship?: whether a financial means test is used to eliminate victims who can "afford" their losses
 Grants Emergency Loans?: whether immediate reimbursement is allowed, before claims are resolved
 Pays Attorney Fees?: whether the expenses of hiring a lawyer are reimbursed, in addition to other losses
 Pays Out-of-State Residents?: whether visitors and commuters are covered as well as residents
 —: information was not available.

†Georgia has had a compensation program for injured Good Samaritans since 1967. During 1983, compensation programs began to operate in Iowa, Louisiana, Rhode Island, and South Carolina. The District of Columbia and the Virgin Islands have programs, but Puerto Rico doesn't.

*From Austen et al., 1979; Gaynes, 1981; Leepson, 1982; McGillis and Smith, 1983; Meurer, 1979; NOVA, 1983.

Source: Reprinted with permission from Andrew Karmen, *Crime Victims: An Introduction to Victimology* (Monterey, Cal.: Brooks/Cole, 1984), pp. 208–209.

These figures have led experts to predict the growth of gray power. The term was coined during the 1970s, and it refers to the growing political influence of our nation's elderly. According to some experts, gray power will create greater public awareness of the problems of the aged, including provisions for improving conditions in homes for the elderly and the safety of the elderly from crime (Harris and Cole, 1980; Newman and Newman, 1984; Whitaker, 1987).

A growing area of concern is the victimization and abuse of elderly persons by their own children. The elderly may be physically assaulted, verbally insulted or degraded, starved, or deprived of needed health services. Because much elderly abuse is unreported, accurate and reliable estimates of its occurrence cannot be made. However, human services and other interested agencies report annual increases in the number of cases involving elderly abuse (Pillemer, 1987). Why would adult children abuse their elderly parents? One hypothesis is that the abuse is an outlet for financial frustration (Clayton and Baird, 1987). The cost of caring for aging parents is increasing annually, but many families cannot afford to place their parents in homes or hospitals for the elderly. Instead, the children must bear this burden. Similar to child abuse, elderly abuse will continue to be an important social and criminal issue well into the 1990s.

The elderly often suffer abuse from others besides family members. Because they are often unable to defend themselves and live alone, they are targeted by muggers and other criminals for various crimes. The actual number of elderly victims is small in proportion to victims in other age categories, but the numbers of elderly victims are growing proportionately each year. Table 1.5 shows the distribution of crimes of violence and property by age of victim.

With the exceptions of purse snatching and pocket picking, the 1983 NCS revealed that the elderly have the lowest crime rates of any age category. However, elderly victims are different in several respects from their younger counterparts. First, elderly victims pose little or no physical threat to criminal offenders who prey upon them (Goldsmith and Goldsmith, 1976). Second, elderly females are increasingly the targets of rapists because of their greater physical vulnerability (Baldassare, 1986). Third, elderly victims are often unable or unwilling to appear in court and testify against their assailants for fear of retaliation. Fourth, elderly victims heal less quickly when physically attacked. This means that their victimization is frequently more serious and of longer duration compared with that of younger victims.

TABLE 1.5 Crimes of Violence and Property per 1,000 Persons by Age of Victim, 1985

Age	Violent Crimes	Property Crimes
12–15	54.1	108.3
16–19	67.2	122.1
20–24	60.2	107.6
25–34	37.4	82.7
35–49	19.9	62.9
50–64	9.9	37.5
65 and over	4.5	17.2

Source: U.S. Department of Justice, *Sourcebook of Criminal Justice Statistics, 1986* (Washington, D.C.: U.S. Government Printing Office, 1987), p. 160.

While the elderly are the least likely age group to become crime victims, they are easy prey for muggers on the streets. They are injured easily, most don't fight back, they seldom report the incident to police, and they seldom prosecute when suspects are apprehended.

Perhaps the greatest problem confronting elderly crime victims is the fear of being victimized (Clemente and Kleiman, 1976). Threats of mugging, purse snatching, robbery, and assault make many elderly persons avoid routine trips to the store or places of entertainment ordinarily available to others.

Elderly Criminals

As the proportion of elderly increases in our population, the frequency of crimes committed by the elderly increases (Shichor, 1984; Champion, 1988). Estimates of the number of elderly who commit crimes range from 300,000 to 500,000. This is less than 1 percent of all crimes in the United States. While the elderly currently have no significant impact on the amount of crime in the United States, their numbers are growing (Hucker and Ben-Aron, 1984). The situation is problematic for judges sentencing elderly offenders. Ordinarily, a convicted robber or drug dealer might receive a 5- or 10-year sentence. For a 90-year-old thief or drug dealer, a 10-year term would be the equivalent of a death sentence. The convicted elderly offender would probably die in prison.

Currently, the criminal justice system makes no distinction between adults of different ages who commit similar offenses. If anything, judges are often more lenient in sentencing elderly offenders than in sentencing their younger counterparts when identical offenses are committed (Champion, 1988a: McCarthy and Langworthy, 1988). For example, an 80-year-old woman was arrested in Kentucky for growing one hundred marijuana plants. She claimed the marijuana helped her glaucoma and that she was growing the illegal plants for her health. The judge gave her a small fine, a lecture, and a suspended sentence. In a similar Kentucky case, a 26-year-old person was convicted of growing thirty marijuana plants and received a 3-year-sentence in the state penitentiary from the same judge who sentenced the 80-year-old woman.

Most judges attempt to dispense justice impartially for all offenders, regardless of age (with noted exceptions), but police officers are reluctant to arrest elderly citizens for offenses, even serious ones. However, by the year 2000, the sheer numbers of elderly offenders will be such that police and judicial discretion will have to be modified. There are no easy answers to the question about how to punish elderly offenders.

Child Abuse

Child abuse is any form of cruelty to the physical, moral, or mental well-being, sexual abuse or exploitation, negligent treatment, or maltreatment of a child under the age of 18 by a person who is responsible for the child's welfare (42 U.S.C., Sec. 5101-5105, 1989). In many states, child abuse is a felony and appropriate punishment is imposed upon conviction. In a few states, it is a misdemeanor. Child abuse is a problem of interest to many agencies and organizations. Health departments and child welfare services try to identify and prevent child abuse. The UCR and NCS do not collect data about child abuse, but child abuse may involve child pornography or sexual abuse, including prostitution.

At present, little is known about how much child abuse occurs nationally. Media-reports and human services agency data suggest that child abuse is an increasingly pervasive phenomenon. It is not clear whether this is because there is more child abuse today than in earlier years or public awareness of child abuse is increasing because of greater media coverage of child abuse incidents. Statistically, estimates of child abuse range from 1 million to 5 million abused children each year (Finkelhor, 1984; McNeese and Hebeler, 1977). Some of these estimates are that 95 percent of all parents have

CRIME BEAT

What is child sexual abuse? How do you decide when affectionate touching becomes abusive fondling? As reports of child sexual abuse become more frequent, we are not necessarily seeing an escalation in the incidence of this crime. Rather, more people are saying something about it. Greater public awareness of child sexual abuse has made adults and children increasingly sensitive to this phenomenon. No particular profile typifies the child molester. The kindly woman down the street, the local minister, the playground director, the owner or manager of a day school, parents, and older siblings may be child molesters and commit child sexual abuse.

Once such abuse is detected by others, however, there are prosecution problems, according to many prosecutors. Unless the defendants possess considerable tangible evidence, such as photographs of small children posing nude or performing various sex acts, prosecutors must often rely on the testimony of children themselves as witnesses. Children in their early

years, ages 3–5, often cannot or will not disclose to others what has occurred between them and child sexual abusers. They have learned to avoid talking about these "dirty" topics, or they are afraid or embarrassed.

The witness stand in court can be most traumatic for these children. Prosecutors use a wide variety of props to extract the truth of what occurred from them. Using anatomically correct dolls, they can ask children to show where they were touched and what the abuser did. Some courts have even permitted closed-circuit television cameras in rooms adjacent to the courtroom, where children give testimony without fear of being observed by large crowds of spectators. However, defense attorneys argue that their clients have a right to cross-examine child witnesses in open court. Should small children be compelled to testify in open court about sexual abuses they have suffered? Is their testimony accurate and relevant, or will it be distorted by the questions from prosecutors and defense attorneys?

The amount of child abuse in the United States is unknown. Much of it is not reported because family members are reluctant to report their spouses or relatives to police.

physically abused their children on one or more occasions in their children's lives, although this figure may be exaggerated (Gelles and Strauss, 1979).

In 1978, the Child Abuse Prevention and Treatment Act was passed. This Act provides for a national center to collect and disseminate information regarding child abuse and neglect, and the operation of a national adoption information exchange system to facilitate the adoptive placement of children (42 U.S.C., Sec. 5107, 1989). In 1981, the federal government appropriated $30 million to deal with this growing problem.

An attempt to profile child abusers has been made. Abusive parents have been described as "low in self-esteem, emotionally immature and self-centered, and feeling incompetent as parents" (Straus, Gelles, and Steinmetz, 1980). Child abuse cuts across all socioeconomic sectors and occurs in all types of families (Spinetta and Rigler, 1975).

Missing Children

Missing children make up a category that is different from abused children. Unless the child is quite young (under 5 or 6 years of age), the missing child is assumed to be a runaway. While missing infants are sometimes victims of kidnapping, the most common form of abduction occurs when divorced noncustodial parents take their children from the custodial parents without their knowledge or permission.

Missing children are any individuals under 18 years of age whose whereabouts are unknown to such individuals' legal custodians and the circumstances of disappearance are such as to indicate removal without consent of the legal custodian or with strong indications of abuse or sexual exploitation (42 U.S.C., Sec. 5772, 1986). Sexual exploitation may include prostitution as a means of surviving and paying for necessities where runaways are involved, or the exploitation may be child pornography.

Under the provisions of the Missing Children's Assistance Act of 1984, an Advisory Board on Missing Children provides information about and coordinates the efforts of child welfare agencies to locate missing children (42 U.S.C., 1986). In 1985, $10 million was appropriated by Congress for this Advisory Board. In 1984, the United States Department of Justice reported that there were over 300,000 missing children. The Department of Justice maintains computerized files of missing children and assists agencies in locating them (U.S. Department of Health and Human Services, 1984).

■ TECHNOLOGY AND THE CRIMINAL JUSTICE SYSTEM

Widespread technological developments in electronics and computer innovations have contributed to significant improvements in our ability to monitor crime and criminal activity. Initiated by the FBI in 1967, The **National Crime Information Center (NCIC)** is a central source for information on stolen vehicles, accidents, stolen property of every description, arrested persons, fingerprints, criminal offenses, and convicted offenders and their whereabouts.

High technology is now a common feature of law enforcement organizations. Routine checks for stolen vehicles among states take only a few seconds. Technological developments have improved the effectiveness of every law enforcement agency.

If a driver is stopped for a minor traffic violation in New York City, for instance, information may be quickly relayed to the NCIC and back to help the officer determine whether the driver is wanted in another jurisdiction, such as California, for a criminal offense or whether the automobile is stolen. Information exchanges between police departments occur in seconds. The computerization of record keeping applies to all jurisdictions in the United States, regardless of their remoteness or size (Johnson, 1981).

The United States Bureau of Prisons, under the direction of the attorney general of the United States, supervises the management and regulation of all federal penal and correctional institutions. Information about any federal prisoner can be retrieved immediately. All prisoner locations, projected parole dates, and other relevant prisoner information is available at the touch of a button.

The criminal justice system is becoming increasingly streamlined with the use of computerized record keeping. Although a gradual transformation to computerized record keeping has been helpful in some respects, it has created some new problems. For instance, a proliferation of rules and regulations for processing alleged offenders has created courtroom backlogs. Judges are increasingly overworked, with crowded dockets and ever-expanding legal paperwork.

■ SUMMARY

The criminal justice system of the United States is rooted in the common law of Great Britain. Common law has evolved through judicial decrees and decisions, whereas statutory laws are established through legislative action. Laws are always being changed to reflect the customs and preferences of society. Law regulates social conduct in a particular jurisdiction at a given point in time. It facilitates dispute resolution and assures the preservation of individual freedoms.

Crime is a violation of criminal laws by persons held accountable by those laws. It is also a form of deviant behavior. Crimes differ according to greater offenses, known as felonies, and lesser offenses, known as misdemeanors. Measures of crime include the Uniform Crime Reports and the National Crime Survey. These measures are only approximations of the actual amount of crime that exists in the United States. Most authorities consider them underestimates of the actual amount of crime committed.

Victims of crimes include persons of all ages. Most crime victims are young, single people, although crimes committed against the elderly are increasing. Elderly criminals are increasingly problematic, as judges, police officers, and others must decide appropriate punishments for them. Victims of crime also include children, who are frequently abused physically or mentally by their parents or legal guardians. Missing children and child abuse account for a $40 million expenditure by the federal government annually. The criminal justice system is streamlining its efforts to monitor the frequency of crime and to control it.

KEY TERMS

actus reus

child abuse

common law

concurrent jurisdiction

crime

crimes against property

crimes against the person

criminal justice system

criminology

deviance

felony

index offenses

jurisdiction

law

mala in se

mala prohibita

mens rea

misdemeanor

National Crime Information
  Center (NCIC)

National Crime Survey (NCS)

procedural laws

property crimes

statutory law

substantive laws

tort

Uniform Crime Reports
  (UCR)

victim compensation programs

Victim's Bill of Rights

victimless crimes

victimology

violent crimes

QUESTIONS FOR REVIEW

1. What is meant by common law? Who makes the laws and decides how they should be applied?
2. Differentiate between *mala in se* and *mala prohibita*.
3. Discuss how at least one of our laws has undergone change in the last two decades.
4. What are three functions of law? What are the significance of time and jurisdiction in defining the law for a given community or state?
5. Are crime and deviance the same thing? Give an example of deviant behavior that is not criminal.
6. What are some potential sources of error in crime measurement in the UCR and NCS?
7. Which measure of crime do you prefer: the Uniform Crime Reports or the National Crime Survey? Why?
8. Differentiate between crimes against persons, or violent crimes, and crimes against property, or property crimes. If a person commits robbery, which type of crime has the person committed?
9. What are some of the characteristics of crime victims in the United States? Is a victimization the same as an incident?

10. When a crime is cleared by arrest, does that necessarily mean the crime has been solved? Does the fact that crimes are cleared by arrest mean that we are cutting down the actual amount of crime in the United States? Explain.
11. What are some of the major reasons victims do not report crimes to police officers?
12. What crimes are committed by elderly criminals? Is there any reason to believe that crimes committed against the elderly are more serious than crimes committed against younger victims?
13. What is child abuse? What is the government doing about it? Why is the issue of missing children of concern to authorities in the criminal justice system?
14. How is the bureaucratization of our criminal justice system both a help and a hindrance to effective law enforcement and processing of offenders in the courts?

SUGGESTED READINGS

Fairchild, Erica S., and Vincent J. Webb (1985). *The politics of crime and criminal justice.* Beverly Hills, Cal.: Sage.

Karmen, Andrew (1984). *Crime victims: An introduction to victimology.* Monterey, Cal.: Brooks/ Cole.

Newman, Graeme R. (1980). *Crime and deviance: A comparative perspective.* Beverly Hills, Cal.: Sage.

O'Brien, Robert M. (1985). *Crime and victimization data.* Beverly Hills, Cal.: Sage.

Sheley, Joseph F. (1985). *America's crime problem: An introduction to criminology.* Monterey, Cal.: Wadsworth Publishing Co.

Criminal Justice and the Influence of Criminology

CHAPTER

2

■ INTRODUCTION

About 11:30 P.M., Mrs. Lloyd was awakened by Leonore's crying, "Oh, God, John. You're going to kill me. Help, Mother. Help. John is killing me." Mrs. Lloyd jumped out of bed, opened the door, and saw Leonore in bed and John standing over her, his right hand raised and his left hand on her throat. When Mrs. Lloyd got her daughter Leonore to the hospital, she was dead. The doctor counted forty-three stab wounds on her body—nineteen in the chest, five on the face, five on the right hand, thirteen on the left hand, and one on the left thigh. There was a laceration of a large vein and there were two lacerations on the trachea, any one of which could have caused her death. (*Government of Virgin Islands v. Lake,* 1966). John Lake, husband of Leonore Lake, pled not guilty to a charge of first-degree murder because he claimed his state of mind ruled out the criminal element of premeditation. He was subsequently convicted of first-degree murder, and his conviction was upheld by the United States Court of Appeals.

Such bizarre events are abundant in our society. We often refer to these events by media-generated labels, as the "Manson family murders," the Tylenol killer, the McDonald's massacre, the Hinkley affair. The common thread of these tragic incidents is the question, Why?

For several centuries, scientists have wrestled with the question of why people commit crime. This chapter describes several theories for a criminal act, or an *actus reus.* In order for an act to be defined as criminal, it must be accompanied by criminal intent, or *mens rea.* There are exceptions, however. Corporations may be held strictly liable for harm to others. For example, if power companies make inadequate provisions for the safety of citizens when they are installing high-tension power lines in remote areas, children may climb power poles and be electrocuted. The blame is ordinarily placed on the power companies for failure to take precautionary measures against such occurrences. Furthermore, if those under the age of consent agree to sexual intercourse, criminal acts may be alleged without the offenders having the actual intent to do wrong. In the case of John Lake, was the *actus reus* of stabbing his wife, Leonore, accompanied by the requisite *mens rea,* or guilty or criminal intent to inflict wounds sufficient to cause death? The courts determined that the circumstances of the killing (forty-three wounds) were sufficient to infer that Lake possessed the necessary *mens rea.*

However, an important contrast is made between the criminal justice system's handling of Lake in determining his guilt or innocence, and the criminologist's explanation for Lake's behavior. The criminal justice system processed Lake for his crime. The criminologist might attempt to account for Lakes' actions by asking questions about Lake's sanity or mental state when the crime was committed. This chapter looks at several explanations for criminal behavior that have influenced the criminal justice system in different ways.

■ THEORIES OF CRIMINAL BEHAVIOR

A **theory** is a set of assumptions that attempts to explain and predict relationships between phenomena. The primary functions of theories are to explain and predict.

Conformity comes in many forms. So does deviance. The influence of peer group associations may lead members to commit deviant acts or adhere strictly to legal codes.

Regarding crime rates, we are interested in explaining why certain crimes are committed. We are also interested in predicting the occurrence of crime. Criminologists conduct statistical studies to identify high-crime areas, or situations most conducive to crime, such as dark streets or bad neighborhoods. If someone robs a bank, criminologists might theorize that the person needed the money or that the person was mentally ill and didn't know what he or she was doing. If an adolescent joins a delinquent gang and commits burglaries or engages in gang fights, criminologists might say that this adolescent had a poor home life, was not doing well in school, or needed peer companionship and esteem. Thus, several theories may account for criminal behaviors.

Questions asked by criminologists include, To what extent does criminological research influence juries in determining the guilt or innocence of defendants accused of crimes? Do judges adjust the leniency or harshness of the sentences they impose according to what they believe prompted the offender to commit the crime? Are alternative punishments influenced by criminological theories emphasizing free will and evil intent of criminals or their need for medical help or social assistance? A judge who believes criminal behaviors were inspired by an offender's environment or social circumstances may hospitalize rather than incarcerate the offender. However, a judge who believes an offender acted maliciously, with the intent to cause harm to others, may impose incarceration in a jail or prison for the crimes committed.

Experts disagree about the objectives of corrections. Some see corrections as rehabilitative, while others see it as purely punitive. Yet others see the objective of corrections as a deterrent to crime. There are those who believe that corrections embraces all of these objectives. Understanding the causes of crime and criminal behavior is useful in designing effective strategies for the corrections process.

The criminal justice system of the United States, including the statutes applicable to sanctioning criminal offenders, has evolved over several centuries. The influence of various theories of criminal behavior is apparent. Theories of criminal behavior can be grouped into three general categories that stress different causal factors: (1) biological theories; (2) psychological theories; and (3) sociological, or sociocultural, theories.

Between 1890 and 1990, there has been a major theoretical shift in the thinking of criminologists about why people commit crimes. Early theories of crime emphasized factors inside the individual. Bad blood, malfunctioning glands, physical deformities, criminal personality, criminal drives or tendencies, possession by evil spirits, heredity, and mental illness are some of the many internal concepts advanced to explain deviant behavior generally and criminal behavior specifically (Hooton, 1939; Mednick and Volavka, 1980; Montagu, 1968; Yochelson and Samenow, 1977).

During the 1940s and 1950s, some criminologists changed their thinking about criminal behavior to phenomena occurring outside the individual, such as social status (sociocultural position), group pressures and gang conformity, antisocial criminal patterns, association with criminals, labeling of oneself as criminal, or learning to be a criminal (Cohen, 1955; Nettler, 1984; Thornton, James, and Doerner, 1982). While this shift has not been overtly acknowledged, the emergence of violent delinquent gangs and certain adult offenders have undermined existing internal explanations of criminal behavior. Another indication of this shift is the subtle change in the research literature that explains crime and describes criminality. Although interpretations of trends in the criminological research literature are largely impressionistic, today's explanations of crime emphasize causal factors that differ from those emphasized in the 1920s and 1930s.

This shift does *not* mean that professionals have abandoned inside explanations for outside ones. Rather, external theories are currently more popular than internal theories. This popularity may be seen in the treatment of criminal offenders. Manipulating the external environment of criminals seems easier than modifying their genetic structure, driving out evil spirits, or erasing criminal propensities, whatever they might be. Of course, there are other explanations for this shift. Recent theoretical developments in sociology and psychology have emphasized the importance of social or external factors in determining criminal behavior.

In addition, criminologists have learned more about genetic makeup, the role of diet in personality, and the medical control of various psychological disorders. Interestingly, these and similar developments have recently renewed interest in some of the more popular internal explanations for criminal behavior. For example, sociobiologists believe that body chemistry and genetic makeup are crucial in determining all human behavior, including deviance and criminal conduct (Jeffrey, 1978; Wilson, 1975; Wilson and Herrnstein, 1985). **Sociobiology** is the scientific study of the causal relations between genetic structure and social behavior. Some of the treatment programs currently used for offenders are based, in part, upon this biological explanation for criminal behavior.

An important issue common to all of the theories of criminal behavior, regardless of their intuitive value, innovativeness, or general interest, is whether they can explain and predict criminal behavior. How can each theory be applied? Can effective rehabilitative programs be developed for criminals? Can any of these theories be used to control criminal behavior or prevent crime? Such practical questions are often used to judge the *adequacy* of theory.

Some of the theories of criminal behavior may seem farfetched in view of current scientific knowledge, but their impact may be evaluated by their influence on correctional policies and other criminal justice issues. Thus, while a theory of criminal behavior may be refuted and found to be false, it nevertheless may have important implications for the policies of various agencies within the criminal justice system. For instance, one theory of criminal behavior shown to be false is that heredity transmitted criminal characteristics among generations, but in the 1930s and 1940s, thousands of state and federal prisoners were sterilized because it was believed that their sterilization would prevent the birth of new generations of criminal offspring.

Evaluations of theories are not limited to strictly pragmatic criteria. Sometimes, explanations of criminal behavior are abstract and provide contextual backgrounds for other, more practical theories. For instance, sociologists say that the social class structure of the United States explains certain kinds of crimes. Crime fluctuates among neighborhoods as well as social classes, so evidently, there is *some* connection between the social class structure and crime. Because major changes in the social class structure of the United States that affect crime or crime rates are unlikely to occur soon, criminologists use social class as an explanation for crime and crime trends, and police officers spend more of their patrol hours in less affluent neighborhoods where higher crime rates are observed.

Biological Theories

Biological theories of criminal behavior include (1) abnormal physical structure, (2) hereditary criminal behavior, and (3) biochemical disturbances.

Abnormal Physical Structure. One biologically based set of theories attempts to link **abnormal physical structure** with criminal behaviors. A pioneer of the school of thought that criminals may be identified by their abnormal or unusual physical characteristics was the Italian physician Cesare Lombroso (1835–1909). He coined the expression, "born criminals." Lombroso said that (1) criminals are, by birth, a distinct type; (2) this type can be recognized by asymmetrical craniums, long lower jaws, flattened noses, scanty beards, and low sensitivity to pain; (3) these characteristics do not themselves cause crime but assist in our identification of personalities disposed toward criminal behavior; (4) such persons cannot refrain from criminal behavior except under unusual social circumstances; and (5) different physical features are associated with different kinds of crime (Vorenberg, 1981:33–34).

Originally, Lombroso argued that 100 percent of the prison population was comprised of born criminals, but in subsequent years, he modified this figure to about 40 percent. His treatise on the subject was published in 1876 and was expanded into three volumes (Lombroso, 1918). His views later were known as the Italian school, or the positive school, because direct empirical indicators of criminal tendencies could be identified (that is, cranium shape, jaw angle, body hair, and so forth) compared with other speculation about criminality.

Lombroso's studies of Italian prison inmates led him to observe that many had long, sloping foreheads, pointed ears, narrow or shifty eyes, receding chins, and overly long arms. Subsequent comparisons of other prisoners with the population at large have revealed no significant differences in physical characteristics between criminals and noncriminals. However, an explanation for Lombroso's views about physique and criminal behavior is that often, persons with odd appearance are rejected by others. This rejection may lead them to follow deviant or criminal paths.

Lombroso's views still enjoy popularity in the media whenever particularly bizarre events occur. For instance, the late Truman Capote wrote a nonfictional work entitled

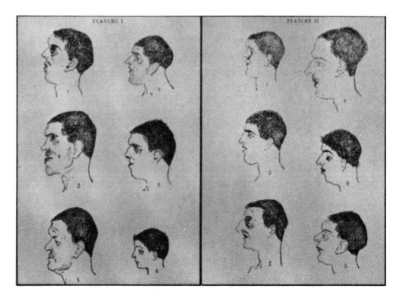

Lombroso emphasized physical features as indicators of criminal propensities.

In Cold Blood. This book detailed the murder of an entire Kansas family by two drifters. The men were apprehended, tried, convicted of murder, and executed. At or about the time of their execution, their photographs appeared in several popular magazines. The writer of one article called the reader's attention to the "fact" that one of the murderers had a face "made up from two parts where the two parts did not quite match up with one another." The article drew attention to portions of that murderer's photograph, showing that one eye was not level with the other, the mouth curved down on one side and up on the other, and the ears were unevenly matched.

A popular outgrowth of Lombroso's positivist thinking was Sheldon's concept of various body types. Sheldon (1949) classified persons into three distinct categories: (1) **endomorphs** (fat, soft, plump, jolly), (2) **ectomorphs** (thin, sensitive, delicate), and (3) **mesomorphs** (strong, muscular, aggressive, tough). Sheldon wrote extensively about the behavioral characteristics of each body type, eventually developing crude indices from which generalizations about criminal behavior could be made. He said that ectomorphs tend to commit forgery, fraud, or burglary (passive, nonviolent crimes),

A DAY IN COURT

One of the most infamous studies in criminology was conducted by Professor Henry H. Goddard in 1912 (Goddard, 1912; Nassi and Abramowitz, 1976). Engaging in some questionable research, Goddard conducted a study of Martin Kallikak, allegedly a Revolutionary War hero. According to Goddard, Kallikak came from a "religious, God-fearing, and prominent" family, went to war, and had an illicit sexual union with a feebleminded girl. Later, he returned home and married a Quaker woman of "proper upbringing." These two sexual unions produced two distinctly different family lines.

The descendents of the feebleminded girl were allegedly thieves and criminals of every variety, while the descendents of the Quaker woman were allegedly wholesome, virtuous, and socially prominent conformists. Goddard's conclusion was that bad genes from the feebleminded girl produced one lineage, while good genes from the Quaker woman produced the other lineage. Subsequent reexamination of Goddard's information by later researchers revealed that he had invented a great deal of the history of both lineages. His pronouncements about the genetic transmission of good and bad behaviors were based largely upon his own imagination.

In spite of a lack of scientific support for Goddard's claims and the work of others linking criminal behavior with heredity, several states made significant policy decisions that appeared to be influenced by such studies and beliefs. For instance, Oklahoma established an Habitual Offender Sterilization Act, which required the automatic sterilization of all offenders convicted of three or more felonies. In 1942, the constitutionality of this act was challenged in the case of *Skinner v. Oklahoma.* In this case, Arthur Skinner was convicted of a third felony (larceny) and incarcerated. He was scheduled for sterilization but appealed to higher courts, arguing that such an act was a violation of certain constitutional rights. The United States Supreme Court eventually heard Skinner's case and ruled in his favor. Oklahoma was forced to abandon its sterilization law. Other states with similar laws, including Virginia, were obligated to abolish them as well.

while mesomorphs tend to commit robbery, rape, murder, assault, and other physically demanding crimes. Sheldon believed that body type was a *cause* of particular types of criminal conduct. Subsequent studies and extensive research by criminologists and others have failed to support Sheldon's theory.

Hereditary Criminal Behavior. The theory of **heredity** as a cause of criminal conduct suggests the inheritance of certain physical and behavioral characteristics from parents or ancestors. According to this theory, whether people become criminals depends upon their hereditary background. If one's ancestors were cattle rustlers, thieves, or rapists, then the offspring would also tend to be cattle rustlers, thieves, or rapists. Little scientific evidence exists supporting this theory.

A more recent heredity-based theory of criminal behavior is the **XYY syndrome.** *X* and *Y* are labels assigned to the human sex chromosomes. Males are *XY,* while females are *XX.* The sex chromosomes, *X* and *Y,* are inherited from the mother and father. The father transmits the *Y,* or aggressive, chromosome, while the mother transmits the *X,* or passive, chromosome. Occasionally, infants are born with an *XYY* (doubly aggressive?) chromosomatic pattern.

In the 1960s, researchers were intrigued by the discovery that Richard Speck had an *XYY* chromosomatic pattern. At that time, Speck was in prison for the brutal murder of eight student nurses in Chicago. Could this extra *Y* chromosome have caused his violent behavior? Geneticists have investigated the *XYY* syndrome in selected, captive-audience situations: prisons (McClearn, 1969; Mednick and Volavka, 1980; Shah and Roth, 1974). Their studies show that (1) there appear to be more *XYY* people in the criminal population compared with the general population and (2) less than 5 percent of the prison population has the *XYY* chromosome pattern (Shah and Roth, 1974). Thus, the *XYY* syndrome is not a consistent cause of criminal behavior (Sarbin and Miller, 1970).

Biochemical Disturbances. A third group of biologically based theories of criminal behavior focuses upon biochemical disturbances and glandular malfunctions for inducing criminal acts. The thyroid, adrenal, pituitary, and hypothalamus glands have been linked with different kinds of aggressive and antisocial behavior. Glands have been shown to control metabolism, growth, and activity levels. Hyperactivity, or abnormally active behavior, is often associated with oversecretions or undersecretions of various hormones (Hippchen, 1981; Yaryura-Tobias and Neziroglu, 1975).

Recent medical developments have led to a greater understanding of our biochemical functions and to the development of drugs and synthetic chemicals that can control abnormal behavior. Thorazine is administered to mental patients to control various psychotic disorders. Valium (diazepam), an antidepressant, is used to treat severe alcohol withdrawal or to help patients manage severe anxiety or stress. These products alter hormonal states and permit some regulation of deviant and criminal behavior.

Psychological Theories

Another set of theories about criminal conduct is based in psychology, the study of individual behavior. By studying individual behavior, psychologists try to explain the inner workings of the mind. Since various components of the criminal justice system must determine criminal intent and a defendant's mental competence to stand trial, prosecutors and defense attorneys often turn to psychologists for help. Psychologists and psychiatrists, physicians who specialize in treating mental disorders, are often asked to examine defendants and give their expert testimony in court. Psychological theories of criminal behavior have also influenced correctional and rehabilitative programs. Psychological counselors and psychiatrists play key roles in contemporary criminal rehabilitative therapy. This section presents three psychological theories. They include (1) psychoanalytic theory, (2) cognitive development theory, and (3) social learning theory.

Psychoanalytic Theory. **Psychoanalytic theory** was created by Sigmund Freud (1856–1939), an Austrian neurologist. Frustrated by the primitive technology of his day, Freud tried to explain the human personality and mental disorders through the interaction of four concepts: (1) the id, (2) the ego, (3) the superego, and (4) the libido. The **id** is the "I want" associated with the behavior of infants. Getting 2-year-olds to *share* their jellybeans or ice cream is nearly impossible. As children grow, they learn that the id cannot always be satisfied. They cannot have everything they want. Therefore, the id is eventually controlled by the **ego,** which embodies society's standards. As children mature into adolescence, moral values are incorporated into their personalities. Moral values are the domain of the **superego.** The **libido** is the sex drive, which Freud believed was inborn.

Freud explained criminal behavior as a function of an inadequately developed ego, the controlling mechanism for the id. When persons fail to control their impulses and disregard the rights and feelings of others, their aggressive behaviors often follow deviant or criminal paths. Thus, according to Freud, rape may be the result of an uncontrollable libido, and theft may be the result of a poorly developed ego.

Some counseling centers and rehabilitative agencies work with offenders to assist them in improving their self-concepts as well as their abilities to function normally around others. They encourage offenders to talk out their problems and exchange personal information with others through group therapy and encounter sessions in order to gain greater control over their behaviors.

Cognitive Development Theory. **Cognitive development theory** stresses cognitive development, or a learning process involving various stages. Jean Piaget (1896–1980) was one of the first to stress the importance of cognitive stages of development and the idea that all "normal individuals pass through the same sequential periods in the growth or maturing of their ability to think or to gain knowledge and awareness of themselves and their environment" (VanderZanden, 1984:116–117). As children move through various stages of development, they acquire awareness of people, objects, and standards of behavior or judgments of right and wrong (Boehm, 1962; Piaget, 1948).

Kohlberg (1981) modified and expanded Piaget's notions of cognitive development. Kohlberg described three levels and six stages in the development of a person's moral judgment. According to Kohlberg, the three levels (**preconventional, conventional, and postconventional**) and six stages reflect different relationships between the individual and society (VanderZanden, 1984:123). See Table 2.1 for Kohlberg's levels and stages of development.

Kohlberg says that very young children, some adolescents, and many criminals are in the preconventional stage of development. Thus, psychologists supporting this

TABLE 2.1 Kohlberg's Stages in Children's Development

Level	Stage
Level one:	Preconventional
	1. *Obedience and punishment orientation.* Child obeys rules to avoid punishment.
	2. *Naive hedonistic and instrumental orientation.* Child's actions motivated by desire for reward.
Level two:	Conventional
	3. *Good boy morality.* Child seeks approval of others.
	4. *Law and authority maintain morality.* Child does his or her duty.
Level three:	Postconventional
	5. *Morality of contract, individual rights.* Child desires to protect society.
	6. *Morality of individual principles of conscience.* Child is concerned with self-condemnation for violating own principles.

Source: From L. Kohlberg, "The Development of Children's Orientations Toward a Moral Order," *Vita Humana* (June 1963), pp. 11–33. Reprinted with permission of S. Karger AG, Basel.

theory associate criminal behavior with inadequate moral development during childhood. Some gender bias is inherent in Kohlberg's scheme, because conventional role conformity encourages males in our culture to acquire protective and aggressive behaviors and females to be more submissive and nurturing.

Yochelson and Samenow (1976) devised a different perspective. These researchers reject the notion that criminal behavior is the direct result of one's environment. Rather, they believe that those who become criminals do so because they want to. At a very early age, some youths seek associations with others who are delinquent. The excitement of committing delinquent acts becomes a self-perpetuating influence in their lives. As these youths graduate to more serious offenses as adults, the same excitement urges them to carry out criminal acts.

Yochelson and Samenow believe that free will rather than one's environment determines whether a criminal career pattern is pursued. Thus, if criminal behavior is to be decreased or eliminated by any conventional treatment program, it is imperative that psychologists and others try to dissuade delinquents from thinking about committing crimes. Changing their thoughts about crime will lead to a cessation of their criminal behaviors. Unfortunately, Yochelson and Samenow do not answer the question of why some people think about engaging in criminal acts. In short, little support exists for their position. However, their theorizing is an interesting contrast with the work of Kohlberg and others who stress environmental experiences as primary ingredients for stimulating criminal behavior.

Experts disagree about the causes of criminality. One theory is that some children who eventually become criminals fail to make conventional role adjustments at crucial periods in their early years. Another theory is that some children think about committing crimes and that their future criminality is unrelated to developmental stages or adjustments.

Social Learning Theory. Applied to criminology, **social learning theory** states that criminals learn their behavior by modeling the behaviors of others who are criminal. In social learning theory, deviant conduct and criminal conduct, as well as conventional conduct, stem from the process of reinforcement. In external reinforcement, people perceive others being rewarded by goods, money, or social status for conforming to certain rules or being punished for deviating from those same rules. External reinforcement is a crucial social mechanism, but people also derive reinforcement from internal sources. In internal reinforcement, people engage in self-punishment when they perceive themselves behaving badly and reward themselves when they perceive themselves conforming or behaving appropriately.

Reinforcement comes from the environments in which people are socialized, either conventional or unconventional. Those who observe criminals being rewarded may be motivated to emulate their behavior. Likewise, people who do not fit in with certain social groups, are unsuccessful in adapting to social situations, or perceive little or no reward for their conventional behavior may try other behaviors. If such conduct is criminal and it yields rewards from others who are criminal, the rewards can dissuade them from adopting more conventional modes of behavior.

Social learning theory fails to explain the roles played by close friends, family, and other agencies of socialization in modifying conventional or unconventional conduct. It stresses psychological factors and alludes to certain stimulus-response behavior patterns. Its main value is that it focuses attention upon the social contexts in which conventional or unconventional conduct is acquired. However, it does not adequately explain the process of acquiring these behaviors.

Sociological and Sociocultural Theories

Sociological and sociocultural theories are as diverse as psychological theories. There is considerable interplay between the psychological and sociological perspectives. Sociologists, however, focus more closely upon the social processes involved in criminal conduct, as well as the importance of social structure. They believe that forces or processes in the external social environment lead people to commit criminal acts. Sociological theories stress external forces, in contrast to the internal forces empha- sized by biological and psychological theories. Popular sociological theories of criminal behavior include (1) differential association; (2) anomie; (3) labeling; (4) social control; and (5) conflict/Marxist theory.

Differential Association Theory. The sociologist Edwin Sutherland (1893–1950) is credited with formulating perhaps the best-known sociological theory of crime. Sutherland's theory, known as **differential association,** was formally presented in the 1920s, and a few researchers still use it to explain some forms of adult crime (Fannin, 1984). Sutherland used the differential association concept to explain the process by which persons become criminals. As the name implies, association with criminals is an important part of this process.

However, it is an oversimplification of Sutherland's theory to state that simple association with criminals causes a person to become a criminal. The theory is more complex than that. In some respects, Sutherland's theory is an outgrowth of cultural transmission theory developed by Shaw and McKay (1929), who believed that criminal behavior patterns are transmitted in much the same manner as culture is transmitted, through socialization. **Socialization** is learning through contact with others, or social learning.

Expanding on the work of Shaw and McKay, Sutherland outlined a multidimensional social interaction process that would induce a person to adopt criminal behaviors. The dimensions of differential association theory include (1) frequency, (2) duration, (3) priority, and (4) intensity. The transmission of deviant and criminal cultural values and behaviors occurs in a social context. In this context, the potential criminal has frequent contact with criminals. These frequent contacts are of some lasting duration. Priority and intensity are more elusive concepts in Sutherland's scheme. Priority refers to behavior learned in early childhood. This persists throughout a person's life to reinforce criminal behaviors whenever associations with criminals occur. Intensity is the degree of emotional attachment to either conventional or criminal groups and the prestige allocated to each. Thus, criminal behaviors acquired at an early age and reinforced through frequent and lengthy emotional attachments with one or more criminals are seen as primary contributing factors.

Professionals involved in corrections programs have shown some respect for Sutherland's differential association ideas over the years. In some jurisdictions, first offenders are not placed in the same cells with repeat offenders. However, this policy is a luxury, and it is relinquished when incarceration rates are high and prison funding is low. Thus, because of overcrowding, penal authorities sometimes mix all inmates, regardless of the nature or seriousness of the crimes they have committed. This overcrowding has caused some observers to label prisons and jails as "institutions of higher criminal learning," where more seasoned criminals teach first offenders how to avoid being apprehended next time.

Critics of differential association theory have said that Sutherland's terms are difficult to define and understand. What is meant by an intense relation? How frequent is frequent? Also, Sutherland's theory does not explain all types of criminal conduct. Although Sutherland intended his theory to account for most criminal behavior, numerous exceptions to his scheme caused him to believe that additional factors, such as opportunity and individual needs, are equally important. Therefore, he eventually adopted multiple-factor theoretical explanations for criminal conduct and gave less attention to differential association.

Anomie Theory, or Innovative Adaptation. The use of *anomie* in anomie theory is a misnomer. *Anomie* literally means normlessness, or a condition when the norms or behavioral expectations are unknown, undefined, or in conflict. People seldom experience true normlessness.

Robert K. Merton (1938, 1957) is credited with developing anomie theory, which was originally proposed by the French sociologist Emile Durkheim (1858–1917). **Anomie theory** states that all people in society are taught to pursue certain culturally approved goals. These people are also taught socially acceptable means by which these goals may be achieved. Merton's theory of anomie emphasized ways that persons adapt to goal attainment and the means they use to achieve these goals. As Merton has said, persons either accept or reject the goals of their society. Also, they either accept or reject the approved means to achieve those goals. Table 2.2 shows Merton's modes of adaptation and the categories he subsequently developed and described.

According to Merton, conformity is the most common adaptation. In conformity, people accept culturally approved goals and socially approved means to achieve them. Thus, most people who want a new car or a new home will work patiently at socially acceptable jobs to eventually acquire these possessions.

On the other hand, some people accept the culturally approved goals but reject the means to achieve those goals. For instance, a trustee at a state prison once confided that he had been an A student at a large California university. He was majoring in business administration and planned a business career. At the end of his third year, however, he decided the educational process was too slow and that his calculations of future earnings were too low for his particular desires. He said, "I decided that to get what I want fast, I've got to have a lot of money. The best place to get a lot of money

TABLE 2.2 Merton's Modes of Adaptation

Mode of Adaptation	Cultural Goals	Socially Approved Means
Conformity	+	+
Innovation	+	−
Ritualism	−	+
Retreatism	−	−
Rebellion	+ and −	+ and −

+ equals acceptance of goals or means

− equals rejection of goals or means

Source: Adapted with permission of The Free Press, A Division of Macmillan Inc. from SOCIAL THEORY AND SOCIAL STRUCTURE by Robert K. Merton. Copyright © 1957 by The Free Press, renewed 1985 by Robert K. Merton.

fast is a bank. So I started robbing banks." His adaptation to the goals-means relation was innovation. His criminal behaviors were the innovative means that he substituted to achieve his culturally approved goals. Merton's theory of anomie is particularly relevant for explaining property crimes, such as burglary and larceny. The people who commit these crimes may want material wealth or expensive possessions but be unwilling or unable to earn money through socially acceptable occupations. Thus, they seek goal attainment through innovative means.

Acording to Merton, much criminal behavior is innovative behavior, and this mode of adaptation was the focus of his theory of anomie. However, Merton's theory also tried to explain drug abusers and alcohol users, who have been labeled as retreatists because they withdraw from others and reject the culturally approved goals as well as the means to achieve them. Such people may be unemployed, vagrant, or otherwise indifferent to achieving the culturally approved goals sought by others. Other adaptation forms included in Merton's scheme are ritualism (rejecting the goals, accepting the means) and rebellion (accepting and rejecting some of the goals and means and substituting new goals and means). Ritualists include people who conclude that they will never have the nice home and new car but nevertheless work at their socially approved jobs until retirement. In contrast, rebels reject the goals and the means and are interested in creating new societal goals through revolution or rebellion.

Merton's theory is economically based and concerned with gaining access to certain success goals. Some critics say that Merton made an erroneous assumption that poor persons are more prone toward criminal behavior than rich persons (Thio, 1975, 1983). Furthermore, Merton has not explained the embezzlement or tax fraud of successful business executives (Thio, 1983). It might be, however, that such criminals are simply seeking culturally approved goals through innovative means. Another criticism is that the theory does not explain noneconomic crimes, such as aggravated assault and rape. However, anomie is not intended to explain these offenses. Finally, some critics have said that Merton's scheme does not deal with criminal behavior as a process (Gibbons, 1968).

Merton's scheme presents several adaptations that persons can make in attaining goals and choosing the means to achieve those goals. It is a *static* theory rather than a dynamic one. Merton's innovative mode is a more or less automatic response that is almost always regarded as deviant or criminal. By comparison, differential association theory analyzes such dynamic processes as duration and intensity of social associations that encourage and condone criminal acts.

Sutherland's differential association theory about white-collar criminals and Merton's innovative mode of adaptation may be linked theoretically to the **theory of opportunity.** According to this theory, middle- and upper-class persons have more opportunities to gain access to and achieve success goals, whereas lower-class persons lack these opportunities. Therefore, lower-class persons tend to achieve success by achieving certain objectives that are respected by other criminals.

Labeling Theory. A third popular sociological theory of criminal behavior is labeling theory. It is associated with the work of Edwin Lemert (1951), although Howard S. Becker (1973) and John Kitsuse (1962) have also been credited among its early advocates. **Labeling theory** is concerned with the social definitions of criminal acts rather than the criminal acts themselves. Labeling theory attempts to answer at least two questions: (1) What is the process whereby persons become labeled as criminals or deviants? and (2) How does such labeling influence the persons labeled as deviant? The basic assumptions of labeling theory are that (1) no act is inherently criminal, (2) persons become criminals by social labeling or definition, (3) all persons at one time or another conform to and deviate from laws, (4) getting caught begins the labeling process, (5) the person defined as criminal will develop a criminal self-definition, and (6) the person will seek others similarly defined and develop a criminal subculture (Bernstein, Kelly, and Doyle, 1977; Schrag, 1971; Wellford, 1975; VanderZanden, 1984:206).

According to Lemert (1967), there are two types of deviation: (1) primary and (2) secondary. **Primary deviations** involve violations of law that can be and frequently are overlooked. College students who pull pranks, such as disassembling the university president's car and reassembling it on the roof of the women's dormitory, are mildly chided by police rather than arrested for criminal vehicular theft. **Secondary deviations** occur when violations of the law have become incorporated into a person's life-style or behavior pattern. Usually, by the time secondary deviations have occurred, the offender has accepted the label of deviant or criminal and is on the road toward joining a criminal subculture.

Slum areas of large cities and large, run-down apartment complexes are considered by some criminologists as high-crime areas and logical breeding grounds for delinquents and criminals.

Many labeling theorists say they are not interested in explaining criminal acts. Instead, they want to explain the social process of labeling and reactions to being labeled. Nevertheless, a strong explanatory element persists. The labeling theorist is saying, in effect, that persons who react to social labeling by defining themselves as deviant or criminal will not only engage in further criminal activity but also seek out others like themselves and form criminal subcultures. This subculture development is the equivalent of rejecting the rejectors (Schrag, 1971).

Some evidence of the influence of labeling may be found by examining arrest rates by race and social class. Labeling theorists argue that the most likely targets of labeling are persons who are young, nonwhite, and of lower socioeconomic status. Such persons are most likely to be labeled by police and others as deviant or inclined to be criminal. Statistics support this point. While blacks and Hispanics make up 18 percent of the population, for instance, they account for up to 60 percent of all arrests for murder and rape and 65 percent of those arrested for assault and robbery. Persons in the lower socioeconomic classes account for nearly 90 percent of all murder and rape arrests. Again, arrests do not necessarily mean that convictions will be obtained; not everyone who commits crimes will be arrested, and others may be charged with lesser crimes. For example, whites who commit rape may be arrested and charged with assault.

Researchers disagree about the meaningfulness of arrest rates and their relation to social class and race. Some say that social class is an important predictor of criminal behavior; that is, lower-class persons will commit more crimes than upper-class persons (Braithwaite, 1981; Thornberry and Farnworth, 1982). Others argue that there is no association between criminal behavior and social class or that the relation is a weak one at best (Johnson, 1980; Krohn et al., 1980). Instead, they claim that arrest rates are a function of the area a person lives in. More arrests tend to be made in high-crime areas, which are the same areas that tend to attract larger numbers of police, who may be more inclined to take advantage of persons of lower socioeconomic status. When compared to middle- or upper-class citizens, lower-class individuals have fewer resources and lack the legal sophistication needed to resist or to retaliate within the legal system (VanderZanden, 1984:206).

On the surface, labeling theory is an external explanation for criminal behavior. Criminal behavior is whatever lawmakers—an external source—say it is. A criminal is whomever a society labels as criminal. An offender's acceptance of the label of criminal merely completes the process and leads the offender to seek the companionship of others who are similarly labeled. In some respects, labeling theory involves interplay between the social and psychological realms. An offender reacts to social definitions, interprets or defines himself or herself as deviant or criminal, and forms a subculture with others in an effort to win acceptance and preserve a sense of self-worth.

However, labeling theory fails to account for the people who either reject deviant or criminal labels or successfully unlabel themselves as deviants or criminals. It also inadequately explains occasional offenders, or weekend deviants, persons leading two morally different lives by associating with diverse community elements. For instance, a socially prominent woman, the Mayflower madam, operated a high-class brothel for wealthy clientele in New England for several years, effectively concealing this double life from her close friends. When detected and arrested for prostitution and operating a call-girl service, she treated the notoriety as inconvenient rather than embarrassing.

A DAY IN COURT

Labeling theory has attracted considerable attention, especially from the courts and certain correctional institutions. The late J. Edgar Hoover wanted to prevent adult crime by attacking juvenile delinquency. He believed that most adult offenders had had previous records as juvenile delinquents. Therefore, reducing juvenile delinquency would be tantamount to reducing overall adult crime. Decreasing juvenile delinquency was given high priority during his administration. Under his direction, the FBI generated considerable information that it made available to educators and law enforcement agencies across the nation. Some of the material that he supplied to teachers concerned the importance of *not* labeling an adolescent as delinquent. Among the materials provided were articles about how certain jurisdictions dealt with juveniles who had committed relatively minor offenses.

One article furnished by Hoover described an incident involving two young boys who let the air out of tires on seventy-five automobiles in a New York City parking lot. The lot attendant caught the boys and held them for the police. In that particular jurisdiction, juvenile offenders were processed through an adolescent court. In fact, the adolescent court wasn't a court at all. The boys were taken to the home of the juvenile judge. The boys' parents were summoned, and in a very informal meeting with the boys, the judge determined their punishment: Return to the parking lot with hand pumps and pump up all of the flat tires. After the boys worked for several hours with the pumps, the police finally permitted them to use an air compressor to remedy the remaining flats. The boys had had their punishment.

According to Hoover, the good thing about the whole incident was that the boys avoided the formal trappings of the juvenile courtroom: black-robed judge, a prosecution, a defense, and a listing of criminal charges. Especially important was the fact that the boys avoided the label of delinquency. Only the juvenile judge maintained records of the adolescent court proceedings, and these never became a matter of official record. This interrupted the deviant career pattern outlined by Lemert and Becker by eliminating any formal record keeping that would further label them as delinquents. Avoiding the taint of being labeled delinquents probably did much to deter those boys from committing subsequent delinquent acts. Of course, the logistical problems involved in administering such an informal program for dealing with youthful offenders are staggering.

Finally, persons who engage in victimless crimes, or crimes where the victim is a willing participant (such as gambling and prostitution) seem to escape the psychological effects of being labeled deviant. The theory does not explain the mental compartmentalization such people seem to use in refusing to define themselves as deviants.

Social Control Theory. Sometimes referred to as **bonding theory, social control theory** focuses upon the process aspects of becoming bonded, or attached, to the norms and values of society (Hirschi, 1969). As the bonds between society and people become stronger, the possibilities that people will engage in deviant or criminal behaviors becomes weaker. Bonding consists of several dimensions (Hirschi, 1969). These include (1) attachment, the emotional or affective dimension linking us with significant others whose opinions we respect and whose admonitions we follow; (2) commitment, the energy expended by an individual in particular activities, either

These gang members have a turf, or territory. They share many beliefs and have developed strong attachments among one another. Bonding theory might conclude that their attachments with conventional society have weakened, and they have acquired strong involvements with others who are less conventional.

conventional or unconventional; (3) belief, a person's moral definition of the propriety of a particular conduct, that the laws and rules should be obeyed; and (4) involvement, the degree of intensity with which one is involved in conventional conduct or with which one espouses conventional values.

Persons who have strong attachments with conventional groups and their opinions, manifesting beliefs in the values of the groups, intensely involved in the groups' activities, and expending considerable energy in these activities, will probably not become deviant or exhibit criminal conduct. If, however, one or more of these bonding dimensions are weakened, people stand a better chance of deviating from the expectations of conventional society. For instance, when people cease to believe that the groups they associate with are important or exhibit the right values or standards, weakening of the bonds occurs. It may be that a delinquent gang can lure youths away from conventional groups by permitting them to develop close attachments and involvements in delinquent gang activity so that a type of rivalry occurs between conventional bonds and the developing bonds of less conventional social groups.

Hirschi's social control theory builds upon the differential association theory developed by Sutherland. Sutherland's dimensions of intensity and priority appear closely related to Hirschi's notions of attachment, commitment, and involvement. While Sutherland attempted to account for white-collar crime, Hirschi has used his bonding theory to explain juvenile delinquency. In an investigation of a sample of junior and senior high school youth in California, Hirschi found that students who exhibited strong attitudes and attachments to teachers and school officials were less inclined to engage in delinquent activity. These students were also earning higher grades and making more successful adjustments to the rigors of schoolwork than were students with weaker bonds. As for youths engaged in delinquent activity, Hirschi found that they frequently performed poorly academically, disliked school, and had few positive experiences with school faculty and officials (Hirschi, 1969).

Hirschi's theory has been criticized for several reasons. First, it fails to specify the precise relation between the bonding dimensions and conventional and nonconventional conduct. Many youths have attachments to both conventional and nonconventional groups, yet no clear pattern of delinquency or nondelinquency emerges. Which dimensions have the greatest weight in predicting deviant conduct? Hirschi's emphasis on school experiences is an inherent weakness, since it does not account for bonding processes that take place outside school settings. What are the roles of parents and church officials in the lives of such youths? How does social class function as an explanatory variable (Nettler, 1984)?

Social control theory is strongly psychological, since it holds that the individual's mental attachments and beliefs are critical in linking the individual to society's conventional norms. This theory may explain why certain individuals reject conventional behavior for deviant conduct, but it cannot be used to predict which youths among large groups will turn to crime (Nettler, 1984). Finally, its application is restricted to explaining deviance among adolescents who are in school.

Conflict/Marxist Theory. Sometimes called Marxist criminology, conflict criminology, or radical criminology, this theory explains criminal conduct by focusing attention on the people who have the political power to define crime for the rest of society. According to **conflict,** or **Marxist, theory,** the masses can be divided into the have-nots (the poor people who are manipulated and controlled by the haves) and the rich and powerful people who have vested interests in capital, industry, and business.

Statistically, persons in the lower socioeconomic strata are arrested more frequently than those in the upper socioeconomic strata. These facts do not mean that those in the lower socioeconomic categories commit more crimes. Instead, according to Marxist theory, these statistics show that the ruling elite have targeted the poor for harassment. This harassment is a strategy for maintaining the status quo, preserving societal arrangements that perpetuate and legitimize the power of the haves (Manning, 1977; Sykes, 1974). This theory also asserts that one reason for the formal creation of the police in 1829 was to protect the interests of those in power (Manning, 1977). These interests exert considerable influence on how crime is defined. Vagrancy and loitering laws were created, in part, as means for keeping people from wandering about, looking for better jobs and work (Manning, 1977).

Conflict, or Marxist, theory is a general scheme to account for societal characteristics. It does not explain individual behaviors or the behaviors of small groups. It is not linked with any particular social process of acquiring criminal behaviors, and it considers criminal behavior as the result of legislative definitions created by the rich and powerful. To use this theory for creating a specific plan to deal with crime, we would have to change our basic social and economic structures.

■ AN EVALUATION OF THE THEORIES

There is no best theory. Each theory has strengths and weaknesses and has exerted varying degrees of influence on the criminal justice system in processing offenders. An important criterion for evaluating theories of criminal behavior is the extent to which they enable us to explain and predict that behavior. An evaluation of the theories suggests that creating a satisfactory theory stringently meeting this criterion is quite difficult. Most of the theories, regardless of whether they are biological, psychological, or sociological, emphasize single-factor causation. One factor (for example, glands, genes, improper or inadequate ego development, or anomie) is usually featured as the chief cause of criminal behavior, and all other factors are either subordinated or ignored.

One problem with evaluating the theories is that often, the historical context in which they were generated is overlooked. Cesare Lombroso's work on the relation between physique and criminal behavior was devised during the time when Charles Darwin's *Origin of the Species* was popular. Biological evolution was considered to be an important explanation for certain kinds of social behaviors in the 1870s, as well as for the next several decades. Assessing Lombroso's work in view of our current knowledge makes his theorizing seem comical. In contrast, psychologists investigated the influence of an air pollutant, ozone, on criminal behavior in 1987. James Rotton, a psychologist at Florida International University, has estimated that every year, ozone provokes hundreds of cases of family violence in large cities with bad air (Londer, 1987:6). How will this theory be viewed by criminologists and others 100 years from now?

In all likelihood, criminal behavior is the result of a combination of factors. It is insufficient to rely entirely upon a single cause for such a complex phenomenon. There are criminals of every size, shape, and variety. Crimes such as murder or robbery are committed by many different kinds of people for many different reasons. In time of war, murdering the enemy may cause someone to be a hero, whereas murder in other contexts and at other times is punished severely. However, there is a problem with developing conglomerate, or holistic, theories, because they may not be theories at all in the formal sense.

Obviously, the explanations advanced by Lombroso and Sheldon attaching significance to one's body structure have little or no predictive value. We cannot look at someone and determine from physical features whether the person is criminal or will become criminal. Also, genetic structure fails to explain and predict criminal behavior.

Theories emphasizing the id, ego, and superego as crucial determinants of social conduct are difficult to test empirically. Such phenomena cannot be extracted from persons, dissected, and examined microscopically. If we rigorously apply the standards of science and empiricism and subject all explanations advanced to the most scrupulous experiments and tests, *all* theories of criminal behavior presented in this chapter fail such tests.

One way of evaluating theories is to examine the successes that have resulted when the theories have been applied at various stages of the criminal justice process. Which theories seem to be most influential in formulating policies in our various correctional institutions? Which theories seem to be most persuasive in the courtroom when a defendant's guilt or innocence must be decided by a judge or jury? Which theories receive the most consistent emphasis and support from foundations that underwrite research projects examining the causes of criminal behavior?

To identify which theories are most popular, it might be helpful to study parole board hearings. **Parole boards** are groups that determine whether incarcerated prisoners should be released before serving their full sentences. Parole boards consider many factors in deciding whether an offender should be released (Hoffman and Adelberg, 1980). Did the inmate behave properly in prison? Did the inmate exhibit any unusual behavioral disorders? What is the likelihood that an offender will be able to cope effectively with life on the outside? Halfway houses, places where ex-prisoners can stay temporarily in the community until they can find appropriate employment and housing, were created to help offenders adjust to life outside prison. Have inmates had vocational training or group therapy or rehabilitative counseling? What are the reports of the counselors who interacted with these inmates and listened to their problems? The answers to these questions combine to form a release quotient, or salient factor score, which is a numerical value that predicts an inmate's chances of living in the community and not committing new crimes (Hoffman, 1983; Hoffman and Adelberg, 1980; O'Leary and Nuffield, 1972).

Differential association theory seems influential in parole decisions and the conditions prescribed for parolees. For instance, persons who are paroled cannot associate with other known criminals as one of several parole conditions. However, many parolees violate this condition because the community has labeled them as ex-convicts. Thus, community rejection makes it difficult for such former criminals to obtain employment. In a sense, society compels such persons to seek social attachments with other criminals, frustrating their efforts to refrain from further criminal activity.

■ SUMMARY

Theories explain and predict relationships between various phenomena. Criminologists theorize about criminal behavior and describe the characteristics of persons convicted of crimes as well as their motives. Efforts are made to determine whether or not criminals have the necessary *mens rea,* or guilty mind or criminal disposition, in the crimes they commit.

Nineteenth century biological theories of criminal behavior stressed the importance of physical characteristics as indicators of criminal propensities. One biological theory determined that criminal behavior was hereditary. Other biological explanations focused upon body type as a predictor, but these theories have been discounted. Biochemical imbalance or glandular problems are also believed linked with criminal conduct, although no consistent evidence exists to support such beliefs.

Psychoanalytic theory, developed by Freud, emphasizes early selfish behaviors of infants that sometimes remain uncontrolled as children grow older. The id, or I want part of the personality, remains unchecked by the ego, or that part of the personality that includes the standards and conventional rules of society. Again, criminal behavior is one predictable result. The psychological theory of moral development emphasizes developmental stages in the lives of children. As they grow and mature, they incorporate into their personality systems certain socially acceptable behavior patterns. Sometimes, however, disruptions occur in these stages, and criminal conduct results.

Sociological and sociocultural theories of criminal behavior stress social and environmental factors in promoting criminal conduct. One sociological theory, anomie, is that people experience conflict between aspiring to achieve socially acceptable goals and the culturally approved means to achieve those goals. People adapt to this conflict in different ways. Some persons engage in innovative or unconventional behavior to achieve their desired objectives. A third sociological theory is labeling. According to this theory, deviance is whatever a group says it is. Labeling theory involves no moral judgments of criminal actions. Rather, it directs attention at social definitions of criminal behavior and a person's responses to being labeled criminal.

An evaluation of theories may be made according to several criteria. Can we predict criminal behavior by using them? Which are most useful for helping us to understand why people commit crimes? In addition to evaluating their usefulness in predicting crime, we can evaluate the theories by considering the importance each is given in various sectors of the criminal justice system. Counseling programs, group therapy, and rehabilitative practices in prison settings are strongly influenced by psychological theories. Correctional institutional policies and guidelines are influenced strongly by differential association theory and labeling theory. Finally, single-factor explanations of criminal behavior have inherent weaknesses, because they highlight one variable and ignore others. The best explanations combine the best elements of several theoretical schemes.

KEY TERMS

anomie theory

bonding theory

cognitive development theory

conflict theory

conventional level of cognitive
  development

differential association

ectomorphs

ego

endomorphs

heredity

id

labeling theory

libido

Marxist theory

mesomorphs

parole boards

postconventional level of
  cognitive development

preconventional level of
  cognitive development

primary deviations

psychoanalytic theory

secondary deviations

social control theory

socialization

social learning theory

sociobiology

superego

theory

theory of opportunity

XYY syndrome

QUESTIONS FOR REVIEW

1. Which theory of criminal behavior most appropriately applies to the case discussed at the beginning of the chapter, *Government of Virgin Islands v. Lake?* Explain your reasons by citing the theory characteristics and the nature of the crime committed by Lake.

2. Compare and contrast labeling theory with differential association theory. Which theory directs attention to the nature of the crime committed?

Which theory directs attention to the societal reaction toward the offender? Which theory do you feel is the most sociological of the two?

3. What evidence supports the idea that body type has something to do with the causes of criminal behavior? Give supporting information, regardless of its scientific benefits or lack of them.

4. What is a theory of criminal behavior? What are some important objectives of such theories? Can

these objectives be used to evaluate whether certain criminal theories are good or bad? Why or why not? Give an example.

5. Of the three different categories of criminal behavior theories, which one do you prefer? Why? Name your favorite theory discussed in the category you have chosen. Explain why it is your favorite.

6. What is meant by the shift from internal to external explanations of criminal behavior? What emphasis is placed on each perspective? Which perspective is popular currently? Why do you think this is so?

7. How do psychoanalytic theory and developmental theory differ?

8. Some people read about differential association theory and decide that Edwin Sutherland meant that associating with criminals would make someone turn out to be a criminal. Is this what Sutherland was really saying? What are the characteristics of differential association theory? Why are they important in explaining criminal conduct?

9. Discuss the labeling process of becoming a deviant or criminal. What factors seem to be most impor-

tant in this theoretical explanation of deviant or criminal behavior? What are the assumptions or principles of labeling theory?

10. Differentiate between primary and secondary deviation. Give examples of situations where two different persons would commit the same criminal acts but one person is arrested and convicted and the other is only scolded. Why do you think situations like this occur?

11. What is a victimless crime? Is there really a victim? Why or why not? If yes, who is the victim?

12. How do parole boards help in determining which theory of criminal behavior is most acceptable to persons in various sectors of the criminal justice system?

13. In determining prisoner living arrangements and policies in various correctional institutions, which theory or theories of criminal behavior appear to be most influential? Why?

SUGGESTED READINGS

Albanese, Jay S. (1986). *Myths and realities of crime and justice.* Niagara Falls, N.Y.: Apocalypse Publishing Company.

Currie, Elliott (1985). *Confronting crime: An American challenge. Why there is so much crime in America and what we can do about it.* New York: Pantheon Books.

Erikson, Kai T. (1986). *Wayward Puritans: A study in the sociology of deviance.* New York: John Wiley & Sons.

Morris, Norval (1982). *Madness and the criminal law.* Chicago: Univ. of Chicago Press.

Walker, Samuel (1985). *Sense and nonsense about crime.* Monterey, Cal.: Brooks/Cole.

An Overview of the American Criminal Justice System

■ INTRODUCTION

In 1986, 40 million crimes were committed in the United States (National Crime Survey, 1986). The task of investigating these crimes, dealing with and processing alleged offenders, and ultimately housing or rehabilitating convicted offenders is performed by the criminal justice system. The criminal justice system is an interrelated set of agencies and organizations designed to control criminal behavior, to detect crime, and to apprehend, process, prosecute, punish, or rehabilitate criminal offenders.

Consider the following comments of E. Z. Thief, arrested by police for automobile theft in New Jersey in October 1987:

> I stole an '85 Ford from a supermarket parking lot in late September 1987. In early October, I got pulled over by the cops, who said I was speeding. I didn't have a driver's license, and when they checked the registration of the car, they found it was reported stolen by the owner. They arrested me and took me to jail. They booked me and charged me with vehicular theft. They set my bail at $5,000. I called my brother and he came down and bailed me out. They set my preliminary hearing for December 5th. They let me have a public defender because I couldn't afford a regular attorney.
>
> I met with my public defender before the preliminary hearing and he asked if I wanted to cop a plea. I didn't want to do that, and so they had my hearing and set my trial date for January 20, 1988. We went to trial, and they had a jury there. The trial went on for about 2 days, and there were all kinds of people who testified. Anyway, the jury found me guilty of vehicular theft, and the judge sentenced me to 4 years in prison. When I went to prison, I was there for about a year, but they let me out early because of my good behavior, and they put me on parole. I had to report to a parole officer every month for the rest of the 4-year sentence. Now it's all over.

While this story is hypothetical and omits significant stages of criminal processing, E. Z. Thief's narrative indicates contact with most agencies or components of the criminal justice system. A crime was committed when the automobile was stolen. A report was filed and the crime was investigated by police. Subsequently, a suspect, E. Z. Thief, was found and arrested. At this point, Mr. Thief entered the criminal justice system.

After a preliminary hearing determined that sufficient evidence and probable cause existed to proceed with a prosecution of Mr. Thief, a trial date was established and a trial was held. The issue of Mr. Thief's guilt or innocence was ultimately decided by an impartial jury, after considering evidence and arguments from both a prosecutor and a defense attorney. The sentence was pronounced by the judge, and E. Z. Thief was incarcerated for a period of time in a prison facility. Finally, Mr. Thief was paroled and assigned to a parole officer. Upon completion of the term of parole, Mr. Thief exited the criminal justice system.

This chapter is about the different components of the criminal justice system for adults in the United States. It is not intended to be an in-depth description of all agencies and organizations associated with the system. Later chapters provide detailed coverage of the functions and operations of other aspects of the criminal justice system.

■ THE ORGANIZATION OF THE CRIMINAL JUSTICE SYSTEM

The basic components of the criminal justice system include (1) the legislatures, (2) law enforcement agencies, (3) the prosecution and defense, (4) the courts, and (5) corrections.

Legislatures

Although some authorities object to considering legislatures as part of the criminal justice system, there is a sound basis for including them. Legislatures are largely responsible for creating the criminal laws. Accordingly, legislatures modify existing laws or repeal them. Law enforcement agencies enforce the laws, while the prosecution, courts, and corrections further process alleged offenders or violators of these criminal laws.

Criminal laws come from several different sources. State and federal constitutional provisions give legislatures the authority to enact civil or criminal laws. The United States Code (U.S.C.) contains all civil and criminal laws of the United States. The United States Code contains over 220 volumes setting forth all United States statutes governing almost every aspect of citizens' lives (United States Code, 1986). Title 18 of the United States Code contains all federal crimes and criminal procedures. It consists of seventeen volumes.

Among the states, legislatures enact similar codes containing state statutes. These are identified as statutory compilations, including the Oregon Revised Statutes, the Oklahoma Statutes Annotated, the Code of Alabama, the Annotated California Code, the Hawaii Revised Statutes, the Idaho Code, and sometimes simply, the Laws of Nebraska. Such laws are continually undergoing change. Every time a state legislature convenes, legislators enact new laws or modify or eliminate old ones. In 1986, it was a violation of one of Oregon's criminal statutes to possess marijuana for resale or personal consumption. The Oregon legislature has considered the legalization of marijuana possession in recent years. Should the legislature decide to decriminalize marijuana possession, the old Oregon statute prohibiting this substance would be eliminated. Such action is sometimes termed decriminalization.

Decriminalization is legislative action by which an act or omission, formerly criminal, is made noncriminal and without punitive sanctions. Prostitution in Nevada is an example of decriminalization. While prostitution is illegal in almost every United States jurisdiction, it has been decriminalized in certain Nevada counties. In these counties, considerable revenues accrue because of this previously illegal activity. Nevada authorities contend that state-regulated prostitution decreases the likelihood of the spread of infectious diseases such as AIDS. Since prostitution exists everywhere in the United States anyway, some Nevada officials believe that state control of this activity is safer than outright prohibition.

Sometimes, acts that were formerly noncriminal may be defined as criminal through legislative action. Marijuana possession and distribution was lawful until legislation prohibited it in the 1930s. In contemporary society, the use of new drugs or modifications of the use of existing ones (for example, smoking various herbal substances) may not be officially classified as harmful or illegal by the Food and Drug Administration. However, legislative action eventually addresses such activity and either sanctions or prohibits it.

United States Supreme Court decisions also influence state legislative actions. Until 1985, for example, it was permissible for police officers to use deadly force to apprehend those committing serious crimes. If a burglar ran from police officers to avoid apprehension, officers were authorized by state statutes to use deadly force as a means of catching the burglar. Deadly force includes shooting at those fleeing from crime scenes. This was known as the fleeing felon rule. In 1985, however, the United States Supreme Court declared the fleeing felon rule unconstitutional *(Tennessee v. Garner,* 1985). Since then, deadly force may only be used in defense of a police officer's life or the life of a bystander. The fleeing felon rule remains on the books of many state codes, simply because the state legislatures have not acted to repeal it. In many states, laws that are no longer enforced continue to exist in state codes. Again, this is largely the result of legislative inattention or the triviality of the law.

Once laws are in place, certain mechanisms come into play to ensure that the laws will be upheld or enforced. At the threshold of the criminal justice system are several law enforcement agencies established to detect crime and apprehend offenders. Figure 3.1 shows the movement of cases through the adult criminal justice system.

The Police

The law enforcement agencies in the United States make this the largest of all of the components of the criminal justice system. The most visible law enforcement officers are the uniformed police who enforce the laws of cities and townships. Less conspicuous law enforcement officers include FBI agents, IRS agents, city and county detectives, agents of the Bureau of Alcohol, Tobacco, and Firearms, and agents of the Drug Enforcement Administration.

All law enforcement agencies give their officers arrest powers. Police officers have the authority to make arrests whenever law violations occur within their jurisdictions. These arrest powers include apprehending those suspected of committing crimes. Offenses justifying arrest range from traffic violations, such as driving recklessly, to first-degree murder, forcible rape, and kidnapping.

Law enforcement officers are empowered to enforce the laws and statutes of their jurisdictions. Different law enforcement agencies enforce local, state, and federal criminal laws. Each agency has a jurisdiction commensurate with its courts. Primarily an investigative body, the FBI has arrest powers covering violations of over 200 federal laws and statutes. FBI agents observe all appropriate jurisdictional boundaries associated with their position. These agents do not issue traffic citations or monitor speeders on interstate highways. Accordingly, state troopers do not ordinarily investigate and arrest counterfeiters or conspirators in interstate gambling.

In the criminal justice system, those with arrest powers investigate and apprehend persons suspected of criminal activity. An **arrest** involves taking a suspected law violator into custody. Such a suspect is ordinarily taken to a jail, where he or she is booked. **Booking** is the process of making a written report of the arrest—including the name and address of the suspect, the crime(s) alleged, the arresting officer(s), the time

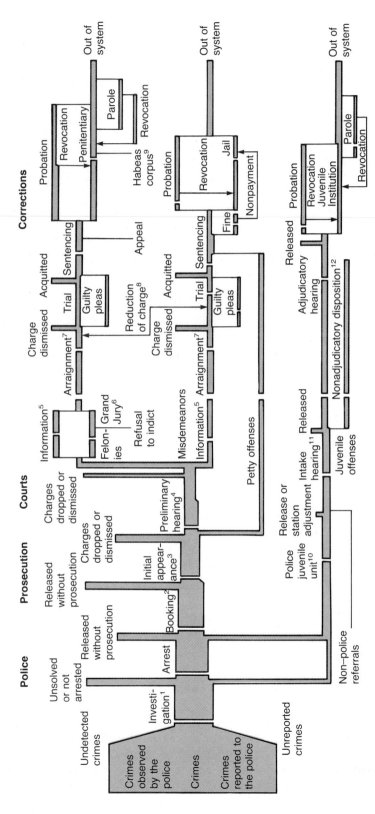

Police

Unreported crimes

Crimes observed by the police

Crimes

Crimes reported to the police

Undetected crimes

Investi-gation[1]

Unsolved or not arrested

Released without prosecution

Arrest

Prosecution

Booking[2]

Released without prosecution

Initial appear-ance[3]

Charges dropped or dismissed

Non-police referrals

Police juvenile unit[10]

Release or station adjustment

Courts

Charges dropped or dismissed

Preliminary hearing[4]

Information[5]

Felonies — Grand Jury[6]

Refusal to indict

Misdemeanors

Information[5]

Petty offenses

Intake hearing[11]

Released

Juvenile offenses

Charge dismissed[7]

Arraignment[5]

Trial

Guilty pleas

Reduction of charge[8]

Charge dismissed[7]

Arraignment[5]

Trial

Guilty pleas

Nonadjudicatory disposition[12]

Adjudicatory hearing

Acquitted

Sentencing

Appeal

Acquitted

Sentencing

Fine

Nonpayment

Released

Corrections

Probation

Revocation

Penitentiary

Parole

Revocation

Habeas corpus[9]

Out of system

Probation

Revocation

Jail

Out of system

Probation

Revocation

Juvenile Institution

Parole

Revocation

Out of system

[1] May continue until trial.

[2] Administrative record of arrest. First step at which temporary release on bail may be available.

[3] Before magistrate, commissioner, or justice of the peace. Formal notice of charge, advice of rights. Bail set. Summary trials for petty offenses usually conducted here without further processing.

[4] Preliminary testing of evidence against defendant. Charge may be reduced. No separate preliminary hearing for misdemeanors in some systems.

[5] Charge filed by prosecutor on basis of information submitted by police or citizens. Alternative to grand jury indictment; often used in felonies, almost always in misdemeanors.

[6] Reviews whether government evidence sufficient to justify trial. Some states have no grand jury system; others seldom use it.

[7] Appearance for plea; defendant elects trial by judge or jury (if available); counsel for indigent usually appointed here in felonies. Often not at all in other cases.

[8] Charge may be reduced at any time prior to trial in return for plea of guilty or for other reasons.

[9] Challenge on constitutional grounds to legality of detention. May be sought at any point in process.

[10] Police often hold informal hearings, dismiss or adjust many cases without further processing.

[11] Probation officer decides desirability of further court action.

[12] Welfare agency, social services, counseling, medical care, etc., for cases where adjudicatory handling not needed.

FIGURE 3.1 The Criminal Justice System

Source: President's Commission on Law Enforcement and Administration of Justice, *The Challenge of Crime in a Free Society* (Washington, DC: U.S. Government Printing Office, 1967), pp. 8–9.

The most visible component of the criminal justice system is the police. Uniformed law enforcement officers have arrest powers and enforce local and state laws. Other law enforcement personnel are responsible for the enforcement of federal statutes and other jurisdictional matters.

and place of the arrest, and a physical description of the suspect—and taking photographs (so-called mug-shots) and fingerprints. At the time of the booking, arresting officers often run a computer check of the suspect to determine if the person has any priors, or prior arrests or convictions.

A bail bond is a monetary amount required for a pretrial release as a surety for a suspect's court appearance. Bonding companies are located near jails in various cities to post bail bonds for suspects who require bond. A suspect's community standing, prior record, and other relevant factors are considered in bond setting and posting. Most defendants are released on their own recognizance, without having to post bail. Usually, these defendants have established ties with the community, have jobs, and are considered unlikely to flee from the jurisdiction before trial occurs.

If the charges are extremely serious, such as murder, robbery, or some other aggravated offense, bail may be set quite high. In some cases, authorities hold a suspect without bail if it is likely that pretrial release will result in further harm to others or the suspect will flee the jurisdiction to avoid prosecution. This is known as preventive detention. After suspects have been arrested and booked, they have an opportunity to contact an attorney, if desired, and reply to the charges alleged. The next major step in the criminal justice system is the prosecution.

The Prosecution and the Defense

Arresting and booking a suspect for a violation of the law does not automatically mean that the suspect eventually will be prosecuted for the alleged offense. Sometimes those

FIGURE 3.2 Funneling Effect of 500 Serious Crimes from Arrest to Imprisonment

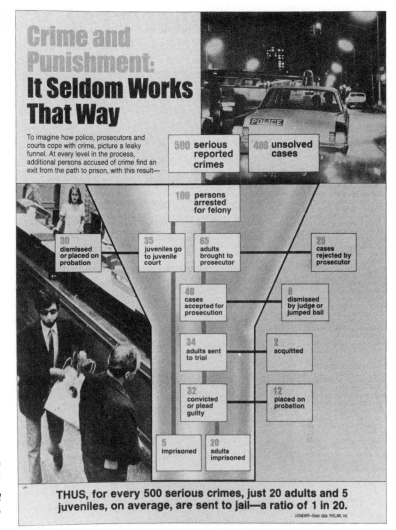

Crime and Punishment:
It Seldom Works That Way

To imagine how police, prosecutors and courts cope with crime, picture a leaky funnel. At every level in the process, additional persons accused of crime find an exit from the path to prison, with this result—

500 serious reported crimes

400 unsolved cases

100 persons arrested for felony

30 dismissed or placed on probation

35 juveniles go to juvenile court

65 adults brought to prosecutor

25 cases rejected by prosecutor

40 cases accepted for prosecution

8 dismissed by judge or jumped bail

34 adults sent to trial

2 acquitted

32 convicted or plead guilty

12 placed on probation

5 imprisoned

20 adults imprisoned

THUS, for every 500 serious crimes, just 20 adults and 5 juveniles, on average, are sent to jail—a ratio of 1 in 20.

USN&WR—Basic data: INSLAW, Inc.

Source: "American Justice: The ABCs of How It Really Works," *U.S. News & World Report* (November 1, 1982), p. 4. Reprinted from *U.S. News and World Report.* Copyright 1982 by U.S. News & World Report, Inc.

believed to be law violators are arrested but later released. Arrests made by police are often made where the evidence against the defendant is insufficient to pursue the case. Furthermore, not all prosecutions result in convictions (see Figure 3.2).

Figure 3.2 compares the process of arrest and subsequent punishment to a leaky funnel. Beginning with 500 serious crimes in an average community, 400 of those cases remain unsolved. Felony arrests are made in the remaining 100 cases. Of these, 35 are juveniles and 65 are adults brought to the prosecutor's attention for a prosecution decision. The prosecutor actively pursues 40 of these cases. Of these, 8 result in a trial, 2 are acquitted, and the remaining 32 plead guilty without a trial and are convicted. Only 20 of these 32 convicted offenders are incarcerated. In short, only 1 in 20 is incarcerated from an initial sample of 500 felonies reported.

Prosecutors. City and county attorneys (frequently called district attorneys, DAs, prosecuting attorneys, and prosecutors) and their assistants act in their jurisdictions to determine which cases should and should not be prosecuted. A **prosecution** is the carrying forth of criminal proceedings against a person, culminating in a trial or other final disposition, such as a plea of guilty in lieu of a trial. A prosecuting attorney screens cases and determines which ones have the highest probability of conviction. Many factors influence a prosecutor's decision to prosecute, including the sufficiency of evidence against the accused, the seriousness of the crime, the availability of witnesses, and the general circumstances associated with the arrest (Cole, 1970). A prosecutor also determines the priority given particular cases, such as child sexual abuse and petty theft. Other methods leading to prosecution are independent of prosecutorial discretion. These are described in Chapter 8.

The prosecution represents the government in any criminal proceeding. It is not always necessary that a specific victim be available to press charges against the accused. As a representative of the state, a prosecutor may prosecute any suspect, even if the victim is unwilling to press charges or there is no apparent victim. For instance, the action of the government against Spinelli (*Spinelli v. United States,* 1969) involved alleged interstate gambling. On behalf of the government, United States attorneys prosecuted Spinelli and supported their case against him with evidence seized at the site of the alleged gambling and bookmaking.

Defense Attorneys. A **defense attorney** is a licensed lawyer who is retained by a defendant for his or her defense or is appointed by the court to defend a suspect who is unable to afford an attorney. Acting to protect the defendant's interests, a defense attorney opposes the prosecuting attorney, who protects the government's interests. A defense attorney has access to much of the evidence against the accused and can usually determine the probable course of action to be taken by the prosecution.

If the evidence against the accused is weak or only circumstantial, a defense attorney may attempt to persuade the prosecutor to drop formal proceedings against the client. On the other hand, if the evidence against the accused is strong enough to likely result in a verdict of guilty by a criminal court jury or judge, a defense attorney may try to negotiate with the prosecutor for a reduction in charges or punishment against the client in exchange for a guilty plea. This is known as **plea bargaining** (Alschuler, 1976, 1979; Boland and Forst, 1985; Meeker and Pontell, 1985). Plea bargaining accounts for 90 percent of all criminal convictions where formal trial proceedings are avoided (Stitt and Siegel, 1986).

The Courts

Judges, especially those in courts of appeals, including the United States Supreme Court, contribute to lawmaking in certain ways. A hierarchy of authority exists at both state and federal levels within the court system. The highest court in the land is the United States Supreme Court. In each state, a similar court exists.

Normally, a lower court in the judicial hierarchy must rely on rulings from higher courts under the doctrine of stare decisis. **Stare decisis** is the policy of courts to stand by a particular precedent and not disturb a settled point of law (Black, 1979:1261). For instance, at the federal level, there are thirteen judicial circuits, which are the courts of

A DAY IN COURT

In 1965, an informant advised the FBI that a Mr. William Spinelli was engaging in illegal gambling in violation of federal statutes. Acting on this tip and previous knowledge of Spinelli's history of bookmaking and gambling activity, the FBI undertook surveillance of his actions. They observed Mr. Spinelli during a 5-day period in August, traversing a bridge between Illinois and St. Louis, Missouri. On each occasion, they saw him entering a particular apartment in St. Louis. Subsequently, the FBI obtained a search warrant for the apartment premises, where they found evidence of gambling activity. Spinelli was later convicted of "interstate . . . travel . . . with the intention of conducting gambling activities" (*Spinelli v. United States,* 393 U.S. 410, 1969).

Spinelli later appealed his conviction to the United States Supreme Court, which examined the procedure whereby the search warrant was originally obtained. The court concluded that probable cause did not exist for the warrant to be issued, and overturned Spinelli's conviction. In this respect, the Supreme Court dealt with a procedural law and effected an appropriate ruling. In spite of the fact that the evidence obtained supported the notion that a substantive law had been violated, the court concluded that such evidence was inadmissible against Spinelli because it had been obtained without probable cause. On procedural grounds, Spinelli's conviction was erased.

The case of *Spinelli v. United States* (1969) is interesting for several reasons. First, it demonstrates how the Supreme Court can establish precedents that lower courts are obliged to follow in obtaining search warrants and satisfying the requirements of probable cause. It is also interesting because in recent years, the precedent of *Spinelli* has undergone a certain amount of modification. For instance, in 1983 in the case of *Illinois v. Gates,* the United States Supreme Court modified the *Spinelli* test for probable cause by creating a less rigid totality of circumstances approach (McLaren, 1986). One result of this court action is to make the test for probable cause less stringent. Thus, police officers have less trouble securing search warrants where they suspect criminal activity.

The change says something about the current composition of the Supreme Court compared with its earlier composition. In the l960s, the Warren court triggered a number of sweeping reforms in our criminal laws. More recently, the Burger court has divested itself of some of the power the earlier court had created (McLaren, 1986). Again, this underscores the fact that our laws are in a state of flux and subject to change and differing interpretation.

appeals for decisions rendered in federal district courts. In the Ninth Circuit are the states of Alaska, Arizona, California, Idaho, Montana, Nevada, Oregon, Washington, and Hawaii. In a case brought before the Ninth Circuit, the judges are obliged to follow any ruling of the United States Supreme Court that pertains directly to issues involved in the present case.

As a general rule, lower-court judges have the prerogative of interpretating a decision by a higher court as it applies to a case before their courts. Is the case on point? Does it contain most of the same characteristics of the case decided by the higher court? If, in the opinion of the lower-court judge, the case does not conform to the one decided earlier by the higher court, then the judge is not bound to abide by it. Later, however, that particular interpretation may be appealed by the defendant.

If the issue has not been addressed by the United States Supreme Court, a Ninth Circuit ruling will be made. This ruling can either affirm or overturn a decision from one of several lower federal district courts. As a result, *all* district courts within the Ninth Circuit will be obligated under the policy of *stare decisis* to adhere to the decision of the Ninth Circuit whenever a case is heard involving the same issue of law. No district court in the Ninth Circuit is obliged to follow precedents established by any other circuit, however. Likewise, Ninth Circuit rulings have no effect on courts in the Sixth or Eighth circuits. Courts at the same level of authority do not create precedents for each other to follow, although a court may be influenced by a decision made by another court at the same level. The Ninth Circuit may choose to *rely* upon another circuit court's decision in a particular case to justify its own decisions.

Only the United States Supreme Court can overturn decisions made by circuit courts. The Supreme Court can also act to create uniformity among circuits on certain issues. If one circuit court decision is to permit a certain type of evidence to be introduced in a criminal trial and another circuit decision is to prohibit that same evidence from being introduced, the United States Supreme Court can act to create uniformity as it pertains to the admissibility of that kind of evidence.

Judges do not propose legislation for the legislatures to consider, but their rulings and interpretations often have the same impact. As a part of their lawmaking authority, for instance, legislators deal principally with substantive criminal laws. Substantive criminal laws are all activities defined by statute as criminal as well as the punishments accompanying such activities. The judiciary is often, though not always, concerned with procedural laws. Procedural laws pertain to the implementation of substantive laws.

The courtroom is the place where a defendant's guilt is ultimately determined. It functions as a public forum for all relevant information in a case. The government presents its evidence against the accused, and the defense presents its side. Witnesses are called to testify both for and against the accused, and defendants have the right to cross-examine their accusers. The courtroom is also the place where the sufficiency of evidence against the accused is tested.

The operations of the state and federal court systems are similar. Violations of federal laws are usually prosecuted in federal district courts. Violations of state and local criminal laws are prosecuted in either courts of general jurisdiction or in criminal courts. Each state has a different court organization, with a particular nomenclature applying to the courts performing the different functions. For example, California has superior courts, while Tennessee has circuit courts and criminal courts. Minor offenses in each state jurisdiction are tried before magistrates, justices of the peace, sessions judges, or municipal judges.

When a prosecutor persists in a prosecution against a particular suspect, the suspect becomes a **defendant** in the subsequent criminal proceeding. A defendant is entitled to a jury trial in any criminal proceeding as a matter of right if the charges are serious and could result in incarceration for a period of 6 months or more. This applies to either misdemeanors or felonies. A **jury** is an objective, impartial body of persons who convene to hear the case against the accused and make a determination of guilt or innocence on the basis of the factual evidence presented. Jury members are ordinarily selected from the community and are unrelated to the accused. They are sworn to be objective and impartial in their assessment of the facts presented to them by the defense and prosecution.

The United States trial proceeding is adversarial. A prosecutor presents the case against a defendant, and a defense attorney represents the interests of the client. A judge or jury decides the fate of the accused. Some witnesses testify incognito in order to protect their identities and avoid reprisals from defendants who may have threatened them.

A defendant may waive the right to a trial by jury and elect instead to permit a judge to make a determination of guilt or innocence on the basis of the facts presented. Sometimes the accused is charged with a crime that is so emotionally charged that there is ample reason to believe that no jury could be objective and return an impartial verdict. In such cases, a judge may better consider the facts than a jury. A defendant in a criminal proceeding who is found not guilty (acquitted) is freed by that court action. While the government may appeal to a higher court in a case where the judge has decided in favor of the defendant, such government appeals are relatively rare.

A defendant who is found guilty may appeal the verdict and request a new trial. At the federal level, the thirteen circuit courts of appeal exist to evaluate decisions rendered in the federal district courts. At the state level, the decisions of lower criminal courts may be challenged at courts of criminal appeal. Beyond these appellate bodies are supreme courts. The United States Supreme Court is the highest appellate body. Most states have supreme courts, where decisions made by the criminal courts of appeal may be challenged.

A defendant convicted of the crime alleged is sentenced by the court in a manner prescribed by law. Several options are available to the judge in sentencing. Someone who has committed previous offenses may receive a harsh sentence, while a first offender may receive a light sentence. A judge who decides not to incarcerate a defendant may place the defendant on probation for a prescribed period. **Probation** is a sentence involving a conditional release from incarceration, usually with a number of behavioral provisions or conditions. These conditions include not associating with other known criminals, refraining from further criminal acts, obtaining employment, and participating in medical or counseling programs.

Corrections

The last component of the criminal justice system is corrections. **Corrections** includes all of the agencies and personnel who deal with a convicted offender after a court proceeding. Even in situations where plea bargaining has occurred and a formal

CRIME BEAT

"L.A.Law" is a popular television program. It highlights dramatic events in courtrooms. As in the old "Perry Mason" series, the courtroom is a scene with many players. In an increasingly legalistic society, television has sought to exploit our interest in the law and the events transpiring within courtrooms, with last-minute declarations and confessions by unlikely witnesses. In many respects, real courtrooms emulate their television counterparts. Prosecutors and defense attorneys alike groom themselves to maximize their jury appeal. They may rehearse their roles with star witnesses. In some instances, they even hire acting coaches to assist them in developing more persuasive gestures and speech. In increasing numbers attorneys are enrolling in drama classes, which highlight body language and voice as critical elements of persuasion and believability.

Some critics of our legal system say that we have strayed from dealing with the crucial issue of guilt and the actual facts of the case. Should the fates of defendants be left up to the acting ability of their defense attorneys? Should guilty verdicts be rendered because prosecutors are authoritative and charismatic? Should jurors be persuaded toward a verdict of guilty or not guilty by the clothes worn by defendants or legal adversaries?

courtroom trial has been avoided, one correctional agency or another becomes involved in the further processing of a convicted person.

Typically, corrections is associated with jails and prisons. **Jails** are confinement areas associated with local city and county police departments. They are usually used for persons sentenced to short-term confinement for misdemeanor offenses or for persons charged with more serious offenses who are awaiting trial. **Prisons** are much larger facilities, owned and operated by the state or federal government. Such facilities house criminals sentenced to terms of 1 or more years in length.

Prisons and jails are the most visible corrections facilities. Most are staffed by government employees, who guard and monitor offenders sentenced to those facilities, although there have been some efforts within the private sector to take over selected prison operations (National Institute of Justice, 1985). Such places of confinement have their own rules and regulations, which are rigidly enforced. The custodial functions of jails and prisons are apparent, although some citizens would prefer to see these facilities accomplish more rehabilitative objectives (MacKenzie and Goodstein, 1985; Peak, 1985).

While prisons and jails are important in the corrections process, they are not dominant. In 1985, for instance, 1.7 million adults were on probation in the United States. This is four times the number of inmates in United States prisons (Bureau of Justice Statistics, 1986). In 1987, the prison population consisted of about 446,000 inmates, while the jail population consisted of 235,000 inmates (Bureau of Justice Statistics, 1987).

Convicted offenders who are sentenced to either jail or prison for a specified period may be released early. Early release from prison is known as parole, and parolees are routinely assigned to parole officers. In many instances, there is no difference between a parole officer and a probation officer. The same officer may supervise both parolees and probationers. Probation and parole work includes correctional personnel beyond

Correctional institutions are designed to provide varying degrees of control over inmates. While rehabilitation may be accomplished under some incarcerative circumstances, the preliminary function of prisons is to isolate criminals from the general public.

those who staff jails and prisons. Such officers are responsible for monitoring the behaviors and progress of probationers and parolees for a fixed period of time. This is usually the remainder of the original sentence imposed by the judge in court.

■ GOALS OF THE CRIMINAL JUSTICE SYSTEM

Each of the major components of the criminal justice system performs specific functions. Apart from individual organizational goals and agency objectives, the criminal justice system itself has a set of identifiable aims that serve to shape its policies and practices. While not everyone agrees about these goals, several common concerns can be listed. These include (1) crime prevention and deterrence, (2) crime detection and control, (3) criminal punishment and societal retribution, (4) criminal rehabilitation, and (5) assurance of due process.

Crime Prevention and Deterrence

Criminal laws are derived from several sources. The expected result of establishing criminal laws is regulation of social conduct and protection of citizens' rights. Crime infringes on these rights to varying degrees. Establishing criminal laws and accompa-

Many authorities consider the certainty of punishment to be more effective than the amount of punishment.

nying punishments serves to deter most people from committing crimes. Obviously, however, not everyone is equally deterred from committing crimes through the threat of punishment. Some information shows that increasing the severity of punishment is unrelated to whether people commit crimes (Currie, 1985; Fattah, 1985; Shavell, 1985). Many authorities consider the certainty of punishment to be more effective than the amount of punishment.

In addition, counselors and therapists spend much time with first offenders who are on either probation or parole. They advise them to develop constructive strategies to cope with their problems rather than to resort to crime.

Crime prevention is improved through the efforts of criminal justice agencies that help people avoid circumstances where they stand a good chance of becoming crime victims (Persico and Sunderland, 1985). Crime prevention strategies also include ways of making homes more secure against burglars (Mayhew, 1984). This is known as **target-hardening,** and it includes several new concepts of home or building design (Hope, 1985). Police officers assist communities in developing self-help crime prevention programs and community patrols (Titus, 1984). Preventive strategies include Operational Identification, where citizens imprint their personal possessions with electronic identification labels, such as social security numbers. The imprinting minimizes the chances that thieves will be able to resell such stolen property easily (Reppetto, 1984).

Crime Detection and Control

Other goals of the criminal justice system are to detect the occurrence of crime and to control it. However, the National Crime Survey indicates that only about a third of all crimes are reported to the police annually (Bureau of Justice Statistics, 1985).

One of the more popular crime detection organizations in the United States is the FBI. The FBI maintains files on most convicted felons, including their prior arrests, fingerprints, and other pertinent identification information. The extensive laboratory facilities of the FBI assist interested law enforcement agencies in materials identification, analysis of numerous substances, missing persons identification, and investigative techniques.

Criminal Punishment and Societal Retribution

The criminal justice system seeks to punish offenders for the crimes they have committed. The courts dispense justice and impose sentences on those convicted of crimes. The fines and sentences imposed are punishments for the crimes. The more serious the offense, the more severe the sentence, or at least this is how it is supposed to work.

All criminal offenses have punishments established by statute. The United States Code or any compilation of state criminal laws shows maximum penalties for all criminal acts. For instance, Title 18, Section 1953 of the United States Code (1989) indicates the following punishment for interstate transportation of wagering paraphernalia: "[The offender] . . . shall be fined not more than $10,000 or imprisoned for not more than five years or both." For an offense against personal property belonging to the United States, 18 U.S.C., Sec. 2112 (1989) provides, "Whoever robs another of any kind or description of personal property belonging to the United States, shall be imprisoned not more than fifteen years."

Even illegal weather forecasting is prohibited by federal statute. Under 18 U.S.C., Sec. 2074 (1989), "Whoever knowingly issues or publishes any counterfeit weather forecast or warning of weather conditions falsely representing such forecast or warning to have been issued or published by the Weather Bureau, United States Signal Service, or other branch of the Government service, shall be fined not more than $500 or imprisoned not more than ninety days, or both." All states and territories of the United States have similar statutory provisions addressing various crimes and their accompanying punishments.

No other punishment has aroused as much controversy as the death penalty. The United States Supreme Court has debated the capital punishment issue for years, and it is no closer to resolving this issue now than it was in the 1970s. In cases involving treason or first-degree murder, courts may impose the death penalty. The death penalty has been investigated extensively as a possible deterrent to capital crimes. Opponents argue that the death penalty fails as a crime deterrent and is cruel and unusual punishment. Those favoring the use of the death penalty say that retributive value is derived from executing criminals who deprive others of life (Nathanson, 1985; Reiman, 1985). While the United States Supreme Court has not resolved all controversies about the death penalty, it has specified the manner by which the death penalty may be invoked. It is unlikely, however, that the death penalty issue will ever be resolved to everyone's satisfaction, despite all legal efforts. Chapter 12 discusses the capital punishment issue in greater detail.

Criminal Rehabilitation

Rehabilitating criminals has been a dominant correctional goal, but critics say that prisons and jails do not rehabilitate; rather, they are basically dehumanizing institutions of higher criminal learning (Flanagan and Caulfield, 1984; Irwin, 1985; New York State Defenders Association, 1985). Alternative sentencing, or sentencing offenders to some nonincarcerative program, such as home confinement, electronic monitoring, community service, or restitution, has become popular in recent years, not only as a method

CRIME BEAT

The United States Constitution extends to citizens many rights and privileges, including the exercise of freedom of speech. However, despite the apparent liberal right of free speech the First Amendment conveys, boundaries created by the Supreme Court define when the exercise of free speech by one citizen infringes on the rights of others. In fact, certain types of speech may be deemed unlawful. Advocating the overthrow of the government of the United States, or sedition, is a felony under 18 U.S.C., Sec. 2385 (1989), otherwise known as the Smith Act, and convicted offenders may be sentenced to 20 years in prison and fined $20,000, but seditious-sounding speech may not be unlawful.

In the case of *Brandenburg v. Ohio* (395 U.S. 444, 1969), Clarence Brandenburg, a Ku Klux Klan leader in Cincinnati, Ohio, was convicted of violating the Ohio Criminal Syndicalism Act, established in 1919. This act forbade, among other things, "advocating . . . the duty, necessity, or propriety of crime, sabotage, violence or unlawful methods of terrorism as a means of accomplishing industrial or political reform." Brandenburg allegedly called a Cincinnati television station and announced that there would be a Ku Klux Klan rally at a farm in Hamilton County, Ohio, at a specific time and place. Newspersons attended the rally, photographing and recording Brandenburg stating, "We are marching on Congress July the Fourth, four hundred thousand strong. From there we are dividing into two groups, one group to march on St. Augustine, Florida, the other group to march on Mississippi. Thank you." Brandenburg was charged with violating the act, convicted, sentenced to 1–10 years' imprisonment, and fined $1,000.

Although the Ohio Supreme Court upheld Brandenburg's conviction by a lower court, the United States Supreme Court overturned the conviction. It reasoned that in order for Brandenburg to be guilty of a crime, his advocacy of political rebellion through a march on Congress would have to be directed at inciting imminent lawless action and would have to actually produce such action. According to the United States Supreme Court, Brandenburg was being punished for mere advocacy, without actually "preparing a group for violent action and steeling it to such action." Thus, in the judgment of the Supreme Court of the United States, the State of Ohio infringed on Brandenburg's right to free speech in its prosecution of him under the Criminal Syndicalism Act.

State and federal regulatory agencies may establish their own definitions of permissible speech for broadcasters on television and radio and even for operators of citizens band radio. The Federal Communications Commission (FCC) regulates the airwaves and the nature and content of radio and television transmissions. Although liberal policies govern such transmissions, some newscasters have been held to account for allegedly indecent speech and conduct. In 1987, the FCC warned several radio stations in Philadelphia and New York City about exceeding the limits of freedom of speech by the obscene and indecent nature of their broadcasts. The FCC warned one Philadelphia broadcaster, Howard Stern of WYSP-FM, to refrain from using sexually explicit language during his broadcasts. Stern is noted for his racial, ethnic, religious, and sexist slurs, regularly offending one group or another during his transmissions. However, should the FCC elect to revoke the station's license in a move to silence Stern, defining obscenity and indecency could prove insurmountable in a criminal courtroom.

of easing prison and jail overcrowding but also as a means of establishing more humane, noncustodial environments where true rehabilitation may occur (Lovell, 1985; Medler, 1985; Smith, 1984). Alternatives, such as the private financing and operation of jails and prisons, have also been considered in recent years (Anderson, 1985; Babcock, 1985; Fenton, 1985). Some authorities believe that private enterprise can do a better job in treating criminals and furnishing them with needed educational, vocational, and counseling services than bureaucratic governmental agencies can (Babcock, 1985).

Rehabilitation is concerned in part with providing incarcerated offenders with useful vocational and educational skills to assist them in finding good jobs when they are released from prison. Many prisons have counseling programs where offenders can discuss their problems with trained therapists and psychological counselors. Special counseling programs exist in many prisons for child sexual abusers, drug and alcohol abusers, and those with various psychological disorders. Incarceration fulfills a custodial objective, but it fails to achieve the rehabilitative ideal for most offenders.

While the rehabilitation of criminals has been a major correctional goal, many critics have concluded that existing offender programs are coercive rather than rehabilitative. Inmates may enroll in educational courses or engage in extensive counseling, but these activities are cosmetic, that is designed primarily to impress those who decide about early release from prison—parole boards. Other experts argue that rehabilitation has not succeeded on a large scale primarily because treatment programs have lacked the financial resources and personnel to be effective in changing inmate lives (Cullen and Gilbert, 1982).

Before any rehabilitation program is rejected outright, it should be examined closely to see whether its objectives are being implemented or the program description is being followed by program personnel. High rates of recidivism among offenders who have been enrolled in rehabilitation programs have created some skepticism among correctional critics and the public, but there is evidence to show that rehabilitative programs that are properly managed do assist some offenders (Cullen and Gilbert, 1982).

Assurance of Due Process

Due process is the basic constitutional right to a fair trial; a presumption of innocence until guilt is proven beyond a reasonable doubt; and the opportunity to be heard, to be aware of a matter that is pending, to make an informed choice whether to acquiesce or contest, and to provide the reasons for such a choice before a judicial official. The accused is entitled to the full protection of the law in any criminal proceeding. Several constitutional safeguards exist to ensure that a suspect's rights are respected at every stage of the criminal justice process.

Law enforcement officers must have probable cause whenever they arrest a criminal suspect. Prosecutors must observe all criminal defendants' rights to due process. They must undertake no action that will violate these rights. By the same token, judges must ensure in subsequent court action that all courtroom procedures are carefully observed. Some evidence may not be admissible against a defendant and thus may violate the defendant's rights, permitting a subsequent conviction to be reversed or overturned. If defendants are convicted and incarcerated or placed on probation, all of the officials with whom the convicts interact must continue to ensure that their rights are not violated. At any stage in this process, defendants may challenge any procedure or decision affecting them.

■ SUMMARY

The criminal justice system is a vast network of agencies, organizations, and individuals who attempt to control crime through detection and apprehension of criminals. It processes alleged criminals through a sequence of legal events, culminating in a determination of their guilt or innocence. Eventually, it may oversee and enforce punishment or rehabilitation.

Most criminal laws originate in legislative action through the creation of statutes. All federal laws are listed in the United States Code. These laws are continually subject to revision; some laws are dropped or revised, and new laws are developed as society requires. The courts interpret the laws and establish precedents. Stare decisis is the policy of courts to stand by a precedent. The United States Supreme Court is the final arbiter of actions pertaining to constitutional law, and it reviews decisions made by all lower courts.

The largest component of the criminal justice system is law enforcement. Law enforcement officers are empowered to arrest suspects for crimes, to investigate crimes, and to enforce all laws within their jurisdictional boundaries. Prosecuting attorneys decide which cases should and should not be prosecuted. In a trial, a defendant is tried, and guilt or innocence is determined, often by a jury. A defendant may waive the right to a jury and permit a judge to decide the case or may plea bargain with prosecutors at an earlier stage in the proceeding. If a defendant is found innocent or the charges are dropped, he or she is free from the criminal justice system. If a defendant pleads guilty or is found guilty by the court or a jury, a judge disposes of the case through a sentence prescribed by law.

Corrections is the part of the criminal justice system concerned with supervising convicted offenders. Corrections may include probation or incarceration in jail or prison and parole, depending upon the offense. The goals of the criminal justice system are to prevent and deter crime, to detect and control it, to punish and monitor criminal offenders, to rehabilitate offenders and accelerate their return to society, and to assure that all who enter the criminal justice process receive due process under the United States Constitution.

KEY TERMS

arrest

booking

corrections

decriminalization

defendant

defense attorney

due process

jails

jury

plea bargaining

prisons

probation

prosecution

rehabilitation

stare decisis

target hardening

QUESTIONS FOR REVIEW

1. Identify the major components of the criminal justice system. Are they independent of one another or related? Why?
2. Do judges hand down statutes? Why or why not? Where do statutes come from? Do judges make laws? Do judges modify existing laws?
3. What is the difference between a jail and a prison?
4. What is meant by decriminalization? What kinds of criminal acts are most likely to be decriminalized?
5. When a lower court makes a decision, what principle governs that decision to the extent that a precedent or a similar ruling affects the decision? Is one federal district court bound to observe decisions made in another federal district court?

6. Differentiate between substantive law and procedural law. How is *Spinelli v. United States* related to substantive law?

7. Which component of the criminal justice system is the largest? What law enforcement agencies at the federal level represent the government's interests?

8. Why is probable cause important in the criminal justice process?

9. What is plea bargaining? How much is plea bargaining used in the United States? Is plea bargaining increasing or decreasing? What are some positive benefits of plea bargaining for the criminal justice process?

10. Distinguish between probation and parole.

11. What does corrections involve? Are probation officers part of the corrections process?

12. What is recidivism? Why is recidivism important in the corrections process?

13. What are some ways that law enforcement officers control crime?

14. What are the major objectives of the criminal justice system? How is due process related to the aims of criminal justice?

SUGGESTED READINGS

Cramer, James A. (Ed.) (1981). *Courts and Judges.* Beverly Hills, CA: Sage.

Greene, Jack R. (1982). *Managing police work: Issues and analysis.* Beverly Hills, CA: Sage.

Johnson, Robert (1987). *Hard time: Understanding and reforming the prison.* Monterey, CA: Brooks/Cole.

McDonald, William F. (Ed.) (1979). *The Prosecutor.* Beverly Hills, CA: Sage.

Van den Haag, Ernest (1975). *Punishing criminals: Concerning a very old question.* New York: Basic Books.

PART II

Is the government always fair to those accused of crimes? On Thanksgiving weekend in 1976, Randall Adams, a Columbus, Ohio, resident, was traveling in Texas near Dallas. When his automobile ran out of gas, Adams hitched a ride with 16-year-old David Harris. They rode around Dallas during the day and, according to Adams, Harris dropped him off at his motel at 10:00 P.M.

A police officer, Robert Wood, stopped the Harris vehicle about midnight. He was promptly shot five times by the occupant. Wood's death triggered an extensive investigation that led to Adams' arrest by Dallas authorities. Also apprehended was Harris, who told police that Adams had killed Officer Wood. Adams was convicted of first-degree murder by a Dallas criminal court and sentenced to death. The sentence was later commuted to life imprisonment.

CONSTITUTIONAL CRIMINAL LAW AND PROCEDURE

In 1985, a filmmaker, Errol Morris, was making a documentary about psychiatrists who testify in death penalty cases. He was granted access to Dallas files and became interested in Adams' case. Eventually convinced that Adams was innocent, Morris filmed The Thin Blue Line, a story of Adams' plight in Dallas.

Subsequent disclosures by witnesses, government prosecutors, and investigating police show that Adams was not given a fair trial. Allegedly, Doug Mulder, the Dallas prosecutor who prosecuted Adams, proposed a deal to 16-year-old Harris if he implicated Adams in Wood's murder. Later, several felony counts against Harris were dropped by Mulder. At one point during Adams' trial, Mulder prevented Adams' attorney from cross-examining a state's witness, because, according to Mulder, "She

was traveling." However, the witness was allegedly staying at a local Dallas motel with the full knowledge of Mulder. On March 1, 1989, the Texas Court of Criminal Appeals overturned Adams' conviction.

Despite overwhelming evidence that government witnesses against Adams had lied under oath, the district attorney's office recommended a high bail, $100,000, for Adams. "We have witnesses and we are ready to (re)try this case immediately," said an assistant district attorney, Winfield Scott.

The new district attorney for Dallas, John Vance, was advised of Adams' release on bail. "I don't think Randall Dale Adams ought to be out on the street," Vance declared to reporters, but later in the week, Vance said that his office lacked sufficient credible evidence to retry the case.

In the meantime, Randall Adams was reunited with his family after a 13-year nightmare and incarceration for a crime he never committed. "No offense, but I hate Texas," said Adams.

Part II explores the foundations of our legal system by examining selected amendments of the United States Constitution. Additionally, it examines the general nature, history, and functions of law enforcement at the federal, state, and local levels. Criminal suspects are entitled to certain constitutional rights. Their processing by law enforcement officers must generally comply with procedural safeguards consistent with the constitutional guarantees and Supreme Court rulings.

Chapter 4 closely examines the elements of crime and criminal law. Simply violating a criminal law is insufficient to justify the criminal label. A mental disposition to commit illegal acts must accompany prohibited acts. Criminal conduct is viewed within the context of the United States Constitution and selected amendments pertaining to the rights of those accused of crimes. The processing of criminal suspects must coincide with the rules of criminal procedure in place in all United States jurisdictions. Furthermore, several legal defenses are frequently used in the courtroom to justify apparent criminal conduct or to mitigate its seriousness.

Chapter 5 identifies several key law enforcement agencies at the federal, state, and local levels and discusses the functions of each. Law enforcement agencies are not required to coordinate their activities with other agencies, although considerable interagency cooperation exists in most criminal investigations. The chapter presents an overview of selected law enforcement issues, including the nature of police selection, training, and professionalism; police discretion, deception, and entrapment; police-community relations; police violence and the use of deadly force; police administration and corruption; and overlapping jurisdictions.

Chapter 6 explores the history and role of police in society and discusses how police orga-

nizations are administered. It is evident that the role of police in American society has changed during the past century. Today, recruitment practices of police departments are increasingly standardized, stressing greater amounts of education and more extensive on-the-job training. Human relations skills are more important compared with physical strength and prowess. Minorities and women are hired more frequently in response to affirmative action policies and greater pressure to ensure more equitable representation of the nation's diverse cultures and interests. Police work is stressful, and it is often accompanied by burnout and high turnover among officers, so this chapter describes the police personality and subculture as well.

Chapter 7 presents an in-depth portrayal of police procedures and law enforcement practices. It describes various patrol styles. In addition, it reviews police officer discretion as it pertains to arrests and detentions, searches and seizures, and the use of deadly force. Recent Supreme Court rulings have limited the discretionary powers of police officers and have generated extensive controversy. Furthermore, more sophisticated accountability systems within police departments have disclosed various forms of police misconduct and corruption. Internal investigative bureaus deal with reported misconduct and corruption. A growing law enforcement component is private police, a nongovernmental contingent of officers privately employed by companies and individuals for security and protection purposes.

Chapter 8 focuses upon the arrest and booking process, and it examines alternative procedures for making arrests. Prosecutors and grand juries may also bring suspects into the criminal justice system through indictments and criminal informations, and the chapter discusses these procedures. When suspects are arrested and accused of crimes, their constitutional rights are triggered. These rights are said to attach at virtually every stage of their processing by the criminal justice system. This chapter follows the defendant through the system up to the point of trial.

The Elements of Crime and Criminal Law

CHAPTER

4

■ THE NATURE OF CRIMINAL LAW

This chapter is about the constitutional foundation of United States criminal laws. All criminal laws are contained in local ordinances and state and federal statutes. They specify criminal acts as well as punishments. The criminal justice system deals exclusively with individuals accused and/or convicted of violating these criminal laws. Several important constitutional amendments ensure the basic rights of United States citizens to fair treatment by the police and the courts. Some of these amendments have been prominent in United States Supreme Court decisions in recent years, so this chapter describes several of the landmark cases that have changed or modified laws.

■ THE BILL OF RIGHTS AND STATE AND FEDERAL LAW

The violation of criminal laws is a serious threat to not only the safety and security of citizens but also the perpetuation of an orderly social, political, and economic arrangement. The criminal justice system exists, in part, to punish the guilty and protect the innocent. If someone is accused of committing a crime and is innocent, numerous safeguards exist to ensure due process. Ideally, all have their day in court, where guilt or innocence can be established. However, the system is far from perfect. Occasionally, guilty defendants are acquitted and freed, and defendants who are not guilty are found guilty and punished.

At the foundation of the criminal justice system is the United States Constitution. This document has established several guarantees, or rights, for all United States citizens. Some of these guarantees are explicit in the first ten amendments to the Constitution. These guarantees are known collectively as the Bill of Rights. Table 4.1 shows each of these amendments.

An earlier document, developed in 1781 by the Continental Congress, was the Articles of Confederation. While these articles contained statements about personal liberties and freedoms, they failed to make explicit the respective powers of the states in relation to the federal government. The Congress convened later and devised the United States Constitution to make these powers more explicit.

TABLE 4.1 The Bill of Rights of the United States Constitution

Amendment	Provision
Article I	Congress shall make no law respecting an establishment of religion, or prohibiting the free exercise thereof; or abridging the freedom of speech, or of the press; or the right of the people peaceably to assemble, and to petition the Government for redress of grievances.
Article II	A well-regulated militia, being necessary to the security of a free State, the right of the people to keep and bear arms, shall not be infringed.
Article III	No soldier shall, in time of peace, be quartered in any house, without the consent of the owner, nor in time of war, but in a manner to be prescribed by law.
Article IV	The right of the people to be secure in their persons, houses, papers, and effects, against unreasonable searches and seizures, shall not be violated, and no warrants shall issue, but upon probable cause, supported by oath or affirmation, and particularly describing the place to be searched, and the persons or things to be seized.
Article V	No person shall be held to answer for a capital, or otherwise infamous crime, unless on a presentment or indictment of a Grand Jury, except in cases arising in the land or naval forces, or in the militia, when in actual service in time of war or public danger; nor shall any person be subject for the same offense to be twice put in jeopardy of life or limb; nor shall be compelled in any criminal case to be a witness against himself, nor be deprived of life, liberty, or property, without due process of law, nor shall private property be taken for public use without just compensation.
Article VI	In all criminal prosecutions, the accused shall enjoy the right to a speedy and public trial, by an impartial jury of the State and district wherein the crime shall have been committed, which district shall have been previously ascertained by law, and to be informed of the nature and cause of the accusation; to be confronted with the witnesses against him; to have compulsory process for obtaining witnesses in his favor, and to have the assistance of counsel for his defense.
Article VII	In suits at common law, where the value in controversy shall exceed twenty dollars, the right of trial by jury shall be preserved, and no fact tried by a jury shall be otherwise reexamined in any court of the United States, than according to the rules of the common law.
Article VIII	Excessive bail shall not be required, nor excessive fines imposed, nor cruel and unusual punishments inflicted.
Article IX	The enumeration in the Constitution, of certain rights, shall not be construed to deny or disparage others retained by the people.
Article X	The powers not delegated to the United States by the Constitution, nor prohibited by it to the States, are reserved to the States respectively, or to the people.

It is important to understand the historical context in which the Constitution was created. The colonists were being exploited by Great Britain in different ways. They were denied trials by jury. Taxes were levied upon them without their consent. In a bill of particulars prepared by the colonists about the tyranny of the king of England, they accused the king of cutting off their trade with other countries, ravaging their coasts, plundering their seas, burning their towns, and destroying their lives.

The provisions of the United States Constitution, including the Bill of Rights and the other amendments, were originally developed in the context of the prevailing common law, the law of tradition and precedent. The constitutional provisions were intended to secure existing guarantees and not necessarily to create new ones (United States Code, *Constitution of the United States,* 1968:62–63). Only in the last few decades has the Bill of Rights been extended to the states, and some of these rights continue to be the subject of United States Supreme Court action.

■ THE FOURTEENTH AMENDMENT: RIGHT TO DUE PROCESS

Shortly after the Civil War, in 1868, Congress ratified the Fourteenth Amendment, which made explicit a citizen's right to due process. It also made a clear distinction between state and federal law. A portion of the Fourteenth Amendment follows:

> All persons born or naturalized in the United States and subject to the jurisdiction thereof, are citizens of the United States and of the State wherein they reside. No State shall make or enforce any law which shall abridge the privileges or immunities of citizens of the United States; nor shall any State deprive any person of life, liberty, or property, without due process of law; nor deny to any person within its jurisdiction the equal protection of the laws.

The significance of this portion of the Fourteenth Amendment is twofold. First, it assures all citizens of due process. In any criminal matter where charges are brought, the Fourteenth Amendment gives any citizen an absolute right to a trial. There are some limitations governing when citizens have the right to a trial by jury, however (see Chapter 8). The second important provision is that no state shall make or enforce any law that abridges or deprives citizens of the United States of their rights as provided under the Constitution.

The original intent of the Fourteenth Amendment was to extend the right to due process, as well as equal protection under the law, to all citizens, particularly former black slaves. Prior to this amendment, slaves did not enjoy the same citizen status as other people. After the Civil War, slavery was abolished. Shortly thereafter, the Fourteenth Amendment technically gave the full rights of citizenship and the full protection of the law to former slaves. In reality, however, racial discrimination was not abolished. Despite changes in the law designed to repair previous injustices against blacks and other minorities, injustices continue today in various forms.

Disparities in judicial sentencing decisions are attibutable, in part, to racial and ethnic factors, gender differences, and socioeconomic variables. Evidence also suggests that discrimination based on race, ethnicity, gender, and socioeconomic differences continues to be prevalent in law enforcement, police discretion, officer recruitment practices, prosecutorial decisions, and corrections.

A DAY IN COURT

An example of a state statute's conflicting with Constitutional guarantees is *Duncan v. Louisiana* (1968). Gary Duncan, a 19-year-old black youth, was driving on a Louisiana road in Plaquemines Parish on the evening of October 18, 1966. There had been recent racial incidents between blacks and whites at the local high school. Duncan drove until he saw two of his cousins having a conversation with four white male teenagers by the side of the road. He stopped his car and advised his cousins to leave. They got into his car, and as he attempted to enter his car also, some of the white youths shoved him. Testimony in court later disclosed that he allegedly slapped one of the white teenagers on the elbow. The white trial judge said that the state had "proved beyond a reasonable doubt that Duncan had committed simple battery," and found him guilty. Although Duncan was sentenced to only 60 days and paid a $150 fine, the Louisiana law Duncan had violated provided a *possible maximum punishment of up to 2 years' imprisonment and a $300 fine.*

Duncan had earlier requested a jury trial but was denied one. At that time, the Louisiana constitution provided jury trials only for cases where either capital punishment or imprisonment at hard labor could be imposed. Duncan appealed to the United States Supreme Court, contending that his Sixth and Fourteenth Amendment rights had been violated. The Supreme Court reversed Duncan's conviction, holding that the Constitution was violated by the Louisiana court when Duncan's demand for a jury trial was refused. Even though Duncan was given only 60 days in jail, the Supreme Court concluded that the penalty authorized for a particular crime *is of major relevance in determining whether it is a serious crime.* The court said, "[A] crime punishable by two years in prison is, based on past and contemporary standards in this country, a serious crime and not a petty offense. [Duncan] was entitled to a jury trial and it was error to deny it."

One purpose of the Fourteenth Amendment is to create consistency and uniformity in state and federal civil and criminal statutes. The main effect of this amendment is to bar any state from passing a law inconsistent with federal law. Furthermore, no state may pass a law that infringes on any federal law applying to United States citizens. However, this amendment does not deny a state the right to enact laws that conflict with those of other states. In one state, it may be a crime to serve liquor to persons under 21 years of age. In an adjacent state, it may be lawful to serve liquor to those age 18 years or older. Citizens of the United States must adhere to all federal laws as well as those of states where they reside and those of states they enter on a temporary basis (such as other states they visit for business or pleasure).

■ SUPREME COURT INTERPRETATION OF SELECTED RIGHTS

From time to time, the United States Supreme Court is petitioned to hear cases requiring an interpretation of one or more constitutional amendments. Ordinarily, the petitioners have been convicted of violating local ordinances or state statutes. The cases are appealed to higher courts within the state, and if the petitioners do not receive favorable judgment in any of the lower courts, they may petition a higher court to hear

Each year brings Fourteenth Amendment issues before the United States Supreme Court. The gap between applying the law equally and disparately continues to haunt law-makers and courts. Hope for full equality under the law has not faded, however.

the matter. The state supreme court decides which cases it will hear. If petitioners exhaust all state court remedies available and receive unfavorable judgment from the supreme court of the state in which they reside, then they may appeal to the United States Supreme Court, especially if the appeal involves constitutional issues.

Depending on the composition of the United States Supreme Court, different interpretations of constitutional amendments are made. Justices are appointed by the president of the United States, subject to Senate confirmation. While the United States Supreme Court receives at least 5,000 appeals a year, it only hears oral arguments and writes opinions about only 150 of them.

Among the first ten amendments to the United States Constitution, six have been frequent topics for criminal appeals to the United States Supreme Court. These include the first, second, fourth, fifth, sixth, and eighth amendments. This section examines each of these amendments and provides sample cases associated with them.

The First Amendment: Freedom of Speech, the Press, and Religion

Regarding the rights to exercise free speech or to assemble peaceably, when does such speech become defamatory and injure others? When does a group's assembly become unlawful and harmful? When does religious expression become criminally harmful? It has been determined that verbally soliciting for purposes of prostitution is not within the right of free speech under the First Amendment *(Eissa v. United States,* 1984). In a 1969 free speech case, a Mr. Brandenburg was arrested, tried, and convicted of "advocating . . . the duty, necessity, or propriety of crime and . . . voluntarily assembl[ing] with [a] society, group, or assemblage of persons formed to teach or advocate the doctrines of criminal syndicalism" *(Brandenburg v. Ohio,* 1969). Brandenburg was believed to be a member of the Ku Klux Klan, and he publicly advocated a march on Congress on the Fourth of July to protest a racial issue. He was prosecuted under a controversial 1919 Ohio statute, the Criminal Syndicalism Statute. The United States Supreme Court reversed his Ohio conviction, noting, "[W]e are here confronted with a statute which . . . purports to punish mere advocacy, and to forbid, on pain of criminal punishment, assembly with others merely to advocate the described type of action. Such a statute falls within the condemnation of the First and Fourteenth Amendments."

In another case, several black police officers in Columbus, Georgia, removed the American flags from their uniforms to protest racially discriminatory hiring practices by the city's police force *(Leonard v. City of Columbus,* 1983). City officials dismissed them from their jobs, and they appealed their dismissal on the grounds that their symbolic speech rights had been violated by the city under the First Amendment provision. The United States Supreme Court ruled the city's action unconstitutional and ordered reinstatement of the officers.

In Vermont, a defendant was convicted of using marijuana, but he claimed the marijuana was for religious purposes and part of the doctrine of Tantric Buddhism *(State v. Rocheleau,* 1982). He claimed that his freedom of religion rights were violated by the marijuana conviction. The United States Supreme Court disagreed. It said, "Assuming that the defendant fully subscribed to the doctrines of Tantric Buddhism and that such is a genuine religion which includes the use of marijuana for spiritual purposes, compelling state interest in regulating marijuana use was of sufficient magnitude to override [the] defendant's interest claiming protection under this clause, particularly where [the] defendant did not assert that he would be unable to practice his religion without the use of marijuana and it was doubtful that he was actually practicing his religion while in the restroom of a nightclub" *(State v. Rocheleau,* 1982).

The Second Amendment: Right to Keep and Bear Arms

This amendment is frequently misunderstood and misinterpreted. Each state has the power to regulate the possession and registration of firearms. The original intent of this amendment was to preserve the right of the states to maintain armed militia. Hence, it refers to a collective right rather than an individual one *(United States v. Warin,* 1976). In 1981, the United States Supreme Court held that it was not a violation of the Second Amendment for the city of Morton Grove, Illinois, to ban the possession of handguns *(Quilici v. Village of Morton Grove,* 1981).

The United States Supreme Court also held in a 1983 case that it was not unconstitutional for Texas to bar a defendant from carrying two swordlike weapons in his belt for going armed for self-protection *(Masters v. State,* 1983). All states have the right to regulate the possession and distribution of firearms and to license and oversee their ownership. The Second Amendment places no limitation on the power of states to enact their own gun control legislation *(People v. Morrill,* 1984), and it does not prohibit

A DAY IN COURT

A leading case involving an unreasonable search and seizure is *Mapp v. Ohio* (1961). In May 1957, three Cleveland, Ohio, police officers went to Ms. Mapp's residence, allegedly seeking information about a person who was wanted in connection with a recent bombing. When they arrived, they knocked on the door and demanded admittance. Ms. Mapp immediately called an attorney and advised the officers she would not admit them without a search warrant.

The officers returned later, without a warrant, and forcibly entered Ms. Mapp's home. The police "ran roughshod" over Ms. Mapp and her young daughter, grabbing Ms. Mapp, twisting her hand, and placing her in handcuffs. Their search extended from the living room to adjacent bedrooms and the kitchen, and eventually to the basement, where they located an obscure trunk. They opened the trunk, rifled through it, and found some "obscene" materials in the bottom of the trunk. Ms. Mapp was charged with possession of obscene materials and convicted.

The United States Supreme Court reversed the Supreme Court of Ohio and said, "We can no longer permit [the Fourth Amendment] to be revocable at the whim of any police officer who, in the name of law enforcement itself, chooses to suspend its enjoyment." The warrantless search was invalidated on the grounds of both unreasonableness and insufficient showing of probable cause, two fundamental guarantees of the Fourth Amendment.

However, warrantless searches are not always unconstitutional. Exceptional circumstances almost always permit different interpretation of each of the amendments. In a 1966 case, a Mr. Schmerber petitioned the United States Supreme Court alleging his Fourth Amendment rights had been violated when police obtained a blood sample after he had been charged with driving while intoxicated *(Schmerber v. California,* 1966). Schmerber claimed that obtaining the blood sample over his objection was an "illegal search and seizure" and "brutal and offensive." The United States Supreme Court ruled otherwise, and it indicated that there was nothing "brutal or offensive" about obtaining the blood sample that was later used as evidence against him.

In a 1952 case, however, a particular search and seizure was determined by the United States Supreme Court to be brutal and offensive. In *Rochin v. California* (1952), Mr. Rochin was suspected by the police of being a narcotics dealer. They entered his two-story house and found him in bed upstairs. They noticed some capsules on his nightstand and asked, "Whose stuff is this?" Rochin immediately grabbed the capsules and swallowed them, despite the preventive efforts of the police. They immediately took him to a hospital, where they induced vomiting and had his stomach pumped. This search uncovered two capsules containing morphine. He was convicted of "possessing a preparation of morphine" in violation of California Health and Safety statutes, where the chief evidence against him was the two capsules. The United States Supreme Court reversed Rochin's California conviction and compared the methods used by police to the rack and screw tactics used in medieval times. They said "[T]his is conduct that shocks the conscience." They further said, "[T]his course of proceeding by agents of government to obtain evidence is bound to offend even hardened sensibilities."

state statutes from defining the crime of unlawfully carrying a weapon *(State v. Young,* 1985).

The Fourth Amendment: Regulation of Search and Seizure

The key phrases of the Fourth Amendment are "**unreasonable searches and seizures**" and "probable cause." This amendment has frequently been interpreted as imposing restrictions on law enforcement officers rather than as protecting the rights of private citizens *(Green v. United States,* 1981). It has also been applied to searches of home, automobiles, the body, lunch boxes, dormitory rooms, and blood and urine specimens.

The United States Supreme Court has broadly construed the Fourth Amendment and has created several exceptions to it. Not all warrantless searches are illegal, and not all seizures of personal possessions violate the amendment. For instance, under the **plain view doctrine,** illegal contraband may be seized if it is in plain view during a police officer's investigation. In one case, a man called the paramedics for assistance when his wife stopped breathing. When the paramedics arrived, they accidentally dislodged a closet curtain, which revealed some illegal firearms and controlled substances. The paramedics called a detective to the scene, and the detective arrested the defendant for possession of controlled substances. This search and seizure was not illegal under the Fourth Amendment, and the evidence obtained was used in court to obtain a conviction *(State v. McAlpin,* 1984).

In another case, police officers stopped a motorist for speeding. When the officers approached the vehicle, they could see illegal drugs and other drug materials on the front seat of the automobile. These illegal objects were in plain view and were admitted

The United States Supreme Court has ruled that any law enforcement officer may stop and frisk, or pat down, suspicious individuals where the officer has probable cause to believe that the person is armed or is capable of inflicting substantial harm upon the officer (Terry v. Ohio, *1968). This does not violate the search and seizure provisions of the Fourth Amendment.*

Warrantless searches of vehicles may lead officers to discover illegal substances such as narcotics. Illegal contraband of any kind may be seized if it is in plain view to officers conducting the search. Officers must have probable cause to stop a vehicle initially, although the United States Supreme Court has ruled that seizure of illegal substances may be evidence against an accused later in court, even if the original search was held to be illegal.

as legally seized evidence against the defendant *(State v. Field,* 1985). The plain view doctrine states that evidence in plain view, or within the immediate visual range of officers, may be lawfully seized and used against a defendant for prosecution purposes. Anything that is unlawful or illegal may be seized by the police in the course of their investigations, provided it is in plain view.

Police officers must legally be where they can view illegal contraband, however, and they must have reasonable certainty that the contraband observed is illegal. It is insufficient for police to confiscate a brown paper bag that they believe might contain an illegal substance unless there is substantial supporting evidence associated with the seizure. Furthermore, even if the search and seizure is later held to be unlawful, illegal drugs or other contraband, such as counterfeit money, seized are illegal per se and will not be returned to the defendant *(United States v. Low,* 1966).

The Fifth Amendment: Right Against Self-Incrimination and Double Jeopardy

This amendment guarantees at least two important rights: (1) the right against self-incrimination, and (2) the right against double jeopardy. In criminal cases, defendants cannot be compelled to testify against themselves, and if those charged with crimes are subsequently acquitted, they cannot be charged again with and tried for those same crimes. In federal courts, the Fifth Amendment also protects citizens from being charged with capital offenses without first having those charges presented to a grand jury. A grand jury is convened to determine probable cause that a crime was committed and that the defendant probably committed it. Individual states do not have to abide by this provision. About half of the states do not use the grand jury system; rather, they employ other means for filing serious charges against suspects.

When police officers have reason to believe that a felony has been committed and that a particular person committed it, they may make an arrest. At the time of criminal arrest, when suspects are taken into custody and charged, the police must advise the

suspects of their constitutional rights. These rights include (1) the right to remain silent, (2) the right to an attorney if the person cannot afford counsel, (3) the right to have the attorney present during all questioning, and (4) the right to give up the right to remain silent. Anything suspects say after being placed under arrest can and will be used against them later in a court of law. The police are not required to advise suspects of their rights as long as the criminal case they are investigating is in the investigatory phase. However, once the investigation progresses to accusation, or the critical phase, the rights are in effect. Placing suspects under arrest and restricting their movements (such as placing them in a patrol car or in jail) are part of the accusatory phase, but authorities must advise suspects of their rights before formally interrogating them.

Interrogations are not always conducted in the immediate presence of the police, and police officers do not have to be physically present. A case of illegal interrogation is *Massiah v. United States* (1964). Massiah and another codefendant were formally charged with violating federal narcotics laws. Massiah pled not guilty and was released on bail. While Massiah was out of jail on bail and after retaining counsel, his codefendant, Colson, decided to cooperate with the police and agreed to spy on Massiah.

On November 19, 1959, Colson had a lengthy conversation with Massiah while sitting in Massiah's automobile. By an earlier arrangement, an FBI agent sat in a car parked near Massiah's automobile. Massiah's automobile had been secretly outfitted with a small radio transmitter, and the FBI agent was able to overhear and record the entire conversation between Colson and Massiah. In that conversation, Massiah made several incriminating statements that led to his federal conviction on the narcotics charges. The United States Supreme Court reversed his conviction, however, saying that Massiah was actually under interrogation by the FBI agent, even though the FBI agent was not physically present in Massiah's vehicle. While under interrogation, Massiah had the right to the presence of his attorney. The court also said that if the rule against self-incrimination "is to have any efficacy, it must apply to indirect and surreptitious interrogations as well as those conducted in the jailhouse."

Sometimes, confessions or admissions are obtained from suspects indirectly. In a 1983 Washington, D.C., case, a suspect was told by police that unless he admitted ownership of a gun found in his apartment, his wife would be arrested and taken to jail along with him *(United States v. Griffin,* 1983). His admission was voided by the United States Supreme Court because it was not voluntarily given. His statements about the gun and its ownership could not be used in court against him.

A DAY IN COURT

One of the earlier cases influencing present police arrest standards is *Escobedo v. Illinois* (1964). On the night of January 19, 1960, the brother-in-law of Danny Escobedo was fatally shot. At 2:30 the next morning, Danny Escobedo was arrested by the police and interrogated until 5:00 the next afternoon. During this period of interrogation, he repeatedly requested an attorney but was denied one.

On January 30, 1960, Escobedo was rearrested and taken into custody after being implicated in the killing by another person, Benedict DiGerlando. Escobedo's lawyer arrived shortly at the police station and asked to see his client. His request was refused. Later testimony by the police revealed that during the second interrogation period, Escobedo was handcuffed in a standing position and that he was nervous, had circles under his eyes, and was very upset and agitated because he had not slept well in the past week.

At one point in this second interrogation, Escobedo was permitted to confront DiGerlando, whom he accused of lying about the murder. Shortly after this confrontation Escobedo made a number of incriminating statements to police that led to his conviction. On petition to the United States Supreme Court, Escobedo claimed that his Fifth Amendment rights had been violated. The court agreed and reversed his conviction for the Illinois murder. The court ruled that Escobedo had been deprived of the right to counsel during a critical phase of the police investigation. Specifically, when the investigation moved from *investigatory* to *accusatory,* Escobedo's rights should have been observed. His confession, extracted over a long period of interrogation and without the benefit of advice from counsel, was ruled inadmissible.

The landmark case governing present police procedures in arrests of criminal suspects is *Miranda v. Arizona* (1966). Ernesto Miranda was charged with kidnapping and rape in Phoenix, Arizona. He was taken to a police station, where he was held incommunicado for over 2 hours and interrogated. He subsequently signed a confession. During this period, he was denied legal counsel, nor was he warned that statements he made could and would be used against him in court. Also, he was not advised of his right to counsel or to have his counsel present during questioning. Finally, he was not advised that he did not have to talk to the police and could terminate the interrogation at any time.

The United States Supreme Court reversed Miranda's conviction and held that his Fifth Amendment rights had been violated. His confession was invalidated by the methods of interrogation. Currently, all criminal suspects are advised of their rights through the Miranda warning when the case advances to a critical phase.

The case of Ernesto Miranda (on the right) led to the establishment of the Miranda warning, by which suspects accused of crimes are informed of certain rights.

The Sixth Amendment: Right to Speedy Trial, Legal Counsel, and Witnesses

The provisions of the Sixth Amendment include the right to a speedy trial by an impartial jury, the assistance of counsel, and the right to confront one's accusers in open court. The term **speedy trial** is vague. In order to make it more explicit, the Speedy Trial Act of 1974 was passed (United States Code, 1989). Amended several times since 1974, this act provides a 70-day period between the time an accused is formally charged with a crime and the date of the trial. While there are exceptions to this fixed time period, ordinarily a defendant being charged with a crime on September 1, 1990, will be tried no later than November 10, 1990, as an example.

This act overcomes certain delays and limits the period within which a defendant's guilt is in question. However, sometimes defendants may be granted additional time between indictment and trial in order for their attorneys to prepare adequate defense. In a 1984 Maine case, a defendant changed attorneys three times, causing a 30-month delay between his indictment and trial. The United States Supreme Court held that his Sixth Amendment speedy trial rights were not violated *(State v. Spearin,* 1984).

The Sixth Amendment includes the provision for the assistance of counsel. Some defendants have raised the issue of the competence of counsel as ground for reversing their convictions. In a Nevada first-degree murder trial, a defense attorney failed to introduce critical evidence that might have lessened the sentence imposed on the defendant *(Mazzan v. State,* 1984). The attorney also made several antagonistic remarks to the jury and criticized them for returning a guilty verdict. In that case, the United States Supreme Court ruled that the defendant was deprived of competent or effective counsel.

The Sixth Amendment also guarantees defendants the right to cross-examine witnesses. All have the right to confront their accusers and to cross-examine them. If this right is denied, it may be the basis for the reversal of a conviction. In a 1984 Rhode Island case, a defendant was tried for voluntary manslaughter *(State v. Freeman,* 1984). His attorney called the man's wife to testify. Since she was the only eyewitness to the events relating to the manslaughter charge, the attorney tried to have her describe her arrest status at the time she made statements to the police. The trial judge refused to allow such questioning, which could have informed the jury about her biases and motives in the case. The United States Supreme Court overturned the man's conviction for manslaughter and said his Sixth Amendment rights had been violated. He was denied the opportunity to cross-examine one of his accusers—his wife.

The Eighth Amendment: Prohibition of Excessive Bail and Cruel and Unusual Punishment

The Eighth Amendment pertains to excessive bail and cruel and unusual punishment. A common misconception is that all citizens have an absolute right to bail, regardless of the offense alleged. In some cases, it might be harmful to society to release suspects on bail; therefore, **preventive detention** is used to confine dangerous offenders and those likely to flee the jurisdiction to avoid prosecution. Judges may use their discretion to deny bail to such persons and keep them confined in jails until their trials. In a case involving a violent crime with sufficient evidence, such as a murder case where several persons observed the suspect brutally murdering someone, permitting the alleged murderer to go free while awaiting trial could result in additional murders. In a case involving a nonviolent crime, someone who is likely to flee the country may be denied bail, such as a banker who has a home in Spain and has been accused of stealing $20 million in negotiable securities from a New Jersey bank.

For those who are entitled to bail, bail should not be excessive, but *excessive* is a subjective term. It varies according to the financial means of a suspect. While the right to reasonable bail is based on the presumption of innocence and is protected by the United States Constitution, the right to bail under the Eighth Amendment is not absolute, and Congress may restrict the categories of cases where bail is allowed *(United States v. Bilanzich,* 1985; *Ex Parte Goosby,* 1985). Bail is also discretionary in every jurisdiction. For burglary, for instance, bail might be set at a higher level for an habitual or an especially dangerous offender than for a first offender.

Issues about **cruel and unusual punishment** include police brutality, prison overcrowding, indifference of prison officials, and capital punishment *(Morgan v. Wilkinson,* 1985; *Williams v. Henry,* 1984; *Estate of Davis v. Johnson,* 1984). For example, inmates do not lose all of their rights as the result of being confined in a jail or prison. The Eighth Amendment guarantees that prisoners have the right to be treated in a reasonable manner. However, courts are consulted about the kinds of treatment that may be unreasonable or cruel and unusual. These terms are highly subjective and elusive. The United States Supreme Court has never explicitly clarified them. Each case is decided on its individual merits.

■ THE RULES OF CRIMINAL PROCEDURE

At the heart of the criminal justice system is a set of rules of criminal procedure. Just as debating societies and public forums are conducted according to established rules of procedure, such as *Robert's Rules of Order,* the processing of criminal defendants is governed by established **rules of criminal procedure.** These rules apply from the time a crime comes to the attention of police and they arrest a criminal suspect.

At the federal level, the United States Code has established the Federal Rules of Criminal Procedure under Title 18, United States Code (1989). As the code has specified under the Federal Rules of Criminal Procedure 1 and 2, "[T]hese rules govern the procedure in all criminal proceedings in the courts of the United States. . . . [T]hese rules are intended to provide for the just determination of every criminal proceeding. They shall be construed to secure simplicity in procedure, fairness in administration and the elimination of unjustifiable expense and delay" (United States Code, 1989:11).

Each state and all United States possessions have rules of criminal procedure, as well. In many states, the Federal Rules of Criminal Procedure have been reproduced with only minor variations and exceptions to reflect local customs or crimes unique to particular jurisdictions (such as shooting alligators in Florida or rustling cattle in Wyoming). Each state has statutory compilations of laws. For instance, Maine has the Maine Revised Statutes Annotated, Alabama has the Code of Alabama, and Oregon has the Oregon Revised Statutes. Included in these statutory compilations are state rules of criminal procedure that govern the processing of defendants in the criminal justice system.

Presently, there are sixty federal rules of criminal procedure. These apply to various stages of the process of dealing with alleged criminal offenders. Table 4.2 shows selected rules applying from preliminary proceedings through judgments. It is beyond the scope of this book to examine all of the rules in detail. Rather, several of the rules have been selected for discussion on the basis of their relevance for criminal defendants.

Table 4.2 shows that a federal criminal action is commenced by filing a complaint under Rule 3. The **complaint** is a written statement of the essential facts constituting the offense charged. Rule 4 applies to issuing arrest warrants or summonses. Included in arrest warrants or summonses are statements of probable cause. Once arrest warrants or summonses have been issued by the court, arrests are made and defendants are brought before United States magistrates. Rule 5 covers every aspect of the procedures to be followed from the arrest through the trial and subsequent appeals. Also included are special forms for making motions, such as calling witnesses to court. State courts follow similar procedures in processing criminal defendants. The rules and procedures vary among jurisdictions, but all state jurisdictions follow a general procedural pattern.

TABLE 4.2 Selected Federal Rules of Criminal Procedure and Stages of the Criminal Justice Process*

Federal Rules	Subject	Stage
3	Complaint	Preliminary proceedings
4	Arrest warrant	Preliminary proceedings
5	Appearance	Preliminary proceedings
5.1	Preliminary examination	Preliminary proceedings
6	Grand jury	Indictment/information
7	Indictment	Indictment/information
8	Joinder/offenses	Indictment/information
9	Warrant/summons	Indictment/information
10	Arraignment	Arraignment/trial preparation
11	Pleas	Arraignment/trial preparation
12	Pleadings/motions	Arraignment/trial preparation
15	Depositions	Arraignment/trial preparation
16	Discovery	Arraignment/trial preparation
17	Subpoena	Arraignment/trial preparation
23	Trial by jury	Trial proceedings
24	Trial jurors	Trial proceedings
26	Taking testimony	Trial proceedings
30	Instructions	Trial proceedings
31	Verdict	Trial proceedings
32	Sentences/judgments	Judgments
33	New trial	Judgments
34	Arrest judgment	Judgments
35	Corrections/sentences	Judgments

*Several rules have been omitted because of their incidental nature to this process or because of their special application to particular motions or technicalities.

Source: 18 United States Code, 1989.

■ THE FUNCTIONS OF CRIMINAL LAW

Criminal law performs two important functions. These are (1) defining criminal conduct, and (2) prescribing the punishment for such conduct.

Defining Criminal Conduct

All criminal conduct is specified in federal, state, and local statutes. Criminal conduct is defined according to violations of criminal laws in each jurisdiction. Sometimes, however, local laws and state statutes conflict with constitutional guarantees extended to citizens.

Although all criminal laws are defined in statutes, they are subject to modification, change, elimination, or amplification, and these changes affect the definition of criminal

A DAY IN COURT

In Jacksonville, Florida, one evening, several persons were arrested and charged with vagrancy (*Papachristou v. Jacksonville,* 1972). In 1971, Jacksonville Ordinance Code 26–57 provided:

> Rogues and vagabonds, or dissolute persons who go about begging, common gamblers, persons who use juggling or unlawful games or plays, common drunkards, common night walkers, thieves, pilferers or pickpockets, traders in stolen property, lewd, wanton and lascivious persons, keepers of gambling places, common railers and brawlers, persons wandering or strolling around from place to place without any lawful purpose or object, habitual loafers, disorderly persons, persons neglecting all lawful business and habitually spending their time by frequenting houses of ill fame, gaming houses, or places where alcoholic beverages are sold or served, persons able to work but habitually living upon the earnings of their wives or minor children shall be deemed vagrants and, upon conviction in the Municipal Court shall be punished as provided for Class D offenses. [Class D offenses were arrests and convictions punishable by 90 days' imprisonment, $500 fine, or both.]

When they were stopped and arrested by police, Margaret Papachristou and Betty Calloway (white females) were driving down the streets of Jacksonville in the company of Eugene Melton and Leonard Johnson (black males). They had just dined at a local restaurant and were on their way to a nightclub. On their way to the nightclub, they had stopped briefly near a used-car lot that had been burglarized several times recently, but there was no evidence of breaking and entering that particular evening. The officers arresting them denied that the racial composition of the group had any bearing on the arrest.

The United States Supreme Court reversed the conviction for vagrancy and chided Jacksonville authorities for their unconstitutionally vague ordinance. The Supreme Court justices declared, "[T]he statute is void because of vagueness, and because it encourages arbitrary and erratic arrests and convictions and fails to give a person of ordinary intelligence fair notice that his contemplated conduct is forbidden by statute." The Supreme Court also said that the statute implicated pillars of the community who have married rich wives and don't work. Also, women under this statute are prevented by implication from being affected by a portion of it (that is, living upon the earnings of their *wives*).

conduct in any given jurisdiction. For example, in 1987, Los Angeles, California, prosecutors filed attempted murder charges against Joseph Markowski, age 29. He was accused of selling his blood and engaging in male prostitution even though he knew he was suffering from AIDS. At that time, no statute prohibited "knowingly transmitting AIDS" *(Time,* July 20, 1987:63), but the lethal nature of AIDS and Markowski's knowledge of this fact brought Markowski's conduct within the context of an attempted murder statute.

Prescribing Appropriate Punishment for Criminal Conduct

Criminal law prescribes punishments for violations of the law. From time to time, there are revisions of punishments prescribed for various criminal offenses. States differ in the ways they define crimes as well as the punishments they prescribe for the same crimes. One state may recognize third degree burglary, whereas another state may not have an equivalent burglary category. The punishment for simple breaking and entering varies among states from 10 years to probation. Offense seriousness and previous records are considered in determining the degree of punishment.

In a Texas case, a murderer and his accomplice received widely different punishments when sentenced. Together, they had abducted and murdered a victim, but at the trial, one of the accomplices testified for the government and received 10 years' probation. The other defendant was sentenced to death. The United States Supreme Court held that this disparity did not violate either accomplice's rights under the Eighth Amendment *(DeGarmo v. State,* 1985).

It is well documented that when judges sentence offenders, they consider such factors as the gravity of the offense, harshness of the penalty, sentences imposed on offenders in the same jurisdiction, and sentences imposed on offenders in other jurisdictions *(State v. Brand,* 1985; *United States v. Hernandez,* 1985; *Rhoden v. Israel,* 1983). Sentences are considered excessive if they are grossly disproportionate to the severity of the crime *(State v. Turner,* 1984; *State v. Roberts,* 1985), but decisions about excessiveness of punishment are subjective, depending on court discretion.

The American Bar Association, the American Law Institute, and several states have created uniformity in their penal sanctions for all major criminal offenses. However, uniform punishment guidelines for all jurisdictions have not been adopted on a national scale. One attempt to introduce uniformity and systematization into criminal justice systems in various jurisdictions is the American Law Institute's Model Penal Code (American Law Institute, 1962). The penal code outlines types of offenses and prescribes uniform punishments for each of them. Fines of $10,000 are provided for first- and second-degree felonies, and fines of $5,000 are provided for third-degree felonies. A $1,000 fine is prescribed for petty misdemeanors.

■ THE ELEMENTS OF A CRIME: *MENS REA* AND *ACTUS REUS*

A crime is a violation of the criminal law by anyone held accountable by that law. Simply committing an act defined as criminal is insufficient. The criminal intent associated with criminal conduct is known as the *mens rea.* The criminal act is the *actus reus.* Combining these two elements, the *actus reus* and the *mens rea*, criminal acts occur, and people may be subject to criminal penalties.

In a California case, Lawrence Robinson was arrested and charged with the willful and unlawful use of narcotics *(Robinson v. California*, 1962). A California statute said it was a criminal offense for a person to be "addicted to the use of narcotics." Under this statute, Robinson was convicted and sentenced to jail. Robinson's attorney argued that Robinson had not committed a crime, but rather, he was being punished for a disease. The United States Supreme Court agreed and reversed his California conviction. The Court said, "[I]t is unlikely that any State at this moment in history would attempt to make it a criminal offense for a person to be mentally ill, or a leper, or to be afflicted with a venereal disease. . . . [E]ven one day in prison would be a cruel and unusual punishment for the 'crime' of having a common cold." In this case, narcotic addition was a status or condition, not an act in the traditional sense. Without an *actus reus*, or a criminal and overt act, there is no crime. Also,thinking about committing a crime but not actually carrying out or attempting to carry out the act is not a crime.

Lacking the requisite criminal intent makes it difficult for prosecutors to convict defendants. This is true in cases where one's sanity or ability to differentiate between right and wrong is at issue. Mental illness and diminished capacity are sometimes defenses for negating the *mens rea*, or guilty mind. In an unfortunate 1969 Idaho case, a woman was charged with voluntary manslaughter after she picked up her 3-month-old infant and threw her on the floor, causing fatal cranial damage *(State v. White*, 1969). The defendant, Janet White, claimed, "[M]y mind snapped, and I threw her [the baby] to the floor." Mrs. White then picked up her baby and put her in the crib. The baby died a few hours later from massive head injuries. Subsequently, Mrs. White was tried and acquitted of voluntary manslaughter charges, relying on the defense of insanity. The State of Idaho appealed the case, but the United States Supreme Court upheld the acquittal. In that instance, a jury had determined that Mrs. White lacked the necessary *mens rea* to sustain a guilty verdict for the alleged criminal offense.

In recent years, several plea options have been proposed to relieve the state of the burden of proving defendants' sanity in criminal cases. The American Psychiatric Association has proposed a "guilty, but mentally ill" alternative to the "not guilty by reason of insanity" plea (American Psychiatric Association, 1984; Ingram, 1986; Pasewark, 1981). States such as Kentucky currently use the "guilty, but mentally ill" option as an acceptable plea in response to criminal charges.

■ CRIMINAL DEFENSES

What defenses explain a person's alleged criminal conduct? Besides insanity, other defenses include (1) self-defense, (2) protection of property, (3) duress, (4) ignorance or mistake, and (5) intoxication.

Self-Defense

The successful use of **self-defense** in criminal proceedings must show that defendants have the reasonable belief that they are in danger. Not only must defendants believe that they were in fear of death or great bodily harm but also that such fear was real and that the actions taken to repel the aggressor were absolutely necessary.

In a 1975 Massachusetts case, a woman was convicted of homicide in the shooting death of her estranged husband (*Commonwealth v. Shaffer,* 1975). On the morning of the homicide, her husband came to her home and threatened her. The defendant ran downstairs to her basement and picked up a .22 caliber rifle. She began to telephone the police but hesitated. Five minutes later, her husband came down the stairs and she fired the rifle, mortally wounding him. The Massachusetts Supreme Court upheld her conviction, saying that she had the means to escape but did not do so. A basement door was available for escape or retreat, and she could have escaped with her children. Because of the totality of circumstances, the court decided she was not in grave peril. Therefore, they concluded the killing was not justified by self-defense.

In a Missouri case, a man pleaded self-defense in the stabbing death of another, but he was convicted of murder in the second degree anyway (*State v. Mayberry,* 1950). In this case, Mr. Mayberry was chased around his own home by Charles Talley, the ex-husband of his present wife. Mayberry made a substantial effort to escape from the home and ran from one room to another, seeking an exit. Finally, he was cornered and pulled a knife to defend himself. In the final confrontation, he stabbed Talley with the knife. The trial court convicted him of murder, but the Missouri Supreme Court reversed the conviction on the ground of self-defense. While they did not absolve him from all blame, they said "[The] defendant in good faith sought to withdraw from the encounter" and that the original charge should be reduced in seriousness because of self-defense.

In noncapital cases, where loss of life does not occur, self-defense might excuse someone from criminal liability if that person fights to avoid personal bodily injury. A court would probably not convict a defendant of assault if it could be shown that the defendant was acting only to protect himself or herself from bodily harm from another.

Protection of Property

Sometimes a defendant may be freed of criminal liability because of **protection of property.** If someone damages another's automobile or home, it is proper for the automobile or home owner to protect the property by any force necessary under the circumstances short of taking the life of the aggressor. Killing someone else to prevent property damage is never justified (*Tennessee v. Garner,* 1985).

A Washington case illustrates the improper use of lethal force in the protection of personal property. In *State v. Marfaudille* (1907), a man rigged a gun to discharge inside his trunk when anyone tried to open it without his permission. He stored his personal valuables and possessions inside the trunk. The landlady entered his apartment one day and opened the trunk. The spring gun inside the trunk discharged and killed her. Marfaudille was convicted of second-degree murder, and the Washington Supreme Court upheld his conviction on the ground that "[Marfaudille] had no greater right to take the life of the deceased by indirect means than he would have had to take it by direct means under the same circumstances if personally present."

Duress

Duress is a defense for criminal conduct under circumstances of coercion. If people are overpowered, coerced, or constrained to perform particular criminal acts against their will, duress is a defense for the criminal conduct. In a 1974 California case, two women escaped from the California Rehabilitation Center, where they were inmates (*California v. Lovercamp*, 1974). They were later captured and convicted of felonious escape. They appealed the conviction and argued that they were placed in a hazardous situation, involving fifteen lesbian female inmates who had threatened them with great bodily harm unless they submitted to sexual advances. They fought with some of the women and were further threatened that the group would "see them again." Therefore, they believed their lives were in danger and fled the prison. The California Court of Appeals believed their argument and accepted the duress defense in that situation. While this action did not necessarily excuse all acts of escape from California penal facilities by inmates who believed their lives were in danger, the court said "[T]he prisoners were faced with a specific threat of forcible sexual attack in the immediate future." The court also noted a phrase applied in seventeenth century England, saying "Some conditions excuseth the felony."

Patty Hearst, who was kidnapped and held hostage by the Symbionese Liberation Army in 1967, was photographed robbing a California bank. She claimed duress and argued that her life was in danger if she didn't cooperate with her captors, but other evidence indicated that she actively and willingly participated in one or more robberies without coercion or threats. The duress defense was unsuccessfully used in her case.

The Model Penal Code recognizes duress as one defense for criminal conduct. The code states that duress excuses criminal conduct where a person "was coerced to do [a criminal act] by the use of, or a threat to use, unlawful force against his person or the person of another, which a person of reasonable firmness in his situation would have been unable to resist."

Patty Hearst obviously posed for this picture, but was her subsequent participation in a bank robbery voluntary or the result of duress?

Ignorance or Mistake

The old adage "ignorance is no excuse" is frequently applied to law violators who claim ignorance of the law when apprehended by police. However, sometimes ignorance of the law *is* a defense that may mitigate punishment or eliminate the *mens rea*. In *Morissette v. United States* (1952), Morissette was hunting deer one afternoon on a government practice bombing range in Michigan. Although there were signs stating "Danger—Keep Out—Bombing Range," the area was known as good deer country and Morissette hunted there anyway. In the course of his hunting, he came across a number of spent copper shell casings that appeared to be discarded.

After a frustrating day of hunting, Morissette decided if he couldn't find a deer, he would offset some of his trip expenses by taking some of these casings and selling them for their copper value. He was arrested and charged with stealing United States government property, convicted, sentenced to imprisonment for 2 months, and fined $200. The United States Supreme Court reversed Morissette's conviction, holding that because Morissette didn't know that he was violating the law by removing the copper casings, he had no intention of committing a crime. In addition, through his good character and his openness in the taking of the casings, he demonstrated that his action was not deliberately criminal.

Intoxication

The American Law Institute and the Model Penal Code position concerning intoxication as a defense to criminal behavior is that it should not be used unless it negates an element of some other offense. For instance, in order for defendants to be convicted of first-degree murder, they must carry out the act with premeditation. It is insufficient that they commit the murder. Thought and planning (premeditation) must be proved before a first-degree murder conviction may be obtained.

In a 1983 Tennessee case, Wayne Adkins was convicted of first-degree murder in the shooting death of Junior Adams *(State v. Adkins,* 1983). Evidence submitted by the defendant showed that on the day of the shooting, Adkins had been drinking large quantities of beer. In fact, witnesses testified that Adkins had consumed at least twenty-four cans of beer before the shooting. The victim of the shooting, Adams, was also a witness to a shooting involving Adkins a few month earlier, where Adkins shot a girlfriend in the stomach. It was common knowledge that Adams planned to testify against Adkins in a future trial. Coupled with Adkins' intoxicated state, these facts led to an argument between Adkins and Adams, resulting in Adams' death. The Supreme Court of Tennessee affirmed the conviction for murder, but it reversed the death penalty, holding, "[Adkins'] drunkenness may be considered in determining whether he specifically intended (premeditated) the particular act for which he is on trial."

Other Defenses

Defendants may use other defenses when charged with crimes. Defendants may act out of necessity. If a home is on fire and the owners are out of town, a neighbor may break and enter in order to put out the blaze and save the home from certain destruction. A charge of burglary against the neighbor will not be upheld in court because the neighbor acted out of necessity.

Sometimes people are entrapped into committing crime. **Entrapment** is the act of law enforcement officers to induce people to commit crimes not contemplated by them. In the case of John DeLorean in California, DeLorean was acquitted of cocaine dealing charges in federal court when it was shown he was induced to participate in a cocaine sale by undercover FBI agents who offered him a large sum of money. This was considered entrapment. DeLorean had no history of cocaine dealing and was not known for any involvement in the drug community; therefore, he was induced to do something that he had not contemplated and that he was not ordinarily disposed to do.

If suspects can prove they were not in the vicinity of a crime when it supposedly occurred, they have an **alibi.** Usually, police interview friends and acquaintances of suspects or others familiar with their whereabouts at the time of the crime. If it is reasonably determined that the suspects were not in the vicinity and could not possibly have committed the crime in question, then alibi is a strong defense against subsequent prosecution.

The common defenses used in criminal actions to explain and condone otherwise criminal conduct are not always successful, but they are considered by jurors and the court. Alibis, especially good ones, may result in exoneration from all charges. Other defenses tend to mitigate the seriousness of punishment; judges and juries tend to punish offenders less harshly if they believe that plausible circumstances contributed to the commission of the crime.

■ CRIMINAL LAW REFORMS AND DECRIMINALIZATION

An examination of federal and state criminal statutes reveals the legal equivalent of culture lag: Criminal laws do not keep pace with an everchanging society. In some states, there are still statutes on the books prohibiting cattle rustling. Of course, in some farming areas, cattle rustling still occurs and is a serious crime, but in large urban centers, such laws are irrelevant.

Likewise, federal criminal laws continue to prohibit selling alcoholic beverages to Indians on their reservations and committing piracy on the high seas. For instance, 18 United States Code, Section 1154 (1989) provides that anyone who sells beer or wine to any Indian on any government land shall be fined $500 and sentenced to 1 year in prison. Subsequent offenses are punishable by a fine of $2,000 and imprisonment up to 5 years. The most recent case cited by the United States Code concerning a criminal violation involving intoxicating beverages on Indian land is 1943!

There is also little uniformity in criminal laws and prescribed punishments among states. In thirty-four states, public drunkenness is not a criminal act, whereas other states include it in one or more of their criminal statutes (Finn, 1985).

That criminal laws and their accompanying statutory punishments should be revised and standardized is evident when examining judicial sentencing practices. Judges vary considerably in sentencing criminal offenders and setting bail (Feeley, 1983; Frazier and Bock, 1982; Gertz and Price, 1985; Goldkamp and Gottfredson, 1985). In most jurisdictions, about 90 percent of the criminal offenders avoid jail or prison sentences and are placed on probation. These arrangements are usually negotiated through plea

CRIME BEAT

An elderly patient is lying in a Prince Georges, Maryland, hospital room in agony, suffering from terminal cancer, near death. A nurse who has been at the patient's side for months cannot bear to watch another minute of suffering. She shuts off all of the life support equipment keeping the patient alive, and the patient dies quietly. After waiting several minutes, the nurse reconnects the life support equipment. She leaves the room to report the expiration.

In Cincinnati's Drake Memorial Hospital a male nurse injects a lethal dose of cyanide into the arm of a patient who was seriously injured in a motorcycle accident 8 months earlier and has been lying in a coma since. Shortly after the injection, the patient dies. The male nurse reports the death to the floor supervisor.

In a Long Island hospital, a male nurse injects a patient with a muscle-paralyzing drug, Pavulon, and immediately runs from the room to summon help. Doctors arrive quickly, administer appropriate medicine, and the patient lives. The male nurse is praised by all staff members for saving the patient's life. A few week later, the male nurse injects another patient with a mild dose of a colostomy cleaner. He runs from the room to alert doctors about the patient's condition. The doctors arrive and find the patient dead.

These incidents are increasingly common. Hospital personnel motivated by one factor or another seek to put dying patients out of their misery or seek recognition for "saving" lives. Richard Angelo, a male nurse at the Good Samaritan Hospital in West Islip, New York, wanted recognition. Therefore, he brought many patients near death only to revive them in a heroic manner. Unfortunately, over twenty-five patients are estimated to have died as the result of Angelo's heroics. At Prince Georges Hospital in Maryland, Jane Frances Bolding, a nurse, allegedly induced cardiac arrest among numerous elderly patients by injecting them with potassium. "My motive was mercy," said Bolding, after admitting injecting potassium into at least two of her patients. In Cincinnati's Drake Memorial Hospital, Donald Harvey, a 35-year-old male nurse, confessed to murdering John Powell, a comotose accident victim who had not regained consciousness for 8 months. "I injected him with cyanide," confessed Drake. "I didn't want to see him suffer."

In each of these cases, the nurses involved may possibly receive the death penalty if convicted. However, it is more likely that plea bargaining will result in lengthy prison terms rather than capital punishment. In Donald Harvey's case, at least, defense attorneys negotiated with the prosecutors to permit their client to plead guilty to lesser charges and avoid having the death penalty imposed. Despite his confession, Harvey stood a good chance of being hospitalized rather than incarcerated and executed, although court-appointed psychiatrists could find little evidence of mental illness to support an insanity plea.

bargaining, an arrangement where defendants plead guilty to one or more charges and have their sentences reduced in severity in exchange for the guilty plea.

With more offenders avoiding prison or jail and the probationer population growing, questions arise about the reality of the punishment provisions that accompany criminal offenses. One trend in sentencing practices is creative sentencing (Czajkoski and Wollan, 1986; Miller, 1986). **Creative sentencing** applies to a broad class of punishments that are alternatives to incarceration and are designed to fit particular crimes. A creative sentence may compensate victims for their losses and injuries or require doing good works. Florida uses such creative sentencing alternatives to incarceration as aiding the handicapped and participating in rehabilitation or counseling programs.

However, there are problems with creative sentencing. Some persons say creative sentencing encourages judicial abuse of sentencing discretion (Czajkoski and Wollan, 1986:228). In one situation, a judge noted that a woman convicted of a marijuana offense was receiving considerable public assistance and had several children out of wedlock. He placed her on probation for the marijuana offense, but as a part of her probationary requirements, he forced her to undergo sterilization. Analysts observed, "[T]he sterilization could not be justified, however, as relating to her marijuana offense or to her personal rehabilitation, and so the judge must have had in mind some benefit to the community by reducing the number of illegitimate children and welfare recipients" (Czajkoski and Wollan, 1986:228).

As a part of criminal law reform, decriminalization has also occurred. Decriminalization is the elimination of certain acts from the body of criminal laws or the removal or lessening of sanctions applied to particular criminal conduct.

One example is the decriminalization of public drunkenness in various states (Finn, 1985). Offenses such as prostitution or minor drug violations have also been considered for removal, modification, or decriminalization.

Critics are skeptical about the effectiveness of decriminalization or the legalization of offenses, such as the use and possession of marijuana, and they believe decriminalizing this conduct will lead to substantial increases in the consumption rate of potentially harmful substances. However, a historical investigation of the decriminalization of marijuana use and possession in eleven states between 1974 and 1979 revealed only small increases in marijuana use when the threat of incarceration was removed for that offense (Harrell, 1983).

■ SUMMARY

Criminal laws have been developed as means of protecting society from the harmful acts of others. Criminal laws define criminal conduct and prescribe appropriate punishments. Criminal laws change as society changes. Such laws and sanctions are applied in the context of certain United States constitutional guarantees to citizens. The Bill of Rights guarantees several rights that must be observed by the criminal justice system whenever accusations of crime are made. Defendants are guaranteed the right to trial by jury in major criminal actions. They have the right to speedy trial, to the benefit of counsel, and the opportunity to confront their accusers in court. They are protected against self-incrimination as well as unreasonable searches and seizures of their persons and property.

The basic elements of a crime are the *mens rea*, or guilty mind or guilty intent, and the criminal act itself, or the *actus reus*. All citizens are presumed innocent until their conduct is judged impartially in court. Certain defenses may explain and excuse criminal conduct at particular times and under particular circumstances. A person may be intoxicated or mentally ill. A person may engage in criminal conduct while under duress or while performing an act necessary for self-defense or protection of property.

As society changes, certain laws become outmoded. These are eventually eliminated or revised. At the same time, new laws are created to fit newly acquired societal needs and interests. Among the problems confronting the criminal justice system are sentencing disparities among jurisdictions and decriminalization issues. Legal reforms through legislation and the actions of organizations such as the American Law Institute attempt to resolve these disparities and issues.

KEY TERMS

alibi	entrapment	self-defense
complaint	plain view doctrine	speedy trial
creative sentencing	preventive detention	unreasonable searches and seizures
cruel and unusual punishment	protection of property	
duress	rules of criminal procedure	

QUESTIONS FOR REVIEW

1. Which of the amendments to the United States Constitution covered by this chapter pertain to due process? What is due process? What importance does it have for alleged offenders entering the criminal justice system?
2. Who is entitled to bail under the Bill of Rights? Under what circumstances might a person not be considered for bail?
3. What are the primary functions of criminal law? What is decriminalization? How is decriminalization related to criminal laws specifically?
4. Does a person have to testify against himself or herself in court? Why or why not? What constitutional provisions are relevant here?
5. Under the Fourteenth Amendment, is it lawful for a state to enact a law that is different from and contrary to a federal law? Why or why not?
6. What is meant by an unreasonable search and seizure? Is evidence obtained by an unreasonable search and seizure necessarily excluded from court? Why or why not?
7. Some persons think that the Second Amendment gives them the right to carry a lethal weapon such as a firearm anytime they want. What does the Second Amendment provide in this regard?
8. What is meant by probable cause? Which of the amendments discussed in this chapter includes probable cause as an integral feature?
9. Identify and discuss two important cases having to do with police interrogation of suspects and leading to major changes in police procedures in this regard.
10. What is the difference between the investigatory phase and the accusatory phase when police are investigating a crime?
11. What two elements must exist in order for a crime to occur? What defenses are available to negate one or the other of these two elements?
12. Is intoxication a defense in excusing criminal conduct? Why or why not? What can a jury or judge do when the defense of intoxication is raised by a defendant?
13. What is meant by creative sentencing? Discuss the potential usefulness of creative sentencing in the sentencing of offenders. What are some of the logistical problems in implementing creative sentencing on a national scale?

SUGGESTED READINGS

Abraham, Henry J. (1977). *Freedom and the court: Civil rights and liberties in the United States.* New York: Oxford Univ. Press.

Cullen, Francis T., and Karen E. Gilbert (1982). *Reaffirming rehabilitation.* Cincinnati, OH: Anderson Publishing Co.

Friedman, Lawrence (1984). *American law.* New York: Simon & Schuster.

Scheb, John M., and John M. Scheb II (1989). *Criminal law and procedure.* St. Paul, MN: West Publishing Co.

Vago, Stephen (1988). *Law and society.* Englewood Cliffs, NJ: Prentice-Hall.

Law Enforcement: Forms and Functions

CHAPTER

5

■ INTRODUCTION

This chapter identifies and examines several law enforcement agencies at the local, state, and federal levels. It describes their major functions and operations. One troublesome feature is that these agencies have overlapping jurisdiction in many criminal matters, and this overlapping jurisdiction fosters competitiveness that sometimes lessens agency effectiveness. In addition, as law enforcement agencies expand their services and functions, questions arise about their goals and purposes, as well as the ways in which these goals and purposes are fulfilled.

■ FEDERAL LAW ENFORCEMENT AGENCIES AND ORGANIZATIONS

Over 20,000 public law enforcement agencies exist at the local, state, and federal levels (Michalowski, 1985:176; Office of Management and Budget, 1982; U.S. Department of Justice, 1981). These agencies employ over 600,000 personnel and have budgets of $37 billion. About 471,000 of the employees are sworn law enforcement officers. In the private sector, over 4,000 private police and security agencies employ an additional 1 million personnel with an annual payroll of $21 billion (Cunningham and Taylor, 1984).

Considering all law enforcement personnel in the public sector, it is ironic that 70 percent to 90 percent of their time is spent performing activities only incidentally related to law enforcement itself (Bittner, 1975:42; Bohm, 1986; Manning, 1978; Pepinsky, 1980). The bulk of their activities includes traffic control, public service, social services, crowd control, supervision of licensed establishments, settling of citizens' disputes, emergency health assistance, and ceremonial work (Bittner, 1975:41; Bohm, 1986). It is a long-held myth that these persons are primarily crime fighters (Bohm, 1986).

At the federal level, several government departments and bureaus oversee a number of law enforcement agencies. Three organizations are presented here. These include (1) the Department of Justice, (2) the Treasury Department, and (3) the Central Intelligence Agency.

The Department of Justice

The United States **Department of Justice** is headed by the attorney general, who is appointed by the president with Senate approval. The president also appoints the attorney general's assistants as well as United States attorneys for each of the judicial districts. Figure 5.1 shows the organization of the Department of Justice. United States

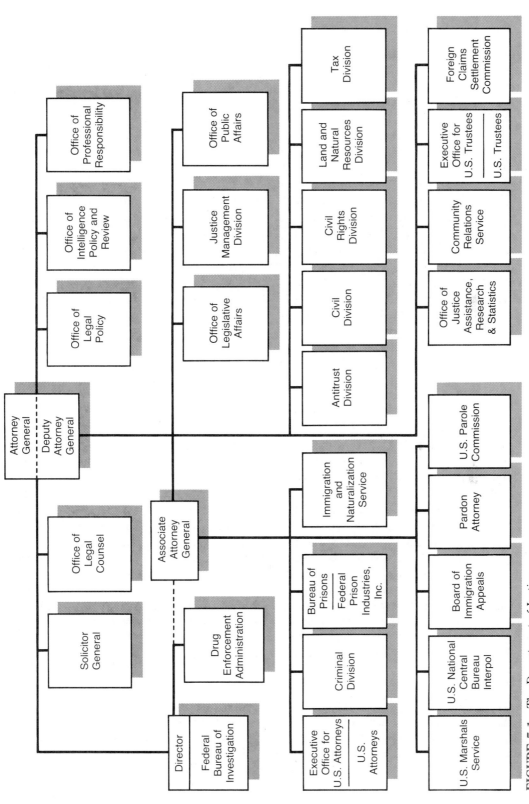

FIGURE 5.1 The Department of Justice

Source: Adapted from the United States Code (1989).

attorneys in each judicial district control and supervise all criminal prosecutions and represent the government in legal suits where it is a party. They may appoint committees to investigate other governmental agencies or offices when questions of wrongdoing are raised or when possible violations of the laws of the United States are suspected or detected.

The Department of Justice is the official legal arm of the government of the United States. Within this department are several law enforcement organizations that investigate violations of federal laws. Among these are (1) the Federal Bureau of Investigation (FBI), (2) the Drug Enforcement Administration (DEA), (3) the Immigration and Naturalization Service (INS), and (4) the United States Marshals Service (USMS).

The Federal Bureau of Investigation (FBI). The **Federal Bureau of Investigation (FBI)** was created and funded through the Department of Justice Appropriation Act of May 22, 1908 (United States Code, 1989). It was originally known as the Bureau of Investigation. It had no specific duties or responsibilities other than the broad charge of the Appropriation Act, which made funds available to the Department of Justice "for the prosecution of crimes." Since the Department of Justice was established to enforce the laws of the United States, the Bureau of Investigation assumed the general responsibility of enforcing these laws, especially the criminal statutes.

In 1933, all of the bureau's functions, including those of the old Bureau of Prohibition, were consolidated and transferred to a Division of Investigation headed by a Director of Investigation. Finally, the Division of Investigation became the Federal Bureau of

CRIME BEAT

The Federal Bureau of Investigation (FBI) becomes involved in any violation of federal criminal laws. When those who commit crimes in one state cross the line into other states, the FBI has an interest in the case. Often, prison escapees who elude police and subsequently relocate in other states become the objects of FBI manhunts. Claude Dallas, Jr., was the subject of an extensive manhunt when he escaped from an Idaho prison and was spotted in California. Originally convicted of manslaughter in the shooting deaths of two game wardens who caught him poaching on a farm in Idaho in 1981, Dallas was reapprehended in early 1987 in Riverside, California, by FBI agents.

In a more bizarre vein, FBI agents are investigating the disappearance of Leo Evoniuk and the death of Daniel Ben Jordan, who are presumed to be on a death list prepared by Ervil Morerel LeBaron, the so-called Mormon Manson, who died in a Utah prison in 1981. The polygamist had thirteen wives who committed various crimes at his order. As FBI agents note,

LeBaron was originally convicted of masterminding the murder of Rulon Allred, a Utah doctor and leader of a polygamist sect consisting of 5,000 members. Although LeBaron did not actually commit the murder, it was clear that he had ordered Allred's death by others.

LeBaron's imprisonment in 1980 led him to devise a list of persons he believed had betrayed him. He died in prison in 1981, but his followers apparently have seen fit to carry out his last wishes. At least two persons from his list have been murdered or have disappeared under suspicious circumstances. Leo Evoniuk, a LeBaron disciple, disappeared from his Watsonville, California, home in May 1986. Left behind were his dentures, numerous shell casings from a 9mm weapon, and a pool of his blood. The disappearance of Evoniuk brought FBI agents into the matter, when it became apparent that the case was related to LeBaron and that its base of operations was Utah. Another disciple, Daniel Ben Jordan, was ambushed during a deer hunt with nine of his wives in a national forest in Utah.

John Edgar Hoover became Director of the Federal Bureau of Investigation in 1924. Under his leadership, the FBI acquired notoriety through the arrests of George "Machine Gun" Kelly in 1933, and John Dillinger and Charles "Pretty Boy" Floyd in 1934. He was responsible for establishing the FBI National Academy at Quantico, Virginia, as well as the Identification Division, a national depository for millions of fingerprints.

Investigation through congressional action on March 22, 1935, Chapter 39, Title II, United States Code. The FBI investigates cases involving at least 200 federal criminal statutes. FBI objectives include the reduction of criminal activity through its investigative efforts. It investigates civil matters and intelligence cases of national security; cooperates with other federal, state, county, and local authorities in cases of mutual interest and assists them with information or laboratory services; and provides extensive professional training to all interested law enforcement officers (Torres, 1985:135–136).

Although the FBI is primarily an investigative agency, it has also been one of the more colorful law enforcement organizations, capturing the attention of the media. During Prohibition, the FBI was instrumental in bringing to justice several infamous criminals such as George "Machine Gun" Kelly in 1933, John Dillinger in 1934, and Charles "Pretty Boy" Floyd in 1934. More recent FBI activity has included the investigation of the murder of Congressman Leo J. Ryan at Bob Jones' People's Temple in Jonestown, Guyana, in November 1978; the murder of United States District Court Judge John H. Wood of San Antonio, Texas, in May 1979; and the investigation of public corruption in the Abscam operation in the early 1980s, which led to the conviction of several congressmen and state government leaders (Torres, 1985:136).

The FBI has not always had an untarnished reputation, however. In 1986, the federal racketeering trial of John DeLorean, a former carmaker, disclosed evidence of FBI misdeeds, including perjured testimony and the concoction of incriminating materials intended to make DeLorean appear guilty to federal jurors. DeLorean was acquitted of all criminal charges, and numerous instances of FBI misconduct were disclosed in posttrial interviews.

More favorably, FBI assistance to other law enforcement agencies throughout the country is unsurpassed. In April 1983, about 177 million fingerprints were on file with the FBI, including about 80 million fingerprints of criminals. The Identification Division

George "Machine Gun" Kelly kidnapped Charles F. Urschel, an Oklahoma oil millionaire, on July 22, 1933. In 2 short months, Kelly was captured by federal agents in a Memphis, Tennessee, hotel room. During his capture, he reportedly shouted, "Don't shoot, G-Men!" The government-men label stuck, probably encouraged by J. Edgar Hoover, who was much concerned with FBI image building.

of the FBI has assisted state and local police departments in identifying not only criminal suspects but also missing persons and accident victims.

The FBI also maintains an Instrumental Analysis Unit, where samples of various substances are stored. In criminal investigations, almost any type of material evidence can be examined and identified by this unit. In 1982, over 800,000 scientific examinations of physical evidence were conducted for various interested agencies.

The Criminal Investigation Division of the FBI is most directly involved in combating criminal activity. In 1982, for instance, about 20 percent of the time of special agents of the FBI was devoted to organized crime investigations, leading to the conviction of over 700 individuals. There were also about 4,000 white-collar criminal convictions (Torres, 1985:139–140).

The Drug Enforcement Administration (DEA). The **Drug Enforcement Administration (DEA)** is an outgrowth of the former Bureau of Narcotics, established in 1930 under the direct control of the Treasury Department. In 1968, the Bureau of Narcotics was transferred from the Treasury Department to the Department of Justice and renamed the Bureau of Narcotics and Dangerous Drugs. This transfer occurred, in part, because Bureau of Narcotics special agents were accused of selling a quantity of the drugs that they had confiscated (Torres, 1986:126–127).

In 1973, the DEA was established under a general reorganization plan that combined the functions of several agencies. In January 1982, the DEA was given primary responsibility for drug and narcotics enforcement, sharing jurisdiction with the FBI in

A DAY IN COURT

Significant is the FBI's conduct (or misconduct) in its investigation of Dr. Martin Luther King, Jr. (Garrow, 1981). From December 1963 until his death in 1968, Dr. King was the target of an intensive campaign by the FBI to neutralize him as an effective civil rights leader (Sorrentino, 1985:108). In January 1964, for instance, William C. Sullivan, assistant to Director J. Edgar Hoover, wrote the following memorandum to Deputy Associate Director Alan Belmont:

> It should be clear to all of us that Martin Luther King must, at some propitious point in the future, be revealed to the people of this country and to his Negro followers as being what he actually is—a fraud, demagogue, and scoundrel. When the true facts concerning his activities are presented, such should be enough, if handled properly, to take him off his pedestal and reduce him completely in influence. When this is done, and if it can and will be done, obviously much confusion will reign, particularly among the Negro people. . . . If this thing can be set up properly without the [FBI] in any way becoming directly involved, I think it woulds [sic] be not only a great help to the FBI, but would be a fine thing for the country at large. (Sorrentino, 1985:120)

The FBI then embarked upon a course of action designed to discredit Dr. King at every turn—bugging his motel rooms, using the Internal Revenue Service to audit his income tax returns, and writing anonymous letters alleging infidelity and other improprieties to his supporters. Clearly, these actions are not within the scope of the proper activities outlined by law for the FBI to follow.

Some critics have suggested that a feud existed between FBI Director J. Edgar Hoover and Dr. King during the era of civil rights activism and that this feud prompted many FBI indiscretions during the period (Garrow, 1981; Sorrentino, 1985). Current evidence suggests that in spite of numerous internal safeguards to the contrary, the FBI continues to harass selected investigative targets.

---

this regard (Torres, 1985:126). The major responsibilities of the DEA include (1) the development of an overall federal drug law enforcement strategy, including programs, planning, and evaluation; (2) full investigation of and preparation for the prosecution of suspects for violations under all federal drug trafficking laws; (3) full investigation of and preparation for the prosecution of suspects connected with illicit drugs seized at United States ports of entry and international borders; (4) conduct of all relations with drug law enforcement officials of foreign governments; (5) full coordination and cooperation with state and local law enforcement officials on joint drug enforcement efforts; and (6) regulation of the legal manufacture of drugs and other controlled substances (28 U.S.C., Sec. 509, 1989). In 1984, the DEA employed over 4100 persons. About half of these are special agents authorized to carry firearms, make arrests, and seize property when violations of federal drug laws occur.

The Immigration and Naturalization Service (INS). Congress was given power to establish a naturalization service originally under Article I, Section 8 of the Constitution (Torres, 1985:178). In 1798, the Alien Act gave the president the power to expel aliens

CRIME BEAT

In 1986, Congress passed the Anti-Drug Abuse Act. This act authorized an initial $1.7 billion appropriation to combat drug trafficking on an international scale. Many law enforcement agencies became involved in an effort to at least slow, if not stop, the flow of drugs from countries such as Colombia. The magnitude of the problem was such that in 1985 alone, Americans consumed 72 metric tons of cocaine. About 80 percent of this cocaine is believed to have been manufactured in and transported from Colombia by the notorious Medellin Cartel.

One of the principal figures in the Medellin Cartel was Carlos Lehder Rivas, formerly a small-time marijuana dealer in New York City. In the early 1980s, Carlos Rivas rose to head perhaps the largest drug-smuggling operation in the world. In fact, U.S. attorney Robert Merkle characterized Rivas as the "Henry Ford of cocaine." Rivas allegedly used airplanes and boats to transport an estimated 15 tons of cocaine into the United States every month.

As the result of a Colombia–United States pact for enforcing a ban on drug production and distribution, Colombian police arrested Rivas in February 1987 to face extradition to Florida to face drug-smuggling charges. At the time of his arrest, Rivas, age 38, boasted that he controlled over 300 Colombian police and government officials who knew about and condoned his drug-smuggling operations.

In November 1987, Rivas went on trial in a federal district court in Miami, Florida. United States prosecutors believed that the case would be concluded within 3 months and that over 200 witnesses would be called by both the prosecution and defense. Actually the trial lasted 7 months, and Rivas was convicted of smuggling hundreds of millions of dollars worth of cocaine into the United States. Although his attorneys filed appeals, Rivas was sentenced to life imprisonment for his crime. Despite the snaring of this drug kingpin, officials are skeptical that his arrest and conviction will have a perceptible impact on the flow of drugs from Colombia.

who were considered a threat to United States security. The Office of Commissioner of Immigration was created in 1864 under the Department of State, and in 1898, the Commissioner of the Bureau of Immigration was established. In 1903, this bureau was placed under the control of the Department of Commerce and Labor. By 1913, it was divided into a Department of Labor and the Bureau of Naturalization, and these two bureaus were placed under the control of the Department of Labor. Later, the two bureaus were recombined into the **Immigration and Naturalization Service (INS).** The INS was transferred to the Department of Justice in 1940.

Perhaps the best-known agency of the INS is the Border Patrol (BP), which was established in 1924 with 450 officers (Torres, 1985:178). The BP was originally created to police the borders between the United States and Canada and Mexico. Under the McCarran-Walter Act of 1952, the INS was charged with three goals: (1) the reunification of families; (2) the immigration of persons with needed labor skills; and (3) the protection of the domestic labor force. The BP is most visible today in its fight against the illegal entry into the United States of persons from countries including Cuba and Mexico.

The BP is responsible for more than 8,000 miles of international boundaries. An example of the magnitude of the enforcement activity by the BP is that in 1982, it apprehended 819,919 aliens. Many of these aliens were involved in illegal activities, including drug smuggling and theft—3,112 of them were convicted of smuggling-related

The Border Patrol arrests thousands of persons each year who cross the United States borders illegally. With 8,000 miles of international boundaries to patrol, the Border Patrol snares only a handful of illegal aliens. In 1982, 800,000 illegal aliens were apprehended and returned to their countries of origin.

charges (Torres,1985:182). The budget for the INS is $450 million. INS agants have the power of arrest and search and seizure under 8 United States Code (1989).

The United States Marshals Service (USMS). The **United States Marshals Service (USMS)** is one of the oldest federal law enforcement agencies in existence (Torres, 1985:360). The office of United States Marshal was established under the Judiciary Act of 1789, and George Washington appointed 13 marshals, one for each of the original thirteen states. In the Old West, Wyatt Earp was one of the more famous United States marshals.

In 1969, the United States Marshals Service itself was established. It formally became a bureau in 1974. In 1984, it had ninety-four judicial districts and 93 United States marshals, with at least one marshal per state. The budget for the USMS in 1984 was $117.7 million. In 1984, in addition to the United States marshals, it had 93 chief deputy marshals, 1,600 deputy marshals, and over 400 staff employees (Torres, 1985:363).

Duties of the United States marshals include serving process for federal judges, serving criminal and civil subpoenas and civil summonses, arresting fugitive felons, serving federal arrest warrants, handling international extraditions, and providing secure detention for approximately 75,000 federal law violators (Torres, 1985:363). United States marshals also are empowered to seize and dispose of land or goods under federal court orders to secure judgments.

Another important function of United States marshals is the operation of the Witness Protection Program. Federal witnesses are sometimes threatened by defendants or their friends, and depending upon the case (such as when testifying in a conspiracy trial against a member of the Mafia or other organized crime figure), United States marshals sometimes provide complete changes of identity for witnesses and their families, new Social Security numbers, new residences, and new employment. The Witness Protec-

CRIME BEAT

The six-year prison term handed last week to the former head of the International Telecommunications Satellite Organization in a bid-rigging and kickback scheme was just the latest example of an intensified federal drive against *white-collar crime*.

A new Justice Department report shows convictions are up nearly 20 percent since 1980. Leading categories are *fraud, forgery* and *embezzlement*. Dropping slightly were counterfeiting, tax and regulatory cases. Prison terms also are edging up as prosecutors seek *stiffer sentences* to deter potential lawbreakers. Average sentences rose from 24 months in 1980 to 29 months in 1985. Still, only 40 percent of white-collar convicts *ever go to jail*—a figure that hasn't changed

much in recent years. But prosecutors predict the figure will rise dramatically—to as much as 60 percent—if federal sentencing guidelines go into effect November 1, as expected. The rules set standard minimum sentences, including *mandatory terms* for many white-collar offenses.

Meanwhile, Justice officials say they are targeting two areas of white-collar crime for special attention in coming years: Fraud in *banking and in the defense industry.* But critics charge that the prosecution numbers are misleading—that many of those arrested are *little fish,* not major corporate perpetrators.

Source: Reprinted with permission from *U.S. News and World Report* (October 5, 1987), p. 34.

tion Program was established in 1984. Within a year, the program had afforded protection to 15,000 individuals, including the successful relocation of 4,250 witnesses.

Other Department of Justice Divisions. The Department of Justice also has a Civil Rights Division, which is authorized to investigate allegations of civil rights violations. In 1982, the Civil Rights Division prosecuted fifty-six criminal actions against ninety-eight defendants for discriminatory acts and other civil rights violations (Torres, 1985:31).

The attorney general is also empowered to conduct investigations of organized crime and racketeering under the amended Racketeer Influenced and Corrupt Organizations Act (RICO) of 1984. *United States v. DiCaro* (1985) challenged the right of the attorney general to conduct such investigations, but the court upheld the attorney general's right under the act. In recent years, the American Bar Association has attempted to coordinate state and federal antiracketeering efforts by developing some common objectives to be adopted by interested law enforcement agencies (American Bar Association, 1985; Marcus et al., 1983).

The Treasury Department

Many agencies with law enforcement functions are under the direct control of the **Treasury Department.** Those of interest here include (1) the Bureau of Alcohol, Tobacco, and Firearms, (2) the Customs Service, (3) the Internal Revenue Service, and (4) the United States Secret Service.

The Bureau of Alcohol, Tobacco and Firearms. The **Bureau of Alcohol, Tobacco and Firearms (BATF)** has its origin as a subunit within the Internal Revenue Service in 1862, when certain alcohol and tobacco tax statutes were created (Torres, 1985:63). It was originally called the Alcohol, Tobacco, Tax Unit. The organization was later named the Alcohol, Tobacco, and Firearms Division within the IRS. In 1972, it became the current BATF under the direct control of the Treasury Department.

Like the FBI, the BATF has a fairly colorful history. There are numerous episodes of disposing of illegal whiskey stills in remote mountain regions. In 1919, Congress ratified the Sixteenth Amendment, prohibiting the manufacture, sale, or transportation of intoxicating liquors into the United States. For a 12-year period, the United States underworld thrived on illegal liquor sales and the operation of speakeasies or secret bars where the public could purchase liquor. This era bolstered the popularity of such persons as Elliot Ness, a BATF agent who led federal authorities after bootleggers and organized gangsters who were profiting from illegal liquor sales. "The Untouchables," a television program in the 1960s, was based upon Ness's exploits of the 1920s and 1930s.

The BATF has a budget of $150 million and employs 1,200 special agents. Its law enforcement functions extend to not only liquor, tobacco, and firearms trafficking but also arson, high explosives including bombs, and automatic weapons. It is illegal for a private citizen to own or possess an automatic weapon, such as a submachine gun, without official authorization from the Treasury Department and the purchase of an expensive tax stamp. The BATF approves such possessions only after thoroughly investigating the character and background of the applicant. Unauthorized possession of an automatic weapon in any state is a felony. The BATF also authorizes licenses for firearms dealers, importers and exporters, and ammunition manufacturers. In 1983, nearly 1 million firearms were imported into the United States, and this figure does not include the number of weapons domestically manufactured!

The BATF's general mission in combating crime is to reduce the illegal use of firearms and explosives. It also seeks to curtail arson-for-profit schemes, and its agents investigate scenes of fires with mysterious origins (Torres, 1985).

The Customs Service. The first Customs Service officers and agents were created under the Tariff Act of 1789, when Congress authorized them to collect duties on goods,

Illegal automatic weapons and explosives that were seized in a raid on a Symbionese Liberation Army (SLA) headquarters in California are exhibited by a BATF agent. The SLA had claimed credit for kidnapping Patty Hearst, daughter of wealthy newspaperman, William Randolph Hearst.

wares, and merchandise (Torres, 1985:353). Under Title 19 of the United States Code (1989), the **Customs Service** is authorized to conduct searches and inspections of all ships, aircraft, and vehicles entering United States borders. Customs personnel may seize any illegal merchandise or wares, and agents are empowered to arrest suspects engaging in illegal activities.

The Customs Service employs over 14,000 persons in both enforcement and nonenforcement positions. In 1984, Customs Service officers and agents made substantial seizures of narcotics and engaged in numerous narcotics arrests. They seized almost 20,000 pounds of cocaine, 2.7 million pounds of marijuana, 2,200 pounds of hashish, and 6,000 pounds of heroin, worth about $8 billion. They seized and impounded nearly 10,000 vehicles and 200 aircraft as a part of illegal drug trafficking (Torres, 1985:355–356).

Normally, the Customs Service maintains a close liaison with other law enforcement agencies, particularly in the area of international drug trafficking and smuggling. It interfaces with the National Crime Information Center operated by the FBI as well as with the Drug Enforcement Administration (Torres, 1985:356)

Customs patrol officers enforce the federal laws at airports and in cargo areas, piers, and terminals. They perform their duties on foot, on horseback, in helicopters, by boat, and by airplane. They use dogs to locate contraband emitting odors, such as marijuana. Customs personnel also investigate the illegal smuggling of firearms. In close cooperation with the Immigration and Naturalization Service under the Department of Justice, they also investigate illegal aliens.

The Internal Revenue Service. Another agency within the Treasury Department is the **Internal Revenue Service (IRS).** The main role of the IRS is to monitor and collect federal income taxes from individuals and businesses. However, the IRS has a Criminal

CRIME BEAT

The Customs Service and the Drug Enforcement Administration have their work cut out for them in tracking down drug smugglers. Casual trips by tourists to Mexico and other countries result in amateurish attempts to smuggle small quantities back to the United States in shaving cream cans, cosmetic cases, and toothpaste tubes. Large-scale smuggling of marijuana has involved large shipments in cans purportedly containing refried beans and destined for anonymous supermarkets in various states.

At the John F. Kennedy Airport in early 1987, a highly sophisticated network of airlines, airport, and baggage handling personnel were involved in large-scale cocaine smuggling. Baggage handlers emptied cocaine from luggage destined for customs inspection and passed it through emergency exits not checked by

the customs officials. When the smuggling ring was broken and diagramed, over forty persons employed by the airport and various airlines were involved in the operation.

Drug enforcement efforts by various government agencies seemingly uncover only a small portion of the drugs that actually enter the United States annually. Even the arrest and subsequent conviction of the "Henry Ford of drug trafficking," Carlos Lehder Rivas of Colombia, is believed by many officials to have little long-term impact on the flow of drugs from other countries into the United States. Unfortunately, as long as those engaged in public transportation and baggage handling continue to be involved in drug smuggling at Kennedy and other airports, the flow of illegal drugs will continue.

Investigation Division (CID), which investigates possible criminal violations of income tax laws and recommends appropriate criminal prosecution whenever warranted (Torres, 1985:97). The first chief of the Special Intelligence Unit, Inspector Elmer I. Irey, gained notoriety by participating in investigations including the income tax evasion charges against Al Capone and the kidnapping of Charles Lindbergh's baby (Kennedy, 1985:104–105).

The Criminal Investigation Division cooperates with the United States Attorney's Office of the Department of Justice in investigating possible criminal violations of federal income tax laws and recommending criminal prosecutions and civil penalties against taxpayers. In 1983, the CID conducted 5,785 investigations and recommended 2,610 individuals for criminal prosecutions that resulted in 1,492 convictions. In over 60 percent of these convictions, prison terms were imposed (Torres, 1985:101–102). CID agents carry weapons and are authorized under 18 United States Code, 26 United States Code, and 31 United States Code (1989) to execute search warrants, make arrests without warrant for offenses relating to internal revenue laws, and make appropriate seizures of property in relation to criminal offenses relating to internal revenue laws.

The United States Secret Service. The **United States Secret Service (USSS)** originated in 1865 as the Secret Service Division (SSD). It had a primary responsibility to capture and punish counterfeiters. In 1908, the SSD was transferred to the Department of Justice. From 1912 to 1918, the SSD made numerous arrests and secured over 1,000 counterfeiting convictions, involving about $250,000 in fake coins and currency. Presidential security became an SSD function in 1917 in addition to its anticounterfeiting duties. In 1965, shortly after President Kennedy was assassinated, the SSD was placed under the Treasury Department and renamed the United States Secret Service (Torres, 1985:370).

The USSS has been helpful in preventing several presidential assassinations. In 1975, President Gerald R. Ford was the target of an assassination attempt by Lynette "Squeaky" Fromme in Sacramento, California. USSS personnel intervened successfully to prevent his assassination. USSS agents also overpowered John Hinckley when he attempted to assassinate President Ronald Reagan in Washington, D.C., in 1981.

USSS personnel are authorized to carry firearms and to make arrests for violations of any federal laws. They have jurisdiction in counterfeiting activity. They also are empowered to investigate credit and debit card frauds and frauds related to electronic fund transfers, such as bank automatic teller machines (18 U.S.C., Sec. 3056, 1989). In a Texas case, the USSS was responsible for the arrest and prosecution of persons who had stolen Treasury Department checks and were attempting to cash them in various stores (*United States v. Collins,* 1982).

The Central Intelligence Agency

Under the National Security Act of 1947, the National Security Council was established. The congressional purpose of the act was to provide a comprehensive program for the future security of the United States, and to provide for the establishment of integrated policies and procedures for the departments, agencies, and functions of the government relating to the national security. Under the CIA Act of 1949, the National Security

Council established a subordinate organization called the **Central Intelligence Agency (CIA)**. The CIA is considered one of the more clandestine government services, participating in undercover and covert operations on an international scale. The CIA has been linked with such covert actions as the ill-fated Bay of Pigs fiasco and the supply of arms to Nicaraguan rebel forces.

The functions of the CIA include (1) the collection, production, and dissemination of foreign intelligence and counterintelligence, including information not otherwise obtainable and (2) the collection, production, and dissemination of intelligence on the foreign aspects of narcotics production and trafficking. The second function is of particular interest to criminal justice. The CIA transmits information it obtains to other interested agencies, including the FBI and the Customs Service, as a part of a nationwide program to curtail the distribution of illegal narcotics. However, the intelligence gathering functions of the CIA have greatly overshadowed the agency's participation in the investigation of illegal drug trafficking on an international scale. For instance, in 1985, the CIA was directly responsible for the seizure of over 1,000 pounds of cocaine and other narcotics having a value of $3 million.

Other Federal Agencies

The federal agencies and organizations just described are only a few of the many federal law enforcement agencies that exist. Although each agency has specific functions and goals, some overlap occurs in critical areas, such as drug trafficking and contraband smuggling. These overlapping responsibilities sometimes create internal conflicts, where one organization attempts to steal the show from another. If the FBI became involved in an illegal international drug transaction, it probably would proceed independently. Most likely it would not involve the Customs Service or the Bureau of Alcohol, Tobacco and Firearms in its operations. By the same token, the Bureau of Alcohol, Tobacco and Firearms sometimes would take action without notifying other interested agencies.

Inasmuch as the United States Code provides that each agency should maintain an effective liaison with other interested agencies in the enforcement of federal laws, it is organizationally inefficient for these agencies to fail to share valuable information with others when violations of the law occur. However, it is unlikely that anything can be done administratively in the immediate future to remedy such interorganizational jealousies.

■ STATE POLICE AGENCIES

About a fourth of all law enforcement officers (117,000) are members of the state police (U.S. Department of Justice, 1986:242). One of the most publicized state police organizations is the Texas Rangers, the first state police department, established in 1835. However, some historians argue that the Pennsylvania State Police, established in 1905, was the first true, or modern, state police agency.

The Pennsylvania State Police organization was one of several different models of state law enforcement. The Pennsylvania State Police model required all officers to function as a uniformed force. Throughout the state, Pennsylvania troopers continue to enforce all state laws. In addition, these officers have arrest powers similar to local police, have the authority to perform investigatory functions when major crimes are committed, and have teams of specialists who engage in forensic and laboratory work. Other states, such as Delaware and New York, have emulated the Pennsylvania model.

However, different models focus almost exclusively on the enforcement of state highway laws. Highway patrols in such states as Utah, Kansas, Georgia, and Kentucky spend most of their time enforcing state traffic laws, although they sometimes perform additional functions. The police in each state jurisdiction perform different tasks, although the public sterotype of state police is the contingent of uniformed officers of **state highway patrols.** With the exception of Hawaii, most states have a highway patrol or its equivalent. The responsibilities of highway patrol officers, often known as state troopers, include enforcing state motor vehicle laws on major state roads and federal interstate highways.

In some states, state police conduct training for local, city, and county officers. Training centers offer courses on crime detection, personal safety, and weapons. In New Mexico, for instance, traffic enforcement is only one of several functions of the state police, who are trained in techniques of criminal investigation and cooperate with other authorities in cases that cross jurisdictional boundaries.

As a part of their official duties in some states, state troopers and other state police are empowered and obligated to assist in collecting state taxes and other revenue. In Tennessee, state troopers establish roadblocks to determine whether motorists have appropriate driver's licenses, and they utilize dogs in searches of automobiles to detect marijuana and other substances prohibited by statute. They carry weapons and make arrests for various law violations.

Some states have bureaus of identification similar to the FBI. Agents of these state bureaus perform routine criminal investigation functions. When state police become involved in such operations, they usually assist state investigative agents. They assist these agents by making arrests of criminal suspects, interviewing witnesses, and gathering and securing evidence from crime scenes.

■ COUNTY AND METROPOLITAN POLICE

The history of the modern police department can be traced to nineteenth century England, although the *notion* of police may be traced to earlier periods, such as ancient Rome, which used centurions as quasi-military personnel. During the nineteenth century, a magistrate, Patrick Colquhoun (1745–1820), made several innovative proposals, several of which were influenced by an earlier writer, Henry Fielding (1707–1754). Colquhoun proposed the establishment of a bureaucratic law enforcement organization with full-time, paid personnel specializing in particular detection, prevention, and deterrence functions (Becker and Whitehouse, 1980). In 1806, Colquhoun outlined his proposals in his work, *Treatise on the Police in the Metropolis*. This treatise presented the following idea:

> Police in this country may be considered as a new science; the properties of which consist not in the judicial powers which lead to punishment, and which belong to magistrates alone; but in the prevention and detection of crimes; and in those other functions which relate to the internal regulations for the well ordering and comfort of civil society. (Colquhoun, 1806:preface)

In 1829, England's home secretary and political reformer, Sir Robert Peel, established the Metropolitan Police of London through the Act for Improving the Police in and Near the Metropolis (Lee, 1901). This act created two justice of the peace positions to conduct the business of the police office, and it also framed a number of regulations for the management of the force (Manning, 1977:77–78). Two police commissioners gave considerable substance and direction to early English police work: (1) an army officer, Charles Rowan (1783–1852) and (2) a lawyer, Richard Mayne (1796–1868), appointed by Peel to head his new force (Becker and Whitehouse, 1980:6–8; Miller, 1985:49). Modern police organization in the United States has been patterned from the Metropolitan Police of London of 1829 (Becker and Whitehouse, 1980:34). The first police force was established in Boston in 1838, and the next in New York City in 1845 (Miller, 1985:49–50).

Currently, there are 12,200 local police agencies in the United States (U.S. Department of Justice, 1986:242). Table 5.1 shows the number of full-time law enforcement officers per 1,000 inhabitants of United States cities in 1987. The national average for all cities is 2.6 officers per 1,000 inhabitants. Geographically, the highest rate of officers to population occurs in the Northeastern states, where there are 2.9 officers per 1,000 inhabitants. The lowest rates occur in the Western states, where there are 2.4 officers per 1,000 inhabitants (U.S. Department of Justice, 1988:227).

CRIME BEAT

Noted police historian Charles Reith has said that the following principles should be reviewed and considered as measurable behavioral objectives to be achieved and maintained for proper police efficiency, effectiveness, and economy of operation (Reith, 1952):

1. The primary objective of an efficient police force is the prevention of crime as an alternative to the repression of crime and disorder by military force and severity of legal punishment.
2. To recognize always that the power of the police to fulfill their functions and duties is dependent on public approval of their existence, actions, and behavior, and on their ability to secure and maintain public respect.
3. To recognize always that to secure and maintain the respect and approval of the public means also the securing of the willing cooperation of the public in the task of securing observance of the law.
4. To recognize always that the extent to which the cooperation of the public can be secured diminishes proportionately the necessity of the use of physical force and compulsion for achieving police objectives.
5. To seek and preserve public favor . . . by constantly demonstrating absolute impartial service to law . . . by ready offering of individual service and friendship to all members of the public without regard to their wealth or social standing; by ready exercise of courtesy and good humor; and by ready offering of individual sacrifice in protecting and preserving life.
6. To use physical force only when the exercise of persuasion, advice and warning is found to be insufficient to obtain public cooperation to an extent necessary to restore order.
7. To maintain at all times a relationship with the public that gives reality to the historic tradition that the police are the public and that the public are the police; the police being only members of the public who are paid to give full-time attention to duties which are incumbent on every citizen in the interests of community welfare and existence.
8. To recognize always the need for strict adherence to police-executive function, and to refrain from even seeming to usurp the powers of the judiciary of avenging individuals or the State, and of authoritatively judging guilt and punishing the guilty.
9. To recognize always that the test of police efficiency is the absence of crime and disorder, and not the visible evidence of police action in dealing with them.

TABLE 5.1 Full-time Law Enforcement Employees[1], Rate per 1,000 Inhabitants, Region and Population Group, October 31, 1987 [1987 Estimated Population]

Region	Total (9,255 Cities: Population 133,087,000)	Group I (60 Cities, 250,000 and Over; Population (43,916,000))	Group II (123 Cities, 100,000 to 249,999; Population 17,977,000)	Group III (300 Cities, 50,000 to 99,999; Population 20,402,000)	Group IV (650 Cities, 25,000 to 49,999; Population 22,291,000)	Group V (1,604 Cities, 10,000 to 24,999; Population 25,115,000)	Group VI (6,518 Cities, under 10,000; Population 23,387,000)
Total 9,255 cities; population 153,087,000: Average number of employees per 1,000 inhabitants	2.6	3.5	2.4	2.2	2.1	2.1	2.8
Northeastern States 2,352 cities; population 39,141,000: Average number of employees per 1,000 inhabitants	2.9	4.6	3.2	2.4	2.3	2.0	2.1
Midwestern States 2,490 cities; population 37,927,000: Average number of employees per 1,000 inhabitants	2.5	3.9	2.2	1.9	1.8	2.0	2.5
Southern States 3,164 cities; population 43,070,000: Average number of employees per 1,000 inhabitants	2.8	3.0	2.5	2.6	2.4	2.4	3.5
Western States 1,249 cities; population 32,950,000: Average number of employees per 1,000 inhabitants	2.4	2.6	2.0	1.8	2.0	2.1	3.7

Population Group

[1]Includes civilians. Population figures were rounded to the nearest thousand. All rates were calculated before rounding.

Source: Reprinted from U.S. Department of Justice, *Uniform Crime Reports* (Washington DC: U.S. Government Printing Office, 1988), p. 227.

Police organization varies considerably among jurisdictions in the United States. Some police departments in rural areas are staffed by one police officer or sheriff, whereas in New York City, there are over 25,000 police officers. There is also great variation in the functions performed by the police in each city and county jurisdiction. In some jurisdictions, police perform only civil functions, such as regulating traffic and serving warrants for magistrates. In other jurisdictions, police conduct criminal investigations.

■ CONTEMPORARY LAW ENFORCEMENT ISSUES

Law enforcement officers at the federal, state, and local levels experience moral and ethical dilemmas, conflicting expectations, and organizational problems that influence their job performance and effectiveness. Over the last decade, several areas have emerged as law enforcement issues. This does not mean that these problems did not exist earlier; rather, these particular issues are currently receiving much attention from criminal justice professionals, law enforcement personnel, and the public.

The following issues are not an exhaustive compilation of all of the problems of law enforcement, but they do touch upon several areas investigated heavily in the current literature. The issues include (1) police training and professionalization; (2) police discretion in law enforcement; (3) police deception and entrapment; (4) police-community relations; (5) police violence and the use of deadly force; (6) police administration and corruption; and (6) overlapping jurisdiction and lack of interagency cooperation.

Police Training and Professionalism

In 1967, the President's Commission on Law Enforcement and Administration of Justice recommended that all police officers be required to possess, as a minimum, a college degree. The average police officer received less than 200 hours of formal training compared with teachers and other professionals. Teachers, for example, receive more than 7,000 hours of training, while barbers receive more than 4,000 hours (McLeod, 1979:201). In spite of improvements in police training and the efforts to raise minimal education requirements for law enforcement officers generally during the 1980s, most agencies are far from achieving their minimum educational objectives for new recruits (Fyfe, 1985; Meadows, 1985; Pugh, 1985; Witham, 1985).

In 1976, the Police Foundation established the National Advisory Commission on Higher Education for Police Officers, which identified six critical questions: (1) What should be the objectives of education for police officers? (2) What should the curriculum be for preemployment and in-service police education in proportion to vocational subjects and liberal arts subjects in the education program? (3) What preparations (such as academic or police experience) should police instructors have? (4) What kind of student should receive federal funding? (5) Should an associate degree or bachelor's degree be required for entry or promotion? and (6) How can curriculum be changed, if necessary, within the many instructional institutions? (Becker and Whitehouse, 1980:50).

One of the early advocates of education for police was August Vollmer, the chief of police in Berkeley, California. Vollmer and law professor Alexander M. Kidd developed the first criminology curriculum at the University of California-Berkeley in 1916. Since then, hundreds of programs in colleges and universities in the United States have been established. Some experts say that the transition from apprentice police officer to master is more assured if formal training programs stress the problem-solving nature of policing, if master police officers act as field instructors for rookie police recruits, and if such training involves developing skills related to experience (Bayley, 1984).

However, experts disagree about the effectiveness of greater police professionalization and decreasing the incidence of crime. The prevailing view is that better-educated police officers are more likely to observe their responsibilities and to violate fewer rules (Heffernan, 1985). Most police reform movements stress improvement through professionalization and more rational policy making. Unfortunately, recent evidence indicates that many professionalization reforms have given the *appearance* of change without actually increasing police officer professionalization (Sykes, 1985).

Police Discretion in Law Enforcement

Police are authorized to enforce all laws. However, police officers often enter situations where formal law enforcement conflicts with community attitudes and expectations. The President's Commission on Law Enforcement and Administration of Justice identified several factors that influence a police officer's discretion. These include (1) the sheer volume of technical violations, (2) the limited police resources to handle this volume of activity, (3) the overgeneralized nature of many legislative enactments, and (4) various local pressures that reflect community values and attitudes (Johnson, Misner, and Brown, 1981:28).

For officers, **police discretion** is not an option; it is a necessary and unavoidable part of their jobs (Cohen, 1985:27). Yet discretion is very much an area calling for wisdom and judgment (Cohen, 1985:29; Hanewicz, 1985:52–53). Frequently, seasoned police officers say that in discretionary situations, they must use common sense (Cohen, 1985:28). Situations often do not present clear choices for police officers to follow. For example, when officers are attempting to disperse a crowd in a bar, it is difficult to distinguish between the "good guys" and the "bad guys."

Legislatures have been reluctant to limit the discretionary powers of police officers. This reluctance stems from the prevailing myth that police officers have no choice in determining how and against whom to enforce the law (Williams, 1985). Prosecutors prefer to avoid criticism of police discretion in arrests because prosecutors also have broad discretionary powers (Sherman, 1984; Williams, 1985).

Police Deception and Entrapment

Closely related to the problem of police discretion is **police deception**. To what extent is it proper for law enforcement officers to employ deceit in their law enforcement practices (Elliston and Feldberg, 1985:73)? Is there an acceptable level of perjury by police officers testifying in court to increase the chances of obtaining a criminal conviction? Where should a police officer draw the line when participating in illegal activities to obtain incriminating evidence against a suspect?

Deception usually occurs at three stages of the police detection process: (1) investigation, (2) interrogation, and (3) testimony in court (Skolnick, 1985:76). Particularly objectionable is the idea that a police officer would not be truthful when testifying under oath in court. However, much evidence suggests that there are "tolerable" levels of perjury among police officers when testifying in court (Skolnick, 1985:76–77).

Columbia University law students described evidence of police officers lying under oath in court. In their study, they analyzed the effect of the *Mapp v. Ohio* decision on police practices in the seizure of narcotics (Comment, 1968; Skolnick, 1985:77–78). The law students found that before the *Mapp* decision, police officers typically testified that they found narcotics hidden on the defendants. After the *Mapp* decision, police officers testified that the narcotics they found were dropped on the ground by the defendants. This became known as *dropsy testimony.* Prior to the *Mapp* decision, narcotics evidence obtained from suspects by police, even when illegally seized, was admissible in court. After the *Mapp* decision, it was no longer so. Hence, police officers began to commit perjury to circumvent the illegal seizure of evidence rule to ensure that their testimony and evidence would be admissible against defendants charged with narcotics possession (Barker and Carter, 1986; Skolnick, 1985:78–79).

Fabrication of a case when there is no case or creation of evidence where none exists also is done by some law enforcement officers. These behaviors are not restricted to uniformed police officers in city and county police departments. The FBI and other organizations have been caught engaging in deceptive practices on various occasions, much to their embarrassment. FBI agents have also resorted to perjury as witnesses in federal court in order to ensure convictions against particular defendants (Poveda, 1985).

Entrapment is the act of a law enforcement officer or agent of the government in inducing a person to commit a crime not otherwise contemplated by him or her for the purpose of instituting a criminal prosecution against him or her. Consider the following scenarios:

- □ A businessman has just checked into a hotel. He is unpacking when an attractive young woman dressed in a very short skirt and halter knocks on his door. She asks him to invite her in for a drink. A little later, when he offers her money to engage in sexual intercourse, she pulls out a badge, identifies herself as a policewoman, and arrests him for soliciting for prostitution. (Stitt and James, 1985:129)
- □ A customer in a bar asks the bar owner if he would like to buy a color television set very cheaply and adds, 'Don't ask me how I got it.' The owner purchases the television set and is then arrested for receiving stolen property. (Stitt and James, 1985:129)

The preceding are obvious entrapment situations. Or are they? The decision whether the situation is entrapment is made by determining if the police planned, suggested, encouraged or aided an individual in the commission of a specific crime that would not have occurred otherwise in order to make an arrest (Stitt and James, 1985:130).

The earliest case recognizing and applying the entrapment defense in a criminal prosecution was *Sorrells v. United States* (1932). In this case, a federal prohibition agent posed as a tourist, approached Sorrells, and engaged him in conversation about their common war experiences. After gaining his confidence, the agent asked Sorrells for some liquor (liquor was prohibited in Sorrells' community). Sorrells refused several times, but eventually, he agreed to supply the agent with illegal liquor. Sorrells was promptly arrested, but subsequently, the United States Supreme Court overturned his conviction on the ground of entrapment. In a later case, a government investigator was "so enmeshed in the criminal activity" himself that the United States Supreme Court found his behavior "repugnant to the American criminal justice system" *(Greene v. United States,* 1970).

Two tests are used to evaluate whether a government activity is entrapment. These are (1) the subjective test and (2) the objective test. The subjective test is that if suspects have criminal records or are possibly disposed toward a particular criminal activity, then whatever means the police want to use to elicit their criminal behavior are permissible; individuals are responsible for their own actions. The objective test is that regardless of what record a person may have, certain police conduct is reprehensible in itself and should not be tolerated (Park, 1976; Rossum, 1978; Stitt and James, 1985:132).

Police entrapment does little to increase police prestige in the community view. The action causes mistrust of the police among citizens. Besides, the victims of entrapment must admit an unlawful act in court if they elect to use the entrapment as their defense (Stitt and James, 1985:133).

Police-Community Relations

Police-community relations as an operational concept originated in the St. Louis, Missouri, Police Department in 1957 (Geary, 1975:211). Since then, community relations has been popularized among police departments throughout the nation. **Police-community relations** is the philosophy of administering police services so that members of the community and the police determine (1) what police services will be provided, (2) how police services will be provided, and (3) how the police and members of the community will resolve common problems (Attorney General's Advisory Commission, 1973).

The desire to develop better police-community relations has been stimulated by several factors. First, police officers have been accused of selectively enforcing the law against certain racial or ethnic groups (Barker and Carter, 1986; Blumberg, 1986:222–244; Carter, 1985). In a study of the attitudes of 312 Hispanics in Texas toward the selective enforcement of laws by police, most respondents perceived police officers as having bad attitudes, believed that police should be more responsive to emergency calls, and said there should be less discrimination against Hispanics (Carter, 1985).

At least two important factors have shaped citizen attitudes toward police officers. These are (1) the actual experiences citizens have had with police, and (2) the impressions that citizens have relative to police fairness, bias, or prejudice. Citizen participation in sanctioning police for alleged misconduct is a sensitive issue. Many community residents believe that more citizens should be involved in the review process when police misconduct is alleged, police departments should adopt more effective means of encouraging complaints, and police should provide better feedback about the status of investigations of citizen complaints.

One strategy for improving police credibility among citizens is through the establishment of civilian complaint review boards, which are boards comprised of certain community residents and businesspersons that independently monitor police conduct or misconduct. When community residents complain about being mistreated by particular police officers or make allegations about police misconduct, the civilian complaint review board conducts its own investigation of the allegations and recommends actions to be taken by police chiefs and other officials. However, in most jurisdictions, civilian complaint review boards are primarily cosmetic and have no direct sanctioning powers or authority. Since these citizen review boards have little or no independent investigative capabilities, they ordinarily rely on what police tell them anyway. In addition police response to civilian complaint review boards is that police officers are accountable and responsible only to the chief of police. Civilian review boards are perceived by police officers as infringing on police authority and involving laypeople with little knowledge of police work (Fyfe, 1985).

Police Violence and the Use of Deadly Force

A subject of interest to the community and police officers alike is the use of deadly force and excessive violence in the apprehension of criminal suspects. **Deadly force** is any force likely or intended to cause death or great bodily harm (Black, 1979:359).

Consider these hypothetical examples. A 15-year-old boy has just stolen a jacket from a department store. He runs from the store and flees in a stolen car, which he took a few hours earlier. The police are notified of the car theft and shoplifting incident and observe the fleeing boy. They follow in their cruiser at high speeds in excess of 90 miles per hour through congested city streets, firing at the suspect with .357 magnum revolvers. Eventually, they succeed in wounding the boy, stopping the vehicle, and retrieving the stolen goods. In the process, they have damaged fifteen automobiles, caused considerable damage to their own cruiser, and endangered the lives of many innocent pedestrians.

In another incident across town, a suspect has shot and killed two bank employees in a holdup and is being pursued by police, again at high speed. The suspect fires at the pursuing police with a shotgun, and they, in turn, return the suspect's fire. Eventually, they wound the suspect and capture him.

Are either of these incidents justified? Are the lives of the pursuing officers in jeopardy where the 15-year-old shoplifter is involved? Is there any difference in either of the two hypothetical cases?

Civil rights groups and concerned citizens have expressed disapproval over police use of deadly force in situations which are not life threatening. In 1984, twenty-four states permitted police officers to use deadly force to apprehend fleeing felons (Griswold, 1985). However, in view of the *Tennessee v. Garner* (1985) decision, the fleeing felon rule is no longer valid. All states must modify their deadly force policies and statutes when police officers attempt to apprehend fleeing felons. The defense of life standard has replaced the fleeing felon rule. It specifies the use of deadly force whenever the life of a police officer or a bystander is in jeopardy.

Police officers in Washington, D.C., are required to use only soft-lead bullets rather than copper-jacketed rounds in their revolvers, which must be no larger than .38 Special. (Rationale: Such lead bullets are less powerful, have lower velocities, and travel at slower speeds. Thus, they are less likely to penetrate and pass through more than one body, compared with jacketed higher caliber ammunition, which may pass through as many as five or six persons. In crowds where shooting occurs, fewer innocent people will be wounded if police must fire their weapons.) Yet, when these police officers face suspects using a .357 or .44 magnum revolvers, they justifiably feel that they are disadvantaged in firepower.

Police Administration and Corruption

Police corruption received national attention in the United States when the Knapp Commission investigated New York City Police Department corruption (Knapp,1972). One New York City police officer, Frank Serpico, testified extensively about payoffs to police at various ranks by business owners and organized crime figures. His story was popularized in the movie, *Serpico*.

Corruption is the acceptance of money or the equivalent of money by a public official for doing something he or she is under a duty to do anyway, that he or she is under a duty not to do, or to exercise legitimate discretion for improper reasons (Elliston and Feldberg, 1985:251). For example, police officers engage in corruption when they permit pimps and prostitutes to operate for a share of the profits and when they accept bribes to permit illegal gambling and bookmaking (Barker and Roebuck, 1983).

Corruption in police departments and government is neither uncommon nor recent (Geller, 1985; Heffernan and Stroup, 1985). It undermines public faith in law officers

Al "Scarface" Capone, a Chicago gangster and racketeer, had many public officials and police officers on his private payroll. "Public service is my motto," he claimed. His business cards listed him as a used furniture dealer. In 1931, he was convicted for income tax evasion, for which he served a term in prison. Capone died of syphilis a few years after his release.

whenever it is detected and publicized (Feldberg, 1985; Sherman, 1985). Al Capone bragged that he "owned" a number of police officers in Chicago during the 1920s, and that much of his criminal activity was permitted to flourish in exchange for police payoffs. Corruption still exists in many police departments, including such cities as Indianapolis, Denver, and Dallas (Geller, 1985; Heffernan and Stroup, 1985; Sherman, 1985).

Several stages of moral decline of police officers have been identified: (1) officers engage in minor "perks" (e.g., free meals from restaurants); (2) officers overlook bar closing hours; (3) officers accept gratuities from motorists and other persons involved in minor law violations; (4) officers permit more serious crimes, such as gambling, to occur in exchange for larger financial payoffs; (5) officers permit prostitution and other more serious offenses to flourish; and (6) officers permit narcotics trafficking to occur and other more serious crimes in exchange for bribes (Sherman, 1985:258–260). These stages are controversial, and not all corrupt police officers follow this pattern. Sometimes, too, it is difficult to distinguish between genuine gifts (such as Christmas gifts), gratuities, bribes, and corruption (Feldberg, 1985:267). At times, however, accepting any kind of gift is the beginning of the slippery slope syndrome, where the path is paved for accepting other, larger gratuities in the future, and eventually bribes (Feldberg, 1985:267–268). Greater citizen involvement in police administration is one community response to police corruption, and citizen review boards may have merit, despite the negative sentiments of some police chiefs (Fyfe, 1985; Reiss, 1985).

Overlapping Jurisdiction and Lack of Interagency Cooperation

Historically, there has always been rivalry among various branches of law enforcement. When Charles Lindbergh's baby was kidnapped in 1932, several law enforcement agencies became involved, including the New Jersey State Police, local officials, and the FBI. In November 1933, when the FBI asked the New Jersey police what progress was being made in their investigation, they were told, "None" (Kennedy, 1985:203). Actually, they had made extensive progress in their investigation, and they certainly could have used FBI laboratory assistance in their identification of various objects associated with the kidnapping incident. In the Lindbergh kidnapping, the New Jersey State Police wanted to solve the crime and not rely on assistance from the FBI or any other agency. When John Dillinger was confronted and killed by FBI agents, the assistance of other law enforcement agencies was refused. The FBI wanted the Dillinger apprehension to be "their show."

One troublesome feature about the organization and responsibilities of all law enforcement agencies is considerable jurisdictional overlap. Narcotics trafficking is within almost every law enforcement agency's jurisdiction, including that of the FBI, the Bureau of Alcohol, Tobacco and Firearms, the Customs Service, and even the CIA! Although these agencies are supposed to coordinate their activities with other agencies, they frequently do not. During J. Edgar Hoover's FBI administration, Hoover deliberately advocated noncooperation with local police agencies whenever the FBI was involved in a major investigation. His personal views, policies, and biases opposed interagency cooperation; he wanted the FBI to solve crimes without the assistance of other agencies. Some experts say that law enforcement agencies must overcome their turf jealousies and develop more effective anticrime alliances (Shanahan, 1985:449–452).

■ THE LAW ENFORCEMENT ASSISTANCE ADMINISTRATION

In 1968, Congress established the **Law Enforcement Assistance Administration (LEAA)** (United States Code, 1989). Under 42 United States Code, Section 3701, Congress declared that it "finds that the high incidence of crime in the United States threatens the peace, security, and general welfare of the nation and its citizens. To reduce and prevent crime and juvenile delinquency, and to insure the greater safety of the people, law enforcement and criminal justice efforts must be better coordinated, intensified, and made more effective at all levels of government."

The purpose of the LEAA was to provide necessary resources, leadership, and coordination to various state and local law enforcement agencies to prevent or reduce adult crime and juvenile delinquency. The LEAA recognized crime as a local problem and stressed the value of the financial and technical resources of the federal government in assisting local jurisdictions in combating the crime problem. The LEAA attempted to more effectively coordinate the anticrime activities of law enforcement agencies at local, state, and federal levels and to reduce interagency rivalries. Congress authorized grants to state and local agencies, as well as other financial and technical assistance, to devise new crime prevention and reduction methods and to improve methods of detecting, apprehending, and rehabilitating criminals. Unfortunately, the goals of the LEAA were not realized within the period originally projected, and funding for the program was gradually withdrawn in the early 1980s.

In 1983, a project was undertaken to evaluate the effectiveness of the LEAA in improving criminal justice (Hudzik, 1984). Data were obtained from thirty-three state planning agency directors through questionnaires and in-depth interviews. One disappointing finding was that LEAA-assisted programs continued to thrive in only about a third of the states, but in the states where the LEAA did not succeed, independent funding was not made available when LEAA funds were discontinued.

After October 1984, references to the LEAA were changed to refer to the new Bureau of Justice Assistance, a grant-making body within the Department of Justice. Also established was the Office of Justice Programs, headed by the assistant attorney general of the United States. These new agencies assumed some of the functions of the earlier LEAA, such as the research and grant activities relating to criminal justice.

In 1979, the **National Institute of Justice (NIJ)** was established to provide for and encourage research for (1) improving federal, state, and local criminal justice systems, (2) preventing and reducing crimes, (3) ensuring citizen access to appropriate dispute-resolution forums, and (4) identifying programs with proven effectiveness or high probability of improving the functioning of the criminal justice system (United States Code, 1986).

The **Bureau of Justice Statistics (BJS)** was also established in 1979 to provide for and encourage the collection and analysis of statistical information concerning crime, juvenile delinquency, and the operation of the criminal justice system. Currently, much information concerning local and federal criminal justice systems is distributed by the National Institute of Justice and the Bureau of Justice Statistics. In addition, these bureaus provide grants to persons and interested organizations for studying criminal victimization and crimes against the elderly and for gathering statistical information.

■ SUMMARY

Most federal law enforcement agencies are located in two major departments: (1) the Department of Justice, and (2) the Treasury Department. Within the Department of Justice are the Federal Bureau of Investigation (FBI) and Drug Enforcement Administration (DEA). The FBI investigates violations of over 200 federal statutes involving both criminal and civil offenses, and the DEA investigates a variety of narcotics violations. Within the Treasury Department are several law enforcement agencies, including the Bureau of Alcohol, Tobacco and Firearms (BATF), the Customs Service, the Internal Revenue Service, and the United States Secret Service. Within the Internal Revenue Service the Criminal Investigation Division (CID) investigates and recommends for prosecution any person who violates federal income tax laws or engages in tax fraud. The Secret Service, originally assigned to investigate cases of counterfeiting of federal currency and coin, also has the responsibility for protecting the president and governmental dignitaries. In addition, it investigates any fraud involving electronic funds transfers in banking institutions.

State police agencies operate primarily to enforce state traffic laws, although their duties vary considerably from one state to another. County and metropolitan police are charged primarily with enforcing local laws and conducting local criminal investigations.

Law enforcement in the United States suffers from several continuing problems. Currently, little coordination between major agencies exists at the federal, state, and local levels. Critics have questioned the quality of police training, police professionalism, the use of deadly force by police officers in making arrests, police corruption, and the use of police deception and entrapment. Many people encourage greater cooperation between the community and law enforcement agencies and greater citizen participation in police affairs.

The Law Enforcement Assistance Administration (LEAA) was established in 1968 to coordinate many of the anticrime activities between local, state, and federal agencies, but it failed to achieve its goal over the next 15-year period. It has been replaced by the Office of Justice Programs and the National Institute of Justice, which currently fund criminal justice research and compile statistics relating to crime trends and criminal characteristics.

KEY TERMS

Bureau of Alcohol, Tobacco and Firearms (BATF)

Bureau of Justice Statistics (BJS)

Central Intelligence Agency (CIA)

corruption

Customs Service

deadly force

Department of Justice

dropsy testimony

Drug Enforcement Administration (DEA)

Federal Bureau of Investigation (FBI)

Immigration and Naturalization Service (INS)

Internal Revenue Service (IRS)

Law Enforcement Assistance Administration (LEAA)

National Institute of Justice (NIJ)

police-community relations

police deception

police discretion

state highway patrols

Treasury Department

United States Marshals Service (USMS)

United States Secret Service (USSS)

QUESTIONS FOR REVIEW

1. What program was initiated in 1968 to coordinate police activities in local and state jurisdictions? Explain briefly the functions of the program.
2. What are the responsibilities of the Criminal Investigation Division of the Internal Revenue Service? What department oversees the IRS?
3. Identify the major law enforcement agencies supervised by the United States Department of Justice. Briefly discuss the functions of each.
4. What law enforcement agencies have jurisdiction over illegal drug trafficking? Discuss briefly some of the problems associated with overlapping jurisdictions.
5. What agency investigates arson-for-profit and illegal possession of automatic weapons? What other duties and responsibilities are associated with this agency?
6. What are the various duties and responsibilities of the United States Secret Service? Which department oversees the Secret Service?
7. Differentiate between state and local police in terms of their respective functions. Are all state police in the United States assigned identical functions? What are some of the duties of state police beyond traffic control?
8. Discuss briefly the history of the modern police department. Are police departments today based on a particular historical model?
9. What were some of Colquhoun's proposals for a proper police agency? Discuss the importance of these proposals for modern police work.
10. Who was Sir Robert Peel, and what was his contribution to the subsequent development of police departments?
11. What police department is the oldest in the United States? Contrast the functions of today's police departments with those of state police organizations.
12. Under what circumstances do you feel that police officers should be permitted to use deadly force to apprehend suspects?
13. What problem areas have been identified by the National Advisory Commission on Higher Education for Police Officers?
14. Why are personality inventories and assessment measures used in the recruitment of police? Do they appear to be of value?
15. Why is the crime-fighter image of police considered by some critics to be a myth?
16. What pressures experienced by police officers make it difficult to enforce all laws vigorously?
17. What is meant by entrapment? Under what circumstances is entrapment justified? Identify two court cases where entrapment was used as a defense. Briefly discuss the outcome of each case.
18. Differentiate between the objective and subjective test for entrapment.
19. What is meant by dropsy testimony? What court case has contributed to dropsy testimony? What was the significance of the court case? What is meant by the exclusionary rule?
20. Discuss briefly the stages in a police officer's moral decline.
21. What agencies currently dispense grants for the purpose of conducting criminal justice research?

SUGGESTED READINGS

Fogelson, Robert M. (1977). *Big city police*. Cambridge, MA: Harvard Univ. Press.

Goldstein, Herman (1975). *Police corruption: A perspective on its nature and control*. Washington, DC: The Police Foundation.

Sherman, Lawrence W. (1978). *Scandal and reform*. Berkeley, CA: University of California Press.

Westley, William A. (1970). *Violence and the police*. Cambridge, MA: MIT Press.

Wise, David (1976). *The American police state*. New York: Random House.

The Police: History and Operations

■ INTRODUCTION

This chapter describes the history of police in the United States. Police organization in the United States has been influenced by the police organization of Great Britain, although United States police departments have evolved into several different operational styles.

Important functions of police department administration are recruitment, selection, and training of police officers. Police organizations use various selection criteria and training efforts. One increasingly important objective of all law enforcement agencies is professionalization, so this chapter describes professionalism of police officers, as well as some of the means whereby professionalism is achieved.

Among police officers, an esprit de corps has been traditionally exhibited, leading many citizens to conclude that there is a distinctive police personality. Thus, the chapter presents a description of police personality and subculture. Finally, a continuing organizational problem is labor turnover. Police departments and other law enforcement agencies share this problem, as stress and burnout negatively influence officer efficiency and work performance and cause officers to resign.

■ THE HISTORY AND ROLE OF POLICE IN SOCIETY

The word **police** stems from the Greek word *polis,* meaning city, and it has been applied historically to the exercise of civil or collective authority (Manning, 1977:39). In 1800, the French viewed police unfavorably because the police secretly surveyed the citizens to control them (Manning, 1977:39; Reith, 1938). In England, however, the police force was originally created to maintain state security and protect citizens. In 1829, Sir Robert Peel (1788–1850) passed a bill through the British Parliament, establishing the first formal police department, the Metropolitan Police of London (Becker and Whitehouse, 1980:6; Manning, 1977:39–40).

For two centuries prior to the Metropolitan Police of London, England had many political, social, and economic problems. Historians say that the development of police in England can best be understood by examining certain societal structural changes in England, including various reforms of its political and legal systems (Manning, 1977:52–71). Between 1750 and 1820, the London population doubled from 676,000 to 1.3 million. In fact, between 1801 and 1831, England's population grew from 8.9 million to 13.9 million. The population changes resulted, in part, from growing birthrates, sharp reduction in the death rate, and extensive citizen migration from the rural areas to the cities (Manning, 1977:53–54).

Simultaneously, several significant occupational changes occurred, including a shift of many persons from agricultural to nonagricultural employment, a growing number of skilled workers and artisans, and the formulation of a middle class (Manning, 1977:54). There was also similar growth among the professions, medicine, law, and the clergy. However, the Napoleonic Wars during the first years of the nineteenth century eroded England's economy to a critical level (Manning, 1977:57–59). Prices of goods skyrocketed. Postwar unemployment levels were extraordinarily high, with large numbers of soldiers and sailors looking for work, committing fraud and petty crime to support themselves. From 1770 to 1828, at least six major political and legal reforms involved struggles for power and competition for political domination between various British classes.

In the late 1700s, London "was a hell of a place at night. There was almost no street lighting and no police worth the name. Burglary and robbery with violence were widespread, and the roads on the outskirts of London were infested with highwaymen" (Pringle, 1955:29–30). Thus, in the context of great social, economic, and political problems, Peel made his idea of an organized, professional force of metropolitan police a reality. His thinking about the organization and functions of the Metropolitan Police of London was influenced by other reformers, such as Patrick Colquhoun (1745–1820) and Henry Fielding (1707–1754).

The original plan for the **Metropolitan Police of London** in 1829 included provisions for personnel to detect crime. **Bobbies** (named after Sir Robert "Bobby" Peel), or constables, walked the streets 24 hours a day (Becker and Whitehouse, 1980:34). Patrolling officers wore special uniforms, and detectives wore street clothing. Police officers tried to minimize crime by their visibility and arrests of suspects observed engaged in criminal activity, while detectives collected evidence of a suspect's guilt when crimes were committed and presented the evidence in court (Becker and Whitehouse, 1980:34–35).

British bobbies acquired their nickname from Sir Robert "Bobby" Peel, who originated the first formal police department, the Metropolitan Police of London, in 1829.

Early recruitment for the Metropolitan Police of London emphasized such criteria as sex, height, weight, character, and ability to read and write. Training was mandatory, although it consisted mainly of close-order drill similar to military training (Gorer, 1955). Size and strength were considered important, because police were often required to quell public disorders and make arrests by sheer physical force. Their military-type training was useful for instilling discipline among them and making it easier to function as a unit when confronting large numbers of lawbreakers or rioters.

Modern police department organization strongly resembles military organization, with a central command structure and many rules of police conduct rooted in the military ethos. There are some obvious differences, however. Modern police are increasingly trained to think for themselves and to exercise discretion in arrest situations. They are not directly and continuously supervised as are the military, and they do not engage in military maneuvers. The aim of the Metropolitan Police of London was simple: to protect citizens and their property (Manning, 1977:82–83). To guide the Metropolitan Police of London, Sir Robert Peel outlined the following principles:

> . . . to prevent crime without resort to repressive legal sanctioning and to avoid military intervention in domestic disturbances; to manage public order nonviolently, with the application of violence viewed as an ultimate means of coercing compliance; to minimize and indeed reduce, if at all possible, the schism between police and public; and to demonstrate efficiency by the absence of crime and disorder, not visible evidence of police action in dealing with them. (Manning, 1977:98–99)

During the same period, some of the larger cities in the United States, such as Boston and New York, were also experiencing the problems of rapid population growth and increased urban density from migration and industrialization. Formal police departments were created in Boston in 1838, New York in 1845, and successively Chicago in 1851, Cincinnati and New Orleans in 1852, Philadelphia in 1854, and Newark and Baltimore in 1857 (Manning, 1977:123). Boston experienced widespread thievery, drunkenness, vagabondage, lewd and lascivious behavior, assault and battery, and other forms of unruly conduct (Lane, 1967:6). New York City faced similar problems, its streets called "pathways of danger" (Richardson, 1970:25).

Policing in the United States was not unknown prior to 1838, however. In 1643, New Amsterdam (later New York) had a burgher watch, which used constables, marshals, and watches (guards or lookouts on duty) who were appointed or elected (Bayley, 1985:32). In 1789, the new government of the United States created specialized federal marshals, carryovers from earlier appointments made by the king of England. In the various counties and districts of England in the 1500s, called shires, various jurisdictions were overseen by law enforcement officers known as reeves. Reeves were the chief law enforcement agents, and each shire had its reeve. Hence, the more contemporary word **sheriff** is used to describe the chief law enforcement officers in most United States counties.

The early development of police departments in the United States was patterned largely from England's 1829 model of the Metropolitan Police of London. The objectives of these police departments were similar to those of their British counterparts (Johnson, 1981). Boston and New York City police officers had responsibilities for keeping the peace (hence, they were called peace officers), being visible deterrents to criminals by patrolling the streets. Their effectiveness as deterrents to crime was measured by the absence of crime in their jurisdictions.

United States police departments have undergone many reforms since their origins in Boston and New York. One reason for these reforms was that the original police role in the United States was related to conflicting moral codes and political interest groups. The Prohibition era was a turning point in police organization in the United States (Manning, 1977:96–98). Three major changes occurring in the 1930s profoundly affected the nature of the police role: (1) the development of a systematic collecting, gathering, and publishing of crime statistics through the *Uniform Crime Reports,* a bulletin distributed by the FBI, commencing in 1930; (2) the linking of criminal statistics published in such reports to the notion of professionalism among police; and (3) police use of radios, automobiles, and dispatch/control/supervision systems that permitted more immediate response whenever crime incidents were reported.

The motto, "To serve and to protect," is printed on police automobiles in many cities. This motto symbolizes the major functions police officers perform—service and protection. However, while the police serve and protect the citizenry, most of their time is consumed by activities such as public service and traffic control (Bohm, 1986; Pepinsky, 1980). Therefore, conflicting images of police work and the functions of police officers exist.

One image is the Joseph Wambaugh, *Blue Knight,* Hollywood image (although not necessarily the potbellied, cigar-chewing, billy club toting beat cop), with police officers as crime fighters, spending much of their time on the streets catching criminals, seeing to their prosecution and conviction, and clearing most crimes. Whenever police officers are not engaged in fighting crime, they are preventing crime by their high visibility (Bradel, 1979:151).

The second image is more realistic, based on the actual things police officers do while they are on duty. In reality, police officers spend only a fraction of their time fighting crime. Some studies show that police officers spend less than 10 percent of their work time on crime-related business (Bittner, 1975:42; Bohm, 1986; Pepinsky, 1980:107). The rest of a police officer's time involves controlling traffic, leading funeral processions, lecturing high school students about police methods, fetching cats out of trees, counseling husbands and wives in family disputes, and filling out daily service reports. Persons directly aware of the noncrime nature of most police work have attempted to dispel certain myths about law enforcement—see, for example, "Crime, Criminal and Crime Control Policy Myths" (Bohm, 1986), "The Mythology of Law Enforcement" (Bradel, 1979), "The Functional Nature of Police Reform: The Myth of Controlling the Police" (Sykes, 1985), and *Sense and Nonsense About Crime: A Policy Guide* (Walker, 1985).

Why, then, is there a prevailing public misconception about police work? Why are the myths about crime and crime control by police perpetuated? According to some critics, "[M]yths about crime, criminals, and crime control policy are perpetuated because they serve a variety of interests. Among the interests served are those of the general public, the media, the politicians, academic criminologists, criminal justice officials, and social elites" (Bohm, 1986:199–209). The public itself perpetuates myths about crime and crime control because the myths help to forge a sense of community. The community distinguishes between the "good guys" and the "bad guys" and takes pride in the "fact" that the police, through law-and-order campaigns, are doing something about crime (Bohm, 1986:204).

The media and politicians benefit from perpetuating many of the myths about crime control. The media sell more papers, get higher television ratings, and market more of a sponsor's product, while politicians get more votes from a reassured constituency by "doing something about the crime problem" (Bohm, 1986:205–206). Even academicians and those conducting police research benefit from perpetuating certain myths about crime control. For instance, considerable grant money is allocated annually by the National Institute of Justice and the Bureau of Justice Statistics to support research projects for improving crime detection methods and stimulating crime prevention. Many criminologists in colleges and universities are awarded these grants and derive professional benefits from them.

Police department budgets, salary increments, and other allocations are made often on the basis of the effectiveness of a department's crime-fighting efforts (Bohm, 1986:206–207). To dispel some of the myths about the police and crime control would only undermine the rationale for a larger crime-control budget. Does spending more money on crime control actually decrease crime? This question is difficult to answer. One widely held view is that changing a police department's budget has little or no perceptible impact on the level of crime in any jurisdiction (Bayley, 1985; Bohm, 1986; Bradel, 1979; Decker and Kohfeld, 1985).

■ THE ADMINISTRATION OF POLICE ORGANIZATION

The structural features of police organization and administration in the United States and other countries have been remarkably consistent over time (Bayley, 1985:60–61). Early organizational models of police departments were patterned after the Metropolitan Police of London, and many United States police departments have several similarities with their 1829 counterpart in England (Becker and Whitehouse, 1980:34–36). However, public demand for greater police efficiency in reducing crime, together with internal administrative concerns for organizational effectiveness and the elimination of corruption, have resulted in significant reforms in recent years.

Figure 6.1 shows an organizational chart of the offices and divisions of the Washington, D.C., Metropolitan Police Department. This department is headed by a chief of police, who oversees several bureaus. In turn, each bureau supervises divisions such as the field operations bureau, which oversees patrol, traffic, and criminal investigations. This type of organization is traditional, reflecting a highly centralized operating unit, where four bureau heads report directly to the chief of police, who is responsible to a commissioner or some other public official.

Police organization is divided into line, staff, and auxillary functions (Becker and Whitehouse, 1980:38). Line functions are patrol, traffic, juveniles, and detective work. Staff functions are performed by both civilians and police officers, who may work in clerical or public relations jobs (where they are responsible for improving police-community relations). Staff personnel are professionally trained to coordinate the internal organizational activities and law enforcement assignments among different

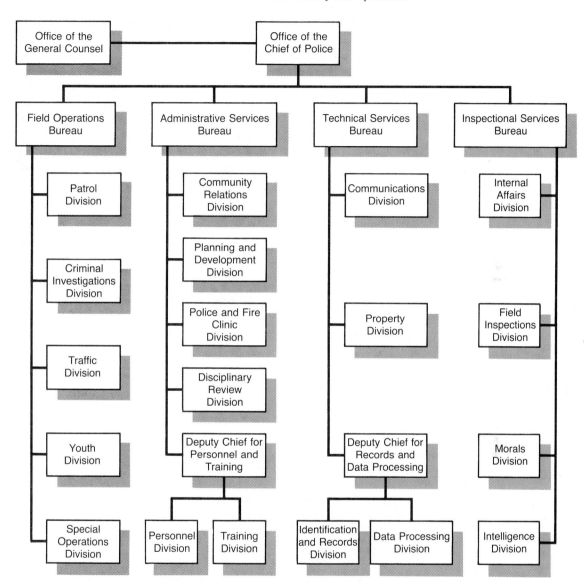

FIGURE 6.1 Traditional Department Organization: An Outline of the Washington, D.C., Metropolitan Police Department

Source: "The Shadow of the Past—The Light of the Future: 1974 Annual Report" (Washington, D.C.: Metropolitan Police Department, Planning and Development Division), p. 4.

police divisions. Auxillary personnel include maintenance employees and jail guards (Becker and Whitehouse, 1980:38–40).

Police departments in most cities are municipal agencies under the direct control of the chief executive, such as a mayor or city manager. In Chicago, Illinois, the police superintendent is appointed by the mayor, but in Los Angeles, California, the commissioner of police is appointed by a Board of Police Commissioners (Ruchelman,

1973:6). In Indianapolis, Indiana, the mayor appoints a public safety director, who in turn, with the mayor's approval, appoints a police chief, who serves at the pleasure of the director and mayor (Hudnut, 1985:21).

Historically, police departments in the United States have been political bodies, extensions of the municipal political authority (Brzeczek, 1985:48; Ruchelman, 1973:5–6). Because of the close relation between police departments and the political leadership of the community, some abuse of political power by mayors in various jurisdictions has occurred (Frazier, 1985; Fyfe, 1985; Goldstein, 1977; Walker, 1977). Because the political systems in cities developed at about the same time as the police agencies, there has always been a close relation between the two bodies. Also, some mutual exploitation has furthered certain vested interests of political groups as well as police organizations. A former Superintendent of Police of Chicago, Illinois, Richard J. Brzeczek, wrote:

> Historically, mayors abused their power over the police department, placing inept cronies on its payroll and using its members as footsoldiers in political skirmishes. Remnants of such inappropriate mayoral meddling can be found in modern times in a number of cities. For example, Minneapolis, during the 1970s, suffered from mayoral abuse of the police personnel structure, and Chicago only within the past decade (1975–1985) ceased the unconstitutional use of police for surveillance of the mayor's political enemies. (Brzeczek, 1985:51)

In 1982–1983, a nationwide study of 493 police chiefs examined the training and background of chief executives of police (Witham, 1985). This study described chiefs of police in state, county, or municipal agencies employing seventy-five or more persons. Typical respondents were about 49 years old, had been police chief for about 5 years, and had an average of 24 years' experience as law enforcement officers. Furthermore, 50 percent had a bachelor's degree, and most had experience with at least one other law enforcement agency. However, the police chiefs' credentials were unimpressive compared with those of administrators of corporations employing similar numbers of persons (Witham, 1985). Nearly 50 percent of the police chiefs lacked a bachelor's degree, compared with about 20 percent of the administrators studied in the private sector. The police chiefs often defined their roles too narrowly. Often, too, they were not involved directly in formulating the policies affecting their department officers.

The study recommendations for improvement included establishing and enforcing minimum educational standards for police chiefs, as well as recruiting police chiefs from outside law enforcement. Other critics of police management and administration suggest that police chiefs have exposure to the practices and principles of business management to familiarize them with a variety of managerial strategies to meet their particular departmental needs (Tannehill, 1985; Quarles, 1985).

Because of the limited training and effectiveness of many police chiefs and administrators, police department administration has been the subject of law enforcement reforms for several decades (Fyfe, 1985; Geller, 1985; Reiss, 1985). Several public concerns for administrative reform were contained in the 1967 report of the President's Crime Commission. This report reflected a traditional approach to police reform: (1) greater administrative efficiency, (2) more expert leadership, and (3) higher qualifications for police officers (Walker, 1979:166).

Other reforms being implemented in most major police departments in the United States were described in the 1981 United States Civil Rights Commission report, "Who

Is Guarding the Guardians?" (Hanewicz, 1985:50–51). The report recommended that police departments develop clear and restrictive rules governing the use of force, better regulation of weaponry and training, and stricter procedures for reporting firearms discharges. However, some experts say that policy statements about the use of firearms and other issues often have little effect on how police officers act on the job when confronted with hazardous situations (Mays and Taggart, 1985). In addition, police reforms have not eliminated mayoral interference in the operations of police departments. Mayors continue to influence police actions, including how police respond to disturbances, when police use deadly force, and how police enforce certain laws (Brzeczek, 1985:51; Kuykendall, 1985).

A current trend in police reform is greater police-community interaction (Reiss, 1985). Many communities are moving away from the traditional view of police and toward a definition of police skills more consistent with the service nature of the police role (Guyot, 1985; Reiss, 1971). Specifically, contemporary reforms are directed at (1) improving police-public communication, (2) emphasizing the service functions of the police and rewarding officers for doing well in that area, and (3) democratizing police departments by involving rank-and-file police officers in policy making to a greater degree (Walker, 1979:168). One effort to increase police-community interaction is team policing, a patrol experiment where several officers work intensively in a small geographical area, but the public and police reactions to this concept have been mixed (Bloch and Specht, 1973; Sherman, et al., 1973; Vera Institute of Justice, 1984).

■ THE SELECTION OF POLICE OFFICERS

Police officer recruitment practices have greatly improved since the days of the Metropolitan Police of London in 1829 and the Boston and New York City police departments of the 1830s and 1840s. While more sophisticated selection methods have been devised in recent years, some of the original criteria, such as physique, continue to attract researcher interest. A 1985 Florida study examined the relation between one's height and potential for aggression. It was found that shorter officers had greater aggression potential, issuing more warnings than their taller counterparts (Willoughby and Blount, 1985).

Police recruitment programs vary considerably among police departments. In rural areas with small police departments, no formal selection criteria may exist. Applicants off the street may be hired as police officers with only cursory checks of their backgrounds, or nepotism may result in appointments of relatives or close friends to law enforcement positions, because usually, no great deal of competition exists for these jobs. In most of the larger municipal police departments, however, where there are numerous applicants for positions, the selection process is more formal (Burbeck and Furnham, 1985). It may include completing numerous personal data forms, submitting college transcripts or records of university work completed, taking several psychological personality and abilities tests, submitting to polygraph, or lie detector, tests, and responding to situational screening (Aylward, 1985; Gettys and Elam, 1985; Hargrave, 1985; Inwald, 1985; National Institute of Justice, 1985; Prior, 1985; Pugh, 1985;

Silverstein, 1986). The primary objective of such screening procedures is to select the persons who will make the best police officers.

Some psychological tests are designed to identify well-adjusted officers, or those who can handle stressful situations. Since police officers inevitably are exposed to stressful situations when enforcing the law, the recruits who demonstrate a better ability to handle stress may make better police officers than those who have a low stress capacity. The Minnesota Multiphasic Personality Inventory (MMPI) and the California Personality Inventory (CPI) are administered to prospective police recruits in California and other states, as well as in some foreign countries, including Canada (Hargrave, 1985; Pugh, 1985). These instruments purportedly measure personality dimensions, such as anxiety, sociability, personal adjustment, and social adjustment.

Surveys of state and local law enforcement employees emphasize personality characteristics related to coping with personal stress (Phillips, 1984). Psychological clinicians frequently interpret personality test results, indicating various levels of recruit potential, such as acceptable, unacceptable, and marginal (Hargrave, 1985). Therefore, sometimes, paper and pencil personality tests are used as negative predictors, that is, police departments sometimes utilize these tests to determine applicants they do *not* want to hire, identifying problem, or maladjusted personalities (Aylward, 1985). However, in instances where the Minnesota Multiphasic Personality Inventory and the California Personality Inventory have been used as screening tools, the recruits selected have less attrition (that is, a lower dropout rate) than those selected by alternative selection procedures, including personal interviews and review boards (Hargrave, 1985; Hargrave and Berner, 1986).

A problem with paper and pencil personality tests is that answers can be faked. However, the Minnesota Multiphasic Personality Inventory, the California Personality Inventory, and other personality assessment devices incorporate lie factors. Usually, these lie factors are statements that have obvious answers or are typical of most people, such as, "I never question my ability to accomplish difficult tasks" or "I never worry about my work quality or social relations with others." Since most persons occasionally worry about their skills in relation to difficult job assignments or have occasional interpersonal problems, disagreement with such items may indicate attempts by applicants to present their images of ideal police recruits. In short, such items may indicate that the applicants are deliberately making untrue statements.

Of course, several methodological problems are associated with the administration of paper and pencil psychological tests (Burbeck and Furnham, 1985). In some jurisdictions, these instruments are used by highly trained professionals, skilled in selecting applicants for different types of jobs. In other jurisdictions, they are administered with little or no professional interpretation of the test results.

In spite of methodological drawbacks, such devices are used increasingly to select police recruits (Inwald, 1985). If psychological tests are to be part of an agency's personnel selection process, then the agency should be prepared to experiment with various tests in order to establish selection criteria that can be reasonably quantified, to identify the tests having the highest predictive potential for job performance, and to refine existing procedures for selection to meet the particular staffing needs of the agency (Gettys and Elam, 1985). In any case, the results of any personality assessment device are subject to different kinds of error and should be cautiously interpreted. Such devices should be supplemented with interviews and other situational criteria; they should not be relied upon as the sole criterion for officer selections.

In some jurisdictions, prospective police recruits are asked how they would handle certain situations on the job, certain community statutes, and simple traffic directions. Such situational selection methods successfully predicted good job performance in a study of sixty-one police recruits in Alberta, Canada (Pugh, 1985). Situational tests also permitted recruiters to identify prospective candidates with high verbal expression skills, which are valuable to police officers in their early years of service.

Another popular supplement to psychological tests for screening purposes is the polygraph, or lie detector, test (Garwood, 1985). While the results of polygraph tests are inadmissible in court, their use in police recruit screening is widespread. In 1983, for instance, the Vermont State Police administered polygraph tests to 181 applicants and rejected 109 of them. The two major reasons for rejecting them were (1) former drug offenses and (2) undetected larcenies (Prior, 1985). Polygraph tests are used to identify persons who attempt to deceive recruiters about their backgrounds and police records, if any (Garwood, 1985), and such persons are excluded as candidates for police positions.

Some agencies make available materials to help prospective police recruits. They answer questions about selection criteria, salaries, fringe benefits, and career advancement. The *Police Employment Guide,* published by the National Employment Listing Service in Huntsville, Texas, permits recruit prospects to compare the entrance requirements and employee benefits of different police departments from a variety of regions (National Employment Listing Service, 1982).

In 1979, the United States Equal Employment Opportunity Commission raised several important ethical and legal issues about the prevailing police selection criteria. It proposed the "Uniform Guidelines on Employment Selection Procedures" (Inwald, 1985). These guidelines are (1) using psychological screening as only one component of

Is there a distinctive police personality, or are police officers like members of any other profession? Is their camaraderie a function of their unusual working hours and the stressful aspects of their work?

the overall selection process, (2) devising sufficiently reliable validation schemes to determine the usefulness of test results, (3) selecting a variety of tests and procedures for verification purposes, (4) avoiding arbitrary cutoff scores on psychological tests, (5) documenting all selection procedures with written progress reports available for public inspection, (6) educating all appropriate staff members on testing procedures in interpretive guidelines, (7) interviewing all candidates subjected to written psychological tests, (8) using well-defined and reliable psychological tests, (9) manifesting flexibility in the use of various evaluative procedures, and (10) sharing information with other agencies through networking on a state or local level (Inwald, 1985).

All states require a license or certification for a person to practice the profession of policing, using the Peace Officer Standards and Training (POST) Commissions or their equivalent (Levinson, 1983; Shigley, 1987). Florida requires prospective police recruits to acquire a certificate that essentially guarantees that the person has never committed a felony or misdemeanor involving moral turpitude and that the person has a high school diploma, as well as other standards (Levinson, 1983). In order to maintain officer certification, police officers must avoid insubordinate conduct, gross immorality, habitual drunkenness, or gross misconduct (Levinson, 1983). The principal objectives of POST licensing procedures used in such states as Minnesota and California are (1) to keep bad officers (such as those with felony convictions or disciplinary problems) out of law enforcement and (2) to contribute to quality law enforcement personnel by requiring certain basic training (Minnesota Board of Peace Officer Standards and Training, 1980; Shigley, 1987:10).

■ MINORITY HIRING PRACTICES

In 1968, the National Advisory Commission issued its *Report on Civil Disorders.* According to the report, one cause of civil disorders was the discrimination that minorities perceived being directed against them by police. The commission noted that despite the fact that blacks made up at least 12 percent of the United States population, their proportionate representation among police officers was less than 5 percent.

The problem of underrepresentation of minorities in police departments has been a reason for many racial conflicts in the United States. Before 1948, blacks were not allowed to be members of the Atlanta, Georgia, Police Department (Kuykendall and Burns, 1983:64), and when some blacks were hired in 1948, they were not permitted to wear uniforms similar to those worn by white officers. By 1981, black police officers in the Atlanta Police Department made up 46 percent of all city police officers, compared with an Atlanta black population of 67 percent (Hochstedler, Regoli, and Poole, 1984; Kuykendall and Burns, 1983; Stroup, 1985).

The underrepresentation of minorities in police departments has not been limited to Southern cities. Every major municipal jurisdiction in the United States has had the same problem for decades. In 1981, the Los Angeles Police Department had a black police officer membership of 9 percent, even though 17 percent of the city consisted of blacks. And even in Washington, D.C., where the black population is 70 percent, the police department in 1982 had only 50 percent black membership. Among the fifty largest cities in the United States in 1982, only Toledo, Ohio, had a proportion of black

A DAY IN COURT

In the case of *United States v. Paradise,* (107 S.Ct. 1053, 1987), the National Association for the Advancement of Colored People (NAACP) filed a racial discrimination suit alleging that although the Alabama Department of Public Safety employed blacks as troopers in the Alabama Highway Patrol, no blacks held officer ranks. Initiated in 1972, the suit continued until 1981, when it was shown that the Alabama Department of Public Safety had not complied with federal court orders to obtain a certain proportion of black highway patrol officers.

The Supreme Court found that as of November 1978, out of 232 state troopers at the rank of corporal or above, *"there is still not one black"* (emphasis theirs). Thus, it ordered Alabama officials to have at least 50 percent of all promotions extended to black officers until 25 percent black proportionate representation in rank was achieved. Despite protests and legal arguments from Alabama officials on various grounds, the court ruled that this measure fulfilled the equal protection clause of the Fourteenth Amendment of the United States Constitution.

How far must Alabama go to comply with the Supreme Court's decisions? Will other states be obligated to fulfill quotas of minorities in various law enforcement ranks? Can this decision be extended to other forms of employment?

police officers (18 percent) commensurate with the proportion of blacks in that city generally (17 percent). In the other forty-nine cities, the discrepancy was sizable (Walker, 1983:5).

In 1973, the National Advisory Commission on Criminal Justice Standards and Goals adopted the following standard:

> Every police agency should engage in positive efforts to employ ethnic minority group members. When a substantial ethnic minority population resides within the jurisdiction, the police agency should take affirmative action to achieve a ratio of minority group employees in approximate proportion to the makeup of the population. (National Advisory Commission on Criminal Justice Standards and Goals, 1973:329)

Between 1973 and 1983, this affirmative action proposal resulted in only one of the fifty largest cities in the United States being able to achieve a racially representative balance in its police ranks. Table 6.1 shows the black and Hispanic police employment in the United States' fifty largest cities for 1981–1982. Regarding Hispanic employment compared with blacks in police ranks throughout these cities for the 1981–1982 period, Table 6.1 shows that only five cities (Toledo again, Minneapolis, Milwaukee, Omaha, and Oakland) had employment of Hispanics in their police department ranks equivalent or approximately equivalent to their actual proportionate community representation. For blacks and Hispanics, at least, affirmative action is making progress, although most cities do not have proportionate racial and ethnic balances in their police officer representation (Hertig, 1985).

One investigation of the proportion of racial minorities in police departments revealed that between 1967 and 1981, the average increase in minority police officer membership was 330 percent (Hochstedler, Regoli, and Poole, 1984). Concerning

TABLE 6.1   Black and Hispanic Police Employment in the Fifty Largest Cities

Rank Order by Population 1980	City	Sworn Officers	Black Officers		Percent of Blacks in Community	Index	Hispanic Officers		Percent of Hispanics in Community	Index
			Number	Percent			Number	Percent		
1	New York	23,408	2,395	10.2	25.2	0.40	1,704	7.2	19.9	0.36
2	Chicago	12,472	2,508	20.1	39.8	0.51	432	3.4	14.0	0.24
3	Los Angeles	6,928	657	9.4	17.0	0.55	943	13.6	27.5	0.49
4	Philadelphia	7,265	1,201	16.5	37.8	0.44	46	0.6	3.8	0.16
5	Houston	3,629	355	9.7	27.6	0.35	314	8.6	17.6	0.49
6	Detroit	4,032	1,238	30.7	63.1	0.49	32	0.7	2.4	0.29
7	Dallas	2,053	169	8.2	29.4	0.28	96	4.6	12.3	0.37
8	San Diego	1,363	76	5.5	8.9	0.62	107	7.8	14.9	0.52
9	Phoenix	1,660	48	2.8	4.8	0.58	156	9.3	14.8	0.63
10	Baltimore	3,056	537	17.5	54.8	0.32	10	0.3	1.0	0.30
11	San Antonio[a]	1,164	54	4.6	7.3	0.63	384	32.9	53.7	0.61
12	Indianapolis	936	123	13.1	21.8	0.60	1	0.1	0.9	0.11
13	San Francisco	1,957	159	8.1	12.7	0.64	159	8.1	12.3	0.66
14	Memphis	1,216	268	22.0	47.6	0.46	0	0.0	0.8	0.00
15	Washington, D.C.	3,851	1,931	50.1	70.3	0.71	40	1.0	2.8	0.36
16	Milwaukee	1,438	168	11.6	23.1	0.50	66	4.5	4.1	1.09
17	San Jose	915	20	2.1	4.6	0.46	159	17.3	22.3	0.78
18	Cleveland[a]	2,091	238	11.3	43.6	0.26	6	0.2	3.1	0.06
19	Columbus	1,197	133	11.1	22.1	0.50	0	0.0	0.8	0.00
20	Boston	1,871	248	13.2	22.4	0.59	40	2.1	6.4	0.33
21	New Orleans	1,317	276	20.9	55.3	0.38	26	1.9	3.4	0.56
22	Jacksonville[a]	1,263	78	6.1	25.4	0.24	9	0.7	1.8	0.38
23	Seattle	1,011	42	4.1	9.5	0.43	18	1.7	2.6	0.65
24	Denver	1,379	82	5.9	12.0	0.49	180	13.0	18.8	0.69
25	Nashville	969	114	11.7	23.3	0.50	3	0.3	0.8	0.38

26	St. Louis	1,763	346	19.6	45.6	0.43	0	0.0	1.2	0.00
27	Kansas City, Mo.	1,140	123	10.7	27.4	0.39	18	1.5	3.3	0.45
28	El Paso	650	13	2.0	3.2	0.63	370	56.9	62.5	0.91
29	Atlanta	1,313	602	45.8	66.6	0.69	9	0.6	1.4	0.43
30	Pittsburgh	1,222	175	14.3	24.0	0.60	4	0.3	0.8	0.38
31	Oklahoma City	662	27	4.0	14.6	0.27	5	0.7	2.8	0.25
32	Cincinnati	971	89	9.1	33.8	0.27	1	0.1	0.8	0.13
33	Fort Worth	766	43	5.6	22.8	0.25	51	6.6	12.6	0.52
34	Minneapolis	672	20	2.9	7.7	0.38	8	1.1	1.3	0.85
35	Portland	688	19	2.7	7.6	0.36	9	1.3	2.1	0.62
36	Honolulu	1,557	11	0.7	1.2	0.58	4	0.2	5.2	0.04
37	Long Beach	637	20	3.1	11.3	0.27	35	5.4	14.0	0.39
38	Tulsa	695	30	4.3	11.8	0.36	4	0.5	1.7	0.29
39	Buffalo	1,018	86	8.4	22.6	0.37	21	2.0	2.7	0.74
40	Toledo	757	139	18.3	17.4	1.05	28	3.6	3.0	1.20
41	Miami[b]	1,051	181	17.2	25.1	0.69	413	39.2	55.9	0.70
42	Austin	607	43	7.0	12.2	0.57	73	12.0	18.7	0.64
43	Oakland	636	147	23.1	46.9	0.49	59	9.2	9.6	0.96
44	Albuquerque	561	14	2.4	2.5	0.96	184	32.7	33.8	0.97
45	Tucson	549	17	3.0	3.7	0.81	95	17.3	24.9	0.69
46	Newark	1,144	275	24.0	58.2	0.41	55	4.8	18.6	0.26
47	Charlotte[b]	644	144	22.3	31.0	0.72	0	0.0	1.1	0.00
48	Omaha	551	46	8.3	12.0	0.69	12	2.1	2.3	0.91
49	Louisville	673	68	10.1	28.2	0.36	1	0.1	0.7	0.14
50	Birmingham	646	109	16.8	55.6	0.30	0	0.0	0.8	0.00

[a]1980–1981 data. *Source:* Police Executive Research Forum, *Survey of Police Operational and Administrative Practices 1981* (Washington, D.C.: PERF, 1981).

[b]1982 data. *Source:* Peggy Triplett, The Police Foundation.

Source: Sam Walker, "Employment of Black and Hispanic Police Officers," *Academy of Criminal Justice Sciences Today* (November 1983), p. 5. Reprinted by permission.

affirmative action progress for nonwhites generally compared with blacks specifically, the average affirmative action index for nonwhites in 1981 was 52.5, whereas it was only 32.1 for blacks. This suggests that affirmative action progress has been greater for other nonwhites than for blacks over the last few decades (Hochstedler, Regoli, and Poole, 1984). While current recruitment priorities of law enforcement agencies emphasize, among other things, matching department needs with the existing applicant pool and personnel forecasts, there is a concerted effort to infuse minorities into police ranks through affirmative action procedures (McChesney, 1986; Stroup, 1985; Walker, 1985).

A significant trend in the employment of minorities in police officer roles is the growing number of women in law enforcement (Gross, 1984; National Institute of Justice, 1985; Pogrebin, 1986; Potts, 1983; Walker, 1985). Prior to 1967, a negligible percentage of female police officers performed patrol work in most United States jurisdictions. Many female officers were meter maids, and their activities were largely restricted to issuing parking tickets or performing routine clerical tasks in municipal police departments (Hochstedler, Regoli, and Poole, 1984). By 1981, affirmative action increased the employment of women to 6 percent of all law enforcement officers

While the recruitment of women and other minorities in law enforcement has improved in recent years, there is high labor turnover among women, who find the type of work performed stressful or unchallenging.

nationally. This percentage is well below the proportionate representation of women in the United States, although few critics propose the creation of a 50-50 balance of males and females in law enforcement.

Many police departments find it difficult to attract, hire, and retain women (as well as certain racial and ethnic groups) for police work. Operating to influence the numbers of women in police work is the self-selection process. An investigation of the motivation of women for entering police work reveals that little is known about it (Powers, 1983; Pogrebin, 1986). The little existing information shows that women are attracted to police work because of salary and opportunity to help others (Powers, 1983). In short, they do not appear to be challenged by the ERA or the women's movement to enter a male-dominated career field.

Many women who enter police work are initially self-confident and idealistic about their roles and interactions with their male coworkers, but after eight weeks of training, many become disillusioned, experiencing sex-role conflict, self-doubt, repressed anger, and confusion (Gross, 1984). Also, in some instances, female recruits report sexual harassment by male officers (West, 1986). However, in jurisdictions such as Miami, Florida, veteran female police officers form support networks and function as role models for less experienced female recruits who otherwise might be inclined to quit (Gross, 1984).

In spite of critics' predictions, women experience overall job success rates equal to their male counterparts. Field training officers in the Los Angeles Police Department in 1983 gave male recruits more than twice as many unsatisfactory ratings as their female counterparts during their probationary training period (Hickman, 1983), and women performed better than men in every major category of patrol activity.

In a study of policewomen in Texas and Oklahoma in 1984, researchers determined that the female officers were more authoritarian than were the male police officers (Davis, 1984). Additionally, in spite of the idea that women make fewer arrests than men, policewomen in the jurisdictions investigated made more arrests and were more inclined to intervene than were their male counterparts whenever law violations occurred in their presence (Davis, 1984).

Generally, affirmative action policies influence positively the proportion of minorities and women in police departments throughout the nation (McCoy, 1984). The use of quotas in establishing appropriate racial, ethnic, and gender balances is legally justified, particularly when there is a compelling interest in rectifying past discrimination in any particular municipal department. Most police executives are complying with the general principles of affirmative action in their hiring practices (McCoy, 1984; Stroup, 1985). While percentage levels of women and other minorities may never be achieved equivalent to their proportional representation in the population, significant affirmative action efforts continue to promote greater equality for all minorities.

■ PROFESSIONALISM: POLICE EDUCATION AND TRAINING

Little progress occurred in developing better police training until the establishment of the first police training school in the United States in 1908 by Berkeley, California, chief of police, August Vollmer. Vollmer is considered the father of scientific police investigation. He pioneered such innovations in law enforcement as fully mechanized patrol systems and two-way radios for more efficient police communications. In 1916, Vollmer and Professor Alexander M. Kidd developed the first criminology curriculum in the United States at the University of California at Berkeley. This program became a division of the Department of Political Science in 1939. In 1963, the University of California established a doctor of criminology program (Becker and Whitehouse, 1980:49–51). Other institutions, such as the University of Southern California, the University of Chicago, and Michigan State University, developed law enforcement programs during the late 1920s and 1930s.

The development of degree programs was stimulated largely by the recommendations of the National Commission on Law Observance and Enforcement, chaired by George W. Wickersham. President Herbert C. Hoover appointed Wickersham, who published several reports in 1931 on the state of police training in the United States. These documents were known as the **Wickersham Reports.** In 1979, over 700 academic degree programs in law enforcement were offered in community colleges and universities throughout the United States (Becker and Whitehouse, 1980:51). It is difficult to know for sure how many degree programs in criminal justice exist today, because so many of these programs are intertwined with the programs of such departments as political science, public administration, and sociology. Estimates of the number of programs range from 800 to 1,200.

Vital to the growth and development of law enforcement programs in colleges and universities in the United States were the educational recommendations of the Commission on Law Enforcement and the Administration of Justice and the Omnibus Crime Control and Safe Streets Act of 1968. In 1969, the federal government established the Law Enforcement Assistance Administration (LEAA), which allocated billions of dollars toward the development of law enforcement education and criminal justice programs during the 1970s (Becker and Whitehouse, 1980:51–52).

In 1973, the National Advisory Commission on Criminal Justice Standards and Goals strongly recommended that by 1982, all police agencies require as a condition of employment a bachelor's degree from an accredited college or university (Becker and Whitehouse, 1980:51). Interestingly, in 1940, over 50 percent of the police officers in the New York City Police Department (NYPD) had college degrees. However, the general level of education among law enforcement officers nationwide was not equivalent during the same time period (Geary, 1975:87). One explanation for the higher educational level of the NYPD officers compared with that among police officers of other jurisdictions in 1940 is that the NYPD paid its officers well. Thus, the NYPD was not only able to attract numerous applicants but also to be highly selective in its officer recruitment. Another reason for the higher NYPD educational level is that during the Depression years, many college graduates were unable to find work in their chosen professions. Thus, some of them turned to law enforcement.

Early police reformers such as August Vollmer sought to do at least four things: (1) to eliminate political influence from police administration, (2) to secure expert leadership in police management, (3) to modernize the organizational structure of police departments, and (4) to raise the quality of the rank and file police officers (Walker, 1979:164). It is doubtful whether political influence has been eliminated from police administration. It is also doubtful that profound changes have occurred in the organizational structure of police departments. Furthermore, it is doubtful whether reform efforts have been successful in infusing the offices of police executives with expert leadership. However, there *have been* substantial improvements in the quality of the rank and file police officers.

Professionalism ordinarily signifies the attainment of at least five general objectives. These include (1) a clearly defined body of knowledge, (2) a code of ethics, (3) ongoing education, (4) uniform standards of excellence for selection, education, and performance, and (5) an unequivocal service orientation (Shigley, 1988). If these standards are stringently applied to law enforcement, it is questionable whether professionalism among police officers has been fully realized. Increasingly, law enforcement officers are expected to acquire minimal educational levels and fixed amounts of in-service training, but in many jurisdictions, educational courses relevant for police officers are recommended but not required. Greater amounts of training are equated with greater professionalism, but the type and amount of training are often vaguely defined or unspecified.

Improving the quality, or professionalism, of the rank and file police officer means several things. Most municipal police departments have minimum educational requirements for employment. In addition, most large police departments use psychological screening devices, and many of these departments employ professional psychologists on their oral screening boards to assist in candidate interviews and selections (Silverstein, 1986). Also, candidates must meet stringent physical standards and pass thorough investigations and background checks. The law enforcement code of ethics (see Figure 6.2) contains many provisions, including honesty and integrity; therefore, investigative checks sometimes include lie detector tests. Finally, in most states, recruits must be certified by a regulatory board before being hired.

Some critics of police professionalism question whether the requirements and restrictions necessarily are appropriate for police work and its many responsibilities (Shigley, 1988). How do we know that any psychological screening device necessarily measures accurately one's ability to handle stressful situations? How does being able to run a mile in less than 7 minutes make a police officer more qualified to assist in promoting effective police-community relations? Does the possession of a college degree mean that a police officer will act more decisively when being fired upon by a bank robber than an officer facing the same situation but possessing only a high school diploma?

Currently, a majority of police officers in large municipal police departments have either completed college or have acquired the equivalent of some postsecondary educational training (Fischer and Golden, 1985; Scott, 1986). An argument can be made that college-educated police officers communicate more effectively with the public as a result of their acquisition of greater verbal skills. Those possessing college degrees may also have better promotional potential within their departments, but a study of Illinois police departments showed that being promoted to higher ranks may be more a function of politics than merit or education (Fischer, Golden, and Heininger, 1985). In the Illinois study, 537 police officers above the rank of patrol officer who had more than eight years' experience completed questionnaires. The majority of the veteran police officers who sought promotion and who had college educations were unable to achieve higher ranks. Most officers believed that education or merit had little or nothing to do with who gets promoted and who doesn't (Fischer, Golden, and Heininger, 1985).

Law Enforcement Code of Ethics

As a Law Enforcement Officer, my fundamental duty is to serve mankind; to safeguard lives and property; to protect the innocent against deception, the weak against oppression or intimidation, and the peaceful against violence or disorder; and to respect the Constitutional rights of all men to liberty, equality and justice.

I will keep my private life unsullied as an example to all; maintain courageous calm in the face of danger, scorn, or ridicule; develop self-restraint; and be constantly mindful of the welfare of others. Honest in thought and deed in both my personal and official life, I will be exemplary in obeying the laws of the land and the regulations of my department. Whatever I see or hear of a confidential nature or that is confided to me in my official capacity will be kept ever secret unless revelation is necessary in the performance of my duty.

I will never act officiously or permit personal feelings, prejudices, animosities or friendships to influence my decisions. With no compromise for crime and with relentless prosecution of criminals, I will enforce the law courteously and appropriately without fear or favor, malice or ill will, never employing unnecessary force or violence and never accepting gratuities.

I recognize the badge of my office as a symbol of public faith, and I accept it as a public trust to be held so long as I am true to the ethics of the police service. I will constantly strive to achieve these objectives and ideals, dedicating myself before God to my chosen profession . . . law enforcement.

FIGURE 6.2　The Law Enforcement Code of Ethics

Among police officers themselves, ideas of professionalism reflect a concern for acquiring knowledge about police operations, the ability to cope with a wide range of problems requiring the exercise of discretion, and a degree of pride in uniform and appearance not unlike the military (Brown and Vogel, 1983). In jurisdictions where computer-assisted instruction is used in police training, police officers have prided themselves in acquiring essential information concerning criminal justice procedures, such as use of the exclusionary rule for evidence gathered during police investigations (Wilkenson and Chattin-McNichols, 1985). Most police officers are genuinely concerned with a professional image and support programs designed to enhance that image (Brown and Vogel, 1983; Fischer, Golden, and Heininger, 1985; Frost and Seng, 1983; Hunt and McCadden, 1985).

In some jurisdictions, such as White Plains, New York, a 40-hour in-service training program is required of all personnel below the rank of captain. The program is designed to increase job proficiency and to enhance self-image and motivation (Bradley, 1986). Training in human relations skills is increasingly a part of a recruit's instructional activities in most departments as well (Das, 1985). The relatively new human relations emphasis dovetails nicely with the trend toward greater police-community interaction, and it says something about the priority given to the tasks and problems confronting police officers in over 75 percent of their daily routine (Bohm, 1986). However, some training programs are faulted for being too structured and for not cultivating the necessary flexibility police officers must have in making split-second, on-the-spot decisions in the midst of an increasingly diverse public (Bayley, 1984; Fowler, 1985;

Goodroe, 1985; Jones and Joss, 1985; Steinman and Eskridge, 1985; Stratton, 1984; Wiatrowski, 1985).

■ POLICE PERSONALITY AND SUBCULTURE

Apart from the military-like uniforms that typify police officers and the regimentation they observe in their routine activities, some writers note a police personality, which can readily be identified as different from other personality systems in the general public (Franz and Jones, 1987; Gorer, 1955; Manning, 1977). Does a particular police subculture, with its own set of norms and belief systems, exist apart and distinct from, yet within, the larger culture of the American public? Social psychologists have portrayed police as having a distinct set of personality characteristics, including cynicism, aggressiveness, conventionalism, and authoritarianism (Krug, 1961; Watson and Sterling, 1969; Wilson, 1974).

The term *working personality* has been used to describe similar and distinctive cognitive tendencies, behavioral responses, and life-style of police officers (Skolnick, 1966). This working personality emerges through a combination of two principal variables—danger and authority. Police officers are trained to be suspicious, and the element of danger inherent in the police role sets them apart from those not exposed to it. Furthermore, arrest powers and authority set police officers apart from others; officers are required to enforce laws that regulate the flow of public activity and morality (Baker and Meyer, 1980:102–103). A pervasive *esprit de corps* binds police officers to one another (Bittner, 1970:63). Bittner (1970:63–64) notes, "Police officers often remark that one of the most cherished aspects of their occupation is the spirit of 'one for all, and all for one'. To the extent that the fraternal spirit binds members of the police, it also segregates them from the rest of society." Police develop a code of secrecy and exhibit a high degree of fraternal loyalty.

Most close friends of police officers are other police officers, although this is not particularly atypical of other professions or occupational categories (Skolnick, 1966). This pattern of social interaction, however, gives outsiders the impression that police do, indeed, have their own subculture. This view is reminiscent of Homans' notion of interactions, activities, and sentiments (Homans, 1950). Although somewhat oversimplified, this view is that persons who engage in similar activities and interact with one another frequently develop similar sentiments. Applied to police officers and the associations they develop with one another, it suggests a rather unique police subculture, or police family (Drummond, 1976; Niederhoffer and Smith, 1978).

Several factors seem to account for a police subculture and its perpetuation over time. For one thing, police officers are selectively recruited and screened through interviews and psychological tests and measures. Most officers are conservative and conventional. Unconventional persons are probably excluded from the selection process. It may be, too, that certain types of persons are attracted to police work (such as persons who want to exert authority over others, who want to control the actions of people, or who want absolute power). Also, because police are obligated to enforce the law, they are often regarded as the enemy by citizens who exceed the speed limit on our nation's highways or engage in other minor law violations. They are alienated from many

Skolnick (1966) says that a working personality for police officers is stimulated largely by their possession of authority and exposure to danger. They are trained to be suspicious, and citizens sometimes view them as the enemy.

people because they are sworn to uphold a code of conduct that is supposedly higher than the code expected of others. In addition, they work shifts that cause them to observe unusual hours. Thus, they are not in a position to socialize on a continuous basis with persons who hold down routine jobs.

However, there probably is the same degree of *dissimilarity* among police officers that exists among the general public, and serious efforts to identify a particular type of police personality have not been successful (Broderick, 1987). Police officers in every jurisdiction in the United States engage in social relationships with persons from every walk of life. It is probably most accurate to say that police officers manifest their working personality primarily when they are working in their police roles, and while instances of social aggregation among police officers may give the impression of a police subculture, it is more likely that police officers maintain loose social ties with many persons, so that a particular subculture as such is not apparent.

■ POLICE STRESS AND BURNOUT

In recent years, two psychological phenomena have appeared to affect police officers to a critical degree. These are stress and burnout. **Stress** is the body's nonspecific response to any demand placed on it (Selye, 1974). While stress may be either positive (such as the challenge of a sports event or preparation for an examination) or negative, police stress specifically refers to negative stress, which is accompanied by an alarm reaction, resistance, and exhaustion.

Sevier County, Tennessee, sheriff's deputy Dave Clayton was shot in the shoulder as he approached an old Ford van without license plates on a lonely county road early one morning. Had it not been for his hand-held radio and quick action by paramedics, Deputy Clayton's wound would have been fatal.

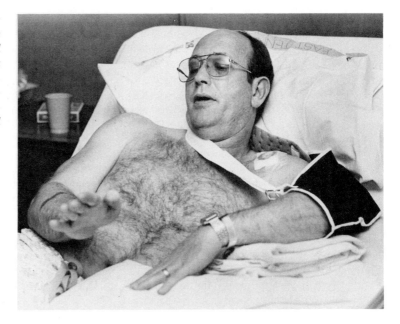

Stress is not unique to police work. All jobs have some degree of stress. Most studies of police stress have been theoretical, speculative, and full of conjecture. Comparatively little empirical research data exists on police stress directly and the problems such stress creates for police officers (Terry, 1981; Malloy and Mays, 1984). Nevertheless, several police stressors appear to cause an increase in the incidence of coronary heart disease, ulcers, high blood pressure, headaches, and gastric disorders. Such stressors inherent in police work include the constant threat to an officer's health and safety; boredom alternating with the need for sudden alertness and mobilizing energy; responsibility for protecting others' lives; continual exposure to people in pain or distress; the need to control one's emotions even when provoked to anger; the presence of a gun, sometimes even during off-duty hours; and the fragmented nature of police work, with only rare opportunities to follow a case to its conclusion or to obtain follow-up information (Goolkasian, Geddes, and DeJong, 1985:4–5; Selye, 1974; Stratton, 1978).

Stressors also come from the police department itself, from the criminal justice system, or from society at large. Poor administrative supervision, few rewards for good job performance, insufficient training and experience, excessive paperwork, and inadequate job opportunities often are cited as major causes of stress for police officers within their departments (Dantzker, 1986). Court decisions, such as the exclusionary rule and legal restrictions on the use of firearms when attacking crime, also contribute to stress. Finally, a conspicuous lack of public support for police work is yet another source of stress (Goolkasian, Geddes, and DeJong, 1985:5–7).

Police officers sometimes experience stress from personal and internal sources, too. They may worry excessively about their ability to cope with certain assignments or they may have fears about dangerous assignments. For instance, over 950 police officers were killed in the line of duty between 1976 and 1983 (Schmidt, 1985). Of course, the

CRIME BEAT

One of the most routine duties of police officers is the enforcement of traffic laws. Thus, officers devote a considerable amount of their time to stopping speeding or reckless motorists and citing them for their violations. These citations normally involve nominal fines. It takes either a major traffic violation (driving while intoxicated) or many minor violations before one's license is suspended for 6 months or more. Ordinarily, the stops for traffic citations are harmless, although motorists leave the scene upset over receiving a traffic citation.

However, in some instances, police stops for traffic offenses can be lethal. On the afternoon of January 1988, Officer John Chase, a 25-year-old white police officer with the Dallas Police Department, stopped a speeding vehicle and determined that the driver did not have a valid driver's license. Soon, an angry shout was heard from behind Chase. A black vagrant with mental problems, Carl Williams, observed the stop and citation and yelled out a protest against the officer's action. Officer Chase argued with Williams, and soon a scuffle broke out. Williams grabbed Chase's service revolver and trained it on Chase. People nearby shouted "Shoot him, shoot him" to Williams, urging him to shoot the unarmed officer. Williams accommodated the crowd, walking up and shooting Officer Chase three times, once directly in the face.

Dallas has one of the highest death rates among police officers of all large cities in the United States. The stresses of police work and the potential for situations such as that as encountered by Officer Chase foster burnout and high labor turnover among police officers. As one officer has said, "You never know who you are pulling over. It could be a mass murderer or serial killer, an escaped convict, robbery suspects, or someone who is mentally deranged. You never know."

probability of an officer's death from a traffic accident is much greater than that of death in the line of duty. The unusual working hours, as well as the life-threatening risks, also affect a police officer's family, which is another stress source. Female police officers have especially high stress levels, as they strive to compete physically with male officers in difficult police roles (Bass, 1982; Goolkasian, Geddes, and DeJong, 1985:6; O'Brien, 1986; Wexler and Logan, 1983).

Closely associated with stress is burnout. **Burnout** is a disorder characterized by the loss of motivation and commitment related to task performance. Police burnout is the loss of commitment to the job, that is, the loss of motivation to be successful in the accomplishment of police work (Burke and Deszca, 1986). Burnout is frequently measured by the Maslach Burnout Inventory, a psychological device consisting of a number of subscales, each designed to tap selected psychological dimensions (Maslach and Jackson, 1979).

Stress and burnout are important because they influence the quality of a police officer's job performance. High absenteeism, low morale, inefficiency in the performance of tasks, and poor judgment are direct results of stress and burnout. Other phenomena related to burnout and stress are high suicide rates among police officers, high divorce rates, and alcoholism (Fabriacatore and Dash, 1977; Schreiber and Sietzinger, 1985; Terry, 1985; Violanti, Marshall and Howe, 1985; Wallace, 1980; Wallace, Roberg, and Allen, 1985; White, 1985).

Suicide rates among police officers have been reported as high as six and one half times that of other individuals (Friedman, 1968). While authorities disagree about the accuracy of these figures among jurisdictions and nationally, evidence suggests higher suicide rates among police officers than the general population (Terry, 1985:406–408). One problem noted by Terry (1985:407) is that police departments are reluctant to keep accurate records of their police suicides. The unfavorable image that such statistics convey to the general public seems to account for some of the reluctance to disclose any information about officer suicides.

Attempts to profile the police officers who commit suicide disclose little. For example, Danto (1978) studied twelve Detroit police officer suicides between February 1968 and January 1976. He concluded that the officers were ". . . young men, married and for the most part, fathers . . . with backgrounds of unskilled employment prior to their police appointment or military service, high school or better, and some stable family life. . . . The majority of officers were white and had not been employed as police officers for many years. . . ." (1978:36). However, it is impossible to use these characteristics as predictors of future suicide victims among police officers, since many of these characteristics are descriptive of a majority of the nation's police officers.

It has been postulated that police suicides are higher than those for the general population because most police officers are male, and males have higher suicide rates than females. Furthermore, police have access to firearms, are constantly exposed to death in the line of duty, have unusual working hours, are publicly criticized, and suffer setbacks from judges who nullify their effectiveness by their inconsistent rulings and contradictions (Nelson and Smith, 1979). However, no reliable information profiles suicide-prone police officers to distinguish them from other police officers who are exposed to the same problems.

Investigations of how police officers cope with the stressful aspects of their work have led researchers to view alcohol as the most convenient and socially acceptable coping alternative to stress (Violanti, Marshall, and Howe, 1985). In fact, there is evidence that a police subculture accepts and reinforces the use of alcohol. Other coping alternatives have been identified, such as cynicism and deviance, although such stress responses often trigger even greater stress levels (Violanti and Marshall, 1983).

Narcotics officers appear to be especially susceptible to burnout and stress (Wallace, Roberg, and Allen, 1985). They deal with dangerous situations (such as drug rings and illicit drug buyers and sellers) on a fairly frequent basis, sometimes working undercover, where they pose as drug buyers in order to make arrests. This undercover work creates additional stress (Wallace, Roberg, and Allen, 1985).

Several strategies have been used to combat stress and burnout among officers. These strategies include employee assistance programs, home visits, and peer counseling programs. **Employee assistance programs** offer diagnostic, referral, and treatment services for police officers suffering from job stress (Besner, 1985). In Florida, employee assistance programs are involved in prevention, intervention, and aftercare counseling. They assist police officers with such problems as substance abuse; family, child, or interpersonal difficulties; legal concerns; and emotional problems (Besner, 1985).

Indiana has an employee assistance program, as well. Originally created in 1978, the Indiana State Police Employee Assistance Program (EAP) assists officers or their family members with such problems as alcoholism, drugs, or emotional difficulties. It was the first of its kind in any state police department or agency in the country, and it has enjoyed a fairly high success rate for those receiving treatment (Lambuth, 1984). In fact, in 1984, the program began training all state police recruits to recognize stress, to handle coworkers' problems, and to become acquainted with the hazards and pressures of their jobs (Lambuth, 1984).

The Los Angeles Police Department has experimented with a limited home-visit program that uses an outreach approach, utilizing in-house mental health specialists who work with distressed officers to reduce sick time, medical costs, and civil liability (Petrone and Reiser, 1985). During a 4-month evaluation period, eighty-eight officers were questioned concerning their views about the program. Over 50 percent were supportive of such a program, and many indicated a willingness to accept home visits (Petrone and Reiser, 1985).

Peer counselors are police officers who counsel other police officers suffering from work stress (Goolkasian, Geddes, and DeJong, 1985:64–66). Police departments in Rochester, New York; New Haven, Connecticut; and Tucson, Arizona, have experimented with peer counselors, and they report favorable results. In Tucson, only one officer acts as a peer counselor. This officer is a sergeant, but the patrol officers he counsels look up to and feel comfortable with him in the counseling role. In order for the program to be effective, it is important for peer counselors to have the trust and respect of their fellow officers. The costs of these programs range from $10,000 to $200,000 annually, depending on the sophistication, operations, and services provided.

■ SUMMARY

The organization and operation of modern police departments in the United States is based largely on the 1829 British model of the Metropolitan Police of London, established by Sir Robert Peel. The police were originally protective bodies, whose functions included the general security of the state and individuals. The first police departments in the United States were created in Boston in 1838 and New York City in 1845, although policing activities were known in earlier periods under different names.

The modern police officer performs many functions similar to those of the officers in the early New York and Boston police departments. While some of an officer's time is spent in crime-fighting activity, a much larger portion is devoted to a variety of service activities.

There is similarity in the organization and administration of large municipal police departments. They are usually headed by a chief of police who is appointed by the mayor or other city executive. The influence of politics in police operations is generally acknowledged, and police reformers such as August Vollmer have sought, among other things, to provide police departments with some independence from political influences.

The selection and recruitment of police officers has resulted in a general upgrading of officer quality, particularly in educational attainment and physical fitness. Psychological tests and measures are used to an increasing degree to make more acceptable officer selections. While their use has not been without controversy, it appears that such tests, together with additional selection criteria, result in more informed officer appointments.

Studies of police subculture and personality have failed to define consistent police officer traits, although police are often viewed as conventional, cynical, and authoritarian. Selecting other police officers as friends contributes to the notion of a police subculture, although little empirical evidence supports the idea of a pervasive subculture of police officers.

Police officers are subject to stresses not ordinarily encountered by other citizens. Life-threatening situations and other anxieties create police stress and contribute to burnout among officers. Various programs, including peer counseling and employee assistance, are utilized by police departments to help their police officers cope with the strains of police work.

KEY TERMS

bobbies

burnout

employee assistance programs

Metropolitan Police of London

police

professionalism

sheriff

stress

Wickersham Reports

working personality of police officers

QUESTIONS FOR REVIEW

1. Distinguish between the words *police* and *sheriff*. Where does each originate? What were their earlier meanings?

2. What model is used as the basis for early police department organization in the United States? Briefly discuss the political and social context within which this original model was created.

3. What were some of the early criteria used to recruit police in England and the United States? What changes have occurred in the recruitment of police officers in modern municipal police departments?

4. What policing activities were used in the United States prior to the creation of the first police departments in Boston and New York? How was police officer effectiveness measured by the police departments of Boston and New York?

5. What are two conflicting images of the police role in the United States? What is the basis for each of these images?

6. Why are certain myths about police work perpetuated by the public, the media, and politicians? Does spending money on crime control actually result in lessening the amount of crime? Why or why not?

7. Differentiate between line and staff in police organization. Who controls the police department administratively? What is a key source of political influence in police departments?

8. What have been some of the objectives of police reforms since 1900? Have these objectives been achieved in recent years?

9. Who is the father of scientific police investigation? What innovations did this person introduce into police departments? What educational programs did this person introduce?

10. Evaluate the effectiveness of psychological screening devices in the selection of police officers. Is everyone in agreement concerning their usefulness? Why or why not? Identify some of the problems associated with the psychological measures used in police recruitment.

11. Do current recruitment practices in police departments necessarily upgrade police officer quality? Why or why not? What supplements to psychological screening devices are recommended as a part of the hiring process in the "Uniform Guidelines on Employment Selection Procedures"?

12. Are large municipal police departments fully integrated and fairly represented in the hiring and retention of women and minorities? Why or why not? Which city or cities in the United States appear to be racially balanced in the employment of black police officers?

13. What are some reasons for the underrepresentation of blacks and other minorities in police departments historically? What are some objectives of affirmative action?

14. How do women compare with men in the police role? What are some of the findings of studies comparing male and female police officers?
15. What is meant by police professionalism? Have police departments been able to achieve professionalism among their police office ranks? Why or why not?
16. Is there a distinct police personality? Is there a police subculture? Why or why not?

17. What characteristics of police officers lead some persons to believe that there is a police personality?
18. What is meant by stress? What is meant by burnout? What are some of the sources of police stress and burnout?
19. What are three programs designed to alleviate police stress and to treat burnout? What is the general effectiveness of these programs?

SUGGESTED READINGS

Barker, Thomas, and David L. Carter (1986). *Police deviance*. Cincinnati, OH: Pilgrimage Press.

Broderick, John J. (1987). *Police in a time of change* (2nd ed.). Prospect Heights, IL: Waveland Press.

Hageman, Mary J. (1985). *Police-community relations*. Beverly Hills, CA: Sage.

Rubinstein, Jonathan (1973). *City police*. New York: Farrar, Straus & Giroux.

Wilson, James Q. (1968). *Varieties of police behavior: The management of law and order in eight communities*. Cambridge, MA: Harvard Univ. Press.

Police Procedures and Police Work

■ INTRODUCTION

This chapter discusses what police officers do and how they do it. Police work means many things. Police officers spend much of their time on patrol, and they make frequent decisions about arrests and when to intervene in citizen affairs. Sometimes, citizens who are dissatisfied with these decisions raise the issues of police discretionary powers and the mechanisms that exist for monitoring the police themselves.

In recent years, improving police-community relations has been advocated by commissions, agencies, and politicians to help the public gain a better understanding of the police officer role. By the same token, police may obtain from citizens a better concept of their own role and how it ought to be performed. This chapter describes police patrol as well as police-community relations.

A growing component of law enforcement is private police. Private police agencies and private police are performing greater numbers of law enforcement functions, but this raises issues about the training and professionalism associated with private police work. This chapter discusses some of those issues and examines some of the private agencies and personnel that perform policing activities.

■ REAL POLICE WORK

James Q. Wilson says for police officers, real police work is catching real criminals or felons, preferably while the crime is in progress (Wilson, 1968:68). However, such work happens for the average police officer only about 10 percent or 20 percent of the time on duty (Bohm, 1986:198). Depending upon the jurisdiction, police officers spend from 50 percent to 90 percent of their time on patrol (Terry, 1985). During all hours, isolated or in pairs, on foot, on motorcycles, or in cruisers, police officers patrol. Most routine police work (such as giving first aid, counseling, mediating, citing, investigating auto accidents, and locating lost children) is unrelated to crime fighting, but the small fraction of crime-fighting time that police officers spend while on patrol is the type of work that brings suspects into the criminal justice system for processing.

Real police work goes well beyond catching criminals and enforcing the law. Police officers are involved in many community service functions, including the distribution of teddy bears to young victims of crime.

Crime fighting begins when one of two things happens. First, and most often, police officers are notified by a dispatcher that a crime has been committed or is in progress when silent alarms in banks are triggered and the police department is notified by alarm companies such as ADT or when citizens call the police and report victimizations, crimes being committed, or someone's suspicious behavior, which may or may not be criminal. Police officers investigate these reports nevertheless. The second thing that may happen is that police officers observe crimes being committed. This is relatively rare compared with receiving reports of crimes because criminals wish to avoid encounters with police. Criminals usually plan their crimes at times and in places where police are unlikely to appear. Patrolling officers may drive by a liquor store and see someone in a ski mask pointing a pistol at a store clerk, they may see a woman being attacked by a street gang, or they may hear a burglar alarm in a nearby building and suspect that a burglary is in progress. When any of these events occurs, the police officer's crime fighting begins.

Police officers have broad discretionary powers when making arrests. However, the courts have restricted the types of things they can do while patrolling their community. Thus, the rights of suspects and the responsibilities of police officers sometimes conflict. Most officers attempt to walk a fine line, balancing their job expectations with those of the community residents. Finally, other types of officers, private police, supplement the routine tasks performed by regular police officers on patrol. Private police make up a growing law enforcement component that contributes to community welfare in several ways.

CRIME BEAT

Some uniformed police officers work in undercover operations from time to time. These operations require that officers wear regular street clothes and attempt to infiltrate a drug ring or obtain information about organized crime. Obviously such work involves the calculated risk of being detected. The implications of detection for an undercover officer may be fatal. For example, in the fall of 1987, a Midlothian, Texas, police officer, George Raffield, Jr., 21 years of age, enrolled in the local high school as a senior. He enrolled under the name of George Moore, and his youthful appearance enabled him to pass for a high school student.

A drug ring was known to be circulating various illegal substances among the high schoolers, including cocaine, LSD, marijuana, crack, and heroin. Although Raffield seemed to blend in with other students, possibly those connected with the drug trafficking saw danger signals. The school officials gave Raffield three lunch periods in order to permit him the freedom to mingle and gain the confidence of other students. Unfortunately, students' suspicions were immediately aroused, and word spread that Raffield might be an undercover officer. On October 24, 1987, Raffield's body was found. Raffield had died as the result of a gunshot wound to the head. Students who were acquainted with Raffield said that he tried too hard to fit in and that his three lunch periods undermined his cover. It is likely also that his lack of experience in undercover work increased the risk of his detection.

This case raises the question of whether police administrators should place rookie police officers in such hazardous situations. What are the moral and ethical issues? While it is likely that Raffield volunteered for this duty when asked, it is clear that drug dealers have much to lose and will do virtually anything, including commit murder, to avoid apprehension.

■ PREVENTIVE PATROL AND GOLF CARTS

The Houston (Texas) Police Department believes that crime prevention is its most important goal and that it should "vigorously pursue those who commit serious crimes" (Brown, 1984). Among other aims of the Houston Police Department are that (1) it will involve the community in all policing activities that directly impact the quality of community life, (2) it is committed to managing its resources carefully and effectively, (3) it believes that it must structure service delivery to reinforce the strengths of the city's neighborhoods, and (4) it believes that its policing strategies must preserve and advance democratic values (Brown, 1984).

The Houston Police Department is not much different from other large municipal police departments in its goals. All police departments attempt to prevent crime and apprehend criminals, but all police departments share a common problem: They must operate within the limited budgets established by community leaders. These budgets are based upon community resources and needs. Police departments with greater financial resources are able to hire more highly qualified police officers than are those with limited financial resources. In addition, some police departments patrol vast geographical territory, while others patrol small areas. Population density also varies greatly among jurisdictions.

Preventive patrol is the belief that high police officer visibility will effectively deter crime, but evidence shows that the size of a police department and officer visibility have little deterrent effect on criminals and the amount of crime. In a study of crime rates in 252 United States suburbs and 269 United States cities in 1960 and 1970, the amount of crime and police visibility were correlated. It was originally believed that increasing the number of police officers in selected community areas would lessen crime in those areas, but investigators found no evidence that either violent crimes or property crimes were reduced as the result of greater police officer visibility (Greenberg, Kessler, and Loftin, 1983). Although the cities and suburbs described in this research reacted to violent crime by greatly increasing the size of their police forces during the 1960s, this response was ineffective in reducing the amount of crime.

What type of patrol scheme is best suited for a city such as this? How many officers are required to effectively patrol so-called high-crime areas? Limited resources and vast territories to cover serve to limit police effectiveness.

The Kansas City Preventive Patrol Experiment

One of the most controversial studies to test the effectiveness of preventive patrol and its influence on the crime rate occurred in 1972 in Kansas City, Missouri. This study, called the **Kansas City Preventive Patrol Experiment,** was controversial because it rejected the rhetoric of police administration and public relations personnel that spending more money on police services and increasing police visibility through more patrolling would decrease crime (Kelling, Pate, Dieckman, and Brown, 1974). In fact, it showed that increasing or decreasing the number of police patrols in Kansas City suburbs had no effect on the amount of crime in those suburbs where the experiment was conducted.

Funded by a grant from the Police Foundation, the Kansas City Police Department varied the numbers of routine preventive patrols within fifteen of the Kansas City police **beats,** or the habitual patrols conducted by police officers. The fifteen beats were divided into three groups of five each. In the control beats, routine preventive patrol was maintained by the usual one-car patrol. In the reactive beats, routine patrols were eliminated. Instead, police officers responded only to calls for assistance from citizens. In the proactive beats, routine preventive patrols were increased to three cars per patrol. The Kansas City Police Department randomly dispersed 1,300 police officers throughout the southern district of the city of 500,000 according to these different beat groupings.

The duration of the experiment was from July 1972 to September 1973. Then, the results were compiled, including data about crime rates during that period, citizen perceptions of police service and visibility, police response time to citizen calls, and the satisfaction of citizens with police services. Surprisingly, the presence or absence of police patrols had no effect on the number of residential and nonresidential burglaries, auto thefts, larcenies, robberies, and vandalisms. This finding was important because these crimes are usually considered deterrable through preventive patrol. Furthermore, the fear among citizens about crime was unaffected. The attitudes of businesspersons toward crime and police services were unaffected also, as was the level of citizen satisfaction with police services and response time.

These findings do not necessarily mean that preventive patrol doesn't prevent crime. Also, these findings do not mean that preventive patrols in large cities should be discontinued. However, the citizen satisfaction with police officer responses to their calls suggests that preventive patrols did enhance police-community relations. It has been suggested that one reason Kansas City police officers found no differences in the amount of crime in the geographical areas with or without patrols was because of the phantom effect. Thieves, robbers, and burglars may have thought that patrols were present because of the previous police patrols in those community areas. However, this is only speculation.

This experiment has been faulted in other respects. To what extent is Kansas City representative of other cities? Would the same results be observed in small communities or in larger cities? No investigations examined the effectiveness of one- or two-officer patrol cars. Team policing was not tested, and neither were a number of other experimental patrolling styles being used during that period. Nor did the findings suggest that police forces should be reduced or that police should be withdrawn from certain areas within cities. Nevertheless, the findings challenged traditional beliefs about police visibility as a crime deterrent. The findings were neither conclusive nor absolute, and further experimentation with the nature of police patrols was strongly suggested.

Patrol Alternatives

It is not clear whether the Kansas City research caused increased interest in police management and effectiveness studies of police patrols in later years, but many studies were conducted during the 1970s (Davis, 1978, Mastrofski, 1979, 1981; Maxfield, 1979; Muir, 1977; Parks, 1979, 1980; Police Executive Research Forum; Police Foundation, 1978; Schwartz and Clarren, 1977, 1978; Wilson, 1975). One topic investigated was the scale of police patrol. Although the size of the police organization (that is, number of employees and budget) is often used as a measure of organizational scale, in this case the **scale of patrol** is the scope of a police officer's routine geographical patrol responsibilities (Mastrofski, 1981).

It is unsettled whether the scale of police patrols should be extensive or limited. Those favoring the use of large-scale police patrols believe that officers will be deterred from becoming too attached to any given community area, reducing the likelihood of police officer corruption by those engaging in clandestine gambling or other illicit activities in those areas and decreasing officer potential for becoming complacent or stale (Vanagunas and Elliott, 1980:346). Those favoring small-scale police patrols believe that a neighborhood will benefit more because of the police officer's continuous contact with citizens in the beat area, enhancing a police officer's understanding of the citizens' problems and customs. Officers having greater familiarity with those citizens on the beat would be less likely to stereotype them or misinterpret their actions and would be less likely to use unnecessary force to make arrests and uphold the law (Davis, 1978:134–137; Gay et al., 1977:17–19; Murphy and Plate, 1977:264).

Reductions in the scale of patrol are designed to link police officers with small populations of citizens (Whitaker, 1984:25). Programs emphasizing close contact with citizens are known as back-to-the-people programs. Among such programs are neighborhood, territorial, and team policing. In Tampa, Florida, the Tampa Police Department experimented with a community-based patrol concept, the Neighborhood Sector Patrol System (Smith and Taylor, 1985). Under **sector patrolling,** police officers were assigned to sector commanders in city areas where police-citizen relationships were most vital because of economics, population, crime, and crowd behavior. Sector offices were manned 18 hours daily, and police officers were permanently assigned specific areas to "become familiar with the characteristics of individual neighborhoods and to become acquainted with the inhabitants and the problems peculiar to the area" (Smith and Taylor, 1985:pp. 39–40). Reported crime in those sectors decreased significantly during the first 6 months of the experiment, and greater police-citizen cooperation occurred (Smith and Taylor, 1985).

In another Tampa experiment, the permanent patrol assignment system, the back-to-the-people program was supplemented with **golf cart patrols** (Morrill, 1984). The golf cart patrols responded more rapidly to citizen calls than did the old system and increased dispatcher efficiency in dealing with citizen complaints.

In Flint, Michigan, a foot patrol program was started in 1979 (Payne and Trojanowicz, 1985). The Flint Police Department assigned twenty-two officers to **foot patrol** in selected neighborhoods as supplements to officers in patrol cars. Administrative concerns about the foot patrols related to program costs, attitudes of officers toward their work, and potential communication problems resulting from patrolling on foot rather than in cruisers. However, first, the Flint community supported the foot patrol program. The taxpayers agreed to increased property tax assessments in exchange for the expansion and continuation of the foot patrol (Trojanowicz, Steele, and Trojanowicz, 1986). Between 1981 and 1985, Flint residents appeared increasingly satisfied with the deterrent value of foot patrols in neighborhoods with formerly high crime rates (Trojanowicz, Steele, and Trojanowicz, 1986). Second, a comparison of work satisfactions of cruiser officers and those assigned foot patrol showed that foot patrol officers believed that they were doing a more important job in their patrol areas, dealing with crime and other local problems more effectively, improving police-community relations, and doing work that their department considered important (Trojanowicz and Banas, 1985b). Third, both foot and motorized patrol officers said that although foot patrol officers found it more difficult to communicate with their dispatchers and with other patrolling units, motor officers had greater difficulty maintaining high morale and work satisfaction (Trojanowicz and Banas, 1985b).

By 1984, foot patrol strength had been increased to sixty-four officers, and other cities, such as Newark, New Jersey, experimented with similar foot patrols (Trojanowicz and Banas, 1985). When the sixty-four foot patrol officers were interviewed and their responses were compared with fifty motorized officers, the foot patrol officers believed they were safer in the neighborhoods they patrolled. They also sensed greater closeness to community residents and believed these residents would come to their aid if necessary (Trojanowicz and Banas, 1985a).

One interesting implication of this foot patrol research involved attitudes of blacks and whites toward the foot patrol program (Trojanowicz and Banas, 1985c). Interviews

Officers often patrol neighborhoods on foot. This familiarizes them with local residents and resident problems and enhances police-community relations. It also reassures citizens that the police are taking an active interest in their problems.

were conducted with 1,220 blacks and whites in Flint in 1979, 1981, 1982, and 1983. While the 1979 interviews showed that blacks perceived police officers less favorably than whites, by 1983, blacks not only viewed the foot patrol program and police officers favorably, but they also viewed police more favorably than whites (Trojanowicz and Banas, 1985c).

Disagreement exists about whether small-scale police patrolling is the most effective means of combating community crime. Some experts believe an emphasis upon neighborhood sector patrols creates localism, which isolates communities rather than unites citizens in working on solutions to common problems, including crime (Einstadter, 1984). Despite this disagreement, more active citizen involvement in policing has occurred where foot patrol programs have been implemented. In Boston, for example, citizens actively participate with police officers in neighborhood crime and street patrol committees (Graves et al., 1985). In Atlanta, a Bureau of Police Services Partnership Against Crime Program has actively involved citizens with police in devising ways of attacking the crime problem through more aggressive prevention and control (Napper, 1986).

One innovative type of police patrol scale is team policing. **Team policing** is the assignment of a small geographical area of a community to a team of police officers who are, in turn, commanded by a team leader (Greenwood, Chaiken, and Petersilia, 1977). Terry (1985:346) says, "[T]he basic concept of team policing involves assigning complete responsibility for police service in a small geographical area to a team of police officers, commanded by a team leader. Using this pattern a city of several hundred thousand may be divided into six to ten team areas, with each area covered by a team of 20 to 40 police officers." Team policing gives special officer teams complete responsibility for the police services in any area assigned. Decentralization of police authority is maximized, as it is distributed among numerous teams. Team policing has been implemented in Rochester, Hartford, Los Angeles, and St. Louis. Its most extensive use has occurred in Cincinnati, where team policing experimentation has been conducted on a large scale (Schwartz and Clarren, 1977).

The goals of team policing are similar to those of foot patrolling: to bring police officers closer to citizens and to be more effective in providing police services. However, it is unclear whether team policing has achieved this objective (Brown, 1981; Gay et al., 1977; Mastrofski, 1981). In Los Angeles, police officers have been found to be more aggressive in law enforcement under team-policing arrangements than under nonteam-policing arrangements (Brown, 1981). In Cincinnati, after a 30-month experiment with team policing, the degree of informal citizen contact with police had not changed significantly, and the police had developed a proprietary interest in their patrol areas (Schwartz and Clarren, 1977).

James Q. Wilson and other criminologists have said that police patrol practices should return to the watchman style of policing that was typical of pre-1930 police patrols. According to Wilson, during the 1930s, patrol practices were changed toward more crime-control-oriented policing. One type of crime-control-oriented policing put police officers in cars patrolling specific geographical beats. It is claimed that this type of policing tended to depersonalize officers and isolate them from their communities.

Wilson and a colleague, Kelling, have recommended strengthening police officer ties with the community through closer contacts with citizens in small business and

Police patrols are not exclusively confined to automobiles and foot beats. The recent increase in boating accidents on many of the nation's lakes and waterways has resulted in greater numbers of officers assigned to enforce water safety laws and arrest drunk boaters.

residential sectors (Kelling and Wilson, 1982). Known as the **broken-windows approach,** this form of police patrol emphasizes developing better communication between police and citizens. Managing neighborhood juveniles and preventing them from pestering store owners and customers, investigating suspicious persons, and paying occasional visits to store proprietors and others to check on their personal safety are indicative of the broken-windows approach. Foot patrols, team policing, and other back-to-the-people programs are consistent with the broken-windows approach espoused by Kelling and Wilson.

Walker (1984) disagrees with Wilson, saying that any depersonalization that has occurred through crime-control-oriented policing is greatly exaggerated. Innovations such as the telephone have helped promote more intimate police-citizen contact rather than less of it.

The police patrolling trend is toward more extensive experimentation with alternative forms. Police administrators are pragmatic, and eventually, they will adopt the most economical and efficient patrol alternative for their community needs. In the meantime, no single patrol style is considered the best style for *all* communities. The prospects are that continued experimentation by police departments will lead to the discovery of more productive patrol styles for each jurisdiction (Boostrom and Henderson, 1984; Ferguson, 1985; Guyot, 1985; Schuiteman, 1985; Trojanowicz and Harden, 1985; Walker and Kratcoski, 1985).

■ DISCRETIONARY POWERS OF POLICE

According to Bittner (1970:46), "Police roles are best understood as mechanisms for the distribution of non-negotiably coercive force employed in accordance with the dictates of an intuitive grasp of situational exigencies." In plain English, this means that police officers have the authority to use force and they will use it to enforce the law if they feel that the situation demands it.

A key objective of police professionalization is producing officers who can make informed choices in everyday encounters and properly exercise their discretionary powers. A critical part of such professionalization is learning about and understanding their responsibilities as well as the reasonable limits of their discretion. Real police work and service activities confront police officers with the public mandate to enforce the laws of the community. However, an overwhelming number of technical violations are committed. With the limited police resources, police officers must exercise discretion (Hanewicz, 1985:44; Johnson, Misner, and Brown, 1981:28–29). This means that police officers will enforce some laws but not others. However, this situation is not necessarily what police officers desire; the nature of their position demands it. Therefore, police officers create enforcement priorities, where more serious offenses have higher priority than lesser offenses. Officers are more likely to chase a speeding, weaving driver rather than to cite a plodding motorist with a broken taillight, unless there is nothing better to do at the time.

According to some authorities, how police exercise their discretion is the most pressing and complex problem confronting twentieth-century American policing (Hanewicz, 1985:43; Ryan and Williams; 1986). There are at least three ways of examining police discretion. These are (1) the legal approach, (2) the organizational approach, and (3) the behavioral approach. The legal approach is to codify discretion according to specific legal proscriptions and to measure discretionary behavior by the amount of deviation from these rules. The organizational approach is to follow lists of organizational priorities created by the police administrators to clarify explicitly how to handle a wide array of police-citizen encounters. Finally, the behavioral approach, a blend of management, sociology, psychology, and political science, is to negotiate through each encounter with alternative behavioral choices that seem to fit the situation (Hanewicz, 1985:43–47). The behavioral approach uses the highly subjective word, *depends*. Whether to arrest a drunk in a bar depends on the drunk's attitude. Whether to cite a speeding driver depends on how the driver reacts to the officer's lectures about speeding and traffic safety. Whether to arrest juveniles who are having a loud party and disturbing their neighbors depends on their cooperation with officers.

Arrests and Detentions

The **Model Penal Code (MPC)** is the voluntary code developed by the American Law Institute to clarify crimes and their punishments. It also outlines the authority of law enforcement officers to make arrests without warrants. Under Section 120.1 of the MPC, officers may arrest suspects without warrant whenever they have reasonable cause to believe that the suspects have committed a felony. The MPC further provides that officers may arrest suspects without warrant for committing misdemeanors if the officers have reasonable cause to believe that the suspects will not be apprehended unless immediately arrested, the suspects may cause injury to themselves or others, or the suspects may cause damage to property. Also, police may make arrests without warrant for misdemeanors committed in an officer's presence. Most jurisdictions follow these guidelines in arrests without warrant.

Suppose police officers patrolling on First Avenue in a large city are notified that a food market has just been robbed by two suspects, one white and one black, and that they escaped in a blue, 1967 Ford station wagon with broken taillights. They were last seen headed west on First Avenue. At that moment, suppose a blue, 1967 Ford station wagon with broken taillights, driven by a black with a white passenger, speeds west past the officers. While this is not absolute proof these suspects committed the robbery, the

Vagrancy ordinances in cities give police broad discretionary powers to arrest persons for suspicious activities. Disorderly conduct, public drunkenness, and other offenses also encourage arrests by officers. These are most frequently considered nuisance offenses by police, because they are not particularly serious and involve considerable paperwork.

A DAY IN COURT

In the Supreme Court case of *Henry v. United States* (1959), Mr. Henry was convicted of unlawfully possessing three cartons of radios, valued at more than $100, that had been stolen from an interstate shipment. In this case, agents of the FBI received a report of a theft from an interstate shipment of whiskey from a terminal in Chicago. While in an adjacent neighborhood investigating the theft, the agents observed Mr. Henry and another person loading three boxes marked Admiral into their automobile. Their observations were made at a distance of 300 feet, and they could not at first identify or determine the size, number, or contents of the boxes. The agents stopped the car, searched it, placed the boxes marked Admiral in their own car, and held Henry and his friend for about 2 hours, until they ascertained that the boxes contained the stolen radios. Then, they formally arrested both men.

The United States Supreme Court reversed Henry's conviction, because "an arrest is not justified by what the subsequent search discloses." The rationale also included the following factual information. Henry and his friend were in a residential area, not near a loading terminal. The fact that packages had been stolen does not make every person who carries a package subject to arrest nor the package subject to seizure. The police must have reasonable grounds to believe that the particular package carried by a citizen is indeed contraband. Supreme Court Justice Black concluded by observing, "[I]t is better, so the Fourth Amendment teaches, that the guilty sometimes go free than that citizens be subject to easy arrest."

A United States Supreme Court precedent was set in the landmark case of *Terry v. Ohio* (1968). This was another case involving a police-citizen confrontation as the result of a police officer's observations. In this case, on October 31, 1963, at 2:30 in the afternoon, Terry and some friends were standing on a Cleveland, Ohio, street corner conversing. While one of the men waited at the corner, the other walked up the street, looked in several store windows, and then returned. After conversing some more, the other man walked up the street and repeated the other's actions. While continuing to converse on the corner, the two men were soon joined by a third person.

Observing these men engaging in "measured pacing, peering, and conferring" was a plainclothes Cleveland Police Detective, Martin McFadden. McFadden had been a police

circumstances give the officers reasonable cause to make an arrest. The officers do not have to see the crime committed by these suspects in order to make an arrest.

In the second instance, suppose someone is traveling to Denver and has just exited a bus stopped at a terminal in St. Louis. The person is drunk and disorderly and steals a magazine from the terminal gift shop. Police officers are summoned to the terminal, where they discuss the situation with the gift shop owner, who points out the disorderly bus passenger. In this situation, the officers are empowered to make an arrest because there is a good chance that if they don't, the disorderly drunk will board the bus to Denver and never return to the St. Louis jurisdiction. Also, there is a good chance that the drunk bus passenger may injure himself or others. These conditions permit arrests without warrant, even though the crime is a misdemeanor and has been committed outside the officers' presence. In the third instance, if police officers are standing in the bus terminal and observe the drunk passenger steal a magazine from the gift shop, they officer for 39 years and a detective for 35 years. On the basis of his experience, he interpreted their actions as casing a job for a possible stickup. He considered it his duty as a police officer to investigate further, and fearing that these men might be armed, he approached them, identified himself as an officer, and asked for their names. According to McFadden, they mumbled something. McFadden grabbed Terry, spun him around, and patted down his clothing. In the left breast pocket of Terry's coat, McFadden felt a pistol. He ordered Terry to remove his coat, and this action revealed a .38 caliber pistol, which McFadden removed. He arrested Terry, and Terry was subsequently convicted of carrying a concealed weapon.

The United States Supreme Court heard Terry's case on appeal. Terry claimed that McFadden did not have reasonable grounds to stop him and search him for weapons, and therefore, McFadden's seizure of Terry's pistol was unconstitutional under the Fourth Amendment. For this reason, Terry sought to suppress the pistol seized as evidence against him. The Supreme Court disagreed, upholding Terry's conviction. It argued that McFadden did, indeed, have probable cause to stop these men and question them concerning their behavior. More important, the court endorsed McFadden's right to pat down these men, because on the basis of his experience, he had probable cause to believe that they were armed and dangerous, and "it was necessary for the protection of himself and others to take swift measures to discover the true facts and neutralize the threat of harm if it materialized." Thus, the foundation for the stop and frisk, or pat down, prerogative of police officers was established.

Why was this case different from the case of *Henry?* After all, the FBI eventually determined that Henry possessed a number of stolen radios and Terry possessed a concealed weapon, but Henry's conviction was reversed, while Terry's was upheld. The answer is that in Henry's case, the FBI did not have probable cause to detain him. He was not acting suspiciously or engaging in any apparently illegal activity. No legitimate grounds existed for his arrest and detention, even though the radios turned out to be stolen. In Terry's case, Terry and his friends exhibited considerable suspicious behavior.

may make an arrest immediately and without warrant because the crime was committed in their presence.

Stops and Frisks. In many cities, municipal ordinances prohibit vagrancy, including loitering without any visible means of support or for no worthwhile purpose. Police officers have accosted persons who appear to be loitering or vagrant. They have arrested and detained them without warrant. While these vagrancy ordinances have been held unconstitutional because they fail to define prohibited behaviors, they illustrate discretionary abuses by police. Vagrancy ordinances give officers license to harass citizens because of their race, ethnic background, or general appearance.

In warrantless arrests and stops and frisks, police discretionary power is influenced by the element of probable cause. Is there probable cause to believe that a crime has been committed and that a specific suspect has committed it? Police officers learn that each case has its own merits, and there are often fine lines between cases, regardless of their factual similarities.

Limitation of Stop and Frisk. The following incident illustrates police excesses relating to stop and frisk. In *Sibron v. New York* (1968), Sibron was convicted of unlawful possession of heroin. He moved to suppress the heroin seized, claiming that the police officer stopped and frisked him without probable cause. The incident occurred on the afternoon and evening of March 9, 1965, in Brooklyn, New York. While patrolling his beat, Brooklyn Patrolman Anthony Martin observed Sibron continually between the hours of 4:00 P.M. to 12:00 midnight in the vicinity of 742 Broadway. Sibron had casual conversations with six or eight persons, whom Martin recognized as known narcotics addicts. Later in the evening, Martin observed Sibron enter a restaurant, sit down, and order pie and coffee. Sibron was later joined by three more known addicts inside the restaurant.

During this 8-hour period, Martin observed nothing passed between Sibron and these addicts, and he overheard nothing of their conversations. Patrolman Martin entered the restaurant, approached Sibron, and ordered him outside. Once outside, Martin said, "You know what I want." Sibron started to reach into his jacket and Patrolman Martin thrust his own hand into Sibron's pocket and pulled out several glassine envelopes containing heroin. Sibron's conviction for heroin possession was overturned by the United States Supreme Court because officer Martin lacked probable cause to stop and frisk Sibron. Futhermore, Sibron's "mere act of talking with a number of known narcotics addicts over an eight-hour period no more gives rise to reasonable fear of life and limb on the part of the police officer than it justifies an arrest for committing a crime."

The court distinguished between Sibron's case and the matter of *Terry v. Ohio* by noting that the search for Terry's weapon consisted solely of patting down the suspect's outer clothing, not thrusting hands into his pockets. The court concluded that Martin's search of Sibron violated the Fourth Amendment and was not an act of self-protection, such as disarming a potentially dangerous man. Had officer Martin patted down Sibron, it is unlikely that the heroin envelopes would have been found. Certainly, these envelopes of heroin would not feel like a .38 caliber revolver to the officer. Therefore, no cause would exist for officer Martin to search Sibron further for a dangerous weapon.

Searches and Seizures

Ordinarily, police officers may make arrests without warrant under the conditions outlined earlier, when (1) they have reasonable cause to believe that a felony has been committed and that the suspect has committed it, (2) they have reasonable cause to believe that a misdemeanor has been committed and that the suspects may injure themselves or others if not immediately arrested, and (3) a misdemeanor is committed in the officers' presence. In the cases recently examined here, suspects were stopped, questioned, frisked, or searched. The evidence seized and used later in court to convict these suspects was either suppressed or not suppressed by the United States Supreme Court. This decision depended on whether the officers had reasonable cause to detain the suspects initially and whether the officers believed that clear and present danger existed regarding a suspect's possible possession of a dangerous weapon.

CRIME BEAT

In 1963 Gregory Powell and Jimmy Lee Smith were cruising Los Angeles streets looking for an easy place to rob. Their suspicious actions attracted the attention of two police officers, Ian Campbell and his partner. The officers stopped Powell and Smith to question them, but they were immediately subdued by Powell and Smith, who drew weapons and forced them into their car. Powell and Smith drove the officers north to Bakersfield. Late that night in a remote field, Powell and Smith shot Ian Campbell at point-blank range, killing him. Campbell's partner managed to escape into the darkness.

Later Powell and Smith were apprehended, and Campbell's partner identified them as Campbell's executioners. Both were convicted of murder and sentenced to death. However, because of a 1972 United States Supreme Court decision relating to the death penalty, California commuted their sentences to life imprisonment. (Joseph Wambaugh eventually described this incident in his book *The Onion Field.*) When California authorities commuted Powell's and Smith's sentences to life imprisonment, they became eligible for parole at a later date. Although subsequent parole boards in California declared Powell and Smith eligible for release in 1982, protesting citizens caused the parole board to deny them parole. In early January 1987, the Chief Justice of the California Supreme Court, Rose Bird, voted to uphold the parole of Gregory Powell. While Bird's action did not mean immediate release of Powell, it did provide his defense attorneys with sufficient legal muscle to press the parole board for a favorable early release decision.

Who should decide whether murderers should be granted early release from incarceration? Should life imprisonment mean imprisonment for life?

Rose Bird lost her position as chief justice of the California Supreme Court after losing a reconfirmation election in 1985.

These cases involved personal encounters with suspects on the street, searches and seizures of items on their person, and arrest and detention without warrant. Ordinarily, when police officers stop a suspect in an automobile or contact a suspect at a residence, they are prevented from searching the automobile or home and from seizing contraband found in the course of the search unless they have a warrant authorizing the search and seizure, but several important exceptions exist to this requirement. Before examining these exceptions, two contrasting cases are presented that involve warrantless searches of a suspect's premises.

Warrantless Searches of Private Dwellings. The first landmark case involving a warrantless search of a dwelling is *Payton v. New York* (1980). On January 14, 1970, New York detectives pieced together sufficient evidence to have probable cause that Theodore

Payton had murdered the manager of a gas station 2 days earlier. On January 15, six police officers and detectives went to Payton's apartment in the Bronx, where they intended to arrest him. They did not have a warrant. They knocked on Payton's door, and after receiving no reply, they used crowbars, forcibly entering his apartment. At that point, they observed in plain view a .30 caliber shell casing, which they seized and subsequently introduced as evidence against Payton in a murder trial.

The United States Supreme Court reversed Payton's murder conviction because neither an arrest nor search warrant had been issued. The police had time to obtain warrants, but they failed to do so. When the police entered Payton's apartment illegally and seized evidence used against him later in court, the evidence was suppressed because it had been unlawfully seized. Without the incriminating evidence, Payton's conviction was overturned.

Exigent Circumstances. In an earlier landmark case, *Ker v. California* (1963), Ker and his wife were convicted of unlawful possession of marijuana. Like Payton, they claimed that a warrantless search of their home revealed evidence that they claimed to be illegally seized. The Los Angeles County Sheriff's Office had several undercover narcotics officers who purchased some marijuana from a man named Murphy. Undercover officers observed Murphy contact Ker on several occasions, and they eventually learned that Ker was engaging in marijuana sales in his apartment. Without either an arrest or search warrant, Los Angeles police officers went to Ker's apartment building, obtained a key from the building manager, and without warning entered Ker's apartment, where they discovered a large quantity of marijuana. The marijuana was seized and eventually used as evidence at Ker's trial, where he was convicted.

In Ker's case, the United States Supreme Court upheld his conviction. The court reasoned that the police officers were justified in not giving Ker notice of their intent to arrest him and search his premises, because narcotics dealers are known to quickly dispose of their drugs by flushing them down the toilet or throwing them out the window. The officers had to act quickly, because exigent circumstances required fast action to prevent destruction of the incriminating narcotics evidence.

Justices Warren, Douglas, and Goldberg dissented from the majority and argued, "[N]ot only were the Kers completely unaware of the officers' presence, but there was absolutely no activity in the apartment to justify the officers in the belief that anyone was attempting to destroy evidence." Also, the police had ample time to secure the necessary warrants to effect an arrest of the Kers as well as a search of their premises, given informant reports as well as their own observations supporting reasonable cause. The fact that they didn't take the time to secure warrants undermines the legitimacy of their subsequent actions. Nevertheless, by a narrow margin, the United States Supreme Court upheld Ker's conviction for the reason noted.

In the search of Payton's premises, however, no exigent circumstances existed to justify the warrantless search. Also, no arrest warrant had been issued. In Ker's case, the warrantless search was allowed because of exigent circumstances. Police officers receive training and learn to discern between situations where exigent circumstances exist. As the two cases illustrate, the decision to search without a warrant often involves police officer discretion. Warrantless searches of premises depend on the personal judgment of police officers. If police lack the requisite grounds to conduct these searches, the case against a suspect may be thrown out.

Searches Incident to an Arrest. Another discretionary situation arises when police officers possess an arrest warrant. Whey they make their arrest of the suspect, they sometimes search the premises without a specific search warrant. This is a **search incident to an arrest.** The purpose of a search incident to an arrest is to enable police to determine if suspects possess any weapons or fruits of the crime, either on their person or somewhere on their premises. No police officer has liberal license to conduct a warrantless search of a suspect's entire premises.

In a landmark case involving a search incident to an arrest, an officer's discretion to search an entire dwelling incident to the arrest of that suspect was challenged. In the case of *Chimel v. California* (1969), police suspected Chimel of committing a burglary of a coin shop. On September 13, 1965, three officers armed with an arrest warrant came to Chimel's apartment in Santa Ana, California, where they were admitted to the apartment by Chimel's wife. They waited for Chimel to return home from work, and when he did, they handed him the arrest warrant and asked if they could look around. Chimel objected, but the police said that on the basis of the lawful arrest, they had the right to conduct a search anyway. No search warrant had been issued, but the officers searched through the entire three-bedroom house, including the attic, the garage, and a small workshop. Eventually, they found some coins that might have come from the coin shop burglary. Chimel was convicted of burglary largely on the basis of the evidence seized by these officers.

The United States Supreme Court reversed his conviction, because the arrest warrant did not entitle the officers to search the entire premises. They were limited by the arrest warrant to search only the suspect and the area in the immediate control of that suspect. The high court indicated that a gun on a table or in a drawer in front of one who is arrested is just as dangerous as a gun concealed on his person, but there is no justification for routinely searching any room other than that in which the arrest occurs. The court maintained that Chimel could have been arrested at his place of work or outside his apartment. Letting Chimel's conviction stand would give officers license to wait conveniently for suspects to return home and search their entire premises. This would eliminate completely the step of obtaining a proper search warrant.

Warrantless Searches of Automobiles. In the case of warrantless searches of automobiles, a police officer's discretion to conduct a search must be based upon reasonable cause *(Carroll v. United States*, 1925; *Chambers v. Maroney,* 1970). By the same token, if police officers stop a vehicle for a traffic violation and observe a pistol or illegal narcotics in plain view on the seat inside the vehicle, they have the reasonable cause needed to conduct a more extensive search of the car without a warrant (*Cooper v. California,* 1967; *Harris v. United States,* 1968).

Warrantless Searches as the Result of Hot Pursuit. Sometimes, police officers are in hot pursuit of a fleeing suspect. Hot pursuit may be ample justification for officers to search a suspect's premises and seize evidence related to a crime. In the case of *Warden v. Hayden* (1967), for instance, a cab company in Baltimore, Maryland, was robbed on the evening of March 17, 1962. A suspect was chased by the cab company employees and police to his residence. Police officers were admitted to the dwelling by Mrs. Hayden, the suspect's wife, and they conducted a search of the premises. Hayden was found pretending to be asleep in an upstairs bedroom. In the bathroom, police found a shotgun and pistol. Other officers found trousers and a jacket in a washing machine in another part of the home. These items matched those worn by the robber. The United States Supreme Court upheld Hayden's conviction, holding that the police officers' warrantless search in the course of hot pursuit was justified. In some respects, the notion of hot pursuit is similar to that of exigent circumstances; it is imperative that officers act quickly to prevent a suspect from secreting or destroying evidence of a crime.

Warrantless Searches by Consent. Finally, there are occasions where suspects voluntarily permit officers to search their premises or automobiles. Warrantless searches and seizures are permissible in cases where suspects voluntarily give their consent to the search. Of course, the circumstances must be scrutinized carefully to determine if, in fact, the suspects voluntarily consented. If police officers threaten to arrest suspects unless they allow a search, then the discretionary action by police officers may be successfully challenged.

In the case of *Schneckloth v. Bustamonte* (1973), for instance, a police officer stopped a car at 3:00 in the morning because a headlight and the license plate light were burned out. The driver could not produce a driver's license and the officer asked permission to search the car. One of the occupants, a brother of the car owner, said, "Sure, go ahead." With this consent, the officer opened the car trunk and discovered three checks that had previously been stolen from a car wash. This evidence was used in obtaining a conviction against Robert Bustamonte, one of the passengers, who had hidden the checks in the trunk initially.

The Court of Appeals for the Ninth Circuit in California reversed Bustamonte's conviction, saying that the government failed to establish that Bustamonte "knew that he had a right not to consent to the search." But the United States Supreme Court reversed the Court of Appeals decision, stating that when a subject is not in custody and consent is given in the absence of duress or coercion, voluntariness is presumed. Bustamonte's conviction was upheld.

Summary of Search and Seizure Without Warrant Options. Officer discretion to search a suspect's premises and seize evidence of crime without warrant is influenced, in part, by probable cause. Officers may be in hot pursuit of suspects, or they may observe evidence in plain view. Officers may determine that exigent circumstances justify a warrantless search as well. Finally, suspects may voluntarily consent to a search. These are several of the options available to officers when they exercise their discretionary powers in arrests, searches, and seizures.

Deadly Force

Perhaps the most sensitive issue about police discretionary powers is the use of force to make an arrest (Bittner, 1985). Whether police can use force is not the issue, however. Rather, the matter is, *how much* force can they use? Public reaction to the use of force by police is mixed (Williams et al., 1983). In 1980, the National Opinion Research Center in Chicago surveyed 1,468 respondents. Would they approve a police officer's striking an adult male under any of the following circumstances: (1) if the suspect was being questioned as a suspect in a murder case, (2) if the suspect had said something that was vulgar or obscene, (3) if the suspect was attempting to escape from custody, and (4) if the suspect was attacking the officer with his fists? Those interviewed condoned the use of physical force by police if suspects were attempting to escape from custody or if they were attacking the officer. Although most of those surveyed did not approve of the use of physical force by police against suspects who made obscene remarks or against suspects in a murder case, some respondents did condone such force in these situations (Williams et al., 1983).

A Force Continuum. A force continuum has been devised. Among the weapon or technique options available to officers, which range from no force to extraordinary force, are (1) controlled confrontation, (2) body language, (3) verbal persuasion, (4) contact controls, (5) joint restraints, (6) nerve center controls, (7) weapon-assisted pain compliance techniques, (8) chemical irritants such as mace, (9) electrical devices, (10) intimate impact weapons, (11) extended impact weapons, (12) weaponless techniques with debilitating potential, (13) weapon techniques with debilitating potential, (14) service firearms, and (15) supplemental firearms and shotguns (Conner, 1986). Some experts also recommend indexing and reporting the use of all force used by police officers in any given department to perhaps protect the department and the officer from lawsuits by persons subjected to officer force (Patti, 1984).

The Use of Deadly Force. Of interest to criminal justice researchers and citizens alike is the discretionary power of police officers to use deadly force in making arrests. In recent years, this topic has stimulated much controversy and has been the subject of important court decisions (Alpert and Anderson, 1986; Brown, 1984; Elliston, 1985; Fyfe, 1986; Fyfe and Blumberg, 1985; Geller, 1985; Griswold, 1985; Scharf and Binder, 1983; Waegel, 1984).

Deadly force is any force likely or intended to cause death or great bodily harm, and it may be reasonable or unreasonable, depending upon the circumstances (Black, 1979:359). For many years, law enforcement officers followed the **fleeing felon rule,** which permitted them to exercise deadly force to apprehend anyone believed to have committed a felony and who was attempting to elude police. Officers were authorized to use any necessary means to make the arrest, including deadly force (*Cunningham v. Ellington,* 1971; *Beech v. Melancon,* 1972; *Smith v. Jones,* 1973).

During the 1970s, several studies examined the nature of police shootings and the implications of the fleeing felon rule. The Police Project of the Philadelphia Public Interest Law Center compiled information on all police shootings in the city for the years 1970–1978 (Waegel, 1984a). Many of the lethal force incidents were not split-second reactions to life-threatening situations. About 20 percent of the incidents during the 1974–1978 period were violations of legal standards for the use of deadly force, which Philadelphia had statutorily changed in 1973. Burglary suspects and purse snatchers were shot and killed while running away from police officers after being ordered to halt. Suspicious persons were occasionally shot and killed by police after attempting to elude police for minor speeding violations. Despite more restrictive provisions governing firearms use, many officers continued to use deadly force in legally impermissible circumstances, and several officers faced serious penalties for doing so.

Police use of deadly force has been largely situational, consisting of a series of interactional stages between officers and suspects (Scharf, 1983). The outcome of the potential deadly force situation is influenced by the type of suspect (such as a criminal or an insane person), the mode of contact (such as off-duty, regular patrol, or planned

Would you try to use deadly force if you were a police officer confronted by a gun-wielding suspect? Rules cannot be written to cover every circumstance under which deadly force ought to be used to subdue a suspect. Many situations involve judgment calls by officers, who may legitimately feel that their lives are in jeopardy.

apprehension), and the number of police officers present. Using the phase model of police decision making, Scharf (1983) proposed (1) an anticipation phase, (2) an intitial confrontation, (3) dialogue and information exchange, (4) a final decision to shoot or not to shoot, and (5) the aftermath. When backup officers are present, other officers have been dissuaded from shooting at suspects. Psychological measures in the early training of officers help them to learn several alternatives to deadly force in police-suspect confrontations.

Deadly force is not limited to shooting at suspects or fleeing felons. High-speed police chases such as those seen on popular police television programs are examples of deadly force as well (Alpert and Anderson, 1986). When police officers conduct high-speed chases of suspects, their cruisers become instruments that can injure or kill innocent bystanders. Thus, deadly force is not exclusively limited to shooting at suspects to apprehend them.

Prior to 1985, twenty-five states permitted police to use deadly force to arrest fleeing felons. Seven other states had restrictions on police use of deadly force, and seven other states adopted the Model Penal Code provision (Griswold, 1985). The Model Penal Code provision states, "[T]he use of deadly force is not justifiable . . . unless the . . . officer . . . believes that such force is necessary to protect himself against

CRIME BEAT

A police officer sees someone lurking in the shadows late at night while on patrol. She shines a spotlight on the person in the shadows and sees what appears to be a pistol pointed in her direction. Immediately she unholsters her service revolver and shoots at the person with the pistol. The suspect falls to the ground and dies. On close inspection, the pistol is determined to be a toy weapon sold in department stores. No charges are filed against the officer, who believed that she was acting in self-defense.

This scene is repeated with some frequency in many cities, as juveniles and some adults carry toy weapons to intimidate potential muggers and others. However, police officers are trained to defend themselves and to make split-second decisions. All too

often, persons lurking in shadows may have real weapons and kill police officers if the officers do not take immediate defensive action. In early 1987, in Rancho Cucamonga, California, a 19-year-old youth, Leonard Falcon, was shot and killed by police when they believed that he was firing at them with a real pistol, but the pistol turned out to be a Lazer Tag pistol, which emits a flash at night. Believing the flash to be the flash made by a discharged bullet from a pistol and acting on their instincts and best judgment, officers shot and killed Falcon. Only too late did they realize that the pistol was a toy. If police officers believe suspects have weapons and are intending to use them, should they act defensively and shoot at these suspects?

death, serious bodily harm, kidnapping, or sexual intercourse compelled by force or threat." (Griswold, 1985).

A significant change in the police use of deadly force occurred in the 1985 case of *Tennessee v. Garner*. Garner was a 15-year-old youth who was allegedly burglarizing a house in Memphis, Tennessee. Police were called to the neighborhood, and Garner fled from the scene on foot. Police fired several shots at Garner after ordering him to halt. One of the bullets struck Garner in the back of the head, killing him instantly.

The suit against the Memphis Police Department filed on behalf of Garner upheld an old, 1858 Tennessee statute, TCA 40-7-108, which stated, "If, after notice of the intention to arrest the defendant, he either flee or forcibly resist, the officer may use all the necessary means to effect the arrest" (*Garner v. Memphis Police Department*, 1979). The Tennessee courts interpreted the statute as the codification of the common-law rule allowing officers to kill fleeing felons rather than permitting them to escape apprehension. This rule applied to fleeing felons suspected of property crimes and not endangering human life. It applied also to life-endangering crimes and to felons who posed threats of bodily harm to others if not apprehended immediately and to felons dangerous to others if left at large (*Garner v. Memphis Police Department*, 1979).

The case was appealed, and the United States Sixth Circuit Court of Appeals ruled that the Tennessee statute was unconstitutional and violated the Fourth Amendment because it constituted an unreasonable seizure of the person (*Garner v. Memphis Police Department*, 1983). The State of Tennessee appealed the case to the United States Supreme Court, which eventually greatly restricted the use of deadly force by all law enforcement officers and others to situations involving the defense of one's life (*Tennessee v. Garner*, 1985).

Until the *Garner* decision, the right of police officers to use deadly force in apprehending suspects had been taken for granted by most police departments in the

United States under the fleeing felon rule. However, the fleeing felon rule raises an important ethical question. The principle of justice may, indeed, be undermined when police officers are licensed to kill people before trial, people who ordinarily would not be executed anyway if eventually convicted (Elliston, 1985). Application of the death penalty, even in capital cases, is extremely limited. Authorizing police officers to make death penalty decisions when attempting to arrest low-risk property offenders or even fleeing violent felons raises the question of the right to due process under the Constitution of the United States, but the issue cannot be settled here. Because of the *Tennessee v. Garner* (1985) decision, many police departments have revised their deadly force provisions. The defense-of-life standard set forth in *Garner* currently takes precedence over state statutes that authorize deadly force under the fleeing felon rule or other justifications.

■ POLICE MISCONDUCT, CORRUPTION, AND INTERNAL AFFFAIRS

In the early 1970s, police dishonesty and corruption in New York were the targets of a major investigation by the Knapp Commission, which uncovered evidence of large-scale graft, together with numerous incidents of police misconduct (Knapp Commission, 1973). The Knapp investigation led to anticorruption reforms during the following decade, including several important administrative changes designed to increase police accountability (Gelb, 1983).

While police misconduct and dishonesty are often linked with individual police officers, misconduct also originates within the police organization itself (Lundman, 1979:218). Three conditions must be present in order for police misconduct to be organizationally condoned:

1. The misconduct must be supported and encouraged by peer norms situated at some level within the police organization.
2. Mechanisms must exist to teach new officers the norms of misconduct.
3. The misconduct must be supported by police administrators.

In this context, abuse of police discretionary powers is supported either overtly or covertly by the entire department. This means that in certain jurisdictions, there are no organizational penalties for such abuses.

If police organizations covertly support police misconduct, more effective departmental monitoring systems are needed. As we have seen, civilian complaint review boards in police departments have been used as independent monitoring mechanisms for police conduct. These boards are also designed to increase police accountability. Theoretically, they independently and objectively judge the grounds underlying citizen complaints alleging police misconduct (Fyfe, 1985). While many municipalities, such as New York City, Philadelphia, and Detroit, have civilian complaint review boards, such boards are sometimes considered ineffective because of (1) police resistance, especially from police chiefs who regard these boards as infringing on their authority, (2) police resentment, caused by feelings of being singled out for close scrutiny by citizens with little or no knowledge of police work, and (3) unrealistic expectations of what these boards can accomplish (Fyfe, 1985).

An alternative to citizen review boards is to improve the mechanisms for the receipt, investigation, and review of citizen complaints against police officers. A thorough documentation of complaints is required, including the involvement of several officers at different administrative levels in the review process. Most important, citizens must be provided with meaningful feedback about what has been done about their complaints (Fyfe, 1985). The major citizen complaint is that no action is taken regarding allegations. Establishing a feedback system increases police credibility and ensures greater fairness for both citizens and officers.

Increasing police accountability is a major aim of **internal affairs divisions (IADs)**, internal affairs units, which are police officers who investigate allegations of misconduct against other police officers. In many cities, IADs maintain files of complaints against all officers. These files are reviewed when the administrators are making retention and dismissal decisions.

Victims of police misconduct can seek damages against the police officers themselves. Also, the United States Supreme Court has made it possible for citizens to pursue legal action against the employing municipal agency under the **municipal liability theory** embodied within 18 U.S.C., Sec. 1983 (Elliott, 1986). Awards to victims of police brutality and other forms of officer misconduct have reached $1 million, and such suits have done much to improve and modernize police operations and procedures, but victims of police brutality and misconduct find it difficult to win their cases in court.

The Philadelphia Police Department was involved in several federal civil suits during the 1970s, when many allegations of police brutality against minorities were made (Anechiarico, 1984). The outcomes of these suits for the various plaintiffs (*COPPAR v. Rizzo,* 1973; *Rizzo v. Goode,* 1976; *United States v. Philadelphia,* 1979) were unsuccessful. The fact that the plaintiff citizens in these actions against the Philadelphia police had to prove intentional discrimination and injury seriously weakened their cases. Sometimes, too, lawyer apathy or unwillingness to sue police officers causes delays in civil actions alleging police misconduct. If the legal delays are excessive, the statute of limitations expires and the cases are dismissed outright (Harrison, 1985).

■ POLICE-COMMUNITY RELATIONS

A major priority of many police departments is promoting positive community relations. Many large municipal police departments have special public relations divisions and bureaus, which are staffed by persons who try to harmonize the interests of the police and the community.

Police patrols are increasingly oriented toward community policing (Guyot, 1985; Holland, 1985; Pierce, 1984). The Dallas, Texas, Police Department arranged with local business leaders, as well as organizations such as the Dallas Housing Authority, to hold monthly meetings (Pierce, 1984). These meetings include members of business associations, apartment managers, and other parties who want to learn about various new crime prevention techniques, basic security measures, area crime information, and reporting to the police.

In Detroit, Michigan, the Detroit Police Ministation Program places police officers in neighborhood **ministations,** or smaller versions of police precincts (Holland, 1985). These ministations are staffed by officers 24 hours a day. They provide all of the regular services a regular precinct provides except detention facilities. In order to build better police-community relations, the police department has encouraged citizen participation and involvement in staffing these ministations. Nearly forty ministations serve the neighborhood needs of Detroit residents. As community residents have perceived police officer interest in these ministations as genuine, their participation has increased. In fact, citizen volunteers have become a valuable asset to the operation of the ministation program (Holland, 1985).

Police-community relations are enhanced through the implementation of community crime control programs, such as the one in Dallas, Texas. A successful police-community relation is established by tailoring police anticrime programs directly to community needs and expanding citizen participation in the policing role (Bennett and Baxter, 1985). In some jurisdictions, however, police-community relations programs have been nothing more than public relations gimmicks. In these instances, police departments have wanted to promote only the appearance of working with the community. In reality, the police continue to operate as they have previously, without community intervention or involvement.

■ PRIVATE POLICE

In the mid-1980s, 4,000 agencies employed over 1,000,000 as **private police,** or private security police, in the United States, with a budget of over $22 billion (Cunningham and Taylor, 1984). In contrast, there were about 471,000 public police officers in 12,200 local police agencies throughout the United States in 1985 (U.S. Department of Justice, 1986:242).

One reason for the rapid growth of private security police in the United States in recent years is that the cost of crime has risen to over $20 billion per year (Kakalik and Wildhorn, 1977:17). Among the reasons cited for the growth of private security forces are (1) increasing public awareness and fear of crime, (2) the trend toward specialization of all services, (3) more sophisticated electronic surveillance devices and monitoring systems, (4) lower insurance rates when private police are on the business premises, and (5) a lack of confidence in the ability of regular police officers to protect business interests (Kakalik and Wildhorn, 1977:19).

In fairness to police departments, however, private security forces are proprietary, or operated on a contractual basis. As such, they can devote unlimited time to certain types of crime problems associated with the industries and businesses they serve. One result is that their effectiveness in crime control is greater than that of many public police departments, who must perform diverse police tasks. Private police include private detectives and investigators, but over 90 percent of the private security force consists of guards, doorkeepers, crossing guards, and bridge tenders.

The oldest security firm in the United States is Pinkerton's, established in 1850 by Allan Pinkerton. Pinkerton's continues to provide contract guard and investigative services. It currently has over 30,000 personnel and revenues of over $150 million. Other private companies marketing crime-protection services are Brink's, American District Telegraph Company (ADT), Baker Industries, Burns, Wackenhut, and Globe Security Systems.

Compared with municipal police, most private guard and police training is less organized. Its quality varies in extensiveness and quality among companies. The training most guards receive is considered inadequate by critics (Buikema, Horvath, and Dodson, 1983; Kakalik and Wildhorn, 1977:119; Shearing, Stenning, and Addario, 1985). North Carolina and several other states have developed fairly stringent private security licensing and regulation codes. These statutory provisions professionalized the security work in these jurisdictions, but most other jurisdictions do not have licensing mechanisms or regulations to ensure training consistency and quality among recruits for private guard positions.

Union organization exists among some types of security personnel. Among plant guard workers there is a Union of Plant Guard Workers of America, with a membership of over 25,000 guards, or about 10 percent of all private sector guards in the United States. One positive feature of unionization is that union members are encouraged to upgrade their skills and improve their training pertaining to various kinds of guard duty.

Private security guard training programs are available in all major cities. Table 7.1 summarizes the training programs of 188 industrial plants that are considered typical, as well as data obtained from 275 security workers surveyed (Kakalik and Wildhorn, 1977:127–129). In almost all of the programs, there is little, if any, in-class instruction and almost no on-the-job training. Bank guards and in-house guards in research organizations tend to receive the most on-the-job training, and this is usually acquired from their immediate supervisors while at work.

For the average company offering guard-training programs, 12 hours is allocated to seventeen topical areas at the discretion of the local trainer. Table 7.2 shows the percent of time allocated to special subjects. Table 7.2 shows that more time is spent on uniforms and appearance than using firearms. According to most sources this unusual priority scheme is indicative of the quality of these training programs (Brennan, 1975; Kakalik and Wildhorn, 1977).

All states have regulations governing handgun ownership, registration, and possession. California follows a model statute specified by the Uniform Firearms Act, which does not require a license to purchase a handgun. Instead, it requires handgun sellers to provide the local police with descriptions and identifying information about all purchasers of handguns and to refuse sales to minors, drug addicts, or criminals. California requires a permit to carry a concealed weapon. Therefore, the state can check the backgrounds of private investigators and off-premises security guards for prior arrest records, if any.

Security regulations lack uniformity among the states. In 1976, a national advisory committee on criminal justice standards and goals released a report encouraging improvements in licensing requirements and regulations for three major types of private police services: (1) guard services, (2) private police investigators, and (3) alarm system contractors. In 1981, Buikema, Horvath, and Bodson (1983) investigated the

TABLE 7.1 Current Private Security Guard Training Programs

Program	Initial Prework Training								Initial On-the-Job Training				Total Initial Training (Hr)
	Talking with Supervisors (Hr)	Read Manual	View Films/ Slides (Hr)	Class (Hr)	Test	Firearms Range	Trained on Previous Job	Total (Hr)	By Supervisor (Hr)	By Fellow Employee (Hr)	Written Post Orders	Total (Hr)	
Company A: Small contract guard firm	$\frac{1}{2}$–1	None	None	None	None	N/A[a]	None	$\frac{1}{2}$–1	8–16	None	Yes	8–16	$8\frac{1}{2}$–17
Company B: Small contract guard firm	1–2	Yes	None	None	Yes	Yes	None	$2\frac{1}{2}$–$3\frac{1}{2}$	8–16	None	Yes	8–16	$10\frac{1}{2}$–$19\frac{1}{2}$
Company C: Medium contract guard firm	1–3	Yes	$1\frac{1}{2}$	None	Yes	Yes	None	5–7	8–16	None	Yes	8–16	13–23
Company D: Large contract guard firm (full and part-time)	1–2	Yes	2	None	Yes	Yes	None	$6\frac{1}{2}$–$7\frac{1}{2}$	1–8	None	Yes	1–8	$7\frac{1}{2}$–$15\frac{1}{2}$
Company E: Large contract premium guard firm	1–2	Yes	2	40–80	Yes	Yes	None	$46\frac{1}{2}$–$87\frac{1}{2}$	1–8	None	Yes	1–8	$47\frac{1}{2}$–$95\frac{1}{2}$
Company F: Large contract guard firm													
a. Regular	None	Yes	1	9	None	Yes	None	12	1–8	None	Yes	1–8	13–20
b. Temporary	3–4	None	1	None	None	None	None	4–5	$\frac{1}{2}$	None	None	$\frac{1}{2}$	$4\frac{1}{2}$–$5\frac{1}{2}$
Company G: Large contract guard firm													
a. Regular	None	Yes	None	10	Yes	Yes	None	11	$\frac{1}{2}$–1	None	Yes	$\frac{1}{2}$–1	$10\frac{1}{2}$–11
b. Temporary	None	None	None	8	None	None	None	8	$\frac{1}{2}$	None	None	$\frac{1}{2}$	$8\frac{1}{2}$
Company H: Small contract patrol guard firm	1–2	None	None	None	None	Yes	None	3–4	16	None	Yes	16	19–20
Company I: In-house guards (bank)	2–4	Yes	None	None	None	Yes	Occasionally	5–7	80–120	None	Yes	80–120	85–127
Company J: In-house guards (research)	1–4	Yes	None	None	None	N/A	None	3–6	None	160	Yes	160	163–166
Company K: In-house guards (manufacturing)	$\frac{1}{2}$–1	Yes	None	None	None	N/A	Mandatory	$\frac{1}{2}$–2	None	24	Yes	24	$25\frac{1}{2}$–26

N/A: not applicable.

Source: Reprinted from pp. 128–129 of *The Private Police: Security and Danger* by James S. Kakalik and Sorrel Wildhorn (New York: Crane, Russak, 1977). Copyright The RAND Corporation. Used with permission.

TABLE 7.2 Typical Training Course for a Guard Training Program

Subject	Time Spent (Percent)
History and description of company	5
List of guard duties	3
Uniform and appearance	6
Written orders at each post	3
Use of telephone and guard station	3
Legal (arrest, search, use of force, etc.)	15
Keys and watch clocks	3
Report writing	9
Fire fighting and prevention	30
Firearms—how to use	18
Firearms—when to use	5
Total	100

Source: Reprinted from p. 131 of *The Private Police: Security and Danger* by James S. Kakalik and Sorrel Wildhorn (New York: Crane, Russak, 1977). Copyright by The RAND Corporation. Used with permission.

licensing requirements in all states. Of the forty-seven states responding through various officials and agencies, thirty-seven states said their jurisdictions regulate at least one of the three types of security services mentioned above. The most common requirement for licensing is not having a felony conviction. Grounds for revoking licenses include previous felony convictions, false statements made on job application forms, and dishonesty or fraud associated with the clients served. Most respondents indicated that their jurisdictions are reviewing current licensing requirements and considering proposals for upgrading licensing criteria.

Private police perform several law enforcement and protection functions (Meadows, 1985). They can make arrests, detain suspects, search suspects, interrogate persons, and use force in their actions. The use of force and suspect searches occur most often in shoplifting incidents and break-ins of businesses or residences, but because of several United States Supreme Court decisions concerning search and seizure, the legality of the arrests and searches remains troublesome (Meadows, 1985).

Private guards and other law enforcement personnel in the private sector have the same arrest powers as citizens. Citizens may make arrests when they observe suspects committing crimes. Of course, there are inherent dangers when untrained citizens attempt to subdue and detain criminal suspects. Whereas a police officer is trained to deal with suspects who may be armed, the average citizen runs the risk of sustaining serious or fatal injury when attempting to make a citizen's arrest.

Business establishments also have certain rights relating to the arrest and detention of those suspected of crimes. A department store may detain anyone suspected of shoplifting for a reasonable period without fear of liability. There is nothing to prevent citizens from filing suits against these businesses for false arrest or imprisonment, however, even when the arrest and detention appeared justified. In some jurisdictions, private security forces must be deputized by the county executive (such as the county sheriff) in order to carry a concealed firearm or to simply go armed, even on private premises, such as large industrial plants or businesses.

Private policing will probably continue to grow at a rate similar to that of past years. A more security-conscious public is increasingly concerned about security services. Certainly, the training and employment requirements for those performing guard services will improve in the near future. This is particularly true for services where firearms are required and where tasks are performed similar to those of the regular police. Regular police still perceive their private police counterparts as deficient in professional police training, however. Sometimes, regular police officers must intervene to rescue private police from dangerous criminals. However, negative impressions of private police will change as greater regulation is incorporated into the initial recruitment, education, and training of private police (Shearing, Stenning, and Addario, 1985).

■ SUMMARY

Police officers spend a fraction of their time catching felons and investigating criminal activity; they spend most of their time on patrol. They also perform many necessary community services, including first aid and various types of citizen assistance.

Criminologists disagree about the value of patrol as a crime deterrent. The Kansas City Preventive Patrol Experiment showed that more patrols in high-crime areas did not reduce crime as originally expected.

Police officers have considerable discretionary powers, but the public sometimes criticizes them for abusing such powers. Police officers have conflicts of interest between doing their jobs as they believe the jobs ought to be performed and respecting community sentiments that seek to limit their discretion. Police may make arrests without warrant under certain conditions. They may also conduct searches and seizures of suspects and their dwellings or automobiles when certain conditions prevail. Probable cause must exist in all search situations. Police may also conduct searches while making arrests or while engaging in the hot pursuit of suspects. Warrantless searches are permitted, too, if there is a strong likelihood that the evidence of the crime will be destroyed or if life-threatening circumstances prevail.

One important issue is the discretion of police in using force in making arrests. The fleeing felon rule was previously observed in many states, but it has been replaced by the defense-of-life standard. The United States Supreme Court has declared that officers may use deadly force only when their own lives or the lives of others are in danger.

Police misconduct and corruption have prompted the creation of citizen review boards. Entire police organizations may covertly support departures from proper procedures when their officers deal with citizens, so greater involvement of police and citizens in anticrime activities is occurring. Also, the increased use of community policing strategies is promoting greater closeness between police and citizens.

Finally, the numbers of law enforcement officers are growing in the private sector. Private police are often poorly trained or undertrained, although most states are making efforts to remedy this situation through greater regulation. The concern for greater security and the feeling among citizens that regular police cannot adequately protect them is causing many businesses, industries, and private citizens to seek private assistance for security work.

KEY TERMS

beats

broken-windows approach

fleeing felon rule

foot patrol

golf cart patrols

internal affairs divisions (IADs)

· Kansas City Preventive Patrol Experiment

ministations

Model Penal Code (MPC)

municipal liability theory

· preventive patrol

· private police

scale of patrol

· search incident to an arrest

sector patrolling

· team policing

QUESTIONS FOR REVIEW

1. What is real police work as far as regular police officers are concerned? What functions do police perform most of the time?
2. What was the Kansas City Preventive Patrol Experiment? Did it reduce crime in Kansas City? Why or why not?
3. What is a beat? What were the three types of beats in the Kansas City Preventive Patrol Experiment?
4. What is meant by the scale of police patrol? Do researchers agree about whether the scale of police patrols should be extensive or limited? What are the arguments in favor of each?
5. What is neighborhood patrolling? Where would you expect to find such patrols in the United States? How successful are such patrols?
6. What is a foot patrol? Briefly compare the effectiveness of patrol car officers and foot patrol officers and their ability to communicate with headquarters.
7. What is team policing? Does team policing foster better police-community relations? Why or why not?
8. James Q. Wilson favors a return to watchman style patrolling. Other researchers disagree. Briefly discuss Wilson's rationale and the opinions of his critics about patrol styles.
9. Do police officers enforce all laws? Do you think that the community expects them to enforce all laws? Why or why not? How do officers often react when faced with enforcing minor laws and major ones?
10. What are three approaches to police discretion?
11. When can a police officer make an arrest without a warrant?
12. Suppose a police officer sees a person he doesn't like driving down the road. The officer pulls him over for no reason and searches his car. He finds some marijuana in a small bag in the person's trunk and arrests the person for possession of marijuana.

Criticize the officer's action in view of the Supreme Court cases discussed in the chapter. Should the marijuana found in the car be used as evidence against the person? Why or why not?
13. Suppose a police officer sees a person sitting in a bus station at 3:00 A.M. He walks over to the person and makes him stand against the wall. The officer thrusts his hands into the persons' pockets and finds a pocketknife. He arrests the person for going armed. Criticize his action here in view of the cases discussed in this chapter.
14. What was significant about *Terry v. Ohio?*
15. Briefly discuss two cases that involved warrantless searches of a person's dwelling. Was evidence suppressed in court in either of these cases? If so, why was it suppressed? If evidence was not suppressed in court, why not?
16. What are exigent circumstances? Give some examples of exigent circumstances that would justify a police officer's breaking into a person's home to seize evidence.
17. What is meant by deadly force? Under what circumstances are officers permitted to use deadly force? How does deadly force relate to the fleeing felon rule?
18. What is the significance of *Tennessee v. Garner* (1985)? Briefly discuss the case and its results.
19. How can it be argued that police corruption is an organizational problem associated with an entire police department? What factors must be present?
20. What can citizens and police departments do to reduce police misconduct or police dishonesty? Discuss some of the plans and proposals suggested in the chapter.
21. Discuss briefly two plans to promote more effective police-community relations.
22. Who are private police? What are some types of private police? Do they have the same arrest powers as regular police?

SUGGESTED READINGS

Broderick, John J. (1987). *Police in a time of change* (2nd ed). Prospect Heights, IL: Waveland Press.

Cohn, Alvin W. (Ed.) (1978). *The future of policing.* Beverly Hills, CA: Sage.

Hageman, Mary Jeanette (1985). *Police-community relations.* Beverly Hills, CA: Sage.

Lynch, Ronald G. (1986). *The police manager: Professional leadership skills* (3rd ed.). New York: Random House.

Shearing, Clifford, D., and Phillip C. Stenning (1987). *Private policing.* Beverly Hills, CA: Sage.

Pretrial Processing
of Defendants

CHAPTER

8

■ INTRODUCTION

You are in a shopping mall store and see someone produce a weapon and take money from the sales clerk by force; you can arrest the robber. You observe a woman chasing a young man with a purse down the street, and the woman is shouting, "Stop that man. He stole my purse!" Again, you can arrest the purse thief. These are citizen's arrests. A **citizen's arrest** is an arrest that occurs whenever a private citizen makes an arrest of another (1) who has committed a public offense or attempted one in the citizen's presence; (2) who has committed a felony, although not necessarily in the citizen's presence; or (3) who the citizen has reasonable cause to believe has committed a felony (Black, 1979:222). Police have these arrest powers as well. As we have seen, their powers also include stop and frisks (pat downs), searches of dwellings and automobiles without warrant under certain circumstances, and searches incident to arrest, which are not extended to citizens in general. Arrests of criminal suspects by either citizens or police set in motion a sequence of pretrial events.

This chapter discusses the pretrial processing of defendants. Besides the arrest powers of police, defendants may be brought into the criminal justice system for processing several other ways, including complaints, bench warrants, indictments, presentments, and criminal informations. Succeeding actions may include arrest and booking of a defendant, a preliminary hearing, an arraignment involving a specification of the charges against the accused, a plea by the defendant to the charges, and bail for the suspect's pretrial release.

Whenever a police officer arrests a suspect, with or without a warrant, the officer must bring the suspect before a magistrate or other judicial officer without undue, or unnecessary, delay (*United States v. Duvall,* 1976). Most jurisdictions have provisions for bringing suspects before magistrates or local judicial officers *without unnecessary delay.* The primary purposes of these rules are to (1) prevent the unlawful detention of suspects, (2) protect suspects' rights, and (3) satisfy courts, juries, and the public that coercion has not been used and that the defendants know their rights (*United States v. Carignan,* 1951; *Naples v. United States,* 1962; and *United States v. Smith,* 1962).

The provision, **without undue delay,** upholds the suspect's constitutional right to due process. The words, *without undue delay* do not mean instantly or immediately. Rather, they mean as quickly as possible or as soon as is reasonable *(Muldrow v. United States,* 1960; *Mallory v. United States,* 1957). The reasonableness of delay is not measured in terms of hours or days (*United States v. Gorman,* 1965). In fact, there is much variation in how undue delay is interpreted by the courts, which look at circumstances leading to delays of suspect appearances before magistrates.

In a California case, a defendant was not taken before a magistrate for 17 hours following his arrest, despite the fact that a magistrate was available at the time and in the building where the suspect was taken following his arrest. In that case, the police questioned the suspect and subjected him to a grueling interrogation. They eventually obtained a confession from him, but the confession was ruled inadmissible by the trial judge (*United States v. Mayes,* 1969).

In contrast, there was a 37-hour delay after an arrest of a Kansas defendant before taking him to a magistrate, but in that instance, the arrest occurred on a weekend, and the magistrate was not available until the following Monday morning (*Davis v. United*

Police officers may make warrantless arrests whenever a law is violated in their presence. Demonstrators who block major thoroughfares and otherwise interfere with the rights of others may be taken into custody without warrants.

States, 1969). Arrests made on holidays, weekends, or other special occasions, arrests of intoxicated suspects, or arrests where there is considerable distance between the point of arrest and the nearest magistrate are exceptional circumstances. Most courts will hold that suspects were not subject to undue delay under these circumstances (*Wakaksan v. United States*, 1966; *United States v. Blocker*, 1973; *United States v. Sterling*, 1971; *United States v. Burke*, 1963).

■ ALTERNATIVE PROCEDURES LEADING TO ARRESTS

Besides a direct arrest by police or a private citizen, a suspect may be taken into custody other ways. These ways include (1) the issuance of a warrant or summons based upon the filing of a criminal complaint; (2) the issuance of an indictment or a presentment; and (3) the issuance of a criminal information.

Warrants and Summonses

When a crime has been committed and a suspect has been identified, a complaint is filed. A complaint is a written statement of the essential facts constituting the offense alleged, and it is made under oath before a magistrate or other qualified judicial officer. On the basis of the facts contained in the complaint, the oath of the citizen making the

When a judge issues an arrest warrant, police officers usually serve it. The officers determine the location of the person named in the warrant, identify the person, and take the person before the judge without undue delay.

complaint, and a general consideration of all relevant circumstances by a presiding judge, a warrant or a summons is issued.

One question is whether the citizen filing the complaint or supplying the information supporting it is trustworthy. The test for determining the trustworthiness of a citizen or information supplied is whether a reasonably prudent person would be persuaded that an offense has been committed and that the suspect named in the complaint committed the offense (*United States v. Cooperstein,* 1963). If police officers receive a tip from a reliable informant that cocaine and heroin are being exchanged in an airport lobby by several suspects, these officers assert this information under oath before a judicial officer. Thus, probable cause exists to support the issuance of a warrant (*United States v. Salliey,* 1966; *United States v. Casanova,* 1963). The magistrate is persuaded by the officers' presentation of facts from reliable informants. However, if an irate citizen storms into the courthouse demanding that his neighbor be arrested for vehicular theft, and it is determined that (1) no one saw the vehicle stolen and (2) both neighbors have been feuding for several weeks, a magistrate will be unable to support an arrest warrant solely on the word of the hostile neighbor.

If a magistrate determines that probable cause exists to support the complaint and the information contained in it, a warrant is issued for the arrest of the suspect named in the complaint. A **warrant** is a written order directing a suspect's arrest and issued by an official with the authority to issue the warrant. A warrant commands a defendant to be arrested and brought before the nearest available magistrate; it does not necessarily have to be the same magistrate who issued the original warrant. Sometimes, a magistrate will issue a summons instead. A **summons** is in the same form as a warrant, except that it commands a defendant to appear before the magistrate at a particular time and place. A summons based on a complaint is shown in Figure 8.1.

A warrant permits an officer to arrest the defendant named in the warrant, but a summons is merely served, and the suspect named in the summons is not formally arrested. Instead, the suspect is required to appear before a magistrate at a later time and place. Often, suspects are issued summonses for traffic violations. If these suspects

FIGURE 8.1 A Summons on Complaint

FORM 2.
SUMMONS ON COMPLAINT
(RCr 2.04, 2.06)

DISTRICT COURT OF KENTUCKY

Franklin County

COMMONWEALTH OF KENTUCKY
      V.   SUMMONS

_____
              Defendant.

TO THE ABOVE NAMED DEFENDANT:

    You are hereby summoned to appear before the District Court, in the Franklin County Court House at Frankfort, Kentucky, at 9:00 A.M. (Eastern Standard Time) on Wednesday, October 31, 19   , to answer a complaint made by _____ charging you with the offense of reckless driving.
    Issued at Frankfort, Franklin County, Kentucky, this _____ day of _____, 19__.

                              _____
                              Judge, District Court of Kentucky
                              Franklin County
(Amended October 14, 19   , effective January 1, 19   .)

FORM 3. SUMMONS ON INDICTMENT
             (RCr 6.52, 6.54)

(Caption)

TO THE ABOVE NAMED DEFENDANT:
    You are hereby summoned to appear before the Franklin Circuit Court in the Franklin County Court House at Frankfort, Kentucky, at 9:00 A.M. (Eastern Standard Time) on Wednesday, October 31, 19   , to answer an indictment charging you with the offenses of (1) malicious shooting and wounding with intent to kill and (2) carrying concealed a deadly weapon.
    Issued at Frankfort, Franklin County, Kentucky, this _____ day of _____, 19___.

                              Clerk, Franklin Circuit Court
                              By _____
                              Deputy Clerk

fail to show up at the particular time and place indicated by the summons, *then* judicial officers may issue a bench warrant on their own authority to cause the immediate arrest of the suspect.

    Police officers serve arrest warrants on suspects when criminal offenses are alleged. They take these suspects into custody and before a local magistrate or judicial official. If the name of the person to be arrested is unknown or if the person is known by some other name, such as an alias, a particularized description of the defendant is sufficient. In some cases, the magistrate issues a **John Doe warrant,** which is a warrant that contains an adequate description of the defendant (*United States v. Jarvis,* 1977; *United States ex rel. Savage v. Arnold,* 1975; *Clark v. Heard,* 1982). An arrest warrant based on a filed complaint is shown in Figure 8.2.

An arrest warrant can be held invalid if it lists an alias by which the defendant is *not* known. In a Tennessee case, an arrest warrant was prepared against a person described as "John Doe alias Bud Ferguson." The defendant had never been known as Bud Ferguson, even though other facts of the description on the arrest warrant were accurate. The warrant was declared invalid because "the defendant had never been known or called by the alias of 'Bud Ferguson' and was not himself a party to the officer obtaining such a misnomer" (*United States v. Swanner,* 1964).

When a criminal complaint is filed either by police officers or private citizens against others for committing crimes, the government takes the initiative of either pursuing the case or not pursuing it. A magistrate determines whether probable cause exists for issuing an arrest warrant after the complaint has been filed. If the complaint has been filed in Philadelphia by Jim Jenkins who has said that Fred Smith has stolen his car, and if there are reasonable grounds to support the complaint, an arrest warrant will be issued against Fred Smith and police officers will attempt to arrest him. Eventually, when Fred Smith is brought to trial for vehicular theft, the state (through the district attorney in Philadelphia) will prosecute Fred Smith, and Jim Jenkins will be called as a witness against him. Jim Jenkins does not personally prosecute Fred Smith, however. An offense has been committed, but it was a violation of a Philadelphia criminal law. Through its prosecutors, Philadelphia, not Jim Jenkins, prosecutes Fred Smith.

FIGURE 8.2   An Arrest Warrant Based on a Filed Complaint

FORM 4.
WARRANT OF ARREST ON COMPLAINT

(RCr 2.04, 2.06)
(Caption)

TO ALL PEACE OFFICERS IN THE COMMONWEALTH OF KENTUCKY:

You are hereby commanded to arrest _____ _____
(Name of defendant)
and bring him forthwith before a judge of the District Court in Franklin County, Kentucky (or, if he be absent or unable to act, before the nearest available magistrate), to answer a complaint made by _____ charging him with the offense of reckless driving.

Issued at Frankfort, Franklin County, Kentucky, this _____ day of _____, 19__.

_____
Judge, District Court of Kentucky
Franklin County

(Indorsement as to bail)
The defendant may give bail in the amount of $_____.

_____
Judge, District Court of Kentucky
Franklin County

(Amended October 14, 19   , effective January 1, 19   .)

This principle is frequently misunderstood. For example, a woman alleges that she has been raped, and she files a complaint against the alleged rapist. Later, as it turns out, the alleged rapist is a close friend and the woman wishes to drop the charges against him, but the state may decide to prosecute anyway. If a criminal law has been violated, the jurisdiction where the law was violated is the final arbiter in deciding whether or not to prosecute. A similar situation exists in child sexual abuse cases. If a father sexually abuses his daughter and the incident is reported to the police and a complaint is filed, it is a public offense and the public is entitled to appropriate action by authorities. In this type of situation, however, it is often difficult to get close friends or families to testify against one another, and if no one testifies, pursuing the case is pointless. However, in some situations, incriminating physical evidence may permit the prosecutor to develop and support a convincing case against the defendant without relying on the testimony of witnesses.

Indictments and Presentments

Since there is such great diversity among states about how criminals are processed, the federal system is discussed here as an example. Many states and local jurisdictions emulate the federal system in their processing of criminal defendants. However, other jurisdictions have quite different criminal processing systems. Throughout this discussion, some of these exceptions are noted.

In federal proceedings and many state jurisdictions in the United States, grand juries are convened. A **grand jury** is an investigative body whose number varies from state to state and whose duties include determining whether probable cause exists that a crime has been committed and whether formal charges should be returned against a suspect. Federal grand juries consist of no fewer than sixteen nor more than twenty-three citizens selected from within the jurisdiction of each federal district court. These are United States citizens representing average socioeconomic levels in their respective communities, since their names and addresses are selected from voter registration lists or property tax records.

Grand juries convene at different times and meet for periods such as 90 days or 120 days. They hear complaints and consider the government evidence against defendants (Neubauer, 1979). They deliberate and return either a no bill or a true bill. A **no bill** means that in their opinion, the government did not produce sufficient evidence to determine that probable cause exists that a crime has been committed. If the grand jury returns a **true bill,** this means that it was convinced that probable cause exists that a crime was committed and that the defendant should be charged with that crime. The true bill is an indictment. An **indictment** is a charge or written accusation found and presented by a grand jury that a particular defendant has committed a crime. It is the means whereby defendants are brought to trial to answer the charges against them.

Normally, a government prosecutor presents a complaint to the grand jury, alleging that a certain crime has been committed by a particular suspect. This presentation is accompanied by government evidence that a crime has actually been committed. Such evidence links an accused with a crime, and the prosecutor tries to convince the grand jury that sufficient probable cause exists to issue an indictment against the accused. Once a true bill, or indictment, has been issued by the grand jury, either an arrest warrant or a summons is prepared. Then, police apprehend the defendant and bring him or her before a magistrate without unnecessary delay or serve the summons, which directs the defendant to appear before a magistrate at a particular time and place.

Grand juries are not juries in the sense that they convene to determine the guilt or innocence of suspects. They determine whether probable cause exists to support charges, and some grand juries perform investigative functions to determine if crimes have been committed. Many citizens mistakenly believe that if a grand jury decides to indict someone, then the indicted individual must be guilty of the crime alleged. This is not true. An indictment is simply a charge, and one's guilt remains to be proved in a court of law. A presumption of innocence underlies all charges of crimes, but the price of an indictment can be quite high, even for those who are subsequently acquitted of crimes.

If a defendant is indicted by a grand jury and eventually tried in court, another jury will hear the case and decide the guilt or innocence of the defendant. This kind of jury is the one with which we are most familiar. It is called a **petit jury** to distinguish it from the grand jury (Black, 1979).

Procedurally, a government representative or prosecutor prepares an indictment or bill of particular charges, including any supporting evidence. Suspects do not appear before the grand jury and do not have the opportunity to present exculpatory evidence that would otherwise clear them of the offenses alleged. Indictments are fairly easily obtained because usually, only the most incriminating evidence is presented and materials favorable to the defendant are excluded from the grand jury (Champion, 1988).

Grand juries may make recommendations independent of the prosecutor, however. When considering evidence against a defendant, a grand jury may determine that others have committed crimes as well. In some jurisdictions, grand juries issue their own indictments against defendants. These indictments are called presentments. A **presentment** is an accusation, initiated by a grand jury on its own authority, from its knowledge or observation, that functions as an instruction for the preparation of an indictment (Black, 1979:1066). A government prosecutor does not seek a presentment. In effect a presentment bypasses the prosecutor. A presentment has the same effect as an indictment. Once issued, an arrest warrant or summons is prepared.

Criminal Informations

A criminal information is to a prosecutor what a presentment is to a grand jury. In the case of a presentment, a grand jury could, on its own authority, prepare an indictment against a suspect. In the case of a criminal information, a prosecutor can bypass the grand jury and obtain the equivalent of an indictment against an accused. A **criminal information** is a written accusation made by a public prosecutor against a person for some criminal offense, without an indictment. An information is formulated against a suspect by a prosecutor where a minor offense is involved and the punishment by imprisonment is less than 1 year (18 U.S.C., Rule 6, 1989). If a crime is punishable by imprisonment of 1 year or more, a prosecutor may use an information if an indictment is waived by the criminal suspect. Otherwise, an information cannot be used to prosecute.

CRIME BEAT

Many citizens believe that indictments are equivalent with guilty verdicts. A jury has found someone guilty of something, and therefore, the person must be guilty. However, facts presented by the defense attorney in court may show that the indicted defendant could not possibly have committed the crime. The verdict from the jury is not guilty, but where does this leave the acquitted victim of the criminal justice system?

By themselves, indictments suggest guilt, even though our system is based upon the principle that one is presumed innocent until proven guilty beyond a reasonable doubt. Defendants who are innocent in reality suffer socially, financially, and psychologically from indictments. If judges are so inclined, they may order that indicted defendants be held without bail until trial. Incarceration removes innocent defendants from the community and often spells the loss of jobs and prestige.

An example of the detrimental effects of indictments is Raymond Donovan, labor secretary of former president Ronald Reagan. In 1985, Donovan was indicted on charges of fraud involving phony billings related to a New York City Transit Authority subway building project. In late May 1987, Donovan was acquitted of the fraud charges after an 8-month trial. Donovan's legal fees exceeded $13 million, and the prosecution purportedly spent over $4 million. Donovan was quoted as saying, "Where do I go to get my reputation back?"

One problem with indictments is that practically any prosecutor in the United States can persuade a grand jury to issue them against practically anyone. Prosecutors have almost absolute control over the information disclosed to a grand jury about defendants, and almost always, this information is inculpatory. Defendants are not permitted to rebut this adverse information. Defendants cannot testify before the grand jury in their own behalf. Thus, prosecutors slant any case as they wish. Grand juries see only what prosecutors want them to see. On the basis of this one-sided information, grand juries usually issue indictments.

Experts have noted the tremendous powers possessed by prosecutors in securing indictments against various suspects. However, there is a substantial gap between indictments and convictions. In any case, there are no winners. Even when an accused is acquitted, there is little or no recourse. Suing a prosecutor for legal fees incurred is almost always out of the question. Besides, the prosecutor was just "doing his job." Therefore, someone who is acquitted is regarded by many people as having beaten the system. After all, a jury found the person not guilty rather than innocent.

In most states, informations prepared by prosecutors may be used in place of grand juries to bring defendants to trial, provided the possible punishment of imprisonment is less than 1 year (Black, 1979:701). When an information is obtained, an arrest warrant or a summons is prepared, and officers bring the accused before a magistrate without undue delay (or they command the accused to appear before the magistrate at a particular time and place at some later date). Again, criminal informations are most often issued for minor offenses, such as misdemeanors.

In many jurisdictions, indictments, presentments, and criminal informations result in the issuance of a **capias** (this is a term for several kinds of writs). A capias has the same effect as an arrest warrant in that it requires an officer to take an accused into custody and bring the accused before a magistrate. The capias describes the offense charged and commands an officer to bring the accused before the court where the charge is pending.

Summarizing, a suspect may be arrested and brought before a magistrate in the following ways: (1) a citizen's arrest without an arrest warrant; (2) a direct arrest by a police officer with or without an arrest warrant; (3) the issuance of an arrest warrant from a judicial official following a complaint; or (4) the issuance of a criminal summons, a capias, or an arrest warrant by the court as the result of grand jury action leading to indictments, presentments, or informations. Normally, before an arrest warrant is issued by a magistrate or judicial official, a determination of probable cause is made by the official according to the information accompanying a criminal complaint. In the case of grand jury action, the grand jury itself or a prosecutor determines whether probable cause exists to proceed with an indictment, presentment, or an information. If these documents are forthcoming, arrest warrants, summonses, or capiases are prepared and suspects may be taken into custody.

■ BOOKING

Once a suspect has been taken into custody with or without a warrant or capias or presents himself or herself to law enforcement officers after being served with a criminal summons, the suspect is usually booked. Booking is simply an administrative procedure designed to furnish personal information about a suspect to a bonding agency. Booking includes the compilation of a file for a suspect, including name, address, telephone number, age, place of work, relatives, and other personal data. The extensiveness of the booking procedure varies among jurisdictions. In some jurisdictions, a suspect may be photographed and fingerprinted, while in others, a suspect may answer a few personal, descriptive questions.

Arrested suspects are taken to jail and booked. Booking may include photographs, fingerprinting, and gathering of other pertinent information.

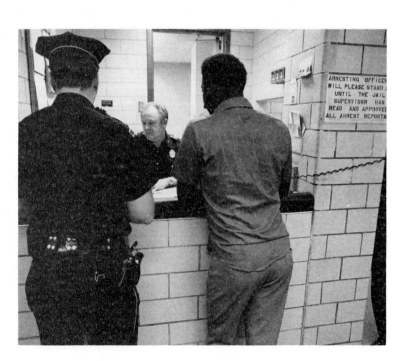

At the federal level, booking is performed by federal marshals, who require a suspect to be photographed. Frontal and lateral pictures are often taken, fingerprints obtained, and an extensive questionnaire completed, including the identification of one's close associates and social habits. "Just in case we have to track you down," remarked one federal marshal when interviewed by this author and asked why such extensive identification material was obtained.

■ THE INITIAL APPEARANCE

The **initial appearance** of a defendant before a magistrate is a formal proceeding during which a judge advises the defendant of the charges. This proceeding usually follows the booking process, and the presiding judicial official determines from a reading of the charges whether or not they constitute petty offenses. Petty, or minor, offenses vary in interpretation among states. Indicators of petty offenses are usually the maximum fine imposed or length of sentence associated with the criminal offense.

In *Duncan v. Louisiana* (1968), the United States Supreme Court discussed this issue in the matter of a 19-year-old man who was convicted and sentenced to serve 60 days in jail and pay a $150 fine for simple battery. Duncan had requested a jury trial

Arrested suspects are brought before magistrates for their initial appearance. At these appearances, suspects are advised of the charges against them and bail is determined.

but was denied one. The State of Louisiana claimed that Duncan's crime was a petty offense and did not qualify him for a jury trial. The United States Supreme Court disagreed. It noted that Louisiana's law pertaining to battery, although a misdemeanor, carried a 2-year maximum possible sentence and a $300 fine. The Supreme Court observed that most states define petty offenses as punishable for terms less than 1 year, and in some jurisdictions, the maximum sentence is no more than 6 months and a $50 fine. Without defining precisely the meaning of a petty offense, the Supreme Court concluded, "We need not . . . settle in this case the exact location of the line between petty offenses and serious crimes. It is sufficient for our purposes to hold that a crime punishable by two years in prison is . . . a serious crime and not a petty offense." Duncan's conviction was overturned.

More recently, 18 United States Code, Section 3401 (1989) has specified the right of an accused to a trial by jury in petty cases when initially appearing before a federal magistrate:

> Any person charged with a misdemeanor may elect . . . to be tried before a judge of the district court for the district in which the offense was committed. The magistrate shall carefully explain to the defendant that he has a right to trial, judgment, and sentencing by a judge of the district court and that he may have a right to a trial by jury before a district judge or magistrate. (18 U.S.C., Sec. 3401(b), 1985:14)

Under the Sixth Amendment, in all criminal prosecutions, all accused are entitled to the right to a speedy and public trial by an impartial jury, but this is interpreted differently in different jurisdictions. Some prosecutors resent an accused's requesting a jury trial for a petty offense. In a New Jersey case, a man was indicted by a federal grand jury on federal misdemeanor charges, and the prosecutor for the government expressed strongly the opinion that the man ought to waive his jury trial rights. The man refused, and so the prosecutor brought felony charges against the man in retaliation. This created such an atmosphere of coercion that the court dismissed all indictments against the man as the fairest remedy, and the prosecutor was criticized for his improper conduct (*United States v. Lippi,* 1977).

In felony cases, however, the initial appearance of the defendant is extremely important. This is not intended to detract from the seriousness of misdemeanor charges, but for felonies, the penalties are substantially more severe, and it is crucial that defendants be advised of the specific charges against them as well as their rights under the circumstances.

For those arrested by police on either misdemeanor or felony charges, the initial appearance before a magistrate is the formal proceeding where they are advised of the charges against them and their rights, and bail is considered. This is also the occasion where magistrates determine the date for a preliminary examination, or a preliminary hearing, to establish whether probable cause exists to move forward toward a trial. The time interval between the defendant's initial appearance and the date of the preliminary hearing or examination permits defendants the opportunity to secure legal counsel for their defense.

A defendant's initial appearance may also be ordered by an indictment, presentment, or criminal information (in a case where indictment has been waived by a defendant or the crime is punishable by possible imprisonment of less than 1 year). The defendant's initial appearance is for advising the defendant of the indictment, presentment, information, or specification of the charges and allegations, and furnishing the defendant with a copy of it. It is also the occasion where the conditions for bail are determined and bail, if any, is established. Finally, it sets a time for the defendant to appear for a preliminary hearing (which may be waived as a defendant option).

■ BAIL

When a defendant has been arrested, a determination is made concerning whether the defendant will be brought to trial. If a trial is likely because of the circumstances of the case, most defendants can obtain temporary release from detention. They may be released on their own recognizance. If their reputation in the community is such that it is unlikely that they will flee from the jurisdiction, a **release on own recognizance (ROR)** will be ordered by the presiding magistrate or judicial officer (Bynum, 1977; Toborg, 1981).

In a situation where the character of a defendant is unknown or the offenses alleged are quite serious, the magistrate often establishes bail or a bail bond. **Bail** is a surety to procure the release of those under arrest, to assure that they will appear to face charges in court at a later date. A **bail bond** is a written guarantee, often accompanied by money or other securities, that the person charged with an offense will remain in the court's jurisdiction to face trial at a time in the future. A bail bond form is shown in Figure 8.3.

For minor traffic offenses, motorists may be required to post a cash bond which guarantees their appearance in court later to face the charges of violating traffic laws. If the motorist fails to appear, the cash bond is forfeited. The bond set is often the exact amount of the fine for violating the traffic law anyway.

Near most jails in cities throughout the United States are bail bond companies. These companies function for those arrested for various offenses, and company representatives appear at the jail and post bond for defendants. A defendant is required to pay the bonding company a fee for this service, often 10 percent of the bail bond established by the magistrate. For instance, if the bond set by a magistrate for a particular offense is $5,000, the bonding company may post this bond for the defendant if the defendant is considered a good risk and the defendant or an associate of the defendant pays the bonding company a nonrefundable fee of $500. If defendants are unable to pay the fee and no one will pay it for them, they must remain in jail until trial is held.

Bonding companies provide bond for some defendants, but not for others. Some defendants are considered poor risks, and they will likely jump bail, that is, attempt to escape prosecution by leaving the vicinity. Many bonding companies employ **bounty hunters,** who track such persons down for a fee and bring them to court. If a defendant escapes the jurisdiction of the court and is not found, the bonding company forfeits the bond it has posted. If a defendant has real property, the court may accept a written pledge from the defendant of this real property as a bail bond for release from detention. The court may also accept other assets as bond, such as bank deposits, securities, or valuable personal property (Black, 1979).

FIGURE 8.3 A Bail Bond Form

BAIL BOND

(Caption)

_____ being in custody charged with the offense of
   (Name of defendant)
_____ and being admitted to bail in the sum of $_____, we under-
take that he will appear and be amenable to the orders and process of this
and any other court in which this proceeding may be pending hereafter for
any and all purposes and at all stages of the proceeding (including, in event
of indictment, proceedings thereafter) in accordance with
(Name of defendant)
   Executed this _____ day of _____, 19__.

_____
(Name of defendant)   (Address)

_____
(Name of surety)   (Address)
   Taken and subscribed before me this _____
_____ day of _____, 19__.

                        _____
                        (Signature)

                        _____
                        (Title)

   I, _____, by entering into the (above) bond obligation, do
hereby submit to the jurisdiction of the courts of   in which any
forfeiture proceeding arising out of my bail obligation may be pending, and
do further irrevocably appoint the clerk of such court as my agent upon
whom any process affecting my liability on such bond may be served, such
clerk to forthwith mail copies to me at _____ City
                        (Street address)

of _____, County of _____, State of
_____, or at my last known address.
   Date this _____ day of _____, 19__.

                        _____
                        (Name)

Under the Eighth Amendment, citizens are advised that excessive bail shall not be required, nor excessive fines imposed. Some citizens believe that regardless of the offense alleged, bail will be set and defendants will be permitted to remain free until the date of trial. This is not true. Some defendants have a very high bail, while others are not granted bail at all; they are required to remain in jail until trial.

The constitutional prohibition against excessive bail means that bail will not be excessive in cases where it is proper to grant bail (*United States v. Giangrosso,* 1985). The right to bail is not absolute under the Eighth Amendment (*United States v. Bilanzich,* 1985; *United States v. Provenzano,* 1985; *United States v. Fernandez-Toledo,* 1984). In some cases, suspects are detained for trial without bail (*United States v. Acevedo-Ramos,* 1984), while in others, defendants are subject to detention if they are unable to pay high bail, ranging from $25,000 to $1 million (*United States v. Szott,* 1985; *United States v. Jessup,* 1985). A murder suspect caught in the act, a habitual offender, or other such defendant is often denied bail, because it is likely that the person will

CRIME BEAT

Denial of bail is not always restricted to persons charged with violent crimes. Often, bail is denied in cases where white-collar crime is involved. Income tax evasion charges were filed against Marc Rich, a New York commodity trader, but he evaded apprehension and is now living in Switzerland. It is alleged that he failed to pay $48 million in taxes from profits on stock trading. Bankers and others charged with embezzlement are sometimes considered high risks for bail, because they may attempt to flee the jurisdiction or country to avoid prosecution.

attempt to escape prosecution for the offenses alleged. Do suspects pose a danger to the community? Not all states permit judges discretion for making this determination, but in thirty-one states and the District of Columbia, this judicial consideration often results in preventive pretrial detention (Gottlieb, 1984).

Violent criminals aren't the only defendants denied bail, however. The magistrate considers the totality of circumstances in setting bail for any person. A former bank president was denied bail in a case alleging fraudulent manipulation and theft of depositors' funds. While the former bank president had substantial community ties and property interests to protect, he had a recently acquired passport and travel visas to several foreign countries where he also maintained property and business interests. In addition, several million dollars in bank funds were unaccounted for after a federal audit. In this case, he was considered a poor risk for bail.

The American Civil Liberties Union and a number of other groups have challenged the bail provisions of the United States Constitution. Their efforts, as well as those of a variety of special interest groups have prompted a number of bail reforms over the years. Some of the reasons given for such bail reforms are (1) bail is inherently discriminatory against the poor or indigent defendant (Goldkamp, 1984), (2) those who are unable to post a bail bond and must remain in jail cannot adequately prepare a defense or correspond effectively with their attorneys, (3) there is considerable variation from one jurisdiction to the next and from one case to the next within the same jurisdiction for establishing a bail bond for similar offenses, (4) withholding bail or prescribing prohibitively high bail offends one's presumption of innocence until guilt is proven in court, and (5) those who pose no risk to the community may suffer loss of job or other benefits from detention as the result of their inability to meet bail (Gibbs, 1975).

Although bail reform first received widespread national attention during the 1960s, attempts were made to reform local, state, and federal bail provisions in earlier years (Goldkamp, 1984:104). Beeley (1927) was critical of the bail system of Chicago during the 1920s, for instance, and the Wickersham Commission (1929–1931) also urged substantial bail reforms. At the basis of the bail reform movement is the argument that bail is inherently discriminatory. In 1966, the Bail Reform Act provided, "[T]he purpose of this Act . . . is to revise the practices relating to bail to assure that all persons, regardless of their financial status, shall not needlessly be detained pending their appearance to answer charges." The most recent federal action relating to bail has been the passage of the **Bail Reform Act of 1984,** which increased substantially the flexibility of magistrates and judicial officers in setting bail and releasing persons on their own recognizance.

One of the more innovative conditions of the 1984 act was a provision for judicial officers to release suspects subject to certain conditions, such as (1) complying with a curfew; (2) reporting on a regular basis to a designated law enforcement agency; (3) abiding by specific restrictions on one's personal associations, place of abode, and travel; (4) maintaining or commencing an educational program; and (5) maintaining employment or actively seeking employment if currently unemployed.

Preceding the Bail Reform Act of 1984 and possibly contributing to its subsequent passage were several studies in the 1970s and early 1980s. First, the National Bail Study was conducted in twenty jurisdictions in the United States (Thomas, 1976, 1977) between 1962 and 1971. Significantly fewer felony and misdemeanor defendants were detained in jails during those years, and increased numbers of defendants were released

---

A DAY IN COURT

The Bail Reform Act of 1984 authorized judges to prescribe preventive detention for defendants deemed serious risks to the public or otherwise dangerous. This means that bail is denied and such offenders must remain incarcerated until their trial. Opponents of preventive detention say that this confinement is the equivalent of a sentence and punishment, and thus, it is inconsistent with the presumption of innocence until guilt is proved beyond a reasonable doubt. Those favoring preventive detention believe that certain suspects are dangerous and pose definite risks to public safety.

It is well established that bail is available only for those entitled to bail. Thus, the question is, Who is entitled to bail? What criteria should judges use to determine whether preventive detention should be imposed or release on one's own recognizance should be permitted? These are difficult questions to answer. John Hinckley was observed by millions of television viewers in the act of attempting to assassinate former President Ronald Reagan. While being transferred from one Dallas jail to another, the alleged assassin of President John F. Kennedy, Lee Harvey Oswald, was gunned down before millions of viewers by Jack Ruby. Clearly, these men committed violent acts and numerous witnesses observed them, but when only circumstantial evidence suggests a suspect is a crime perpetrator, how do we decide whether the suspect is entitled to bail?

The Bail Reform Act of 1984 was designed in part to remove some of the discrimination inherent in the bail regulations of various jurisdictions. Many persons who had many ties with the community and who were employed at legitimate work were being held without bail. Often, those in the lower socioeconomic strata, particularly blacks, are unable to afford bail for their temporary release before trial. Thus, the act made it possible for judges to grant release on one's own recognizance instead of levying a prohibitively high bail that would cause poorer offenders to remain incarcerated. Despite this act, however, jail inmate populations continue to be represented by many pretrial detainees who cannot afford bail.

on their own recognizance. It was concluded that judges were relying more on ROR for pretrial release of defendants, resulting in a sizable reduction in the use of cash bail, a primary target of bail critics.

In the mid-1970s, the use of release on own recognizance in lieu of cash bail was investigated in Duluth, Minnesota; San Mateo, California; and Salt Lake City, Utah (Bynum, 1977). ROR usage was most frequently used for defendants with good incomes and strong employment records. The economically disadvantaged were not benefited at all through the greater use of ROR by participating judges.

Between January 1981 and March 1982, the Philadelphia Experiment conducted a test with bail guidelines in the Philadelphia Municipal Court (Goldkamp and Gottfredson, 1984). Twenty-two judges were selected for the experiment. One objective was to create visible guidelines for judges to follow in using release on own recognizance in lieu of bail in pretrial release decisions. When bail was established, median bail figures for judges not following prescribed guidelines was $2,000, whereas the median bail figure was $1,500 for the judges adhering to the guidelines provided.

While the findings regarding the use of release on own recognizance were mixed (such as more guidelines judges used ROR for misdemeanor cases than nonguidelines judges, and more nonguidelines judges used ROR for felony cases than guidelines judges), the researchers said that the experiment yielded significant improvements in the equity of bail decisions for defendants generally. The study also encouraged greater use of the supervised or conditional release programs outlined within the Bail Reform Act of 1984. The Philadelphia Experiment suggested that this alternative would provide some degree of relief for jail overcrowding at the very least.

Since a suspect has not been convicted of a crime, the constitutionality of preventive detention of suspects for long time periods has been challenged. In some cases, suspects have been detained in city and county jails for up to 2 years before being tried for and acquitted of crimes. In 1987, however, the United States Supreme Court upheld the constitutionality of preventive detention for suspects considered to be dangerous or likely to flee.

In preventive detention, defendants found likely to be hazards to their community are kept in jail prior to their trials. In June 1987, the United States Supreme Court upheld the Bail Reform Act of 1984 and held that courts may "disable" defendants, at least until after trial. In one case, a defendant was "disabled" for 71 days in jail before a federal jury found him innocent of all charges.

CRIME BEAT

Under the Bail Reform Act of 1984, courts are required to detain prior to trial arrestees charged with certain serious felonies if the government can demonstrate by clear and convincing evidence after an adversarial hearing that no release conditions will reasonably assure the safety of persons in the community (18 U.S.C., Sec. 3142(e), 1989). On March 21, 1986, Anthony Salerno and Vincent Cafaro were arrested and charged in a twenty-nine count indictment alleging various Racketeer Influenced and Corrupt Organizations Act (RICO) violations, including mail and wire fraud, extortion, gambling, and conspiracy to commit murder. The government moved to detain both of these arrestees on the grounds that they were reputed to be mob bosses of La Cosa Nostra and posed definite risk to public safety. The federal district judge granted the detention motion, whereupon defense attorneys for Salerno and Cafaro filed appeals. The essence of these appeals was that the Bail Reform Act itself is unconstitutional, because it authorizes detention of suspects on the basis of their likelihood to commit future crimes. Thus, arrestees are punished in advance for criminal acts they have not committed. The United States Court of Appeals for the Second Circuit overturned the district judge's detention decision consistent with this argument.

United States Attorneys appealed to the Supreme Court, contending that preventive detention of these men was regulatory and not related to punishment. In a vote of 8–3, the Supreme Court reversed the Second Circuit Court and declared that in this instance, preventive detention was regulatory rather than punishing. Furthermore, the Supreme Court declared that the authorization of pretrial detention on the ground of future dangerousness was not unconstitutional and did not violate their Eighth Amendment rights (*United States v. Salerno,* 107 S.Ct. 2095, 1987). Thus, it is likely that preventive detention will be used with greater frequency in the future to control those deemed public risks if released on their own recognizance.

Among the justices opposing the ruling was Thurgood Marshall. He warned that upholding such an act could create a police state that would operate to the disadvantage of blacks and the poor particularly. Black defendants comprise a disproportionately large number of those held under preventive detention.

■ PRELIMINARY HEARINGS AND ARRAIGNMENTS

Preliminary examinations, or hearings, are held after defendants have been arrested and have had their initial appearance before a magistrate. A preliminary hearing is a hearing conducted by a magistrate or judicial official to determine whether a suspect charged with a crime should be held for trial. It permits a magistrate to determine if probable cause exists that a crime has been committed and if probable cause exists that the person charged committed it. A preliminary hearing is the first screening of charges against a defendant (Black, 1979:1062).

A preliminary hearing does not establish a defendant's guilt or innocence, as does a trial. The government is required to present evidence or proof that (1) a crime has been committed and (2) the defendant committed the crime. If the government fails to present a convincing case to the magistrate, the charges against the defendant are dismissed. The option of dismissal by the magistrate does not preclude the possibility that the prosecutor will take the case to a grand jury for their consideration. In jurisdictions that have grand juries, this is sometimes done. However, if the magistrate believes the case presented by the prosecutor is weak, the grand jury probably will not issue an indictment either.

However, there is an important difference between a preliminary hearing and a grand jury proceeding. In a preliminary hearing, a defendant has the right to present facts and evidence supporting innocence of the crimes alleged. A defendant may even cross-examine witnesses and bring in witnesses to support his or her own position. Again, this is an opportunity for a magistrate to determine probable cause that a crime has been committed and that the defendant committed it. In a grand jury proceeding, however, a prosecutor presents only the government's side of the matter. If a magistrate determines that the accused should be released for lack of probable cause, a subsequent grand jury may issue an indictment or presentment against the defendant.

In some jurisdictions, preliminary hearings are used instead of grand juries for the purpose of establishing probable cause. Defendants have the right to retain counsel, to be fully informed of the complaint against them, and to be informed of the general circumstances under which they may secure pretrial release. If a defendant cannot afford counsel, an attorney is appointed to consult with and represent the defendant. When a defendant appears before a magistrate, the magistrate will determine whether the defendant wishes to waive the preliminary hearing. With the exception of certain petty offenses, which may be tried by the magistrate directly, the defendant may either (1) waive the right to a preliminary hearing or (2) not waive that right.

Waiving the Right to a Preliminary Hearing

If a defendant waives the right to a preliminary hearing, the magistrate or judicial official will bind over the defendant to the grand jury. The grand jury will hear evidence from the prosecutor against the defendant and issue either a true bill or a no bill. If a no bill is issued, the criminal charges are dismissed and the defendant is discharged. If a true bill is issued, the defendant faces arraignment on the charges.

Not Waiving the Right to a Preliminary Hearing

If a defendant does not waive the right to a preliminary hearing, then the hearing is held. A magistrate will determine that probable cause either exists or does not exist. If probable cause does not exist in the opinion of the magistrate, then the defendant is discharged. However, the defendant may be subject to a subsequent indictment or presentment from the grand jury. On the other hand, if probable cause exists in the opinion of the magistrate, the defendant faces arraignment on the criminal charges.

Grand Jury Action

The result of a grand jury charge alleging certain criminal offenses on the part of a defendant through indictment or presentment brings the defendant to the arraignment stage of the justice process. Thus, the arraignment stage is reached through (1) a finding of probable cause in a preliminary hearing (possibly resulting from a criminal information filed by the prosecutor) or (2) an indictment or presentment from grand jury action. Figure 8.4 shows a summary of events leading to an arraignment stemming from preliminary hearings, informations, or grand jury action.

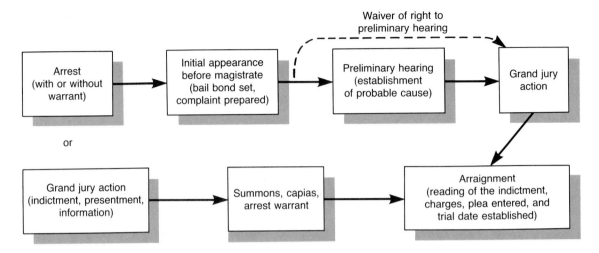

FIGURE 8.4 Alternative Procedures Leading to Arraignment

Arraignment

At the federal level and in many state and local jurisdictions, the **arraignment** is the official proceeding where a defendant is informed of the formal criminal charges and must enter a plea of either (1) guilty, (2) not guilty, or (3) nolo contendere. An alternative set of pleas in the state of Kentucky is (1) not guilty, (2) guilty, and (3) guilty, but mentally ill. Pleas of nolo contendere in Kentucky are prohibited (*Commonwealth v. Hillhaven Corp.*, 1984).

If the arraignment stems from grand jury action rather than a preliminary hearing, a copy of the indictment or presentment is given to the defendant. In many arraignments, indictments or presentments are read to the defendants by either magistrates or clerks of the court. At this stage, defendants are usually, although not always, represented by counsel. Figure 8.5 is an example of a federal arraignment order.

Guilty Pleas. A guilty plea is the equivalent of a confession of guilt in open court (Black, 1979:1036). While the procedures vary among jurisdictions, judges usually are expected to inquire of defendants if their plea is voluntary, if they understand the nature of the charge or charges, and if they know the mandatory minimum penalty under the law, the possible maximum penalty under the law, and that they are still entitled to an attorney if they have not obtained one. Furthermore, the judge will likely inquire if the plea of guilty has been obtained through threats or coercion from anyone and will tell defendants that the plea can be withdrawn and a plea of not guilty entered, that the defendants are entitled to a trial if desired, that they have the right to confront witnesses against them and cross-examine them, that they have the right not to incriminate themselves, and that there is a factual basis for that plea. In short, judges usually extend every opportunity to defendants to exercise all possible constitutional rights to which they are entitled.

Not Guilty Pleas. A plea of not guilty obligates the judge to fix a date for trial. The judge also determines whether or not to continue bail if the defendant is currently out of jail on bail, or the judge may permit the defendant to continue release on own recognizance

FIGURE 8.5 A Federal Arraignment Order

```
DC 15
(Rev. 1/62)
                NOTICE OF SETTING OF CASE FOR ___ ARRAIGNMENT _____

═══════════════════════════════════════════════════════════════════════

                         United States District Court
                                  FOR THE

                         _____


    THE UNITED STATES OF AMERICA               ⎤
                    vs.                        ⎥
                                               ⎥   Criminal No.
                                               ⎥
                                               ⎥
      To                                       ⎦


         ☐¹    TAKE NOTICE that the above entitled case has been set for   arraignment   in said
    Court at  Federal Courtroom   , on              , 19    , at

         ☐¹    As surety for the said defendant
    you are required to produce               ² in said Court at said time, otherwise the bail may be
    forfeited.

    --------------------------------, 19 ____              ------------------------------------------

    1 Sentences following boxes which have been checked are applicable.
    2 Insert "him," "her," as appropriate.
```

if that is the defendant's current pretrial release status. These options are available to the judge at this stage. The primary decision reached in an arraignment proceeding after a plea of not guilty has been entered is the establishment of a trial date, however.

Nolo Contendere Pleas. A plea of **nolo contendere** is the legal equivalent of a guilty plea. Technically, however, it is not a plea of guilty, but rather, a plea of no contest. The defendant is not contesting the facts as presented by the prosecution. However, the defendant may take issue with the legality or constitutionality of the law allegedly violated. For instance, the defendant may say, "Yes, your honor, I do not question the facts presented by the prosecution that I possessed two ounces of marijuana, but I also do not believe that the law prohibiting marijuana possession is constitutionally valid."

Sometimes, businesspersons enter pleas of nolo contendere. Even though these pleas are treated as equivalent to guilty pleas in criminal proceedings, they are not considered admissions of guilt in possible future civil proceedings. If a builder is charged with the criminal offense of fraud in the construction of a large building, a plea of nolo contendere, or no contest, results in criminal penalties. The plea is treated as though the builder had actually plead guilty. However, if the building collapses and persons are injured, they may sue the builder for damages in a civil action later, but they are prevented from using the nolo contendere plea as evidence of an admission of guilt on the fraud charges. In the case of a guilty plea to the same fraud charges, the builder could have the plea of guilty used in the subsequent civil action as evidence not only of guilt in the fraud scheme but also as evidence of negligence. Therefore, a nolo contendere plea is sometimes a strategic option for a person wishing to avoid civil liability connected with criminal activities, traffic accidents, or some other law infraction where civil liability may be incurred.

■ SPEEDY TRIAL

Many options are available to defendants from the time they are arrested to the time they are arraigned and a trial date is set. In fact, many contingencies are available to defendants even during the trial and after the conclusion of it. This last section focuses upon only the trial option. A plea of not guilty by a defendant obligates the presiding judge to set a trial date and eventually conduct a trial. This is the case unless some alternative plea is entered, the prosecution elects to drop charges against the defendant, or the defendant and prosecutor can reach an agreement whereby a formal trial can be avoided. The last contingency is usually referred to as a plea-bargain agreement. In a plea-bargain agreement, the objective of the prosecutor is to secure a guilty plea from the defendant, usually in exchange for a reduction of the charges or a lessening of the severity of penalties associated with the alleged offenses.

To illustrate some important pretrial requirements and procedures, assume that a defendant does not wish to enter a guilty plea and persists in a plea of not guilty to all offenses alleged. Federal courts are bound by law to observe the **Speedy Trial Act** of 1974 and its subsequent 1979 and 1984 amendments. The purposes of the Speedy Trial Act are (1) to clarify the rights of defendants, (2) to ensure that (alleged) criminals are brought to justice promptly, and (3) to give effect to a citizen's Sixth Amendment right to a speedy trial (*Klopfer v. North Carolina,* 1967; *United States v. Pollock,* 1984; *United States v. Horton,* 1983; *United States v. Nance,* 1982; *United States v. Tunnessen,* 1985; *United States v. May,* 1985).

The leading case relating to a speedy trial is *Klopfer v. North Carolina* (1967). In this case, Klopfer was charged with criminal trespass. Klopfer eventually went to court, and his case resulted in a mistrial. Klopfer then tried to find out if the government intended to prosecute him again for the same crime, but government officials declined to make a commitment. Instead, they formally entered upon the court record a nolle prosequi with leave, which meant that while they were permitting the defendant to be discharged, they were allowing themselves an opportunity to retry Klopfer at a later, unspecified date. This case eventually came before the United States Supreme Court, which declared that the government violated Klopfer's Sixth and Fourteenth Amendment rights and that it was unconstitutional to indefinitely postpone his trial without providing an adequate reason. The Supreme Court cited some of the reasons for their decision to endorse a speedy trial provision, which included the facts that (1) witness testimony would be more credible through an early trial; (2) a defendant's pretrial anxiety would be minimized; and (3) a defendant's ability to defend himself or herself and the fairness of the trial would not be jeopardized through extensive, adverse pretrial publicity.

Notwithstanding certain delays for a variety of reasons attributable to either the defense, prosecution, or both, the Speedy Trial Act provides:

1. In a case where a plea of not guilty is entered, the trial will commence within 70 days from the date when an information or indictment was made public or from the date of the defendant's arraignment, whichever date was last.
2. Unless the defendant consents in writing to the contrary, the trial will not commence less than 30 days from the date on which the defendant first appeared through counsel or expressly waived counsel and elected to proceed on his or her own.

These provisions not only make it possible for a criminal defendant to receive a speedy trial, but they also eliminate delays otherwise caused by crowded court dockets (*United States v. Nance,* 1982). Some courts have been notorious for their slowness in conducting trial proceedings. Federal judges have considerable power in deciding what evidence to admit and what evidence to exclude, for example. One judge may permit lengthy tape recordings of conversations between an FBI agent and a defendant. These recordings may consume many hours. In another district court, however, the judge may deny the admission of such tape recordings and insist that such materials be presented through more direct and brief testimony from witnesses. With the provisions of the Speedy Trial Act in force, all federal judges are obligated to comply in spite of the "general congestion of the court's calendar" (18 U.S.C., Sec. 3161(h)(8)(C), 1989). Certainly one consequence of this provision is a more rapid trial proceeding.

The not less than 30 nor more than 70 days provision of the Speedy Trial Act is designed to permit a defendant, together with defense counsel, adequate time to prepare a defense and to spare the defendant any undue delay in coming to trial. If a defendant wishes to consent to an earlier trial date, however, the defendant may do so under the act. Many factors affect the 70-day requirement, however. Defendants may discharge one attorney and appoint another. New attorneys need sufficient time to examine the case and prepare for a defense of their clients (*United States v. Darby,* 1984). The defendant may be ill (*United States v. Savoca,* 1984), or an important witness for either the prosecution or defense must be called and requires additional time to arrive (*United States v. Strong,* 1985). The judge may even request a psychiatric examination of a defendant if the judge has reason to believe that the defendant is not competent to stand trial (*United States v. Howell,* 1983; *United States v. Crosby,* 1983).

Many local and state jurisdictions follow the federal provisions set forth in the Speedy Trial Act, although they are not bound to do so. For example, North Carolina has a 90-day limit from the time of arrest or arraignment to trial, while New Mexico has a 180-day limit. The speedy trial provision of the Sixth Amendment is construed differently from one jurisdiction to the next. Federal courts are bound by the Speedy Trial Act provisions, however.

■ SUMMARY

Defendants are brought into the criminal justice system through arrests by police officers or private citizens. Complaints are filed alleging law violations. Grand juries and prosecutors can also bring defendants into the system through indictments, present-ments, and criminal informations. When suspects are arrested, they are booked, and records are compiled concerning personal data.

Usually, a magistrate or other judicial officer establishes a bail bond for a defendant in order for the defendant to gain pretrial release. A date for a preliminary hearing is usually established, unless the defendant wishes to waive that right. If that right is waived, the magistrate binds over the defendant to a grand jury, which evaluates the particular case. Grand jury action leads to either a no bill or a true bill. A true bill means that the grand jury has determined that probable cause exists to charge a defendant with a crime.

A person who is brought into the justice system through grand jury or prosecutor action is arraigned before a magistrate. When a defendant is subject to a preliminary hearing before a judicial official, the official determines if probable cause exists to support the criminal charges against the defendant. If probable cause is determined to exist, the defendant is subject to arraignment.

An arraignment is a proceeding where a defendant is confronted with formal criminal charges, enters a plea, and has a trial date established by the court. The plea may be guilty; not guilty; guilty, but mentally ill; nolo contendere; or some other plea consistent with the rules of criminal procedure followed in that particular jurisdiction. A plea of not guilty obligates the presiding judge to set a trial date for the defendant.

Under the Speedy Trial Act of 1974 and its 1979 and 1984 amendments, defendants in federal court proceedings must have a trial date set not less than 30 days nor more than 70 days from the date that the charges are placed against them, but many circumstances except these requirements. Federal judges are bound by the provisions of the Speedy Trial Act, whereas local and state judges follow rules for setting trial dates particular to their own jurisdictions.

KEY TERMS

- arraignment
- bail
- bail bond
- Bail Reform Act of 1984
- bounty hunters
- capias
- citizen's arrest
- criminal information

- grand jury
- indictment
- initial appearance
- John Doe warrant
- no bill
- nolo contendere
- petit jury
- presentment

- released on own recognizance (ROR)
- Speedy Trial Act
- summons
- true bill
- warrant
- without undue delay

QUESTIONS FOR REVIEW

1. What are the arrest powers of citizens? Do police officers have the same arrest powers as citizens, or do they have more arrest powers?
2. What does without undue delay mean in reference to bringing arrested persons before magistrates?
3. Under what circumstances is it not necessary to have a warrant to make an arrest?
4. Differentiate between a summons and a complaint. How does a magistrate evaluate the trustworthiness of a person filing a complaint?
5. If a person is cited for a speeding ticket and is given a summons, what does a summons usually provide?
6. If you file a complaint against another person for stealing your automobile, and that person is later arrested and charged with vehicular theft, does the government necessarily have to drop the charges against the person if you decide not to persist in your initial complaint? What are some of the options of the government?
7. Differentiate between an indictment and a presentment. If a prosecutor wants to avoid a grand jury altogether and file charges against a particular defendant, what does the prosecutor file?
8. Distinguish between a true bill and a no bill. In a grand jury action, does a defendant usually get a chance to present his or her side of the story regarding pending criminal charges?
9. John Doe was just indicted for mail fraud. A grand jury indicted John Doe after seeing the government evidence. Is John Doe guilty of mail fraud? Why or why not?

10. Is the Supreme Court of the United States agreed on what a petty offense is? Is there an established money limit on fines to be imposed for petty offenses or an established term in jail or prison for these crimes?
11. Which amendment of the United States Constitution pertains to speedy trials? Has the federal government enacted any legislation pertaining to speedy trials? If so, what is the essence of this legislation?
12. What is bail? What is the primary purpose of bail? Does bail always have to be in the form of money? Why or why not?
13. What is bail supposed to guarantee?
14. The Constitution of the United States says that citizens should be free from excessive bail. Does this mean that all persons are entitled to have bail set so that they can enjoy pretrial freedom? Why or why not? What is the intent of this constitutional provision?
15. Are violent criminals the only persons likely to be denied bail in certain situations? What are other offenses and conditions where citizens are denied bail?
16. Briefly discuss some of the major studies investigating bail from 1960 to 1985. What was the Philadelphia Experiment?
17. What is a preliminary hearing? What is it designed to determine?
18. What generally happens to a defendant at an arraignment proceeding?
19. What is meant by a plea of nolo contendere? Why is it used in some criminal cases?
20. Do all states have pleas of guilty, not guilty, and nolo contendere? What is another plea used in some states, such as Kentucky?
21. Under the federal law, is it likely that a person will be forced to trial within 5 days after an arraignment? Why or why not? What are the general guidelines for setting trial dates at the federal level? Are all states and local jurisdictions obligated to follow the federal procedure?

SUGGESTED READINGS

Gregory, Jeanne (1987). *Sex, race, and the law: Legislating for equality.* Beverly Hills, CA: Sage.

Jenkins, Philip (1984). *Crime and justice: Issues and ideas.* Monterey, CA: Brooks/Cole.

Nagel, Stuart S. (Ed.) (1972). *The rights of the accused in law and action.* Beverly Hills, CA: Sage.

Price, Barbara R., and Natalie J. Sokoloff (1982). *The criminal justice system and women.* New York: Clark Boardman Co.

Warren, Carol A. B. (1982). *The court of last resort: Mental illness and the law.* Chicago: Univ. of Chicago Press.

PART

III

In 1973, the United States Supreme Court declared that pregnancies in early stages may be terminated lawfully. The classic Roe v. Wade case involved an anonymous Jane Roe, who was later identified as Norma McCorvey of Texas. McCorvey's case began with an unwanted pregnancy in 1969; she claimed that she had been raped. Under Texas law, abortions were illegal. Thus, to obtain an abortion McCorvey would have been forced to travel to the nearest state where abortions could be performed (California), but because she was poor, this was not an option. Thus, when her baby was born, she gave it up for adoption. In the meantime, she contacted Sarah Weddington and Linda Coffee, two attorneys who aided her in pursuing her right to an abortion all the way to the United States Supreme Court.

THE COURTS

The Roe v. Wade *case did not have the effect intended. Rather than settle the abortion issue once and for all, it created a minor civil war, including sit-ins, clinic bombings, extortion, and intimidation, pitting pro-life forces against pro-choice forces. In 1989, the United States Supreme Court heard another case, which many believed would overturn the* Roe v. Wade *decision.* Webster v. Reproductive Health Services *involved a St. Louis clinic where abortions were performed. Again, the Supreme Court failed to resolve the abortion issue once and for all. Rather, it basically declared that states must decide when life begins and whether early-term abortions should be performed. The saga continues.*

Part III is an overview of court organization at the federal, state, and local levels. It includes a description of various court officers, including judges, clerks, bailiffs, and prosecutors. It describes pretrial proceedings, plea bargaining, and trial procedures generally, including the selection of juries, jury deliberations, and jury verdicts.

Chapter 9 is an examination of court organization. First, it describes the federal court system in detail, commencing with the United States Supreme Court and ending with a description of federal district courts and United States magistrates. It also describes state and local court systems. Common to the court systems are various functionaries who maintain court decorum and ensure the continuity of trial proceedings. The chapter describes several of these roles, including those of the court reporter, court clerk, bailiff, and prosecution. It examines judicial selection and reviews alternative plans for determining who should fill judicial posts. In recent years courts have been the target of criticism by the public and others, and this has prompted numerous court reforms. Some of these reforms are identified and discussed.

Chapter 10 investigates prosecutorial functions, including the screening of cases for prosecution. Prosecutors present various cases before grand juries and negotiate with defense attorneys to elicit guilty pleas from defendants through plea bargaining. The chapter discusses defense attorneys, including court-appointed public defenders, who assist indigent defendants. It also presents several alternatives to criminal court, including police cautioning, diversion of criminal cases to civil courts, pretrial diversion, and plea bargaining.

Chapter 11 identifies different kinds of trial proceedings, including bench trials and jury trials. It describes juries and jury selection and discusses several important jury functions. It presents the actual trial process, including excerpts of trial transcripts from selected cases. The chapter illustrates the processes of direct examination and cross-examination and describes eyewitness and expert witness roles. It includes jury deliberations and verdicts and their implications.

Court Organization: Structure and Process

■ INTRODUCTION

A popular television program tells viewers, "[T]he next time you feel that someone has violated your rights, don't try to get even by taking the law into your own hands. Take them to court!" The daily soap operas saturate the public with courtroom dramas, as hero and heroine alike are subjected to trials where every word may determine their survival. Newspapers and films also highlight court actions of all kinds. Law is at the height of media popularity, and attorneys and judges are consistently portrayed as idealistic, pristine purveyors of justice and the American way.

It is no coincidence that attention is directed at courtrooms from diverse sources. Courts are at the hub of the criminal justice system. Courts have been called the fulcrum of the justice system (Rubin, 1984). In order to understand the operations of the criminal justice system, a working familiarity with courts, court structure, and court procedures must be acquired. This chapter describes court organization in the United States, including the organization and procedures of the federal and state courts as well as those of lower courts.

Federal courts and their functions are complex. This complexity applies also to every state and local court (Sheskin, 1981). There is as much variation in federal, state, and local court organization and operation as there is in automobile makes, body styles, options, and accessories. Just as automobile manufacturers change their body styles, options, and accessories, courts at all levels change their procedures. Sometimes, these changes occur through legislative enactments. Sometimes, judges themselves dictate how their courts will be conducted. This chapter describes some of this court diversity.

■ LEVELS OF COURT SYSTEMS

Considering the three branches of United States government, citizens know the *least* about the judiciary (Davis, 1985; Gordon, 1985). It would require an entire book to describe adequately the courts of all states. The federal government and fifty state governments make and enforce criminal laws. Therefore, fifty-one systems co-exist, side by side (Abraham, 1968:138–139; Neubauer, 1979). Abraham (1968:139) says, "The character, jurisdiction, quality, and complexity of these (state) courts vary considerably from state to state in accordance with the myriad considerations of public policy, need, size, and constitutional practice that characterize the heterogeneous component parts of the nation."

Despite the diversity among state court organizations and operations, several common features are applicable to all of these systems. The Fourteenth Amendment forbids any state to create laws that conflict with the United States Constitution or that "abridge the privileges and immunities of citizens of the United States." Frequently, local and state laws are challenged regarding their constitutionality. On such occasions, higher courts consider possible conflicts between federal and state statutes.

In both the federal and state court systems, there are higher and lower courts. Each court has a jurisdiction, or power and authority to hear and resolve certain matters or controversies. Figure 9.1 describes the federal and state court systems.

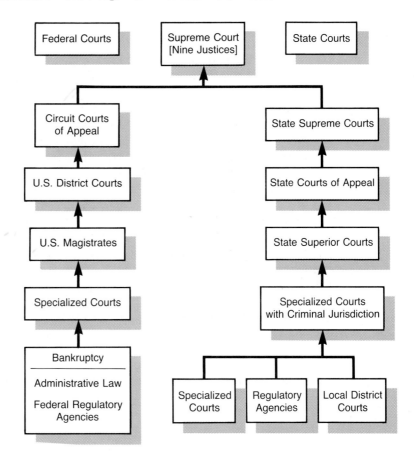

FIGURE 9.1 The Federal-State Court System

Figure 9.1 shows that the highest of all state and federal courts is the Supreme Court of the United States. Beneath the Supreme Court of the United States in power are lesser federal and state courts. These comprise two parallel, yet separate and distinct, court systems, each with a particular jurisdiction (Lieberman, 1984). The federal side of Figure 9.1 has jurisdiction over all federal laws, while the state side has jurisdiction over state and local statutes and ordinances. While these two parallel court systems are conceptually distinct for analysis purposes, there is some interplay between them. Areas of stress occur when federal courts intervene in state court proceedings or remove cases from state to federal jurisdiction (Kenny, 1984). For purposes of this chapter, however, the federal and state court systems are discussed separately.

■ FEDERAL COURT ORGANIZATION

Many state courts copy federal court structure and process (Coffin, 1980). In fact, some states have adopted the Federal Rules of Criminal Procedure contained in the

United States Code almost verbatim, with only slight changes or modifications to fit state needs.

Most courts in the United States trace their roots to the actions of colonists during the Constitutional Convention in the 1780s. Prior to the final vote on the Bill of Rights, convention delegates passed the Judiciary Act of 1789, which was influenced by the **Virginia Plan** (sometimes called the **Randolph Plan**) (Carp and Stidham, 1985:2).

The Virginia Plan presented the concept of superior and inferior courts, with the former having considerable appellate authority over the latter (Goebel, 1971). Interestingly, the Virginia Plan stemmed from England's royal court system. When the colonists created the new court system through the Judiciary Act of 1789, they continued the provision of life appointment for federal judges. Royal judges in England had served "at the King's pleasure during good behavior," or the equivalent of life appointments. This practice is still followed in all United States courts and some state courts, where judges are appointed to serve for life or until they choose to retire.

The provisions of the Judiciary Act of 1789 created three tiers of courts: (1) thirteen **federal district courts,** each presided over by a district judge; (2) three higher-level **circuit courts,** each comprising two justices of the Supreme Court and one district judge; and (3) a **Supreme Court,** consisting of a chief justice and five associate justices (Carp and Stidham, 1985:2–3). The federal district courts were given jurisdiction in all civil and criminal cases. The circuit courts reviewed decisions of federal district courts, although they had some limited original jurisdiction (Coffin, 1980:35). Finally, the Supreme Court was given jurisdiction that included interpreting federal legislation and balancing the interests between the state and nation through the maintenance of the rights and duties of citizens (Hughes, 1966:1). Figure 9.2 shows the structure of the federal judicial system.

The United States Supreme Court

The United States Supreme Court has both original and exclusive jurisdiction over (1) all actions or proceedings against ambassadors or public ministers of foreign states and (2) all controversies between two or more states. **Original jurisdiction** means the court may recognize a case at its inception, hear that case, and try it without consultation with other courts or authorities. **Exclusive jurisdiction** means that no other court can decide certain kinds of cases except the court having exclusive jurisdiction. A juvenile court has exclusive jurisdiction over juvenile matters, for example. The adult criminal courts have no juvenile jurisdiction.

The United States Supreme Court also has original, but not exclusive, jurisdiction over (1) all actions or proceedings brought by ambassadors or other public ministers, (2) all controversies between the United States and other states, and (3) all actions or proceedings by a state against citizens of another state or aliens (United States Code, 1989). The Supreme Court is also the ultimate reviewing body regarding decisions made by lower appellate courts or state supreme courts. The United States Supreme Court is primarily an appellate court, since most of its time is devoted to reviewing decisions of lower courts (Carp and Stidham, 1985:9–10). It is the final arbiter of lower court decisions unless Congress declares otherwise. Congress may change existing constitutional amendments or other acts. The United States Supreme Court meets 36

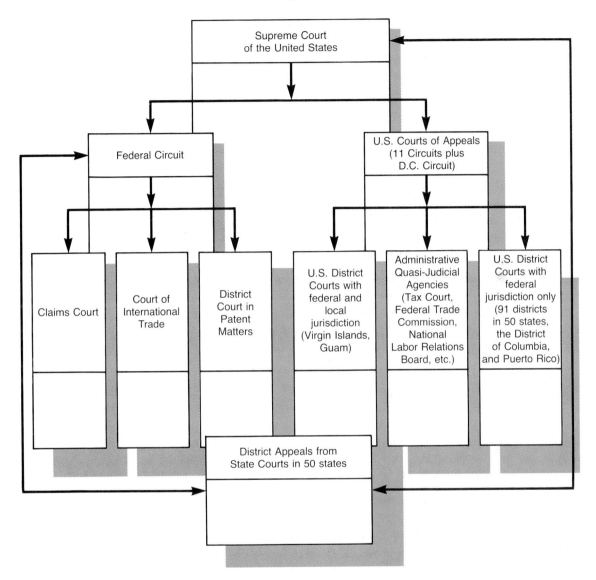

FIGURE 9.2 The Federal Judicial System

Source: American Bar Association, *Law and the Courts* (Chicago: American Bar Association, 1974), p. 21.
Updated information provided by the Federal Courts Improvement Act of 1982 and West Publishing Company.

weeks annually from the first Monday in October until the end of June. Annual salaries of the chief justice and associate justices were $104,700 and $100,600 in 1985.

Supreme Court justiceships are appointments by the president of the United States, subject to congressional approval. They are life appointments. Because these judgeships are presidential appointments, they often reflect a president's vested interests. Therefore, judges with judicial philosophies consistent with those of the president are

A DAY IN COURT

The president of the United States recommends judicial appointees to the United States Supreme Court. These recommendations must be approved by Congress. Despite this congressional safeguard, however, United States presidents have a profound impact on American social and legal policy for decades. Logically, presidents of the United States select judges who will likely support their presidential policies, programs, and interests, and prospective Supreme Court justices are usually from the same political party as the president.

Some indication of the long-range influence of United States presidents is the fact that in 1989 an Eisenhower appointee and the justice with the most Supreme Court longevity, Justice William J. Brennan (appointed in 1956), was still a member of the court. Two of ex-President Richard M. Nixon's appointees, Justice William Rehnquist and Justice Harry Blackmun, were still on the court. Gerald Ford appointed Justice John Paul Stevens. Ronald Reagan appointed the first female justice, Sandra Day O'Connor, as well as Justices Anthony Kennedy and Antonin Scalia. John F. Kennedy appointed Justice Byron White, while Lyndon B. Johnson appointed the only black member, Justice Thurgood Marshall, in 1967. In 1989, all of these justices were still serving on the high court.

In turn, the United States Supreme Court interprets the laws of the United States. During the 1960s, it rendered several important decisions that police regarded as overly restrictive in their efforts to enforce the law. The court was criticized as tying the hands of police officers in relation to their arrestees. The 1960s was an era of advocacy for the rights of criminal suspects. In later years, when the Supreme Court composition changed, it seemed to restrict the rights of criminal suspects and liberalize police arrests, searches, and seizures.

While the Supreme Court seldom reverses itself, it often creates exceptions to rulings by former courts. For example, in 1896, the separate but equal doctrine was declared constitutional by the Supreme Court (*Plessy v. Ferguson,* 163 U.S. 537, 1896). The original 1892 incident prompting this decision was an attempt by a Louisiana black man ("seven-eighths Caucasian and one-eighth African blood . . . the mixture of colored blood was not discernible in him" [at 538]), Plessy, to enter a railway passsenger coach area specifically designated for white passengers. He was arrested for entering the white section of the railroad car and attempted to enjoin the trial judge, Ferguson, from proceeding with the charge against him. The United States Supreme Court stressed that Plessy's constitutional rights were not violated, since the railroad did, in fact, provide separate but equal accommodations for black and white passengers. This broad doctrine was eventually extended by states to apply to all situations involving interaction of blacks and whites.

In 1954, the Supreme Court heard the case of *Brown v. Board of Education* (347 U.S. 483, 1954), a class action suit filed by several minor blacks in four states (Kansas, South Carolina, Delaware, and Virginia) seeking admission to all-white schools under laws mandating segregation. The court did not overturn the separate but equal doctrine. Rather, it ruled in favor of the black students by declaring that the separate but equal doctrine does not apply to education. The court said, "We conclude that in the field of public education the doctrine of 'separate but equal' has no place. Separate educational facilities are inherently unequal."

Numerous challenges of the separate but equal doctrine have been made since the *Brown* decision, and in each case, the court has declared the doctrine not applicable to the subject matter of these specific suits. Pendulum swings by the high court are indicative of the importance of the composition and political views of the justices. The shifts are also indicative of the influence of United States presidents on public policy and the law.

appointed instead of other, sometimes more qualified, judges who hold contrary philosophies (Goldman, 1985; Solomon, 1984). When former President Ronald Reagan nominated Robert Bork to fill a United States Supreme Court vacancy, the nomination was rejected by Congress after it examined Bork's views on various issues. Political differences were influential in Judge Bork's rejection as a Supreme Court justice.

The composition of the United States Supreme Court is considered crucial in interpretations of the United States Constitution and amendments relevant to citizens. Since the president of the United States appoints justices subject to congressional approval, these appointments influence Supreme Court decision making in favor of liberal or conservative interests. When Earl Warren was chief justice of the United States Supreme Court, the court rendered decisions that were directed at minimizing the abuse of police discretion in arrest and search and seizure matters. That court introduced stringent requirements to emphasize the rights of criminal suspects and minimize police misconduct. The exclusionary rule and pat down doctrines were parts of the Warren court heritage. The Warren court instituted the *Miranda* doctrine, whereby defendants were advised of their right to counsel and against self-incrimination. Law enforcement officers perceived these Supreme Court decisions as restrictive and favoring the interests of criminals. However, the American Civil Liberties Union and other rights groups were pleased with these decisions, because they demonstrated concern for the rights of individuals, regardless of their guilt or lack of guilt.

In 1969, Warren Burger became chief justice of the United States Supreme Court, and the Supreme Court introduced several exceptions to the Fourth Amendment rights of citizens, liberalizing former police search and seizure regulations and policies. These exceptions broadened police powers and eased restrictions that the Warren Court had imposed earlier. In 1986, William H. Rehnquist became chief justice, replacing Warren Burger. No doubt his philosophies and opinions will influence Supreme Court decision making for his tenure as chief justice.

One issue significant to most citizens is the imposition of the death penalty for capital crimes. The United States Supreme Court has never banned the death penalty, although it has narrowed the circumstances under which the federal government and the states may apply it. Another issue is whether abortion should be declared illegal. The Warren court issued the dramatic *Roe v. Wade* (1965) ruling which ruled unconstitutional the state statutes that prohibited abortion.

The composition of the Supreme Court is vital to whether capital punishment will eventually be abolished in the federal and state systems. Two justices, William J. Brennan and Thurgood Marshall, have consistently opposed the majority of justices by declaring their belief that the death penalty is cruel and unusual punishment and violative of the Eighth and Fourteenth Amendments under all circumstances (*Monroe v. Butler*, 1988). These justices were appointed in 1956 and 1967 respectively. In fact, seven of the justices on the Court in 1989 were appointed prior to 1980 (four of these prior to 1965). While later Supreme Courts have not been inclined to reverse previous Supreme Court decisions, they have decided narrow issues that have the effect of law. Capital punishment and abortion are two issues that may be affected by subsequent Supreme Court decisions.

A DAY IN COURT

Justices Thurgood Marshall and Sandra Day O'Connor represent only two of the nation's many minority elements. Yet, their presence influences the legal practices employed by police against criminal suspects and a wide variety of public policy issues. Justice Marshall, a black, might be expected to take positions favoring blacks whenever the Supreme Court convenes and votes in applicable cases. Justice O'Connor, a woman, might be expected to take positions favoring females whenever the Court votes in gender-relevant cases. However, being black or female does not mandate that Supreme Court justices vote one way or another.

Supreme Court justices are supposed to be impartial arbiters and interpreters of the laws of the United States. Their rulings affect millions of citizens each year. Yet, every volume of the *Supreme Court Decisions,* published opinions of the United States Supreme Court dating back to the late 1800s, contains personalized and emotional arguments from each justice. The Supreme Court has left a long trail of subjective decision making, and it no doubt will continue to be influenced by the personal sentiments and political views of its membership.

In 1973 the Supreme Court ruled in *Roe v. Wade* (410 U.S. 113, 1973) that a Texas criminal statute that prohibited abortion at any stage of a pregnancy was unconstitutional. The Jane Roe in the case was Norma McCorvey, a Texas resident who could not obtain a legal abortion in Texas at the time and could not afford fare to California. As the result of lower court action in Texas, McCorvey had her baby and eventually allowed others to adopt it. The Supreme Court opinion nullified the Texas statute and permitted abortions to be performed at various stages of pregnancy at the discretion of the physician. In its ruling, the court stressed that discretionary abortions should be made primarily in cases involving the preservation of life or health of the mother. Thus, it established a groundwork that permitted women to have abortions if they desired them, provided the unwanted pregnancy was performed within the first trimester or shortly thereafter in consideration of the life or health of the mother.

Various religious and political interests have sought to reverse this ruling by attacking the *Roe* decision. Until 1989, these attacks have proved unsuccessful. A battle has raged continuously between the forces. The battle has been a bitter one. Clinics where abortions are known to be performed have been picketed and even bombed. Lives of physicians who perform abortions have been threatened by anonymous callers, and some physicians and their families have suffered physical assault and other forms of harm.

In April 1989, the Supreme Court heard the case of *Webster v. Reproductive Health Services* (_____ U.S. _____, 1989), a Missouri case triggered by several "right-to-life" activists. This case dealt with the question of whether life begins at conception. Experts analyzing potential Supreme Court votes suggested that Justice O'Connor could be the pivotal justice in the case. However, overturning previous Supreme Court rulings is atypical of most Supreme Court holdings. Accordingly, the 1989 decision made by the Supreme Court about this abortion issue merely shifted to the individual states the responsibility for determining the legality of abortion and the conditions under which it should be performed.

President George Bush reviews the qualifications and credentials of various persons before making federal district judge appointments.

When George Bush became president of the United States in 1989, his personal political philosophies and interests as well as those of the Republican Party became increasingly significant in shaping the future of various United States policies. Selecting justices who favor capital punishment or abortion or who favor their abolishment will sway future Supreme Court decisions toward or away from vested interest groups advocating opposing views. It is the responsibility of justices to be objective in their resolution of any constitutional issue, but personal views of individual justices are evident frequently as dissenting opinions. The rationales underlying such dissenting opinions are often as persuasive as the rationales accompanying majority opinions. Thus, the composition of the Supreme Court is the primary force in interpreting the United States Constitution, and it affects the rights of all United States citizens.

The caseload of the United States Supreme Court has grown considerably since the early 1960s. In 1963, the Supreme Court was presented with 2,294 case filings. In 1973, these filings had grown to 5,079 cases, or an increase of 121 percent. In 1983, the caseload was similar to that of 1973, but these figures are misleading. Congress has given the Supreme Court considerable power to determine which cases to hear and which ones not to hear. The appearance of a case on the Supreme Court docket is not a guarantee that it will be heard. The United States Supreme Court hears only a few hundred cases per year, and it writes opinions for only about 150 of these cases. This means that 95 percent of all appeals to the United States Supreme Court annually are never heard (Carp and Stidham, 1985:44–45).

Circuit Courts of Appeal

In the early years of the United States, there were only three circuit courts of the United States and these were without permanent personnel (Goebel, 1971). Two Supreme Court justices and a federal district judge comprised the transient judiciary of the circuit courts. These judges were called circuit riders. The circuit riders were obligated to hold twenty-eight courts per year. This created considerable hardship because transportation was poor and it was difficult to travel great distances. Furthermore, since federal district judges were a part of the original circuit judiciary, they were in the prejudicial position of reviewing their own decisions (Goebel, 1971).

The activity of the United States circuit courts in their early years may be gleaned by examining the number of criminal prosecutions handled. From 1790 to 1797, the circuit courts handled a total of 143 criminal prosecutions, with half of these originating in Pennsylvania. A majority of the Pennsylvania cases were connected with the Whiskey Rebellion (Henderson, 1971:70–71). With the exception of insurrection cases in Pennsylvania during that same time period, most of the criminal prosecutions could have been conducted in the courts of the states where the crimes were allegedly committed (Henderson, 1971:71). By comparison, over 2,800 civil or common law cases were handled by these circuit courts during the 1790–1797 period.

The activity of circuit courts soon increased. From 1797 to 1801, there were 3,316 civil cases handled. Criminal cases for the same 5-year period doubled to 283.

Over the next century, numerous changes occurred in the circuit court structure. Several reforms, such as the Judiciary Act of 1891 (Evarts Act), were introduced to create the current scheme for federal appellate review. In 1989, there were thirteen judicial circuits at the federal level (these include the District of Columbia and federal circuits) with 168 circuit court judges in practice (28 U.S.C., Sec. 41, 1989). Table 9.1 lists the thirteen judicial circuits. Figure 9.3 shows these circuit court geographical boundaries.

All circuit court judges are appointed by the president of the United States, with the advice and consent of the Senate. These appointments are for life or until a circuit judge retires. In 1986, annual salaries of circuit court judges were $85,700.

Each of the circuit courts of appeal has appellate jurisdiction for all federal district courts in the particular circuit. For instance, the Eleventh Circuit Court of Appeals includes Alabama, Florida, and Georgia. These states are divided into several divisions, each containing one or more federal district courts. When a defendant wishes to appeal a decision of any federal district court within Alabama, Florida, or Georgia, the appeal is directed to the Eleventh United States Circuit Court of Appeals.

While all circuit courts of appeal have appellate jurisdiction from the district courts, there are occasions where a direct review may be made by the United States Supreme Court. Panels of three circuit judges must convene at regular intervals to hear appeals from federal district courts. Of course, if a defendant disagrees with the decision of a circuit court, the United States Supreme Court is the court of last resort for appeals.

The caseload for the United States Courts of Appeals has increased substantially from the early 1960s to the 1980s. Table 9.2 shows the number of cases commenced in the United States Courts of Appeals from 1963 to 1983. In 1963, 5,437 were cases filed. Of these, 965 (17.7 percent) were criminal cases. In 1973, these figures had risen

TABLE 9.1   The Thirteen Judicial Circuits of the United States and Numbers of Circuit Judges, 1986

Circuits	Composition	Number of Circuit Judges
District of Columbia	District of Columbia	12
First	Maine, Massachusetts, New Hampshire, Puerto Rico, Rhode Island	6
Second	Connecticut, New York, Vermont	13
Third	Delaware, New Jersey, Pennsylvania, Virgin Islands	12
Fourth	Maryland, North Carolina, South Carolina, Virginia, West Virginia	11
Fifth	Canal Zone, Louisiana, Mississippi, Texas	16
Sixth	Kentucky, Michigan, Ohio, Tennessee	15
Seventh	Illinois, Indiana, Wisconsin	11
Eighth	Arkansas, Iowa, Minnesota, Missouri, Nebraska, North Dakota, South Dakota	10
Ninth	Alaska, Arizona, California, Idaho, Montana, Nevada, Guam, Oregon, Washington, Hawaii	28
Tenth	Colorado, Kansas, New Mexico, Oklahoma, Utah, Wyoming	10
Eleventh	Alabama, Florida, Georgia	12
Federal	All Federal Judicial Districts	12
	TOTAL	168

Source: 28 United States Code, Section 44, 1988.

to 15,629 total cases. About a fourth of these were criminal cases. In 1983, the total number of cases had virtually doubled to 29,630, but only 4,790 (16 percent) of these cases were criminal. Civil case filings accounted for most of the increase in caseload between 1973 and 1983.

The litigation explosion of the 1980s has increased the use of the appeals process. Some analysts believe that if the appellate judiciary are not increased substantially over the next few years, a watering down effect will probably occur in circuit courts. That is, judges will increasingly rely on professional staff for case processing (Meador, 1983). One proposed solution to the problem of growing caseloads is subject matter specialization,

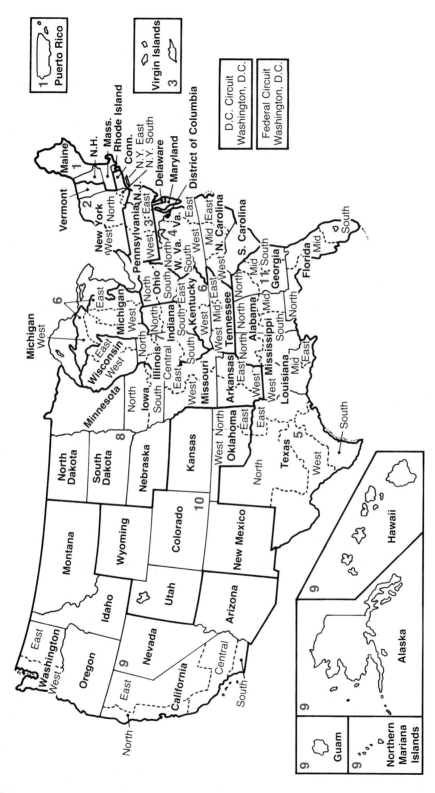

FIGURE 9.3 District and Appellate Court Boundaries

Note: The large numerals indicate the Courts of Appeals, and the broken lines represent jurisdiction boundaries of district courts.

Source: Administrative Office of the United States Courts.

TABLE 9.2 Cases Commenced in the United States Courts of Appeals: 1963, 1973, and 1983

	1963	1973	1983	Percent Change 1963–1973	1973–1983
Criminal	965	4,453	4,790	361.4	7.5
U.S. civil	1,054	1,703	4,562	61.5	167.8
Private civil	2,030	4,344	10,360	64.7	138.5
Prisoner petitions					
Federal	N/A	1,001	1,258		25.6
State	N/A	1,828	4,069		122.5
Bankruptcy	144	338	688	134.7	103.5
Administrative					
appeals	1,141	1,616	3,069	41.6	89.9
D.C. Court					
of Appeals	3		N/A		
Original proceedings	99	346	834	249.4	141.0
Other	1				
Total criminal	965	4,453	4,790	361.4	7.5
Total civil	4,472	11,176	24,840	149.9	122.2
Total	5,437	15,629	29,630	187.4	89.6
Number of authorized					
judgeships	78	97	132	24.3	36.0

Source: *Annual Reports of the Director of the Administrative Office of the United States Courts* (1963, 1973, and 1983).

where certain circuit judges will have exclusive control over particular areas of the law. Currently, three-judge panels preside over all appeals, regardless of the subject matter. Introducing a certain amount of organization into the subject matter of each appeal may maximize the efficiency of the current appellate judiciary (Meador, 1983).

In 1982, the United States Ninth Circuit Court of Appeals incorporated several innovations suggested by the Federal Judicial Center to improve the processing of the backlog of cases awaiting argument (Cecil, 1985). The **Innovations Project** was a submission-without-argument program, where cases were presented without oral argument. A prebriefing conference program was also implemented, where attorneys filing appeals met with court-designated staff members to discuss the length and structure of appeals briefs. The median time involved from filing an appeal to its final disposition was reduced from 17.4 months in 1980 to 10.5 months in 1983. The average number of case participations by active circuit judges increased by 27 percent from 229 cases in 1981 to 291 cases in 1982, greatly improving court case processing (Cecil, 1985).

Federal District Courts

In 1986, there were 558 federal district judges in practice in the United States within the various circuits. Federal district judges are also appointed by the president of the United

States and they also serve life terms. The annual salaries of federal district court judges in 1986 were $81,100. Federal district judges who serve 10 or more years with good behavior are entitled to retire at their option anytime thereafter and receive their annual salary for life. Although judicial appointments are ideally made without regard to one's race, color, sex, religion, or national origin, the appointments are primarily political. Thus, they reflect the interests and views of the president. The advice and consent of Congress is required for all such appointments.

The jurisdiction of federal district courts is considerable. The federal district court is the major trial court for the United States. All violations of federal criminal laws are tried in the district court. Besides criminal cases, federal district courts have the following jurisdictional authority:

1. To hear all civil actions where the matter exceeds $10,000 and arises under the laws, Constitution, or treaties of the United States.
2. To try a diversity of citizenship matters and determine amounts in costs in controversy.
3. To entertain bankruptcy proceedings.
4. To hear interpleaders, or third-party complaints.
5. To enforce Interstate Commerce Commission orders.
6. To hear commerce and antitrust suits.
7. To hear cases involving patents, copyrights, trademarks, and charges of unfair commercial competition.
8. To hear internal revenue cases and customs duty matters.

Sandra Day O'Connor was the first woman in history to serve on the United States Supreme Court. This photograph shows her being sworn in by Justice Warren Burger, while her husband, John J. O'Connor, is holding two family Bibles.

9. To judge tax matters by states.
10. To hear civil rights cases.
11. To hear matters where the United States is a plaintiff or defendant.

Criminal cases heard in federal district courts are commenced in the same ways as are cases in local and state courts. Federal law enforcement officers arrest suspects directly, federal grand juries issue indictments or presentments, or federal prosecutors issue criminal informations. The defendants appear before magistrates, who set their bonds or release them on their own recognizance. Federal judges conduct arraignment proceedings in federal district courts. Since arraignments include the entry of pleas by criminal defendants and the determination of trial dates, the federal judges who will eventually try the cases schedule the trials to fit their court dockets, or calendars.

Table 9.3 provides caseload figures for the United States district courts. The table shows the number of cases commenced in the United States district courts for 1963, 1973, and 1983. In 1963, 95,376 cases were filed in United States district courts. Of these 31,746 (33 percent) were criminal cases. In 1973, 140,994 cases were commenced, with 42,434 (30 percent) of these criminal cases. In 1983, the caseload had nearly doubled to 277,714 cases. Of these, only 35,872 (not quite 13 percent) were criminal cases. One explanation for the decline in the percentage of criminal cases commenced may be that more of these cases are plea-bargained, avoiding trial proceedings at the time of arraignment (Alschuler, 1979; Champion, 1987; Farr, 1984). Another explanation for this decrease is that many cases are returned, or remanded, to state courts for processing. Certain United States Supreme Court decisions have directed state courts to handle particular criminal cases involving previously resolved constitutional issues (*Stone v. Powell*, 1976).

TABLE 9.3   Cases Commenced in the United States District Courts: 1963, 1973, and 1983

	1963	1973	1983	Percent Change 1963–1973	Percent Change 1973–1983
Criminal	31,746	42,434	35,872	33.6	−15.4
U.S. civil	19,755	22,949	91,449	16.1	298.4
Private civil	39,621	58,393	119,618	47.3	104.8
Prisoner petitions					
Federal	1,630	4,535	4,354	178.2	−3.9
State	2,624	12,683	26,421	383.3	108.3
Total criminal	31,746	42,434	35,872	33.6	−15.4
Total civil	63,630	98,560	241,842	54.8	145.3
Total	95,376	140,994	277,714	47.8	96.9
Number of authorized judgeships	289	400	515	38.4	28.7

Note: The 1963 statistics exclude the District of Columbia, the Canal Zone, Guam, and the Virgin Islands.
Source: *Annual Reports of the Director of the Administrative Office of the United States Courts* (1963, 1973, and 1983).

■ STATE COURTS

State court systems are diverse, and no generalization is applicable to all of them. One factor contributing to this diversity is the number of reforms that have been directed at the state court systems (American Bar Association, 1967, 1973, 1975; Ashman and Parness, 1974; Brennan, Jr., 1971; Champion, 1981; Saari, 1976; Sheskin, 1981). Figure 9.4 is a general sketch of state court organization. The figure shows a state supreme court to which all appeals from lower courts are directed. There are also intermediate courts of appeal, a superior court, and lesser courts, including probate, county, municipal, magistrate, and domestic relations courts.

Not all states follow this model. Some states do not have justices of the peace. And even though the same kinds of courts exist in most states, they may have different names. Some states have courts of equity, or chancery, where civil matters are litigated. Other states refer to these courts as courts of common pleas, or circuit courts. The highest courts are called supreme courts in most states, but there are exceptions. In Massachusetts, the highest court is called the supreme judicial court. In New York, this court is called the court of appeals. In West Virginia, this court is called the supreme court of appeals (Harvard Law Review Association, 1981).

Beneath the state supreme court are intermediate appellate courts. Over two thirds of the states have intermediate appellate courts. These courts hear appeals directly from local trial courts. For example, Tennessee has a court of appeals and a court of criminal appeals, which function as the civil and criminal conduits through which trial court cases must pass on their way to the Tennessee Supreme Court.

Figure 9.4 shows a **superior court.** This is sometimes known as a circuit court or court of common pleas. New York calls this court a supreme court to add confusion to an already confusing nomenclature. At the lower levels of court organization are probate courts, county courts, municipal courts, and domestic relations courts. Sometimes these are known as courts of limited jurisdiction. Limited, or special, jurisdiction means that the court is restricted to handling certain kinds of cases, such as probate matters or juvenile offenses. Criminal courts deal only with violations of criminal laws. Often, the amount of money in controversy limits the court's jurisdiction. Therefore, courts of domestic relations do not conduct murder trials, and lawsuits for negligence demanding $1 million in compensatory damages are not within the jurisdiction of a justice of the peace. In 1986, there were over 13,000 courts of limited jurisdiction in the United States.

Another common classification of court is **general jurisdiction.** Trial courts are courts of general jurisdiction in many states, because they are not restricted to certain kinds of cases. Some states have both civil and criminal trial courts, or even more elaborate court systems to perform a wide variety of jurisdictional functions. When applied to jurisdiction, the term *general* indicates a legal authority including an entire subject and *special* indicates one limited to a part of it (Black, 1979:616). In 1986, there were 4,000 courts of general jurisdiction in the United States.

In many county jurisdictions, there are no criminal trial courts. In those counties, the circuit court concept functions the way it did in federal circuits in the 1790s. Circuit courts convene at regular intervals in certain areas of a state, hearing both civil and

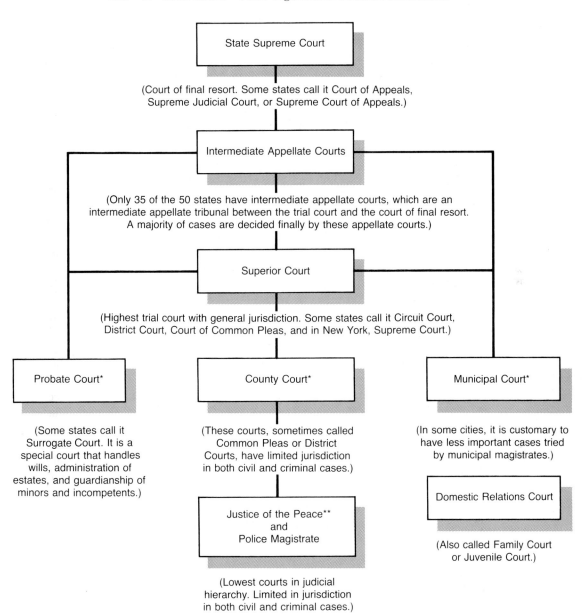

*Courts of special jurisdiction, such as probate, family, or juvenile courts, and the so-called inferior courts, such as common pleas or municipal courts, may be separate courts or part of the trial court of general jurisdiction.
**Justices of the peace do not exist in all states. Where they do exist, their jurisdictions vary greatly from state to state.

FIGURE 9.4   The State Judicial System

Source: American Bar Association, *Law and the Courts* (Chicago: American Bar Association, 1974), p. 20. Updated information provided by West Publishing Company, St. Paul, Minnesota.

CRIME BEAT

When we hear the phrase, "assault with a deadly weapon," we are inclined to conjure up an image of one attacking another with a gun or knife. Even the fists of professional boxers are considered "deadly weapons" in the commission of a crime. However, the range of deadly weapons has been extended in recent years to include the knowing transmission of AIDS (Acquired Immune Deficiency Syndrome—a fatal disease) to others.

In 1987, Pfc. Adrian G. Morris, Jr., stationed at Fort Huachuca, Arizona, tested positive for the AIDS virus. Shortly after this diagnosis, he went on a date with his girlfriend, Patricia Pruitt. She disclosed that she was pregnant with his child, although she probably would not want to marry him. He was upset and distraught. Thus, he sought the companionship of a fellow soldier, Pfc. Anthony L. Baldwin. In the course of their conversation, they became intimate, fondled one another, and engaged in mutual oral sex. Another

soldier overheard them and reported the incident to officers. In time, charges of conduct that would bring discredit to the armed services were filed against Morris. These charges also included aggravated assault as the result of knowingly transmitting the AIDS virus to another soldier, Baldwin, since oral sex is one of several ways AIDS can be transmitted.

In other cases, prostitutes have been charged with aggravated assault by knowingly transmitting AIDS to their customers. In yet other instances, arrestees have been charged with aggravated assault as the result of biting arresting officers and declaring that they have AIDS. No doubt such cases will introduce new dimensions to the meaning of aggravated assault. Is it possible that attempted murder charges might be filed against persons who have AIDS and knowingly donate their blood to blood banks? Yes. Attempted murder charges have been filed against AIDS carriers in California and elsewhere.

criminal matters. A wide variety of cases, including domestic relations and juvenile adjudication proceedings, are heard in these circuit courts.

The most popular model of state court organization is the **traditional model,** or the **Texas model.** Figure 9.5 shows the Texas model. The major features of the Texas model include two courts of last resort: (1) the supreme court, which hears cases of a civil nature and juvenile matters, and (2) the court of criminal appeals, which has final appellate jurisdiction in criminal cases. In both courts at this level, there are nine judges just as there are nine judges in the United States Supreme Court.

Between the major trial courts and the supreme court, there is a court of civil appeals. This court hears all civil appeals from lower trial courts. These trial courts are designated as district courts, and each is assigned a jurisdiction. A family district court oversees matters having to do with child custody questions, juvenile delinquency, and child abuse cases. A criminal district court has exclusive criminal jurisdiction. Finally, a general district court has general jurisdiction, and it hears both civil and criminal cases. At the lower levels of the Texas court system are various county courts and municipal courts. Texas also has a justice of the peace court, which is staffed with 1,000 judges. These are courts of limited jurisdiction.

More simplified versions of state court systems have been suggested. Pound (1940) proposed a three-tiered system of state court organization. He outlined four principles that influenced his model: (1) unification, (2) flexibility, (3) conservation of judicial power, and (4) responsibility. Pound said:

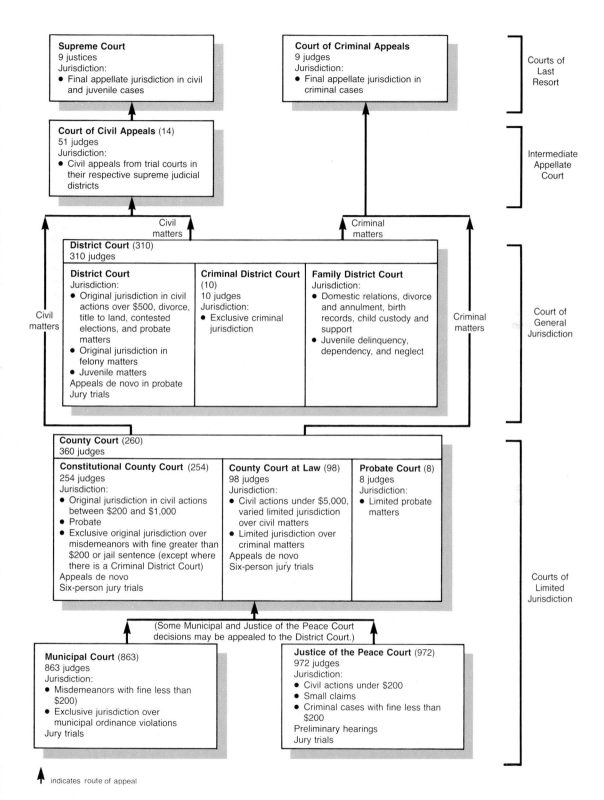

FIGURE 9.5 The Texas, or Traditional, Court Model

Basic to the achievement of these principles is the establishment of a single three-tiered state court system. At the top sits the ultimate court of appeal (the supreme court). A trial court of general jurisdiction for all major civil and criminal proceedings constitutes the second level. Depending upon the volume of litigation or on the traditions of the state, this tier might be organized into divisions specializing in certain types of litigation. Finally, the lowest tier of the court, a minor trial court, hears cases of lesser magnitude. (Pound, 1940:230).

The American Bar Association has submitted many state court organizational proposals over the last several decades. In 1962, it proposed a model with a four-tiered system, including a supreme court at the top, an intermediate appellate court, a major trial court, and a minor trial court. In 1974, it modified this model somewhat by combining the major and minor trial courts into a trial court designation as the lowest part of a three-tiered court system. Figure 9.6 shows Pound's model and the two ABA models.

■ FUNCTIONS OF STATE AND LOCAL COURTS

State and federal laws consume many volumes on judges' shelves. While rules of procedure in administering the law are reasonably clear and prescribe behaviors for judges to follow while they are on the bench, judges have considerable authority over the conduct of their courts and the behaviors of the litigants. Each case has unique aspects, and it is difficult for judges to promote fairness, regardless of the precision of the procedural rules and court administrative policies (American Bar Association,

FIGURE 9.6 Pound's Model, the ABA Model of 1962, and the ABA Model of 1974

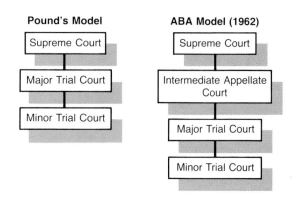

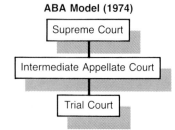

Source: Henry R. Glick and Kenneth N. Vines, *State Court Systems* (Englewood Cliffs, NJ: Prentice-Hall, 1973), p. 32.

1975:1). Judges decide on the admissibility of evidence. These decisions are often subjective, since there are so many exceptions to the rules of evidence in federal and state courts. Sometimes, a judge's ruling about the admissibility of evidence may be appealed to a higher court.

The diverse functions of state and local courts are closely linked with their jurisdictions. The American Bar Association described standards relating to state trial courts and their administration (American Bar Association, 1975). While these standards are not binding on individual trial courts, judges have been persuaded to abide by them because of their objectivity and clarity. According to these standards, the trial court performs three primary functions:

1. It is required to decide conflicting contentions of law and disputed issues of fact.
2. It is required to formulate sanctions and remedial orders.
3. It is required to supervise the activity of persons subject to the authority of the court.

The Texas model is a good example of the diverse functions performed by various courts of limited jurisdiction. At the county court level, the constitutional county court consists of 254 judges on a statewide basis. This court has jurisdiction over civil actions involving amounts between $200 and $1,000. It hears probate matters, where wills are read and estates are settled. It also has jurisdiction over misdemeanors involving fines greater than $200 or where jail sentences can be imposed. It conducts six-person jury trials, and can also grant appeals for new trials where the original jury verdicts are unfavorable.

The county court at law has 100 judges and jurisdiction over civil actions where the amount is less than $5,000. It may conduct six-person jury trials and grant appeals for new trials. It also has jurisdiction over certain types of criminal matters. The probate court has fewer than ten judges and deals exclusively with probate matters, such as wills and estates.

The municipal and justice of the peace courts make up the largest number of Texas courts. They have jurisdiction over misdemeanors involving fines of less than $200, traffic offenses, and violations of municipal ordinances. They can settle small claims in civil actions, and they may also conduct preliminary hearings to determine probable cause.

■ COURT PERSONNEL

In most jurisdictions in the United States, there is consistency regarding court personnel and their respective functions. Besides the judge, there are several other positions, including (1) the court reporter, (2) the court clerk, (3) the bailiff, and (4) the prosecutor.

Court Reporters

All **courts of record** maintain a written or tape-recorded record of all court proceedings. The trial court in most states is a court of record. At the federal level,

United States district courts are courts of record. Typically, **court reporters** make verbatim, or word-for-word, transcriptions of court proceedings. In criminal trials, transcriptions of what is said are often quite important, particularly if defendants appeal their convictions to higher courts.

In criminal cases before United States district courts, federal judges must follow the Federal Rules of Criminal Procedure and the Federal Rules of Evidence, but judges are not perfect decision makers. Frequently, they commit errors of judgment in their decisions about evidence or their rulings on motions made by the defense or prosecution. Much of the time, these errors are harmless. On some occasions, however, these errors are serious. Serious errors committed by judges are termed harmful errors and reversible errors. A **harmful error** is often prejudicial to a defendant's case, and the jury may render a guilty verdict because of such judicial errors. The same is true about reversible errors. **Reversible error** is considered by an appellate court when reviewing a transcript of lower court proceedings. If a judge has committed a reversible error, the judgment may be reversed by higher courts. A record of court proceedings made by the court reporter is essential for determining whether harmful or reversible errors have been made. Appeals by defendants often allege such errors for jury verdicts.

For instance, in a 1981 Tennessee case, Larry Hamm and some friends stole a truck belonging to Don Bailey and drove it around for about an hour (*State v. Hamm*, 1981). Later, police recovered the truck and found evidence that linked Larry Hamm to the theft. At his trial later, Hamm contended that he was only joyriding, although he was charged with grand larceny, a more serious offense. When the judge gave instructions to the jury, he failed to charge the jury concerning the joyriding statute, which carried less severe penalties. Hamm was convicted of grand larceny and sentenced to 6 years in prison. Hamm's lawyers appealed on the grounds that the judge had erred by failing to instruct the jury about the joyriding statute. When the court reporter's transcript of the proceedings was reviewed, the error was apparent, and the Tennessee Court of Criminal Appeals reversed Hamm's conviction.

Court Clerks

In most local jurisdictions, court clerks are elected officials. In federal district courts, the court clerk is often the district judge's secretary or personal aide. The **court clerk** is a court officer who may file pleadings, motions, or judgments, issue process, and may keep general records of court proceedings. In the United States district courts, each district court may appoint a clerk who in turn may appoint (with the approval of the court) necessary deputies, clerical assistants and employees. These court clerks keep records of court dockets for federal judges and advise them concerning the scheduling of cases for trial.

Bailiffs

Bailiffs are court officers who have charge of maintaining order while the court is in session. The bailiff is often placed in custody of the jury in a trial proceeding, and sometimes the bailiff has custody of prisoners while they are in the courtroom. Bailiffs, known also as criers and messengers in United States district courts, may be given additional duties by federal judges, including the duties of law clerks, if they are qualified. These criers call the court to order, attend to the needs of jury members while deliberations are taking place, and generally serve the various interests of the federal judge (28 U.S.C., Sec. 751–755, 1989).

Prosecutors

A key figure in any court proceeding is the **prosecutor.** At the state and local levels, the prosecutor may be called the district attorney, city attorney, county attorney, or simply, the prosecuting attorney. At the federal level, each of the United States districts has a United States attorney appointed by the president of the United States with the advice and consent of the Senate. These attorneys are appointed for 4-year terms and are subject to removal by the president. The attorney general of the United States appoints one or more assistant United States attorneys (AUSAs), depending on the caseload of any particular district. These AUSAs are subject to removal by the attorney general.

Following are the duties of the United States attorney for any given district. Except as otherwise provided by law, each United States attorney, within his district:

1. Prosecutes all offenses against the United States.
2. Prosecutes or defends, for the government, all civil actions, suits or proceedings in which the United States is concerned.
3. Appears on behalf of the defendants in civil actions and suits or proceedings pending in the district against collectors or other officers of the revenue or customs for things they have done or for the recovery of any money exacted by or paid to them.
4. Institutes and prosecutes proceedings for the collection of fines, penalties, and forfeitures incurred for violation of any revenue law.
5. Reports as the attorney general directs.

At the state and local levels, district attorneys, or DAs, decide which cases to prosecute, and they represent their respective local governments in all civil and criminal matters. Like their federal counterparts, DAs initiate prosecutions of defendants and seek indictments from grand juries or they issue criminal informations. Prosecutors have considerable power and discretion in determining which cases to prosecute. They appoint assistant district attorneys according to their respective caseloads and city or county budgets. They are also pretrial intermediaries between judges and criminal defendants. Prosecutors may negotiate plea agreements. In the courtroom, prosecutors present evidence against defendants and seek convictions for crimes.

■ JUDGES AND JUDICIAL SELECTION

The key figure in any courtroom is the judge. Judges are all-powerful within their courtrooms, and their decisions affect defendants as well as decisions made by lower courts. Judges sometimes make decisions that are reversed by higher courts. A judge may allow introduction of incriminating evidence against a defendant, or the judge may

CRIME BEAT

A new twist has been given to the list of defenses used by the accused in crimes of violence. Common defenses, such as mistake, duress, insanity, and necessity, have been joined by "blame the victim" and "she asked for it." Some rapists have contended that rape victims asked for it by dressing provocatively. See-through clothing and scanty apparel have been cited by defendants accused of rape. According to the rapists, the victims enticed them to commit their acts of violence. In some cases, such defenses have been successful to the extent that rape charges have been changed to simple assault.

In recent years several deaths have purportedly resulted from "rough sex." The most publicized case in recent years was the 1986 killing of Jennifer Levin by 21-year-old college student Robert Chambers in Manhattan's Central Park. Chambers' defense was that he and 18-year-old Levin were engaging in rough sex, and that things got out of hand. He claimed that Levin hurt him during their sexual interlude, and that he squeezed her neck in retaliation. He claimed it was an accident, and that he "went too far." Known as the preppie murder trial, the case lasted over 11 weeks. Defense lawyers conferred with the prosecution, and eventually through plea bargaining, Chambers entered a guilty plea to first-degree manslaughter. The maximum penalty, which was imposed by the judge, was 5–15 years in prison.

In another case, 17-year-old Joseph Porto wrapped a rope around his girlfriend's neck, choking 17-year-old Kathleen Holland to death. "She asked me to do it," he claimed during his videotaped confession. Charged with second-degree murder at first, Porto claimed that the death was accidental and that he did not intend to kill Holland. Again, "rough sex" was the explanation for going too far in the encounter. The prosecutor of Nassau County, New York, where the murder occurred dubbed it the oops defense. In any case, the jury found Porto guilty of criminally negligent homicide, punishable by a maximum incarcerative term of 4 years. In both the Porto and Chambers cases, it is likely that neither of these convicted offenders will serve much time in prison for their crimes. In cases where murderers and their victims are allegedly close through engagement or lengthy periods of dating, it is likely that increasing numbers of deaths will be explained away in court as the result of "rough sex."

---

decide to exclude such evidence. The judge decides what testimony is relevant. The judge controls the conduct of all trials. Harmful error or reversible error may result in the overturning of judicial decisions by higher appellate courts, but not all errors are detected in a trial, not all guilty verdicts are appealed, and not all appeals are heard on their merits by higher courts. The United States Supreme Court hears only about 4 percent of the appeals it schedules annually.

It is assumed by all appellate courts that the original judgment or verdict rendered by a lower trial court was the correct one. Therefore, clear and convincing evidence must be presented by the defendant supporting a reversal of a verdict by the trial judge or jury. It is insufficient simply to prove that errors were committed. Even harmful errors are insufficient under certain conditions when attempting to overturn a judge's decision. In a murder case, a judge admitted into evidence photographs of the murder victim. These photographs showed the mutilated corpse of the victim, and they had absolutely no bearing on the guilt or innocence of the accused. There were eyewitnesses to the murder, and the defendant's guilt had been proven beyond a reasonable doubt without the photographs, but the photographs obviously inflamed the jury and influenced their decision to impose the death penalty. The murder conviction was appealed, but the verdict was affirmed by the higher court. In that case, the court said there was so much evidence against the accused that the admission of these inflammatory materials into evidence resulted in harmless error. Under other circumstances, however, the admission of inflammatory photographs might persuade the jury to render a guilty verdict in an otherwise weak case against a defendant. Again, the trial judge controls the courtroom and influences the general course of the trial as well as the defendant's chances for conviction or acquittal.

One misconception is that all judges are lawyers and know the fine points of the law (Gordon, 1985; Provine, 1986). However, many judges have no legal training and are not former lawyers. For instance, among the 2,000 judges who serve in the various townships and villages in New York state, 1,600 are nonlawyers. Only 400 of these have passed the New York state bar (Zimmerman, 1981:265–268). Similar distributions of nonlawyer judges are found in most other states (Provine, 1986).

Judges are either appointed or elected (Abraham, 1968). Alfini (1981:253) has identified five methods of judicial selection as basic variations on appointments or elections: (1) popular election by partisan ballot, (2) gubernatorial (or presidential) appointment, (3) popular election by nonpartisan ballot, (4) legislative election, and (5) selection through a merit plan.

At the federal level, the president recommends judges for district, circuit, and Supreme Court judgeships, with Congressional sanction (that is, advice and consent) (Solomon, 1984). Supreme Court appointments have not necessarily depended upon previous judicial experience, however. From 1930 to 1967, twenty-three Supreme Court justices were appointed. Of these, only seven had previous federal judge experience, with all but one serving 5 or fewer years on the federal bench. Only four of these twenty-three appointments had experience as state judges. Only Justice Cardozo, appointed in 1932, had more than 8 years' experience, having served 18 years in state courts.

During President Reagan's administration, the judicial selection process was increasingly formalized (Goldman, 1985). Compared with previous administrations, President Reagan shifted the appointment emphasis toward greater judicial experience. During President Carter's administration, there were many judicial appointments of law school professors to federal judgeships. In contrast, the Reagan administration made proportionately fewer appointments of law school professors to such positions. Under the Reagan administration, more women (9 percent) were appointed to district court judgeships than in previous administrations with the exception of President Carter's. However, the partisan nature of presidential appointments is clearly shown by President Reagan's selection of district court judges, where 97 percent of them were Republicans (Fowler, 1984; Goldman, 1985).

In most states, the governor appoints judges to high court posts. In many other jurisdictions, persons campaign for judgeships, much as candidates run for political offices. In fact, politics is the primary reason for large numbers of nonlawyers as municipal judges, justices of the peace, and county court judges. There has been considerable debate about whether judges should be appointed or elected, although no judicial selection method has been found superior to others (Alfini, 1981; American Judicature Society, 1983; Feeley, 1988).

Politically appointed or elected judges raise several important issues. Are the most qualified persons selected for the judgeship? An investigation of elected and appointed

Greater numbers of women are being appointed or elected to judgeships at the local, state, and federal levels.

judges for the California superior court from 1959 to 1977 compared their demographic characteristics, educational backgrounds, and pre-judicial career experiences (DuBois, 1983). Of the 739 judges investigated, 662 of them had been appointed. Most of these had had earlier careers as attorneys or some previous legal experience. When their decisions were examined for technical accuracy and legal justification, however, no significant differences between elected or appointed judges were found (DuBois, 1983).

Another issue is whether political appointments contribute to corruption among the judiciary (Forer, 1984; Gershman, 1985). Because of their powerful positions, judges may influence trial outcomes, dismiss cases, or find innocent defendants guilty. They also regulate the harshness of penalties imposed whenever a jury verdict of guilty is rendered. All states have judicial sanctioning boards, which are usually operated through state bar associations. Thus provisions exist for officially questioning judicial behavior.

The American Judicature Society has shown that thirty-three states and the District of Columbia have used nominating commissions to help select judges (American Judicature Society, 1983). However, no one has ever determined which qualities judicial applicants must possess and how those qualities should be used for selecting judges. The Report of the Committee on Qualification Guidelines for Judicial Candidates indicated nine criteria for judicial selection: (1) age, (2) communication skills, (3) health, (4) industry, (5) integrity, (6) judicial temperament, (7) justice (impartiality, fairness, objectivity), (8) professional skill, and (9) social consciousness (American Judicature

Society, 1983). However, this general list is used only in the primary screening phases of judicial nominations.

A popular method of judicial selection which as been adopted by several states is the Missouri Plan. Originally proposed in 1940, the **Missouri Plan** is a method of judicial selection using the merit system for appointments to judgeships (President's Commission on Law Enforcement, 1967:66–67). The essential features of the Missouri Plan are:

1. A nominating committee consists of lawyers and nonlawyers appointed by the governor and chaired by a judge.
2. A listing of qualified candidates is nominated by the committee for each judicial vacancy.
3. Each judicial vacancy is filled by the governor by referring to the list of candidates nominated by the committee.
4. Any appointed judge seeking reelection will run only on the issue of whether or not to be retained on the basis of merit.

The Missouri Plan is a variation of the much earlier Kales Plan (Kales, 1914). The Kales Plan has survived in various forms in several states over the years, and its influence on the Missouri Plan is obvious. For instance, the **Kales Plan** requires a nonpartisan aggregate of lawyers, judges, and nonjudicial personnel to acquire a list of the most qualified candidates on the basis of their records and expertise. This list is then submitted to the governor for use in making appointments. Vacancies because of death, retirement, removal for incompetence, or any other reason can be filled without reference to political affiliations or associations. Ideally, any choice a governor makes from the list provided by nonpartisans is, by definition, a good choice. The important point is that the selection process minimizes the element of politics.

Some critics question whether *any* merit plan, including the Kales and Missouri versions, can eliminate politics from judicial selection (Adamany and DuBois, 1976; Hannah, 1978; Melone, 1977; Watson and Downing, 1969). However, other analysts find the merit plan useful for promoting greater accountability and fairness among judges (Griffin and Horan, 1983).

■ COURT REFORMS

The courts of the United States have been criticized for their assembly-line justice (Blumberg, 1967; Feeley, 1983). Among other criticisms, the courts have been depicted as overworked, inadequately staffed, glutted with case overloads, unsympathetic, unfair, and extremely lethargic in resolving legal disputes. There are indications that at least some of these accusations are true. Recent legislative action of Congress during the past few decades has introduced bail reforms, speedy trial rules, sentencing reforms, and pretrial diversionary measures for low-risk defendants.

Within the courtroom, trial court delay is investigated extensively (Feeley, 1983; National Institute of Justice, 1986; Mahoney, Sipes, and Ito, 1985). Perhaps the concern about trial delays encourages the court's image as an assembly-line process. Courts have extensive caseloads, but United States courts are dispatching cases today with greater frequency than in previous years (Flango, Roper, and Elsner, 1983). A major problem is the great increase in the number of case filings that consume valuable court time.

An investigation of misconceptions about state trial courts found that traffic cases make up the bulk of court activity (Flango, Roper, and Elsner, 1983). Civil cases make up most of the activity in courts of general jurisdiction. In criminal cases, most defendants plead guilty. Where not guilty pleas are entered, about half the cases are heard by judges and about half are decided by juries. Between 1972 and 1977, filings of civil cases increased more than three times as rapidly as the general population (Flango, Roper, and Elsner, 1983). Between 1977 and 1983, civil case filings in the United States increased by 20 percent, while criminal filings increased by 23 percent. Between 1977 and 1981, however, the number of trial judges increased only 7 percent, while the number of appellate judges increased by only 15 percent (National Institute of Justice, 1986:2).

Several states have implemented alternative strategies for preventing trial court delays. In New Jersey, Hudson County has a central judicial processing (CJP) court (Conti et al., 1985). This court handles all initial appearances of defendants charged with indictable offenses. The main goal of the CJP is to eliminate municipal court delays and free judges to deal with more serious cases. Since the program was implemented in 1980, court backlogs of over 3,800 cases have been eliminated. Furthermore, the program has (1) assured greater consistency of defendant treatment, (2) controlled paperwork more effectively, (3) improved the efficiency of the grand jury operation, and (4) greatly enhanced prosecutor and defense services (Conti et al., 1985).

The emphasis of court reform programs is upon better coordination and management of court resources (Feeley, 1983). In the United States district court for the western district of Missouri, district judges have developed a **joint trial calendar system** for processing various cases (Stienstra, 1985). For example, all judges share a common trial calendar for cases that have been developed to a point where they are ready for trial. Only cases ready for trial are placed on the calendar. A criminal joint calendar is used for all but the most complicated cases, and a civil calendar is used for jury cases that can be tried in four days or less. During a particular 2- to 3-week period, judges suspend all of their activities and try all of the cases on the calendar. This procedure guarantees a trial. At the same time, it stimulates pretrial settlements by defense attorneys who are unsure about the particular district judge who presides. Some attorneys wish to avoid judges who have a history of dealing harshly with particular offenses (Champion, 1987; Stienstra, 1985).

One of the more successful programs is the use of volunteer lawyer-judges to bolster court resources (Aikman, 1986:2). A project undertaken by the National Center of State Courts has examined the influence of judicial adjuncts on reducing caseloads and backlogs for regular judges. **Judicial adjuncts** are lawyers who assist courts on a temporary basis while maintaining an active law practice. They are considered attorneys rather than full-time judicial officers. The study found judicial adjuncts of significant benefit in (1) assisting in alternative dispute resolution, (2) assisting in settlement conferences, (3) filling quasi-judge positions, (4) filling commissioner and magistrate positions, (5) and providing temporary trial and appellate judge services. In civil cases where arbitration is necessary, a judicial adjunct can save valuable court time by getting the litigants to agree on a settlement figure. Judicial adjuncts also conduct preliminary hearings and arraignments, and set bail. They are empowered to sign warrants and subpoenas, preside over nonjury misdemeanor cases, and decide small claims issues (Aikman, 1986:2–3).

For several years, a **community dispute resolution program** has been used in New York state to resolve legal matters that would otherwise have to be heard in courts (New York State, 1984). Currently, thirty-five dispute resolution centers serve thirty-seven different counties in New York. In 1982–1983, these centers handled 54,254 cases, resulting in 15,280 conciliations, mediations, or arbitrations. Most of the referrals to the centers (81 percent) were from the courts. The average cost per conciliation was only $67, including the state administrative costs. In 90 percent of the cases reaching the mediation stage, successful resolutions of problems were made. Thus, the expense and time of a trial were avoided.

One of the more useful mechanisms for eliminating trial court delays occurs prior to a defendant's entering the courtroom, however. This is a pretrial settlement or plea-bargain agreement reached between the prosecution and defense attorney.

■ SUMMARY

Courts are the cornerstone of the criminal justice system. The major court systems exist at the federal and state levels. These are parallel systems, each having particular jurisdictions and responsibilities. On the federal side, the court organization is headed by the United States Supreme Court, which consists of nine justices. This court is the highest appellate body in the United States. Beneath the Supreme Court are thirteen circuit courts of appeal. These are intermediate courts with appellate jurisdiction over the United States district courts. The United States district court is the federal trial court. It has exclusive jurisdiction over many subjects, including all violations of federal criminal laws. All major federal court appointments are made by the president of the United States, with the advice and consent of the Senate.

State court organization is similar to federal court organization. However, considerable variation in court operations and the number of different courts exists from one state to the next. Most state courts have a supreme court, a court of appeals (criminal, civil, or both), several trial courts, local municipal courts, and justices of the peace. While a number of models have been advanced and promoted over the years by such groups as the American Bar Association, no single model of court organization typifies our state court systems.

Court officers include the court reporter, who makes and maintains verbatim records of court proceedings in courts of record. The bailiff is responsible for maintaining order in the courtroom, while the court clerk maintains the judicial calendar and serves the needs of particular judges. The prosecutor is a court officer who commences cases against particular defendants and represents the state's interests in prosecutions.

Judges at both the federal and state levels are either appointed or elected. Critics of judicial appointments cite political favoritism and corruption as reasons for rationalizing the judicial selection process. Among the many court reforms suggested over the years are appointing judges with legal expertise and law backgrounds, centralizing the trial court decision-making procedures, unifying court rules on a statewide basis, using judicial adjuncts to stimulate the processing of cases and reduce trial backlogs, and creating delay-reduction programs using community resources.

KEY TERMS

- bailiffs
- circuit courts
- community dispute resolution program
- court clerk
- court reporters
- courts of record
- exclusive jurisdiction
- federal district courts

- general jurisdiction
- harmful error
- Innovations Project
- joint trial calendar system
- judicial adjuncts
- Kales Plan
- Missouri Plan
- original jurisdiction

- prosecutor
- Randolph Plan
- reversible error
- superior court
- Supreme Court
- Texas model
- traditional model
- Virginia Plan

QUESTIONS FOR REVIEW

1. What is the jurisdiction of the United States Supreme Court? Who appoints judges to the United States Supreme Court? Can these appointments be challenged? If so, by whom?

2. Among the different federal judgeships discussed in this chapter, which ones are life appointments? How long does a district judge have to serve before retiring with full federal judge salary benefits?

3. What did the Virginia Plan provide concerning court organization?

4. Approximately how many cases does the United States Supreme Court actually hear during any given year? What proportion of cases is this in relation to the total number of cases submitted to the court for its consideration annually?

5. Why were early circuit judges known as circuit riders? Do any states have circuit judges?

6. What is the Innovations Project implemented by the Ninth Circuit Court of Appeals? What is it designed to accomplish?

7. What is the jurisdiction of the United States district courts? Can these courts hear matters having to do with copyright infringement and patent controversies?

8. What are the major differences between the Texas model of state court organization and the ABA model of 1962?

9. Describe the functions of the following court personnel: (a) court reporters, (b) court clerks, (c) bailiffs, and (d) prosecutors.

10. Do most judges have law degrees? Do most of the justices on the United States Supreme Court today have extensive backgrounds as federal or state judges?

11. What is the community dispute resolution program run by New York state officials? What are some of its objectives?

12. What is the Missouri Plan? What is its purpose? What plan preceded it?

13. What are some major court reforms to deal with trial court delays? Describe each.

14. What are so-called areas of stress between state and federal courts? Why are they called areas of stress?

15. What is a joint trial calendar? What is its purpose? Where is it used? What is its success thus far?

16. What are some of the characteristics cited by the American Judicature Society for the selection of judges?

17. What is a judicial adjunct? What functions does a judicial adjunct perform?

SUGGESTED READINGS

Kirp, David L., Mark G. Yudof, and Marlene Strong Franks (1987). *Gender justice.* Chicago: Univ. of Chicago Press.

McDonald, William F. (1983). *The defense counsel.* Beverly Hills, CA: Sage.

Thomas, Charles W., and Donna M. Bishop (1987). *Criminal law: Understanding basic principles.* Beverly Hills, CA: Sage.

Wrightsman, Lawrence, Saul M. Kassin, and Cynthia E. Willis (1987). *In the jury box: Controversies in the courtroom.* Beverly Hills, CA: Sage.

Wrightsman, Lawrence S., Cynthia E. Willis, and Saul M. Kassin (1987). *On the witness stand: Controversies in the courtroom.* Beverly Hills, CA: Sage.

Processing Defendants: More Pretrial Procedures

■ INTRODUCTION

This chapter describes the interval between arraignment and trial. Suspects charged with one or more criminal offenses may consider several pretrial options. A defense attorney represents the client's interests, while a prosecutor represents the state's interests. When suspects are arrested, bail is arranged or denied, depending upon the seriousness of the crimes alleged, the strength of the evidence, and the adequacy of the defendant's financial resources. Frequently, a defendant cannot afford bail and must remain in jail, often for prolonged periods, while awaiting trial (Lay and DeLaHunt, 1985).

The delay in jail can be lengthy. A study was conducted of felony cases processed by twenty-eight United States urban prosecutors' offices for the years 1980–1982 (including Iowa, Massachusetts, Michigan, Missouri, and Colorado). The median case processing time from arrest to final disposition ranged from 57 days to 246 days (Boland and Brady, 1985). Even under certain state speedy trial programs, delays averaging 6 months or more from arrest to final disposition are not uncommon (Langdon, 1983; Klemm, 1986). It has been found, for example, that over a third of New Jersey's felony cases were over 6 months old, while the mean case processing times were 106 days in Atlanta, Georgia, and 171 days in Oakland, California, based on studies of large samples of felony cases (Klemm, 1986; Langdon, 1983). The final disposition of a case is not necessarily a trial, however.

While some criminal defendants never have an attorney to represent them, each defendant is guaranteed access to a lawyer at every stage of the criminal proceeding

CRIME BEAT

According to several eyewitnesses, Ricardo Armstrong robbed two banks in Springfield, Ohio. He was photographed by bank cameras in the act. Armstrong was sent to jail to await trial. A cursory check of Armstrong's background showed that he worked as a custodian, had eight children, and did not possess a criminal record, but because of the evidence from bank cameras and eyewitnesses, Armstrong was denied bail. He stayed in jail for 71 days. When his case finally came to trial, the jury rapidly acquitted him. He was the wrong man and could prove that he was elsewhere when the robberies occurred. In this instance, authorities were certain that Armstrong was their man. They could see plainly the person being photographed by bank cameras; he looked just like Armstrong. On this basis, they recommended that he posed a significant public risk and recommended that he not be granted bail. Although it was determined that he was innocent of the crimes alleged, he was punished for something he had not done. He served over 2 months behind bars.

Judges have been given the discretion to jail any defendant that they believe poses a serious risk to public safety. However, many so-called public risks are likely not to be dangerous if released on their own recognizance. Confining them in jails to await trial exacerbates jail overcrowding. Furthermore, it limits their chances of assisting in their own defense, because their time with defense attorneys is limited and they cannot be free to locate persons willing to testify in their behalf. In short, deprivation of freedom prior to trial enhances the likelihood that defendants will be convicted. Should judges have this sort of discretion? How accurate are assessments of future dangerousness or risk?

under the Sixth Amendment. If a defendant cannot afford an attorney, one will be appointed at the state's expense. Arrest of a suspect does not mean prosecution of that suspect, however. In many United States jurisdictions, over half of all felony arrests are rejected by prosecutors because they lack "prosecutorial merit" (Boland and Brady, 1985).

In instances where a suspect is formally charged with a crime, a Miranda hearing is often conducted to determine if the suspect's rights were observed by the police when conducting their interrogation. This is especially crucial in cases where serious crimes are alleged and where suspects have given up the right to silence and consented to a formal interrogation. While the number of suspects who waive their rights and do not want an attorney is unknown, estimates suggest fairly large numbers (Florida Law Review, 1970; Forst, Lucianovic, and Cox, 1977).

The importance of pretrial proceedings is measured by the number of convictions obtained by prosecutors without formal trial. Although estimates vary, about 90 percent of all criminal convictions are obtained without trial (Alschuler, 1979; Mather, 1979; McDonald, 1985; Meeker, 1984; Miller, Cramer, and McDonald, 1978; Stitt and Siegel, 1986). In many of these cases, a defendant simply pleads guilty after discussing the situation with a prosecutor. In other instances, negotiations occur between a defendant's attorney and the prosecutor to work out an agreement satisfactory to both sides. The mean processing time is lengthy between the arrest and final disposition of the case to enable the prosecutor to evaluate the strength of the evidence and the probability of obtaining a conviction, if the case were to go to trial. This includes time spent conferring with defense attorneys about the disposition of the case and the defendant's feelings and intentions in the matter.

A prosecutor's reputation is measured by his convictions. United States Attorney Rudolph Giulliani, of the Southern District of New York, has gained notoriety by putting important figures behind bars, including organized crime leaders and corrupt public officials.

■ THE PROSECUTION AND ITS FUNCTIONS

Local, state, and federal prosecutors represent the government's interests whenever criminal laws are violated. When federal laws are broken the United States Attorney's Office decides which cases to prosecute and which ones lack prosecutive merit. At the state and local levels, city and county attorneys make similar decisions.

Jurisdictions vary considerably. In some states, the state supreme court appoints a state attorney general for a specified term. In Tennessee, the Tennessee Supreme Court appoints an attorney general for a term of 8 years. In New Mexico, the state attorney general is elected through a partisan election and serves one 4-year term. In other states, the attorney general is appointed by the governor. In city and county government, district attorney is often an elected position.

The functions of prosecutors at the local, state, and federal levels include, but are not limited to, the following: (1) deciding, or screening, cases slotted for prosecution, (2) representing the government in presenting cases against suspects before the grand jury, (3) conferring with police participating in the initial arrest and ensuring the suspect's right to due process, (4) evaluating the sufficiency of evidence against the accused, (5) conferring with defense attorneys in pretrial conferences in an effort to avoid a trial proceeding, and (6) presenting the case against the defendant in court.

Screening Cases

A prosecutor must look at each case in terms of how it will appear to a judge and jury if it comes to trial. This view often differs from that of arresting officers, who are directly familiar with the crime scene and the circumstances leading to a suspect's arrest. The following dialogue between an El Paso, Texas, prosecutor and an interviewer serves as an example of the process:

> *Q:* What types of things do you look for in deciding if a case should be screened out?
> *A:* We look for elements that constitute that particular penal offense.
> *Q:* What if you have an 18-year-old kid who is with his date and pulls off her underwear then she jumps out of the car screaming? What do you do with that?
> *A:* Well, it's attempted rape. But, how are you going to prove it? What were his intentions? Well, you can't prove he intended to rape her. Maybe he wanted to look at her. Attempted rape is an impossibility to make. . . . We'd probably have an assault by contact case. When it boils down to it, that's all we've got. That's assuming she'll press charges. (McDonald, 1985:41)

In that situation, the officers making the arrest at the crime scene observed the woman's torn and disheveled clothing and listened to the suspect as he made admissions to them, but the prosecutor reviewing the arrest report considers how a jury would react to the evidence presented several months after the incident. In the meantime, the woman may change her mind about prosecuting, and she may even marry the accused. The El Paso Screening Bureau, consisting of two attorneys with some trial experience and two investigators from the police department, uses as its standard of case strength whether the case can be won at trial. In that jurisdiction, the screening bureau rejects 60 percent of all cases forwarded to it (McDonald, 1985:42).

CRIME BEAT

Date rape is increasingly frequent and poses several legal issues. People who date one another often take for granted a certain amount of sexual license. Under the most innocent of circumstances, aggressive males may force themselves upon passive or submissive females, despite the females' protestations to the contrary. Afterwards, the males explain their actions by claiming that their partners were willing participants, wanted them to do it, and offered little, if any, resistance to ward off their advances.

More women annually are verbalizing their fears and frustrations, their rape experiences with persons they know and have trusted. Rape crisis centers on many college campuses report a greater incidence of date rape today than in past years. However, such rape allegations are difficult to sustain in court. Frequently, the couple had been drinking, using drugs, or both. "She gave her consent but doesn't remember" is a typical response from male defendants charged with raping their dates, and when it is disclosed that both were drinking or taking drugs, the prosecution's case is weakened considerably.

Between 90,000 and 100,000 forcible rapes are reported annually. This is believed by many experts to be only half of the actual number of rapes that occur. One reason that many rapes are not reported is that the female knows the male and is afraid that a case of rape would never hold up in court. Of the rapes that are reported, the victim knows the assailant in over a third of the cases. If the rape occurs during a dating encounter, it is quite difficult for a prosecutor to prove that the female did not consent to the male's advances. A psychologist at Auburn University, Barry Burkhart, has reported that a large proportion of women who reported being forced to have a sexual encounter avoid using the term "rape" in their account of what occurred. Only a handful of date rape victims, probably less than 5 percent, report the rape to police. What criteria should prosecutors use to differentiate between date rape and mutual consent "rough sex"?

Presenting Cases Before a Grand Jury

A prosecutor presents cases to grand juries. If a defendant waives the right to a preliminary hearing, the prosecutor must present the evidence obtained and try to obtain a true bill or an indictment from the grand jury. Of course, the prosecutor can act independently of grand jury action and secure a criminal information against the accused. This is sufficient to start proceedings that may eventually lead to trial.

Conferring with Police Concerning a Suspect's Right to Due Process

Part of the screening process of a criminal case is consulting with the arresting officers to determine the circumstances surrounding the arrest. Were the accused informed of their constitutional rights, and did the police give the suspects the Miranda warning? While a hearing on this matter may be held at a later date, the prosecutor usually conducts an independent investigation before recommending prosecution of a case.

Evaluating the Sufficiency of Evidence Against an Accused

The evidence linking a suspect with the crime itself is crucial to a successful prosecution. Sometimes the evidence against an accused is purely circumstantial. A person with a red shirt and jeans robbed a food store. He used a "silver-looking" pistol, according to eyewitnesses. Later, a suspect wearing jeans and a red shirt is stopped and

Make-my-day laws are the legislator's answer to liberal United States Supreme Court decisions that limit police discretion in combatting crime and obtaining evidence legally against criminals. Although deadly force is not justified to protect personal property, the Oklahoma legislature passed a bill in 1987 authorizing residents to kill anyone they feared might use force after entering their homes unlawfully. Such laws make screening cases for prosecution difficult, because prosecutors know that juries tend to condone defendant actions such as Bernhard Goetz's against New York Subway muggers.

questioned. The suspect is frisked, and a nickel-finished ("silver-looking") pistol is found tucked inside his belt. Although eyewitnesses can't make a positive identification of the suspect, there is circumstantial evidence connecting that suspect with the robbery.

Some suspects are homeowners who have acted to protect their property. Some states have passed "make-my-day" laws, which authorize citizens to defend their homes against persons entering unlawfully. These are difficult cases to screen and unpopular to prosecute. The jury almost always sides with the homeowner.

A prosecutor must examine all witnesses who have relevant information about the case. Will they be willing to testify in court later? Sometimes a conviction hinges on the availability or unavailability of a witness. Depending upon the sufficiency of evidence against the accused, the prosecutor either drops the case or prosecutes.

Conferring with Defense Attorneys

A suspect is entitled to certain information from the prosecution. This is known as **discovery** (*Brady v. Maryland*, 1963). For instance, a defendant is entitled to see the results of any tests conducted, including blood tests and psychiatric examinations. A defendant also has the right to see any statements that he or she made to the police at the time of arrest or during any custodial interrogation. The defense attorney will seek to obtain these discoverable materials (sometimes referred to as Brady materials). This information gives the defense attorney a more accurate picture of the state's case against the clients.

Another purpose of a pretrial conference with the defense attorney is to attempt to work out an arrangement whereby a trial can be avoided. The prosecutor may feel that the suspect is guilty of the crime alleged, based on the sufficiency of the evidence. If the evidence is strong and incriminating, the prosecutor may ask the defendant through the defendant's attorney to plead guilty to the offenses alleged. A guilty plea will save the state considerable time and expense of a trial. The prosecutor may offer leniency or a reduction in the seriousness of charge against the defendant as an inducement to plead guilty. This process is known as plea bargaining.

In any event, the prosecutor's meeting with the defense attorney is one way of testing the water. In many criminal cases, a defendant may possess information that is unknown to the prosecutor. The information and evidence may be exculpatory or favorable to the defendant. It even may support the innocence of the defendant. Witnesses unknown to the prosecution may be able to testify to the true whereabouts of the defendant at the time the offense was committed. Both the prosecution and the defense exchange limited information in an effort to work out the most equitable arrangement for everyone concerned.

A further inducement for a defendant to plead guilty, especially when the incriminating evidence is strong, is that sentences imposed after a jury trial are from two to three times as severe as those imposed by the judge after a plea of guilty and the waiver of a trial (Champion, 1987; Eisenstein and Jacob, 1977; LaFree, 1985). The message from the prosecution is, If you force us to take you to trial by pleading not guilty, prepare yourself for a stiffer sentence if you're convicted. Sometimes, this tactic works, and a defendant pleads guilty in exchange for lenient treatment by the court.

Presenting the Case Against a Defendant

A prosecutor presents the government's case against the accused in court. The responsibility includes calling witnesses who can give incriminating testimony supporting the defendant's guilt. It also involves coordinating the presentation of other relevant evidence with the detectives, police officers, and laboratory experts. In a jury trial, the prosecutor must persuade the jury that the defendant is guilty beyond a reasonable doubt. In fact, the beyond-a-reasonable-doubt standard of guilt makes the prosecutor's role especially difficult to perform. The finder of fact is the jury, who after weighing all of the evidence presented must find the evidence against defendants sufficient to support guilt beyond a reasonable doubt. In a weak case, a prosecutor must give serious thought to the jury's opinion of the evidence that will be presented. In a borderline case, the prosecutor may eventually decline to prosecute, simply because the probability of a conviction is not strong enough.

■ DEFENSE ATTORNEYS AND THEIR FUNCTIONS

A defense attorney's job is not easy. For one thing, the attorney comes into contact with every sort of unsavory criminal defendant imaginable. Burglars, child sexual abusers, murderers, rapists, robbers, drug dealers, arsonists, prostitutes, thieves, and organized crime figures appear at the defense attorney's doorstep desiring legal aid and

A DAY IN COURT

In the precedent-setting Florida case of *Gideon v. Wainwright* (1963), Mr. Gideon was charged with entering a poolroom with intent to commit a misdemeanor. Under Florida law, the offense was a felony. Mr. Gideon appeared in court without a lawyer and advised the court that he was indigent and wanted counsel. The following dialogue took place:

> *Mr. Gideon:* "The United States Supreme Court says I am entitled to be represented by counsel."
> *The Court:* "Mr. Gideon, I am sorry, but I cannot appoint counsel to represent you in this case. Under the laws of the state of Florida, the only time the court can appoint counsel to represent a defendant is when that person is charged with a capital offense. I am sorry, but I will have to deny your request to appoint counsel to defend you in this case."

Gideon went on to represent himself in a trial by jury, and he was convicted and sentenced to 5 years in the state prison. He appealed his conviction to the Florida Supreme Court, but it upheld the verdict of the lower court. Gideon then appealed to the United States Supreme Court. The justices heard the case and reversed his conviction on the grounds that he was entitled to the benefit of counsel. Among other things, the United States Supreme Court said:

> [T]he right to be heard would be, in many cases, of little avail if it did not comprehend the right to be heard by counsel. . . . [The defendant] requires the guiding hand of counsel at every step in the proceedings against him. Without it, though he be not guilty, he faces the danger of conviction because he does not know how to establish his innocence.

The United States Supreme Court decision in Gideon's case was initially interpreted by state courts as applicable to felony cases only. However, the right to counsel was eventually applied to misdemeanors, where a conviction could result in imprisonment.

In 1972, a case came before the United States Supreme Court involving another Florida defendant who was indigent, had not been represented by counsel even though he requested such representation, and had been convicted of carrying a concealed weapon (*Argersinger v. Hamlin,* 1972). The offense carried a maximum punishment of 6 months in jail and a $1,000 fine, or both, if the defendant were convicted. Argersinger was convicted by a trial judge and sentenced to 90 days in jail, but he appealed his case to the Florida Supreme Court. Again, the Florida court upheld the decision of the trial judge and held that "court-appointed counsel extends only to trials for 'non-petty offenses punishable by more than six months imprisonment.' " Again, the United States Supreme Court reversed the Florida high court stating:

> We reject . . . the premise that since prosecutions for crimes punishable by imprisonment for less than six months may be tried without a jury, they may also be tried without a lawyer . . . the requirement of counsel may well be necessary for a fair trial even in a petty-offense prosecution.

In a later Illinois case, in 1979, a defendant was tried and convicted for shoplifting goods worth less than $150, for which the statute authorized a maximum penalty of a $500 fine, 1 year in jail, or both (*Scott v. Illinois,* 1979). Scott was convicted of the offense and fined $50. He argued that he should have been represented by counsel, and thus, his conviction ought to be overturned. The United States Supreme Court reviewed his case and affirmed the decision of the Illinois high court by concluding:

> [W]e . . . hold . . . that the Sixth and Fourteenth Amendments to the United States Constitution require only that no indigent criminal defendant be *sentenced to a term of imprisonment unless the State has afforded him the right to assistance of appointed counsel in his defense.* (Emphasis mine)

Therefore, in instances where petty offenses are alleged, an indigent defendant is entitled to court-appointed counsel only if the possible sentence includes imprisonment.

assistance. In spite of the crime alleged against a defendant, however, every defendant facing felony charges or misdemeanors where imprisonment is a possible penalty is entitled to the benefit of counsel, whether he or she can afford it or not (*Argersinger v. Hamlin,* 1972; *Baldasar v. Illinois,* 1980; *Gideon v. Wainwright,* 1963). While federal courts have always complied with the Sixth Amendment and provided an attorney if a defendant could not afford one, this has not always been the case in the various states.

In a case where a defendant is indigent and cannot afford an attorney, a defense lawyer is appointed by the court. Such a defense attorney is a **public defender.** Each jurisdiction has different arrangements for providing counsel to indigent defendants. In some communities, for instance, courts require attorneys to allocate a certain amount of their time each year to representing indigent clients. These attorneys sometimes perform the defense services without remuneration from the government or other sources. More frequently, however, nominal sums are provided these attorneys. Other communities have public defender offices, where attorneys are employed on a full-time basis. Their exclusive role is to provide legal counsel to all indigent defendants. In yet other jurisdictions, attorneys volunteer as counsels for indigents, and they rotate with other attorney/volunteers as their caseloads vary.

Sometimes, indigent defendants turn to legal aid clinics for assistance. These agencies and organizations are usually operated by persons less trained in legal fundamentals than bona fide attorneys, and they are frequently staffed by law students in their last years of legal training, performing under the direction or supervision of a court-approved attorney. Often, public defenders are new attorneys looking for legal experience. Typically, they are not paid well, and as a result, their motivation to assist criminal defendants may not be as strong as it should be. Some evidence suggests that a privately obtained attorney, compared with a court-appointed one, will do a better defensive job, although the defendant's prior record and the seriousness of the offenses alleged seem more influential in sentencing severity than does attorney quality (Champion, 1987; Willison, 1984).

Criminal defense attorneys work diligently to convince juries of their clients' innocence. Indigent, as well as wealthy, defendants are entitled to competent attorney services. Defendants must be presumed innocent until proven guilty beyond a reasonable doubt by convincing prosecution evidence. Jurors must remain impartial and weigh the evidence presented by both sides.

In legal circles, criminal lawyers are often the targets of criticism by their attorney peers. In particularly brutal murder or rape cases, for instance, or in cases where severe bodily injury has resulted from a criminal offense, defense attorneys who agree to handle the case for the defendant often are asked, How can you defend those people? (Kunen, 1983). Some attorneys reject requests from alleged drug dealers to represent them in court. Many attorneys avoid criminal work altogether.

The major function of a criminal defense attorney is to secure the best possible disposition of a case for the clients. This means either (1) to represent the clients and convince a judge or jury of the accused's innocence if the case goes to trial or (2) to secure the best possible bargain with government representatives for the client in terms of dismissal of all charges, a light sentence, probation, or a general mitigation of punishment associated with the offenses alleged.

To accomplish any of these feats, the attorney must resort to investigative tactics practiced by detectives and police. Defense attorneys should contact all prospective witnesses for the government as well as those supporting their client's case. In short, defense attorneys must place themselves in the place of prosecutor and attempt to formulate a picture of the case from their standpoint. Only then will certain flaws emerge which are crucial to either side. Interviewing witnesses for either the prosecution or defense will lead to disclosures which were unknown earlier to either side. Inconsistencies in recollections will be detected, and the defense attorney will acquire a better grasp of the entire affair.

Sometimes, criminal defense attorneys encourage their clients to persist in a not guilty plea if the case against the client is weak. This is a form of bluffing, and it is practiced by both sides. Frequently, prosecutors drop charges against a criminal defendant at the last minute. Some prosecutors have gone so far as to impanel a jury before dropping a case. This tactic is a means of frightening a defendant into a plea of guilty (McDonald, 1985:50–51).

Some criminal cases do not lend themselves to plea bargaining. Attempted assassinations of United States presidents result in sensational trials. Would-be assassin John Hinckley was prosecuted for the carnage he wrought by attempting to assassinate President Ronald Reagan. His insanity plea earned him a jury acquittal.

■ ALTERNATIVES TO CRIMINAL COURT

Between the time a person is arrested, formally charged with a crime, arraigned before a judge or magistrate, enters a plea, has a trial date determined, and actually goes to trial, a number of things usually happen behind the scenes. Exchanges of information occur between the prosecutor, the prosecutor's staff, and the defendant's attorney. Assuming the prosecutor intends to prosecute the defendant (that is, in the prosecutor's view, the evidence against the defendant is likely to result in a conviction if the case comes to trial), the defendant's attorney attempts to convince the prosecutor to drop or at least reduce the severity of the charges (Adams, 1983).

Some of the alternatives to a formal criminal trial include (1) police cautioning, (2) diversion to a civil court, (3) pretrial diversion, and (4) plea bargaining.

Police Cautioning

Police cautioning is verbally warning an alleged offender of further police action and the certainty of prosecution if the offender commits additional offenses (Marshall et al., 1985). Such a tactic is often useful in reprimanding those caught committing petty crimes, such as voyeurism or soliciting a prostitute.

In jurisdictions where court dockets are overcrowded and prosecutors must heavily weigh the cases that they will prosecute and which cases they will drop, police cautioning may be in order. Of course, this alternative almost always applies to minor offenses, with some exceptions. For instance, a person was arrested for using cocaine at a small party. Others were arrested including the cocaine supplier. However, the police cautioned the cocaine user, permitting her to go free with the stern warning that if she is caught using cocaine again or possessing it, she will be arrested and prosecuted.

Diversion to a Civil Court

Some offenses are on a fine line between civil and criminal violations. For instance, assault and battery is considered a tort in every jurisdiction. It is any unlawful touching of another which is without justification or excuse (Black, 1979). **Assault** may be a verbal threat of harm, whereas **battery** is actual harmful contact with another. Assault and battery is also a crime, although the wording varies between states. Usually, the distinction is *aggravated* assault and battery for the criminal classification.

If two or more persons get into a fight, either person may charge the other with assault and battery. If the charge is filed with the police department and a warrant alleging assault and battery is issued, the person named in the warrant will be arrested and charged with the crime of aggravated assault and battery. A prosecutor may recommend the charge be changed to simple assault and battery and transferred from criminal to civil court, where it can be dealt with as a tort. In that situation, the plaintiffs will not be seeking the defendant's imprisonment, but rather they will seek damages, usually a sum of money for injuries sustained. Transferring the case from criminal to civil status keeps the defendant from acquiring a criminal record and alleviates an already crowded criminal court docket.

Fraud is another tort that is also classified as a crime. Again, there is the prosecutorial option of transferring the case from the criminal court to civil jurisdiction in order to prevent the defendant from possibly acquiring a criminal record.

Pretrial Diversion

Pretrial diversion is a procedure where criminal defendants are diverted to either a community-based agency for treatment or assigned to a counselor for social or psychiatric assistance (President's Commission on Law Enforcement and the Administration of Justice, 1967). Pretrial diversion may involve education, job training, counseling, or some type of psychological or physical therapy (Nardulli, 1979; Zemans, 1979:40).

A pretrial diversion disposition of a criminal case removes the case from the criminal justice system temporarily. For instance, those who have been arrested for **driving under the influence (DUI)** or child sexual abuse involving family members may be granted pretrial diversion by the prosecutor rather than going through a trial and admitting their guilt publicly.

Usually, a pretrial diversion involves a number of conditions. A person with a pending DUI charge may have to attend Alcoholics Anonymous meetings regularly for a year. The person also may have to attend a course in driver's training and see films about the hazards of driving while intoxicated. Child sexual abusers may be required to undergo intensive psychiatric therapy, and their families may have to become actively involved in the recovery program. Usually, if the conditions of the pretrial diversion are complied with, the criminal charges are dropped. In some jurisdictions, the record of the arrest is ordered expunged, or deleted permanently from police files as though it never existed.

Unless the crimes alleged are particularly serious, prosecutors usually try to keep first offenders out of prison. Not all first offenders are considered eligible for pretrial diversion programs, however. Usually, **screening** occurs, whereby the prosecutor evaluates the suitability of a particular alleged offender for pretrial diversion. Does the person have a prior criminal record? Is the person employed? Does the person otherwise have a good reputation in the community? Is the offense inconsistent with the person's character? Did extraneous variables contribute to the offender's conduct, such as financial hardship, divorce, loss of a family member, or some other emotionally traumatic event?

If a defendant is recommended for pretrial diversion, the court must approve the diversion and assign the offender to the supervision of an appropriate agency or service for a specified period. If an offender fails to comply with the terms of the diversionary program, the offender's status reverts to whatever it was when the pretrial diversion was granted. The prosecution of the case will proceed. The importance of pretrial diversion cannot be underestimated. It is designed to help a defendant avoid the criminal label and further involvement in the justice system.

Pretrial diversion is not without its critics, however. Implicit in any pretrial diversionary program is an admission of guilt by a defendant to the particular crime alleged. Technically, a courtroom appearance is avoided (not always), and the defendant must comply with certain terms and conditions for a fixed period. At the end of the diversion period, defendants may have their records expunged, provided they complied with the provisions of the diversion. Diversion is often used for juvenile offenders as well.

Plea Bargaining

The most popular pretrial alternative is plea bargaining. Plea bargaining or plea negotiating is defined as a preconviction bargain between the state and accused whereby the defendant exchanges a plea of guilty or nolo contendere for a reduction in charges, a promise of sentencing leniency, or some other concession from full, maximum implementation of the conviction and sentencing authority of the court (McDonald, 1985:5). The defendant enters a guilty plea with the reasonable expectation of receiving some consideration from the state (McDonald, 1985:6).

Plea bargaining is not new. Evidence of its use can be traced to the twelfth century (Alschuler, 1979). Plea bargaining is so pervasive in the United States today that many persons regard it as a standard feature of our criminal justice system (Alschuler, 1979; Heuman, 1978; Stitt and Siegel, 1986). At the local, state, and federal levels, 80 percent to 90 percent of all criminal convictions are obtained through plea bargaining (Mather, 1979; Maynard, 1982; Miller, Cramer, and McDonald, 1978).

Plea bargaining is controversial. It is regarded as a time-saving device by its supporters. It is viewed as a denial of due process by its opponents. Some states, including Alaska, have prohibited its use altogether in the settlement of criminal cases, although most other states and the federal government condone it (Alschuler, 1979; Bell, 1984; Church, 1979; Iowa Law Review, 1975; Parnas and Atkins, 1978; Rubin and White, 1979; Stitt and Siegel, 1986).

If a defendant pleads guilty to certain criminal charges, the state is spared the time and expense of a trial. In fact, as an inducement to plead guilty where the prosecution has substantial evidence against an accused, there is evidence to indicate that if the defendant were to persist in a not guilty plea and eventually be convicted by the judge or jury at trial, the sentence will be more severe than that proposed by the earlier plea bargain agreement from the prosecution (Eisenstein and Jacob, 1977; Nardulli, 1978; Tiffany, Avichai, and Peters, 1975).

Plea bargaining was officially condoned by the United States Supreme Court in the landmark case of *Brady v. United States* (1970). Brady and a codefendant were charged with kidnapping in violation of 18 United States Code, Section 1201(a). Since the indictment charged that the victim of the kidnapping was not liberated unharmed, Brady faced the maximum penalty of death if the verdict of the jury should so recommend. The trial judge was reluctant to try the case without a jury, and in the meantime, a codefendant pleaded guilty and was available to testify against Brady. Brady entered a guilty plea and was subsequently sentenced to 30 years in prison.

In 1967, Brady petitioned the United States Supreme Court contending that his plea was not voluntary, because government prosecutors put much pressure upon him to plead guilty. The Supreme Court upheld the original verdict and said, "Although Brady's plea of guilty may well have been motivated in part by his desire to avoid a possible death penalty, we are convinced that his plea was voluntary and intelligently made and we have no reason to doubt that his solemn admission of guilt was truthful." In that same case, the Supreme Court declared:

> We cannot hold that it is unconstitutional for the State to extend a benefit to a defendant who in turn extends a substantial benefit to the State and who demonstrates by his plea that he is ready and willing to admit his crime and to enter the correctional system in a frame of mind that affords hope for success in rehabilitation over a shorter period of time than might otherwise be necessary.

Another important case was *North Carolina v. Alford* (1970). Alford was charged with first degree murder, a capital crime in North Carolina at that time. Considerable evidence existed against him. Although Alford protested his innocence, his attorney advised Alford to enter a plea of guilty to second-degree murder, which carried a maximum incarcerative penalty of 20 years. Although continuing to maintain his innocence, Alford entered a guilty plea to second-degree murder and was sentenced to 20 years' imprisonment. Subsequently, Alford sought relief from a court of appeals, arguing that his plea was not voluntary. Rather, he entered the plea in order to escape the death penalty that might have been imposed had he been tried on the first-degree murder charge and found guilty. The court of appeals believed Alford, and overturned his conviction for second-degree murder on the ground that he was coerced into a guilty plea because of the possible imposition of the death penalty. The state of North Carolina appealed, and the United States Supreme Court heard the case.

The Supreme Court reversed the court of appeals, reasoning that Alford was not unconstitutionally coerced into the plea of guilty to second-degree murder. Despite his protestations of innocence, the overwhelming evidence against him suggested that a trial on the first-degree murder charge would have resulted in a verdict of guilty. Thus, Alford had nothing to gain through a trial, but he had much to gain by pleading guilty to a reduced murder charge.

In later years, the Supreme Court has extended to the government wide discretion in the kinds of pressures it may exert on defendants if they do not agree to plea bargain with the government (*Bordenkircher v. Hayes,* 1978; *Santobello v. New York,* 1971). In the case of *Bordenkircher v. Hayes* (1978), the Supreme Court said, "The disposition of criminal charges by agreement between the prosecutor and the accused, sometimes loosely called 'plea bargaining,' is an essential component of the administration of justice. Properly administered, it is to be encouraged."

The frequency of the use of plea bargaining in contrast with taking a case to trial is about four to one (Boland and Forst, 1985; McDonald, 1985). This ratio varies from one jurisdiction to the next and when misdemeanor cases are compared with felony cases. In a study of the misdemeanor disposition process in the municipal courts of Philadelphia, Pennsylvania, one fifth of all misdemeanor dispositions and one half of all guilty verdicts resulted from genuine adversarial trials (Schulhofer, 1985). An examination of 600 misdemeanor cases showed that even routine misdemeanor cases benefit from guarantees of fairness and accuracy afforded by trial. In many other jurisdictions, however, felony as well as misdemeanor convictions from trials are proportionately few in number compared with convictions obtained through plea bargaining (Bell, 1984; Farr, 1984; Stitt and Siegel, 1986).

There are four different systems of plea bargaining in the United States. One system is **implicit plea bargaining,** where a defendant pleads guilty in the expectation of receiving a more lenient sentence. The second is **charge reduction bargaining,** where a prosecutor downgrades the charges in return for a defendant's guilty plea. A third is **judicial plea bargaining,** where the judge offers a specific guilty plea sentence. And the fourth is **sentence recommendation plea bargaining,** where the prosecutor proposes a sentence in exchange for a guilty plea (Padgett, 1985). A plea-bargain agreement may contain promises or provisons for a reduction in charges, leniency in sentencing or recommendation for a specific type of sentence, and proposals *not* to prosecute the defendant for other crimes alleged or seek enhancement of punishment.

Historically, some form of plea bargaining has always been observed in the United States. Plea bargaining occurred in the colonies for many years. After the United States was established, various state courts gradually incorporated plea bargaining into their justice systems. In New York state, for instance, only 22 percent of all criminal convictions for the entire state in 1839 were obtained through plea bargaining. By 1869, this figure rose to 70 percent, and by 1920, it had reached 88 percent (McDonald, 1985:3).

However, federal court rules are not binding on state courts. For instance, the rules governing plea bargaining in federal district courts are not constitutionally mandated for state courts. The United States Supreme Court has held that the rule relating to the acceptance of guilty pleas is a federal procedural rule to be observed scrupulously by the federal courts, but the precise terms of this rule are not constitutionally applicable to state courts (*Roddy v. Black,* 1975; *Osborne v. Thompson,* 1979; *Neeley v. Duckworth,* 1979; *Winegar v. Corrections Dept.,* 1975). Most states use plea bargaining, however, and some states have copied the rules followed by federal district courts into their own plea agreement procedures.

The most prevalent plea bargaining systems offer charge reduction and leniency in sentencing recommendations in exchange for a defendant's plea of guilty, but the final arbiter in a plea bargaining agreement in every jurisdiction is the judge. Judges are not bound to observe the conditions of any plea agreement. Usually, they approve the plea agreement between the prosecution and defense, but they reserve the right to reject the plea agreement as well. Also, they may decide to impose maximum sentences and fines upon a defendant who pleads guilty, in spite of the fact that a prosecutor's recommendation favors milder sanctions or even probation (Littrell, 1979; Nagel, 1982).

Federal prosecutors are limited to four possible concessions in a plea bargain agreement. First, the charge may be reduced to a lesser or related offense. Second, the attorney for the government may promise to move for dismissal of other charges. Third, the attorney for the government may agree to recommend or at least not oppose a particular sentence. And fourth, the attorneys for the government and the defense may agree that a given sentence is appropriate for the case.

Figure 10.1 is an example of an actual plea bargain agreement between the United States Attorney's Office and a defendant in the Eastern District of Tennessee. In this plea agreement, the United States Attorney at that time, John H. Cary, and Assistant United States Attorneys J. Michael Haynes and Edward Wilson offered a defendant in

United States Department of Justice

UNITED STATES ATTORNEY
EASTERN DISTRICT OF TENNESSEE
~~XXXXXXXXXXXXXXXXXXX~~ P.O. Box 872
KNOXVILLE, TENNESSEE ~~XXXXX~~ 37901
July 15,

IN REPLY, PLEASE
REFER TO FILE NO.

Dear

        RE:

        On May 2,   , Ed Wilson and I met with
regarding a proposed plea bargain for the captioned individual. Due
to your absence from the office the original deadline for acceptance
was informally extended "until you had time to discuss the situation
with   ". To date, I have not heard anything relative to
acceptance or rejection.

        As we are now prepared to begin Grand Jury proceedings
in the immediate future on this matter which will involve calling a
number of witnesses from various parts of the country at significant
expense to the Government, I wanted to clarify our offer and set a
firm deadline for action.

        We believe that Mr.   violated 18 U.S.C.   and
as the result of his purchasing, transporting and subsequently
selling certain stolen   begining in the summer of   . This
Office has proposed the following plea bargain which if accepted
would be followed by the filing of an information and subsequent
presentation of the plea bargain to Judge Taylor for approval.
This offer is also contingent upon a proffer by you of your client's
testimony regarding this matter and which, if acceptable to us, would
be followed by the following plea bargain presentation to the Court:

1) $10,000 fine
2) Three year probation (payment of fine condition thereto)
3) Furnish detailed account of his dealings with the
   stolen   to FBI
4) No   prosecution
5) Immunity for any further violations arising from
   transactions from June,   , to date of information.
   (Please note as I have advised you earlier this is not
   as broad as the "transactional immunity" previously
   discussed with Mr.   on May 2nd.)

        If in fact the case is going to be plea bargained, it must
be done so before the Government incurs additional significant expense.
Therefore, I am placing a deadline of July 31,   , on the offer. If
the bargain is not accepted by the end of that date, it will be withdrawn
and terminated. Please discuss this matter with Mr.   and advise
us of your decision.

                  Very truly yours,

                  JOHN H. CARY
                  United States Attorney

                  BY: J. MICHAEL HAYNES
                  Assistant United States Attorney

JMH:sjv

FIGURE 10.1 Federal Plea Bargain Agreement

a criminal prosecution involving several counts of interstate transportation of stolen property and conspiracy a number of concessions in exchange for a guilty plea. The total fines and maximum statutory imprisonment for the original charges totaled $285,000 and 45 years.

In exchange for a plea of guilty to one count of interstate transportation of stolen property having a value in excess of $5,000, the government offered the following plea bargain: (1) the defendant must pay a $10,000 fine; (2) the defendant must accept a 3-year probation term; (3) the defendant must testify against a codefendant in a later trial; (4) the defendant must disclose all transactional details of the stolen property matter; (5) there would be no further prosecution of the defendant for any of the other charges; and (6) the defendant would receive immunity from prosecution for any further violations arising from the original transactions (such as receiving and concealing stolen property, and selling stolen property). In this case, the defendant rejected the plea agreement, went to trial twice in the federal district court (the first trial resulted in a hung jury and a mistrial was declared), and was subsequently acquitted of all charges. The codefendant was offered a similar plea bargain agreement, accepted it, and served 1 year in a medium-security federal prison.

Because a number of important constitutional rights are waived whenever a defendant elects to enter a guilty plea, both federal and state trial courts have been increasingly interested in ensuring that defendants' due process rights are fully observed. When the courts or prosecutors violate one or more of these rights defendants have grounds to appeal to a higher court and obtain reversal of the original conviction.

While state and local trial courts are not bound to comply strictly with the same plea bargaining rules governing federal trial judges and these same courts are not bound to accept plea bargaining in any form as an alternative to trial, these courts are bound to observe defendants' constitutional rights. Constitutional rights override and take precedence over local and state procedures. These rights are guaranteed to every citizen under the Fifth, Sixth, and Fourteenth Amendments of the United States Constitution (*United States v. French,* 1983; *United States v. Carter,* 1981; *Clemmons v. United States,* 1983).

Since the rules followed by federal district judges in plea bargain agreements and the general plea agreement procedure encompass all of a citizen's rights in this regard, it is helpful to examine the substance of these rules. Under the provisions of 18 U.S.C., Rule 11 (1989), whenever a defendant enters a plea of guilty or nolo contendere, a judge must address the defendant personally in open court, informing the defendant of and determining if the defendant understands the following:

1. The nature of the charge(s) to which the plea is offered.
2. The maximum possible penalty provided by law.
3. The mandatory minimum penalty as provided by law.
4. The effect of any special parole term and any special provisions for compensating victims.
5. That a defendant who does not have an attorney has a right to one; and if the defendant cannot afford an attorney, one will be appointed at state expense.
6. That the defendant has the right to plead not guilty and to withdraw a guilty plea at any time.

7. That the defendant has the right to a trial by jury and the right to the assistance of counsel at the trial.
8. That the defendant has the right to confront and cross-examine prosecution witnesses.
9. That the defendant has the right not to incriminate himself or herself.
10. That if the plea of guilty or nolo contendere is accepted, there will be no further trial of any kind; therefore, the plea is a waiver of the right to a trial.
11. That there is a factual basis for the plea.
12. That the plea is voluntarily given and that it is not the result of force, threats, or coercion apart from a plea agreement.
13. That the judge may accept or reject the plea agreement.
14. That the plea is accurate.
15. If the plea is the result of prior discussions between prosecutors and defendants or their attorney.

As specified in 18 U.S.C., Rule 11 (1989), the district judge is prohibited from participating in the plea agreement negotiations between the prosecution and defense. This prohibition protects a defendant from the possibility of a conflict of interest arising from the federal judges' being faced with approving or disapproving a plea agreement that he or she helped to formulate.

All plea agreement hearings and proceedings are recorded. This is a requirement in the event that a defendant wishes to appeal the decision of the trial judge or any portion of the plea agreement to a higher court on various legal grounds. For example, some defendants have appealed to higher courts on the ground that the federal judge did not advise them of all their rights as literally stated in 18 U.S.C., Rule 11 (1989) (*United States v. Thompson,* 1982; *United States v. Cooper,* 1984).

In the Illinois case of *United States v. Thompson* (1982), Thompson claimed in his appeal that the district judge had failed to read verbatim the admonitions for federal judges to follow as set forth by 18 U.S.C., Rule 11 (1989). The United States Supreme Court affirmed Thompson's conviction and held:

> This rule should not be read as requiring litany, or any other ritual which can be carried out by word-for-word adherence as to set script, but rather, it is sufficient if colloquy between the court and the defendant would lead a reasonable person to believe that the defendant understood the nature of the charge.

However, in the 1981 Arkansas case of *United States v. Riegelsperger,* the district judge asked general questions about whether threats or promises had been made, but the judge failed to advise the defendant, Riegelsperger, that the court was not obligated to follow the plea agreement. The judge also failed to ask if the guilty plea was the result of prior discussions between the prosecution and defense. The United States Supreme Court reversed Riegelsperger's conviction on these grounds and sent the case back to the lower court for further processing. At least for the federal judiciary, these rules are extremely important, and everything in these rules pertaining to a defendant's constitutional rights is critical in all state trial courts where plea agreements are arranged.

In state and local trial courts where plea bargaining is permitted, there is considerable interjurisdictional variation in plea agreement hearings as well as in the procedures followed by prosecutors in configuring plea bargains initially. In some jurisdictions, prosecutors engage in overcharging criminal defendants (Baldwin and McConville, 1977:112; McDonald, 1985:20; Utz, 1979:105). **Overcharging** is filing charges against a defendant more serious than the ones the prosecutor believes are justified by the evidence and charging more counts or more serious counts than those on which the prosecutor wants a conviction (Bond, 1981:231; Utz, 1979:105). Overcharging is a crude form of blackmail (Alschuler, 1968). A defendant facing many charges often feels relieved when the prosecution offers to drop all but one in exchange for a guilty plea. The prosecutor's original intention may have been to secure a guilty plea to the single charge anyway (Holten and Jones, 1982).

The American Bar Association (1971) and the American Law Institute (1975) have outlined some of the ethical obligations of prosecutors relating to overcharging. Some of these obligations are that (1) it is unprofessional conduct for a prosecutor to institute criminal charges against someone without probable cause, (2) the prosecutor is not obligated to present all of the charges the evidence might support, (3) the prosecutor should not bring or seek charges greater in number or degree than he or she can reasonably support at trial with evidence, (4) he or she should not seek to obtain a plea of guilty or nolo contendere by charging or threatening to charge a defendant with a crime not supported by the facts believed by the prosecutor to be provable, and (5) charging or threatening to charge a defendant with a crime not ordinarily charged in the jurisdiction for the conduct allegedly engaged in. While overcharging probably occurs in all United States jurisdictions, some critics have cautioned that more often than not, overcharging is a misnomer. This is because the defendant has, in fact, committed all of the crimes alleged (McDonald, 1985), but overcharging does pressure a defendant into more serious consideration of pleading guilty to at least one of the offenses alleged.

The plea bargaining process proceeds unevenly from one jurisdiction to the next. In one jurisdiction, defense attorneys may routinely approach prosecutors with offers from their clients. In another jurisdiction, prosecutors make the initial offers. In a study of dialogues occurring between prosecutors and defense attorneys, it was found that out of the fifty-two cases studied, twenty-seven were settled when one party took a position (made an offer) with which the other aligned (Maynard, 1984). Another twenty-two cases were settled when one party aligned with the other's position after both parties advanced a position. Only three cases were settled by compromise between the two parties' positions.

Some cities have used **criminal bench trials,** where the state promises to drop charges or reduce sentences if defendants waive the right to have a jury determine their guilt (*University of Pennsylvania Law Review,* 1984). While this practice has been challenged as unconstitutional, it continues to be used in a limited number of jurisdictions with results that have significantly shortened case processing time.

Extensive studies of plea bargaining have been made in jurisdictions such as El Paso, Texas; New Orleans, Louisiana; Seattle, Washington; Tucson, Arizona; and Norfolk, Virginia (McDonald, 1985). It has been found that many local and state jurisdictions violate defendants' Constitutional rights regularly, and these violations occur with little or no resistance from the defendants involved.

 **CRIME BEAT**

Some field notes from Norfolk (Virginia) District Court are particularly illuminating. The following cases are considered typical:

Case 1
Charge: Soliciting.
Do you want your case heard today? "Yes."
Rights: Signed waiver of attorney form.
Facts: Police stated the facts.
Sentence: $100 fine.
Time elapsed: 1 minute.

Case 2
Charge: Drunk and disorderly.
Do you want your case heard today? "Yes."
Rights: Signed waiver of attorney form.
Facts: None; no police officer present.
Sentence: $10 and 10 days suspended on good behavior.
Time elapsed: 1 minute.

Case 3
Charge: Possession of drugs.
Do you want your case heard today? "Yes."
Rights: Signed waiver of attorney form.
Facts: Police state the amount.
Sentence: $25 fine.
Time elapsed: 1 minute.

Case 4
Charge: Drunk in public (ten defendants brought into court at same time).
How do you plead? "Guilty."
Rights: None; did not sign waiver of attorney form.

Facts: None.
Sentence: $10.
Note: The judge told this group of defendants that the fine was $10 whether they plead guilty or went to trial.
Time elapsed: 1 minute.

A summary of field observations for the Norfolk District Court follows:

1. No constitutional rights were recited to the defendant.
2. The defendant is not asked if he understands the rights that he is giving up. He simply signs a waiver of attorney form. In most cases, the defendant doesn't even bother to read the form.
3. The defendant is not asked if he is pleading guilty because he is in fact guilty.
4. In many cases no factual basis for the plea is presented.
5. The defendant was not asked if anyone threatened, coerced, or pressured him into pleading.
6. The judge did not specify what maximum sentence was permissible by law.
7. No collateral consequences of the plea were noted.

When the researcher asked the judge about all of these problems, the judge replied, "They are usually so happy that they don't have a felony conviction or that they don't have to go to jail, that they don't care." (McDonald, 1985)

In many jurisdictions, defendants merely sign a waiver form or a plea agreement initialing each right waived. Figure 10.2 shows a standard plea agreement form used by local judges in criminal district courts in New Orleans, Louisiana.

While district judge participation is prohibited in federal plea bargaining negotiations, it is not necessarily prohibited in all state and local jurisdictions. In Tennessee, all state trial judges follow the federal rules rigidly, having adopted them into their rules of criminal procedure. In other states and jurisdictions where plea bargaining occurs, however, trial judges sometimes take part in plea-bargain proceedings (Alschuler, 1976; Ryan and Alfini, 1978). In spite of the obvious conflict of interest problems created by such judicial participation, these jurisdictions continue to condone it.

In view of the wide variation in plea bargaining practices nationwide, the fact that plea bargaining has been banned in some jurisdictions, and present efforts to ban it in others, this controversial practice has both strengths and weaknesses. On the positive side, plea bargaining (1) saves a defendant time and money for attorneys' fees, (2) saves the

FIGURE 10.2 Guilty Plea Acceptance Form for New Orleans, Louisiana: Alternative Procedure for Accepting Guilty Pleas Used by Local Judges

```
                              CRIMINAL DISTRICT COURT
                                 PARISH OF ORLEAN
                                STATE OF LOUISIANA
                                   SECTION "D"

                                  JUDGE: FRANK A. MARULLO, JR.

   STATE OF LOUISIANA
          VS.                          NO. _____

   _____            VIO: _____

                               PLEA OF GUILTY

        I, _____, defendant in the above case

   informed the Court that I wanted to plead guilty and do plead guilty to the crime of

   _____ and have been informed and understand the charge to which

   I am pleading guilty. (_____)

   The acts which make up the crime to which I am pleading have been explained to me as well

   as the fact that for this crime I could possibly receive a sentence of _____.

   (_____)

        I understand that in pleading guilty in this matter I waive the following rights:

        (1)   To a trial by either a judge or a jury and that further the right to a
              trial by judge extends until the first witness is sworn, and the right
              to a trial by jury extends until the first juror is sworn, and if
              convicted the right to an appeal.
              Please specify: Judge trial or Jury trial          (_____)

        (2)   To face and cross-examine the witnesses who
              accuse me of the crime charged.                    (_____)

        (3)   The privilege against self-incrimination or
              having to take the stand myself and testify.       (_____)

        (4)   To have the Court compel my witness to
              appear and testify.                                (_____)

        I am entering a plea of guilty to this crime because I am, in fact, guilty of this

   crime.  I have not been forced, threatened, or intimidated into making this plea, nor has

   anyone made me promises in order that I enter a plea.  I am fully satisfied with the

   handling of my case by my attorney and the way in which he has represented me.  I am

   satisfied with the way the Court has handled this matter.  (_____)


                                             _____
                                             DEFENDANT

   _____
   JUDGE

                                             _____
                                             ATTORNEY FOR DEFENDANT

                                             DATE: _____

            NOTE:     Defendant is to place his initials in the
                      blocks provided for same.
                      Defendant is to block out Judge trial or
                      Jury trial as it applies.
```

state the considerable time and expense of a trial proceeding, (3) makes it possible for prosecutors and defense attorneys alike to handle more cases annually and dispose of more cases with results favorable to both sides, (4) permits the state to deal in trial proceedings with more serious cases warranting more time and attention, and (5) increases the likelihood for leniency toward a defendant for cooperating with the government (Stitt and Siegel, 1986; Wheatley, 1974). On the negative side, critics argue that plea bargaining (1) deprives a defendant of the right to a trial and to due process, (2) results in shortchanging the justice system by depriving society of just and equitable retribution against offenders who are offered leniency when their punishments should be more severe, (3) is inherently coercive in view of the implied coercion from prosecutors through overcharging, (4) involves self-incrimination in direct violation of the Fifth Amendment, (5) is a violation of the ethics attorneys abide by in their professional work, and (6) often induces guilty pleas from innocent defendants.

Interactions in court between prose-cutors, defense attorneys, and judges are not always amiable. Each side seeks to discredit the other. Often, victims themselves are targets of sexual or racial slurs from opposing attorneys. Two black henchmen of a New York City landlord slashed the face of white, 25-year-old model Marla Hanson with razor blades when she asked for the return of her security deposit on an apartment she had rented. She had resisted the landlord's sexual advances and was later humiliated in court by several derogatory sexual slurs. Her ordeal caused New York Mayor Edward Koch to ask in outrage, "How many times must a victim be victimized?"

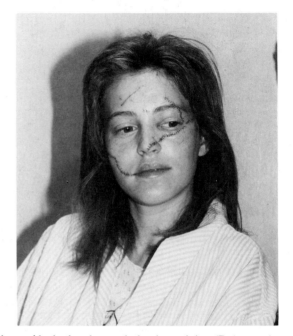

Among other states and jurisdictions, Alaska has banned plea bargaining (Rubenstein and White, 1979). This has effectively eliminated sentence bargaining, where the prosecutor could offer a reduced sentence or no sentence at all. Alaska currently follows what is known as **presumptive sentencing,** where statutes prescribe a specific punishment range for each offense. For example, a conviction for some offense may carry a 5-year prison term. The judge is permitted to vary this term between 4 years and 6 years, depending upon the mitigating or aggravating circumstances of the particular case. A mitigating circumstance might be that the person is elderly. Aggravating circumstances might be that serious bodily harm was inflicted during the commission of the crime or that a firearm was used.

However, Alaska prosecutors have sidestepped the plea-bargaining ban by negoti-ating with defense attorneys about the nature of charges against their clients. Aggravated assault and battery might be reduced to simple assault, for example, if the defendant pleads guilty to that particular offense. Thus, charge bargaining continues in many jurisdictions, including Alaska, and little, if anything, can be done about that. The types and numbers of charges brought against a particular defendant are ordinarily within the discretionary powers of the prosecutors and police.

In all plea-agreement hearings, a judge presides and assesses the fairness of the agreement under the circumstances of the case. From various studies of this process, disparities exist in the judicial supervision of the plea-agreement proceeding. Having a defendant sign a form such as that shown in Figure 10.2, for instance, is not a sufficient guarantee that the defendant realizes fully the rights being relinquished. Furthermore, in that particular form, no provision exists for determining the factual basis for the original guilty plea. Finally, a defendant is signing away the right to an appeal. This is in spite of the fact that certain procedural irregularities might otherwise void the guilty plea.

There is a general national trend toward greater use of plea bargaining, particularly in felony cases. In California, for example, approximately 70 percent of convicted felony offenders are placed on probation rather than incarcerated (Petersilia, 1985). It is important to recognize for the moment that probation is used increasingly as an incentive for alleged offenders to plead guilty (Rosett and Cressey, 1976). Many of the offenses committed by defendants who are eventually placed on probation and not incarcerated are nonviolent and petty crimes, such as theft or burglary.

In situations where the crimes alleged involve aggravating circumstances, such as armed robbery, forcible rape, and homicide, the likelihood for probation is remote. Much of what happens to offenders when they enter the criminal justice system depends on what is occurring in other parts of the system, especially corrections. When prisons are overcrowded and cannot accommodate growing numbers of convicts annually, different sentencing alternatives are more likely to be considered. The plea-bargain phase considers such corrections factors as well as the crime seriousness and the prior record and age of the defendant.

■ SUMMARY

Prosecutors perform many functions, including representing the state when persons are charged with criminal offenses. Prosecutors initially screen cases to determine which ones have prosecutive merit. Like detectives, they evaluate the sufficiency of evidence against the accused and determine the probability of guilt or innocence. Prosecutors represent the state before the grand jury and present evidence of an alleged offender's guilt. They also present the case for the government in a formal trial if the case reaches that stage.

A defense attorney confers with the prosecution and determines the nature of the case against an accused. Defense attorneys attempt to prevent prosecution of their clients, conferring with prosecutors and perhaps working out plea agreements that are acceptable to all concerned.

Several alternatives to criminal court proceedings occur in the pretrial phase. They include police cautioning, transferral of criminal cases to a civil court if possible, and pretrial diversion for those who qualify. These alternatives serve to remove the defendant from the taint of a criminal prosecution and possible conviction. Finally, plea bargaining may occur.

Plea bargaining is an attempt by the prosecution to secure a guilty plea from a defendant in exchange for certain concessions, including a reduced sentence, a reduction in charges, or probation. Plea bargaining is used at the federal level, but there is considerable controversy concerning its use at state and local levels. From one jurisdiction to the next, plea bargaining varies. In some states, such as Alaska, plea bargaining has been banned. It has both proponents and critics. It is seen largely as a time-saving device by prosecutors and defense attorneys alike, but other persons regard plea bargaining as a threat to the right to due process under the United States Constitution.

Between 80 percent and 90 percent of all criminal convictions are obtained through plea bargaining. At the federal level, there are strict safeguards governing the conduct of district judges in approving plea agreements. Much variation occurs at the local and state levels regarding this process, however. This chapter examined some of the major uses of plea bargaining as well as some of its strengths and weaknesses.

KEY TERMS

assault

battery

charge reduction bargaining

criminal bench trials

discovery

driving under the influence (DUI)

implicit plea bargaining

judicial plea bargaining

overcharging

police cautioning

presumptive sentencing

pretrial diversion

public defender

screening

sentence recommendation plea bargaining

QUESTIONS FOR REVIEW

1. What is meant by plea bargaining? Is it followed by all states and jurisdictions?
2. What are the major functions of a prosecutor?
3. What are some of the important functions and duties of a defense attorney?
4. What is pretrial diversion? Do all persons who request it succeed in obtaining pretrial diversion? Why or why not?
5. Who are likely candidates for pretrial diversion?
6. Are federal district judges obligated to follow any particular rules or procedures when they supervise plea agreement hearings?
7. What constitutional amendments are affected when a person enters a plea of guilty?
8. Why does a prosecutor screen cases?
9. What is meant by overcharging? What are some of the functions of overcharging?
10. What are two offenses that might be tried in either criminal or civil courts? How does diversion to a civil court help a defendant?
11. What is meant by police cautioning? Under what circumstances would you expect police cautioning to be used? Give two examples.

12. What was the significance of the case of *Gideon v. Wainwright?*
13. Is an indigent defendant entitled to an attorney if he or she cannot afford one? Under what circumstances has the United States Supreme Court said a person has the right to an attorney?
14. What is a public defender?
15. How do our state and federal prison policies influence the plea-bargaining process, if at all?
16. Suppose that in federal court, John Doe, a criminal defendant, entered into a plea bargain with the government and pleaded guilty to vehicular theft. The prosecutor told John that the plea agreement included a provision that John must serve 1 year in jail. When John appeared before the federal judge, the judge said simply, "John Doe, is everything in this plea agreement okay?" John said, "Yes." Then the judge approved the agreement. Did the judge do anything wrong? If so, cite some of the things that the judge should have done.

SUGGESTED READINGS

Bennett, W. Lance, and Martha S. Feldman (1981). *Reconstructing reality in the courtroom.* New Brunswick, NJ: Rutgers Univ. Press.

Klonoski, James R., and Robert I. Mendosohn (Eds.) (1970). *The politics of local justice.* Boston: Little, Brown & Co.

Maynard, Douglas W. (1984). *Inside plea bargaining: The language of negotiation.* New York: Plenum Press.

Miller, Herbert S., William F. McDonald, and James A. Cramer (1978). *Plea bargaining in the United States.* Washington, DC: National Institute of Law Enforcement and Justice.

Nardulli, Peter F. (1978). *The courtroom elite: An organizational approach.* Cambridge, MA: Ballinger.

Juries and Trial Procedures

■ INTRODUCTION

This chapter discusses the selection of juries for public trials, the functions of juries, and the trial process itself. It also presents the functions and general roles of trial judges at the local, state, and federal levels.

   The landmark case of *Duncan v. Louisiana* (1968) specified objective criteria that restricted the right to a jury trial to offenses other than petty ones where a possible punishment of imprisonment for more than 6 months could be imposed. Other cases, such as *Baldwin v. New York* (1970), have upheld this standard. However, it may be that jury trials in the future will be held for *any* petty criminal offense (*Argersinger v. Hamlin*, 1972; Hans and Vidmar, 1986:31; Kalven and Zeisel, 1971; Schulhofer, 1985; Simon, 1980).

   Several constitutional amendments pertain to jury trials and the right to a trial. The Sixth Amendment guarantees all citizens the right to a trial by jury. The Seventh Amendment provides that the right of trial by jury be preserved in all suits at common law where the disputed value is more than $20. Finally, the Fourteenth Amendment provides among other things that no state make or enforce any law that deprives citizens of due process or enjoying all the privileges or immunities as citizens.

■ BENCH TRIALS AND JURY TRIALS

There are at least 300,000 jury trials annually (Hastie, Penrod, and Pennington, 1983:1). The number of nonjury trials is many times that figure. About 80 percent of all jury trials are civil and 20 percent are criminal. While the system of trial by jury appears first in United States history in 1607 under a charter granted to the Virginia Company in Jamestown by James I, jury trials were prevalent as early as the eleventh century in England (Hyman and Tarrant, 1975; Simon, 1980:5).

   A formal definition of a **criminal trial** is an adversarial proceeding within a particular jurisdiction, where a judicial examination and determination of issues can be made, and where a criminal defendant's guilt or innocence can be decided impartially by either a judge or jury (Black, 1979:1348). Basically, there are two types of criminal trials. These are (1) bench trials and (2) jury trials.

Bench Trials

Bench trials, also known as trials by the court and trials by the judge, are trials conducted in cases where either petty offenses are involved and a jury is not permitted

CRIME BEAT

In recent years, an alarmingly large number of state and federal judges have been removed from their judgeships through impeachment or political writ. Former United States District Judge Alcee Hastings of Miami was impeached in August 1988 and removed from the federal bench. He became the twelfth federal judge in United States history as well as the first black judge to suffer impeachment. Charges against him included conspiracy to obtain a $150,000 bribe in exchange for leniency to two convicted racketeers.

In early 1988, several Texas judges issued rulings that gave the strong appearance of impropriety. A favorable ruling for Pennzoil by a Texas judge was tainted by nearly $250,000 in earlier campaign contributions by Pennzoil to the judge. The case was suffi-ciently serious to prompt Texas legislators to reform their judicial selection scheme.

In Philadelphia, Pennsylvania, fifteen judges, 7 percent of the city's judicial force, were suspended in 1987 for committing crimes and violating public trust. Microphones planted in the judges' offices by federal agents disclosed acceptances of bribes in exchange for various favors, including issuing favorable union rulings and fixing a young man's criminal record in order to permit him to enter the army. If judges are increasingly implicated in illegal schemes, conspiracies, and other allegations, how much corruption exists among prosecutors who initiate the criminal actions against most defendants?

---

or defendants waive the right to a jury trial. A judge presides, hears the evidence, and then decides the case, relying on the rational principles of law.

The popular television shows, "Divorce Court" and "The People's Court," show trials without juries. In those cases, the **litigants** (the parties to the lawsuits) have waived their right to a jury trial and have permitted the judge to decide their cases. In criminal courts, defendants often waive the right to a jury trial and permit a judge to decide their cases on the basis of the evidence.

One explanation for waiving one's right to a jury trial is that juries are sometimes more likely to convict persons for felonies than are judges (Smith and Stevens, 1984). State criminal trial data by the Court Statistics and Information Management Project at the National Center for State Court for 1976–1978 shows that the number of criminal jury trials increased by 70 percent between 1955 and 1978. Nevertheless, two thirds of all felony trials were jury trials. Juries convicted felons more often than did judges, and judges were found to convict nonfelons more often than juries (Roper and Flango, 1983). These differences are partially attributable to the public's growing sensitivity to and fear of serious crime.

There is a negative side to bench trials. When judges are left to their own devices in determining guilt or innocence, there arise temptations and influences from external sources to decide a case either favorably or unfavorably for a defendant. In recent years, judges at the state and federal levels have been charged with corruption and accepting bribes to render decisions favorable to their constituencies. In 1987, the Pennsylvania supreme court suspended temporarily 15 of 105 judges who were under investigation by the FBI and other agencies for suspected bribery.

Jury Trials

A person charged with a felony is guaranteed the right to a jury trial in the United States. In the last few decades, the number of trials by jury has increased for both major crimes and misdemeanors (Schulhofer, 1985). While trials by jury are increasing, the trend is criminal convictions obtained through plea bargaining (McDonald, 1985). In at least one major city, the number of jury trials of *all* dispositions of felony arrests has dropped to 2 percent (Hans and Vidmar, 1986:6).

■ JURIES

A jury supposedly consists of peers of the accused, meaning that a defendant is entitled to a jury of his or her equals. This concept originated with the Magna Carta (Black, 1979:759). Today, tried by a jury of one's peers means tried by a jury of citizens.

Veniremen Lists

Jurors are selected in several ways for federal and state courts. Each federal district prepares a **venire,** or list of persons from which a jury will be selected. Persons selected as potential jurors are veniremen. These persons are drawn from voting registration lists, tax assessors' records, lists of persons with driver's licenses, and other public documents (Knowles and Hickman, 1984). Persons are notified by mail to appear at the courthouse on an appointed date and at an appointed time. Such lists of veniremen may consist of employed or unemployed persons, housewives, fire fighters, doctors, lawyers, police officers, trash collectors, teachers, businesspersons, engineers, and others. The major restriction for almost every list of veniremen is for the persons selected to reside within the jurisdiction of the court where the case is tried.

Functions of Juries

Juries perform a number of functions, including (1) preventing government oppression, (2) determining guilt or innocence of an accused, (3) representing diverse community interests, and (4) buffering between the accuser and the accused.

Preventing Government Oppression. In *Williams v. Florida* (1970), the United States Supreme Court declared, "[T]he chief function of a jury is to safeguard citizens against arbitrary law enforcement." The court also said that one of the primary purposes of a jury trial is to prevent oppression by government (*Duncan v. Louisiana,* 1968).

Determining Guilt or Innocence. Beyond these Supreme Court declarations, *a jury determines the guilt or innocence of an accused on the evidence presented by the prosecution and defense.* In criminal cases, the standard that decides guilt or innocence is belief that the defendant is guilty beyond a reasonable doubt. In civil cases, the standard for determining fault or liability is the preponderance of the evidence presented by the opposing litigants.

Representing Diverse Community Interests. One objective of jury trials is to represent the divergent interests of the community (Zeisel, 1971). In the case of *Williams v. Florida* (1970), the United States Supreme Court said that the jury was a valuable safeguard against the "corrupt or overzealous prosecutor and against the compliant, biased, or eccentric judge."

"We find the defendant guilty of pride, covetousness,
lust, envy, gluttony, anger, and sloth."

Buffering Between the Accuser and Accused. A jury also functions as a buffer between the accused and the accuser (Hastie, Penrod, and Pennington, 1983:4–5). Ideally, they are community participants who help determine a defendant's guilt or innocence. All juries should be free from both internal and external attempts at intimidation (Hastie, Penrod, and Pennington, 1983:5).

Numbers of Jurors

Traditionally, criminal juries consist of twelve members. In federal district courts, twelve persons are impaneled, or selected by the prosecution and defense, with additional persons selected as alternative jurors. Alternate jurors are not required, but they are generally permitted. In case a member of the impaneled jury becomes ill or for some reason cannot continue as a juror, an alternate juror may serve as a replacement (*United States v. Phillips,* 1981; *United States v. Viserto,* 1979). At state and local levels, alternate jurors are optional at the discretion of the presiding judge.

For many years, however, local courts have conducted civil and criminal trials by juries consisting of fewer than twelve persons (Simon, 1980). In many jurisdictions, it is not uncommon to conduct a trial by jury with six jurors. In 1970, a six-member criminal court jury was challenged as unconstitutional in the case of *Williams v. Florida.* Williams was sentenced to life imprisonment for a capital offense and appealed the verdict on the ground that the six-person jury violated his Fifth and Sixth Amendment rights. The United States Supreme Court affirmed the verdict of the lower court and said, "[T]he fact that the jury at common law was composed of precisely 12 is a historical accident." In its decision in the *Williams v. Florida* case, the Supreme Court

An X-rated film was the subject of a
major United States Supreme Court
case, where the operator of an X-rated
theater was convicted by a five-
member jury. The operator's convic-
tion was overturned, thereby estab-
lishing a minimum of six jury
members for constitutionally proper
jury trials.

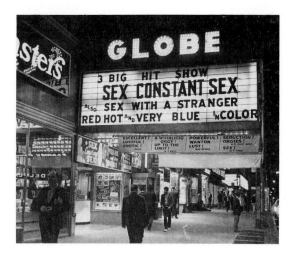

also observed that in some jurisdictions, juries consist of from five to twelve persons, and in one instance (Louisiana), a nine-out-of-twelve-person majority verdict is sufficient for conviction.

In the case of *Ballew v. Georgia* (1978), however, the Supreme Court held that a five-member jury is unconstitutional. Ballew operated the Paris Adult Theatre on Peachtree Street in Atlanta, Georgia, in 1973. In November 1973, he showed an X-rated film, *Behind the Green Door,* to his patrons. Investigators from the Fulton County Solicitor General's Office viewed the film and obtained a warrant to seize it in violation of obscenity laws. Ballew obtained another copy of the film and continued to show it.

Later, investigators seized the second copy of the film and arrested Ballew, charging him with two counts of distributing obscene material. These charges were misdemeanors, and it was common practice in Fulton County to conduct misdemeanor trials with five-member juries. Ballew wanted a twelve-person jury, but the court refused. He was convicted of the charges, sentenced to a year in prison, and ordered to pay a $2,000 fine (imprisonment was suspended upon payment of the fine). Ballew appealed the court's action, and eventually, the case was heard by the United States Supreme Court. Ballew claimed the five-person jury violated his constitutional right to a jury trial.

The United States Supreme Court held Ballew's right to a trial by jury had been violated and said, "We readily admit that we do not pretend to discern a clear line between six members and five. But the assembled data raise substantial doubts about the reliability and appropriate representation of panels smaller than six." For the first time, the Supreme Court of the United States established a constitutional *minimum* number of jurors in any criminal case—six. In a test of the Supreme Court's decision of the six-person jury minimum in Ballew's case, a Colorado man challenged the limit in 1981 by requesting a jury of *one* in a case involving charges of criminal mischief (Hans and Vidmar, 1986:171). The trial judge granted the defendant's motion, but before the proceedings could be completed, a Colorado appellate court overruled the trial judge and declared six jurors the minimum the defendant could have (Hans and Vidmar, 1986:171).

The issue of jury size has been examined extensively by researchers (Lempert, 1975; Saks, 1977, 1982; Simon, 1980; Padawer-Singer, Singer, and Singer, 1977; Zeisel and Diamond, 1974). These investigations have focused on such questions as whether smaller juries have less difficulty reaching agreement on guilt or innocence issues than do larger juries. Also, are smaller juries less representative of the community and more biased than larger juries? The research findings about jury size are disappointing and inconsistent (Hans and Vidmar, 1986; Simon, 1980). Some research shows that six-person juries have fewer disagreements and hung outcomes (where the jury cannot reach a unanimous verdict) than do twelve-person juries (Padawer-Singer, Singer, and Singer, 1977; Zeisel, 1971). Other studies show few, if any, differences in verdict agreements or disagreements between juries of different sizes (Hastie, Penrod, and Pennington, 1983; Lempert, 1975; Saks, 1977).

On the issue of the representativeness of smaller or larger juries, it would seem that greater representativeness of community residents would be found in juries of twelve persons than of six persons. In fact, the following strong argument favoring the greater representativeness of larger juries has been advanced:

> Suppose that 90 percent of the community holds one view and 10 percent holds a minority viewpoint. Further suppose that we draw 100 twelve-member juries and 100 six-member juries from this population randomly. Seventy-two of the 100 twelve-person juries would have at least one person with a minority viewpoint on the jury, while only 47 percent of the 100 six-person juries would have a minority representative. (Zeisel, 1971:720)

Inconsistencies regarding jury size, representativeness, and verdict findings may be caused by certain methodological problems and lack of control over important independent variables, such as the types of cases deliberated, the ages of the jurors, the gender composition of the jurors and the jurors' previous jury experience (Simon, 1980:76–77). Other researchers have made similar observations about juries, their size and composition, and the decision-making process (Craig, 1983; Dillehay and Nietzel, 1985; Kassin and Juhnke, 1983; Miller, 1985).

Jury Selection

It is generally assumed that the composition of a jury influences significantly the final trial outcome. The problem is that jury selection experts differ in their opinions about which juror characteristics are most important and which factors influence a juror's favorable verdict for the defendant (Hastie, Penrod, and Pennington, 1983:121; Simon, 1980; Suggs and Sales, 1978). One visible juror characteristic found to have a critical impact on jury verdicts is race. A high correlation has been found between race of a criminal defendant and sentencing severity, particularly where interracial crimes were involved (for example, white victim-black defendant) (Bullock, 1961). Also, it has been found that racial bias influences jury deliberations and verdicts, although there is inconsistency in this research (Johnson, 1985; Osborne and Rappaport, 1985; Spohn, Welch, and Gruhl, 1985; Turner et al., 1986; Werner et al., 1985). Thus far, it is uncertain about how jury verdicts are influenced by racial bias, although such bias does seem to make important differences in selected cases.

Simon (1980:33–34) has made one of the more extensive investigations of juror characteristics and jury verdicts. She conducted a thorough examination of the trial procedure literature and deduced a number of rules of thumb followed by lawyers as they impanel a jury:

1. A young juror is more likely to return a verdict favorable to the plaintiff than to the defendant.
2. An older juror is more likely to be sympathetic to the plaintiff than to the defendant in civil, personal injury cases.
3. A male juror is more likely to return a verdict favorable to the plaintiff if she is an attractive female.
4. A female juror is more likely to return a verdict favorable to the plaintiff if he is an attractive male.
5. A woman juror is more likely to be intolerant to the complaints of her own sex and thus return a verdict unfavorable to a party of her own sex.
6. A juror belonging to the same fraternal organizations, union, or political party as the client or witness is more likely to return a verdict favorable to that party.
7. A juror is more likely to return a verdict favorable to the party of his own religion.
8. A juror of Nordic, English, Swedish, Norwegian, German, or Scottish descent is more likely to respond to an appeal based on law and order and, thus, to return a verdict favorable to the defendant.
9. A woman juror is more likely to be emotional and sympathetic and to return a verdict favorable to the plaintiff.
10. A juror whose age closely approximates the age of the client, lawyer, or witness, is more likely to give a favorable verdict. (Simon, 1980:33–34)

Whether or not these rules of thumb are factually correct, many attorneys do their best to select the most favorable juries for their clients, and some empirical support for each of these statements exists.

Several strategies have been proposed for the selection and screening of jury members. Some studies suggest that color psychology, dress, body language, space and time usage, and speech patterns are important indicators of attitudinal dispositions and preferences favorable or unfavorable to a defendant (Rasicot, 1983). Nonverbal cues, such as not looking directly at the defendant's attorney during the process of questioning jury members concerning their biases or prejudices, are considered important (Suggs and Sales, 1978).

In recent years, handicapped jurors have been selected with increasing frequency. Deaf jurors require interpreters to convey dialogue between witnesses and counsel. While deaf persons cannot appreciate fully the wavering voice of a criminal defendant or the vocal inflections of critical witnesses, they can make astute observations of a witness's body language that others sometimes overlook. However, selecting jurors with physical impairments that may cause them to overlook audible or visual evidence is controversial.

Some experts employ a jury selection technique known as the Community Network Model, which uses members of the local community or private investigators to provide a defendant's attorney with personal background information about the jurors whose names appear on the jury list from which the jury will be selected (Bonora and Krauss, 1979). Also, some attorneys and prosecutors apply game theory and probability theory to information about prospective jurors in efforts to maximize their advantage (Brams and Davis, 1978; Kadane and Kairys, 1979; Roth, Kadane, and DeGroot, 1977).

A DAY IN COURT

Juries consist of a cross-section of community residents, supposedly a sample of peers of the defendants on trial. However, prosecutors and defense attorneys attempt to structure juries in ways that will increase their chances of winning cases. Some prospective jury members are excluded by both sides through peremptory challenges, where the reasons for their dismissal as jurors do not have to be provided. In recent years, however, the deliberate exclusion of persons because of their race, even through peremptory challenges, has been ruled unconstitutional.

Another aggregate of prospective jurors has been routinely excluded from jury duty. These include persons who are deaf. Should deaf people or those who suffer serious hearing impairment be denied places on juries because of these handicaps? Allen Hammel of Blair County, Pennsylvania, was a 28-year-old postal worker who was called to jury duty. Hammel is deaf and required an interpreter using sign language in order to follow court proceedings. Another deaf person, JoAnn DeLong, residing in the same county, was dismissed from jury duty because of her hearing impairment. She challenged her exclusion by filing suit in federal court.

The inclusion of the deaf on juries raises several issues. For some jurors, the interpreter's hand motions, sign language, may be distracting. When testimony is given, interpreters cannot convey the true tone or expression of the witness. Sometimes the way in which a thought or opinion is expressed or facts are related reflects on the credibility of the witness. Thus, some sounds during testimony are crucial, according to some experts. Very few states have laws prohibiting deaf persons from serving on juries. In most jurisdictions, judges decide whether to permit their inclusion. Certainly one consideration is the cost of hiring interpreters. Some states, such as California and Illinois, have court-appointed interpreters for deaf jurors and pay their fees. Should deaf or blind persons be excluded from jury duty because they may not hear or see crucial audio or visual evidence relating to the guilt of defendants?

Often, defense attorneys hire social scientists to conduct telephone surveys in communities where a client is to be tried. These surveys sometimes reveal prejudicial community sentiment about the case and the client. Several trial consulting firms, such as Litigation Sciences, have emerged in recent years to assist lawyers in their juror selections. Litigation Sciences boasts, "[T]o date, where our advice and recommendations have been employed, our clients have achieved successful results in over 95 percent of the cases in which we have been involved" (Hans and Vidmar, 1986:90).

In a widely publicized 1974 trial, the work of social scientists and jury selection experts appeared instrumental in a verdict favorable to the defendant (McConahay, Mullin, and Frederick, 1977). Joan Little, a black prisoner in the women's section of the Beaufort County (North Carolina) Jail, was allegedly assaulted by a night jailer, Clarence Alligood. Alligood was found dead in Ms. Little's cell in the early morning hours of August 27, 1974, stabbed with an ice pick.

Ms. Little escaped from the jail and could not be found. There was much publicity about the incident, and eventually, Ms. Little turned herself in to authorities. She claimed that Alligood had raped her and she killed him in self-defense. Her attorney hired some social scientists to conduct a survey of local attitudes about the incident, and these researchers found extensive racial and sexist views to be held by most Beaufort County residents questioned. The judge was persuaded and agreed to move the trial from Beaufort County to Wake County, a larger urban location. Pretrial publicity and racism were among the reasons cited by the judge for his decision.

The jury in Wake County acquitted Ms. Little of the murder charge. Defense lawyers claimed the pretrial survey was influential in Ms. Little's acquittal. Jerry Paul, her attorney, boasted afterward that he had bought the verdict with a large defense fund, which was used to support the team of jury selection experts (Hans and Vidmar, 1986:90). These jury selection experts may or may not have influenced the outcome. According to Hamilton Hobgood, the trial judge, the case against Ms. Little was one of the weakest he had seen in 20 years on the bench (Hans and Vidmar, 1986:90).

Education, gender, socioeconomic status, religion, occupation, political affiliation, and any number of other variables obviously influence one's opinions and decision making. Currently, little is known about the relation between juror characteristics and juror attitudes toward criminal defendants. The most frequently examined individual difference is gender (Hastie, Penrod, and Pennington, 1983:140), but even in recent years, satisfactory juror attitude prediction schemes based on gender have not been reliably devised.

In rape cases, some studies have found female jurors to be more prone to conviction than male jurors (Miller, 1985). Most of the research has been conducted with mock jurors and college students, who pretended to be jury members in hypothetical cases and jury simulations (Hastie, Penrod, and Pennington, 1983:140). In one hypothetical rape case, different researchers found different results using the same set of facts with different jurors. In sum, few consistent differences in jury decisions can be attributed to gender (Davis et al., 1977; Kerr et al., 1976; Nagao and Davis, 1980).

Screening Jury Members

Before a trial commences, persons summoned to jury duty are gathered or sequestered either in the courtroom or in a nearby area. They are often drawn at random and take seats in the jury box. Depending upon the judge's rules, the prosecution and defense attorneys may or may not be permitted to ask questions of specific jurors. In certain federal district courts, for instance, the prosecutors and defense attorneys submit lists of questions they would like to ask prospective jurors. The judge reviews these questions and directs these to the jury as a whole. The judge is not obligated to ask the jurors any one or all of the questions submitted by these attorneys.

The judge determines whether any juror is related to any of the trial participants. The defense often wants to know if any member of the jury is a law enforcement officer or related to one. The prosecution wants to know if any jury member is even remotely related to or knows the criminal defendant. Ordinarily, these are grounds for excusing a jury member from that particular jury.

The formal procedure whereby both prosecutors and defense attorneys address jurors and inquire into their backgrounds and potential biases in a case is called the **voir dire.** It is applied to the examination of prospective witnesses as well. Voir dire means "to speak the truth," and it signifies an attorney's inquiry into the qualifications of witnesses to present expert testimony or an oral examination of prospective jurors to discover their impartiality in the pending case. Both the prosecution and the defense can challenge jurors and exclude any of them from the jury for whatever reason. These are called **peremptory challenges.** A peremptory challenge excuses a juror without assigning a reason for the challenge (Black, 1979:1023). In all courts, the prosecution and defense are limited in the number of peremptory challenges they may use. There is wide variation in the number of peremptory challenges attorneys can use from state to state.

In federal district courts, 18 United States Code Rule 24 (1989) provides the following numbers of peremptory challenges available to the prosecution and defense:

1. *Capital cases:* If the offense charged is punishable by death, each side is entitled to twelve peremptory challenges.
2. *Felony cases:* If the offense charged is punishable by imprisonment for not more than 1 year, each side is entitled to five peremptory challenges.
3. *Misdemeanor cases:* If the offense charged is punishable by imprisonment for not more than 1 year, a fine, or both, each side is entitled to two peremptory challenges.

In all courts at the local, state, and federal levels, attorneys for both sides may also challenge and excuse any juror for cause. If an attorney can show good cause why a juror should not be a part of the jury, the judge is obliged to excuse that juror. For example, if prospective white jurors in the case of a black defendant are being questioned by the defendant's attorney, any racist expression uttered by white jurors or any evidence of racial prejudice on their part will be grounds to exclude them from jury service. Attorneys from both sides have unlimited challenges for cause (Johnson, 1985).

In 1986, however, the United States Supreme Court heard an appeal from a convicted black offender (*Batson v. Kentucky,* 1986). James Kirkland Batson, a black defendant, had been convicted of second-degree burglary and receipt of stolen goods by an all-white jury in a Kentucky criminal court. The prosecutor had used his four peremptory challenges to excuse four prospective black jury members. Batson's attorney moved to discharge the jury before it was sworn on the ground that the prosecutor's removal of the black veniremen violated Batson's rights under the Sixth and Fourteenth Amendments. The presiding judge denied the motion and said that prosecutors and defense attorneys were entitled to use their peremptory challenges to strike anybody that they want to.

Batson's attorney formulated an appeal to the Kentucky Supreme Court and argued that the all-white jury had deprived Batson of a fair and impartial jury trial. The Kentucky Supreme Court relied on an earlier United States Supreme Court case and upheld Batson's conviction. The earlier case, *Swain v. Alabama* (1965), also concerned a black defendant who alleged racial discrimination in his jury selection. The United States Supreme Court held in *Swain* that the burden of showing the discriminatory use of peremptory challenges by prosecutors was on the defendant. Furthermore, the defendant would be required to show that discrimination was a systematic pattern in the jurisdiction where the trial was held. In Swain's case, Swain was unable to meet this burden, and his conviction was affirmed by the Supreme Court.

The United States Supreme Court did not directly reverse the position that it had adopted in *Swain.* However, it did modify *Swain* to permit a defendant to raise the question of discrimination in jury selection in his or her own case instead of requiring the defendant to demonstrate discrimination throughout an entire jurisdiction as a general practice among the prosecutors. Batson's case clearly pointed to the discriminatory use of peremptory challenges by the prosecutor. It was significant also because it required prosecutors instead of defendants to show the court why their use of peremptory challenges was not discriminatory once the defense made apparent a discriminatory pattern of jury member selection.

It is important to understand that the *Batson* case did *not* hold that defendants have the right to a jury composed of members of their own race only. Furthermore, it is unnecessary that *any* jury members share racial similarities with defendants in order for fair and impartial jury trials to be held. However, Batson did establish that the jury in his trial was exclusively white because the prosecutor used his peremptory challenges to excuse the only black persons who could have been selected as jury members. Thus, Batson's conviction was reversed because his right to an impartial jury trial had been violated by the Kentucky court. He had been put on trial before a jury from which members of his race had been purposely excluded.

Ordinarily, defense and prosecuting attorneys do not have to explain their use of peremptory challenges. Where clear biases exist among prospective jurors, challenges for cause may be made without limit, but excusing prospective jurors without providing the court with rationales for doing so has seldom been questioned. No doubt, the Batson case will cause prosecutors to consider carefully their use of peremptory challenges in the future. According to the United States Supreme Court, the taint of discrimination will not be tolerated in the courtroom, and such discrimination extends to previously unquestioned peremptory challenges.

In cases where the death penalty may be imposed for the crime alleged, the composition of jury members is especially crucial. If the prosecution asks a prospective juror, "If you found this defendant guilty of murder, would you be able to impose a death sentence on the defendant?" and the prospective juror says, "No, I don't believe in the death penalty," then the prosecutor may ask that the prospective juror be dismissed for cause.

Some evidence indicates that in death penalty cases, such challenges for cause result in a death qualified jury, which is actually biased against the defendant (Fitzgerald and Ellsworth, 1984; Haney, 1984; Kadane, 1984). In a random survey of opinions of 811 eligible jurors from Alameda County, California, Fitzgerald and Ellsworth (1984) found that of the 717 respondents who said they could be fair and impartial in deciding on the guilt or innocence of a capital defendant, about 17 percent said they could never vote to impose the death penalty. These researchers found that significantly greater portions of blacks than whites and females than males are eliminated by the process of death qualification, and that this biases the resulting jury against the capital defendant.

Another argument is that death qualification, or determining whether a juror would vote for the death penalty, creates a set of suggestive conditions (Haney, 1984). A sample of persons in one study appeared influenced by the process of death qualification itself (Haney, 1984). Subjects were led to believe that the judge, the prosecutor, and even the defense attorney were convinced of the guilt of the defendant. Specifically, these subjects were led to believe that the law disapproves of people who oppose the death penalty and that this belief, therefore, leads to a death penalty choice more often

CRIME BEAT

Convicted murderer Billy Ray Irick of Knoxville, who is scheduled to die in the electric chair next year for killing a girl, was sentenced Monday to a 40-year prison term for raping the child.

Knox County Criminal Judge Jim Duncan dismissed a plea for leniency by Irick's attorneys and called the 1985 rape of 7-year-old Paula Dyer of Knoxville the most brutal he had encountered in his six years on the bench.

"Basically, she was more or less ripped apart, based on medical testimony," Duncan said, before sentencing Irick on two aggravated rape counts. "If you disregard the murder case, the court has not heard a rape case so aggravated."

Earlier this month, a Knox County jury found Irick, 27, guilty of the vaginal and anal rape of Paula. The jury also found Irick guilty of the child's murder and sentenced him to die for her slaying.

Duncan Monday also denied Irick a new trial.

Although Duncan sentenced Irick to two 40-year prison terms on both rape counts, he ordered the sentences to be served concurrently. However, they will be served consecutively with Irick's death sentence.

"Sometimes death sentences are converted to life sentences," the judge said, explaining why he imposed the rape sentence even though Irick is facing death. "The 40-year sentence will run consecutively to any sentence Irick serves on his murder conviction."

Irick is scheduled to be executed May 4 in the Tennessee State Penitentiary electric chair. His attor-

neys, Ken Miller and James Varner of Knoxville, plan to appeal the rape and death convictions.

Irick was accused of raping the child twice and suffocating her with his hands while baby sitting with her and her four young brothers in their home in April 1985.

The 40-year rape sentence is the minimum Irick could have gotten for aggravated rape. The state had asked the court to impose the maximum sentence of life.

Irick's attorney said he had been punished enough.

"He has received the death penalty for murder," Miller told Duncan. "There is no need to punish him more."

Irick is the first person to be sentenced to die by a Knox County jury since Terry Lyn King received the death penalty in February 1985.

Irick's attorneys, in asking for a new trial, argued that the court erred in allowing testimony by a Knoxville police officer regarding statements Irick allegedly made.

The attorneys also said the court erred during jury selection and by refusing to provide Irick, who was declared indigent, funds to pay for an expert witness.

Duncan, denying the request, said the court "bent over backward" to give Irick a fair trial.

Source: Reprinted with permission from Clara Whatley, "Convicted Slayer of Girl, 7, Gets 40 More Years," *The Knoxville News-Sentinel* (December 2, 1986), p. A4.

---

as an appropriate punishment. However, other research has found that the death-qualification process has only a negligible effect on prospective jurors (Kadane, 1984).

Agreement of Jury Members

In federal district courts, juries consist of twelve persons. The judge may or may not approve the selection of several alternate jurors. If a juror becomes ill during the proceedings, or if during deliberations, a juror cannot continue to serve, 18 United States Code, Rule 23 provides, "[I]f the court finds it necessary to excuse a juror for just cause after the jury has retired to consider its verdict, in the discretion of the court a valid verdict may be returned by the remaining 11 jurors" (United States Code, 1989). A decision reached by a jury in any federal district court must be unanimous. If one or more jurors disagree and persist in their disagreement with the other jurors, the judge declares a hung jury and a mistrial. This means that the entire case will have to be tried again before a new jury at a later date.

At the local and state levels, however, the federal rule for complete jury agreement does not apply. Under existing United States Supreme Court guidelines, local and state juries may vary in size from a minimum of six persons. While the Supreme Court has established the minimum number of jury members at six in the case of *Williams v. Florida* (1970), no such precedent has been established for an upper limit. Thus, it is conceivable that a defendant may request a jury consisting of more than twelve persons.

Juries consisting of six persons only must be unanimous in their verdict (*Burch v. Louisiana,* 1979). However, if the juries consist of twelve persons, a majority verdict is acceptable, unless such a verdict is prohibited under state or local laws. For instance, in the cases of *Apodaca v. Oregon* (1972) and *Johnson v. Louisiana* (1972), the respective defendants were convicted by a majority of jurors, but there was no unanimity of agreement. In the first case, Robert Apodaca (and several other defendants) were convicted of assault with a deadly weapon. Apodaca was convicted by an eleven-to-one jury vote (in Oregon, the minimum requisite vote by a jury to sustain a criminal conviction is ten to twelve). In the second case, Frank Johnson was arrested, tried, and convicted of armed robbery in 1968. The twelve-person jury convicted him by a nine-to-three vote (the absolute minimum majority required under Louisiana law). Their appeals were heard by the United States Supreme Court, which upheld their convictions and the right of the states to utilize a majority vote in their jury trials.

■ THE TRIAL PROCESS

Trial procedures vary among jurisdictions, although the federal district court format is followed most frequently by the judges in state and local trial courts. Figure 11.1 is a diagram of a typical trial from the indictment stage through the judge's instructions to jury members.

Pretrial Motions

Before the start of court proceedings, attorneys for the government and defense may make a number of **pretrial motions,** or **motions in limine,** which are motions to avoid potentially serious or embarrassing situations that may occur later during trial, such as an attempt by either side to introduce evidence that may be considered prejudicial, inflammatory, or irrelevant. For example, in a brutal murder case, it may be considered inflammatory for the prosecution to introduce photographs of a dismembered body or a mutilated corpse. The jury may be emotionally persuaded to interpret the photographs as conclusive evidence that the defendant committed the crime. In addition, such photographs may enhance sentencing severity if additional and overwhelming evidence exists of the defendant's guilt.

In some instances, a defense attorney will move to suppress certain evidence from being introduced because it was illegally seized by police at the time the defendant was arrested (Bell, 1983). This is known as the **exclusionary rule,** and it provides that

FIGURE 11.1 The Trial Process

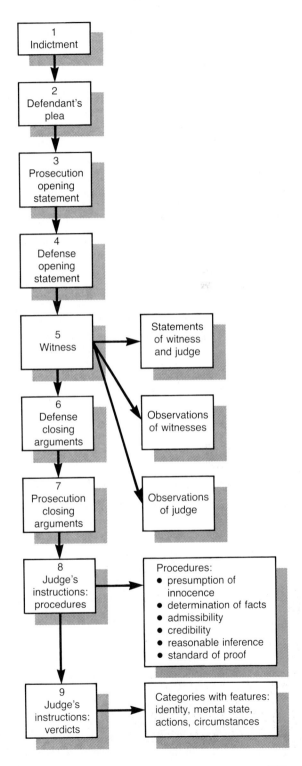

Source: From R. Hastie, S. Penrod, and N. Pennington, *Inside the Jury* (Cambridge, MA: Harvard Univ. Press, 1983), p. 16. Reprinted by permission.

where evidence has been obtained in violation of the privileges guaranteed citizens by the United States Constitution, the evidence must be excluded at the trial (Black, 1979:506). For instance, evidence seized by an illegal search and seizure by police would be within the exclusionary rule. The case of *Mapp v. Ohio* (1961) involved an illegal search of Ms. Mapp's premises by police officers in Cleveland, Ohio, and the illegal seizure of certain obscene material found in an obscure trunk in Ms. Mapp's basement. The United States Supreme Court overturned Ms. Mapp's conviction because of the illegal search and seizure of evidence by police.

In a case involving narcotics sales, a Chinese suspect, Wong Sun, was arrested by police, charged, and convicted of violating federal narcotics laws (*Wong Sun v. United States,* 1963). Earlier, federal agents had acted on a tip, and without a warrant, they broke down the door of James Wah Toy's dwelling and arrested him. They searched his home for narcotics but found none, but Toy told police later under questioning that Johnny Yee was selling narcotics. Yee was arrested, and narcotics were taken from his home. Yee, in turn, implicated Wong Sun, who was also arrested. All of the subsequent action against Wong Sun stemmed from an original unlawful search of James Wah Toy's premises and illegally obtained statements from Toy when immediately arrested.

The United States Supreme Court overturned Wong Sun's conviction and declared that the statements implicating Wong Sun in narcotics sales were fruits of the poisonous tree. The **fruits of the poisonous tree doctrine** provides that evidence spawned or directly derived from an illegal search or an illegal interrogation is generally inadmissible against a defendant because of its original taint. Often, a defense attorney will file a **motion to dismiss,** which is a motion designed to attack the prosecutor's evidence as insufficient or to signify the absence of a key prosecution witness upon which a conviction depends. Such pretrial motions are ordinarily conducted outside of the presence of the jury. The judge rules on the motions and the trial proceeds.

Opening Statements

Unless both the prosecution and defense attorneys agree to waive opening statements, the prosecutor makes an opening statement to the jury. Usually, this statement includes a portion of the state's theory about the case and the defendant's guilt. Often, prosecutors tell a jury what they intend to prove and attempt to persuade them initially to consider certain kinds of evidence to be presented later. This outline or summary of the nature of the case is to advise the jury of the facts to be relied upon and the issues involved (Black, 1979:984).

The defense attorney is also permitted to make an opening statement. The defense is permitted wide latitude by the court in addressing the jury. Basically, the defense's statement is intended to undermine the state's case against the defendant and to indicate that in the final analysis, the accused should be acquitted of all charges.

The State Presentation

The prosecution commences by calling witnesses and presenting evidence that a crime has been committed and that the defendant committed it. Each witness is sworn in by a court officer and is obliged under the law to be truthful in all testimony subsequently presented. This stage is termed **direct examination.**

The defense has the right to challenge any question asked a witness by the prosecution on direct examination. Defense attorneys may object to a question or to an answer provided by a witness. The presiding judge rules on such objections and either sustains (approves) them or overrules (disapproves, or denies) them. The same option is available to defense attorneys pertaining to the introduction of evidence by the prosecution. Objections may be raised at any time, and the judge sustains or overrules such objections.

The Federal Rules of Evidence contain explicit guidelines for judges and attorneys to follow regarding what evidence is admissible and what evidence is not admissible (Saltzburg and Redden, 1986). These rules are rather elaborate and technical. If they are not followed by any of the major participants in a trial proceeding, a violation can be the basis for overturning a guilty verdict on appeal to a higher court. The prosecution is also entitled to appeal a not guilty verdict on similar grounds. If certain evidence rules are violated, a verdict in favor of the defendant can be reversed on appeal.

Cross-Examination

After the prosecution has questioned a witness, the defense has the right to ask the witness questions. The right to cross-examine witnesses is constitutionally prescribed. In addition, it illustrates the adversarial nature of the trial system. The defense attorney tries to impeach the credibility of the prosecutor's witnesses or to undermine their believability to the jury (Graham, 1985). Sometimes, a defense attorney can use a prosecution witness to advantage, eliciting statements that are favorable to the defendant.

While some persons believe that re-cross-examination prolongs an otherwise long trial, each side is entitled to re-cross-examine witnesses and recall witnesses to the stand for further questioning. This tactic is particularly important where new evidence comes to light. Judges may halt extensive cross-examinations and re-cross-examinations if they feel that attorneys are merely covering information disclosed in earlier testimony.

Impeachment is calling into question the truthfulness or credibility of a witness. If either the prosecutor or defense attorney can demonstrate that a particular witness is lying or otherwise unreliable, then that witness's testimony is called into question. Jury members may be inclined to disbelieve such witnesses and the evidentiary information they provide for or against defendants. Of course, defendants themselves are subject to impeachment.

A defense attorney can impeach a witness in several ways. The attorney can obtain inconsistent testimony from the witness or can get the witness to admit confusion over certain facts recalled. The attorney also can introduce evidence of the untruthfulness of the witness based on previous information acquired through investigative sources. Perhaps a witness has been previously fired from a company because of embezzlement. Embezzlement is one form of dishonesty, and jurors may infer that if a witness were dishonest in employment, he or she may not be telling the truth on the witness stand. Of course, when the defense presents its witnesses, the prosecution has the same cross-examination rights and can attempt to impeach the credibility of the witnesses called on the defendant's behalf.

A DAY IN COURT

In the case of *Robinson v. California* (1962), Lawrence Robinson was arrested and charged with being "addicted to the use of narcotics," in violation of a California statute. At his trial, the prosecution introduced as an expert witness Officer Theodore M. Lindquist, a police officer for the city of Los Angeles, who was attached to the narcotics division. Mr. Gage, the prosecutor, conducted the direct examination of Officer Lindquist, a portion of which is shown below:

Q: How long have you been attached to the Narcotics Division?
A: Going on eleven years.
Q: Have you seen addicts in various stages and conditions of addiction?
A: Yes.
Q: Did you have occasion to examine the defendant in this case, Mr. Robinson?
A: I did.
Q: Approximately where and when did you examine the defendant?
A: The defendant was examined on the 5th day of February, 1960, at approximately 10:15 A.M. at the Central Jail, Felony Section.
Q: On that occasion, did you examine his arms?
A: I did.
Q: What, generally, did you note about his arms at that time?
A: In the area of the inner right elbow, I found two scabs. These scabs were over a vein. In the area of the inner left elbow, there was an area of discoloration and scabbing over a vein bearing five scabs.
Q: From your examination of these various scabs and various marks on the defendant's arm, did you form an opinion as to what caused those marks?
A: I did.
Q: What was your opinion?
A: In my opinion, these marks and the discoloration were the result of the injection of hypodermic needles into the tissue into the vein that was not sterile.
Q: Did you form an opinion as to the length of time or the age of these various marks that you observed on the defendant's arm?
A: I did.
Q: Relate that please.
A: Those scabs that appear on the inner right elbow area were estimated to be approximately ten to fifteen days old. The scabbing appearing in the inner left area was estimated to be approximately three to ten days old.
Q: And is there a difference in the appearance of these marks and scabs with age?
A: Yes.
Q: And generally, what did you notice in that connection?
A: Originally, a scab is a pinkish-orange color, and as it grows older, the blood oxidizes and ages, becoming a different color.
Q: When the defendant indicated that he had had his last fix, did he tell you whether it had been the Wednesday just previous to the day that you had examined him or a week previous to that?
A: It was the previous Wednesday.

Then the defense attorney, Mr. McMorris, took over and conducted the cross-examination of the expert witness.

Q: As an expert in the field of narcotics, you know the symptoms of heroin addiction, do you not?
A: Yes, sir.
Q: And among those symptoms are those termed withdrawal symptoms?
A: That is correct.
Q: And at no time did you witness any withdrawal symptoms in Mr. Robinson?
A: No, I did not.
Q: As a matter of fact, he wasn't under the influence at the time you interviewed him at all?

A: No, he wasn't.

Q: So you saw no influence and no withdrawal?

A: That is correct.

Q: You saw on his arms certain discolorations on the veins of each arm?

A: On the inner left arm, I noticed the discoloration.

Q: As a matter of fact, did you observe the whole of Mr. Robinson's body, say, above the belt?

A: You mean the nude torso?

Q: Yes.

A: No, just his arms.

Q: Then you don't—you don't know whether he has all over his body certain discolorations similar to this?

A: No, I do not.

Q: As an expert in the field, you also know there is a Nalline test that can determine conclusively the presence of narcotics?

A: Within limitations.

Q: This test wasn't given to the defendant, was it?

A: No.

Q: As to the freshest scars which you allege you saw, they were how old?

A: Approximately three days.

Q: Did you say three to five?

A: That three- to five-day period was the varying period of time in which they could have been made.

Q: It might have been three to five days that there was an actual injection by your own determination?

A: Yes, sir. The freshest, three days, the oldest being five days.

Q: And you can look at these marks and estimate three to five days or seven by looking at the marks on a person's arm?

A: Yes.

Q: Of a needle?

A: Yes.

Q: Can you, by looking at these marks, tell us whether or not they could have been caused by a blood test?

A: Yes. The blood test, generally, doesn't leave a scabbing for any length of time. It will have a small scab that will disappear rapidly. The needle used is larger and results in a larger scab.

Q: Such a scab might last a day, though, a day or two?

A: Oh, yes.

Q: Simply looking at the scars on a person's arm, if such has been left by a blood test, it would be—the scab would not last as long as one made by a heroin needle, in your opinion?

A: That is correct.

It is apparent from this dialogue that Mr. McMorris, the defense attorney, was calling into question the expert's ability to examine a needle mark and determine its age and cause. The prosecution sought to demonstrate that Robinson had recently used heroin in violation of California statutes, and Officer Lindquist's testimony was designed to support the state's contention that Robinson was, indeed, an addict.

Robinson was subsequently convicted of the offense alleged and sentenced to serve 90 days in the Los Angeles County Jail. He appealed the case to a higher court. The case eventually was heard by the United States Supreme Court, where it was concluded that narcotic addiction was tantamount to an illness. Robinson's conviction was overturned, and the Supreme Court noted, "[E]ven one day in prison would be a cruel and unusual punishment for the 'crime' of having a common cold."

Eyewitnesses and Expert Witnesses

In criminal law expert testimony is solicited often (McCloskey, Egeth, and McKenna, 1986). Experts can testify and identify blood samples, firearms, and ballistics reports. They can comment on a defendant's state of mind or sanity and provide opinions about any number of other pieces of evidence that would link the defendant to the crime. By the same token, defense attorneys can introduce expert testimony of their own to rebut or counter the testimony of the prosecution's experts.

Expert witnesses are intended to interpret the meaningfulness of evidence presented by either the prosecution or the defense (Homant and Kennedy, 1985). Expert testimony can render complex issues understandable (McCloskey, Egeth and McKenna, 1986; Whitcomb et al., 1985). Being an expert witness involves certain hazards or risks, however. Some expert witnesses have reported being harassed by defendants or their attorneys outside the courtroom. Particularly in the case of forensic psychiatrists, who testify to a defendant's sanity or criminal motives, expert witnesses actually may be physically assaulted or threatened with harm (Anderson and Winfree, 1987; Miller, 1985). In a survey of 408 members of the American Academy of Psychiatry (representing 48 percent of the largest United States organizations of forensic psychiatrists), 42 percent of the respondents reported harassment in some fashion from defendants, plaintiffs, victims, the press, and even judges (Miller, 1985). A majority of cases involving harassment involved criminal cases or cases where the insanity defense was raised as a major issue.

Eyewitnesses are also of significant value to both prosecutors and defense attorneys (Konecni and Ebbesen, 1986; Wells and Loftus, 1984). They can provide opinions and interpretations of events they actually experienced, and they can provide accounts of the defendant's involvement in the crime alleged. However, some researchers have explored the impact of eyewitness testimony on jury verdicts and have suggested strongly that any such testimony should be corroborated with supportive evidence in order to be more fully reliable (Jackson, 1986).

A major problem faced by prosecutors is obtaining the cooperation of victims or witnesses to testify in court as to pertinent information they have about a particular case (Davis, 1983). The courtroom is a mystery to many persons, and the thought of enduring questioning on the witness stand is not especially attractive. In an effort to allay fears of victim-witnesses, victim-witness assistance programs have been initiated, particularly by prosecutors and courts in various jurisdictions (Finn and Lee, 1985). **Victim-witness assistance programs** are services that are intended to explain court procedures to various witnesses and to notify them of court dates (Finn and Lee, 1985). Additionally, such programs permit victim-witnesses to feel more comfortable with the criminal justice system generally. One particularly important function performed by such programs is to assist witnesses in providing better evidence in criminal prosecutions, with the result being a greater number of convictions where their testimony is given (Finn and Lee, 1985).

An area that has received much attention in recent years is the reliability of the testimony of child witnesses, especially in cases alleging child sexual abuse (Berliner and Barbieri, 1984; Fote, 1985; Goodman, 1984; Pynoos and Eth, 1984; Whitcomb, Shapiro, and Stellwagen, 1985). The scientific study of child witnesses by psychologists in the United States began around the turn of the century, and some researchers have concluded that children are the most dangerous witnesses of all (Goodman, 1984). One reason for this view is that a child's recall of an especially traumatic event, such as a rape or homicide, has been found to distort what actually occurred (Fote, 1985; Pynoos and Eth, 1984). Many child victims of sexual abuse are under age 12, and nearly a third are under age 6 (Bulkley, 1985). Of primary concern to a judge and other participants in the courtroom scene is the ability of children to distinguish between real and imagined events (Johnson and Foley, 1984).

In addition to the obvious trauma of being asked about emotionally disturbing events, such as sexual molestation, the parents of sexually abused children are often reluctant to allow their children to testify in court. Some persons have suggested that the children be permitted to testify in a location away from the actual courtroom and that their testimony be monitored through closed-circuit television (Bainor, 1985; Fote, 1985; Whitcomb, Shapiro, and Stellwagen, 1985). Under the Sixth Amendment, however, defendants are entitled to a face-to-face confrontation with their accusers (Bainor, 1985). Thus, at least for the present, it seems that the utilization of closed-circuit television in cases of child sexual abuse must undergo close scrutiny by the United States Supreme Court before being approved on a national scale. It has numerous proponents, however.

At the conclusion of the state's case against the defendant, the defense attorney may ask the court for a directed verdict of acquittal. No evidence exists to indicate the frequency with which such a verdict is requested, but it is likely asked for in a large number of criminal cases. If the case is being heard before a jury, the presiding judge is reluctant to grant such a motion. The jury is charged with the responsibility of determining one's guilt or innocence. Judges may grant such a motion, however, if they feel that the state has failed to present a convincing case of the defendant's guilt. Such motions are infrequently granted, however.

The Defense and Summation

The defense attorney presents all evidence and witnesses who have relevant testimony favorable to the defendant. The prosecutor may object to the introduction of certain witnesses or to evidence that the defense intends to introduce. A defendant may or may not choose to testify. This is a right guaranteed under the United States Constitution, and no defendant may be compelled to give testimony in a case against himself or herself. Of course, if a defendant does not testify, the jury may feel that the defendant has something to hide. It is difficult to convey to a jury that a defendant is merely exercising a right under the Fifth Amendment, and that nothing, of either a positive or negative nature, should be construed from a defendant's election not to testify.

The prosecution is prohibited from mentioning a defendant's refusal to testify to the jury (*Griffin v. California,* 1965). If a prosecutor were to say, "Ladies and gentlemen of the jury, if this defendant were innocent, he would get up here on the stand and say so," the statement would be improper, and the judge would order the statement stricken from the record. Both prosecutors and defense attorneys alike are bound by legal ethics when presenting a case or representing a client in the courtroom. Occasionally, however, some attorneys engage in unethical conduct, either deliberately or inadvertently. Sometimes, such conduct results in a mistrial, and the case must proceed from the beginning in front of a new jury.

Each side is permitted a summation at the conclusion of all evidence presented. Ordinarily, a defense attorney presents the final oral argument. This argument is followed by the closing argument of the prosecuting attorney. Sometimes, with court consent, a prosecutor may present a portion of the closing argument of the prosecution, followed by the closing argument of the defense, followed by the remainder of the prosecutor's closing argument. In short, the prosecutor gets in the final remarks to the jury.

Jury Deliberations

After the prosecution and defense have presented their final arguments, the judge instructs the jury on the procedures that it must follow in reaching a verdict, and the jury retires to the jury room to consider the evidence and arrive at a verdict. A judge's instructions to a jury often include a recitation of the charges against the defendant, a listing of the elements of the crime that the prosecution must prove beyond a reasonable doubt, and a charge for them to carefully consider the evidence and testimony of the witnesses. The jury must either be unanimous or comply with the particular rules governing jury verdicts followed locally. Federal juries must be unanimous. If a jury of twelve persons fails to agree, a mistrial is declared by the federal judge. If one jury member becomes ill, an eleven-member federal jury is acceptable with court approval and must render a unanimous verdict as well. In some states, such as Louisiana and Oregon, the particular state rules governing jury verdicts call for a certain majority of votes in order for a defendant to be convicted of the crime alleged. In six-person jury situations, the jury must reach a unanimous decision, according to the United States Supreme Court.

In recent years, social scientists have studied jury deliberations and the process of arriving at a verdict (Craig, 1983; Hans and Vidmar, 1986; Hastie, Penrod, and Pennington, 1983; Miller, 1985; Stasser, Kerr, and Bray, 1982). The chief difficulty confronting those interested in studying jury deliberation processes is that such deliberations are conducted in secret. Some investigators have participated as actual jury members in their respective jurisdictions, and the insight that they gained through such experiences has been instrumental in preparing defense attorneys in presenting more convincing cases to juries on behalf of their clients (Greene, 1986).

Jury deliberations have often been the subject of feature films. The 1957 drama, *Twelve Angry Men,* epitomized the emotion and anger of jurors in a murder case. In that film, Henry Fonda played the lone juror voting not guilty against the other eleven guilty votes. The remainder of the film described the jury's attempt to convince Fonda that he was wrong. As it turned out, Fonda convinced the other jurors that *they* were wrong, and the defendant was acquitted.

Jury deliberations such as that in *Twelve Angry Men* are common (Simon, 1980). Jurors who differ in their estimation of the value of particular evidence attempt to persuade the other jurors to side with them. At the outset, jurors may take an informal vote to see where they stand. More often than not, this initial ballot influences significantly the final verdict by presenting the determination of the majority of jurors (Kalven and Zeisel, 1966).

Hastie, Penrod, and Pennington (1983:119–120) have found that group pressure is responsible for moving minority factions in a jury to an alignment with the majority opinion. In jurisdictions where the majority-rule option is in effect, such as Oregon and

Louisiana, agreement among jurors is achieved more rapidly than in those requiring unanimity of opinion (Foss, 1981). Figure 11.2 shows the jury deliberation task.

When deliberations commence, juries may or may not establish a deliberation agenda. Ordinarily, juries discuss the importance of particular pieces of evidence and witness testimony. If there is an initial vote and the jury disagrees on the verdict, deliberations continue until it reaches a verdict. If the jury cannot agree on a verdict or cannot obtain the required majority, the judge will declare a mistrial.

■ THE VERDICT AND THE AFTERMATH

After deliberating, the jury returns to the courtroom to deliver its verdict to either the judge or an officer of the court. The defendant rises and faces the jury, while either the jury foreman or the judge reads the verdict aloud. If the verdict is not guilty, the defendant is released. In some cases, acquitted defendants may be rearrested for other crimes. Ordinarily, an acquittal removes the defendant from the criminal justice system.

If a guilty verdict is rendered by the jury, the defendant has the right to appeal the verdict. The defense attorney may request the judge to make a directed verdict of acquittal in spite of the jury's decision. The judge may, indeed, exercise this option. However, if the judge sets aside the jury verdict and declares the defendant acquitted, the prosecution can appeal that decision to a higher court.

If the judge does not grant the defense attorney's request, the defendant is sentenced. In some jurisdictions, a defendant will be sentenced in a separate proceeding at a later date, usually following a presentence investigation conducted by court-appointed officials. The presentence investigation functions to determine, in part, a defendant's potential for probation in lieu of incarceration. In any case, a convicted

Jury trials are unpredictable in their duration. Some last a few days, while others last a year or more. After a 10-month trial, John Landis, a movie director, was acquitted of charges that he was indirectly responsible for the deaths of actor Vic Morrow and two children during the filming of an action sequence for Twilight Zone—The Movie *in 1982.*

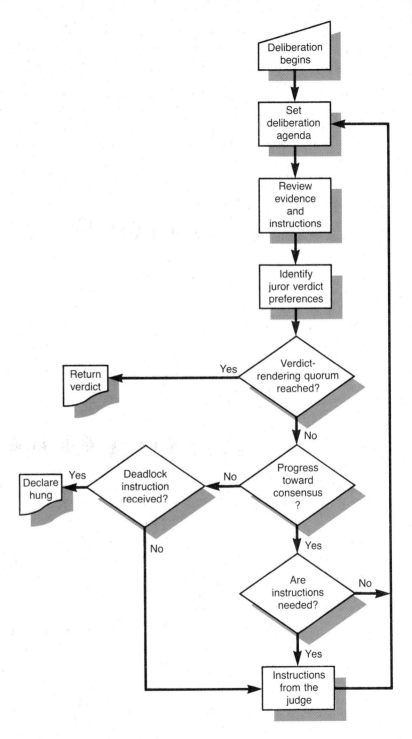

FIGURE 11.2 Jury Deliberation

Source: From R. Hastie, S. Penrod, and N. Pennington, *Inside the Jury* (Cambridge, MA: Harvard Univ. Press, 1983), p. 25. Reprinted by permission.

defendant is entitled to appeal the jury verdict to a higher court on any number of grounds.

The appeal process may take years. In all of the United States Supreme Court cases presented in this and previous chapters, the interval of time between the offense, the conviction, and the United States Supreme Court decision has been several years. Before a case gets before the Supreme Court, however, it must be reviewed by higher courts within the particular state jurisdiction where the original judgment was entered against the defendant. The appeals process consumes much time. Cases presented before the Supreme Court involve constitutional issues primarily; that is, were a defendant's constitutional rights violated at any stage of the criminal proceeding?

■ SUMMARY

A trial proceeding provides a defendant with the opportunity to confront and cross-examine accusers and to offer exculpatory evidence favoring a verdict of not guilty. A trial is an adversarial proceeding where the prosecution attempts to establish a defendant's guilt and the defense attempts to prove the defendant's innocence of any offenses alleged.

Trial procedures vary from one jurisdiction to the next. Where a jury trial is conducted, the number of jurors ranges from six to twelve. At the federal level, a jury verdict must be unanimous. At the state and local levels, however, a unanimous verdict may or may not be required, depending upon the prevailing laws.

Juries are made up of persons from the community or region that has jurisdiction over the crimes alleged. The selection of jury members involves questioning concerning possible prejudices in the case before the court. Both the prosecution and defense attorneys attempt to select jurors favorable to their particular interests. Jurors are excluded from jury duty for illness or other compelling circumstances, and both prosecution and defense attorneys may challenge any juror for cause. Jurors also may be excluded by peremptory challenges, as the prosecutor and defense attorney attempt to construct the most favorable jury. These peremptory challenges may not be used for purposes of discrimination, however.

The science of jury selection is popular. Many attorneys turn to consulting firms that specialize in the selection of jury members. Thus far, however, the results of studies investigating particular jury member characteristics and decision-making propensities have been inconsistent and disappointing.

In a trial proceeding, both the prosecution and defense have specific roles and follow established protocol in presenting evidence and witnesses. Each side is permitted to address the jury with an opening statement. Each side is also entitled to cross-examine witnesses and to object to the introduction and relevance of certain evidence.

Jury deliberations are conducted following the presentation of witnesses and evidence from both the prosecution and defense. If the jury cannot agree on a verdict as local, state, or federal law requires, the presiding judge will declare a mistrial. This will require a new trial before a new jury. If the jury finds the defendant guilty of the crime alleged, the judge will pass sentence either at the conclusion of the trial or in a separate proceeding.

KEY TERMS

bench trials

criminal trial

direct examination

exclusionary rule

fruits of the poisonous tree
   doctrine

impeachment

litigants

motion to dismiss

motions in limine

peremptory challenges

pretrial motions

venire

victim-witness assistance
   programs

voir dire

QUESTIONS FOR REVIEW

1. What is a pretrial motion? What else is it called? What are some examples of pretrial motions?
2. Differentiate between a bench trial and a jury trial. Does any evidence indicate that a defendant is better off having a bench trial than having a jury trial?
3. What is a criminal trial? What are some of the functions of a trial proceeding?
4. Does a criminal defendant have to have a jury trial if he or she is charged with murder? Can the defendant waive the right to a jury trial? What constitutional amendment pertains to jury trials?
5. What is a venire? What is it used for?
6. Identify three functions of juries. What United States Supreme Court decision pertained to setting a lower limit for jury sizes? What was the limit established?
7. Suppose that a six-person jury brought back a verdict of guilty, but the vote was 5 to 1. Evaluate this verdict in view of what you have learned about jury size and unanimity of agreement among jurors.
8. On the basis of some of the research conducted about jury size, is a twelve-member jury more representative of community interests than a six-person jury is? What are some differences between these jury sizes other than the number of jurors?
9. How are juries selected? Where do jurors come from? What criteria do courts use to prepare jury lists?
10. What are five rules of thumb believed by many attorneys and reported by Rita Simon about juror characteristics and accompanying juror attitudes?

11. Do scientific consulting firms appear to make a difference in criminal cases using scientific jury selection methods? Briefly discuss the case of Joan Little and the apparent impact of a consulting firm on the verdict in her trial. What did the presiding judge say about Ms. Little's case?
12. How can a prosecutor or defense attorney reject any juror from serving on the jury? Can either side reject as many prospective jurors at will or are the sides limited in their challenges? What reasons allow both the prosecution and the defense to reject jurors an unlimited number of times?
13. What is a death-qualified jury? Why is it important?
14. At the federal level, must a jury be unanimous in its verdict for conviction? Does it make any difference if there are eleven jurors?
15. In such states as Oregon and Louisiana, is unanimity required to convict someone of a criminal offense? What rules apply in these states?
16. What is meant by the fruit of the poisonous tree? What does it have to do with evidence? Explain briefly.
17. What is the exclusionary rule?
18. How reliable is the testimony of a child witness? Cite some research that has investigated the competency of child witnesses.
19. What is the purpose of a victim-witness assistance program?
20. Who usually gets the last argument in a criminal case before a jury?

SUGGESTED READINGS

Crites, Laura L., and Winifred L. Hepperle (1987). *Women, the courts, and equality.* Beverly Hills, CA: Sage.

Hans, Valerie P., and Neil Vidmar (1986). *Judging the jury.* New York: Plenum Press.

McDonald, William F. (1988). *The defense counsel.* Beverly Hills, CA: Sage.

Van Dyke, J. (1977). *Jury selection procedures.* Cambridge, MA: Ballinger.

Weisheit, Ralph, and Sue Mahan (1988). *Women, crime, and criminal justice.* Cincinnati, OH: Pilgrimage Press.

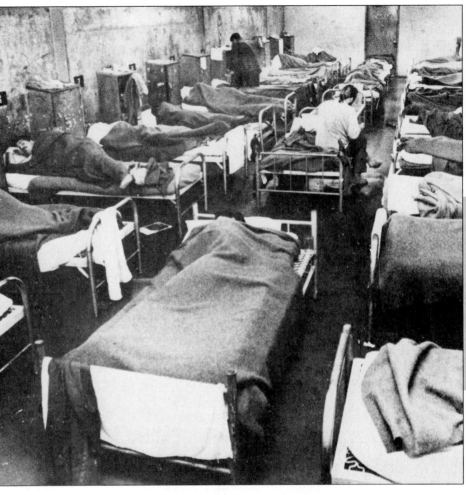

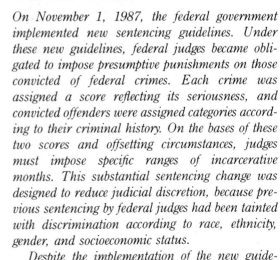

On November 1, 1987, the federal government implemented new sentencing guidelines. Under these new guidelines, federal judges became obligated to impose presumptive punishments on those convicted of federal crimes. Each crime was assigned a score reflecting its seriousness, and convicted offenders were assigned categories according to their criminal history. On the bases of these two scores and offsetting circumstances, judges must impose specific ranges of incarcerative months. This substantial sentencing change was designed to reduce judicial discretion, because previous sentencing by federal judges had been tainted with discrimination according to race, ethnicity, gender, and socioeconomic status.

Despite the implementation of the new guidelines, nearly 150 federal judges balked at abiding by them. On various grounds, judges rejected these

CORRECTIONS

sentencing constraints. One objection lodged by federal judges and many offenders convicted under the new guidelines was that the separation of powers doctrine had been violated. The United States Sentencing Commission, a body created by Congress under the Comprehensive Crime Control Act of 1984, included federal judges as a part of its composition. Thus, federal judges were in the position of making statutory punishments as well as imposing those punishments.

The sentencing guidelines underwent an official United States Supreme Court challenge in the case of Mistretta v. United States *in January 1989. John M. Mistretta and another man were indicted in the United States District Court for the Western District of Missouri on three counts involving a cocaine sale on December 10, 1987. Subsequently, Mistretta was convicted, and he was sentenced*

under the new guideline formula, which carried a more severe incarcerative penalty and allowed for fewer judicial sentencing options than did the previous statutory penalties. This greater severity was consonant with the congressional aim of getting tough on crime in general and those trafficking in illegal drugs in particular. Mistretta's attorney argued that excessive legislative power had been delegated to the commission by Congress, but the eight-to-one Supreme Court opinion (Justice Scalia dissenting) stated:

> [T]he Sentencing Guidelines are constitutional, since Congress neither (1) delegated excessive legislative power to the Commission nor (2) violated the separation-of-powers principle by placing the Commission in the Judicial Branch, by requiring federal judges to serve on the Commission and to share their authority with nonjudges, or by empowering the Pres-

ident to appoint Commission members and to remove them for cause. The Constitution's structural protections do not prohibit Congress from delegating to an expert body within the Judicial Branch the intricate task of formulating Sentencing Guidelines . . . nor from calling upon the . . . wisdom and experience of the Judicial Branch in creating policy on a matter uniquely within the ken of judges.

While this decision did not eliminate other challenges of the guidelines, it indicates the sentiments of the court toward the guidelines and how that court may decide future cases.

Part IV is an extensive examination of sentencing and punishment. It discusses various sentencing options available to judges, as well as some overall objectives of sentencing. It treats correctional institutions for men and women and covers correctional issues extensively. This part also describes probation systems, parole systems, and community-based corrections, together with some of the moral, legal, and ethical issues associated with each.

Chapter 12 explores the sentencing process. Judges may rely upon aggravating or mitigating circumstances when sentencing offenders. Probation officers supply presentence investigation reports for many serious offenders, and these documents fulfill a vital role in the sentencing process. The chapter also describes a variety of sentencing functions, different sentencing schemes, and the implications of the different schemes for convicted offenders. Sentencing reforms in recent years have generated numerous moral and legal issues.

Chapter 13 discusses correctional institutions, which are facilities that accommodate convicted offenders. First, it discusses correctional goals. It distinguishes between jails and prisons and discusses each of these incarcerative facilities in-depth. The chapter also describes jail and prison inmate characteristics, and it includes an examination of women's prisons and some of the problems relating to incarcerating females. Prisons vary in their functions and complexity, and inmate violence is commonplace. Attempts to segregate prisoners according to their dangerousness or risk to others have led to classification systems. The chapter illustrates some of these systems, and it describes prison management and construction.

Chapter 14 investigates prison culture and the lives of inmates within the jail and prison settings. Correctional officers monitor and regulate the lives of these inmates. The chapter discusses correctional officer recruitment and training practices, together with some of the psychological and social problems experienced by these officers in their interactions with inmates. In recent years, the private sector has gradually taken over a limited amount of inmate management and control through the operation of private prisons and aftercare facilities, so the chapter explores the privatization issue. Finally, the chapter highlights several correctional issues, including prison and jail overcrowding, the exploitation of prison labor, education and vocational training programs for inmates, racism in prisons, prisoner rights, and jailhouse lawyers.

Chapter 15 is an overview of probation and parole programs. These are front-door and back-door strategies for easing jail and prison overcrowding. Less serious, nonviolent offenders are often placed on probation rather than incarcerated. Of the offenders who are incarcerated, many are selected for early release through parole. However, the programs have elicited criticism from the public and others as being lenient or discriminatory. The chapter features some of the problems of probation and parole programs. It includes the major functions of probation and parole and a discussion of whether or not these functions are achieved in various jurisdictions. A variety of intermediate punishments are available to convicted offenders, where offenders receive intensive supervision or supervised release in lieu of incarceration. The chapter describes and evaluates furloughs, halfway houses, and intensive supervised probation programs. It also describes relatively new monitoring and incarcerative strategies, such as electronic monitoring and home incarceration, together with some of the criticisms that these programs have prompted.

The Sentencing Process

■ INTRODUCTION

This chapter examines the sentencing process at all levels. Included in this examination are the goals of sentencing, a number of sentencing issues, a defendant's rights in the sentencing process, selected variables and their influence on sentencing decisions and sentencing severity, predicting dangerousness, and several popular sentencing alternatives.

The sentencing process is the penalty phase of the criminal justice system. While sentencing is one of the most important subjects, it is also controversial. In recent years, the sentencing practices of judges at the local, state, and federal levels have been widely criticized as discriminatory, unfair, inappropriate, inconsistent, and ineffective (Figueira-McDonough, 1985; Ghali and Chesney-Lind, 1986; von Hirsch, 1984). Such factors as jail and prison overcrowding, escalating rates of recidivism, increased use of plea bargaining, and obvious gender, racial, ethnic, and socioeconomic influences on sentencing disparity have led to criticisms of the sentencing process generally and judicial sentencing practices specifically (Ebbesen and Konecni, 1985; Kempf and Austin, 1986; Koppel, 1984). Some sentencing reformers favor the selective incapacitation of felons who pose a high risk for recidivism. **Selective incapacitation** is the process of incarcerating certain offenders who are defined by various criteria as having a strong propensity to repeat serious crimes (Greenwood, 1982).

Opponents of selective incapacitation argue that the process is discriminatory, results in undeserved punishment for many offenders, fails to identify the best predictors of criminal behavior, and violates one's constitutional right to due process (Clear and Barry, 1983; Hill, 1985; McGriff, 1985).

■ THE SENTENCING REFORM ACT OF 1984

Faced with a rapidly expanding prison population and overcrowding, Congress passed the **Sentencing Reform Act of 1984** (18 U.S.C., Sec. 3551, 1989). Amended several times in recent years, this act established several significant policy shifts to be implemented by federal trial judges in their sentencing practices. For instance, Section 239 of Public Law 98-473 provided:

Since, due to an impending crisis in prison overcrowding, *available Federal prison space must be treated as a scarce resource* in the sentencing of criminal defendants; since, sentencing decisions should be designed to ensure that prison resources are, first and foremost, reserved for those violent and serious criminal offenders who pose the most dangerous threat to society; since, in cases of nonviolent and nonserious offenders, the interests of society as a whole as well as individual victims of crime can continue to be served through *the imposition of alternative sentences, such as restitution and community service* . . . Federal judges, in determining the particular sentence to be imposed [should] consider (1) the nature and circumstances of the offense and the history and characteristics of the defendant; (2) the general appropriateness of imposing a sentence other than imprisonment in cases in which the defendant has not been convicted of a crime of violence or otherwise serious offense; and (3) the general appropriateness of imposing a sentence of imprisonment in cases in which the defendant has been convicted of a crime of violence or otherwise serious offense. [Emphasis mine] (18 U.S.C., Sec. 3551, 1989:263–264)

This act has given federal judges considerable latitude in their sentencing of criminal offenders. It encourages judges to consider seriously various alternative sentences in lieu of incarceration, such as community service, restitution, and even probation. At the end of 1984, there was a noticeable increase in the federal probationer and parolee populations. The parolee population increased by 3 percent, while the probationer population increased by 5 percent (Greenfeld, 1986:2–4). Also during 1984, forty-five out of fifty-two jurisdictions examined (the fifty states, the District of Columbia, and the federal system) had substantial increases in their populations of probationers (Green-feld, 1986:1).

Among the factors to be considered by the trial judge are (1) the nature and circumstances of the offense and the history and characteristics of the defendant; (2) the need for the sentence imposed to reflect the seriousness of the offense, to promote respect for the law, to afford adequate deterrence to criminal conduct, and to protect the public from further crimes of the defendant; (3) the educational or training services, medical care, or other correctional treatment appropriate for any particular defendant; (4) the sentences available; and (5) the need to avoid unwarranted sentence disparities among defendants with similar records who have been found guilty of similar conduct (18 U.S.C., Sec. 3553, 1989:265).

Congress has been more sensitive to at least some of the criticisms leveled at judicial sentencing practices in recent years. In several jurisdictions, for example, women have received less severe sentences than have men who were convicted for similar offenses (Zingraff and Thomson, 1984). Quite often, black and ethnic minority defendants receive harsher sentences than do whites convicted of similar crimes under similar circumstances (Clayton, 1983; Holmes and Daudistel, 1984; La Free, 1985; Peterson and Hagan, 1984). However, some investigators have reported no significant differences in sentencing severity as the result of racial, gender, or ethnic factors (Ghali and Chesney-Lind, 1986; Tinker, Quiring, and Pimentel, 1985).

Many local and state jurisdictions are influenced by the sentencing standards and provisions of federal courts, because these jurisdictions have similar problems such as prison overcrowding. Several states, including Tennessee and Louisiana, have experienced substantial increases in their parolee populations as the result of court-ordered prison population reductions (Greenfeld, 1986:3). Compared with 1983, Tennessee's

CRIME BEAT

On the evening of March 1, 1982, 31-year-old Sterling Rault, an accountant for the Louisiana Energy & Development Corporation (LEDC), raped, shot, killed, and with gasoline set afire Jane Francioni, a 21-year-old LEDC clerk. Rault had a history of embezzlement with other firms, although he was never prosecuted for his crimes; he had always repaid the companies or made restitution. In one instance, he was suspected of the attempted murder of a coworker who may have turned him in.

When he set Francioni's body on fire in a New Orleans ditch, an off-duty state trooper spotted the blaze and saw Rault running from the scene. He stopped Rault and arrested him after smelling gasoline and seeing the burning corpse. In August 1987, Rault was electrocuted in the Louisiana State Penitentiary at Angola.

In 1990, thirty-two states had the death penalty as a possible punishment for those committing capital crimes. Louisiana is one of those states. The death penalty is one of the most controversial issues in American jurisprudence. There are those who cheer the execution of serial murderers such as Ted Bundy, while an equally vocal aggregate of protesters considers the death penalty barbaric.

One of the most disturbing features of the death penalty is that it seems to be selectively applied, largely to blacks. Of the 1,900 convicted murderers on death row currently, nearly 50 percent are black. Since blacks comprise approximately 12 percent of the United States population, this disproportionate representation of blacks awaiting execution raises questions about the discriminatory nature of the death penalty. This issue has been addressed by previous United States Supreme Courts and has led to bifurcated trials to achieve greater fairness in sentencing. Is the death penalty discriminatory? Should those convicted of capital crimes be executed or incarcerated for the rest of their lives?

1984 parolee population increased by 83 percent, while Louisiana's parolee population increased by 57 percent during the same time interval. Other states, such as New Mexico, have been forced on occasion to either refuse new admissions to its prisons or engage in mandatory releases of inmates. Several of the states do not have parole boards to function as a safety valve to alleviate prison overcrowding.

Court-ordered reductions in prison populations place state and local trial judges in precarious positions, not unlike those of their federal district judge counterparts. Increasingly, trial judges are forced to place convicted felons on probation rather than incarcerating them. Against their better judgment, trial judges at all levels are contributing to a growing probationer population that includes an increasing number of serious offenders (Petersilia, 1985:2). In California, for example, 70 percent of all convicted felons are granted probation. By the end of 1984, 1 percent of California's population consisted of probationers (Petersilia, 1985:2).

One implication of the Sentencing Reform Act of 1984 is that it is causing judges to reconsider their ideas about sentencing and to change their priorities concerning *which* convicted felons pose the *least* public risk if placed on probation. The national recidivism rate is such that about half of those who are released from prison annually commit new offenses within the next 3 years (Greenfeld, 1985:1–2). In an investigation of California felony probationers conducted by the Rand Corporation, 65 percent of those placed on probation committed new offenses within a 40-month period (Petersilia, Turner, Kahan, and Peterson, 1985). These statistics have made judges increasingly sensitive to the question of a felon's dangerousness and the conditions under which dangerousness provisions ought to be invoked in the sentencing process (Gottlieb and Rosen, 1984; Morris and Miller, 1985; Stone, 1985; von Hirsch, 1985). Before examining these and other factors, it is important to consider some of the functions and types of sentencing systems.

■ FUNCTIONS OF SENTENCING

The Sentencing Reform Act of 1984 restated a number of sentencing objectives that have guided sentencing judges in their leniency or harshness toward convicted defendants. Some of these objectives have been made explicit by various states and local jurisdictions in past years, while others have been implicitly incorporated into prevailing sentencing guidelines. Some of the more important functions of sentencing are (1) to reflect the seriousness of the offense; (2) to promote respect for the law; (3) to provide just punishment for the offense; (4) to deter future criminal conduct; (5) to protect the public from the convicted defendant; and (6) to provide the convicted defendant with education or vocational training or other rehabilitative relief. The purposes of sentencing include punishment or retribution, deterrence, custodial monitoring or incapacitation, and rehabilitation.

Reflecting the Seriousness of Offenses

One objective of sentencing is to juxtapose the sentence with the seriousness of the offense. In federal district courts prior to November 1, 1987, offenses were classified according to Class A, B, C, D and E felonies, and Class A, B, and C misdemeanors. Each of these classifications carried a minimum and maximum term of years for the convict's imprisonment. For example, if the maximum term of punishment was life imprisonment or if the maximum penalty was death, then the offense was a Class A felony. If the maximum term of imprisonment was 1 year or less but more than 6 months, then it was a Class A misdemeanor. These sentencing classifications were explicitly provided in 18 U.S.C., Sec. 3559 (1986). Table 12.1 shows the federal sentencing classification of offenses.

All federal criminal statutes had accompanying penalties and variable terms of imprisonment. Federal district judges could consider *any* felon eligible for immediate probation, unless the offense was either a Class A or a Class B felony. These felony classifications provided imprisonment for 20 years or more, life imprisonment, or the death penalty, but in certain exceptional cases, particularly if a sufficient number of mitigating circumstances were present, judges could exercise discretion and impose probation even in Class A and B felony cases. New federal sentencing guidelines changed these sentences and will be examined in a later section of this chapter.

Promoting Respect for the Law

A function of sentencing is to show offenders what can happen to them when criminal laws are violated, but if current recidivism rates are a measure of the respect for the law acquired by convicted offenders, then our sentencing practices are not successfully fulfilling this particular objective. An examination of the recidivism rates for 153,465

TABLE 12.1 Federal Sentencing Classification of Offenses

If Maximum Term of Imprisonment Authorized Is:	Then the Classification and Type of Offense Is:
Life imprisonment, death penalty	Class A felony
20 years or more	Class B felony
Less than 20 years but 10 or more years	Class C felony
Less than 10 years but 5 or more years	Class D felony
Less than 5 years but more than 1 year	Class E felony
1 year or less but more than 6 months	Class A misdemeanor
6 months or less but more than 30 days	Class B misdemeanor
30 days or less but more than 5 days	Class C misdemeanor
5 days or less, or no imprisonment	Infraction

Source: 18 U.S.C., Section 3559 (1986), pp. 268–269.

state prison inmates nationally reveals, for example, that 29 percent of these return to prison for committing new crimes within 1 year of their release; 48 percent return within 2 years of their release; and 60 percent return within 3 years of their release (Greenfeld, 1985:3).

Providing Just Punishment for Offenses

A historical analysis of sentencing reforms in the United States suggests that determining appropriate punishment for offenders has been at the forefront of sentencing issues for the last 2 centuries (Rossi, Simpson, and Miller, 1985; Shane-DuBow, Brown, and Olsen, 1985; Tonry and Zimring, 1983). In the first years of the United States, from 1790 to 1820, capital punishment was gradually replaced by lengthy incarceration. This was regarded as more humane and guaranteed more certain punishment to offenders (Rothman, 1983).

From 1820 to 1900, a general shift in sentencing policy occurred, reflecting the sentiments of various political interest groups and concerned citizens, moving sentencing priorities from deterrence to rehabilitation (Rothman, 1983; Stolz, 1984). In recent years, sentencing policy has shifted to the justice model, which is a legitimatization of the power of the state to administer sanctions (Cavender, 1984; Fogel, 1978; Tonry and Zimring, 1983). The **justice model** is a philosophy that emphasizes punishment as a primary objective of sentencing, fixed sentences, an abolition of parole, and an abandonment of the rehabilitative ideal. Some critics view the justice model as purely symbolic sentencing reform, because any policy that suggests an expansion of the present prison population ignores the fiscal crises facing federal and local governments (Cavender, 1984). Also, the emphasis of the justice model is convenient for avoiding the undesirable connotation associated with retribution or societal revenge (Cavender, 1984). As promoted by its proponents, among the favorable features of the justice model are that it promotes standards of equality and proportionality under the law and it neither overpunishes the poor nor overlooks the crimes of the rich (Humphries, 1984). The justice model seemingly encourages equal treatment in sentencing and avoids the discriminatory and disparate nature of existing judicial sentencing practices (Humphries, 1984).

Deterring Future Criminal Conduct

Evidence of substantial recidivism among first offenders and career criminals suggests that any sentence, even capital punishment, is an insufficient deterrent to future criminal conduct (Fattah, 1985; Hill, 1985; Scarfone, 1986). Does the selective incapacitation of recidivists significantly curb the commission of subsequent felonies? In a study of 3,552 convicted burglars conducted in Dade County, Florida, in 1982 (McGriff, 1985), the convicted burglars were given hypothetical sentences of 1, 3, and 5 years for their previous and most recent felony convictions prior to 1982. It was determined that 5.5 percent of the 1982 burglaries would not have occurred had these felons been given an earlier 1-year sentence. Furthermore, 26 percent of the 1982 burglaries would not have been committed by these burglars had they received and served a 5-year sentence at the time of their last felony conviction (McGriff, 1985), but 77.5 percent of these felons were first offenders and unaffected by the hypothetical sentences. Thus, it is questionable that the gains (absence of burglaries) achieved through incarceration for a 5-year period would seriously offset the financial expenditures associated with imprisoning these offenders (McGriff, 1985).

Protecting the Public from Convicted Defendants

Incapacitating felons by imprisonment or hospitalization effectively isolates them from the public. However, prisons and jails in the United States have become increasingly overcrowded with recidivists and career criminals (Petersilia, 1985:1). The exigencies of state and federal correctional institutions are such that prison construction is simply not keeping pace with the number of felony convictions. For instance, between 1974 and 1983, the national prison population increased by 48 percent, but the probation population increased by 63 percent (Petersilia, 1985:1). Some persons are concerned that excessive use of probation creates a high degree of risk to the public, with increasing numbers of convicted felons permitted to reenter society and escape confinement.

Judges are currently concerned with the potential public risk posed by the felons to be sentenced. Judges would like to be able to turn to specific social and personal background criteria for each convicted defendant and determine with some high measure of certainty the convict's potential for staying clean, or not committing additional criminal acts. The criteria most often used by judges are unrelated to a convicted defendant's prospects for recidivism, however. The record-keeping practices of various jurisdictions are often so unsophisticated that the same defendant may go through the justice system several times as a first offender in different parts of the state. Persons convicted and punished for crimes in one state also may commit crimes in other states. Again, a quick check of state records may fail to disclose that the person has been convicted elsewhere for serious crimes and should be treated differently in sentencing. In short, it is not always an easy matter to identify recidivists.

The contemporary sentencing debate centers around a choice between basing sentences and sentencing severity on the blameworthiness of past criminal acts committed by an offender versus predictions of the offender's future dangerousness (von Hirsch, 1985). Most states have **habitual offender statutes,** which require the imposition of greater sentences on dangerous, multiple, or persistent offenders, but few state jurisdictions enforce such statutes (Hunzeker, 1985). In a survey of all state corrections departments in 1985, for example, Hunzeker (1985) found that three states reported no inmates serving time under these statutes and seventeen other states reported fewer than 3 percent of their inmate populations consisting of such offenders. A likely explanation for a state's reluctance to pursue habitual offender charges against a particular offender is prison overcrowding and the mandatory imprisonment provisions associated with an habitual offender conviction.

Providing Education and Vocational Training

Education and vocational training are the rehabilitative functions of sentencing. Some critics have observed that the rehabilitative ideal has declined over the years as a viable correctional goal (Cavender, 1984; Rothman, 1983). Alternatives to incarceration, alternative sentencing, currently include restitution to victims, community service, and educational or vocational training (Berman, 1983; Cunniff, 1985; Koppel, 1984; Smith, 1984; Stanley and Baginsky, 1984).

■ SENTENCING SYSTEMS

Sentencing systems vary from one state to the next and jurisdictions within each state. There are four basic kinds of sentencing systems. They include (1) indeterminate sentencing; (2) determinate sentencing; (3) mandatory sentencing; and (4) presumptive sentencing.

Indeterminate Sentencing

Indeterminate sentences are sentences of imprisonment by the court for either specified or unspecified durations, with the final release date determined by a parole board (Black, 1979:694). Indeterminate sentences provide judges with maximum flexibility in the discretion they can exercise in sentencing (Goodstein, Kramer, and Nuss, 1984; Nagel and Geraci, 1983). In the federal system, for example, district judges may impose sentences within the ranges for the various classes of felonies and misdemeanors. It is also within a judge's discretion to place a convicted offender on probation in lieu of incarceration, in view of the facts disclosed by the presentence investigation. In addition, indeterminate sentencing provides parole boards with considerable power in determining an offender's release date. For example, in Oklahoma, judges impose fixed indeterminate sentences that are the maximum times offenders may serve, but parole board action can effect a prisoner's release before a third of the sentence is actually served (Koppel, 1984:9). Similar sentencing practices and parole board actions are observed for Oregon and Wyoming, as well. Prisoners may be awarded shorter sentences by parole boards for good behavior or for participating in various prison activities and programs (U.S. Bureau of Justice Statistics, 1983).

Indeterminate sentencing is criticized as contributing to sentencing disparities among judges for offenders of different socioeconomic backgrounds, ethnic and racial identities, and genders (Brantingham, 1985; Griswold, 1985; Koppel, 1984; Zingraff and Thomson, 1984). Therefore, in recent years, state legislatures have limited sentencing discretion by creating statutes that require mandatory sentencing for specific terms for various classes of offenses (California Legislative Analyst, 1985; Hammrock and Santangelo, 1985). For instance, most states have mandatory prison term statutes for at least one of the following categories: habitual crime, violent crime, narcotics violation, and crime involving the use of a firearm (U.S. Bureau of Justice Statistics, 1983).

Determinate Sentencing

Determinate sentences involve sentences by the court to confinement for a fixed period of time, which must be served in full and without parole board intervention, less any good time earned in prison (Black, 1979:405; Koppel, 1984:2). In Minnesota, for example, the judge sets a determinate prison term based on sentencing guidelines that were established in 1980. Although parole release has been abolished in that state, because of good time, a prisoner may be released before actually completing the full term of the sentence (Koppel, 1984:8). In fact, in the jurisdictions where determinate sentencing has been implemented, the average prison term imposed by the court has decreased by 50 percent compared with other sentencing forms (Cunniff, 1985:5). In some states such as New Mexico, however, the average sentence actually *served* has increased. Thus, while judges are inclined to impose shorter terms of incarceration for offenders under determinate sentencing, the offenders are serving longer sentences than they did under indeterminate sentencing.

One objective of determinate sentencing is to provide prisoners with release certainty, and it is ideally designed to increase fairness in the sentencing process (Goodstein, Kramer, and Nuss, 1984). North Carolina utilized indeterminate sentencing guidelines until 1981 (Clarke et al., 1983), but negative public reaction to unjustified sentencing variations in felony cases led to North Carolina's Fair Sentencing Act. Based upon an analysis of data derived from over 15,000 felony judgments between 1979 and 1982, persons convicted of felonies statewide stood a better chance of serving time in prison after the act than before it. The actual chances that offenders would serve prison time increased from 55 percent in 1979 to 63 percent in 1982, yet the median *length* of sentences *decreased* from 60 months to 36 months between the 2 years.

Mandatory Sentencing. Both mandatory sentencing and presumptive sentencing are considered subclasses of determinate sentencing. There are some differences, however. Under **mandatory sentencing,** the court is required to impose an incarcerative sentence of a specified length, without the option for probation, suspended sentence, or immediate parole eligibility (Koppel, 1984:2). This sentencing form allows the court no leeway in deciding whether or not to incarcerate a convicted defendant. Almost every jurisdiction has one or more statutes with mandatory sentencing provisions.

Hawaii's penal code was amended in 1976 to provide for the mandatory imprisonment of repeat offenders (Hawaii Crime Commission, 1984). In 1980, the Hawaii legislature enacted a mandatory sentencing statute for all Class A felonies, including murder, kidnapping, and narcotics trafficking. Between 1976 and 1983, Hawaii's imprisonment rate climbed substantially, possibly as a result of such mandatory sentencing provisions. Repeat offenders are often categorized as habitual offenders and career criminals. Normally, habitual offenders are offenders with two or more previous felony convictions. Career criminals are offenders who make their living from crime. Most states, including Hawaii, have habitual offender statutes, which usually provide mandatory incarceration, possibly life imprisonment, for persistent offenders.

There are several persistent problems with mandatory sentencing of persistent offenders. One is prison overcrowding. Requiring mandatory incarceration may be sound in principle, but it is difficult to implement on a large scale if there is no room in prisons for convicted offenders. Furthermore, habitual offender statutes in most states are not enforced vigorously. Rather, they are used as prosecutorial leverage in plea bargaining; it is not illegal for prosecutors to threaten to prosecute defendants on habitual offender charges if they do not plead guilty to other offenses with which they are charged. Of course, there must be sufficient evidence to provide a factual basis for the guilty plea and a judge makes this determination in a plea agreement hearing, but if all habitual offenders were prosecuted and convicted, the mandatory incarcerative sentences of life imprisonment would soon cause overwhelming prison and jail overcrowding problems beyond those already experienced by correctional authorities in most jurisdictions.

Presumptive Sentencing. Another type of determinate sentencing is presumptive sentencing. Presumptive sentencing is statutory sentencing that specifies normal sentences of particular lengths with limited judicial leeway to shorten or lengthen the term of sentence (Black, 1979:1223; Koppel, 1984:2). Ordinarily, under presumptive sentencing, the sentence prescribed by statute must be imposed in all unexceptional circumstances (Koppel, 1984:2). Depending upon whether there are any mitigating or aggravating circumstances, offenders may have their sentences enhanced or decreased by 1 or more years under such systems. In California, for example, a judge imposes a determinate prison term based upon presumptive sentence lengths that are set by legislation (Koppel, 1984:5). Three presumptive sentence lengths are specified for each class of offense, and the judge is obligated to impose the middle sentence length *unless* there are mitigating or aggravating circumstances. In instances where such factors exist, the greater or lesser sentence length *may be imposed by the judge at his or her discretion.*

For those states that have instituted sentencing reforms of various kinds in recent years, most have changed from an indeterminate to a determinate sentencing system, including presumptive or mandatory sentencing provisions and eliminating or drastically curtailing parole discretion (Koppel, 1984:2). California and Minnesota are examples of states that utilize presumptive sentencing provisions currently.

■ SENTENCING GUIDELINES

In November 1987 the United States government implemented presumptive sentencing guidelines for use by judges in all federal district courts. These guidelines were formulated by the United States Sentencing Commission under a mandate set forth by the Comprehensive Crime Control Act of 1984 (U.S. Sentencing Commission, 1987). While these guidelines have generated considerable controversy (Champion, 1989), they provide federal judges with recommended sentencing ranges for those convicted of any federal crime.

Table 12.2 shows the sentencing table and guideline range recommended by the United States Sentencing Commission. Across the top of the table are Roman numerals ranging from I to VI. These refer to a defendant's criminal history and place the offender in one of six categories. Down the left-hand side of the table are forty-three offense levels that reflect the seriousness of the offense. While it is beyond the scope of this book to provide a comprehensive analysis of how the various sentencing lengths were derived, this section presents some general information about how an offender's criminal history is derived. The criminal history categories across the top of the sentencing table in Table 12.2 are determined as follows:

1. Add 3 points for each prior sentence of imprisonment exceeding 1 year and 1 month.
2. Add 2 points for each prior sentence of imprisonment of at least 60 days not counted in (1).
3. Add 1 point for each prior sentence not included in (1) or (2), up to a total of 4 points for this item.
4. Add 2 points if the defendant committed the instant offense while under any criminal sentence, including probation, parole, supervised release, imprisonment, work release, or escape status.
5. Add 2 points if the defendant committed the instant offense less than two years after release from imprisonment on a sentence counted under (1) or (2). If 2 points are added for item (4), add only 1 point for this item (adapted from U.S. Sentencing Guidelines, 1987:4.1).

An example follows. Suppose an offender has been convicted of perjury in a federal district court. This offense has a base offense level of 12, meaning that the sentencing judge would move down the left-hand column to 12. Further suppose that the convicted offender had served a 2-year sentence for forgery and had been on parole for 2½ years when the new conviction offense occurred. Finally, suppose that the offender had been convicted of two previous felonies in the past 20 years, and in each of those cases, the offender served separate sentences of 1 year. We would arrive at the following criminal history score:

Facts	Points
One prior sentence of at least 1 year and 1 month	3 points
Two prior sentences of at least 60 days' imprisonment	4 points
A new conviction offense committed while on parole	2 points
Sum	9 points

The nine points would place the offender in criminal history category VI. Examining Table 12.2, the offense level for perjury, 12, intersects with criminal history category IV, showing a sentencing range of 21 to 27 months. Thus, the federal judge would

TABLE 12.2 United States Sentencing Commission Sentencing Table

Offense Level	Criminal History Category					
	I 0 or 1	II 2 or 3	III 4, 5, 6	IV 7, 8, 9	V 10, 11, 12	VI 13 or more
1	0–1	0–2	0–3	0–4	0–5	0–6
2	0–2	0–3	0–4	0–5	0–6	1–7
3	0–3	0–4	0–5	0–6	2–8	3–9
4	0–4	0–5	0–6	2–8	4–10	6–12
5	0–5	0–6	1–7	4–10	6–12	9–15
6	0–6	1–7	2–8	6–12	9–15	12–18
7	1–7	2–8	4–10	8–14	12–18	15–21
8	2–8	4–10	6–12	10–16	15–21	18–24
9	4–10	6–12	8–14	12–18	18–24	21–27
10	6–12	8–14	10–16	15–21	21–27	24–30
11	8–14	10–16	12–18	18–24	24–30	27–33
12	10–16	12–18	15–21	21–27	27–33	30–37
13	12–18	15–21	18–24	24–30	30–37	33–41
14	15–21	18–24	21–27	27–33	33–41	37–46
15	18–24	21–27	24–30	30–37	37–46	41–51
16	21–27	24–30	27–33	33–41	41–51	46–57
17	24–30	27–33	30–37	37–46	46–57	51–63
18	27–33	30–37	33–41	41–51	51–63	57–71
19	30–37	33–41	37–46	46–57	57–71	63–78
20	33–41	37–46	41–51	51–63	63–78	70–87
21	37–46	41–51	46–57	57–71	70–87	77–96
22	41–51	46–57	51–63	63–78	77–96	84–105
23	46–57	51–63	57–71	70–87	84–105	92–115
24	51–63	57–71	63–78	77–96	92–115	100–125
25	57–71	63–78	70–87	84–105	100–125	110–137
26	63–78	70–87	78–97	92–115	110–137	120–150
27	70–87	78–97	87–108	100–125	120–150	130–162
28	78–97	87–108	97–121	110–137	130–162	140–175
29	87–108	97–121	108–135	121–151	140–175	151–188
30	97–121	108–135	121–151	135–168	151–188	168–210
31	108–135	121–151	135–168	151–188	168–210	188–235
32	121–151	135–168	151–188	168–210	188–235	210–262
33	135–168	151–188	168–210	188–235	210–262	235–293
34	151–188	168–210	188–235	210–262	235–293	262–327
35	168–210	188–235	210–262	235–293	262–327	292–365
36	188–235	210–262	235–293	262–327	292–365	324–405
37	210–262	235–293	262–327	292–365	324–405	360–life
38	235–293	262–327	292–365	324–405	360–life	360–life
39	262–327	292–365	324–405	360–life	360–life	360–life
40	292–365	324–405	360–life	360–life	360–life	360–life
41	324–405	360–life	360–life	360–life	360–life	360–life
42	360–life	360–life	360–life	360–life	360–life	360–life
43	life	life	life	life	life	life

impose an incarcerative sentence of months ranging from 21 to 27, probably in the middle or presumptive range of 24 or 25 months. These months of incarceration could be raised or lowered, depending upon whether there are any aggravating or mitigating circumstances.

In any case, it is clear that little sentencing discretion is left up to federal district judges under this scheme. In fact, one reason for creating these guidelines in the first place was to reduce disparities among judges. Sentencing disparities observed among federal and state judges in past years have been largely attributable to extralegal and nonrational factors, such as race, ethnicity, gender, and socioeconomic background. While the establishment of sentencing guidelines does not automatically eliminate sentencing disparities, they are intended to minimize them.

■ AGGRAVATING AND MITIGATING CIRCUMSTANCES

A violent crime is one characterized by extreme physical force including murder or homicide, forcible rape or child sexual abuse, assault and battery by means of a dangerous weapon, robbery, and arson (Black, 1979:1408). Sometimes these offenses are referred to as crimes against the person, because persons are directly involved as victims and affected emotionally and physically as a result. Nonviolent offenses include crimes such as burglary, vehicular theft, embezzlement, fraud, forgery, and larceny. These are often referred to as crimes against property, and although persons are indirectly victimized or affected by such offenses, their lives and physical well-being are not directly jeopardized.

Judges are more lenient in the sentencing of those who have committed nonviolent offenses than of those who have committed violent acts (Chaiken and Chaiken, 1984; Petersilia, 1985). Presentence reports include information about the offenses committed and especially aggravating or mitigating circumstances.

Aggravating Circumstances

Aggravating circumstances are those that may increase the severity of punishment. Factors considered by judges to be aggravating include:

1. Death or serious bodily injury to one or more victims.
2. A crime committed while the offender was out on bail facing other criminal charges.
3. A crime committed while the offender was on probation, parole, or work release.
4. Previous offenses for which the offender had been punished.
5. Leadership in the commission of an offense involving two or more offenders.
6. A violent offense involving more than one victim.
7. Extreme cruelty during the commission of the offense.
8. Use of a dangerous weapon in the commission of the crime, with high risk to human life.

If a convicted defendant has one or more aggravating circumstances accompanying the crime committed, the judge is likely to enhance the punishment prescribed. In simple terms, enhancement means a longer sentence, incarceration in lieu of probation, or a

CRIME BEAT

Three men—one of Utah's notorious "Hi-Fi" torture killers and two men who were accomplices to murders—were executed in the United States Friday, the most in a single day since the death penalty was reinstated in 1976.

Five men were to have died, but two received stays.

At 1:18 A.M., Alabama electrocuted Wayne Eugene Ritter. At 3:13 A.M. Dale Selby Pierre died by lethal injection in Utah, and at 7:11 A.M. Beauford White was pronounced dead in Florida's electric chair.

Pierre was one of the "Hi-Fi killers" who in 1974 forced five robbery victims at an Ogden, Utah, stereo shop to drink drain cleaner, then jammed a pen into one victim's ear before shooting all five, killing three.

Ritter died for his part in the murder of Mobile pawnshop owner Edward Nassar during a 1977 robbery.

White, 41, the 17th man executed in Florida since 1976, was the lookout in what at that time was the worst mass murder ever in the Miami area—the drug-related killings of six people in a house in the Carol City suburb on July 27, 1977.

Source: Reprinted with permission from United Press International, "Three Men Executed in 3 States," *The Knoxville News-Sentinel* (August 2, 1987), p. A7.

---

sentence to be served in a maximum security prison rather than a minimum- or medium-security prison facility.

Mitigating Circumstances

Mitigating circumstances are those circumstances considered by the sentencing judge to lessen the crime's severity. Some of the most frequently cited mitigating factors follow:

1. No serious bodily injury resulting from the crime.
2. No attempt to inflict serious bodily injury on anyone.
3. Duress or extreme provocation.
4. Circumstances justifying the conduct.
5. Mental incapacitation or physical condition that significantly reduced the offender's culpability in the offense.
6. Cooperation with authorities in apprehending other participants in the crime or making restitution to the victims for losses they suffered.
7. Motivation to provide necessities for himself or herself.
8. No previous criminal record.

One or more mitigating circumstances associated with the crime committed may cause the sentencing judge to be lenient in the sentence imposed. In view of the current trend toward greater use of felony probation, first offenders and nonviolent criminals are likely to be considered for alternative sentencing that does not involve incarceration. However, recidivists, especially those who have committed a number of violent acts and show every likelihood of continuing their criminal behavior, are likely candidates for punishment enhancement. Aggravating and mitigating circumstances are usually outlined in **presentence investigation reports,** which are documents prepared by probation officers prior to sentencing.

■ PRESENTENCE INVESTIGATIONS AND REPORTS

In all felony convictions in local, state, and federal trial courts, a presentence investigation is conducted. The purpose of this investigation is to assist the judge in determining the most appropriate punishment or sentence for the convicted defendant. This investigation is usually made by a probation officer attached to the court and consists of a check of all relevant background information about a convicted defendant. Similar investigations are conducted for all juvenile offenders as well.

A presentence report is prepared from the facts revealed from the investigation. This report varies considerably in focus and scope from jurisdiction to jurisdiction, but it should contain at least the following items:

1. A complete description of the situation surrounding the criminal action.
2. The offender's educational background.
3. The offender's employment history.
4. The offender's social history.
5. The residence history of the offender.
6. The offender's medical history.
7. Information about the environment to which the offender will return.
8. Information about any resources available to assist the offender.
9. The probation officer's view of the offender's motivations and ambitions.
10. A full description of the defendant's criminal record.
11. A recommendation from the probation officer as to the sentence disposition. (Black, 1979:1066)

Sometimes the report includes other reports from psychiatrists or social workers, indicating their opinions and recommendations concerning the offender.

Figure 12.1 shows a United States Magistrate's Trial Docket Sheet where a defendant has been charged with two counts of willfully obstructing the passage of mail. In this case, the defendant's bail was set at $1,000 at his initial appearance before the magistrate. The "O.R." signifies that he was released on his own recognizance, however, and bail was waived. Later, he entered a plea of guilty to the charges filed against him. The form also shows that the magistrate ordered a presentence investigation. As a result of the investigation, the magistrate sentenced the convicted defendant to two 6-month prison terms, with one 6-month term to run concurrently with the other. No fine was imposed. In this case, where a guilty plea was entered, a criminal information was issued on May 19th, the initial appearance occurred May 26th, the arraignment occurred June 5th, when the guilty plea was entered, and the sentence was pronounced June 30th. At that time, the defendant was taken into custody and imprisoned, presumably for the 6-month term prescribed by the sentence.

Convicted defendants don't always serve the full term prescribed by the sentencing judge. Almost every jurisdiction has a formula whereby a convict may be released after serving only a fraction of the original sentence imposed. As one result of court-mandated reductions in the prison population, some offenders are released within a few weeks after their original confinement, even if they have been sentenced to terms of 1 or more years. Such incidents mean that parole boards and judges are relying

FIGURE 12.1 United States Magistrate Trial Docket Sheet

UNITED STATES MAGISTRATE	FPI LC
TRIAL DOCKET SHEET	
AO 254	

No.

— Docket Number —

OFFENSE [X] Petty [ ] Minor other than Petty — DEFENDANT

Description **willfully obstructing the passage of mail**

Place

U.S.C./C.F.R. Citation

Date

Violation Notice [ ] or Citation	[X] Information [ ] Complaint	ARREST WARRANT ▶	Date issued	Date of Arrest
Number CR-	Date issued 5-19-	If Prosecution from Another District, Give District Name		

Date 5/26/	Tape Number (if recorded)	APPEARED: [X] Voluntarily [ ] In Custody	Arresting Officer

BAIL Amount Set ▶ $ 1,000.00 O. R.

PROCEEDINGS CONTINUED

To (date): | Reason

Date June 5, 19	Tape Number	Verbatim Record Waived [ ] (see reverse)	Testifying Officer or Complainant , AUSA

Attorney for U.S.

, AUSA

Attorney for Defendant

[X] C.J.A.
[ ] Pub. Def.
[ ] Retained
[ ] Waived

DEFENDANT'S CONSENT TO TRIAL BY U.S. MAGISTRATE

The United States Magistrate has explained to me the nature of the offense against the laws of the United States with which I am charged and the possible penalties if I am found guilty. He has fully informed me of my rights to counsel and to a trial before a judge of the United States District Court and of whatever right I may have to a jury trial.

I hereby waive my right to a trial before a United States District Judge and whatever right I may have to a jury trial, and I hereby consent to trial before the United States Magistrate.

_____ _____
(Signature of Defendant) (Date)

PLEA	DISPOSITION
[ ] Not Guilty	[ ] Dismissed [ ] Collateral forfeited $_____
[X] Guilty	[ ] Not Guilty
[ ] Nolo Contendere	[X] Guilty

6/30/ Date (If different from plea or trial)

[X] Presentence Investigation Ordered

Count I - Six months confinement; and
Count II - Six months confinement to run concurrently with sentence imposed in Count I.

FINE ▶ $ XX   Receipt No. _____ Date Committed to Custody 6/30/

Date Filed	Bail Pending $	Certified to be an accurate record of proceedings conducted before the magistrate	6/30/
City Location of Magistrate			(Magistrate or deputy clerk) (Date)

increasingly on a convict's potential risk to the public as a major factor in the decision for an early release.

■ SENTENCING ISSUES

Stimulating a variety of sentencing reforms are several issues that raise a number of moral and ethical questions. These issues pertain to (1) sentencing disparities; (2) predicting dangerousness; (3) selective incapacitation; and (4) alternative sentencing.

Sentencing Disparities

Sentencing disparity takes several different forms. Disparities in sentencing may occur when different judges within any given jurisdiction impose vastly different sentences on offenders charged with similar crimes (Gertz and Price, 1985). Judges may be inclined to be more lenient with female offenders than with their male counterparts. Blacks may receive harsher sentences than whites when the same offenses are involved. Older offenders may receive less harsh sentences from judges than younger offenders, even when the same crimes have been committed.

Promoters of sentencing reforms have been quick to point out deficiencies in our sentencing system (Kramer and Lubitz, 1987; Shane-DuBow, Brown, and Olsen, 1985; Tonry and Zimring, 1983). Many states are modifying their sentencing systems from an indeterminate form to a determinate form. Such changes are almost always accompanied by reductions in sentencing disparities attributable to racial, ethnic, gender, or socioeconomic qualities. The influences of race and gender on sentencing have been investigated extensively.

Race. A study of 4,371 drug offenders in the Southern Federal District of New York revealed, for example, that nonwhite big drug dealers were consistently given harsher sentences than were white big drug dealers during the 1963–1976 period (Peterson and Hagan, 1984).

An investigation of sentencing disparities between whites and Hispanics in El Paso, Texas, and Tucson, Arizona, during the 1976–1977 period revealed inconclusive evidence of ethnic discrimination, however (LaFree, 1985). The investigation looked at a sample of 755 defendants prosecuted for burglary and robbery. In Tucson, being Hispanic made no difference on the type of adjudication received, the verdict, or sentence severity. However, in El Paso, Hispanic defendants were more likely to receive less favorable pretrial release outcomes than white defendants, were more likely to be convicted in jury trials, and consistently received more severe sentences when they were found guilty at trial (LaFree, 1985). Interviews with district attorneys and other officials in both cities indicated that these disparities might be partially attributable to differing language capabilities in the two jurisdictions, different mechanisms for providing attorneys to indigent defendants, and different relations between the established Hispanic-Americans and less well-established Mexican-American citizens and Mexican nationals (LaFree, 1985).

However, in a study of 103 Chicano and 94 Anglo Fresno, California, defendants charged with felonies in 1979, no conclusive evidence of ethnic discrimination in affecting sentencing disparities could be found (Tinker, Quiring, and Pimentel, 1985). In this particular research, the investigators found that the length of the sentence was directly related to the seriousness of the charge rather than to any particular qualitative attributes such as ethnic affiliation.

Sentencing disparities attributable to race differences are particularly noticeable in the South (Kempf and Austin, 1986; Petersilia, 1983). It has been shown, for instance, that for 21,169 convicted felons in Georgia for the years 1973–1980, blacks tended to receive longer sentences than did whites (Clayton, 1983). As a matter of fact, blacks received sentences that were on the average 2.5 years longer than sentences for whites convicted for the same crimes.

Gender. Do women tend to receive more lenient sentences than do men? A study of 1,027 male and female offenders in Minneapolis, Minnesota, who were convicted of theft, forgery, or drug law violations between 1972 and 1976 revealed that gender does have a significant effect on sentencing severity—women receive more lenient sentences

CRIME BEAT

Often, the pace of justice moves slowly. In 1973, Willie Darden, a black, held up a furniture store in Lakeland, Florida. He forced the owner's wife at gunpoint to perform oral sex. He shot the owner point blank in the face, killing him. Shortly thereafter, he was apprehended by police, tried and convicted, and sentenced to death. In 1988, 15 years after his conviction, Darden was executed by Florida officials after exhausting all of his appeals.

In another incident, Georgian Warren McCleskey, a black, was convicted of killing a white police officer and sentenced to death. Many years passed before McCleskey was executed for the crime in 1987. McCleskey's accomplices received 20-year sentences or life imprisonment, while McCleskey received the ultimate punishment. Were Darden and McCleskey victims of racial bias in sentencing?

Supreme Court Justice William Rehnquist has recommended that those concerned about how the death penalty is applied and whether it should be applied at all should write their state legislators. The Supreme Court decides constitutional issues and attempts to ensure equal protection under the law. Justice Powell has written that while statistics may show a correlation between race and the death penalty, the Supreme Court has implemented safeguards to make trials as fair as possible, despite their imperfections. Interestingly, little attention has been given to the conspicuous absence of women from death row. In 1987, for instance, only 21 women out of 1,984 death row inmates (1 percent) were awaiting execution. One of these was Doris Ann Foster, a convicted murderer.

Doris Ann Foster is one of only a few women on death row.

than do men who have committed similar offenses (Kruttschnitt, 1984). Women received not only more lenient sentences but also more lenient treatment related to pretrial release. In a related study of 1,558 convicted males and 1,365 convicted females in Minneapolis between 1965 and 1980, it was found that women were more likely to receive pretrial release than were men, as well as less severe sentences for similar offenses (Kruttschnitt and Green, 1984).

Other research has largely supported the Minnesota study. For example, a study of sentencing severity conducted in Pennsylvania for the years 1970–1975 also showed that women receive more lenient sentences compared with men (Kempinen, 1983), but this research revealed an interesting trend pertaining to decisions to incarcerate women. Proportionately more women were being incarcerated in 1975 than in 1970, with the female incarceration rate increasing from 25 percent in 1970 to 58 percent in 1975. At least in this particular state for the time period investigated, it was concluded that the disparity in treatment between male and female offenders is gradually diminishing (Kempinen, 1983).

As more states adopt reforms, including presumptive and determinate sentencing systems, fewer sentencing disparities may be observed from one jurisdiction to the next. Judges, too, seem to favor greater uniformity in their sentencing practices within the same jurisdictions. The adoption of consistent sentencing standards should gradually eliminate patterns of gender, ethnic, and racial discrimination in sentencing in future years.

Predicting Dangerousness

As the courts move voluntarily or involuntarily toward greater use of felony probation, they increasingly focus on determining which offenders should be incarcerated and which ones should not be imprisoned. Therefore, in recent years several investigators have attempted to devise prediction schemes that would permit judges and other officials to predict a convicted defendant's dangerousness. Obviously, this concern is directed toward preserving public safety and minimizing public risks arising from placing violent and dangerous offenders on probation rather than imprisoning them.

Early attempts to predict the incidence of violent behavior among samples of convicted felons were unsuccessful; the results were inconclusive and highly inaccurate (Monahan, 1984). Behavioral scientists and mental health professionals were involved initially in attempts to identify personality traits or behavioral patterns indicative of one's projected level of dangerousness (Wilbanks, 1985). Initially, much of this research was conducted in Canada. An investigation of 598 criminal defendants in Toronto, Canada, in 1978 failed to disclose which offenders would be more dangerous than others if released (Menzies, Webster, and Sepejak, 1985). Psychiatrists stood the best chance of predicting an offender's potential dangerousness compared with social workers, nurses, psychologists, and corrections personnel. But, unimpressively, psychiatrists' predictions were only 40 percent accurate.

Thirty-one states currently have laws permitting officials to detain criminal defendants on the basis of their perceptions of the defendants' dangerousness (Gottlieb and Rosen, 1984). These include such states as South Dakota, Tennessee, Utah, Vermont, Virginia, Washington, Wisconsin, Arkansas, Arizona, Georgia, Florida, Delaware, Colorado, and Hawaii. The dangerous tendency test used legally is the propensity of a person (or animal) to inflict injury (Black, 1979:355; *Frazier v. Stone,* 1974). Dangerousness is interpreted differently in different jurisdictions. In twenty-one states, for example, dangerousness is defined as a history of prior criminal involvement (Gottlieb, 1984). This history may include a prior conviction, probation or parole status at the time of arrest, or a pending charge when the defendant is arrested. In seven states, the type of crime with which the offender is charged defines dangerousness (for example, a violent crime such as aggravated assault, robbery, homicide). In twenty-two states, judicial discretion determines dangerousness (Gottlieb, 1984).

Current attempts to predict dangerousness have not progressed substantially beyond earlier efforts by clinicians and others. Some researchers and theorists argue that all offenders who have committed the same or similar offenses should be treated similarly (Morris, 1984; Morris and Miller, 1985; Stone, 1985; Wilkins, 1985). In short, is it ethical or moral to incapacitate certain defendants charged with armed robbery and deemed dangerous and yet release others charged with the same offense on their own recognizance?

One of the more successful prediction devices, which has been used extensively by the United States Parole Commission, is the Salient Factor Score (SFS) (Hoffman,

1983). The SFS is an actuarial device that assesses parole success. Using such factors as offense severity and offender characteristics, the SFS yields a customary range of months to be served, assuming appropriate conduct from the offender while incarcerated. The SFS has been used since 1972 and has been revised several times in recent years. In August 1981, a six-item predictive device, designated SFS 81, was established (Hoffman, 1983). This predictive device emphasizes the extent and recency of an offender's criminal history (Hoffman, 1983).

Supporting the view that all felons who commit the same crimes and have the same kinds of records should be treated alike, some authorities contend that *all* felons who have been convicted of violent offenses should serve a term in jail or prison (Conrad, 1985). Of course, a decision to incarcerate violent felons is subject to some leeway, allowing for mitigating or aggravating circumstances and exceptional factors. Currently, the state of the art in accurately predicting dangerousness suggests that researchers should proceed cautiously. Favoring a just deserts view of sentencing, where punishments are based on the gravity of the crime, von Hirsch (1985) argues that persons should be punished according to their degree of fault rather than according to flawed dangerousness prediction devices.

Selective Incapacitation

Closely related to predictions of dangerousness is selectively incapacitating certain offenders who are likely candidates for recidivism (Hill, 1985; Maltz, 1984). On the basis of state prison figures nationally, about 42 percent of all persons entering prison are either on probation or parole for other offenses (Greenfeld, 1985:5). About 60 percent of all persons admitted to state prisons are recidivists (that is, they had served a sentence involving incarceration as a juvenile, an adult, or both) (Greenfeld, 1985:1).

Selective incapacitation means that offenders who are prone to be recidivists or who have prior criminality are incapacitated with relatively long prison sentences (Blackmore and Welsh, 1983). In 1982, the Rand Corporation in Santa Monica, California, devised a classification scheme to enable criminal justice practitioners to determine which offenders should be selectively incapacitated and which should be sentenced to alternative correctional programs (Blackmore and Welsh, 1982; Greenwood, 1982; Wilson, 1983). However, selective incapacitation as a crime control strategy is fraught with theoretical, methodological, and ethical problems (Clear and Barry, 1983). Some researchers argue that the incapacitation of certain offenders simply results in their replacement by newly recruited criminals (Clear and Barry, 1983). In addition, how much predictive error should be permitted in incapacitation decisions? Of course, the issue of fairness is increasingly important, especially as states move toward more determinate and presumptive sentencing forms. It is suggested by some researchers that we must be willing to sacrifice our justice concerns in the interests of crime-preventive utility (von Hirsch, 1984).

Alternative Sentencing

A prevailing view of sentencing equates punishment and control with incarceration (Smith, 1984). In recent years, however, several proposals favor various alternative sentencing forms (Czajoski and Wollan, Jr., 1986; Miller, 1986; Smith, 1984). Sometimes referred to as creative sentencing, **alternative sentencing** offers offenders, especially those who have committed relatively minor or nonviolent offenses, opportunity to serve their sentences outside the prison setting. Usually, alternative sentencing involves some form of community service, some degree of restitution to victims of crimes, involvement in educational or vocational training programs, or affiliation with some good works activity (Czajkoski and Wollan, 1986).

The goals of alternative sentencing are twofold. First, alternative sentencing is aimed at helping certain types of offenders avoid imprisonment. Imprisonment means associating with other criminals, and labeling theorists consider imprisonment as an important factor contributing to one's self-concept as a criminal. Second, alternative sentencing is designed as an alternative to imprisonment. Therefore, it is perceived as a viable means of reducing prison overcrowding and cutting certain costs associated with corrections (Harris, 1983; Wallace and Clarke, 1986:1).

Some of the criticisms leveled at alternative or creative sentencing are that such programs restore to judges considerable power, which they formerly enjoyed under indeterminate sentencing systems. Not all judges favor creative sentencing, and such sentencing alternatives may increase the potential for various kinds of judicial abuses. Czajkoski and Wollan, Jr. (1986:228) describe the judge, for instance, who considered the case of a woman who was convicted for a marijuana offense. The judge placed the woman on probation for her marijuana offense, but he also set as one of her probation conditions that she undergo sterilization (the woman had a number of illegitimate children and was straining the community welfare rolls). Of course, the sterilization had nothing to do with the marijuana offense, but as Czajkoski and Wollan point out, "the judge must have had in mind some benefit to the community by reducing the number of illegitimate children and welfare recipients" (Czajkoski and Wollan, Jr., 1986:228). This is an extreme example, but it serves to illustrate the types of judicial excesses that *might* occur.

In view of the sentencing reforms that are occurring in various states and in the light of prison overcrowding, it is likely that we will continue to see the development and promotion of alternative sentencing programs such as those operating in North Carolina and Florida. The recurring question is how to identify the offenders who will be most responsive to sentencing alternatives or creative sentences. Many of these programs are fairly new, and more data are needed to assess their true impact on crime trends, recidivism rates, and offender rehabilitation.

■ CAPITAL PUNISHMENT—THE MAXIMUM SENTENCE

No other issue in sentencing has been debated as vigorously as the death penalty. This punishment is exacted for such offenses as murder. In many jurisdictions, if a defendant is found guilty of a capital offense, often a separate jury decision is required to establish the actual punishment. This is referred to as a **bifurcated trial.**

All sentences where the death penalty is imposed are subject to an automatic appellate review under all circumstances, although some offenders are willing to waive their right to such a review (Goodpaster, 1983; Kaine, 1983). The purpose of the automatic review is for a higher court to determine if the lower court adhered to proper procedures in arriving at a guilty verdict and if the circumstances of the case warrant the imposition of the sentence of death; that is, were the defendant's rights observed at all stages of the trial proceeding?

The two primary reasons for applying the death penalty in certain capital cases are (1) retribution, and (2) deterrence.

Retribution

Retribution is defended largely on the basis of the philosophical just deserts rationale (Cheatwood, 1985; Draper, 1985; Reiman, 1985; Warr and Stafford, 1984). According to this rationale, offenders should be executed because they did not respect the lives of others. Death is the just desert for someone who inflicted death on someone else. Some citizens regard retribution as the primary purpose of the death penalty. In a study of the opinions of a sample of Seattle, Washington, residents, for example, Warr and Stafford (1984) found that the respondents were most likely to choose retribution as the main purpose of punishment when given a choice between incapacitation, rehabilitation, specific or general deterrence, or retribution. However, these researchers caution that no single adjective adequately describes public opinion about the specific purpose of capital punishment. Some citizens endorse each of these views. Currently, no single dominant ideology of punishment exists nationwide. Theoretically, retribution serves abstract societal interests and has historically been used to justify the nature and severity of punishments imposed on criminals. However, the philosophical and empirical debates over capital punishment as a sound retributive form remain unresolved (Cheatwood, 1985).

Deterrence

The deterrence function of the death penalty is frequently called into question as well. An examination of homicide rates in Illinois during a 48-year period (1933–1980) revealed that the average homicide rates for three different periods did not fluctuate noticeably. These periods included (1) years when the death penalty was allowed, (2) years when the death penalty was allowed but no executions were performed, and (3) years when the death penalty was abolished (Decker and Kohfeld, 1984).

Other investigations of the impact of capital punishment on deterring persons from committing homicide have been conducted in New York, Chicago, and Washington, D.C. (Bailey, 1983, 1984; Fattah, 1985; Forst, 1983; Scarfone, 1986). Most of these investigators categorically conclude that the possibility of the death penalty fails to perform its deterrence function. Persons who commit homicide are going to do it regardless of whether the death penalty exists or does not exist. For instance, Forst (1983) examined the deterrent effects of the death penalty by examining 1960 data from a cross-section of states. In his analysis, Forst considered a full set of variables, which included (1) the probability of execution if convicted, (2) the rate at which homicides result in conviction, (3) the average prison term served by persons convicted of homicide, (4) the proportion of nonwhites sentenced to the death penalty, (5) the median family income of individuals convicted of homicide, and (6) the proportion of males sentenced to the death penalty. None of Forst's formulations showed that the execution rate was a deterrent to homicide.

Bailey (1984) conducted a time-series analysis of the deterrent effect of the death penalty in Washington, D.C., for the periods 1890–1950, 1890–1955, 1890–1960, 1890–1965, and 1890–1970. His findings revealed absolutely no support for the hypothesis that the death penalty deters homicides, regardless of how execution rates or murder rates are measured. In fact, Bailey found that murder rates and execution rates were *positively related* for these time periods. In other words, more executions were associated with more homicides.

Persons favoring the abolition of the death penalty argue that no criminal act ever justifies capital punishment. They further contend that even if capital punishment were an effective deterrent to criminality, abolition would be preferable. Van den Haag and Conrad (1983) have challenged abolitionists to demonstrate the validity of such arguments, however. In the final analysis, neither position can be proven conclusively (Reiman, 1985).

For many years, a majority of states had an assortment of capital punishment laws for special classes of violent offenders. However, the United States Supreme Court declared the application of the death penalty unconstitutional in 1972 in the case of *Furman v. Georgia* (1972), because it was applied in an arbitrary and capricious manner. In that landmark case, the Supreme Court heard appeals that eventually affected three separate cases—(1) a murder case from Georgia, (2) a rape case from Georgia, and (3) a rape case from Texas—in which all three defendants had been convicted and sentenced to death. While the defendants appealed their cases on the ground that the death penalty constituted cruel and unusual punishment under the Eighth and Fourteenth Amendments, other factors were relevant to the issue of the death penalty. These were black defendants, and a disproportionate number of black defendants in capital cases involving crimes other than murder were receiving death sentences and being executed in Georgia and other jurisdictions.

The United States Supreme Court reversed their convictions and held, "[T]he imposition and carrying out of the death penalty in these cases constitutes cruel and unusual punishment in violation of the Eighth and Fourteenth Amendments." The Court also concluded that capital punishment is unconstitutional whenever imposed discriminatorily against certain identifiable classes of people. Justice Douglas indicated, "[I]t would seem to be incontestable that the death penalty inflicted on one defendant is 'unusual' if it discriminates against him by reason of his race, religion, wealth, social position, or class, or if it is imposed under a procedure that gives room for the play of such prejudices." The death penalty was declared to be not only cruel and unusual punishment in such an instance but also discriminatory because it was selectively applied to certain offenders and not to others. This decision caused many states to reexamine their death penalty provisions. For several years, no executions were conducted, as state legislators examined the various implications of the United States Supreme Court's holding in *Furman*. Some states considered the Supreme Court action to be the equivalent of abolishing the death penalty altogether, although this was neither the intent nor the result of *Furman*.

In 1976, however, the United States Supreme Court ruled on another significant case pertaining to the death penalty issue. In the case of *Gregg v. Georgia* (1976), Troy Leon Gregg, a white male, was charged with committing armed robbery and murder. Gregg and a companion, Floyd Allen, allegedly were hitchhiking north in Florida on November 21, 1973. They were picked up by Fred Simmons and Bob Moore. Along the way, they picked up another hitchhiker, Dennis Weaver, who rode with them to Atlanta. Later that evening, they stopped for rest along the highway. The next morning, the bodies of Simmons and Moore were found along the Georgia highway. The hitchhiker, Weaver, read about the incident in the newspapers and reported what he had seen to the police. The next afternoon, Gregg and Allen, while in Simmons' car, were arrested in Asheville, North Carolina. In a search incident to their arrest, a .25-caliber pistol was found in Gregg's pocket. This was later confirmed to be the murder weapon used to kill Simmons and Moore.

Gregg was convicted in a trial, and a separate jury hearing considered the issue of his punishment in accordance with the newly revised Georgia law in view of *Furman v. Georgia* (1972). Gregg appealed to the United States Supreme Court on the issue that the death penalty violated his Eighth and Fourteenth Amendment rights. In this particular case, the Supreme Court held that Gregg's rights had *not* been violated, and that the sentence of death had not resulted from prejudice or any other arbitrary factor. Furthermore, the penalty was not excessive or disproportionate to the penalty applied in similar cases. Thus, in 4 short years, the Supreme Court of the United States had made two important rulings affecting the application of the death penalty. All states were obligated to examine closely their death penalty provisions and determine if, in fact, they complied with the new Supreme Court guidelines.

By 1984, thirty-seven states had provisions for the death penalty in their respective criminal codes (Snellenburg, 1986:7), but only thirty-two states had a prisoner on death row during that year, and only six states carried out an execution (Snellenburg, 1986:7). Between 1976 and 1984, 204,000 persons were killed as the direct result of violent crimes, but during the same period, 2,384 persons were sentenced to death in federal and state prisons. Of these, only 32 were actually executed (U.S. Department of Justice, 1984). By the end of 1984, there were 1,405 persons on death rows in United States prisons, and by the end of 1985, the number of executions in the United States was eighteen (Greenfeld, 1986).

It is unlikely that any United States Supreme Court decision will resolve the capital punishment debate. However, various criminal justice researchers have recommended several alternatives to the death penalty. For instance, commutation of a death sentence to life imprisonment has been suggested (Cheatwood, 1985). Another alternative proposed has been solitary confinement for life (Snellenburg, 1986). Some prisoners have even volunteered for execution rather than suffer in prison as prolonged appeals procedures occur (Strafer, 1983).

In spite of the Supreme Court's proclamation prohibiting the discriminatory application of the death penalty in capital cases, evidence of discrimination continues. In South Carolina, for example, prosecutorial discretion in recommending the death penalty has been found to be race-related in homicides for the years 1977–1981 (Paternoster, 1984). It was found that the race of the victim was significantly related to the decision of whether or not to seek the death penalty even when several legally relevant factors were taken into account. Black killers of whites were more likely and black killers of blacks less likely to have the death penalty requested by prosecutors (Paternoster, 1984). The United States Supreme Court has reviewed allegations that there are racial differences in the imposition of the death penalty in recent years. In 1987, after finding that there were, indeed, racial differences, the Supreme Court concluded that no evidence exists to prove that this is a legally relevant factor, however (*McCleskey v. Kemp,* Docket No. 84-6811).

■ SUMMARY

This chapter described the sentencing process. The Sentencing Reform Act of 1984 was a major attempt to provide judges with greater sentencing consistency and to provide alternatives and options in lieu of incarceration. Judges now have greater latitude to impose alternative sentences on low-risk offenders who otherwise qualify for such sentences. Most states have followed suit in reforming their existing sentencing practices.

The functions of sentencing include reflecting the seriousness of the offense, promoting respect for the law, providing just punishment for the offense committed, deterring future criminal conduct, protecting the public against the actions of the offender, and providing the offender with the means to become rehabilitated through vocational or educational training.

Different sentencing systems are used in different jurisdictions. Indeterminate sentencing gives judges broad discretionary powers over offenders in determining their sentence lengths and sentence severity. Parole boards usually determine when prisoners should be paroled. Determinate sentencing involves fixed terms of confinement without parole board intervention. Mandatory sentencing requires that offenders be incarcerated for specified lengths of time. Presumptive sentencing is a statutory sentencing form specifying normal sentence lengths but permitting judges some leeway for shortening or lengthening sentences depending upon the presence of mitigating or aggravating circumstances.

Current sentencing issues include sentencing disparity, where defendants receive more or less severe sentences depending upon their gender, race, ethnic background, or socioeconomic status. Another issue is predicting an offender's dangerousness. A third issue pertains to selectively incapacitating offenders. Finally, alternative sentencing is used as a means of alleviating prison overcrowding and removing low-risk, nonviolent offenders from imprisonment.

The death penalty is the most severe sentence judges may impose. Most jurisdictions have a bifurcated trial, where two separate hearings by juries are conducted—one to establish one's guilt and another to determine one's punishment.

KEY TERMS

aggravating circumstances	indeterminate sentences	presentence investigation reports
alternative sentencing	justice model	
bifurcated trial	mandatory sentencing	selective incapacitation
determinate sentences	mitigating circumstances	Sentencing Reform Act of 1984
habitual offender statutes		

QUESTIONS FOR REVIEW

1. Differentiate between indeterminate and determinate sentencing. Which sentencing system gives judges more flexibility in the sentence they can impose on offenders?
2. What are two reforms suggested by the Sentencing Reform Act of 1984?
3. What are four functions of sentencing?
4. How does prison overcrowding influence a judge's decision to incarcerate or not incarcerate an offender?
5. What is a presentence investigation? What does a presentence investigation report contain? What is the relation between a presentence investigation and the subsequent sentence a judge imposes on a convicted defendant?
6. Differentiate between aggravating and mitigating factors. List three aggravating and three mitigating factors. How does a judge utilize these factors in the sentencing process?
7. Differentiate between mandatory sentencing and presumptive sentencing.
8. What are the minimum and maximum sentence lengths for Class B, Class C, and Class E felonies?
9. On the basis of recidivism figures, what can be said about the function of sentencing in promoting respect for the law?
10. Discuss two studies where sentencing disparities have been detected. How are sentencing disparities being eliminated or reduced?
11. Identify and discuss briefly two studies involving racial sentencing disparities. What were some of the basic findings?
12. How reliable are predictions of dangerousness? What evidence indicates that we have far to go before devising foolproof predictions of dangerousness of offenders?
13. What is meant by selective incapacitation? What are two issues that can be raised about selective incapacitation?
14. What is meant by alternative sentencing? Is it the same thing as creative sentencing?
15. What are the primary functions of the death penalty?
16. How effective is the death penalty as a deterrent to homicide in the United States? Cite and discuss briefly two studies of homicide and execution.
17. What are two major court cases involving the death penalty? Briefly discuss the cases and the results of these cases. How has each case affected the imposition of the death penalty by the various states?
18. What is a bifurcated trial? Why is it important in death penalty cases? Is there an automatic appeal in all situations where the death penalty is imposed?

SUGGESTED READINGS

Forst, Martin L. (Ed.) (1982). *Sentencing experiments in reducing disparity.* Beverly Hills, CA: Sage.

Goodstein, Lynne, and John Hepburn (1985). *Determinate sentencing and imprisonment: A failure of reform.* Cincinnati, OH: Anderson Publishing Co.

Gottfredson, Michael R., and Don M. Gottfredson (1988). *Decision making in criminal justice: Toward the rational exercise of discretion* (2nd ed.). New York: Plenum Press.

Sellin, Thorsten (1980). *The penalty of death.* Beverly Hills, CA: Sage.

Van den Haag, Ernest, and John P. Conrad (1983). *The death penalty: A debate.* New York: Plenum Press.

Correctional Institutions: Forms and Functions

333

■ INTRODUCTION

Samuel Walker and others say that rehabilitative programs don't rehabilitate, correctional institutions don't correct, and deterrent measures taken by citizens and police don't deter (Walker, 1985). Even retribution and revenge taken against offenders fail to even the score for victims of crime. Maybe the best alternative is to incapacitate offenders whenever feasible for as long as possible, but society picks up the custodial tab and is either unwilling or unable to pay the bills for housing criminals. For better or worse, a majority of convicted offenders spend little or no time behind bars compared with the statutory maximum sentences. Cheap solutions are sought as alternatives to incarceration, but incarceration for some offenders is inevitable.

When convicted felons are sentenced, they go to either prison or jail or are sentenced to probation. This chapter deals exclusively with prisons and jails and the inmates who inhabit them. The first part of the chapter examines the historical development of prisons and jails in the United States and describes correctional goals. Although prisons and jails are intended to serve basically different correctional functions, jails are housing increasing numbers of inmates from prisons as a means of accommodating prison overflow.

An important aspect of this chapter is the description of prison and jail inmate populations. Although prison inmates share many characteristics nationally, many differences exist among prisoners. Thus, as a part of the inmate classification process, different types of prison facilities have been created. Prisons have been targeted by the government and various interest groups for reforms, including more economical construction and better management and operation.

Receiving increased attention from the media as well as correctional officials in recent years are the conditions and operation of jails. Jails have some unique problems associated with their management and inmate control. Finally, the chapter directs attention to the increased importance of women's prisons. United States Supreme Court decisions and other factors have caused dramatic changes in the administration and operation of prisons for women. The characteristics of female inmates and their culture are also described.

■ THE HISTORY OF PRISONS IN THE UNITED STATES

Prisons have existed for all recorded time. The first United States prison systems were patterned after early British penal models and performed similar functions (American Correctional Association, 1983, Harding et al., 1985). Gaols (pronounced *jails*) were established in 1166 A.D. by the assize (constitution) of Clarendon under Henry II (American Correctional Association, 1983:3).

Certain devices to restrain prisoners, such as **body belts** (large belts worn about the waist with wrist restraints at the center of the abdomen), originated in the Middle Ages and are still used to restrain prisoners in state and federal prisons (Prison Reform Trust, 1984). In fact, prison statistics show that between 1981 and 1982, a 35 percent increase in the use of body belts in United States prisons occurred (Prison Reform Trust, 1984).

In the Middle Ages in England and Scotland, there was little planned imprisonment. Clothing and feeding outlaws was considered wasteful, and capital and brutal corporal punishments were the most commonly used punishment methods (Cameron, 1983). Debtors' prisons were abundant. If debtors couldn't pay their debts, they were imprisoned until the debts were paid by family members or friends. Many debtors died in these prisons, unable to pay for their own freedom (Harding et al., 1985). Prisons were places to confine society's undesirables.

Religious organizations influenced the growth and purpose of prisons. Following the Reformation in the sixteenth century, the Church of England frequently used prisons to punish "offenders against morality" together with debtors and secular offenders (Cameron, 1983; Harding et al., 1985). As Great Britain expanded her domination of the colonies and established economic enterprises throughout the world, British penal policy changed to include transporting large numbers of prisoners to remote penal colonies, such as Australia, for cheap labor and general economic exploitation (Smith, 1983).

During the sixteenth and seventeenth centuries, Scottish and English prisons were gradually transformed into industrial centers. Powerful mercantile interests established some of the first formal houses of correction (Dobash, 1983). The type of work performed in these early correctional institutions was intended to achieve several objectives, including improving prisoner "social and moral habits, developing industrial skills, and producing marketable goods to defray confinement costs" (Dobash, 1983). These mercantile interests created the need for trained labor and skilled craftsmen in houses of correction. The Bridewell workhouse was constructed in 1557 to employ and house London's riffraff (American Correctional Association, 1983:4).

Banishment was a popular method of punishing serious offenders. Between 1788 and 1868, 160,000 English prisoners were exiled to Africa and Australia (American Correctional Association, 1983:7; Hughes, 1987). Australia in 1788 was considered the end of the world, and Britain's exile policy was labeled "the long enterprise of social excretion" (Hughes, 1987). Political dissidents as well as the most violent offenders were dispatched in this fashion. Only moral reformers, who developed a comprehensive penitentiary system in England, terminated the Australian banishment experiment.

During the colonial period in the United States, religious interests profoundly influenced corrections programs (Evans, 1982). In 1682, William Penn, a Quaker, deplored the miserable conditions of Pennsylvania's penal system, and he caused the **Great Law of Pennsylvania** to be enacted. Penn was sensitive to the plight of the prisoners in these institutions, because he had once been imprisoned himself for his religious beliefs, which were contrary to the Church of England. Gradually, Penn's enactment eliminated branding irons, gallows, stocks, and pillories and replaced them with fines and a more humane standard of imprisonment.

Penn also ordered each county in Pennsylvania to construct jails to restrain and punish all offenders who violated local laws (Dunn and Dunn, 1982). Several of the other colonies eventually established county jails as well. The county jail concept continues in the United States as evidence of Penn's influence.

When Penn died in 1718, his humane measures used in houses of corrections died with him. His successors eliminated his policies and replaced them with previous correctional philosophies, stressing harsh, corporal treatment and public punishment.

In New England in the early 1800s, stocks and pillories were used as punishments. Because passersby could stare at criminals in them, they were thought to deter young children from criminal conduct.

However, in 1787, a decade after the Revolutionary War, Penn's Quakers reestablished his correctional ideas and created the Philadelphia Society for Alleviating the Miseries of Public Prisons. In 1790, this was followed by Pennsylvania legislative action that created the Walnut Street Jail in Philadelphia.

The **Walnut Street Jail** is important because it represented the first meaningful attempt to classify and segregate offenders according to the crimes they committed and

The Walnut Street Jail in Philadelphia, Pennsylvania, pioneered the concept of solitary confinement in 1790. Considered the first penitentiary, the Walnut Street Jail housed hardened offenders, who could repent of their sins in isolation.

the seriousness of their offenses (American Correctional Association, 1983). Violent offenders were isolated from others and confined in separate cells. Nonviolent offenders were permitted limited movement in common social areas and interaction with other prisoners. Offenders were also segregated by gender. In addition to pioneering the classification of prisoners, the Walnut Street Jail introduced the idea of solitary confinement, a concept that functions in the contemporary United States penitentiary system.

One of the early pioneers to influence the design and operation of Walnut Street Jail was Dr. Benjamin Rush (1745–1813). Dr. Rush was a prominent physician, political leader, and member of both Continental Congresses, as well as a signer of the Declaration of Independence. Dr. Rush believed that prison systems should include areas where prisoners could grow food and exercise. He believed also that punishment should reform the offenders, that it should prevent the perpetration of further crimes, and that it should remove from society offenders who are unfit to live with others (American Correctional Association, 1983:30).

Penal developments in the United States from 1790 to 1914 can be divided into six distinct periods: (1) the postrevolutionary period, 1790–1812; (2) the recession following the War of 1812; (3) the Jacksonian period, 1812–1837; (4) the midcentury period, 1837–1860; (5) the postbellum South, 1865–1890; and (6) the industrial Northeast, 1865–1914 (Adamson, 1984). Changes in United States business conditions and the labor supply were closely linked with these stages in the development of

Dr. Benjamin Rush was a signer of the Declaration of Independence, a physician, and a reformer. His humanitarian ideals did much to improve the health and welfare of those confined in facilities such as the Walnut Street Jail. He believed in health, good food, and exercise, and he encouraged prisoners to cultivate gardens for fresh fruit and vegetables.

penology. General economic changes had a profound impact on prison policies during the nineteenth century, and prison discipline and labor varied in accordance (Adamson, 1984).

Following the example set by the Walnut Street Jail in Philadelphia, New York State established correctional programs that eventually led to the construction of several state prisons. In 1797, Newgate Prison was constructed in New York City. It incorporated several of the penal concepts from Pennsylvania prison systems. In 1816, New York began the construction of a new prison facility at Auburn, New York (American Correctional Association, 1983:48).

The **Auburn State Penitentiary** was another first in United States prison development. Architecturally, Auburn State Penitentiary introduced the **tier system** of cell blocks to alleviate some of the overcrowding typical of other prisons. At Auburn, cells were placed on five floors. Also, the Auburn State Penitentiary adopted a **congregate system,** where prisoners could work and eat together in large, common work and recreational areas. At night, however, prisoners were isolated from one another in solitary cells.

The tier system in the Auburn State Penitentiary was designed to alleviate prison overcrowding. In the Auburn penitentiary, the cells were distributed throughout five floors. Prisoners could congregate in common recreational areas by day, but they were separated in isolated cells at night. However, prison and jail overcrowding remains the number one problem in the United States penal facilities.

The Auburn system became popular because prisoners performed work and produced goods that economically benefited the prison system. The Auburn model was important also because it established separate confinement for various classifications of offenders beyond the criteria developed at the Walnut Street Jail. Prisoners who could not conform to prison norms or were unruly were placed in long-term solitary confinement as punishment. Other, less dangerous, prisoners were given limited freedom, being permitted to work at various skilled and semiskilled jobs. Most prisoners were permitted recreation and opportunities to associate with one another daily in the prison yard. Other states, such as Vermont, New Hampshire, Massachusetts, Ohio, Georgia, and Kentucky, followed the Auburn pattern by building similar correctional facilities. In some respects, the Auburn system created the maximum, medium, and minimum security prison conditions that are found in penitentiaries today.

The national prison population in 1840 was 4,000 prisoners, or about 24 prisoners for every 100,000 persons in the population. In 1850, there were 7,000 prisoners, or 30 per 100,000. In 1860, there were 19,000 prisoners, or about 60 per 100,000. By 1870, this figure had reached 33,000 prisoners, or about 83 prisoners per 100,000 population. Between 1860 and 1870 was an increase of 72 percent in the prison population. With the growing numbers of prisoners, drastic measures were necessary to provide suitable facilities for them (American Correctional Association, 1983:63).

In 1870, the American Correctional Association was founded. Future United States President Rutherford B. Hayes was chosen as its first president. The association then was called the National Prison Association, and later, the American Prison Association. Eventually, it became the **American Correctional Association (ACA)** (American Correctional Association, 1983:73). The goals of the ACA include the formulating of a national correctional philosophy; designing and implementing standards for correctional services and methods for measuring compliance; and providing publications, training, and technical assistance to correctional institutions.

New York State continued its penal innovations by establishing a reform-oriented prison, the **Elmira Reformatory**, in Elmira, New York, in 1876 (American Correctional Association, 1983). Constructed in a social environment of extensive public sentiment against corporal punishment and harsh, violent prison practices, this new prison paralleled developments in England that emphasized prisoner reform and rehabilitation (Glenn, 1984). Priority was given to prisoner educational development and vocational training. An inmate's good behavior and work output meant greater privileges and possibly early release through parole (American Correctional Association, 1983). Among the early advocates of these penal arrangements and ideas were Robert Vaux (1786–1836) and his brother, Richard Vaux (1816–1895). These men belonged to the Philadelphia Prison Society, and their ideas influenced penal philosophy for more than a century.

Hailed by some corrections officials as the new penology and scientific reform, under the direction of Superintendent Zebulon Brockway (1827–1920), Elmira Reformatory stressed individualized treatment, indeterminate sentencing, and parole. Unfortunately, however, historical records and eyewitness accounts of Brockway's methods suggest that Elmira Reformatory was unsuccessful in achieving its goals (Pisciotta, 1983). Some evidence indicates that severe, sometimes brutal, corporal punishment was used by Brockway's staff to coerce conformity to the reformatory norms and maintain order among the inmates (Pisciotta, 1983).

One fourth of the states copied the Elmira Reformatory model between 1876 and 1920. During the 1920s, the United States prisons became increasingly overcrowded, and some of the rehabilitative educational and vocational programs no longer operated effectively. More penitentiaries were built during the 1920–1935 period, but these facilities were primarily custodial rather than rehabilitative in function and operation.

On May 14, 1930, the **Federal Bureau of Prisons** was created. It was charged with managing and regulating all federal penal and correctional institutions and providing suitable quarters and safekeeping of all persons convicted of offenses against the United States. It also provided technical assistance to state and local governments in the improvement of their own correctional systems. The first federal penitentiary was built at Leavenworth, Kansas, in 1895, and it was one of five established by the time the Bureau of Prisons was created. Although it is nearly 100 years old, Leavenworth Penitentiary continues to house federal prisoners.

Among the other functions of the Bureau of Prisons was providing for the "protection, instruction, and discipline of all persons charged with or convicted of offenses against the United States" (18 U.S.C., Sec. 4042, 1989). The Bureau of Prisons interpreted this original charge as a mandate to rehabilitate prisoners besides furnishing them with vocational and educational training. Over the next 20 years, several new treatment-oriented programs were implemented at several federal penitentiaries, including group therapy, individualized psychological counseling, encounter groups, and mental health assistance.

Between 1950 and 1966, over one hundred prisoner riots occurred in state and federal prisons, however. A major contributing factor was prison overcrowding, although the lack of professional leadership and professional programs, inadequate staffing and financial support, and enforced idleness contributed to prisoner unrest as well (American Correctional Association, 1983:209). While numerous correctional reforms have been introduced over the years, prisons and jails still have problems similar to those of earlier times.

■ CORRECTIONAL GOALS

The major goals of corrections include (1) retribution, (2) deterrence, (3) rehabilitation, (4) reintegration, and (5) isolation and incapacitation.

Retribution

Depriving offenders of freedoms through incapacitation is a major function of corrections (Jurik and Musheno, 1986:457; Mullen, 1985). Incarceration is a form of retribution. Early prison reforms stressed rehabilitation through individualized treatment and therapy, but there is evidence that these values are being abandoned in favor of a more primitive purpose—punishment (Nagel, 1984, Pisciotta, 1983). However, inmates seem to be coping more effectively with time served in prison to the extent that they are adjusting to, and even resisting, the unique character of it (Meisenhelder, 1985). Public opinion about the retributive function of correctional institutions is mixed (Flanagan and Caulfield, 1984), and some critics say that the public view of correctional goals is one of social defense rather than retribution.

Deterrence

Encouraging offenders to refrain from future crimes is another correctional objective. However, incarceration does not appear to be a significant deterrent to future crimes. It has been shown that 61 percent of all admissions to prisons in 1979 were recidivists (Greenfeld, 1985). Coupled with earlier research on recidivism, these figures do not support the idea that incarceration is a deterrent to crime.

For example, an investigation studied a 50 percent sample of 1,806 federal prisoners released in 1970. It showed that during the following 5-year period, half of these parolees committed new crimes for which they were incarcerated (Hoffman and Beck, 1985). It is likely that some of these recidivists returned to prison for two or more criminal offenses. In this investigation, recidivism was defined as the presence of a new sentence of imprisonment exceeding 1 year for offenses committed during the follow-up period.

Among the states, recidivism rates are equally high. For instance, a study of 3,257 persons released from Delaware prisons in the 1980–1982 period disclosed that more than half (51.4 percent) were rearrested, and almost 75 percent of these rearrests occurred within the first year following release (Delaware Executive Department, 1984). It is important to note, however, that rearrests do not necessarily result in reconvictions.

In the Delaware sample, officials measured recidivism by rearrests. Different measures of recidivism from different studies make comparisons of statistical information difficult. For example, recidivism is defined as return to prison in a North Carolina study (Clarke and Crum, 1985) and a violation of one or more parole conditions in an Iowa investigation (Boudouris, 1983). The most frequent meaning of the term **recidivist** is a convicted offender who commits a new crime and is convicted of it.

Rehabilitation

A key objective of most prison reforms is rehabilitation. Rehabilitation was one of several correctional objectives of Auburn State Penitentiary in 1816, as well as Elmira Reformatory in 1876. Vocational training and educational programs were intended to upgrade the educational levels of inmates and equip them with work skills that they could use later in performing jobs in their communities. While critics have considered the rehabilitative ideal of correctional institutions ineffective over the years, some analysts see a prison work ethic as a means of providing inmates with work skills and dignity (Cullen and Travis, 1984; Nagel, 1984). One suggestion is to pay prisoners a reasonable wage for the work that they perform (Cullen and Travis, 1984). The argument is that current get-tough-on-crime crusades will continue unless alternative reforms mitigate the consequences of the current correctional policies, which seem only to contain large numbers of offenders. Offender employment may be a way of transforming prisoners into productive citizens, and it may counter the negative effects of prisoner idleness and boredom often associated prison and jail problems.

One consequence of the prison reform movement is correctional education (Muth and Gehring, 1986). Learning deficiencies among prisoners are well-documented (Bell et al., 1983; Duguid, 1984; Holt, 1984). Studies of inmate educational background in the Louisiana, Pennsylvania, and Washington state prison systems revealed, for instance,

CRIME BEAT

A common complaint about prisons is that they do not rehabilitate their inmates. If anything, inmates emerge with greater knowledge than before about escaping detection. Thus, some critics have labeled prisons "institutions of higher criminal learning." The rehabilitative ideal has lost priority during the last few decades, and more legislators are listening to a public concerned with seeing that criminals receive their "just deserts."

In response to criticisms that prisons do little, if anything, to rehabilitate inmates or help them go straight when they are eventually released, various states are implementing meaningful training programs to equip inmates with skills that will make them more employable. In Mississippi, for instance, inmates engage in paramilitary training and receive intensive psychological counseling to help them to cope more effectively with everyday problems. Other prisons, in New York, Iowa, and California, operate programs to train inmates to do telemarketing, deep-sea diving, and automobile licensing.

The Federal Bureau of Prisons administers UNICOR, a for-profit enterprise operated almost exclusively by prisoners. Federal inmates produce marketable goods that are sold to the public. The inmates receive decent wages to help them support their families and dependents. Furthermore, these experiences give them a sense of accomplishment, as they learn to do things that will help them fit into the world of employment later.

The Regimented Inmate Discipline Program (RID) used by Mississippi prison officials seems to be an effective rehabilitative tool. Prisoners learn discipline. They also learn how to reason through personal problems. They are taught reading and other useful skills. When they emerge from Mississippi prisons, many ex-cons seek productive and meaningful solutions to problems, rather than robbery, burglary, or theft.

Should inmates of all prisons be required to participate in rehabilitative and therapeutic programs such as those operated by Mississippi and California prison officials? Who should bear the cost of paying for this rehabilitative training?

---

that 42 percent of the inmates had learning deficiencies, and 82 percent had learning disabilities, especially auditory and visual discrimination problems (Bell et al., 1983). Furthermore, the average inmate had dropped out of high school.

Prisoner response to educational programs has been favorable (Muth and Gehring, 1986; Parker, 1985). Education is a direct path toward self-improvement, and studies show that prisoners develop more positive self-images through participation in education programs (Lawrence, 1985; Priestley et al., 1984). A key factor in ex-offender employment may not be the skills or training acquired, but rather the ability of the ex-inmate to sustain a stable employment record (Duguid, 1984). A stable employment record is acquired through the development of a more favorable self-image, self-esteem, communications skills, good work habits, and cognitive abilities. An effective liberal arts education may be one means of developing these characteristics, but prison overcrowding undermines the efforts of prison educators to offer the individualized instruction needed by inmates.

Reintegration

Reintegration is closely related to rehabilitation as a correctional goal. Inmates must prepare for reentry into their communities because these transitions require significant adjustments to diminish the effects of confinement and rigid compliance with prison

Some college students would love to have dorm rooms like this cell at the Special Offender Center, a maximum security facility at Monroe, Washington. In this center, officials make every effort to remove from prisoners the taint of confinement behind bars. Some persons say the labeling perspective influences such housing innovations, especially in maximum-security facilities.

rules and regulations. Some prisons gradually move their inmates to living quarters that do not have the stigma of the traditional prison environment, including locked cells and bars. Typical cells for inmates in the Special Offender Center, a maximum security facility, in Monroe, Washington, include flowers in the windows, a television set, radio, and small library (American Correctional Association, 1983:252). The North Carolina Central Prison in Raleigh, North Carolina, looks more like a large private college or motor lodge than a prison (American Correctional Association, 1983:249).

Isolation and Incapacitation

A custodial goal of corrections is to isolate inmates from the general public. Isolating offenders is the most direct form of crime control (Warr and Stafford, 1984). Isolation is most frequently used for extremely dangerous and violent offenders. During the 1980s, Charles Manson, convicted of the murder of Sharon Tate and others in California, became eligible for parole. However, public sentiment, usually expressed through the media, strongly opposed Manson's parole. By 1989, Manson's efforts to secure early release through parole had been unsuccessful. In such cases as Manson's, a crucial question is the potential dangerousness of the inmate being considered for parole and the degree of public risk incurred if parole is granted. Most offenders are eventually returned to society, however, and their isolation is temporary. A relatively small number of extremely dangerous criminals serve life terms or are executed.

In the mid-1970s and early 1980s, various researchers examined the implications of incapacitating convicted offenders for affecting community crime rates. For example, Shinnar and Shinnar (1975) estimated that the average number of crimes committed by the average criminal per year was ten (Wilson, 1983:148). Basing these estimates on a complex statistical model, the Shinnars concluded that for a city such as New York, for instance, crimes such as robbery would be reduced by 80 percent each year for each year these offenders were incarcerated.

However, this investigation drew considerable criticism from other researchers. Average figures fail to distinguish between property and violent offenders, adult and juvenile offenders, or male and female offenders or to consider arrest records, racial and ethnic factors, and socioeconomic status (Blumstein and Cohen, 1979; Greenberg, 1975; Van Dine et al., 1977; Wilson, 1975, 1983). For example, using alternative estimates, Greenberg (1975) determined that average offenders commit two serious offenses per year. By contrast, Blumstein and Cohen (1979) found widely different offending rates among criminals in Washington, D.C., according to prior convictions and offenses. They examined adult criminal records for the population of all Washington offenders arrested in 1973 for six major offense categories. The offenders who had been arrested at least twice were estimated to have committed between nine and seventeen serious offenses annually while not incarcerated (Wilson, 1983:149).

Eventually, researchers studied offenders who committed disproportionately large numbers of crimes compared with other offenders. On the basis of the self-reports of over 2,200 inmates in California, Michigan, and Texas prisons, the Rand Corporation found that a small core of offenders in each state committed from eight to twenty-three times the number of crimes of the average offenders for the entire sample (Greenwood, 1982). The small core of criminals were labeled career criminals, chronic offenders, and persistent offenders.

Interestingly, some of this research was stimulated, in part, by two earlier investigations by Marvin Wolfgang and his associates (Wolfgang, 1983; Wolfgang, Figlio, and Sellin, 1972). Popularly known as the Philadelphia Birth Cohort Study, the research identified 9,945 boys born in Philadelphia, Pennsylvania, and tracked them until 1963, when all the boys reached age 18. Furthermore, Wolfgang selected a 10 percent sample of these 18-year-olds and continued to monitor their progress until they reached age 30, in 1975. Wolfgang also investigated a second birth cohort of infants born in Philadelphia in 1958. This cohort included 28,338 children—13,811 males and 14,527 females. Thus, the second cohort was not only larger than the first but also more representative because it included females. The findings from both cohorts were insightful.

Wolfgang found that for the 1945 cohort, one third of the boys had had some contact with police or had acquired records of delinquency by age 18, while two thirds had not acquired records or had police contact. Perhaps the most important finding was that 6 percent (627 out of 9,945 boys) had committed about 52 percent of all the offenses among the entire cohort, including 82 percent of all the robberies, 73 percent of all the rapes, and 71 percent of all the homicides. In his follow-up of these chronic offenders, he found that by age 30, many of these subjects continued their former offending rates and accounted for a disproportionately large share of crimes.

Wolfgang's preliminary investigation of the 1958 cohort of 28,338 boys and girls showed that by 1976, when these subjects reached age 18, a chronic offender aggregate was identifiable. While the proportion of delinquent youths was about the same as that in the 1945 cohort, about 7.5 percent of the entire sample were identified as chronic offenders, accounting for 61 percent of all offenses, including 76 percent of all the rapes, 61 percent of all the homicides, and 73 percent of all the robberies (Wolfgang, 1983). Less than 1 percent of all the females in the 1958 cohort were identified as chronic offenders. One of the more significant differences, however, was that the 1958 cohort had a violent offense rate three times as large as the 1945 cohort. These findings suggest that the nature of delinquency has changed or is changing, and that the change is toward increased violence among juveniles. However, no satisfactory explanation reliably accounts for such differences between the two cohorts (Tracy, Wolfgang, and Figlio, 1985).

The idea that a small core of offenders, both juvenile and adult, accounts for a disproportionately large share of criminal behavior has prompted interest in selective incapacitation, or selective and longer incarceration of those believed to be most likely to commit new crimes (Forst, 1983; Greenwood, 1982; Petersilia, 1987). However, selective incapacitation has been criticized on moral, legal, methodological, and practical grounds (Gottfredson and Gottfredson, 1988; von Hirsch, 1987). Sentencing certain offenders to terms of incarceration or incarceration for longer periods than for offenders convicted of the same crimes under similar circumstances raises the question of fairness. Is it fair to penalize certain offenders more harshly on the basis of what they might do in the future? (von Hirsch, 1987). Are our predictive instruments sufficiently sophisticated to identify offenders who will reoffend? Can we be certain that those who are treated more leniently and sentenced to probation will not reoffend?

Our efforts at identifying high-risk and low-risk offenders have been unsuccessful. Methodological problems undermine our attempts to devise scales that reliably lead to accurate behavioral forecasts. The use of such predictive tools by judges in their sentencing practices raises legal issues that are beyond the scope of this book. However, changing sentencing procedures are narrowing judicial sentencing options. Questions of predicted dangerousness or potential public risk are increasingly irrelevant where sentencing tables are used to determine incarcerative punishments. Nevertheless, a substantial number of states continue to use indeterminate sentencing schemes. In those jurisdictions, at least, selective incapacitation of certain offenders based upon various prediction devices continues to be a viable option for the judiciary.

■ PRISONS AND JAILS: A PRELIMINARY DISTINCTION

By the end of 1987, 581,609 convicts sentenced to terms of 1 year or longer occupied state and federal prisons (Greenfeld, 1988:1). In mid-1987, according to a 1-day count, 290,300 inmates occupied city and county jails in the United States (Kline, 1988:1).

Prisons and penitentiaries are designed to house felony offenders. Usually, offenders who have been sentenced to imprisonment for a year or longer serve that time in a prison or penitentiary. Prisons are self-contained units, usually covering substantial acreage and surrounded by high wire fences, walls, and guard towers. Prisons are financed by state or federal government taxes and are operated by civil employees and administrators.

Jails are city- or county-operated. They are usually administered as a police department facility. Jails house less serious offenders, including misdemeanants (Wayson, Funke, Hamilton, and Meyer, 1977). As the result of overcrowding in federal and state prisons, jails also accommodate federal or state prisoners. Some jails house these prisoners through contractual agreements with state or federal authorities. Those arrested by local police are also initially detained in city or county jails. In addition, those awaiting trial and those who cannot afford bail are placed in jails rather than in prisons or penitentiaries.

Table 13.1 shows the changing number of inmates in state and federal prisons between 1977 and 1987. Inmate populations in state and federal penitentiaries increased by almost 94 percent between 1977 and 1987. State prisons are currently operating at 105 percent of their highest capacities, while federal prisons are operating at 54 percent above their capacity.

In 1985, 621 jails in jurisdictions with large jail populations housed 175,000 inmates, or about 75 percent of the total jail inmate population nationally (Baunach, Sickmund, and Ford, 1986:4). For 1984, jails throughout the United States admitted 7,838,521 persons for various offenses. For the same year, there were 7,716,067 releases. The 621 jails in large jail population jurisdictions are currently operating at 102 percent of their rated capacity.

Prisons

In 1979, there were thirty-seven federal correctional institutions. By 1985, there were over 40,000 inmates in federal penitentiaries (Greenfeld, 1986:2). This was a 17.4 percent increase in the federal prison population compared with the previous year. Table 13.2 shows the distribution of state and federal prisoners for each geographical area in the United States for 1986–1987. Between 1986 and 1987, most state prison systems had inmate population increases. Only four states had reductions in their inmate populations: North Carolina, South Dakota, Washington, and West Virginia.

TABLE 13.1 Changes in the State and Federal Prison Populations, 1977–1987

Year	Numbers of Inmates	Annual Percent Change	Total Percent Change Since 1977
1977	300,024		
1978	307,276	2.4	2.4
1979	314,457	2.3	4.8
1980	329,821	4.9	9.9
1981	369,930	12.2	23.3
1982	413,806	11.9	37.9
1983	437,248	5.7	45.7
1984	464,567	6.2	54.8
1985	503,601	8.4	67.9
1986	545,133	8.2	81.7
1987	581,609	6.7	93.9

Sources: Lawrence A. Greenfeld, *Prisoners in 1985* (Washington, DC: U.S. Department of Justice, 1986), p. 1, and Lawrence A. Greenfeld, *Prisoners in 1987* (Washington, DC: U.S. Department of Justice, 1988), p. 1.

TABLE 13.2   State and Federal Prison Populations, 1986–1987

	Total			Sentenced to More than 1 Year			
	Advance 1987	Final 1986	Percent Change 1986–87	Advance 1987	Final 1986	Percent Change 1986–87	Incarceration Rate 1987
U.S. total	581,609	545,133	6.7%	557,256	522,485	6.7%	228
Federal	48,300	44,408	8.8	39,523	36,531	8.2	16
State	533,309	500,725	6.5	517,733	485,954	6.5	212
Northeast	88,903	82,364	7.9%	85,256	79,066	7.8%	169
Connecticut	7,511	6,905	8.8	4,637	4,326	7.2	144
Maine	1,328	1,316	.9	1,267	1,242	2.0	106
Massachusetts	6,238	5,636	10.7	6,238	5,636	10.7	106
New Hampshire	867	782	10.9	867	782	10.9	81
New Jersey	13,662	12,020	13.7	13,662	12,020	13.7	177
New York	40,842	38,449	6.2	40,842	38,449	6.2	229
Pennsylvania	16,267	15,201	7.0	16,246	15,165	7.1	136
Rhode Island	1,429	1,358	5.2	992	1,007	−1.5	100
Vermont	759	697	8.9	505	439	15.0	91
Midwest	111,095	102,964	7.9%	110,671	102,552	7.9%	185
Illinois	19,850	19,456*	2.0	19,850	19,456	2.0	171
Indiana	10,827	10,175	6.4	10,634	9,963	6.7	192
Iowa	2,863	2,777	3.1	2,863	2,777	3.1	101
Kansas	5,881	5,345	10.0	5,881	5,345	10.0	237
Michigan	23,879	20,742	15.1	23,879	20,742	15.1	259
Minnesota	2,546	2,462	3.4	2,546	2,462	3.4	60
Missouri	11,357	10,309	10.2	11,357	10,309	10.2	222
Nebraska	2,086	1,953	6.8	1,963	1,863	5.4	123
North Dakota	430	421	2.1	380	361	5.3	57
Ohio	24,240	22,463	7.9	24,240	22,463	7.9	224
South Dakota	1,135	1,164	−2.5	1,096	1,133	−3.3	154
Wisconsin	6,001	5,697	5.3	5,982	5,678	5.4	124
South	221,592	214,620	3.2%	214,236	207,308	3.3%	254
Alabama	12,827	11,710	9.5	12,602	11,504	9.5	307
Arkansas	5,443	4,701	15.8	5,443	4,701	15.8	227
Delaware	2,931	2,823	3.8	2,120	1,946	8.9	327
District of Columbia	7,448	6,618	12.5	5,585	4,787	16.7	901

*Offense figures for Illinois for 1986 may not be comparable to previous years.

continued

TABLE 13.2 *continued*

	Total			Sentenced to More than 1 Year			
	Advance 1987	Final 1986	Percent Change 1986–87	Advance 1987	Final 1986	Percent Change 1986–87	Incarceration Rate 1987
Florida	32,445	32,237	.6	32,360	32,228	.4	265
Georgia	18,575	17,363	7.0	17,210	16,291	5.6	274
Kentucky	5,471	5,288	3.5	5,471	5,288	3.5	147
Louisiana	15,375	14,300	7.5	15,375	14,300	7.5	346
Maryland	13,467	13,326	1.1	12,912	12,559	2.8	282
Mississippi	6,831	6,747	1.2	6,669	6,561	1.6	254
North Carolina	17,249	17,698	−2.5	16,151	16,373	−1.4	250
Oklahoma	9,639	9,596	0.4	9,639	9,596	0.4	296
South Carolina	12,664	11,676	8.5	11,862	11,022	7.6	344
Tennessee	7,624	7,591	0.4	7,624	7,591	0.4	156
Texas	38,821	38,534	0.7	38,821	38,534	0.7	231
Virginia	13,321	12,930	3.0	12,931	12,545	3.1	217
West Virginia	1,461	1,482	−1.4	1,461	1,482	−1.4	77
West	111,719	100,777	10.9%	107,570	97,028	10.9%	214
Alaska	2,528	2,460	2.8	1,767	1,666	6.1	339
Arizona	10,948	9,434	16.0	10,558	9,038	16.8	307
California	66,975	59,484	12.6	64,812	57,725	12.3	231
Colorado	4,808	3,804	26.4	4,808	3,804	26.4	145
Hawaii	2,268	2,180	4.0	1,536	1,521	1.0	141
Idaho	1,482	1,448	2.3	1,482	1,448	2.3	149
Montana	1,187	1,111	6.8	1,187	1,111	6.8	147
Nevada	4,434	4,367	1.5	4,434	4,367	1.5	432
New Mexico	2,648	2,416	9.6	2,561	2,306	11.1	169
Oregon	5,482	4,770	14.9	5,482	4,770	14.9	200
Utah	1,888	1,845	2.3	1,872	1,814	3.2	111
Washington	6,131	6,603	−7.1	6,131	6,603	−7.1	134
Wyoming	940	855	9.9	940	855	9.9	195

Note: Prison admissions refer to the number of prisoners received from courts with sentences of more than 1 year. Selected offenses are murder, nonnegligent manslaughter, forcible rape, robbery, aggravated assault, and burglary. Adults are the resident population age 18 and over.

Sources: Data from National Prisoner Statistics; Uniform Crime Reports; Bureau of the Census estimates of population. Reprinted from Lawrence A. Greenfeld, *Prisoners in 1987* (Washington, DC: U.S. Department of Justice, 1988), p. 2.

Prisoner Characteristics. Table 13.3 shows a distribution of selected prisoner characteristics for state and federal prison populations. In the table, males make up 95.6 percent of the inmate population for state and federal prisons. Although blacks comprise only 12 percent of the United States population, they are greatly overrepresented by prison statistics. Nearly half, or 46.9 percent, of all incarcerated state and federal

TABLE 13.3 Sociodemographic Characteristics of State Prison Inmates, 1986

Characteristic	Percent of Prison Inmates
Sex	
Male	95.6%
Female	4.4
Race	
White	49.7%
Black	46.9
Other	3.4
Ethnicity	
Hispanic	12.6%
Non-Hispanic	87.4
Age[a]	
Less than 18	.5%
18–24	26.7
25–34	45.7
35–44	19.4
45–54	5.2
55–64	1.8
65 or older	.6
Marital status	
Married	20.3%
Widowed	1.9
Divorced	18.1
Separated	6.0
Never married	53.7
Education[b]	
Less than 12 years	61.6%
12 years or more	38.4
Military service	
Served	20.2%
Never served	79.8

Note: The state prison population in 1986 was an estimated 450,416. For each of the characteristics listed, data were available for at least 99% of the inmates.

[a]The median age was 28 in 1986.

[b]The median number of years of education was 10 in 1986.

Source: Christopher A. Innes, *Profile of State Prison Inmates, 1986* (Washington, DC: U.S. Department of Justice, 1988), p. 3.

prisoners are black. Almost 73 percent of all inmates are under age 34. Additionally, almost 62 percent of all inmates had dropped out of high school.

According to Table 13.4, 69 percent of all inmates were formerly employed, and over 57 percent were employed full-time. In 1986, about 44 percent of all inmates were sentenced to terms of 9 or fewer years, while 72 percent of all inmates had served at least 3 years of their sentences (Innes, 1988:2–3). Also, 58 percent of all offenders were serving time for violent offenses. This may be explained by the frequent use of

TABLE 13.4 Prearrest
Employment and Income for State
Prison Inmates, 1986

	Percent of Prison Inmates
Prearrest employment	
Employed	69.0%
Full-time	57.4
Part-time	11.6
Not employed	31.0%
Looking	18.0
Not looking	13.0
Income prior to arrest	
Free at least 1 year, annual income:	
No income	1.6%
Less than $3,000	24.7
$3,000–$10,000	33.7
More than $10,000	39.9
Free less than 1 year, monthly income:	
Less than $500	40.1%
$500–$1,000	28.4
More than $1,000	31.5

Note: Prearrest employment data were available for at least 99% of the inmates in 1986. Income data were available for 89% of all State prison inmates in 1986.

Source: Christopher A. Innes, *Profile of State Prison Inmates, 1986* (Washington, DC: U.S. Department of Justice, 1988), p. 3.

plea bargaining, especially felony plea bargaining involving probation for those apprehended for nonviolent and less serious felony offenses (Innes, 1988: 2–4).

Table 13.5 is a profile of all nonviolent offenders by criminal history for 1986. The largest proportions of offenders were convicted of drug trafficking and burglary. Previously convicted burglars were almost evenly divided regarding earlier violent offenses (39 percent) and nonviolent offenses (36 percent), but drug traffickers had fewer prior convictions involving violent crimes.

Types of Prisons. Each state and federal prison or penitentiary may be classified as a maximum-, medium-, or minimum-security facility. Within state prisons and federal penitentiaries are areas that are classified similarly. These security classifications pertain to the degree of custody. Maximum-security prisons maintain the prisoners in the highest degree of custody, and inmate supervision by the guards is intensive. Minimum-security prisons permit considerable freedom of movement among the inmates, and their activities are casually supervised by the guards. The United States Bureau of Prisons uses a scale ranging from Level 1 through Level 6, with Level 1 being an honor farm, or minimum-security camp facility, and Level 6 being a maximum-security penitentiary, or a maxi-maxi penitentiary, such as the one at Marion, Illinois. According to Marion Federal Penitentiary inmates, they represent the "baddest of the bad."

Most inmates in state and federal prisons are classified as medium- to minimum-security risks. Usually, prisoners are assigned to different types of prisons or prison

TABLE 13.5 Current Offense of State Prison Inmates Incarcerated for Nonviolent Crimes, by Criminal History, 1986

Current Offense	First-Timers	Recidivists	
		No Prior Violence	Prior Violence
Total	100%	100%	100%
Property offenses			
Burglary	25.8%	38.6%	35.8%
Larceny/theft	9.8	13.6	14.1
Motor vehicle theft	.7	3.2	3.8
Arson	3.1	1.3	1.8
Fraud	11.0	8.7	6.2
Stolen property	1.0	4.8	4.8
Other property	.9	1.0	1.5
Drug offenses			
Possession	6.6%	6.4%	6.3%
Trafficking	26.1	10.1	9.5
Other drug	.4	.6	.5
Public-order offenses			
Weapons	3.2%	2.2%	5.7%
Other public-order	7.1	8.2	8.8
Other offenses	4.4%	1.1%	1.1%

Source: Reprinted from Christopher A. Innes, *Profile of State Prison Inmates, 1986* (Washington, DC: U.S. Department of Justice, 1988), p. 5.

areas according to their conviction offenses, their propensity for violent behavior, their risk for escape, and the availability of particular programs. Nonviolent prisoners are sentenced to minimum-security prisons, while violent offenders (such as persons convicted of homicide, robbery, or aggravated assault) are housed in maximum-security facilities.

Maximum-security prisons share the following characteristics. The inmates are isolated from one another in single cells. They are monitored constantly by prison guards. The inmates are restricted to the confines of their immediate security housing area, and their privileges, including visitations from family and friends, are severely limited. Although maximum-security prisons provide educational programs and other activities for their inmates, they make no pretense about the fact that they exist to control and contain dangerous offenders (Israel, 1983). About 40 percent of all United States prisons currently are maximum-security facilities (Carney, 1979:116).

Alcatraz, located on an island in San Francisco Bay, was considered the epitome of maximum-security prison institutions. Constructed in 1934, Alcatraz (also known as The Rock) was one of the most feared federal prisons in the nation. The primary aims of Alcatraz were discipline and punishment. Inmates were not allowed to read newspapers, watch television, or listen to radios. Escape from Alcatraz was almost impossible, since the island where Alcatraz is located is in the middle of San Francisco Bay. Inmates who managed to reach the waters of the Bay were drowned by the strong currents. Only eight persons ever escaped from Alcatraz, and of these, three were never recaptured (Carney, 1979:104–105). The popular Clint Eastwood movie, *Escape from Alcatraz,* provides a semifictionalized account of their escape.

About 1,500 prisoners were housed at Alcatraz during 1934–1963. Because of prohibitive prison costs and declining health standards, Alcatraz was closed on March 21, 1963, with an inmate population of 260 (Bennett, 1970:114). Other well-known maximum-security prisons are San Quentin and Folsom prisons in California, Marion Federal Correctional Center in Illinois, Sing-Sing and Attica prisons in New York, and the federal penitentiaries in Atlanta, Georgia, and Leavenworth, Kansas.

One problem with maximum-security prisons is the high level of inmate idleness (Steelman, 1984). Based on site visits to eight maximum-security prisons in New York, 3,100 inmates, or 24 percent of New York's prison population, are idle most of the time. About 1,500 inmates in six of these facilities are partially idle, assigned to menial, unproductive jobs (Steelman, 1984).

Medium-security prisons offer prisoners dormitory-like accommodations. While direct supervision of inmates is limited, inmates may be observed directly in their particular areas of assignment. There are main perimeters where inmates may move, and all inmates are eligible for day and night recreational activities. Prisoners may also be eligible for assignments outside the main perimeter. Visitation privileges are relaxed, and prisoners may move about freely without much supervision or monitoring by guards.

Minimum-security prisons are designed for nonviolent offenders who have either low or no potential for violent behavior. Often, housing is similar to that found in a typical small efficiency apartment. While supervision by guards continues, it is unobtrusive. Inmate privileges are extensive, and family visits, even conjugal visits, are sometimes permitted. Minimum-security inmates are eligible for a variety of work tasks outside of the prison. A positive feature of minimum-security prisons is that inmates may develop higher degrees of self-esteem. Minimum-security facilities maximize trust between prison officials and inmates. Building self-esteem is particularly important for successful prison counseling and rehabilitation programs (Vicary and Good, 1983).

Inmate Classification. A common problem for prison administrators is determining where each new inmate should be housed. In California prisons, for example, a variety of custody levels exists, including Maximum A Custody, Maximum B Custody, Close A Custody, Close B Custody, Medium A Custody, Medium B Custody, Minimum A Custody, and Minimum B Custody. Also used in these prisons are letter classifications to designate special types of offenders: N for narcotics offenders, R for sex offenders, and S for persons who must be confined without cellmates (Carney, 1979:117–118). Prisoners entering the California prison system are initially classified at the Reception Guidance Center, which tries to determine which inmates are most violent and which are most likely to attempt escape.

Psychological assessment inventories are often used for predicting inmate adjustment to prison and propensity toward violence. None of these devices is foolproof, however, although some measures have helped authorities identify the most patholog-ical offenders (Carbonell, 1983). The Minnesota Multiphasic Personality Inventory (MMPI) is a popular psychological predictive instrument used to predict dangerousness and escape risks (Editor, 1984; Johnson, Simmons, and Gordon, 1983). The MMPI consists of over 500 true-false statements, and various combinations of statements form subscales of selected personality characteristics.

The **Megargee Inmate Typology** is also a measure of inmate adjustment to prison life (Megargee and Carbonell, 1985). Using items from the MMPI, Megargee established ten prisoner classifications to predict inmate dangerousness or violent behavior. The typology has been used in several prisons for separating inmates into different custody levels, such as maximum-security or minimum-security categories. For example, 316 inmates at a federal prison in Ashland, Kentucky, were given Megargee's typology and classified into different custody levels according to their assessment scores (Johnson, Simmons, and Gordon, 1983). Of the 316 inmate profiles developed, only 22 failed to meet the criteria for inclusion in at least one of Megargee's types. A final sample of 85 inmates was examined the following year, and only 16 of 85 inmates examined retained their original designation when retested. These results were disappointing and suggest that the Megargee typology may be unreliable as a predictor of dangerousness.

Megargee himself examined the interrelations between a number of popular adjustment scales. Using 1,214 inmates from the Federal Correctional Institute at Tallahassee, Florida, Megargee and Carbonell (1985) correlated eight MMPI subscales with six criteria for subsequent adjustment to prison, including Panton's Adjustment to Prison (revised), Religious Identification, Homosexuality, Habitual Criminalism and Parole Violation, Beall and Panton's Escape, Clark's Recidivism, and Wattron's Prison Maladjustment. Megargee and Carbonell found no significant correlations among the scales, indicating that they had little practical predictive value.

The South Carolina Department of Corrections began using the Adult Inmate Management System (AIMS) in 1984 to comply with a court order to provide for an effective internal classification structure (Leeke and Mohn, 1986; Travisono et al., 1986). AIMS divided prisoners into three groups: (1) alphas, (2) betas, and (3) gammas. These are three levels of aggressiveness which serve to segregate more violent inmates from less violent ones. While approximately 70 percent of all inmates have violent offense records, AIMS has reduced prisoner violence by 18 percent through these segregative measures. In fact, one maximum-security facility had the lowest protective custody population of the prisons in the state (Leeke and Mohn, 1986).

Prison Violence. In October 1983, violence erupted at the Marion, Illinois, federal penitentiary and prisoners killed two correctional officers in the control unit (Mauer, 1985). Ordinarily, this would be considered just another prison riot, such as those occurring during the 1970s and 1980s in other prisons throughout the United States. However, this particular penitentiary was considered an ideal model of prison planning. This facility was considered a maxi-maxi prison for confinement of only the most serious offenders.

The penitentiary was constructed in 1963. At first, it functioned as a maximum confinement facility for federal inmates who were considered incorrigible, vicious, and unmanageable. Later, it housed escape artists, leaders of gangs, and other hardened criminals. There were no newspapers, no entertainment visits from outside groups, and little or no vocational training. Six months' of hearings and a review by a panel of experts are required before inmates are confined there (Satchell, 1980). Marion replaced Alcatraz when it was closed. Currently, Marion receives inmates only from other institutions.

The control unit is a solitary confinement area for nonconformist inmates. It holds 60 inmates, and prisoners must remain in their cells 23 hours a day. The remaining hour is for showering only, and this privilege can be suspended if certain rules are violated. Prisoners must submit to frequent rectal examinations for nonmedical reasons (searches for contraband and weapons) (Ward and Breed, 1985). Such conditions create a great deal of inmate tension and resentment.

As a result of the deaths of the two correctional officers, a lockdown was imposed. **Lockdowns** are complete removals of prisoner privileges and permanent confinement in cells. Among the factors responsible for the violence at Marion were the mental stresses of solitary confinement, interpersonal antagonisms between prison guards and inmates, forced rectal examinations, and the lack of graded confinement units to function as behavioral incentives (Ward and Breed, 1985).

The most common form of prison violence is male rape (Cotton and Groth, 1984). The United States penitentiary at Lewisburg, Pennsylvania, has been the site of much violence in recent years. The Federal Bureau of Prisons conducted a study of violence among inmates and concluded that there are definite links between sexual aggression, homosexuality, and prison violence. Researchers studied 330 inmates in seventeen federal correctional facilities (Nacci and Kane, 1983). They found that 30 percent of all inmate-respondents had been sexually propositioned by other inmates. Seven percent were seduced by other inmates with gifts or favors, but only 1 percent reported that they were forced to engage in sexual relations to protect themselves. However, 9 percent of all inmates reported that they had been prior victims of sexual aggression in their current or previous prison (Nacci and Kane, 1983).

Estimates of the frequency of male rape and other sexual offenses inside prison walls are largely unreliable (Lockwood, 1980, 1982). The Philadelphia Report, an investigation of male rape in the Philadelphia Prison System, concluded that 2,000 out of 60,000 prisoners had been sexually victimized during a 26-month period during the late 1960s (Davis, 1968). However, sexual assault does not always refer to the same phenomenon among studies investigating prison sexual violence. Polite propositions for sexual involvement among prisoners may be interpreted as aggressive (Lockwood, 1980). Besides anal intercourse, sexual assault may be forced oral-genital contact or masturbation.

Prison violence, particularly sexual violence and aggression, has been linked with racial differences and previous violent subcultures in the inmates' communities. Some studies of prison sexual violence describe the targets of sexual aggression as white, while the sexual aggressors are black (Bartollas et al., 1976; Lockwood, 1980). One interpretation is that blacks hate whites and seek to victimize them whenever the opportunity arises (Irwin, 1971). However, little systematic and supportive evidence exists for this view. Another position is that much prison violence is generated by those who were a part of violent subcultures in their communities. Thus, their prison violence is merely a continuation of the violence in their community (Lockwood, 1980). Finally,

Open corridors, recreational yards, and dining halls are frequently sites of inmate fighting. Fighting occurs because of boredom, sexual jealousies, grudges, and desire to establish a pecking order based upon physical strength and brutality.

some authorities say that inmate sexual aggression is prompted more by their quest for power than for sexual gratification (Gagnon and Simon, 1973).

Some experts have drawn parallels between prison architectural features and the frequency of prisoner assaults. Atlas (1983) studied Florida prisons, including Dade and Union Correctional Institutions, Florida State Prison, and the Tallahassee Federal Correctional Institution. While there was considerable variation in the location of assaults and the different prison architectural styles, the most frequent location of prisoner assaults in all prisons was the housing areas. This is despite the fact that all prisoners in those locations are within sight of guards who may intervene. Atlas says that no particular prison design is best at minimizing or preventing prisoner assaults. However, reducing blind spots, such as dead-end corridors and stairwells, and increasing good sight lines assists in more effective supervision of high-risk areas.

Prison Management and Construction. Whenever a prison riot or other inmate disorder occurs, critics cite administrative problems, and many prison reformers suggest changing the management of prison systems (Goodstein and Hepburn, 1985; McEleney, 1985; New York State, 1985). Prison administrators exert power through reward, coercion, and access to information (Stojkovic, 1986). Administrators may impose harsh rules and punishments for rule infractions. Restrictions of yard privileges, mail privileges, visitation privileges, and other inmate amenities may be imposed. Prison officials can also confiscate inmate contraband, whether it is illegal in any context or just in the prison setting (Hill, 1984).

The United States National Advisory Commission on Criminal Justice Standards and Goals has cited several improvements that must be made in state and federal prisons. To alleviate prison overcrowding, more prisons must be constructed. From 1979 to 1983, state corrections budgets were increased by 79 percent. Capital construction in 1984 included 130 new prisons with 52,000 beds, costing over $2 billion, with an additional 52,000 beds slotted for 1985 (Nesbary, 1985).

CRIME BEAT

For centuries, jailers and prison guards have reported rule infractions by inmates. Inmates have always seemed to devise ways of flaunting the rules and regulations, exchanging and possessing illegal goods, drugs, and alcohol. Crimes committed by those under confinement have prompted officials to streamline their detection methods to prevent the influx of illegal goods into their prisons and jails. Nevertheless, despite administrative efforts, safeguards, and procedures, contraband of one form or another inevitably finds its way to prison cells.

Impromptu searches of inmate cells yield a variety of illegal items, including weapons and contraband. While guards, correctional officers, and other jail and prison officials have been involved in illegal smuggling operations in the past and removed from their posts when the smuggling is discovered, it is unthinkable for most persons to conceive that a large number of guards in any single prison might account for most illegal inmate contraband entering their facility. It is even more inconceivable that correctional officers would assist some prisoners in escaping from incarceration. Yet, direct evidence of correctional officer corruption was obtained in October 1988 when almost sixty Philadelphia jail correctional officers and prisoners were arrested.

In 1988, Philadelphia provided seven major jail facilities for over 4,000 inmates. While Philadelphia authorities were aware that inmates were regularly receiving contraband from the outside, they had no direct leads about the origin of these goods or the conduits through which the goods were smuggled. In early 1986, the Philadelphia District Attorney's Office established an undercover operation, codenamed Ferret. Ferret involved the services of several Philadelphia detectives experienced in undercover work.

An early lead came when one of the Ferret team, Detective Joe Rago, met with inmate Albert Harris.

Harris implied that he would be willing to exchange information about illegal drug transactions in prison for leniency in sentencing. Rago learned that a key figure in drug smuggling in Holmesburg (Philadelphia) Prison was the recreational supervisor, Lavier Pounds. Allegedly, Pounds would pick up illegal drugs from outside suppliers and bring them into the prison for sale to prisoners. He smuggled these drugs and other contraband in cases of athletic equipment or motion picture cans. One evening in May 1986, another detective, Cliff Ruley, called Pounds and identified himself as Harris's source for drugs. Subsequently, Pounds agreed to smuggle automatic weapons and money into the prison to assist in an inmate's escape. Surveillance teams recorded the Ruley-Pounds transaction and resulted in Pounds' arrest.

While not all leads obtained by Philadelphia detectives were as easily obtained as the one from Harris, many leads were discovered during the next few years, as undercover officers made over 300 buys of illegal goods with guards and inmates. For instance, at a Halloween party in 1986, several undercover officers were sold $250 worth of cocaine from a correctional officer, Leroy Randolph. Other illicit transactions included bribes, assistance in escaping, and various luxury items. When the Philadelphia District Attorney's Office moved to apprehend and charge all involved in these illicit operations in September 1988, forty-one of fifty-eight arrests involved correctional officers.

While this example is insufficient to typify all correctional officers throughout the United States, it does highlight a major correctional problem—the potential corruption of staff. What screening techniques should jail and prison administrators use in recruiting correctional officers? Should all correctional officers be required to undergo regular drug or lie detector tests to determine their honesty?

The role of architecture in prison construction is increasingly important, particularly in design concepts that are consistent with current correctional philosophies (National Institute of Corrections, 1985). Overcrowding may be eased by improved prison design. Inmate sexual violence and other aggressive behaviors may be controlled more effectively with properly designed prison structures. Prison officials tend to promote building programs that utilize space more efficiently and create greater efficiency among their guards. The cost of building prisons is a key factor influencing prison design. In New York, the cost of imprisoning one inmate is $40,000 per year (Steelman, 1984).

One way of reducing new prison construction costs is to convert existing nonprison facilities into prisons. For example, some government buildings used for state or federal purposes may be converted through remodeling into medium- or minimum-security facilities (Library Information Specialists, Inc., 1984). Projects are being undertaken in Maine, Michigan, Minnesota, New York, Ohio, and Oregon.

Jails

Jails, or gaols (pronounced *jails)*, were inspired by England's Henry II (1154–1189). In sixteenth century England, county sheriffs and justices of the peace in local jurisdictions were charged with the responsibility of building and maintaining jails to imprison local offenders (Wayson, Funke, Hamilton and Meyer, 1977:3–4). These houses of correction originally housed petty offenders and vagrants. Keepers were hired by sheriffs to watch the inmates. Keepers rarely received a salary, however. Rather, they obtained the funds for maintaining inmates through the inmates' own funds, from friends of inmates, or from inmate begging. Some writers observed:

> The schedule of payments under this much criticized . . . system was not uniform . . . but varied with the dreadfulness of events and the prisoner's social station. Beds, mattresses, bedclothes . . . [and other items] were each assigned a price; more striking however, were the charges for admission to the jail and discharge (even if the prisoner was acquitted). (Wayson, Funke, Familton, and Meyer, 1977:3).

In the colonies in 1642, the General Assembly of Virginia initiated an administrative pattern (Wayson, Funke, Hamilton, and Meyer, 1977:4). Six counties in Virginia were required to build jails for the general detention of prisoners awaiting monthly court sessions in Jamestown. The Walnut Street Jail built in Philadelphia in 1790 is recognized as the first modern jail facility.

Jails in the United States house offenders sentenced to short terms and those awaiting trial. Some jails contract with state and federal governments to house their inmate overflow, particularly those who require only short-term incarceration. Also detained in these jails are those arrested for petty offenses who cannot post bond. Ricci (1986:14–15) says that jails also hold convicted offenders who have been sentenced to less than a year. Jails hold mostly young males with poor education, the mentally ill, the retarded, and public inebriates. A majority of persons admitted to jail remain there less than 3 weeks.

Table 13.6 shows a 1-day count of jail inmates in 1986. Approximately 8 percent of the 269,179 inmates were female (21,273), with 53 percent of these (11,306) being detained for reasons other than criminal conviction. Of the male inmates, again, 53 percent were unconvicted of crimes.

In recent years, jails in the United States have been called "festering sores," "cesspools of crime," "teeming houses of horror," and "the ultimate ghetto" (Thompson, 1986:205). Much of the blame for such labels applied to United States jails is attributed to their unique political nature (Thompson, 1986:205). Thompson (1986:206–208) says that our jails are faced with numerous problems. A majority of jails in the United States are old, with many built before the twentieth century. Frequently, too, these facilities are poorly designed and staffed by poorly trained, underpaid, low-status

TABLE 13.6 Detention Status of Adult Jail Inmates, by Sex, 1986

	Number of Jail Inmates (from Annual Survey of Jails)
Total number of adults with known conviction status	269,179
Convicted	127,067
Male	117,100
Female	9,967
Unconvicted	142,112
Male	130,806
Female	11,306

Note: Data are for June 30.

Source: Susan Kline, *Jail Inmates, 1986* (Washington, DC: U.S. Department of Justice, 1987), p. 2.

personnel. Most jails have little public sympathy or support. Jails rely heavily upon county sheriffs for administrative leadership and county government for financial support. Many sheriffs are poorly trained for these important administrative posts.

According to some critics, jails are captives of the criminal justice system (Ricci, 1986:15). The flow of persons in and out of jail is controlled by district attorneys and the courts, not jail administrators. However, sheriffs influence jail populations by the guidelines that they adopt concerning bookings and bail (Ricci, 1986:15–16).

The United States Jail Population. In 1978, the Bureau of Justice Statistics conducted a complete enumeration of jails in the United States. In 1982, the Bureau of the Census began a national survey of jails for the Bureau of Justice Statistics. These surveys are now conducted every 5 years.

By 1987, three fourths of the entire jail population was housed in the 612 jails of 361 city and county jurisdictions (Kline, 1987). Evidence of the short-term nature of jail confinement is the substantial inmate turnover that takes place. For example, total releases in United States jails in 1986 were approximately 8.3 million persons, while new admissions accounted for about 8.2 million persons. Jails are supported largely by city and county funds. In previous years, the Law Enforcement Assistance Administration made funds available to jail personnel for upgrading their skills, augmenting their education, and participating in other enforcement-related activities. Other agencies, such as the United States Department of Justice, continue modest support to jail administrations for research and other purposes.

Table 13.7 profiles some key demographic characteristics of inmates in United States jails in 1986. Ninety-two percent of all jail inmates were male. Blacks accounted for 41 percent of all jail inmates, while whites accounted for 58 percent. In addition, about 1 percent of all jail inmates were juveniles under 18 years of age awaiting transfer to juvenile facilities. About 20 percent of all juveniles in jails had been adjudicated or convicted, while another 49 percent were awaiting adjudication or trial (Kline, 1987:1–2).

TABLE 13.7 Demographic Characteristics of Jail Inmates, 1986

Characteristic	Percent of Jail Inmates
Sex	
Total	100
Male	92
Female	8
Race	
White	58
Male	54
Female	4
Black	41
Male	37
Female	3
Other*	1
Male	1
Female	—
Ethnicity	
Hispanic	14
Male	13
Female	1
Non-Hispanic	86
Male	80
Female	7

Note: Data are for June 30. Sex was reported for all inmates. Race and ethnicity were reported for 98% of the inmates in 1986. Percentages may not add to total because of rounding.

—Less than 0.5%.

*Native Americans, Aleuts, Asians, and Pacific Islanders.

Source: Susan Kline, *Jail Inmates, 1986* (Washington, DC: U.S. Department of Justice, 1987), p. 2.

Table 13.8 shows annual admissions and releases according to legal status and gender for 1983, 1985, and 1986. Between 1983 and 1985, total jail admissions increased by nearly 300,000. Between 1985 and 1986, jail admissions dropped almost imperceptibly. The number of female admissions increased from 708,315 in 1983 to over 850,000 in 1986. Male admissions increased between 1983 and 1985 from 7.3 million to 7.4 million, but a small decline in male admissions occurred between 1985 and 1986. Juvenile admissions jumped from 105,366 to 112,106 between 1983 and 1985, but these admissions plummeted in 1986 to 92,856. Reasons for this significant drop in juvenile admissions may be that (1) jail officials are making a concerted effort to comply with court-ordered inmate population reductions and (2) more accurate classification and identification of juveniles has occurred. Juveniles are increasingly referred to youth services or juvenile detention centers rather than processed initially in adult jails.

Jails are less complex than are prisons. Jails have many of the same features as prisons, such as solitary confinement cells and segregated areas according to the type of inmate incarcerated; however, jails have problems different from those that confront prison administrators. The cost of maintaining inmates varies among jails, depending upon the quality of facilities provided. Steelman (1984) estimates that New York City jail costs are $40,000 per year per inmate, although per inmate figures are lower in other jurisdictions.

TABLE 13.8 Annual Jail Admissions and Releases, by Legal Status and Sex, 1983, 1985, 1986

| | Number of Admissions/Releases | | |
| | National Jail Census | Annual Survey of Jails | |
	1983	1985	1986
Admissions, total	8,084,344	8,364,533	8,354,032
Adults	7,978,978	8,252,427	8,261,176
Male	7,270,663	7,430,148	7,410,057
Female	708,315	822,279	851,119
Juveniles*	105,366	112,106	92,856
Male	86,850	94,579	72,046
Female	18,516	17,527	20,810
Releases, total	7,941,236	8,279,054	8,284,676
Adults	7,837,156	8,169,461	8,193,124
Male	7,145,818	7,359,076	7,342,940
Female	691,338	810,385	850,184
Juveniles*	104,080	109,593	91,552
Male	85,564	92,235	70,442
Female	18,516	17,358	21,110

Note: Data are for the year ending June 30.

*Juveniles are persons of an age specified by State statute (usually under 18) initially subject to juvenile court authority even if tried as adults in criminal court.

Source: Susan Kline, *Jail Inmates, 1986* (Washington, DC: U.S. Department of Justice, 1987), p. 2.

In jails, little concern is given to inmate adjustment problems because of the short-term nature of a jail inmate's confinement. Therefore, little rationale exists for reforming prisoners or developing rehabilitation programs. Only 12 percent of all jails have vocational training programs, and only a third of all jails have work-related programs. There are no guard towers and there is no close supervision of inmate activities. Most jails do not have outside recreational yards, although many jails have recreational areas in special locations within the facility for prisoners to watch television or play cards. Often, these areas are dayrooms.

Inmates are not paroled from jails. When inmates have served their time, they are released without supervision. However, judges may impose short-term sentences for felons, assign them temporarily to jails, and permit them to spend the remainder of their sentences on parole, but these are only occasional cases. In 1984, 24 percent of the jails in all jurisdictions with large jail populations held inmates from state and federal institutions to alleviate overcrowding.

Interestingly, the transfer of state and federal prisoners to local jail facilities to alleviate overcrowding in the larger prisons has created conditions of overcrowding in many local jails. In 1984, 134, or 22 percent, of the 621 jails with large numbers of inmates were under court order to reduce their inmate populations. The leading reason for court-ordered jail inmate population reductions was crowded living units (Baunach, Sickmund, and Ford, 1986:3). Other reasons included fire hazards, staffing patterns, and food services.

The diversity of jail inmates has caused critics to question whether jails are primarily designed for law enforcement purposes (since they are operated by sheriffs) or are major corrections components. The lack of inmate programs and other facilities, together with their poorly trained guards, suggests that they are neither. However, they serve both law enforcement and corrections functions to a limited degree (retribution, deterrence, isolation, and incapacitation).

John Irwin (1985) made one of the more insightful analyses of jails. Irwin studied San Francisco jails extensively. Although he cautioned that his generalizations about jails may be limited because he studied the jails of only one city, he believes that his conclusions apply to most jails in the United States. First, Irwin found that jail clientele are quite different from inmates in prisons. Jail inmates are largely noncriminals. Second, Irwin discovered that jails receive and confine mostly detached and disreputable persons, or rabble (Irwin, 1985:xiii). Third, he concluded that by arresting and holding rabble in jails, society inadvertently increases their number and holds people in a rabble status (Irwin, 1985:xiii).

In view of Irwin's generalizations about jails and the people who are ordinarily confined in them, it is understandable that jails have been neglected by politicians and others. They hold society's undesirables, the unemployed, and minorities. They perpetuate the plight of rabble by continuing to label them as such through arrests and detentions. Jails have been ignored for various improvements primarily because of the inmates they accommodate, individuals who have little or no political power or influence. Citizens are not supportive of programs designed to help them. Irwin believes that there is a large, persistent, permanent rabble population and that jails exist primarily to control them. In recent years, however, jail inmate litigation has increased. The United States Supreme Court has gradually acquired a better understanding of jails and jail problems. Particularly, the high court has mandated substantial jail improvements and inmate population reductions.

Selected Jail Problems. While jail sentences are ordinarily short-term, inmate subcultures nevertheless develop and influence the lives of most of the inmates. When more experienced inmates enter jails for new offenses, they assess their length of stay and readapt quickly to the prevalent inmate subculture (Garofalo and Clark, 1985). In many jails, there are sexual assaults similar to those that occur in prisons (Travisono et al., 1986). Because of inadequate staffing and housing patterns, sexual assaults occur more frequently in jails than prisons.

Chicago's Cook County Jail has been described by some observers as the "worst jail they have ever seen" (Davidson, 1968). Inmate and guard brutality is commonplace, and homosexual rape, narcotics addiction, administrative corruption, and ineptitude are prevalent. One problem is the barn boss system, where certain inmates, because of their wealth, race, or social status, dominate other inmates and even some jail guards.

Another jail problem is a lack of trained jail personnel to supervise inmates. Many local jails are supervised by part-time employees, who have little or no corrections experience. Voluntary reserve police officers sometimes perform routine guard duty and inspect packages brought to inmates on weekends from relatives. Some jails use sheriff's deputies as guards for punishment for inadequate performance on patrol. Other jails use rookie deputies on probationary status as jailers. Such inexperienced jail staff aggravate existing jail problems.

Many of those confined in jails are there unnecessarily. A study of 20,797 booking records of the Milwaukee County Jail in 1983 showed that many of the inmates were housed there temporarily, awaiting transfer to the Milwaukee House of Corrections (Wood, Verber, and Reddin, 1985). Many of those arrested and processed were probationers and parole violators, who had committed technical infractions not ordinarily requiring incarceration. Some offenses, such as disorderly conduct, shoplifting, and possession of small amounts of marijuana, that were treated as ordinance violations in the suburbs, were jailable offenses in the city. Also, suspects charged with nonviolent property crimes were jailed unnecessarily prior to trial.

Jail suicides pose a major problem for jail administrators. Considering the short-term nature of the confinement, authorities cannot explain why certain inmates commit suicide. In 1984, 25 percent of the jails in all jurisdictions with large jail populations reported inmate suicides. Of the 278 jail deaths reported in 1984 in these facilities, 45 percent were suicides. Only 2 percent of the deaths were caused by injuries inflicted by other inmates (Baunach, Sickmund, and Ford, 1986:4). The remaining deaths were due to natural causes, such as age or serious illness.

Studies of jail suicides show no particular racial, ethnic, age, gender, or socioeconomic patterns (Burks and DeHeer, 1986; Kennedy, 1984; Library Information Specialists, 1983). Suicides occur most often within the first few weeks of incarceration, however, and there is a noticeable decline in suicide rates the longer inmates are incarcerated (Kennedy, 1984). Of thirty-nine suicides in Michigan jails and lockups for the 1980–81 period, no significant differences were found attributable to race, age, location, or reason for arrest when the suicide cases were compared with the general arrest trends for the state (Kennedy, 1984).

The Prospects for Jail Improvements. Much of the overcrowding in jails throughout the United States can be eased through better planning, as well as through measures such as those taken by Montana jails. Greater use of probation after sentencing, especially for minor offenses, will ease the jail population to some degree. More efficient bail systems can decrease jail populations as well, particularly if booking for petty or minor offenses occurs without formal incarceration.

Jail improvements are closely linked with political interests and community administrative policies. Determining appropriate jail size is not the technical problem that many persons believe it is. Rather, it is more a matter of public policy (Ricci, 1986:15). Obviously, greater community appropriations will be required to provide jails with better equipment and inmate accommodations, including better bedding, food, and clothing.

It is difficult to forecast jail trends (Ricci, 1986:16). Law enforcement officials, judges, district attorneys, public defenders, and probation officials determine who goes to jail and how long they remain incarcerated. Court-ordered reductions in jail populations help to alleviate overcrowding, but most jails average 102 percent of their maximum inmate capacity. In sentencing, district attorneys are increasingly considering felony probation for less violent felony offenders as court dockets become crowded and state and federal prisons exceed their rated capacities. It is likely that court-ordered inmate population reductions similar to those in Tennessee, Mississippi, Texas, and California will occur in other jurisdictions. No inmate may be put into these state prisons unless another inmate is released. The existing prison populations of these states cannot be exceeded for any reason. This shifts the responsibility of deciding who goes to prison to district attorneys and judges. The same holds true for jails and jail populations. Policy changes about who is to be confined and for how long must be made if significant reductions in existing jail populations are to occur.

■ WOMEN IN UNITED STATES PRISONS AND JAILS

Female prisoners in United States institutions have seldom exceeded 7 percent or 8 percent of the total prison population. In 1985, there were 23,091 female inmates in state and federal prisons, representing 4.6 percent of all inmates. This is three times the number of female inmates incarcerated in United States prisons in 1977. By comparison, the male prison population increased by 68 percent for the same period.

In 1987, there were 3,027 females in federal prisons (6 percent of all federal prisoners) and 25,812 (4.5 percent) in state facilities (Greenfeld, 1988:3). Table 13.9 shows a distribution of females in federal and state prisons with at least 500 female inmates.

Sixteen states had at least 500 female inmates at the end of 1987. However, Table 13.9 shows that between 1986 and 1987, women in prison increased by 8.2 percent. Between 1984 and 1985, the number of female prison inmates increased 11 percent (Greenfeld, 1986:3). This consistent increase suggests a trend toward higher rates of female incarceration (Ryan, 1984).

Until 1790, it was common in colonial prisons and jails to incarcerate everyone in common areas, regardless of age or gender. Men, women, and children were confined together into large rooms (American Correctional Association, 1983; Dobash, 1983). In 1790, the Walnut Street Jail in Philadelphia represented the first segregation of offenders into separate accommodations according to gender as well as other criteria, such as seriousness of the offense and type of crime. Women's prison conditions during the next 30 years did not improve. In 1819, the New York Society for the Prevention of Pauperism characterized the women's quarters at the Bellevue Penitentiary as "one great school of vice and desperation, replete with prostitutes, vagrants, lunatics, thieves, and those of a less heinous character" (Freedman, 1981:7). Troubling the New York Society was the fact that women outside the prison did not seem to care about the terrible conditions being endured by the imprisoned women (Freedman, 1981:7).

Even in more modern prison facilities, such as the Auburn (New York) State Penitentiary, which was constructed in various phases between 1816 and 1820, the well-known tier system and more individualized prisoner accommodations failed to upgrade the treatment of female inmates. At Auburn, women did not have separate cells although male inmates did. Female prisoners were lodged together into one large attic room at Auburn and were left unattended. Their windows were sealed to prevent communication with the men (Freedman, 1981:15). While there were no more than

TABLE 13.9 Women in State and Federal Institutions at Yearend, 1987

Jurisdiction	Number of Women Inmates	Percent of All Inmates	Percent Change in Women Inmate Population, 1986–87
U.S. total	28,839	5.0%	8.2%
Federal	3,027	6.3	6.8
State	25,812	4.8	8.4
States with at least 500 women inmates			
California	4,152	6.2%	16.5%
Florida	1,681	5.2	2.8
Texas	1,555	4.0	− 10.9
New York	1,487	3.6	12.1
Ohio	1,295	5.3	6.8
Michigan	1,183	5.0	16.2
Georgia	928	5.0	−2.0
North Carolina	812	4.7	−2.2
Illinois	779	3.9	2.0
Alabama	732	5.7	18.8
Oklahoma	694	7.2	2.2
Pennsylvania	674	4.1	14.0
Louisiana	673	4.4	7.3
South Carolina	661	5.2	10.0
Arizona	609	5.6	25.3
Missouri	540	4.8	19.2

Source: Reprinted from Lawrence A. Greenfeld, *Prisoners in 1987* (Washington, DC: U.S. Department of Justice, 1988), p. 3.

thirty women at Auburn at any given time, their living conditions were characterized by overcrowding, immobilization, and neglect (Freedman, 1981:15). Between 1790 and 1870, female inmates of most penal facilities in the United States received care inferior to that of the male prisoners (Rafter, 1983). One instance of the scandalous conditions at Auburn involved a young woman, Rachel Welch, who became pregnant while serving a punishment sentence in a solitary cell (Freedman, 1981:15). Welch was flogged brutally by a prison guard (possibly the one who fathered her child), and she died shortly after childbirth. Her death had no influence on a grand jury convened to investigate it, but public uproar led to the appointment of a matron in 1832 to oversee the women's quarters and to replace male guards (Freedman, 1981:15–16).

The Women's Reform Movement began during the 1820s in England and the United States, with small groups of women (frequently affiliated with one religious faith or another) visiting prisons to offer charitable aid to the female inmates. Reflecting the strong Quaker tradition of concern for the unfortunate population of prisoners, Elizabeth Gurney Fry (1780–1845) emerged as the mother of women's prison reform.

Fry was a minister. In that capacity, she entered London's Newgate Gaol frequently to convert inmates through prayer to the Quaker faith (Freedman, 1981:23). However, she soon realized that the female inmates needed better food, clothing, and other amenities that the jail did not provide. She obtained permission from the prison authorities and conducted an experiment in prison reform for women by founding the Ladies Association for the Improvement of the Female Prisoners at Newgate. This association established workshops, Bible classes, and a self-administered inmate monitoring system where women could look after each other (Freedman, 1981:23). To culminate her important reform work, she prepared a treatise outlining her observations and recommendations, entitled *Observations in Visiting, Superintendence, and Government of Female Prisoners,* published in 1827. This work was significant because it elaborated the principles that later dominated United States women's prison reform (Freedman, 1981:23).

Before prisons for women were established, a few institutions offered aid to women recently discharged from prisons or jails. The Dedham Temporary Asylum for Discharged Female Prisoners in Massachusetts was operated from 1864 to 1909. It functioned in much the same way as halfway houses (Bularik, 1984). A privately controlled facility, it provided individualized assistance for women who had recently been discharged from various prisons. Several similar institutions existed in the United States prior to the creation of prisons exclusively for women (Bularik, 1984).

Historians disagree about the first exclusive women's prison in the United States. According to Zebulon Brockway, the first superintendent of the Elmira, New York Reformatory in 1876, he helped to establish the House of Shelter exclusively for female offenders in 1869. He hired Emma Hall, a Detroit school teacher, to serve as matron from 1869 to 1874 (Freedman, 1981:50–51). Michigan historians have labeled this House of Shelter as America's first women's reformatory (Helfman, 1947). However, Freedman (1981:50–51) says that the House of Shelter was not technically a prison. Rather, it was the first penal institution where women had complete control and authority over female inmates.

The Women's Prison in Indiana, constructed in 1873, is considered the first United States facility exclusively for women. One of its major objectives was the instilling of motherhood and sobriety in the women it housed (Gibson, 1973). In New York, the Bedford Hills Reformatory for Women was constructed in 1901, and in 1933, the women at Auburn were housed in their own separate prison, known as the Westfield State Farm (Carney, 1979:201). Federal female prisoners were originally housed in the District of Columbia Women's Reformatory until 1927, when the first federal reformatory for women was opened in Alderson, West Virginia. California did not establish a separate women's prison until 1936 (Carney, 1979:201–202).

Characteristics of Female Prisoners

Glick (1978) has described several demographic and social characteristics of female prisoners in the United States. Over two thirds of the female inmates are under 30 years of age. In 1978, about 50 percent of all female prisoners were black, a significant overrepresentation of black inmates considering their proportionate representation in the overall population. By 1983, these figures had changed significantly, with the female inmate population consisting of 38 percent blacks and 50 percent whites (Ryan, 1984). Between 1975 and 1983, age and educational level remained the same for female offenders.

CRIME BEAT

In recent years, various jurisdictions, including Orlando, Florida, have passed laws that hold pregnant women liable for actions that might harm their fetuses. The American Civil Liberties Union and other interested organizations have challenged the Orlando law, although the United States Supreme Court has never ruled on this specific issue. Orlando officials, as well as those in other cities where similar statutes have been passed, have been mindful of the escalating number of babies born with cocaine in their bodies. In Washington, D.C., for example, a young woman, Brenda Vaughan, was sentenced to 4 months in jail for forging a small check. In the District of Columbia, this sentence is considered harsh for check forgery, but because Vaughan exhibited signs of cocaine use, the judge who sentenced her said that he wanted to protect her fetus from Vaughan's drug use.

Beyond the issue of protecting the fetuses of pregnant women who are likely drug users is the long-term incarceration of women who are pregnant. In states where facilities exist, pregnant inmates are permitted to keep their babies and live with them in separate cottages on prison grounds. In other jurisdictions, however, newborn infants are placed in adoption agencies or receive foster care if the mothers have no family or visible means of providing for them during their incarceration.

Do you believe that special provisions ought to be made for pregnant women in prisons and jails? What are the implications for jail overcrowding, considering the Orlando, Florida, policy? Should all pregnant women who are incarcerated be permitted to keep their babies?

Of the women convicted of felonies, 43 percent are serving time for violent offenses, while the rest are confined for property crimes and narcotics offenses (Glick, 1978). Property crime among females increased significantly between 1978 and 1983, however (Ryan, 1984).

An interesting characteristic of female prisoners is that 70 percent are mothers. Most often, they are single, primary parents (McGowan and Blumenthal, 1978). In many prisons, women are incarcerated while in the early stages of pregnancy. In all prisons, medical services exist for pregnant women, and services are provided for child care until the mothers are released (Smith, Bristow, and Austin, 1985). For example, in 1984 the Massachusetts Correctional Institution at Framingham had more than fifty pregnant women imprisoned. When these mothers' babies were born, community-based services provided placements until the mothers were released.

The Outlook for Women's Prisons

The philosophy of women's prisons since the 1870s has been to promote a more humane environment (Hunter, 1985). Many women's prisons permit inmates to wear their own clothes, and women are more likely to be housed in rooms than cells. They are also permitted to furnish their rooms with personal items (Hunter, 1985). However, guards exercise some authority, conducting frequent headcounts and rigidly enforcing regulations. Thus, these prisons attempt to achieve a delicate balance between security and humanity (Hunter, 1985:131).

Some critics say that female inmates ought to be treated like male inmates, housed in cells, and subjected to similarly harsh confinement conditions. However, most women's prisons have been patterned after early reformatories, and most prison programs continue to perpetuate structurally-induced sexism (Fox, 1984).

A study of the Bedford Hills (New York) Women's Facility during the 1970s showed that although the prison resembled a private women's college campus physically, hostile social relations existed between the administrators, guards, and inmates (Fox, 1984). Fox (1984) suggests that this may have been due to the large influx of younger, more assertive and aggressive women into the prison. Furthermore, many of the older administrators were replaced with less experienced managers, and these new officials instituted internal reforms to conform to men's prison norms to a greater degree. Fox (1984) says that equality of treatment has been interpreted to mean similarity of treatment, and therefore, the new measures introduced created undesirable prison conditions for women as well as men.

A study of female inmates at the Bayview Correctional Facility in New York prompted by inmate incidents in 1983–1984 showed that Bayview was never intended as a correctional facility (Potler, 1985). Bayview was converted into a medium-security women's facility in 1979, and no significant structural changes have been made since then. There were numerous physical problems, including faulty wiring, lack of adequate fire and safety precautions, lack of adequate ventilation, and numerous unsanitary conditions (Potler, 1985). Furthermore, while it eased overcrowding in other women's facilities in New York, Bayview became overcrowded. Insufficient staffing, medical care, and vocational or academic programs for inmates were cited as reasons for inmate discontent. Members of the Bayview Advisory Board were persuaded to make improvements in each of these areas to restore prison order (Potler, 1985).

One problem affecting both men's and women's prisons is that they are sexually segregated. Some critics have advocated the creation of co-ed prisons to reduce homosexuality, lesbianism, and aggravated sexual assaults, which are common features of the prison environment.

In 1971, the first sexually integrated prison in the United States was created in Fort Worth, Texas. It was the Federal Correctional Institution, strictly a minimum-security prison (Smykla, 1980:41). It has a more natural environment, where males can mingle with females in more relaxed social settings. This environment has resulted in lower rates of sexual assaults and a low rate of recidivism. Smykla (1980:45) says that the major disadvantage is the lack of guard control over the sexual activities of inmates. Although the rules permit hand-holding and limited kissing, some prisoners engage in sexual intercourse in areas known to be frequently unguarded and unsupervised. Birth control pills are issued to female inmates on request.

Some experts say that women have been exploited by the male population. Therefore, the time they spend in prison away from men may be what they need to discover themselves and develop realistic understandings of their own needs. One superintendent of a women's correctional facility interprets the establishment of co-correctional institutions as an effort by some prison authorities to ease overcrowding in men's prisons. She says "[O]ne gets a very strong impression—even though it cannot be verified—that institutions are being sexually integrated to please male egos or to smooth out the operation of men's institutions, and not to meet the unique and special needs of the female offender" (Crawford, 1980:268).

Alaska has developed a **coordinate model,** where neighboring female and male prisons share common facilities and programs (Schweber, 1984). Schweber (1984) says that in a co-correctional facility, women are under more intense surveillance for possible sex code violations than if they were in sexually segregated institutions. She thinks that

Alaska's model permits a breakup of female prisons into smaller administrative units. This gives officials more administrative leverage to safeguard and promote the interests of the female inmates. Such a program offers women a greater range of educational programs and other services not otherwise provided in strictly segregated institutions.

While women's institutions have continued to counter stereotypical attitudes about prison operations, they have benefited to some degree because their facilities often have been targeted for experimental programs of various kinds (Hunter, 1985:134). Also, lawsuits filed by female prisoners have resulted in programs in women's prisons more equivalent to those extended to male inmates. However, correctional officials in some jurisdictions have taken steps to drastically modify and curtail the operation of co-ed prisons. In 1988, for instance, the Federal Bureau of Prisons terminated its co-ed prison programs. In their place, the bureau is providing services for the women equivalent to those for the men in separate correctional institutions.

■ SUMMARY

Correctional programs in the United States began in the 1790s and early 1800s with the creation of such facilities as the Walnut Street Jail in Philadelphia and the Auburn (New York) State Penitentiary. Politicians and prison reformers such as William Penn and Benjamin Rush promoted corrections policies that eventually led to the upgrading of United States prisons and jails for the next century.

The Auburn system introduced the tier concept, alleviated prison overcrowding, and produced more individualized inmate treatment. In 1876, the Elmira (New York) Reformatory under the direction of Superintendent Zebulon Brockway promoted individualized treatment even further and fostered indeterminate sentencing and parole programs.

In 1930, the Federal Bureau of Prisons was established, and significant developments in penal reform followed. Programs became increasingly treatment-oriented and many state prison systems tended to copy the federal system.

The major goals of corrections are retribution, deterrence, rehabilitation, reintegration, isolation, and incapacitation, although critics raise questions concerning the degree to which these various goals have been achieved. In 1987, prisons housed over 545,000 inmates, while jails housed approximately 270,000. Prisons are classified according to prisoner dangerousness into maximum-, medium-, and minimum-security institutions. Inmates are classified according to the seriousness of their offenses and the crimes committed. Psychological scales are often used in such classifications. Among the problems associated with prisons are prison violence and the inadequacy of administrative leadership. Architectural influence on prison operation is also increasingly important to corrections personnel.

While prisons house more serious, long-term offenders, jails house inmates for terms of less than 1 year, including those awaiting trial. Sometimes, prisoners from state or federal prisons are accommodated in jails through contractual arrangements to alleviate prison overcrowding. Jail problems include overcrowding, prisoner suicides, and a general lack of prisoner programs to assist the educational and social development of the inmates. Current trends favor greater use of probation and less use of jails as temporary holding facilities for booking and bail.

Women's prisons have recently received considerable attention from corrections personnel. A women's prison reform movement has provided more humane conditions in women's prisons generally and necessary services. Services include temporary shelter and custody of the children of imprisoned women and medical services for women who are pregnant when they enter prison. Efforts are continuing to make women's prisons better and to contribute to the inmates' successful rehabilitation and return to society. Co-correctional, or co-ed, institutions have been proposed as means of reducing sexual aggressiveness among both men and women in prison. These programs have begun in various states, but at present, the results from such programs are inconclusive.

KEY TERMS

American Correctional Association (ACA)

Auburn State Penitentiary

banishment

body belts

congregate system

coordinate model

Elmira Reformatory

Federal Bureau of Prisons

Great Law of Pennsylvania

lockdowns

Megargee Inmate Typology

recidivist

tier system

Walnut Street Jail

QUESTIONS FOR REVIEW

1. Differentiate between jails and prisons. What types of prisoners are each designed to accommodate?
2. What was the first jail constructed in the United States? Why was it an important instrument of prison reform?
3. What was significant about the Auburn (New York) Penitentiary? How did the Elmira (New York) Reformatory improve the correctional goals sought by Auburn?
4. What are four correctional goals? Are United States prisons and jails achieving these goals?
5. What evidence shows that deterrence by imprisonment is somewhat ineffective?
6. What prison activities might be considered part of a rehabilitation program? Do jails have similar programs?
7. What is a halfway house? What is its importance in the correctional process?
8. List three types of prisons and differentiate between them.
9. What inmate classification systems are there? Are these systems effective in classifying prisoners into one type of prison environment or another?
10. What is the significance of prison architectural style in relation to current correctional philosophies?

11. When did jails originate? What were their original functions? In what ways have their functions changed since they originated?
12. What is meant by the statement "Jails are captives of the criminal justice system"?
13. List and discuss briefly two different jail problems. How are these problems to be resolved in the future, if at all?
14. What are the current prospects for improving the plight of jails in the United States?
15. What proportion of the total prisoner population in the United States is female?
16. Who was the leading women's prison reformer in the 1800s? Why was her work on women's prison life important to prison reform?
17. What are some characteristics of female prisoners in the United States?
18. Identify two areas that have been targets of women's prison reform movements.
19. What is a co-correctional prison? What problems are coed or co-correctional prisons designed to eliminate?
20. What were the first exclusively women's prisons in the United States?

SUGGESTED READINGS

Carter, Robert M., Daniel Glaser, and Leslie T. Wilkins (Eds.) (1985). *Correctional institutions*. New York: Harper & Row.

Irwin, John (1985). *Managing the underclass in American society*. Berkeley, CA: Univ. of California Press.

Martin, Steve J., and Sheldon Ekland-Olson (1987). *Texas prisons: The walls came tumbling down*. Austin, TX: Texas Monthly Press.

Thomas, Charles W. (1987). *Corrections in America: Problems of the past and the present*. Beverly Hills, CA: Sage.

Zimmer, Lynn E. (1986). *Women guarding men*. Chicago, IL: Univ. of Chicago Press.

Corrections Operations and Issues

■ INTRODUCTION

One barometer of the effectiveness of prison operations is the number of lawsuits filed by inmates, alleging civil rights violations or challenging the nature and length of their incarceration and treatment (Miller, 1983). Of course, this is also a measure of the responsiveness of the courts to inmate actions. In 1960, 2,000 petitions from state and federal prisoners and jail inmates were filed in United States district courts. In 1970, 16,000 petitions were filed (Allen and Beran, 1977:80). For the 12-month period ending June 30, 1985, 22,000 prisoner petitions were filed in United States district and appeals courts (Hunzeker and Conger, 1985).

Petitions filed in court by prisoners allege a variety of problems. Some of the allegations by inmates include inadequate medical care, staff brutality, inadequate food, gang rape or assault, and few or no recreational opportunities. Other allegations are severe punishment and harsh prison rules, racism, exploitation of prison labor, an absence of or inadequate vocational and educational programs, overcrowding, violations of health and safety standards, and claims for lost or stolen property (Allen and Beran, 1977:80–81; Hunzeker and Conger, 1985). This chapter discusses prison culture and the offenders under correctional supervision. Many problems cited by prisoners in their petitions are traceable to the prison administration and policy decisions. Other problems are grounded in conflicts between the inmates and prison staff.

■ PRISON CULTURE AND TYPES OF OFFENDERS

Prison culture is as diverse as is life in the community, but some important differences make prison culture unique. The most important difference is that the prison population consists exclusively of criminals. All inmates in prison have been convicted of crimes. Another distinction is that strict rules require inmates to adhere to a high standard of conformity. With few exceptions, too, most prisons segregate inmates according to gender and do not permit any type of contact with the opposite sex.

Although a majority of the prisons in the United States are medium- or minimum-security, generalizations about them and their inmate subcultures are often unreliable. There are exceptions to every generalization made. Every prison has an inmate subculture, including an **inmate code** by which most inmates live. These inmate codes are separate from administratively established prison rules enforced by the guards (Carroll, 1974; Clemmer, 1940; Garofalo and Clark, 1985; Jacobs 1974, 1977; Sykes, 1958). Similar to the pecking order in a chicken coop, prisoners develop a social hierarchy based upon several criteria. These include physical strength, race or ethnicity, and political power. Bartering or informal exchange systems exist, not only among the prisoners, but between prisoners and prison staff (Hewitt, Poole, and Regoli, 1984). These bartering systems promote prison stability and make supervising prisoners less stressful for the prison guards.

In 1983, Hewitt, Poole, and Regoli (1984) studied 391 inmates and 44 guards at the Federal Correctional Institution in Fort Worth, Texas. They examined prisoner rule breaking and guard-inmate interactions pertaining to rule violations. These researchers

CRIME BEAT

It is extremely difficult for anyone to penetrate prisoner culture and capture a glimpse of the real life in prison. Superficial descriptions of prisoner idleness or the lack of recreational facilities are commonplace, but on occasions, investigators obtain accurate pictures of what is it like to be a prisoner interacting with other prisoners. In 1979, for instance, James W. Marquart, a social scientist, entered a maximum-security Texas prison as a participant-observer in the role of a prison guard (Marquart, 1986:16–18). Some officials, guards, and prisoners knew Marquart's true identity as a social scientist and the purpose of his observations, because he made no attempt at any time to conceal his actual identity.

Marquart eventually obtained respect from both prisoners and guards alike, and through certain contacts he developed with politically powerful prisoners, he was able to glean much about prison life. All prisons have grapevines, and the prison Marquart studied was no exception. The prisoner grapevine rumored him at various times to be an FBI agent, the son of the director of the prison system, or a Department of Justice official investigating prison conditions.

While playing the role of prison guard, Marquart observed the following incident, which generated several moral, ethical, and legal issues:

I was sitting at the Searcher's desk and Rick (convict) and I were talking and here comes Joe (convict) from 8-block. Joe thinks he knows kung-fu, hell, he got his ass beat about four months ago. He comes down the hall and he had on a tank top, his pants were tied up with a shoelace, gym shoes on, and he had all his property in a large sack. As he neared us, Rick said 'Well, Joe's fixing to go crazy again today.' He came up to us and Rick asked him what was going on and Joe said they (the staff) were fucking with him by not letting him have a recreation card. I told him 'Well, take your stuff and go over there to the Major's office' and there he went. Officer A went over and stood in front of Joe, so did Officer B who was beside Joe, Officer C was in back of A, and two convicts stood next to Officer A. Inmate James, an inmate who we 'tuned up' in the hospital several days before, stood about ten feet away. All of a sudden Joe took a swing at Officer A. A and B tackled Joe. I ran over there and grabbed Joe's left leg while a convict had his right leg and we began kicking his legs and genitals. Hell, I tried to break his leg. At the same time, B

was using his security keys, four large bronze keys, like a knife. The security keys have these points on their ends where they fit into the locks. Well, B was jamming these keys into Joe's head. Joe was bleeding all over the place. Then all of a sudden another brawl broke out right next to us. Inmate James threw a punch at Officer D as he came out of the Major's office to see what was going on. James saw Joe getting beat and he decided to help Joe out. I left Joe to help Officer D. By the time I got there (about two seconds), Officer D and about six convicts (building tenders) were beating the shit out of James. Officer D was beating James with a blackjack. Man, you could hear that crunch noise every time he hit him. At the same time, a convict was hitting him in the stomach and chest and face. These other inmates were kicking him and stomping him at the same time. It was a wild melee, just like being in war. I got in there and grabbed James by the hair and Officer D began hitting him, no love taps. He was trying to beat his brains out and yelling 'you motherfucker, son of a bitch, you hit me and I'll bust your fucking skull.' I think we beat on him alone for ten minutes. I punched him in the face and head. Then Officer D yelled 'take him (James) to the hospital.' Plus we punched and stomped him at the same time. At the hospital, Officer D began punching James in the face. I held his head so D could hit him. Then D worked James over again with a blackjack. We then stripped James and threw him on a bed. D yelled at James 'I'm going to kill you by the time you get off this unit.' Then D began hitting him in the shins and genitals with a night stick. Finally we stopped and let the medics take over. James had to leave via the ambulance. Joe required some stitches and was subsequently put in solitary. (Marquart, 1986:26–27).

As Marquart later observed, "This brutal episode was frightening and certainly went beyond any departmental regulation concerning the proper use of force to subdue an inmate. [But] . . . No civil suits were ever filed against the officers and the incident was 'closed' " (Marquart, 1986:28).

One reason the incident may not have been reported by the inmates involved might possibly be related to the same phenomenon described by Hewitt, Poole, and Regoli (1984), where guards seldom report rule breaking. In the incident described by Marquart, the inmates involved might have anticipated further retaliation or physical reprisals from guards if a prisoner grievance were filed about the guard beatings.

determined that prisoner rule breaking is more widespread than official records indicate. When interviewed, both guards and inmates said that many rule infractions were observed by guards but never reported. Guards said that they failed to report these rule violations in order to preserve stability among the inmates they supervised.

Efforts by wardens and others to classify inmates for suitable prison custody levels and programs are not always successful. Sometimes, prison officials create problems when they misclassify inmates. Webb (1984) investigated the classification process for 2,000 prisoners in a large, state maximum-security prison in the Midwest during 1974–1976. Although appropriate inmate placement was the manifest goal of the reception and classification unit of the prison, the real intention of the unit was to rapidly process all offenders; organizational goals were seemingly irrelevant. The unit wanted to appear efficient and maintain its administrative authority.

In the same study, informal groups of inmates contributed to extensive rule breaking (Webb, 1984). Prisoners either became gang members or were harassed and rejected by other inmates. Inmates who did not affiliate themselves with gangs were frequent victims of assault, robbery, sexual abuse, and extortion. Black inmates not affiliated with gangs were victimized frequently as well. In recent years, however, black gangs have formed in most prisons for self-protection, and these gangs compete with other gangs for prison privileges and power.

Researchers have described various dimensions of inmate environments (Garofalo and Clark, 1985; Marquart and Roebuck, 1987; Zamble and Porporino, 1988; Webb, 1984). Environmental factors, such as inmate privacy, safety, structure, support, emotional feedback, social stimulation, activity, and freedom, have been assessed by instruments such as the Prison Environment Inventory (Wright, 1985). In many maximum-security prisons, several of these environmental features are absent. Inmate idleness, for instance, is frequently associated with rioting and unrest (Steelman, 1984).

Prison culture is affected by not only the presence of violent offenders but also large numbers of inmates who are mentally ill or retarded. Surveys of prisons described numerous inmates who are mentally ill and should be hospitalized rather than imprisoned (Johnson, McKeown, and James, 1984). A study of forty-eight state prison systems in 1984 showed that 13,000 inmates incarcerated for 1 or more years were either mentally retarded or mentally ill and in need of clinical treatment or hospitalization (Denkowski and Denkowski, 1985).

CRIME BEAT

Inmate idleness is particularly apparent in maximum-security prisons, where the most dangerous offenders are often housed. Limited privileges, restricted access to visits from family or friends, limited yard privileges, and a wide range of prohibited behaviors are key conditions for inmate unrest and rioting.

In most prisons, gangs form along racial or ethnic lines. These gangs are instrumental in controlling prison operations, including screening prospective prisoners as racially or ethnically "suitable" for the particular prison. Incarcerating offenders is more complex than assigning inmates to cells and various custody levels. An inmate culture operates to permit relatively easy or difficult prison management.

Sex offenders and narcotics addicts are sometimes diverted from prison to treatment programs or hospitalization. The Sex Offender Treatment and Evaluation Project implemented in California in 1984 has rehabilitated many incarcerated sex offenders (Marques, 1984, 1985). The program treats sex offenders over a 22-month period. It is especially helpful for inmates during the 2-year interval prior to their parole. Currently, prisoner participation in this program is voluntary. While program officials say that too few inmates have volunteered for the program, a major incentive is the possibility of being transferred from the strict prison environment to a less formal hospital setting for treatment.

■ THE CORRECTIONAL STAFF

In the mid-1970s, inmates at the federal prison in Lewisburg, Pennsylvania, complained about prison conditions and sent large numbers of petitions to the Pennsylvania Advisory Committee to the United States Commission on Civil Rights. The complaints cited by inmates included allegations of racial and religious discrimination. Another complaint was staff brutality (Pennsylvania Advisory Committee, 1983). One result of these allegations is that corrections authorities have given greater attention in recent years to their selection and recruitment of prison and jail staffs.

Characteristics of Corrections Personnel

The 1984 survey of the correctional systems in forty-eight states also described the employment status of the correctional officers. Described were 76,000 correctional officers employed in federal and state prisons. Of these, 11 percent were females. The greatest proportion of female corrections personnel was found in Alaska prisons (28.3 percent), while the lowest proportions of female corrections officers were found in Montana and Oregon prisons (3.3 percent in each) (Corrections Compendium, 1984).

Turnover rates among correctional officers during their first year on the job averaged 16 percent. The highest turnover rate among correctional officers, 45 percent, occurred in Arizona prisons. The Federal Bureau of Prisons reports a turnover rate of 35 percent among its first-year correctional officers and 14 percent for officers who have served 1 or more years (Corrections Compendium, 1984).

Recruitment Practices

In many states, candidates for corrections work must complete civil service examinations and possess high school diplomas. Because of the nature of corrections work, several psychological assessment measures that are used to recruit police officers are also used for correctional officer selections. Corrections recruiters use physical attributes (such as size, strength, and gender), security considerations, personal background data (such as prior criminal record and veteran status), and various psychological and personality assessment measures to make officer selections (Wahler and Gendreau, 1985).

The average starting salary for correctional officers in the United States was $13,700 in 1984, with the highest starting salary in Vermont ($22,968) (Corrections Compen-

Correctional officers are increasingly required to have more formal educational training. Their training includes in-service work in prison and jail settings as well as classroom instruction in crucial corrections issues.

dium, 1984). Because these salaries are low compared with those of other occupations, it is difficult for prisons and jails to attract and retain high-quality corrections personnel for any lengthy period. Many correctional officers report that they enter this type of work only temporarily. Those who leave corrections often earn more money in the private sector. Furthermore, these private-sector occupations are less dangerous, because they do not require interactions with criminals.

Many critics consider the training that corrections officers receive inadequate. State, county, and city correctional officers in Georgia, for example, receive widely disparate training for respective jobs. An investigation of the tasks performed by different state, county, and city correctional officers and youth development workers showed three different curricula. For state institutional officers, a 160-hour training program was devised, but an 88-hour course was developed for county correctional officers, and a 36-hour program was created for city and county jailers (Camp, 1985). This shows the priority given to different assignments for correctional officers. In all of the these programs, little or no in-service training was provided.

One problem confronting all corrections personnel who work in prisons is their likelihood for being manipulated by inmates. The American Correctional Association and other agencies have attempted to educate and assist correctional officers in resisting inmate demands or pressures for favors (McGuire and Priestley, 1985). Many prison guards are unskilled in managing potentially hazardous guard-inmate encounters. Although materials exist to educate and inform officers about how to deal effectively with inmate problems, many guards either ignore this information or treat it lightly (McGuire and Priestley, 1985). Currently, only scattered efforts have been made to improve the recruitment and selection for correctional officers. Also, comparatively little interest has been expressed by superintendents, wardens, and other administrators of penal institutions in retaining competent correctional officers and lowering labor turnover.

Job Burnout and Stress

Because of the hazards of correctional work, especially those of supervising inmates in maximum-security prisons, many correctional officers have high stress levels and experience job burnout (American Correctional Association, 1985). A study of 258 Alabama correctional officers in 1984 showed that emotional exhaustion and deperson-alization, characteristics of job burnout, were highly correlated with the officers' perceived work stress, role conflict, lack of support, lack of job satisfaction, and age (Whitehead and Lindquist, 1986). The study used the Maslach and Jackson 22-item Human Services Survey to measure job burnout. Most officers reported that the administrative practices and policies were most responsible for their high burnout levels rather than interactions with the inmates. In fact, these corrections officers said that they had greater feelings of personal accomplishment through their various inmate contacts.

However, a 1983 survey of 250 correctional staff in a large state prison in the South showed that officers believed that job dangerousness and stress were the primary causes of their job burnout (Cullen et al., 1985). Although supervisory support helped to lessen the burnout-inducing effects of stress and job dissatisfaction, an officer's educational level was cited as important as well. More highly educated correctional officers had greater job dissatisfaction and stress than did less educated officers. Female corrections officers exhibited greater stress levels than did their male counterparts.

Women in the Correctional Role

Women were first employed in prisons as matrons. One result of the women's movement was the appointment of women to positions as wardens and guards (Parisi, 1984). Eventually, through public employee unionism and equal opportunity laws, women were hired as correctional officers in male prisons as well as in female penal facilities (Parisi, 1984). In 1984, women made up 11 percent of all correctional officers in the United States.

For many years, women have been subjected to discrimination in correctional work. Stereotypical notions about inability to handle serious prisoner disturbances have made it difficult for women to enter the corrections field in large numbers (Jurik, 1985). One major obstacle is informal organizational resistance among male administrators and officers. Males in correctional work tend to stereotype women as correctional officers (Jurik, 1985). Among the reasons given by corrections authorities that explain their reluctance to hire female officers are that women will endanger the lives of male officers. Some male officers believe that female officers will not be able to back them up when serious inmate disturbances occur. Other reasons are that women use more sick leave, are reprimanded more frequently than men, and are less effective in their task performance. Interestingly, police chiefs and sheriffs have given the same reasons for their reluctance to hire women as law enforcement officers. However, in 1982, researchers examined the records of 386 female correctional officers in California prisons. The investigators found no significant differences between men and women on any performance indicator related to correctional work (Holeman and Krepps-Hess, 1983).

In the same study, women were more likely than male officers to belong to an ethnic minority, to be younger, and to be unmarried. More women had bachelor's degrees than did men. When some inmates were interviewed, they said that female guards invaded their privacy. However, other inmates said that female officers improved the prison environment. Most female officers and about two-thirds of the inmates said that female officers do not endanger the lives of either male officers or prisoners, and a majority of male officers said that female officers backed them up satisfactorily (Holeman and Krepps-Hess, 1983). The United States Supreme Court has upheld the employment of female personnel in prison guard occupations, and it has denied relief to inmates seeking policy changes because of the violence they perceive resulting from the presence of female officers (*Yusuf Asad Madyun v. Thompson,* 1981).

In corrections work, women often seek supervisory or middle-level management positions after serving as corrections officers for several years. In contrast, men tend to aspire to administrative positions (Chapman et al., 1983).

Female employment as corrections officers shows greater occupational discrimination in jails than in prisons. For instance, on-site visits to 554 jails in the United States between 1979 and 1984 showed much gender stereotyping among sheriffs and jail administrators (Kerle, 1985). When local government officials were interviewed, they claimed that women "lacked experience in supervising male prisoners and could not relate to male inmates' problems" (Kerle, 1985). In most of the jails investigated, female officers were employed as matrons for female inmates. There were also significant wage discrepancies between male and female guards.

While it is likely that greater employment equity will occur for women in corrections in the future, it is also likely that court action will be necessary. Currently, administrators are the primary barriers for women who are interested in jail employment (Kerle, 1985). One important factor that may influence significantly the trend toward including larger numbers of women in correctional roles is the privatization of prison and jail management and operation.

■ THE PRIVATIZATION OF PRISON MANAGEMENT AND PRISON DESIGN

Prisoners' petitions filed with United States district courts have included dissatisfaction with the physical conditions of jails and prisons, including unhygienic living quarters, inadequate recreational areas, fire hazards, and overcrowding (*Fischer v. Winter,* 1983; *Inmates, Washington County Jail v. England,* 1980; *Marks v. Lyon County Board of County Commissioners,* 1984; *Mawby v. Ambroyer,* 1983; and *Union County Jail Inmates v. DiBuono,* 1983). A large number of lawsuits are filed against prison officials and administrators as well, alleging several types of misconduct (*McKenna v. Nassau County,* 1982; *Perry V. Walker,* 1984; *Sanders v. St. Louis County,* 1983).

Some analysts believe that if prisons are administered properly, they will generate fewer complaints. Administrative style can create or eliminate many correctional problems. Four types of prison management models have been described. These include (1) the authoritarian model, (2) the bureaucratic lawful model, (3) the shared-powers model, and (4) the inmate control model (Barak-Glantz, 1985). The authoritarian model was dominant during the nineteenth century. The main features of this model were one-person rule and repressive social control.

The bureaucratic lawful model was particularly popular immediately following World War II. Formal chains of command were established within each correctional institution. The objective of this model was to rationalize prison life through the creation of principles, rules, and regulations. Wardens relinquished power through bureaucratization, as supervisors at different levels of prison administration acquired more decision-making power through decentralization.

The shared-powers model was popular during the 1960s. In this management system, prisoners are given limited power and influence in prison operation. This model is characterized by a rehabilitative and democratic philosophy, a recognition of group associations in the prison, and an ongoing, overt attempt by the custodial staff and administration to discuss problems (Barak-Glantz, 1985:48). Inmate government councils were created, and from these, almost every prison policy was increasingly challenged.

In the early 1970s, prisoners formed unions in several state prisons. The goals of the California Union, a major inmate union, offer insight into the internal prison control inmates have acquired: (1) abolition of the indeterminate sentence system and all of its ramifications; (2) establishment of workers' rights for the prisoners, including the right to collectively organize and bargain, and (3) restoration of civil and human rights to the prisoners (Barak-Glantz, 1985:50; Irwin and Holder, 1973).

In California prisons and those of other states, racial and ethnic gangs wield considerable power over other inmates. This power is also exercised over prison guards. At San Quentin and Soledad, a Mexican mafia exists. This inmate organization is so powerful that it controls administrative affairs, such as job classification, housing assignments, and even freedom of movement decisions (Barak-Glantz, 1985:54). Because of powerful inmate gangs and organizations, correctional classification committees often screen incoming convicts' credentials to determine if they will be compatible with existing gang characteristics. Barak-Glantz (1985:54) says, "In California [prisons], the chances of a member of the Nuestra Familia (another Mexican-American mafia-type rival gang) avoiding physical harm or even surviving at San Quentin are not very great. Unfortunately, the gangs have virtually *taken over* the prison and now contribute overtly to its management."

In recent years, private, profit-centered corporations have attempted to acquire control over the financing and operation of local jails and state prisons. This is the **privatization of prison management.** Skyrocketing building costs and maintenance expenses have forced many city and county jail administrators to explore various financing alternatives. Between 1978 and 1983, the population of jail inmates increased by 65,157, or 41 percent. During the same period, beds available for inmates increased by 28,036, or only 11 percent. Figure 14.1 compares prison and jail population growth between 1978 and 1984.

The best estimate of the National Institute of Justice is that correctional institutions require 62 months for construction and that the average cost per bed in new facilities with single-occupancy cells is $50,000 (DeWitt, 1986:4). Assuming an average cost of $50,000 per cell, the current rate of growth is a national building cost of $70 million per

FIGURE 14.1 Prison Versus Jail Population Growth, 1978–1984.

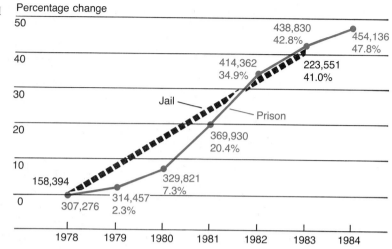

Source: Charles B. DeWitt, *New Construction Methods for Correctional Facilities* (Washington, DC: U.S. Department of Justice, 1986), p. 3.

week—a staggering expense by any standard (DeWitt, 1986:4). Can private corporations with private financial backing operate prisons and jails economically and profitably? There are no clear answers to this question. Some experts say that overcrowding, the undersupply of prison space, the high cost of prison construction, and the use of emergency powers laws to reduce overcrowding (such as court-mandated reductions in inmate populations) are the optimum conditions for competition among private interests and would reduce prison operating costs (Logan and Rausch, 1985).

The success of the privatization of prison ownership and management may be illustrated by comparing the correctional agencies that currently use private services and programs with public agencies. An investigation of private sector agencies was conducted in 1984. Investigators found that thirty-seven adult and twenty-nine juvenile agencies in thirty-nine state jurisdictions and the District of Columbia use thirty-two types of services or programs from the private sector (Camp and Camp, 1985). While these services are provided primarily in juvenile rather than adult agencies, they are more cost-effective than are the same services provided by government agencies. Camp and Camp (1985) found that health services, educational and vocational training, halfway-house and aftercare programs, and staff training programs were most frequently provided by private sources.

No laws forbid the private ownership and management of correctional institutions (Babcock, 1985; Fenton, 1985). Some critics believe that the privatization of correctional institutions is most useful for delivering services to inmates with special needs, including the physically handicapped, those in protective custody or administrative segregation, and those sentenced to the death penalty (Fenton, 1985). It has been recommended that inmates should perform productive work and be paid reasonable wages for their work. They should also be required to defray a portion of their maintenance expenses. This cost-saving feature might also succeed in helping inmates raise their own self-esteem.

The American Civil Liberties Union (ACLU) opposes the privatization of prisons. Although privatization is largely untested and only experimental in some jurisdictions,

Because of the prison and jail over-crowding, authorities have considered housing alternatives. A floating jail, former Staten Island ferryboat Vernon C. Bain, *contains 162 over-flow inmates from New York City jails. Other states with water access are considering similar ship conversions for handling their prison and jail overflows. This is reminiscent of the large prison vessels that once transported exiled prisoners to Australia. For landlocked states, however, the prisoner overflow options include transforming unused public buildings into jails and prisons for short-term and minimum-security inmates.*

the ACLU believes that privatization will limit prisoners' rights unless strong assurances guarantee the adequacy of the prison standards (Elvin, 1985; Roberts and Powers, 1985). Some experts say that privatization will not necessarily reduce prison and jail costs (Immarigeon, 1985). One fear is that privatization of prisons will mean larger numbers of them, and that incarceration as a punishment will dramatically increase in future years (Immarigeon, 1985).

Accountability is an important issue for many correctional critics. Who will monitor the actions and policies of private corporation administrators (Anderson, Davoli, and Moriarty, 1985)? Many of the administrators have been recruited from state or federal prisons. They are often retired or former wardens, associate wardens, or individuals who have served in some other prison capacity. There is little reason to suspect that private prison managers will avoid the same pressures experienced by public prison administrators. Also, there is an inherent conflict between an entrepreneur's interest in maximizing profits from prison operation by maximizing inmate populations and government efforts to provide alternatives to incarceration for low-risk offenders (Keating, 1985). Again, there are no definite answers about the long-range influence of the privatization of correctional institutions and the implications of privatization for inmates (Roberts and Powers, 1985).

Several states are attempting to lower their construction costs for prison and jail facilities by adopting economical construction designs developed by prison architects. Pinellas County, Florida, located near Tampa Bay, is one of the fastest growing regions in the state (DeWitt, 1986). In order to reduce jail construction costs, Pinellas County officials have adopted a precast modular building design. All of the concrete building units are cast entirely at a plant and then transported to the construction site (DeWitt, 1986). Figure 14.2 shows the floorplan of Pinellas County Jail's two main housing wings

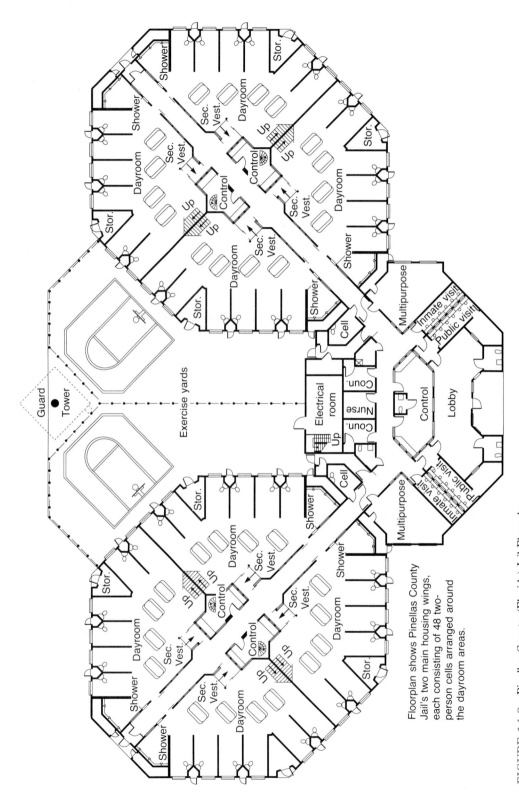

Floorplan shows Pinellas County
Jail's two main housing wings,
each consisting of 48 two-
person cells arranged around
the dayroom areas.

FIGURE 14.2 Pinellas County (Florida) Jail Floorplan

Source: Charles B. DeWitt, *Florida Sets Example with Use of Concrete Modules* (Washington, DC: National Institute of Justice, 1986), p. 2.

using the modular design. The new design reduced construction costs by nearly 10 percent, or $1.2 million. Such new jail designs have several advantages, including more effective utilization of jail guards, greater opportunities to monitor inmate activities, and improved guard safety. Substantial modifications of existing jail designs in future years will try to meet the challenge of growing inmate populations.

■ SELECTED CORRECTIONS ISSUES

Prisoners do not forfeit all of their constitutional rights as the result of being imprisoned (*Cook v. City of New York,* 1984). In 1967, the President's Commission on Law Enforcement and Administration of Justice recommended the establishment of specific inmate grievance procedures in all state and federal prisons (Miller, 1983). By the end of 1982, all state prisons had administrative inmate grievance systems. One consequence of the commission's action was a noticeable increase in the number of petitions filed by state and federal inmates against their prison administrators and others. For the 12-month period ending June 30, 1985, for example, 22,000 prisoner petitions had been filed in United States district and appeals courts (Hunzeker and Conger, 1985). Among the issues raised by prisoners in their lawsuits were (1) prison overcrowding; (2) the lack of vocational, educational, and counseling programs; (3) racism; and (4) basic prisoners' rights.

Prison and Jail Overcrowding

Overcrowding in correctional institutions is correlated with several other administrative problems (Yablon, 1986). Overcrowding in prisons is related to increased rates of natural and violent deaths, suicides, psychiatric commitments, disciplinary infractions, and reconvictions (Paulus, McCain, and Cox, 1985). Most prisoner grievances are connected with prison and jail overcrowding. Factors contributing to prison and jail overcrowding are judicial discretion in sentencing, statutory constraints limiting the flexibility of probation and parole programs, staff shortages, and poor prison administration (Finn, 1984; Gottfredson, 1984; Paulus, McCain, and Cox, 1985). Although there is considerably less overcrowding in women's prisons than in men's facilities, overcrowding is a persistent problem in women's prisons as well (Ruback and Carr, 1984).

Prison and jail overcrowding has been challenged in court as cruel and unusual punishment in violation of Eighth Amendment rights (Herman, 1984). Three landmark cases include *Bell v. Wolfish* (1979), *Rhodes v. Chapman* (1981), and *Ruiz v. Estelle* (1982). In the case of *Bell v. Wolfish,* Louis Wolfish was an inmate awaiting trial and housed at the Federal Metropolitan Correctional Center in New York. The building was fairly new, and all rooms were designed to accommodate one prisoner each. However, an increase in the number of detainees prompted officials to place two persons in each room. This is known as **double-bunking,** and it was to become one of the major issues in the subsequent lawsuit filed by Wolfish.

Among other complaints were the practice of body cavity searches of inmates following visits by friends and relatives and a prohibition against inmates receiving

CRIME BEAT

It was a cramped Thanksgiving for more than 60 inmates at the Metro Nashville jail who were sprawled across a gymnasium floor because of overcrowding, authorities said.

And hundreds more may be moved into the dining room to sleep on mattresses this holiday season if jail officials don't get some relief, said Chief Deputy Billy Lynch.

"We're doing the best we can with a bad situation," he said. "All we can do is find a place to lay them down."

Lynch blamed a huge influx of drunken driving offenders and overcrowding in state prisons as the reason his jail is overflowing. State Correction Department spokesman John Taylor said the state is trying to find 100 extra mattresses to ease the crunch, but rounding them up from state prisons could take at least two weeks.

The Metro Jail held 1,096 inmates Wednesday and 1,081 Thursday, said Deputy Tom Nelson. The jail has a capacity of about 780 inmates, he said.

Elsewhere in the state, other local facilities were blaming state prison overcrowding and bureaucratic hold-ups for filling up county jails.

Lynch said it was like "inviting 50 people over to your house for Thanksgiving dinner and then it snows.

"Nobody can leave your house for two to three weeks, and you have to feed all of them. That is what it's like here. It's a rough situation and there's no getting around it," he said.

There were only 640 prisoners in Metro Jail in October 1985 when U.S. District Judge Thomas A. Higgins ordered a halt to prison admissions until inmate populations at the state's three overcrowded reception centers were below capacity.

The state has since begun accepting more prisoners, but more slowly than county officials had hoped. Taylor said 14 percent to 15 percent of the total number of state inmates are housed in county facilities.

"We have to properly classify inmates before we can place them in certain (state) facilities," he said.

In Memphis, the Shelby County Jail has a capacity of 1,225, but 1,310 prisoners were housed there Thursday and 1,314 Wednesday. In Knoxville, the Knox County Jail inmate population was 316 Thursday and 317 Wednesday in a facility designed for 212.

Source: Reprinted with permission from Associated Press, "Nashville Inmates Sprawl on Floor; Other Jails Have Housing Crunch," *The Knoxville News-Sentinel* (November 28, 1986), p. A12.

---

packages from outside the institution. The government argued that all conditions of pretrial detention at their correctional facility were justified to ensure his presence at trial, security, internal order, and discipline. The United States Supreme Court agreed and upheld the constitutionality of this form of double-bunking (American Correctional Association, 1983:221).

Applied to pretrial detainees, this decision was again upheld in a 1983 New Jersey case, *Union County Jail Inmates v. DiBuono.* The court said that the overcrowded county jail would pass constitutional muster upon full implementation of recommendations by the Commissioner of the New Jersey State Department of Corrections to double-bunk the cells, provide at least 1 hour of recreation daily to each inmate, to provide clean clothing weekly, and to medically screen all new inmates.

In a 1981 Ohio case, *Rhodes v. Chapman,* Kelly Chapman was an inmate of the Southern Ohio Correctional Facility, a maximum-security prison at Lucasville, Ohio. Although this facility was fairly new, double-bunking was used to accommodate 1,400 prisoners (out of 2,300) who were confined two per 63-square-foot cell. This became known as the one man, one cell case, as Chapman argued that two persons per cell violated his constitutional right to be free from cruel and unusual punishment. The

Double-bunking has been a result of prison and jail overcrowding and the subject of numerous case filings by prisoners, but the United States Supreme Court says that double-bunking is not cruel and unusual punishment under the Eighth Amendment.

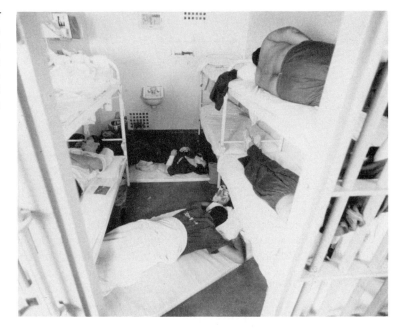

United States Supreme Court disagreed, and ruled in an 8–1 decision that prison overcrowding is not unconstitutional. Justice Powell declared, "The Constitution does not mandate comfortable prisons. . . . To the extent that prison conditions are restrictive and even harsh, they are part of the penalty that criminal offenders pay for their offenses against society."

In the *Ruiz v. Estelle* (1982) case, a class-action suit was filed by a prisoner, Ruiz, and other inmates against the Texas Department of Corrections (Estelle was then the director of the prison system). Among other things, the suit alleged violations of prisoners' constitutional rights relating to prison overcrowding, inadequate health care, guard brutality, and an abusive building tender system (using dominant/aggressive inmates to work with regular staff guards to control other inmates) (Marquart, 1986:17). The Fifth Circuit Court of Appeals held that the overcrowding in the Texas Department of Corrections "was of such a magnitude as to amount to severe punishment." While this may seem to contradict the United States Supreme Court's decision in *Bell v. Wolfish* and *Rhodes v. Chapman,* the Fifth Circuit declared, "Although the Supreme Court stated that there was no 'one man, one cell' principle lurking in the due process clause, the Court specifically reserved judgment on cases presenting *different facts* [italics mine]."

This decision caused massive changes within the Texas correctional system (Martinez and Fabelo, 1985). One change was to establish selective early release procedures for inmates with good records, particularly those with little or no history of alcohol or drug abuse (Eisenberg, 1985). Another change was the passage of the Prison Management Act and the implementation of the Texas Prison Management Plan in 1985. The 1986 Texas prison population was approximately 41,000, and an additional

6,000 cells have been projected as needed between 1987 and 1992, at a cost of $200 million (Martinez and Fabelo, 1985).

Texas is not alone in its prison overcrowding dilemma, however. States with serious overcrowding problems include Connecticut, Oklahoma, Maryland, Louisiana, Tennessee, Massachusetts, Illinois, Maine, Pennsylvania, Oregon, Washington, New Jersey, Rhode Island, and California. The Committee on Prison Overcrowding in Maryland has labeled Maryland's current level of prison overcrowding "intolerable," for example (Maryland Criminal Justice Coordinating Council, 1984). Affecting prison overcrowding in many states are determinate and mandatory sentencing, where the power to parole has been removed from parole boards and sentences of specific lengths have been imposed without time off for good behavior (McCoy, 1984; Phillips, 1983; Rhode Island Governor's Commission, 1984; Thompson et al., 1984; Washington Office of Financial Management, 1985; Westerfield, 1984).

Several solutions to the overcrowding problem have been proposed. Alternative sentencing is used in some jurisdictions, such as Oregon and California (Farbstein and Goldman, 1983; Kapsch and Luther, 1985). Work camps, work release, and a statewide probation department are used in Illinois, Washington, New Jersey, and Pennsylvania (California Joint Commission for Revision of the Penal Code, 1984; Illinois Governor's Task Force on Prison Crowding, 1983; New Jersey Governor's Management Improvement Plan, 1983; Pennsylvania Commission on Crime and Delinquency, 1985; Sims and O'Connell, 1985).

While jail overcrowding is also a problem, the short-term nature of a jail inmate's confinement has caused some authorities to believe that jail overcrowding is easier to control than is prison overcrowding. California has experimented with single-bed cells, double-bed cells, eight-bed cells, and sixteen-bed dormitories (Farbstein and Goldman, 1983). While jail administrators oppose large cell occupancies, a dormitory-style arrangement reduces jail costs and is likely to reduce inmate stress.

Jail overcrowding results also from the classification methods used by jail staff to determine an inmate's length of stay (Brennan, 1985). In a Colorado jail study, misclassifications of inmates caused the needless imprisonment of hundreds of them (Brennan, 1985). In California, 90 percent of all jail bookings involve pretrial defendants. Many of these can be safely released on their own recognizance prior to trial with effective supervisory measures (Kizziah, 1984).

Prison Labor

Many prison reformers have feared inmate exploitation by private enterprise through the production of goods from prison labor (Auerbach, 1982). Also, some labor and business groups are concerned that cheap prison labor will result in unfair competition in the sales of such goods (Auerbach, 1982). Early congressional reaction to these complaints led to the **Hawes-Cooper Act of 1929.** This act provided that any and all prison-made goods transported from one state to another are regulated by the commerce laws of the importing state. In 1940, Congress passed the Sumners-Ashurst Act. This Act made it a federal criminal offense for common carriers to violate state statutes created as the result of the Hawes-Cooper Act of 1929. The result was that thirty states passed laws restricting the transportation of prisonmade goods. For many years, these laws effectively discouraged prison industry (Auerbach, 1982).

Inmates involved in UNICOR, the federal prison industries program, benefit by being less idle and preparing themselves for jobs upon their release.

In 1979, the Prison-Industries Enhancement Act repealed earlier federal laws restricting the movement of prisonmade goods in interstate commerce. While this action has revitalized prison labor and industry, new federal and state statutes have provided that prisoners must be paid reasonable wages for their work.

Today, **Federal Prison Industries (UNICOR)** is a profitable, government-owned corporation that markets numerous products to a variety of federal agencies and employs thousands of prisoners (U.S. General Accounting Office, 1985). Audits and evaluations of UNICOR show that customers are satisfied with the products it markets, and the pricing is competitive with privately owned industries and corporations that market similar goods. While contributing to the economy, prison labor also fulfills other important functions. One major benefit to prisoners is the reduction of inmate idleness. This has been a major cause of inmate unrest. Another benefit is the acquisition of work skills of value to inmates when they are eventually released. Prison labor is also believed to have rehabilitative value, because it restores a prisoner's self-esteem and sense of pride (Funke et al., 1982; Hawkins, 1983).

The use of inmate labor is not restricted to state or federal prisons. In some of the larger jails in the United States, inmate labor is a valuable resource. Inmate industries exist in at least seventy-four jail jurisdictions, and administrators see the reduction of inmate idleness, the training for prisoners, and significant cost reductions as major benefits (Grieser, Crawford, and Funke, 1985).

In 1983 all states had prison industries, and prison industries averaged five per state (Grieser, Miller, and Funke, 1983). In 1983, Florida operated seventeen industries. The numbers of inmates employed in prison industries have ranged from 4,200 in Texas to 52 in Vermont. Wages for inmate workers have varied from $0.32 per day to $8.50, with an average of $3.00. Gross sales from prisonmade products varied from $54,000 in Delaware in 1983 to over $37 million in Texas.

However, prison overcrowding has had an adverse effect on prison industries, creating greater pressure for jobs and greatly reducing the space available for workshops (Grieser, Miller, and Funke, 1983). Prison labor as a major industry has attracted private interests. A study by Abt Associates for the National Institute of Justice shows the degree of interest of private industry in participating in prison work programs (Mullen, 1986:2). Mullen (1986:2) says, "The aggressive participation of private industry in organizing institutions as places of work might go far toward achieving Chief Justice Burger's vision of prisons as 'factories with fences' instead of warehouses with walls." Currently, little has been done in the area of the privatization of prison labor (Mullen, 1982:2), but prisoners' labor unions will no doubt play a significant role when the privatization of correctional institutions occurs on a large scale.

Education and Vocational Training Programs

Correctional education is largely an outgrowth of the prison reform movement (Muth and Gehring, 1986). Reformers such as Zebulon Brockway (Elmira Reformatory) and Austin MacCormick (*The Education of Adult Prisoners,* 1931) helped to develop educational reforms in many prisons and jails in the United States (Muth and Gehring, 1986), but prison overcrowding has seriously interfered with the effective operation of these vocational and educational programs.

Learning deficiencies among inmates of jails and prisons are widespread (Bell et al., 1983). An investigation of 851 inmates of prisons in Louisiana, Pennsylvania, and Washington showed that 42 percent of all inmates scored below the fifth grade reading level on academic achievement and standardized individual intelligence tests (Bell et al., 1983). The average inmate participating in the study had left school by the tenth grade. However, inmates are currently performing academically about 3 years below this level. Average inmate IQs place them in the lowest third of the nation according to national IQ norms.

Jailhouse lawyers are becoming the rule rather than the exception as more inmates learn about the law and how it can help them in efforts to change prison and jail conditions. Inmates learn that they can modify how they are treated by filing appropriate lawsuits against prison officials and others. While most of these suits are unsuccessful, the trend is toward greater consideration and more inmate rights.

In 1982, 297 correctional institutions had postsecondary correctional education (PSE) programs (Peak, 1983). Three fourths of these programs were developed between 1972 and 1982, and about half of the programs offered associate degrees. A fourth of these programs offered bachelor's degrees. Directors of these programs were predominately male, possessed master's degrees, and had spent less than 5 years as directors of the programs. Peak (1983) found that one major accomplishment of PSE was to instill within inmates positive self-concepts. Also, the directors reported that the inmate-student participants experienced many positive personality and social changes.

Not everyone supports prisoner educational reforms, however. For example, a survey of 566 correctional practitioners tried to determine the practitioners' reactions to formal accreditation of inmate educational programs. While most practitioners believed that accreditation helped the individual inmates and that the effectiveness of the programs had improved, 57 percent believed that the programs had had little or no positive effect on the incidence of prison riots or other disturbances. In fact, 50 percent of the respondents believed that accreditation had been disruptive to prison routine and operations (Farkas and Fosen, 1983).

Some authorities say that vocational and educational programs can easily be financed by using prisoners' funds for educational purposes (Chaneles, 1983). At any given time, 200,000 prisoners are serving multiyear sentences and about the same number are serving short-term sentences. Most of these inmates have at least $500 in their prison accounts from which they may draw modest sums for monthly purchases. The aggregate savings are estimated to be $200 million annually. Currently, those accounts draw no interest; however, interest from such accounts invested in a national education money management fund could yield as much as $20 million annually to defray inmate education costs. Using inmates themselves to assist in determining program objectives and spending patterns with advisory boards made up of education professionals and specialists has been suggested.

Some experts believe that expanding a prisoner's education can help that prisoner cope with the stress and strain associated with prison overcrowding (Lawrence, 1985). In fact, prisoner participation in educational programs has been associated with more positive feelings among inmates. Furthermore, inmates in educational programs report fewer headaches and less stress (Lawrence, 1985).

Racism in Prisons

The United States prison system is considered by some as a bastion of racism (Lovejoy, 1983). The number of blacks and other minorities warehoused in United States prisons is alarming, and black persons are incarcerated at a rate ten times that of the white population. Blacks make up nearly half of the total state and federal prison population. Allegations of racism in lawsuits filed by prisoners in United States district courts are frequent. Black prisoners and other minority inmates report discriminatory treatment in prisons and jails similar to what they experience outside of prison (Goetting, 1985). The United States Supreme Court has frequently ruled against prisoner claims of discrimination, and it has stated on more than one occasion, "[F]ederal courts cannot undertake to review every official action taken against a prisoner which results in such prisoner being treated differently from any other prisoner" (*Beatham v. Manson,* 1973).

A 1975 Mississippi case involving allegations of discrimination by a black inmate is typical of lawsuit outcomes filed by inmates in recent years. In the case of *Gates v. Collier* (1975), the Mississippi prison administration was found innocent of any unconstitutional or discriminatory conditions. The United States Supreme Court declared, "[E]vidence established that racial discrimination at the penitentiary had, for all practical purposes, been eliminated." With all due respect to the wisdom of the United States Supreme Court and in view of Marquart's (1986) participant observation experiences as a prison guard, it is doubtful that racial discrimination in the Mississippi penitentiary, or any other state prison for that matter, has been completely eliminated.

The significance of the *Gates* case is not the decision itself, but rather the "fortitude demonstrated in seeing the orders through" (Hopper, 1985). Court action occurred during a period where the public wanted more criminals incarcerated. As a result of this court action, Mississippi shifted toward the construction of larger, brick-and-mortar prisons, thereby dispensing with its old system, which consisted of smaller, more informal, prison units. The fact that some inmates receive more favorable treatment than other inmates is insufficient for basing a claim of racial discrimination (*Fowler v. Graham*, 1979). In order for any court to interpret an administrative policy or action as discriminatory, clear and convincing proof must be offered to support these allegations. The 1967 President's Commission on Law Enforcement and Administration of Justice opened a Pandora's box of prisoner complaints when it mandated the establishment of inmate grievance systems in all state and federal prisons. Although some prisoners file nuisance suits, it is believed that most inmates do not abuse the system through repeated filings (Thomas et al., 1985).

Prisoners' Rights and the Jailhouse Lawyer

The advancement of prisoners' rights through the establishment of formal inmate grievance procedures has become an increasingly important correctional issue. While inmates filed over 22,000 lawsuits between June 1, 1984, and June 30, 1985, very few of those suits resulted in awards of monetary damages (Hunzeker and Conger, 1985). But the success rate of these filings is such that during a 2-year period, only 87 lawsuits were lost. In only 161 suits were monetary damages awarded. The gains from other suits included restoration of certain privileges, the return of confiscated property, and system improvements.

Much prisoner litigation is directed toward the improvement of general prison conditions (Hanson, 1984; Yarbrough, 1984). However, a new federal law passed in 1982 permitted federal district judges to remand or refer prisoner lawsuits back to their state correctional systems for disposition if, in the district judge's opinion, the inmate had not exhausted all internal prison remedies (Miller, 1983). An Indiana case is relevant here. In *Owen v. Kimmel* (1982), a prisoner asserted a claim under 42 United States Code, Section 1983 that prison officials unlawfully confiscated a piece of his furniture during a shakedown. **Shakedowns** are intensive searches of inmate cells for the purpose of discovering weapons or contraband. The district court remanded the case back to the Indiana prison for disposition through the administrative grievance procedure.

Prisoners do not lose all of their rights as the result of being incarcerated. In fact, inmates must be granted access to a law library as a part of their right to petition the courts concerning violations of their constitutional rights or other grievances (*Ganey v. Edwards,* 1985). In an interesting Illinois case, an inmate was segregated from the other inmates and had no direct access to a law library (*Walters v. Thompson,* 1985). He had to rely exclusively on inmate clerks with little or no legal experience, formalized training, or supervision by attorneys, and he was restricted to three hundred pages of photocopied material per year. Furthermore, he was denied telephone access to outside legal counsel. The court ruled that his constitutional rights had been flagrantly violated.

States have the obligation to provide prisoners either with adequate law library facilities or with someone trained in the law (*Lewis v. Faulkner,* 1983). According to the United States Supreme Court, a prison law library that fails to meet the minimum standards set by the American Bar Association and the American Association of Law Libraries violates a prisoner's constitutional rights (*Bouiles v. Ricketts,* 1981). In one case, a prisoner was given access to such an inadequate prison law library that the high court declared that his constitutional rights had been violated (*Borning v. Cain,* 1985).

Prisoners often become proficient at learning the law and understanding the constitutional rights to which they are entitled. These inmates are often called **jailhouse lawyers** because they are self-trained in the law. One of the most famous jailhouse lawyers was Caryl Chessman, author of *Cell 2455, Death Row.* Chessman, a Californian, was convicted and sentenced to death for committing a number of violent offenses as the moonlight bandit in the Hollywood, California, hills in the 1950s. His legal expertise, acquired exclusively while in prison awaiting the death sentence to be carried out, saved him numerous times from the gas chamber. He won one reprieve after another through appeals based upon legal technicalities. Eventually, however, his appeals were exhausted and he was executed.

AIDS is an emerging problem in prison settings. Sexual exploitation of weaker inmates by stronger ones occurs with considerable frequency, despite preventive measures of correctional officers and administrators. Increasingly, those who are diagnosed as having this fatal disease are segregated from others to minimize inmate health risks and promote prisoner safety.

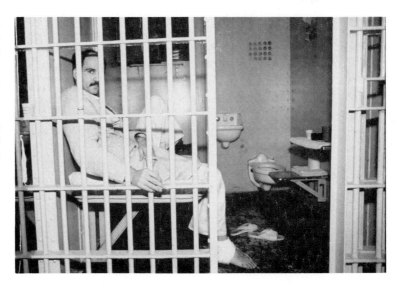

Inmate grievance procedures are intended to provide inmates with an outlet for their frustrations whenever they feel their rights have have been infringed upon by others (Cole, Hanson, and Silbert, 1984). Such dispute resolution diverts many prisoner complaints away from court litigation because prison inmate councils can satisfactorily arbitrate many inmate grievances.

Inmate grievances and their lawsuits are not ignored. The courts, politicians, and prison administrators are influenced in various ways by inmate litigation. In New Mexico, for example, prisoner litigation was successful in bringing about major changes in prison conditions, including the hiring of a new warden (Mays and Taggart, 1985). Also, court action in Alabama as the result of prisoner litigation has stimulated numerous prison reforms in recent years (Yarbrough, 1984). Even though the *Gates v. Collier* (1975) lawsuit was unsuccessful in its charges of racial discrimination in Mississippi prisons, Mississippi officials have made considerable changes and improvements in their state prison system (Hopper, 1985).

■ SUMMARY

Prison culture is diverse. It is unique because it is a population of criminals; all inmates have been convicted of crimes. In this environment, administrators encounter many problems. Prison subcultures exist, and informal inmate codes dominate internal prison affairs.

A contributing factor to prison and jail operations is the quality of the staff. Vast differences exist among jurisdictions regarding training and preparation for correctional work. Jail staff are less adequately trained than prison staff. Recruitment practices result in the selection of applicants who often lack the skills to deal with prisoners effectively.

One factor contributing to high labor turnover among jail and prison personnel is stress. However, more selective recruitment will probably result in hiring individuals better able to cope with the demands of correctional work. Women have been underrepresented in corrections activities. In recent years, however, their numbers in correctional work have increased.

One alternative to prison and jail management is the privatization of prison operations. Private enterprise promises more cost-effective prison operations. However, government officials and concerned citizens suggest that private ownership and operation of prisons may violate prisoner rights and create conflicts of interest.

Contemporary issues in corrections include overcrowding, the exploitation of prison labor by private industry, racism, the inadequacy of prison vocational and educational programs, and prisoner rights. Efforts are under way to remedy these prison problems. Increasing numbers of prisoners are learning about their constitutional rights, and inmates are filing record numbers of lawsuits in state and federal courts.

KEY TERMS

double-bunking
Federal Prison Industries
(UNICOR)

Hawes-Cooper Act of 1929
inmate code
jailhouse lawyers

privatization of prison
management
shakedowns

QUESTIONS FOR REVIEW

1. What is a community-based corrections program? What advantages does it seem to have over regular prison confinement?
2. Are jail problems of overcrowding identical to those of prison overcrowding? Why or why not? Explain.
3. Prison environments have often been compared with outside environments. How are prison environments similar to outside environments? In what ways are prison environments different?
4. What are some of the grounds alleged by prisoners who file lawsuits against jail and prison administrators?
5. What evidence suggests that a prison culture exists?
6. How do the selection and recruitment methods employed by state agencies affect prisoner-staff relationships?
7. What are some general characteristics of corrections personnel?
8. What reasons are cited by corrections personnel for job burnout and stress that lead to labor turnover?
9. What proportion of the correctional staff in prisons and jails in the United States consists of women? What appear to be the prospects for female employment in correctional jobs? What obstacles interfere with the employment of women as corrections officers?
10. What is privatization of prison management? Discuss briefly the pros and cons of privatization.
11. Discuss briefly four different prison management models. Which one is most popular today?
12. What is different about Pinellas County Jail in Florida?
13. Cite and discuss briefly three important court cases relating to jail and prison overcrowding. What were the results of each case?
14. Discuss briefly the federal legislation that has affected the development of prison labor in the United States. What is the significance of UNICOR?
15. Are vocational and educational programs important in prisoner rehabilitation? Why or why not? Do prison officials agree on the importance to be attached to such programs?
16. Is there racism in state prisons? What are two cases having to do with racism?
17. What is a jailhouse lawyer? What rights do prisoners have concerning access to law books, lawyers, and legal materials?
18. What sorts of prisoner complaints stem from overcrowding? Discuss briefly.

SUGGESTED READINGS

Alpert, Geoffrey P. (1980) *Legal rights of prisoners.* Beverly Hills, CA: Sage.

American Correctional Association (1984). *Stress management for correctional officers and their families.* Upper Marlboro, MD: American Correctional Association.

Johnson, Robert (1987). *Hard time: Understanding and reforming the prison.* Monterey, CA: Brooks/Cole.

Parisi, Nicolette (1982). *Coping with imprisonment.* Beverly Hills, CA: Sage.

Zimmerman, Sherwood E., and Harold D. Miller (1981). *Corrections at the crossroads: Designing policy.* Beverly Hills, CA: Sage.

Probation and Parole

CHAPTER

15

■ INTRODUCTION

In January 1987, there were 2,094,405 adults on probation in the United States, an increase of 6.4 percent over the previous year (Hester, 1987:2). Also, 326,752 persons made up the parolee population. This was an increase of 8.9 percent from the previous year.

As larger numbers of offenders are diverted from incarceration through alternative sentencing practices, court-ordered prison population reductions occur, and prisoners are released through parole, pressures increase on an already overworked probation and parole labor force (American Correctional Association, 1986; Bottomley, 1984; Steppe, 1986). Because many of the same agencies that monitor activities of parolees also supervise probationers and these agencies share several common problems, this chapter examines both probation and parole and identifies several key functions of probation and parole programs. The chapter describes current methods of recruiting and retaining probation and parole officers and also examines some of the more popular monitoring programs, including halfway houses and programs using electronic devices for supervision and surveillance. Finally, the chapter discusses recidivism as a method of evaluating the effectiveness of probation and parole programs.

■ PROBATION AND PAROLE DISTINGUISHED

The chief distinguishing characteristics of probation and parole are that (1) **probation** is a sentence imposed in lieu of incarceration, while (2) **parole** is serving some of an imposed sentence in prison and some or all of the remainder under the supervision of designated officials. Probation does not involve confinement. Instead, it imposes conditions and retains authority in the sentencing court to modify the conditions of a sentence or to resentence an offender if the offender violates the conditions. Probation and parole are also distinguished according to the authorities who control probationers and parolees. In the case of probation, judges impose conditional releases when they sentence convicted offenders. In contrast, parole boards control paroles.

By year end 1987, 2.1 million adults were on probation in the United States for various offenses (Hester, 1988). Table 15.1 shows the number of adults on probation from both federal and state prisons according to region as well as state. Table 15.2 shows the number of adults on parole in 1987. Table 15.3 shows the number of adults under some form of correctional supervision in the United States from 1983 to 1987. Table 15.4 shows state prison releases by various methods between 1977 and 1987. While discretionary parole accounts for the largest proportion of releases, it systematically declined between 1977 and 1987. At the same time, supervised mandatory releases increased, largely due to the increased use of the determinate sentencing.

■ THE HISTORY OF PROBATION AND PAROLE IN THE UNITED STATES

Probation in the United States began largely through the actions of John Augustus of Boston, Massachusetts (Allen, Eskridge, Latessa, and Vito, 1985:40). Augustus was much like a bailbondsman in today's society; he acted as a guarantor, or surety, for various offenders. Acting on his own, Augustus appeared in court and offered to supervise various alleged offenders until their cases could be heard later in court. In most instances, judges hearing the case would be so impressed with the "improvement" of offenders that they would impose only nominal fines rather than imprisonment. Between 1841, when he started this practice with court approval, and 1859, when he died, Augustus had obtained probation for 1,956 men and women (Allen, Eskridge, Latessa, and Vito, 1985:40).

Augustus did not commit his trust to *everyone* charged with either petty or serious offenses, however. Primarily Augustus assisted first offenders, or those who had never been charged with criminal offenses. Interestingly, Augustus conducted his investigations in much the same way that a presentence investigation is conducted today. For example, he did a limited amount of research into the offender's background and determined the "previous character of the person, his age, and influences by which he would be surrounded" (Allen, Eskridge, Latessa, and Vito, 1985:41).

In 1901, New York State enacted a statutory probation provision, whereby offenders could be closely supervised by responsible officials. James Bronson Reynolds, an early prison reformer, founded The University Settlement, a private probationary facility designed to alleviate some of the harshness and inequities imposed by a system of severe penal sanctions (Lindner and Savarese, 1984). However, the settlement lacked specific goals and particular implementation methods, and thus it lost a considerable amount of credibility with the public (Lindner and Savarese, 1984).

Parole precedes probation in United States history by several decades (Bottomley, 1984). Sentences in United States courts from 1790 to 1817 were largely mandatory, and they had to be served in their entirety. Within a few years, prisons and jails became overcrowded. New York was the first state to enact legislation giving wardens and other officials the power to parole certain prisoners on the basis of their good behaviors while in prison (Allen, Eskridge, Latessa, and Vito, 1985:26). By 1869, about half the states had good time laws, which authorized reductions of prison terms for prisoners, in order to alleviate prison overcrowding. By 1944, all states had a parole system. In fact, parole

TABLE 15.1 Adults on Probation, 1987

Regions and Jurisdictions	Probation Population 1/1/87	1987		Probation Population 12/31/87	Percent Change in Probation Population During 1987	Number on Probation on 12/31/87 per 100,000 Adult Residents
		Entries	Exits			
U.S. total	2,114,821	1,376,244	1,249,012	2,242,053	6.0%	1,247
Federal	57,337	23,077	20,428	59,986	4.6	33
State	2,057,484	1,353,167	1,228,584	2,182,067	6.1	1,213
Northeast	395,836	215,530	193,093	418,273	5.7%	1,095
Connecticut	41,304	30,841	28,486	43,659	5.7	1,779
Maine	4,620	3,281	3,296	4,605	−.3	521
Massachusetts	94,945	56,390	53,274	98,061	3.3	2,170
New Hampshire	3,583	3,001	2,434	4,150	15.8	525
New Jersey	51,359	27,817	23,389	55,787	8.6	955
New York	107,337	42,724	36,908	113,153	5.4	840
Pennsylvania	78,985	43,977	37,878	85,084	7.7	937
Rhode Island	8,174	4,915	4,908	8,181	.1	1,081
Vermont	5,529	2,584	2,520	5,593	1.2	1,371
Midwest	444,241	349,004	310,189	483,056	8.7%	1,101
Illinois	76,203	51,319	45,190	82,332	8.0	963
Indiana	50,806	51,410	45,238	56,978	12.1	1,403
Iowa	12,584	11,756	11,595	12,745	1.3	606
Kansas	17,125	8,666	7,602	18,189	6.2	997
Michigan	102,653	82,928	71,585	113,996	11.0	1,691
Minnesota[a]	38,901	40,397	34,935	44,363	14.0	1,415
Missouri	33,819	28,700	21,451	41,068	21.4	1,082
Nebraska	11,265	11,514	11,268	11,511	2.2	983
North Dakota	1,544	788	716	1,616	4.7	333
Ohio	72,339	45,316	46,163	71,492	−1.2	900
South Dakota	2,354	4,416	4,176	2,594	10.2	506
Wisconsin	24,648	11,794	10,270	26,172	6.2	740
South	854,043	559,828	527,589	886,282	3.8%	1,441
Alabama	21,371	10,502	8,467	23,406	9.5	789
Arkansas[b]	12,700	2,981	2,206	13,475	6.1	774

as it is known today is considered by many experts to be largely an American invention (Allen, Eskridge, Latessa, and Vito, 1985:27–32).

During the 1850s, Alexander Maconochie, an English reformer, investigated prison conditions in Australia at the request of various reform groups. His investigations and influence led to the passage of the English Penal Servitude Act of 1853, which established certain rehabilitation programs for prisoners and abolished the sale and transportation of prisoners to the Australian colony. One of his Irish supporters, Sir Walter Crofton, created a system where citizens could be assigned various felons for limited supervision in their respective jurisdictions. In several European countries, Crofton is credited with inventing parole.

TABLE 15.1 *continued*

Regions and Jurisdictions	Probation Population 1/1/87	1987		Probation Population 12/31/87	Percent Change in Probation Population During 1987	Number on Probation on 12/31/87 per 100,000 Adult Residents
		Entries	Exits			
Delaware	7,985	5,544	4,241	9,288	16.3	1,927
Dist. of Col.	12,307	9,370	10,880	10,797	−12.3	2,222
Florida	139,859	173,888	160,537	153,210	9.5	1,644
Georgia	109,485	61,235	60,236	110,484	.9	2,463
Kentucky	6,841	4,579	4,239	7,181	5.0	263
Louisiana	27,677	10,134	7,498	30,313	9.5	964
Maryland	69,134	43,700	40,018	72,816	5.3	2,135
Mississippi	6,458	2,930	2,636	6,752	4.6	368
North Carolina	58,644	33,519	29,223	62,940	7.3	1,315
Oklahoma	22,740	12,571	11,758	23,553	3.6	990
South Carolina	21,110	13,406	10,908	23,608	11.8	950
Tennessee	26,291	18,944	18,832	26,403	.4	733
Texas	290,074	146,810	147,194	289,690	−.1	2,454
Virginia	17,126	7,418	6,599	17,945	4.8	404
West Virginia	4,241	2,297	2,117	4,421	4.2	314
West	363,364	228,805	197,713	394,456	8.6%	1,087
Alaska	2,885	1,251	1,195	2,941	1.9	831
Arizona	20,283	10,082	7,767	22,598	11.4	916
California	218,526	139,110	117,785	239,851	9.8	1,178
Colorado	16,335	8,298	10,177	14,456	−11.5	597
Hawaii	8,404	5,983	5,505	8,882	5.7	1,114
Idaho	3,770	2,197	1,821	4,146	10.0	598
Montana	2,943	1,091	866	3,168	7.6	542
Nevada[b]	5,518	2,904	3,084	5,338	−3.3	707
New Mexico	4,175	3,948	4,113	4,010	−4.0	381
Oregon	23,402	10,402	10,833	22,971	−1.8	1,127
Utah	5,620	3,738	3,525	5,833	3.8	555
Washington	49,663	38,740	29,982	58,421	17.6	1,734
Wyoming	1,840	1,061	1,060	1,841	.1	538

[a]The State estimated exits.
[b]The State estimated all of its data.
Source: Thomas Hester, *Probation and Parole, 1987* (Washington, DC: Bureau of Justice Statistics, 1988), p. 2.

Probationers and parolees have several characteristics in common. First, all of these persons have been convicted of criminal offenses. For probationers and parolees alike, these criminal offenses range from nonviolent, petty crimes to violent, serious ones. Parolees and probationers also share a common trust given them by local, state, or federal authorities. For the probationer, the offense may have been committed in the heat of the moment, or the person may have been acting under the influence of drugs or alcohol at the time of the incident. Although voluntary intoxication or drug use does not necessarily excuse a crime, it may be a defense to rule out the specific criminal intent of the defendant when the crime was committed.

TABLE 15.2 Adults on Parole, 1987

Regions and Jurisdictions	Parole Population 1/1/87	1987 Entries	1987 Exits	Parole Population 12/31/87	Percent Change in Parole Population During 1987	Number on Parole on 12/31/87 per 100,000 Adult Residents
U.S. total	326,259	239,752	203,819	362,192	11.0%	201
Federal	17,496	9,956	8,874	18,578	6.2	10
State	308,763	229,796	194,945	343,614	11.3	191
Northeast	88,327	47,830	45,059	91,098	3.1%	238
Connecticut	603	120	257	466	−22.7	19
Maine[a]	...	...	...	...		
Massachusetts[b]	3,998	3,910	3,890	4,018	.5	89
New Hampshire	539	229	128	640	18.7	81
New Jersey	14,064	8,154	6,509	15,709	11.7	269
New York	29,325	15,380	13,461	31,244	6.5	232
Pennsylvania	39,008	19,600	20,210	38,398	−1.6	423
Rhode Island	453	367	397	423	−6.6	56
Vermont	337	70	207	200	−40.6	49
Midwest	43,114	35,344	31,952	46,506	7.9%	106
Illinois	12,311	9,398	8,143	13,566	10.2	159
Indiana	3,273	4,225	4,427	3,071	−6.2	76
Iowa	1,929	1,517	1,480	1,966	1.9	94
Kansas	2,360	1,576	1,260	2,676	13.4	147
Michigan	5,703	4,690	4,028	6,365	11.6	94
Minnesota	1,437	1,580	1,573	1,444	.5	46
Missouri[c]	5,229	3,801	2,672	6,358	21.6	168
Nebraska	304	673	518	459	51.0	39
North Dakota	159	153	161	151	−5.0	31
Ohio	6,147	4,865	5,024	5,988	−2.6	75
South Dakota	408	480	419	469	14.9	91
Wisconsin	3,854	2,386	2,247	3,993	3.6	113
South	124,304	80,726	63,520	141,510	13.8%	230
Alabama[b]	3,038	1,566	1,186	3,418	12.5	115
Arkansas	4,023	1,850	1,941	3,932	−2.3	226
Delaware	978	594	459	1,113	13.8	231
Dist. of Col.	2,980	2,059	1,205	3,834	28.7	789
Florida	3,478	2,325	2,930	2,873	−17.4	31

Probation means forgiveness and derives from a Latin word meaning a period of proving or trial (Allen, Eskridge, Latessa, and Vito, 1985:37–38). Probation was originally intended for offenders who did not pose risks to society and were believed capable of rehabilitation through some type of supervised, productive life in the community (Petersilia, 1985:2). However, there is a trend toward the use of felony probation in the United States. In California, 70 percent of all convicted felons are sentenced to probation rather than incarcerated. In fact, about 1 percent of the entire population of California was on probation by the end of 1984 (Petersilia, 1985:2).

TABLE 15.2 *continued*

Regions and Jurisdictions	Parole Population 1/1/87	1987		Parole Population 12/31/87	Percent Change in Parole Population During 1987	Number on Parole on 12/31/87 per 100,000 Adult Residents
		Entries	Exits			
Georgia	10,421	7,654	7,158	10,917	4.8	243
Kentucky	3,370	2,376	2,408	3,338	− .9	122
Louisiana	4,166	3,748	671	7,243	73.9	230
Maryland	7,494	5,210	4,641	8,063	7.6	236
Mississippi	3,454	1,616	1,614	3,456	.1	189
North Carolina	3,322	6,925	5,601	4,646	39.9	97
Oklahoma	1,670	579	487	1,762	5.5	74
South Carolina	3,066	1,076	923	3,219	5.0	130
Tennessee	8,600	4,714	4,051	9,263	7.7	257
Texas	57,509	31,563	21,764	67,308	17.0	570
Virginia	5,767	6,513	5,996	6,284	9.0	141
West Virginia	968	358	485	841	− 13.1	60
West	53,018	65,896	54,414	64,500	21.7%	178
Alaska	119	99	83	135	13.4	38
Arizona	2,034	3,046	2,856	2,224	9.3	90
California	33,172	51,123	42,960	41,335	24.6	203
Colorado[d]	1,827	1,556	1,703	1,680	−8.1	69
Hawaii	921	522	431	1,012	9.9	127
Idaho	531	355	245	641	20.7	92
Montana[c]	668	310	354	624	−6.6	107
Nevada[c]	1,529	1,272	1,203	1,598	4.5	212
New Mexico	1,147	1,306	1,259	1,194	4.1	113
Oregon	1,973	1,897	1,754	2,116	7.2	104
Utah	1,094	669	626	1,137	3.9	108
Washington[b]	7,666	3,556	776	10,446	36.3	310
Wyoming	337	185	164	358	6.2	105

...Not applicable.

[a]Maine eliminated parole in 1976.

[b]The State estimated entries and exits.

[c]The State estimated all of its data.

[d]The State estimated the number of exits.

Source: Thomas Hester, *Probation and Parole, 1987* (Washington, DC: Bureau of Justice Statistics, 1988), p. 3.

Parole also involves a degree of trust. The government says to an incarcerated offender, "You have behaved well in prison, and if you comply with certain conditions and regulations, we will release you from incarceration into the community under supervision." The expectation is that the parolee will abide by the terms of early release and continue in this status until the full term of the sentence has been served. Early release is a type of sentence commutation. **Commutation** of a sentence means to change or reduce the severity of it in some fashion. Those who have been sentenced to death may have their death sentences commuted to life imprisonment. In the case of inmates, commutation may be parole.

TABLE 15.3 Correctional Populations, Percent of Adult Population under Sanction, and Percent Change, 1983–1987

	1983		1984		1985		1986		1987		Percent Increase in Correctional Populations 1983–87
	Number	Percent of Adult Population	Number	Percent of Adult Population	Number	Percent of Adult Population	Number	Percent of Adult Population	Number	Percent of Adult Population	
Correctional populations											
total	2,475,000	1.44%	2,684,222	1.55%	3,011,494	1.71%	3,239,631	1.82%	3,460,960	1.92%	39.8%
Probation	1,582,947	.92	1,740,948	1.00	1,968,712	1.12	2,114,821	1.19	2,242,053	1.25	41.6
Jail*	221,815	.13	233,018	.13	254,986	.15	272,736	.15	294,092	.16	32.6
Prison	423,898	.25	448,264	.26	487,593	.28	526,436	.30	562,623	.31	32.7
Parole	246,440	.14	266,992	.15	300,203	.17	325,638	.18	362,192	.20	47.0

Note: The following are estimates of the U.S. resident population age 18 and older on July 1: 1983—171,332,000; 1984—173,469,000; 1985—175,727,000; 1986—177,807,000; and 1987—179,856,000. Population counts for probation, parole, and prison custody are for December 31, and jail counts are for June 30. Every year some States update their report; this table uses the corrected counts.

*Estimates of jail populations include convicted and unconvicted adult inmates.

Source: Thomas Hester, *Probation and Parole, 1987* (Washington, DC: Bureau of Justice Statistics, 1988), p. 4.

TABLE 15.4 State Prison Releases by Method, 1977–1987

| | | Percent of Prison Releases | | | | | | | |
| | | Conditional Releases | | | | Unconditional Releases | | | |
Year	Total Releases from Prisons	All	Discretionary Parole	Supervised Mandatory Release	Probation	Other	Expiration of Sentence	Commutation	Other
1977	115,213	100%	71.9%	5.9%	3.6%	1.0%	16.1%	1.1%	.4%
1978	119,796	100	70.4	5.8	3.3	2.3	17.0	.7	.5
1979	128,954	100	60.2	16.9	3.3	2.4	16.3	.4	.6
1980	136,968	100	57.4	19.5	3.6	3.2	14.9	.5	.8
1981	142,489	100	54.6	21.4	3.7	3.1	13.9	2.4	1.0
1982	157,144	100	51.9	24.4	4.8	3.6	14.4	.3	.6
1983	191,237	100	48.1	26.9	5.2	2.5	16.1	.5	.6
1984	191,499	100	46.0	28.7	4.9	2.7	16.3	.5	.9
1985	203,895	100	43.2	30.8	4.5	3.0	16.9	.4	1.2
1986	230,672	100	43.2	31.1	4.5	4.6	14.8	.3	1.4
1987	270,506	100	40.6	31.2	4.4	5.7	16.2	1.0	.9

Note: The data are from the National Prisoner Statistics reporting program. The total releases from State prison are those for which the method of release was reported. Deaths, unspecified releases, transfers, and escapes were not included. Altogether, 305,098 persons were released or removed from State prisons in 1987.

Source: Thomas Hester, *Probation and Parole, 1987* (Washington, DC: Bureau of Justice Statistics, 1988), p. 4.

■ FUNCTIONS OF PROBATION AND PAROLE

The primary functions of probation and parole are (1) to reduce crime; (2) to rehabilitate and reintegrate offenders; and (3) to effect reductions in the prison population.

Crime Reduction

Both probation and parole offer the possibility of reducing crime through the careful supervision of offenders engaged in positive community activities (Harris, 1984; McAnany, Thomson, and Fogel, 1984). Convicted defendants who have been placed on probation in lieu of incarceration should consider themselves fortunate. They should regard probation as a stern warning to avoid committing new crimes. Parolees who have already experienced prison life ideally should consider early release as an opportunity to demonstrate their sincere intent to conform to society's rules.

However, while the deterrent value of probation and parole is supported in scattered studies, it is generally conceded that probationers and parolees exhibit high recidivism rates. During a 40-month period following the probation of 1,672 convicted California felons in 1980, 65 percent were rearrested for new offenses. Of the 1,672 felons, 53 percent had charges filed against them, including violent crimes such as robbery, aggravated assault, and homicide (Petersilia, 1985:3).

In contrast, some studies imply that probation reduces the probationer's propensity to commit further crimes. For example 100 felony and misdemeanor probation cases were studied in the Shreveport, Louisiana Probation and Parole District between 1975 and 1978. Eighty-six percent of those studied successfully completed the terms of their probation and did not recidivate during the study (Roundtree, Edwards, and Parker, 1984). Also, the Massachusetts Department of Corrections examined recidivism rates among parolees between 1971 and 1982. On the basis of annual reports, recidivism rates among parolees, particularly those supervised through prerelease centers and halfway houses, decreased from 25 percent in 1971 to less than 16 percent in 1982 (LeClair, 1985).

Rehabilitation of Offenders

Besides reducing the amount of crime, probation and parole may lead to rehabilitation by enhancing a criminal's reintegration into society. Both probation and parole seek to rehabilitate offenders, although some researchers believe there is a trend away from the traditional rehabilitative ideal (Moran and Lindner, 1985). It is apparent from earlier reports of prison and jail overcrowding, however, that rehabilitation is difficult to achieve under conditions of incarceration. Vocational and educational programs cannot function effectively where overcrowding exists.

However, at Chino Prison in California, for example, criminals who have been convicted of crimes ranging from drug possession to murder participate in a rehabilitation program called Vocational Diver Training (VDT) (Andersen and Andersen, 1984). The program trains participants to become commercial divers, where projected earnings are lucrative. The recidivism rate for persons who have participated in this program is only 6 percent!

The decisions of parole boards are fallible, since many parolees become recidivists. Some states have abandoned the use of parole boards and rely on determinate sentencing system instead.

One major obstacle interfering with the potential rehabilitative value of probation and parole is the influence of the justice model. The justice model favors an abandonment of both probation and parole, a return to incarceration, and a shift to determinate and mandatory sentencing. The justice model focuses upon the crimes an offender has committed and the debt that the offender owes to society, advocating that offenders be punished for those crimes. However, probation and parole philosophically reflect a treatment orientation, which is designed to deter the individual from future criminal activity. The treatment model is rehabilitative, whereas the justice model is retributive and consistent with the "just deserts" position. Supporters of probation, parole, and alternative sentencing programs advocate keeping certain convicted offenders away from association with other criminals. This view also reflects the labeling perspective, which suggests that the more people are involved with the justice system, the more they acquire self-definitions consistent with the criminal label. Both the justice model and the treatment orientation have support among citizens. If the importance of each is assessed in terms of recidivism figures, neither is convincing. A sad commentary on corrections is that incarceration generally is ineffective as a rehabilitation medium or a deterrent to crime, but there are always exceptions.

Reduction of Prison Populations

An intended result of probation and parole is a reduction in prison and jail populations. Figure 15.1 shows parolee, probationer, and prison population changes in the United States for the years 1974 to 1983. Between 1974 and 1983, the number of probationers in the United States increased by 63 percent, while the number of parolees nationally increased by 38 percent (Petersilia, 1985:2). However, during the same period, a corresponding increase of 48 percent occurred in the United States prison population. A large portion of this prison population increase was attributable to the construction and

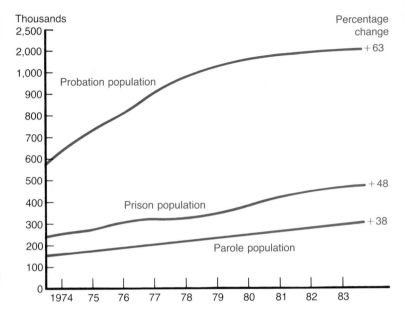

FIGURE 15.1 Change in United States Parole, Probation, and Prison Populations, 1974–83

Source: Joan M. Petersilia, *Probation and Felony Offenders* (Washington, DC: Bureau of Justice Statistics, 1985), p. 2.

development of additional correctional facilities during the 1974–1983 period. At present, the only significant decreases in prison populations have been in states such as Tennessee and Louisiana as the result of court-mandated reductions due to overcrowding.

Programs aimed at reducing prison overcrowding include Florida's Community Control Program. This program was implemented in 1983 as the result of the Correctional Reform Act of that year (Florida Probation and Parole Services, 1984). One of the major goals of the Community Control Program was to help reduce prison overcrowding, but between 1984 and 1985, Florida's jail population has increased by 6 percent. Of course, it may be that if such a program had not been in place by 1983, Florida's prison population by the end of 1985 would have been considerably higher. Following up on the first 1,886 prison and jail probationers, only 93 probation revocations had occurred by the end of 1984.

To the extent that adequate adult intensive supervision programs are in place in various jurisdictions, many judges favor probation over incarceration. A study of 254 Texas district court judges, for instance, found that most judges would be more likely to use probation and diversion in lieu of sentences of incarceration, provided adequate supervision and basic probation services existed to accommodate the offenders (Fields, Field, and Williams, 1983).

Under determinate and mandatory sentencing, parole boards do not determine a prisoner's early release. Critics of parole board decisions cite high rates of recidivism among parolees, although little evidence exists to show that a parole board's decision-making effectiveness concerning who should be placed on probation and who should be incarcerated is any worse than a judge's. No particular sentencing system is more fair, more predictable, or less confusing than parole board decision making (Breed, 1984). Some authorities encourage the preservation of parole board authority to commute

CRIME BEAT

Mary Vincent, a 15-year-old runaway hitchhiker, walked along a San Francisco street one afternoon and accepted a ride from a drunken merchant seaman, Lawrence Singleton. He drove her to a remote rural area, where he raped her repeatedly. Then he cut off her arms below the elbows with a hatchet and left her bleeding and near death in a ditch under a bridge. Somehow, she managed to crawl from the ditch to a farmhouse for help. She lived and was able to identify Singleton as the man who raped her.

Singleton was convicted of the rape, and the aggravating nature of the assault on Vincent was such that the judge declared that he would put Singleton behind bars for the rest of his natural life if he had the power. However, under California law, Singleton was sentenced to the maximum term of 14 years, 4 months in prison. Most onlookers believed that Singleton would be incarcerated until at least 1995. However, on April 25, 1987, Singleton walked away from prison a free man. He was not paroled. The California Department of Corrections had to let him go. According to California statutes, prison inmates may accumulate good time credits for their good behavior behind bars. Singleton had been a good prisoner. Thus, he earned early release after serving less than 8 years for his crime.

Public outrage over Singleton's release prompted California officials and legislators to reexamine their sentencing policies and good time provisions. However, California is one of several states with severe prison overcrowding problems. Longer prison terms mean more long-term occupancy of scarce prison cells. Thus, California currently places on probation nearly 70 percent of all its convicted felons, including some rapists, murderers, and robbers. Furthermore, back-door provisions, such as early release through earning good time credits, create scenarios similar to Singleton's. Should some offenders receive mandatory terms of incarceration and serve the maximum time imposed?

sentences, but they also advocate the establishment of consistent and fair parole guidelines.

■ SELECTING AND TRAINING PROBATION AND PAROLE OFFICERS

In 1958, the National Probation and Parole Association recommended that all probation and parole officers have at least a bachelor's degree from an accredited college or university and that an additional year of graduate study would be desirable (Allen, Latessa, Eskridge, and Vito, 1985:144). By 1982, thirty-one states and the District of Columbia required all entry-level personnel performing probation or parole officer work to possess a bachelor's degree, preferably in a behavioral science. Only one state, Mississippi, required these officers to possess a master's degree in either criminal justice or a behavioral science. Employment as a probation or parole officer at the federal level required a master's degree by 1982 as well (Latessa and Allen, 1982). Most other states required either some college or were not specific. In 1982 in New Jersey, for example, the only requirement to perform parole or probation officer work was possessing a valid New Jersey driver's license.

Some experts see probation and parole as fulfilling court-imposed sanctions rather than performing a mission (McAnany, Thomson, and Fogel, 1984:270). However, probation and parole officers function as liaisons between parolees or probationers and the courts. They monitor convicts' progress and daily, weekly, or monthly activities. They report rule infractions and recommend parole or probation revocation. They help probationers and parolees secure new jobs or adjust to current work roles. At times, they perform the functions of counselors, priests, psychiatrists, and social workers. In sum, probation and parole officers must be flexible, ever able to adapt to new roles and situations (Nielsen, 1984).

The general premise that a college graduate is better able to perform the role of probation or parole officer is widely held in criminal justice circles, but there is little evidence that older probation and parole officers with less education are less effective in their job performance than are younger, more educated officers (Allen, Eskridge, Latessa, and Vito, 1985:148). While it is important for officers to be familiar with the variety of treatment and educational programs available for offenders, no administration or agency has demonstrated a need for officers to possess a formal college degree. While it might be helpful for officers to be able to recognize the behavioral symptoms relative to drug abuse, alcoholism, or mental disturbance, workshops, seminars, and in-service sessions often provide relevant material about these problems.

One unintended consequence of requiring probation and parole officers to have college degrees is that it places greater social distance between them and their clients. Generally, convicted felons lack formal education and certain communicative skills. More highly educated probation and parole officers may have greater difficulty relating to such clients, and this situation may aggravate rather than facilitate the counselor role that these officers perform.

Probation and parole work is stressful. Heavy **caseloads** (that is, numbers of parolees or probationers assigned to each officer) and the exposure of these officers to often hazardous situations create feelings of job stress and lead to burnout (Whitehead and Lindquist, 1985). A study of 108 Alabama probation and parole officers conducted in 1984 showed, for example, that over half reported high job stress, and 20 percent believed they were burned out with their jobs (Whitehead and Lindquist, 1985). In this study, burnout and stress were explained by work overloads and the strains of the officer-client contacts.

In order for probation and parole officers to spend at least 1 hour a month in face-to-face contact with their clients, they should have caseloads of fewer than thirty clients at any given time. In reality, many officers have caseloads far in excess of thirty clients. Ideally, maximum effectiveness of probation and parole programs requires caseloads of between twenty and thirty clients for each officer, but caseloads of three hundred or four hundred clients per officer are not uncommon in some jurisdictions.

It is becoming increasingly difficult for states to attract and retain qualified persons to perform probation and parole officer roles (Davis, 1984; Georgia Department of Audits, 1985). In Ohio, for example, 241 probation and parole officers were surveyed. Salaries for 83 percent of these officers were less than $25,000 per year. In many cases, spouses were required to work in order to supplement the officers' low salaries. Over 70 percent of these officers spent 20 hours per week with probationers or parolees, while paperwork accounted for the remainder of their work time. About 70 percent of these officers spent 4 hours preparing a single presentence report, and most failed to verify the information they reported (Davis, 1984). Most officers said that they obtained experience by doing the probation and parole work.

Considerable role conflict exists among probation and parole officers, often between the role of treatment resource and supervisor (Sigler and McGraw, 1984). A 1978 study of 113 Alabama probation and parole officers examined the influence of police changes that required all officers to participate in mandatory firearms training. This caused many officers to reevaluate their roles and see themselves more as law enforcement officers than rehabilitation-oriented helpers (Sigler and McGraw, 1984). In other studies, probation and parole officers have expressed similar sentiments, as the probation and parole functions shift from rehabilitative to punitive (American Correctional Association, 1986; Moran and Lindner, 1985; Steppe, 1986).

■ INTERMEDIATE PUNISHMENTS FOR PROBATIONERS AND PAROLEES

For both probationers and parolees, several states have intermediate punishment programs (McCarthy, 1987). **Intermediate punishments** are sanctions that exist somewhere between incarceration and probation on the continuum of criminal penalties (McCarthy, 1987:1). One form of intermediate punishment is called **intensive supervision programs,** which provide for low probation and parole officer caseloads and intensive supervision of offenders through frequent visits or telephone communication. For parolees who have been or are about to be released from prison, furlough programs, halfway houses, community-based corrections, and work release programs are utilized to ease these persons back into society.

Intensive Supervision Programs

Decisions to parole offenders who are currently incarcerated, or decisions about which offenders ought to be placed on probation, involve some educated guesswork among sentencing judges and correctional officials. A number of risk assessment devices have been constructed in recent years to determine objectively which offenders pose the greatest public risk. A risk assessment device is intended to predict whether offenders will violate the terms of their parole or probation and recidivate, or commit additional offenses. However, risk assessment measures have not enjoyed the successes originally envisioned by their formulators. For example, the California Department of Corrections operates a Stress Assessment Unit at Vacaville. Between 1962 and 1977, all inmates terminated from that facility were subjected to a follow-up study, where their parole and arrest records were checked over the next 2 to 10 years (Clanon and Jew, 1985). Prisoners received either positive or negative parole recommendations. Incredibly, the offenders receiving positive parole recommendations were more likely to commit new crimes during the follow-up period than those receiving negative parole recommendations. For instance, 43 percent of those receiving positive parole recommendations recidivated compared with 38 percent of those receiving negative parole recommendations.

Gottfredson and Gottfredson (1985) examined the predictive utility of several parole success predictors. Their study of 4,500 offenders released from federal prisons between 1970 and 1972 showed that while there was a high intercorrelation among the various measures examined, the variables ordinarily associated with predicting recidivism, including present and previous offenses, added little to predicting actual recidivism. Other studies examining success predictors have also found inconsistent and disappointing results (Bonham, 1984; Wilbanks, 1985).

In Massachusetts, a risk/need classification system was devised to differentiate the degree of supervision required for any given offender (Brown and Cochran, 1984). A prior record, educational disadvantage, a disorganized family structure, and a history of substance abuse were used to predict subsequent criminal behavior. In 1982, a sample of 1,963 adults and juveniles was placed under the risk/need supervision program in Massachusetts. Offenders scoring high upon their initial assessment were more likely to commit new offenses than were those scoring low on the scale. This suggests that the risk/need classification system is workable, at least for that jurisdiction (Brown and Cochran, 1984).

CRIME BEAT

How do we know that other people might be dangerous to themselves or others? Are there visible signs or verbal cues that should alert us that someone might be disturbed to the point of suicide or murder? In May 1988, Laurie Wasserman Dann, a 30-year-old baby-sitter, walked calmly into Hubbard Woods Elementary School in Winnetka, Illinois, on a cool Friday morning, shot a 6-year-old boy in the bathroom, walked into a classroom and killed an 8-year-old girl, wounded five other students, and then went to a nearby house, held a family of five hostage, and eventually shot herself in the head. The community was shocked. She had baby-sat for several families in Winnetka. They recalled her as a quiet, affectionate young woman who seemed to love children.

Yet, she was known as a psycho to those living near her in student housing at the University of Wisconsin, Madison. She was antisocial according to her student neighbors in the student housing project. According to her ex-husband, Russell Dann, Laurie Dann had numerous disputes with him during 1985 and 1986. One night, Russell Dann was stabbed with an ice pick while he slept. The ice pick missed his heart by an inch. Although the killer was not seen by Dann, he strongly suspected his wife, Laurie. They divorced shortly thereafter. She engaged in various relationships with other men after her divorce, although she was unable to sustain a meaningful relationship with anyone. Soon, several of her previous boyfriends began to receive threatening calls from her. She was reported to authorities in three different states because of her life-threatening calls. Eventually, the FBI was called in, and it intended to interview Laurie. They arrived at her apartment in Madison a day late. She had moved to Winnetka, Illinois, on Chicago's North Shore. Shortly thereafter, she killed and wounded the children at Hubbard Woods Elementary School.

There are many Laurie Danns in the United States. A major problem is diagnosing mental illnesses properly. After a proper diagnosis, what laws are in place to commit such persons to hospitals for psychiatric treatment? Would psychiatric treatment have benefited Dann? Because of her suicide, many unanswered questions remain. Her own life was a trail of circumstantial evidence suggesting possible mental instability. The concrete telephone conversations with her ex-boyfriends provided a foundation for police action, but such action arrived too late.

Perhaps the most important factor influencing the success or failure of an intensive supervision program in any jurisdiction is the size of an officer's caseload (Schumacher, 1985; Steppe, 1986). As a result of the Correctional Reform Act of 1983, Florida created a Community Control Program, which was designed to provide work programs for probationers and parolees and to reduce caseloads to fewer than twenty per officer (an ideal number in view of the original objectives of probation and parole programs generally) (Florida Probation and Parole Services, 1984). During the first year of operation, the Community Control Program had 1,886 clients. Only 93 revocations occurred, with 41 for new crimes and 52 for technical violations (such as failure to communicate with the probation or parole officer at regular intervals or leaving the immediate jurisdiction temporarily). The program is considered successful to the extent that 72 percent of the cases are classified as bona fide diversions from prison (Florida Probation and Parole Services, 1984).

An experiment with intensive supervised pretrial release programs in Miami, Florida; Portland, Oregon; and Milwaukee, Wisconsin, disclosed that between 1980 and 1984, 3,226 persons were randomly assigned to a variety of pretrial release alternatives including (1) release on own recognizance, (2) bail or citation, or (3) supervised release (Austin, Krisberg, and Litsky, 1984). Over 98 percent of those under supervised pretrial release appeared in court later. Those released on their own recognizance, bail, or citation failed to appear much more frequently than did those under the supervised pretrial release plan in those jurisdictions.

Women have much better records under intensive supervised probation or parole than do men. Women are less likely to be charged with new offenses than are males. One explanation for this gender difference may be that probation and parole officers are reluctant to report women because of their family obligations and what the officers feel to be minor problems (Norland and Mann, 1984).

Assisting probation and parole officers in their supervision of various offenders are paraprofessionals and community volunteers (Latessa, Travis, and Allen, 1983). Based on a national survey of the use of volunteers and paraprofessionals in parole, questionnaires mailed in 1979 to fifty-two state parole field supervision departments revealed that volunteer and paraprofessional programs were widely accepted in parole. Although the qualifications for paraprofessionals are more stringent than those for volunteers, both groups appeared to receive positive reports.

Furloughs

For certain low-risk, nonviolent offenders about to be paroled, furlough programs are operated in selected jurisdictions. **Furloughs** are unescorted and unsupervised leaves of prisoners to their homes to be reunited with their families and friends. In jurisdictions where furlough programs exist, absconding rates have been low. One furlough program operating since 1972 for prisoners in Massachusetts correctional facilities has shown that between 1972 and 1982, 81,822 furloughs were granted. Prisoners failed to return in only 585 cases during that 10-year period. This is an absconding rate of only 0.7 percent. Massachusetts has decreased the proportionate number of furloughs per year, however. This was largely the result of growing numbers of parolees rather than absconders. Absconding rates declined each year following 1972 with the exception of 1981, when there was a slight increase (Tobin, 1983).

Furloughs are most often granted to prisoners in minimum-security prisons, although some maximum-security and medium-security prisoners have participated in Massachusetts's furlough program (Tobin, 1983). Massachusetts also operates a number of prerelease centers, where furloughs are being granted to an increasing degree. Prerelease centers are much like halfway houses in their design and operation, and prisoner escape rates from them are well within acceptable levels to support overall effectiveness in this general program (Tobin, 1983).

Despite the successfulness of furlough programs throughout the United States, a few exceptional cases have caused many jurisdictions to reevaluate their furlough programs. During the presidential campaign of 1988, presidential candidates George Bush and Michael Dukakis sought to discredit one another by citing their respective political records. Michael Dukakis, then governor of Massachusetts, was tagged by Bush supporters as soft on crime. Furthermore, Willie Horton, an inmate serving a life sentence for first-degree murder in a Massachusetts penitentiary, was granted a furlough in 1986. He absconded and 10 months later raped a woman and stabbed her companion in Oxon Hill, Maryland. The case received considerable publicity, especially since Dukakis had strongly promoted the Massachusetts furlough plan as one of the most important features of his new criminal justice program. In response to widespread criticism of his furlough program, Governor Dukakis subsequently signed a law that prohibited first-degree murderers from being granted furloughs.

CRIME BEAT

Former United States presidential candidate and Massachusetts governor Michael Dukakis promoted a furlough program in his state for deserving prisoners. During the 1988 presidential campaign, Dukakis drew much criticism from political opponents because a convicted murderer, Willie Horton, had been granted a furlough, or unescorted leave, fled the state, and committed other serious crimes. Horton, convicted of murder and serving a life sentence without the possibility of parole, had been placed on furloughs at least seven or eight times before he escaped his Massachusetts jurisdiction. Dukakis's furlough program was quickly revised to prevent further incidents involving offenders like Horton.

Normally, furloughs are granted to prisoners who are within several months of being released anyway. In Horton's case, there was no logical explanation for officials to grant him numerous furloughs. Ideally,

furloughs are designed to give inmates an opportunity to reestablish themselves in their communities, to become reacquainted with their families and friends outside of the prison setting, and to readjust to the community generally. Many of those granted furloughs use this time to take courses, learn new skills, and look for employment. In some instances, weekend furloughs permit inmates to work at jobs in preparation for the subsequent parole or early release. Furlough programs are operated in most states to alleviate prison overcrowding to a degree. Troubling the public, however, is the fact that these programs may prematurely release inmates such as Horton. Should all furlough programs be terminated? Which inmates should be granted furloughs? What criteria would you use to determine whether a prisoner should be granted an unescorted leave from prison?

The Willie Hortons among prisoners who are eligible for furloughs and other similar forms of release are exceptions. Promoters believe that furloughs assist inmates in becoming reintegrated into their communities. Furloughs are considered therapeutic in a sense, since inmates are given a degree of trust by prison officials. They may visit their families and friends, look for jobs, participate in educational programs, and gradually establish new lives for themselves. However, one inmate such as Willie Horton can contaminate an entire program. The public is inclined to remember rapes, robberies, murders, and other crimes committed by furlough program participants rather than the rehabilitative and reintegrative value of such programs for thousands of other prisoners. Because of the importance attached to the Horton incident, furlough programs in some jurisdictions have been terminated or drastically modified. The same phenomenon occurred when John Hinckley attempted to assassinate President Ronald Reagan and escaped imprisonment by successfully using the insanity defense. That single incident caused many states to revise their insanity plea provisions or abandon them entirely, despite the fact that the insanity plea is used in less than 0.1 percent of all criminal cases, and it is unsuccessfully used in over 99 percent of them.

Halfway Houses

Halfway houses are establishments designed to assist parolees in making smooth adjustments to life outside of prison (Mrad, Kabacoff, and Duckro, 1983; Eisenberg, 1985). Halfway houses have relatively low recidivism rates and offer offenders a more normal, hospitable environment from which they may make a more successful transition to the community. Between January and June 1983, for example, 2,072 prisoners were released from the Texas Department of Corrections. Twenty-five percent, or 536, of these were placed in halfway houses, while the rest were immediately paroled (Eisenberg, 1985). Halfway house offenders recidivated at slightly lower rates than did non-halfway house offenders (14 percent compared with 15 percent). However, offenders with drug or alcohol abuse problems assigned to halfway houses recidivated at a rate of 7 percent compared with 15 percent for non-halfway house cases (Eisenberg, 1985). Careful selection of halfway house participants can lead to significantly lower recidivism rates than those of other release programs, although currently, differences among various types of release programs are not especially significant (Eisenberg, 1985).

Between 1980 and 1982, 409 clients participated in Cope House, a halfway house located in Dayton, Ohio (Donnelly and Forschner, 1984). Program failure was defined as removal from the house for violating house rules or committing new offenses. Cope House clients had a success rate of 65 percent. Also, women did much better than men in their program participation (Donnelly and Forschner, 1984).

One of the best objectives a probation or parole program can achieve is to provide probationers or parolees with effective job placements and work opportunities. Many halfway houses offer such services to offenders about to be released from incarceration. One significant program that has been implemented to assist offenders in securing employment training in various skills is the Community Alliance Program for Ex-Offenders (CAPE) (National Alliance of Business, 1983). In June 1980, this program was created to test a model for ex-offender employment and delivery services.

The program constituted a network of public service organizations, local criminal justice agencies, and private businesses. It was designed to help parolees and probationers secure training and employment by offering them preemployment training and counseling, skill and vocational training, assessment, participant orientation, job development, support services and crisis management, and job placement (National Alliance of Business, 1983). This partnership has been successful in the jurisdictions where it has been used.

Few critics question that halfway houses assist parolees in making the transition to normal society. Some researchers emphasize that participating in a halfway house program tends to give offenders an edge at readjusting to outside life (Orsagh and Marsden, 1985). Failure rates reported by various halfway houses are often attributable to staffing problems and inaccuracies in risk classifications at the outset rather than to defects in the halfway house programs themselves. Most recent halfway house studies reported in the professional literature reveal lower rates of recidivism or reductions in the number and severity of future offenses (Curtis and Schulman, 1984; Dowell, Klein, and Krichmar, 1985; Gotwalt, 1984). Recidivists tend to fall into the younger age categories and are primarily male.

Some jurisdictions resort to shock probation. Shock probation is really a misnomer, because it doesn't provide probation at all. **Shock probation** is placing offenders in prison for a brief period, primarily to give them a taste of prison life (for shock value), and then releasing them into the custody of a parole officer. For instance, the Incarceration Unit of the Lucas County (Ohio) Adult Probation Department, started in 1978, offers intensive probation services to many clients annually (Latessa, 1983). The objectives of the program are to (1) reduce state commitments from the county, (2) provide increased probation services, and (3) maintain community safety at a lower cost than incarceration. Did shock probation do the job it was intended to do? Did offenders exhibit lower rates of recidivism?

No. Despite the fact that caseloads for probation officers were limited to twenty-five, and variables such as risk assessment, race, and sex were controlled, the unit was only able to divert 15 percent fewer cases through shock probation than were units with normal probation caseloads (Latessa, 1983).

Community-Based Corrections and Work Release Programs

Community-based corrections programs are locally operated services offering minimum-security, limited release, or work release alternatives to prisoners about to be paroled (Clear and O'Leary, 1983; Troia, 1983). For example, Iowa passed legislation establishing a locally administered community-based corrections program in 1973 (Iowa Legislative Fiscal Bureau, 1983). The Iowa community-based corrections program provides for (1) pretrial release on own recognizance or release with services; (2) presentence investigation; (3) probation; and (4) residential treatment facilities. Iowa has found community-based adult corrections programs to be inexpensive and effective at reducing recidivism among parolees.

In 1981 in Milwaukee, Wisconsin, a new community residential center was opened for offenders who were within 6 months of prison release (Troia, 1983). The Milwaukee Community Residential Centers are small, urban-based minimum-security prisons that

CRIME BEAT

The conditions accompanying sentences of probation vary among jurisdictions. Probationers may be obligated to pay fines or restitution or to perform public service. They may have to take courses or receive psychological counseling. However, judges may extend their conditions of probation to include unusual penalties. Sometimes, those convicted of driving while intoxicated may be required to display "DUI Driver" on their automobile bumpers for others to see. Some probationers convicted of child sexual abuse may have to display on their automobiles the fact that they are child molesters.

In November 1987, Matthew Zacherl, a 23-year-old former University of Wisconsin-Steven Point student, was convicted of driving while intoxicated and causing great bodily harm by a high degree of negligence in the operation of a motor vehicle. He had driven his car into a building where an inhabitant, Gregory TerHorst, was seriously injured. TerHorst received extensive brain damage and was in a coma.

Zacherl received a split sentence, or split probation from the judge. The entire sentence of 6 years consisted of jail confinement for the first 6 months and escorted visits to the comatose victim, TerHorst, at the hospital on weekends. For the next 6 months of the first year, Zacherl was ordered to visit TerHorst once every 3 months. Finally, for the remaining 5 years, Zacherl was required to visit TerHorst once every 6 months. In addition, the judge ordered Zacherl to pay at least $50 a month to the TerHorst family and assigned Zacherl to 200 hours of community service work. His sentence also included abstinence from alcohol and regular drug-alcohol testing by the probation office. Should those sentenced to probation receive statutory penalties, or should judges be permitted to individualize their sentences such as in the case of Zacherl?

are designed to prepare offenders for reentry into their home communities through work experience, educational opportunities, counseling, and other programming (Troia, 1983). One consequence of being placed in such a center was greater prisoner contact with family members, who could visit more freely than they could with a regular prison facility. It is significant that 83 percent of all persons released from these community residential centers have had successful parole outcomes (Wisconsin Department of Health and Social Services, 1982).

In 1982, Virginia operated six community-based work release units, which maintained an average daily work release population of 314 inmates (Jones, 1982). Persons placed on **work release** are permitted to hold regular jobs in the community during the daytime but must return and spend their evenings at the community-based facility. Assignments to Virginia work release programs according to race have been about 50-50. One significant outcome of Virginia's work release units is that inmates have been able to contribute substantially to the support of their families or dependents. For instance, in 1981, inmate participants in the Virginia program earned $1.1 million and contributed $65,000 to the support of their families. About 14 percent of the program's cost was defrayed by monies paid to the center by the inmates.

The primary aims of community-based corrections programs are to minimize the supervision of inmates, to give inmates increased responsibilities in providing for themselves and their dependents, and to control the risk the offender represents to the community (Clear and O'Leary, 1983). In a study of the effectiveness of a work release program at Fishkill (New York) Correctional Facility, 179 offenders who were released between 1979 and 1983 were tracked from their varying release dates to determine if they had recidivated (MacDonald and Bala, 1984). Only 15.6 percent of all the prison releases had returned to prison, strongly suggesting that work release participation relates to successful postrelease adjustment (MacDonald and Bala, 1984).

■ ALTERNATIVES TO OFFICER SURVEILLANCE

Probation and parole as we know it today will probably be obsolete by the year 2025, as new monitoring systems are incorporated into corrections operations. It is clear that high technology is exerting a profound influence on the future of corrections in the United States (Moran and Lindner, 1985). For example, an automobile stolen in Florida can be driven to California and the driver stopped for speeding. Within seconds, a national computer inquiry can reveal facts pertaining to the theft of the stolen car. By the same token, innovations are taking place regarding the movements and location of probationers and parolees.

Electronic Monitoring

One indication of the influence of technology in probation and parole decisions is the procedure followed by a maverick judge in New Mexico. Judge Jack Love of the Second Judicial District in New Mexico implemented a pilot project in 1983, whereby persons convicted of drunk driving or white-collar offenses are placed on probation, provided that they agree to be electronically monitored during the probationary period (Houk, 1984). Approved by the New Mexico Supreme Court, the GOSSlink system (developed by Michael Goss of the Nimcos Company in Albuquerque, New Mexico) is a bracelet device that electronically monitors the locations of probationers not incarcerated. The purpose of such an electronic monitor is to monitor an offender's presence in a given environment where the offender is required to remain (Schmidt and Curtis, 1987:138).

Some of these devices use miniaturized transmitters which are strapped to the offenders and broadcast encoded signals at regular intervals over a particular range (Schmidt and Curtis, 1987:138). Other devices include wristlets or black plastic modules worn by the offenders. A receiver-dialer, located in each offender's home, detects signals from the transmitter and reports to a central computer.

A central computer can also provide periodic checks (Schmidt and Curtis, 1987:138). When the computer randomly calls, an offender must insert the wristlet into a verifier box connected to the telephone to verify that the call is being answered by the offender being monitored. The central computer accepts reports from the receiver-dialer over the telephone lines, compares them with the offender's curfew schedule, and alerts correctional officials about any unauthorized offender absences (Schmidt and Curtis, 1987:138). Besides the GOSSlink, devices include the BI Home Escort, the Supervisor, the In-House Arrest System, and the Home Incarceration Unit.

The average daily costs for the basic equipment range from $1.29 to $9.04, from $0.95 to $7.00 for lease-purchase agreements, and from $1.91 to $7.00 for straight lease agreements (Vaughn, 1987:158–159). Since jail and prison inmate costs range from $15 to $50 per day, and new construction costs vary from $25,000 to $75,000 or more per bed, depending upon the degree of architectural security, these **electronic monitoring** devices clearly offer inexpensive alternatives (Vaughn, 1987:158–159).

Questions have been raised about the constitutionality of these monitoring systems. However, this issue has not been presented to the United States Supreme Court as violative of Fourth Amendment protection. Houk (1984) says that these devices do not intrude significantly into the lives of offenders, and that it is likely that they will be used to an increasing degree in the future.

Electronic monitoring devices are not new. They were first used as alternatives for incarcerating mental patients in 1964 (Gable, 1986; Schmidt and Curtis, 1987:137; Schwitzgebel, 1964). Personal telemonitoring systems in the United States and other countries are gaining in popularity, and their usefulness in determining whether or not a probationer or parolee is complying with the terms of his or her probation or parole is unquestioned. Interestingly, these devices seem to have a therapeutic effect on those who are required to use them. Their goals of reducing correctional costs, extending public protection, and improving offender rehabilitation are apparently being realized (Gable, 1986).

Should an offender commit a burglary or robbery while wearing a telemonitoring device, it is possible that an electronic in-store device could be designed to receive the signals emitted by the wearer, instantly identifying the offender and solving more crimes. Recidivists required to wear these devices might be deterred from committing new crimes. Removal of the bracelet by the offender would trigger an immediate warning to the central monitoring station, and officials could take appropriate action. Currently, GOSSlink and other similar systems are used in prisons and jails to monitor prisoner whereabouts (Berry, 1985).

Home Incarceration

The idea of incarcerating offenders in their own homes was implemented on a statewide basis in Florida in 1983 (Blomberg, Waldo, and Burcroff, 1987:171). **Home incarceration** has been called **house arrest,** community control, or home confinement. While home incarceration is usually accompanied by some form of electronic surveillance, such as the monitoring systems previously described, it is used without such electronic instrumentation (Blomberg, Waldo, and Burcroff, 1987:169). The Florida program has involved at least 5,000 offenders, making it the largest program of its type in the country (Blomberg, Waldo, and Burcroff, 1987:171). Three categories of offenders are eligible for home incarceration in Florida: (1) those found guilty of nonforcible felonies, (2) probationers charged with technical or misdemeanor violations, and (3) parolees charged with technical or misdemeanor violations—in short, low-risk offenders (Blomberg, Waldo, and Burcroff, 1987:172).

The conditions established by Florida statutes governing the behaviors of offenders placed on the home incarceration program include (1) reporting to the home confinement officer regularly, (2) performing a substantial amount of public service work without pay, (3) remaining confined to their residence when not working at a regular job, (4) making periodic restitution payments to victims, (5) maintaining a daily log of their routine, (6) participating in self-help programs, and (7) submitting to urinalysis or blood specimen tests to determine the presence of alcohol or drugs (Blomberg, Waldo, and

Burcroff, 1987:172). Thus far, the program in Florida appears successful as a rehabilitative measure. However, one issue raised by the Florida selection methods is that those considered for electronic surveillance would probably not be incarcerated anyway. Thus, the idea that Florida is freeing up jail and prison space may be illusory. In effect, Florida may simply be widening the net rather than decreasing serious prison and jail overcrowding problems.

Most of the time, electronic devices are used in conjunction with home incarceration where home incarceration programs are used as intermediate punishments. A Kenton County, Kentucky, experiment was undertaken in late 1984 after the Kentucky General Assembly authorized the use of home incarceration with electronic monitoring. With the cooperation of the county jailer and other local officials, thirty-five offenders were placed in the home incarceration program for a cumulative total of 1,702 days of incarceration outside jail. The savings to the county amounted to almost $18,000, in spite of the fact that only thirty-five offenders were accommodated by the home incarceration program (Lilly, Ball, and Wright, 1987:192).

According to one judge interviewed, "Any time you can save a bed-day in jail, you have done something positive for the criminal system" (Lilly, Ball, and Wright, 1987:192). The objectives of the Kentucky Department of Corrections for home incarceration include minimizing incarceration costs to community residents, contributing to jail depopulation, and assisting offenders in accepting their responsibilities through providing for their families and community service. A control group of parolees was compared with the thirty-five persons participating in the home incarceration program. The control group had a 20 percent recidivism rate, whereas only two persons, or 5.7 percent, of the home incarceration participants were convicted of new offenses. In spite of certain methodological problems encountered, the Kenton County project proved successful and suggested the use of such monitoring schemes in the future on a much larger scale (Lilly, Ball, and Wright, 1987:202).

▪ RECIDIVISM

There is a strong nothing-works sentiment among corrections professionals (Orsagh and Marsden, 1985). While this overstates the case against correctional rehabilitation efforts, it does cause practitioners to reexamine existing rehabilitative schemes, probation and parole programs, and other efforts aimed at reducing recidivism. Education, prior record, and the type of offense committed seem most crucial in predicting future crimes (Roundtree, et al., 1984). Race, gender, age at leaving school, employment at the time of the offense, and marital status do not seem to have much predictive utility regarding recidivism. A fourteen-state study of recidivists during the late 1970s showed that they shared several common characteristics according to offenses committed (Wallerstedt, 1984). Property offenders were more likely to recidivate within 3 years than were violent offenders (36.8 percent compared with 31.5 percent). The median recidivism rate for burglary offenses in the reporting states was 43.2 percent, while the median recidivism rate for all offenders was 34.8 percent (Wallerstedt, 1984). Also, the younger the offender at the time of parole, the greater the likelihood of being returned to prison before the end of the 3-year follow-up period.

A study of 2,072 prisoners released from the Texas Department of Corrections in 1983 showed that race had little to do with recidivism, but that females recidivated less often than males (Eisenberg, 1985). Those with higher recidivism rates also had prior offenses, prior offenses as juveniles, problems with drug abuse and alcoholism, and assaultive tendencies.

In an Oregon study, recidivists were more likely to be rearrested for offenses similar to those for which they were formerly doing time (Oregon Crime Analysis Center, 1984). About 32 percent of the 1,782 offenders released from Oregon prisons in 1979 were rearrested within the next 3 years. In Delaware, more disappointing figures have been reported. For example, of 3,257 persons released from Delaware prisons between 1980 and 1982, 51 percent were rearrested, and 75 percent of these arrests occurred within 1 year of the offender's parole (Delaware Executive Department, 1984).

Out of 9,549 offenders released from North Carolina state prisons between 1979 and 1980, 33 percent returned to prison within 36 months of their release (Clarke and Crum, 1985). While several of the services described earlier in this chapter (such as intensive supervision programs, furloughs, and halfway houses) appear to decrease rates of recidivism among released offenders, no program seems to reduce it substantially compared with the traditional probation and parole methods used by supervisory agencies in recent years. Even the amount of time one serves in prison does not appear to affect recidivism rates appreciably (U.S. General Accounting Office, 1985).

Much work is required in the area of devising more effective strategies for dealing with released offenders. Individualized attention and supervision are helpful. Halfway houses, properly administered and operated, are also productive in a rehabilitative sense. Furloughs to restore an offender's pride and show government trust are instrumental in putting a criminal into the right frame of mind for rehabilitation. However, it may eventually come down to the fact that for some offenders, nothing works. Aging helps to reduce one's involvement in criminal behavior, but new crime control methods are needed to make younger offenders refrain from committing crimes. Perhaps the new technology, especially the GOSSlink and Supervisor systems adopted on a wider scale throughout the United States, can act as deterrents (Berry, 1985).

■ SUMMARY

Approximately 2 million offenders are on probation and parole in various jurisdictions in the United States. These probationers and parolees are supervised under a variety of programs by probation and parole officers. Prison overcrowding and crowded court dockets are causing courts and prison officials to reevaluate their sentencing and release priorities.

Probationers are not incarcerated. Rather, they serve their sentences under some form of intensive supervision. Parolees have served some time in prison, but they have had their sentences shortened so that they may serve the remainder of their time under supervision similar to that of probationers. Parole originated in the early 1820s as a way of alleviating prison overcrowding, but in the early days of the United States, prisoners were required to serve their entire sentences in prison.

Probation and parole perform the functions of crime reduction, offender rehabilitation, and alleviation of prison overcrowding; however, it is questionable whether these objectives have been realized in all jurisdictions. A majority of states require that probation and parole officers have at least a bachelor's degree. Some states have no specific minimum educational provisions, and New Jersey requires only that applicants for probation or parole occupations possess a valid driver's license. Major changes in the recruitment practices for probation and parole officers have occurred since 1960.

Various programs for supervising probationers and parolees exist as alternatives to incarceration. These are called intermediate punishments. These programs include intensive supervised probation or parole, furloughs, halfway houses, electronic monitoring, shock probation, and home incarceration. Recidivism rates among probationers and parolees are high, although intensive supervisory programs, halfway houses, and home incarceration reduce recidivism rates compared with more traditional monitoring methods. Increased use of technology in the surveillance of probationers and parolees suggests further reductions in recidivism rates in the future.

KEY TERMS

caseloads

community-based corrections programs

commutation

electronic monitoring

furloughs

halfway houses

home incarceration

house arrest

intensive supervision programs

intermediate punishments

parole

shock probation

work release

QUESTIONS FOR REVIEW

1. Differentiate between probation and parole. How many probationers are there in the United States?
2. Do all states have minimum educational requirements for persons wishing to do probation or parole work? Do any states require educational attainment beyond the bachelor's degree?
3. Why did Tennessee and Louisiana have large increases in their parolee populations between 1983 and 1984?
4. What were the unofficial and official origins of probation in the United States?
5. What was the original reason for instituting parole in United States prisons? About when did parole first occur in the United States?
6. What are good time laws? How do they affect a prisoner's sentence?
7. What is the Latin meaning of *probation?* Discuss briefly the philosophy of probation as it is used today compared with its Latin meaning.
8. Does the use of probation reduce crime? Why or why not?

9. What is recidivism? Do specific programs always reduce it among probationers and parolees?
10. Why are the justice model and treatment model in conflict?
11. Why has there been a systematic increase in the parolee population, the probationer population, *and* the prison population?
12. What is meant by intermediate punishment? What are three intermediate punishment programs?
13. What is an intensive supervision program? Cite two instances where intensive supervision programs have been used in the United States.
14. What is a risk-assessment instrument? What is its purpose? How successful are risk-assessment instruments?
15. What is the furlough plan? How successful are furlough programs?
16. What is a halfway house? What offenders benefit most from halfway houses?
17. What is shock probation?

18. What is home incarceration? Discuss briefly two studies involving home incarceration as an intermediate punishment.

19. What things cause recidivism rates to decline? How effective are intermediate punishment programs at decreasing recidivism rates?

SUGGESTED READINGS

Archambeault, William G., and Betty J. Archambeault (1982). *Correctional supervisory management: Principles of organization, policy, and law.* Englewood Cliffs, NJ: Prentice-Hall.

Braswell, Michael, Tyler Fletcher, and Larry Miller (1985). *Cases in corrections* (2nd ed.). Prospect Heights, IL: Waveland Press.

Maltz, Michael D. (1984). *Recidivism.* Orlando, FL: Academic Press.

McCarthy, Belinda R., and Bernard J. McCarthy (1984). *Community-based corrections.* Monterey, CA: Brooks/Cole.

Scull, Andrew (1984). *Decarceration: Community treatment and the deviant: A radical view* (2nd ed.). New Brunswick, NJ: Rutgers Univ. Press.

Travis III, Lawrence F. (Ed.) (1985). *Probation, parole, and community corrections: A reader.* Prospect Heights, IL: Waveland Press.

In May 1987 Mathias Rust, a 19-year-old from
Hamburg, West Germany, flew a light plane over
500 miles across Soviet territory undetected by the
most sophisticated radar systems in the world.
Commencing his flight in Finland, Rust made a
perfect landing in Moscow's Red Square, amid the
stares of thousands of Soviet shoppers. Rust
claimed that his stunt was done in the name of
peace and that he merely wanted to catch the
attention of Soviet leaders in order to promote
peace. Rust caught their attention, but his flight
earned him a sentence of 4 years in a Soviet labor
camp for malicious hooliganism.

Hooliganism is a catchall crime category in the
Soviet Union. It includes vagrancy, drunkenness,
prostitution, and even juvenile delinquency. While
Rust's age was considered by the Soviet courts as a

JUVENILE JUSTICE, COMPARATIVE JUSTICE SYSTEMS, AND CRIME PREVENTION

mitigating factor, he soundly embarrassed the Soviet government by defeating all the Soviet air defenses with his flight. With the public looking on, Rust took his sentence in grim silence. Less than 2 years later, Rust was released and returned to West Germany.

Part V examines the processing of juvenile offenders in the juvenile justice system. This part discusses some of the recent trends relating to juveniles and delinquency. Crime also varies in definition and quantity among countries throughout the world. Thus, this part directs attention toward the criminal justice systems of three foreign countries for comparisons. Finally, this part raises the general question of what can be done to prevent crime.

Chapter 16 is an in-depth examination of the juvenile justice system. It defines juvenile delinquency and differentiates it from status offenses. Chapter 16 also discusses the frequency of delinquency throughout the United States, including various ways of measuring delinquency. The juvenile justice system parallels the criminal justice system in many respects, although there are several important differences. This chapter highlights these differences. During the past few decades, juveniles have been granted extensive rights previously extended to adults only. The juvenile court has undergone a transformation that has had significant implications for the criminal justice system generally. Chapter 16 describes some of the more important United States Supreme Court cases involving juveniles. Finally, it illustrates several selected problems in juvenile justice, including juvenile violence, drug and alcohol abuse by juveniles, juvenile corrections, juvenile rehabilitation, and delinquency prevention.

Chapter 17 explores the criminal justice systems of the Soviet Union, Canada, and Great Britain. Each of these countries has a different definition of crime, and each criminal justice system operates in ways different from those of the United States. The punishment of offenders in each country varies, and this chapter makes several interesting contrasts with the United States system of criminal justice. Increasingly important is the development of international law, especially in view of the rising amount of terrorism in recent years. Various international agencies exist to combat crimes that affect two or more countries. One such agency is Interpol, which is headquartered in France.

Concluding, Chapter 18 deals with crime prevention and the victims of crime. Can crime be prevented? What alternatives do crime victims have for protecting themselves from criminals? This chapter describes community programs, such as neighborhood patrols, Crime Stoppers, and Operation Identification. Law enforcement agencies also attempt to prevent crime by operating programs to heighten community resident awareness of victimization potential; therefore this chapter describes various strategies for deterring criminals or at least minimizing the incidence of crime.

The Juvenile Justice System

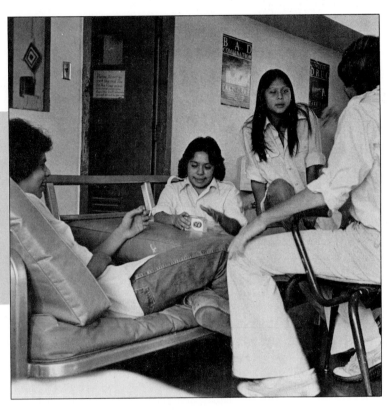

■ INTRODUCTION

One evening in a small suburb of Davenport, Iowa, a 5-year-old girl, Jane, refused to do her assigned chores, was spanked by her father and sent to her room without dinner. She left her room and went into the den where her father kept firearms. She picked up a .38 caliber revolver and walked into the kitchen where her father, mother, and older brother were having dinner. Then, she walked to her father's side, aimed the revolver at his head and pulled the trigger, killing him instantly.

On a bright Sunday afternoon in Indianapolis, Indiana, a farm couple and their daughter drove to the store some miles away for groceries. Left behind at his own request was a 16-year-old boy, James, who had recently been adopted by the couple. James had previously been the target of child sexual abuse by his own parents, who were now in prison. The court had ordered James placed in a foster home, and the farm couple grew to love and care for him very much. In fact, they treated him in every respect as their own son. When the family returned from grocery shopping, James was waiting with two high-powered rifles and a pistol in an upstairs bedroom of the farm home. As the couple and their daughter got out of their car, James shot and killed the entire family.

While both of these scenarios involved homicide, their dispositions were totally different. Jane underwent psychiatric examinations and extensive counseling. She now resides peacefully with her family in a new community and is doing well in school. However, James was apprehended by police and determined by the court to be an adult in the eyes of the law. He is now serving a life sentence in a state penitentiary.

Under the common law, persons under the age of 7 cannot be punished for violating criminal laws (Empey, 1978). In most jurisdictions in the United States, children between the ages of 7 and 18 are considered **juveniles,** or persons who have not achieved the age of majority or their eighteenth birthday (Black, 1979:779). In a third of the states, the upper age limit for juvenile status is either 16 or 17. According to the federal Juvenile Delinquency Act of 1974, *juveniles are persons who have not attained their eighteenth birthday* (18 U.S.C., Sec. 5031, 1989). Federal law defines **juvenile delinquency** as the violation of a law of the United States by a person prior to his eighteenth birthday, which would have been a crime if committed by an adult.

Although significant variations exist between the adult and juvenile justice systems, juveniles are subjected to many of the same experiences faced by adults when arrested for any offense. For example, youthful offenders are apprehended for alleged law violations. They may be taken to jail where their age and identity can be determined. Depending upon the offense(s) alleged, they may be released into the custody of their parents or detained in a juvenile facility. They may be subject to court proceedings, may be formally charged with an offense, and may appear before a juvenile judge or referee. An attorney may defend them. They may be sentenced, depending upon the applicable statutes and juvenile provisions. Ultimately, they will enter some agency associated with juvenile corrections.

This chapter is about the large, bureaucratic apparatus dealing with juvenile offenders, which is known as the juvenile justice system. In all jurisdictions of the United States, there is a juvenile justice system, but this system varies in complexity among jurisdictions. Juveniles who violate laws in New York City are processed differently from juveniles who violate similar laws in a small farming community in Idaho, but all jurisdictions have informal or formal provisions for processing youthful offenders. Generally, the juvenile justice system deals with juvenile delinquency.

■ JUVENILE DELINQUENCY

Because there are significant jurisdictional variations in the juvenile age range, a consistent definition of delinquency applicable to all jurisdictions is difficult to construct. Generally, juvenile delinquency is any illegal behavior or activity committed by a person who is within a particular age range and which subjects him or her to the jurisdiction of a juvenile court or its equivalent. In the legal community, juveniles are referred to as **infants.** A **delinquent child** is an infant of not more than a specified age who has violated criminal laws or engages in disobedient, indecent, or immoral conduct, and is in need of treatment, rehabilitation, or supervision (Black, 1979:385). Delinquent acts include violations of state or local civil or criminal statutes, running away from home, being beyond the control of either one's parents or guardians, or being habitually truant from school or repeatedly violating school rules (Black, 1979:385).

Status Offenses

Status offenses are violations of statutes or ordinances by minors, which if committed by adults would not be considered either felonies or misdemeanors. Some communities have ordinances imposing curfews on persons under a given age. Minors on the streets after 10:00 P.M. are status offenders. An adult would not be penalized for being on the streets after a specific curfew hour for minors. An example of a status offense for an adult is vagrancy (Black, 1979:1264). Other status offenses are running away from home, being incorrigible at either home or school, being habitually truant from school, violating liquor laws, smoking on the school grounds, loitering, and violating a court order (Hahn, 1984; Schneider, 1984b). These infractions place a juvenile within the jurisdiction of the juvenile court, but they are not in the same category as delinquent offenses. Committing robbery or burglary is much more serious than violating curfew or being truant from school.

The Deinstitutionalization of Status Offenses and Net Widening

The United States Office of Juvenile Justice and Delinquency Prevention established by a congressional act in 1974 has promoted legislation designed to narrow the range of

Should this girl be placed on diversion or assigned to community services, where she can receive counseling and specialized attention to meet her needs?

juvenile offenses considered delinquent (Hahn, 1984:182). It encouraged all jurisdictions to limit delinquent acts to violations of federal, state, or local criminal laws. While some jurisdictions have changed their definition of delinquent conduct, many still combine status and delinquent offenders into a catch-all category for legal processing. Thus, status offenders are subject to secure confinement in many jurisdictions, just as a delinquent youth might be securely confined (Schneider, 1984b:410).

Differentiating status offenses from delinquent offenses and treating each class of offender differently is controversial. Eliminating status offenses from the delinquency category and precluding confinement of juveniles in juvenile correction facilities is the **deinstitutionalization of status offenses (DSO).** Some authorities believe that failing to remove minors from juvenile court jurisdiction for committing status offenses and subjecting them to custodial confinement hardens status offenders and increases their likelihood of committing more serious criminal acts (U.S. Senate Judiciary Committee, 1984). Other authorities say that deinstitutionalization of status offenses is pointless and that recidivism rates will remain unaffected regardless of how status offenses are treated legally (Logan and Rausch, 1985).

The principal argument for the juvenile court to retain jurisdiction over status offenders rests on the assumption that delinquent career escalation will occur; that is, if status offenders are left untreated, they will progress to more serious offenses (Rankin and Wells, 1985). However, this argument is challenged by research, which shows that no escalation occurs in jurisdictions where deinstitutionalization has been implemented (Bortner, Sunderland, and Winn, 1985; Datesman and Aickin, 1985; Schneider, 1984a). Yet, no escalation does not necessarily mean that *no* future offenses will be committed. Rather, it means only that the subsequent offenses are no more serious than earlier ones.

A deinstitutionalization program was begun in Connecticut in the 1970s. On the basis of the data examined by researchers for 1977, the primary impact of the DSO program was the diversion of status offenders from the state's only secure facility for juveniles at Long Lane, Connecticut (Logan and Rausch, 1985). The overall detention rate for the juvenile facility remained relatively unaffected, however.

In 1978, Washington passed a divestiture law, which withdrew status offenders from juvenile court jurisdiction. Based on an analysis of 3,200 juveniles in Yakima and Seattle both before and after the legislation, however, deinstitutionalization of status offenses was not successful in removing large numbers of status offenders from juvenile court control (Schneider, 1984). Police officers merely relabeled the youths that they apprehended for various offenses as delinquent and processed them differently than they did in the prereform period. Such relabeling by law enforcement officials created the impression that delinquent acts had more than doubled within a short time period, illustrating how police officers may create crime waves or eliminate them, depending upon the labels they choose to apply to offenses.

On the basis of an extensive analysis of studies investigating the impact of the deinstitutionalization of status offenders, one researcher has concluded that DSO has had little or no impact on recidivism (Schneider, 1984b). However, no adequate test of this particular relationship has been conducted (Schneider, 1984b:427). While the public confinement of status offenders has declined considerably since the mid-1970s, the private confinement of status offenders has increased during the same time period. A number of states, such as Massachusetts and Rhode Island, have contracted with private providers of children's services to confine runaways and other status offenders (Keating, 1984). Deinstitutionalization of status offenses has resulted in (1) **net widening,** or pulling into the juvenile system youths who would not have been involved before and (2) relabeling youths as delinquent who before would have been classified as status offenders, but it has not reduced the overall rate of secure confinement for status offenders (taking into account combined private and public confinement figures), and it has resulted in a general inadequacy of services and juvenile facilities (Schneider, 1984b:411).

Measuring Juvenile Delinquency

Trying to measure the true amount of delinquency is the equivalent of trying to measure the true amount of adult crime. The *Uniform Crime Reports* has numerous methodological inadequacies. If anything, the current delinquency figures for the United States are significant underestimates of the true amount of delinquency. Police officers exercise considerable discretion in determining whether or not to arrest minors for particular offenses. Often, police regard juvenile acts as trivial, and they release youths with stern warnings (Harris, 1986:105; Reiss, 1971). These same youths *could have been* arrested, and if they *had been* arrested and booked, national delinquency figures would obviously be much higher.

For 1985, those under age 18 accounted for 17 percent of all reported felonies and misdemeanors, or about 1.8 million out of 10.3 million reported offenses (U.S. Department of Justice, 1986). Persons under age 15 accounted for about 6 percent of these crimes. Considering index offenses only, persons under 18 accounted for 16.8 percent of all violent crimes, including murder and nonnegligent manslaughter, forcible rape, robbery, and aggravated assault. Persons under 18 also accounted for 34.4 percent of all property crimes, such as burglary and motor vehicle theft.

The most common felonies committed by persons under 18 are burglary and motor vehicle theft or about 38 percent of each. Larceny was the third most frequent felony committed by persons under 18, or about 33 percent. However, persons under 18 accounted for only 8 percent of all homicides and 15 percent of all forcible rapes. In 1985, there were 71,608 curfew or loitering law violations involving persons under 18, and 139,970 runaways were reported. Twenty-five percent of all liquor law violations involved persons under 18.

Self-Reporting of Delinquent Acts

One method of obtaining a more accurate picture of the amount of delinquency in the United States is using self-report surveys (Rowe and Osgood, 1984; Giordano, Cernkovich, and Pugh, 1986). A **self-report survey** is a method whereby researchers ask adolescents or minors directly about various offenses they have committed, regardless of whether they have been arrested or charged with committing those offenses. For a self-report survey, we might enter a cross section of high schools or junior high schools and ask all of the students to respond anonymously to questions about crimes they may have committed. Then we might tabulate and compare these responses with official estimates of delinquency, such as figures reported in the *Uniform Crime Reports.*

Self-reports of delinquent behavior have been utilized by the National Youth Survey Project (Elliot et al., 1983). Between 1976 and 1980, a national probability sample of 1,725 adolescents between the ages of 11 and 17 were surveyed about the extent of their delinquent behavior. Males committed delinquent acts more often than did females. Urban youths were more likely to report delinquency than were rural youths. Generally, the study showed higher rates of delinquency among those surveyed than did official estimates through other sources. Most of those surveyed were involved in some delinquent activity each of the years between 1976 and 1980. However, serious and violent offenses accounted for only a small portion of offenses reported (Elliot et al., 1983).

One flaw of self-reporting delinquency is that juveniles may exaggerate or fantasize about their exploits (Farrington and Tarling, 1985). One survey of teenage smoking behavior among 4,300 students in grades 7–12 conducted in Muscatine, Iowa, showed a discrepancy between self-reported behavior and actual behavior when validated independently by biochemical methods (Akers et al., 1983). For smoking, a biochemical measure of smoking (salinary thiocyanate) can be used in conjunction with self-reports to minimize the deliberate faking of responses that some teenagers might provide.

Regardless of the weaknesses of self-reporting, it is a legitimate alternative to official reports. It may also be used to chart the potential effectiveness of different kinds of delinquency programs. For instance, a federally funded Juvenile Restitution Initiative was established in the late 1970s in various jurisdictions (Griffith, 1983). Participating juvenile delinquents were surveyed in 6-month intervals between 1980 and 1983 to determine whether restitution to their victims had any effect on their behaviors or attitudes. Sites such as Washington, D.C.; Clayton County, Georgia; Ada County, Idaho; Oklahoma County, Oklahoma; and Dane County, Wisconsin, were surveyed. Self-report information showed that restitution groups had lower rates of self-reported reoffending in these jurisdictions than did groups of delinquents who did not participate in the project (Griffith, 1983).

■ THE JUVENILE JUSTICE SYSTEM

The first juvenile court in the United States was created in Illinois in 1899 under the Illinois Juvenile Court Act (McCarthy and Carr, 1980). Prior to the Illinois act, other states tried to establish mechanisms for dealing with juvenile offenders. In 1874, Massachusetts enacted a statute establishing children's tribunals for dealing with children charged with crimes (Hahn, 1984:5), and in 1899, Colorado passed an education law, which created an informal version of today's juvenile court (Hahn, 1984:5; McCarthy and Carr, 1980).

Until these developments occurred in selected jurisdictions, juvenile matters were processed in courts of chancery or equity, which were courts of English origin, dating back to the twelfth century. Such courts were originally created by the king of England and presided over by chancellors or judges appointed by the king. Matters before courts of chancery involved property boundary disputes, trespass, business disputes, and, of course, matters pertaining to children. These courts operated under common law principles and the doctrine of *parens patriae,* which means parent of the country (Black, 1979:1003). The king, through his agents or chancellors, oversaw the welfare of his subjects, especially minors. Several jurisdictions in the United States today have chancery courts to resolve juvenile matters. In many other jurisdictions, however, courts of limited jurisdiction handle only juvenile problems.

An Overview

The uneven development of the juvenile justice system in the United States has occurred for several reasons. First, some jurisdictions have had less need for formal juvenile justice apparatus than have others. Second, some courts have been reluctant to surrender their authority over juvenile matters to more specialized courts. Legislative reluctance to fund specialized juvenile courts has retarded the growth of juvenile justice agencies in some areas. Finally, state and local laws until recently have failed to make express provisions for handling juveniles or to outline their legal rights.

Figure 16.1 is a model of the juvenile justice system developed in 1976 by the National Advisory Committee on Criminal Justice Standards and Goals (National Advisory Committee, 1976:9). The model in Figure 16.1 has been widely adopted in a large number of jurisdictions. While juvenile justice systems vary in complexity among

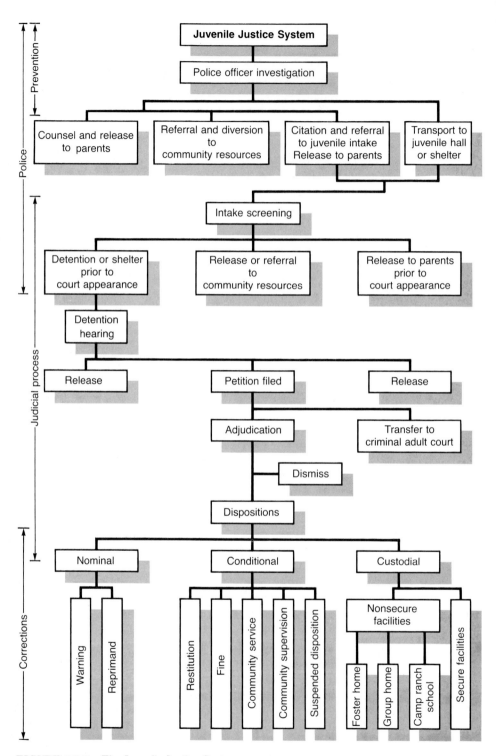

FIGURE 16.1   The Juvenile Justice System

Source: Reprinted from National Advisory Committee on Criminal Justice Standards and Goals, *Juvenile Justice and Delinquency Prevention* (Washington DC: U.S. Government Printing Office, 1976), p. 9.

jurisdictions, this model illustrates the stages through which juveniles are frequently processed from the time they are arrested to their final disposition. There are three stages of the juvenile justice system: (1) prevention and diversion, (2) the juvenile court, and (3) juvenile corrections.

Prevention and Diversion

The prevention and diversion phase of the juvenile justice process involves decisions by both police officers and juvenile intake personnel. Provided that a law enforcement officer makes an arrest of a juvenile suspect instead of a verbal warning and release, one of four things happens. First, the parents or guardians of the arrested youth are notified. For status offenses, youths may be counseled and released to their parents.

A second option is to refer or divert juveniles to community resources, such as residential treatment centers, where they can receive group therapy or counseling (Pierce, 1985). Several states have agencies that deal with special juvenile problems. Missouri's Division of Family Services handles a large number of juvenile referrals and devises particular residential treatment programs for low-risk juvenile offenders prior to any formal court action (Pierce, 1985). A youth's success in either (a) counseling and release or (b) referral and diversion avoids further contact with the juvenile justice system.

If the alleged offense is more serious, however, two remaining options are available to authorities. First, citation and referral to juvenile intake and release to parents may be recommended. This is a temporary release of the juvenile to his or her parents or guardians and is tantamount to bail for an adult offender. At a later date, the juvenile will face an **intake screening,** which is a closer inspection of the juvenile's alleged offense, where a juvenile probation officer or other official determines whether to release juveniles into their parent's custody, detain juveniles in formal detention facilities for a later court appearance, or release them to parents pending a later court appearance. Intake screenings are important because they enable a probation officer to examine closely the facts or circumstances associated with the juvenile's offense. Do the parents appear responsible and capable of controlling the youth's behavior? Does the serious-ness of the offense warrant further legal action? Does the youth appear to be the victim of child abuse? Is the youth mentally retarded? Are there community resources to meet the juvenile's needs as an alternative to court action? Most probation officers try to keep the juvenile out of the juvenile justice process. At this stage, the officers predict the potential risk to society posed by the juvenile offender, but as is the case with any behavioral prediction, there are always errors.

As a result of the Juvenile Justice and Delinquency Prevention Act of 1974, several significant improvements in juvenile detention have been made. Many jurisdictions have provided better services and facilities. The average length of juvenile detention, previously 30 days or longer in some jurisdictions, has been shortened. Also, most jurisdictions now separate juveniles from adult offenders in local jail facilities during the period of the juvenile's detention. Some states continue to engage in controversial juvenile detention practices, however (Dudley, 1983; Keve, 1984; Tomasevski, 1986; U.S. General Accounting Office, 1983).

The diversion of juvenile offenders from further involvement in the juvenile justice system is seen by some as a way of avoiding unfavorable labeling as delinquents and

Police often confine arrested juveniles in jails that are ill-equipped to segregate them from adult arrestees. Many of these temporary holding measures fail to eliminate the potential for adult-juvenile contact and abuse.

ultimately reducing adult criminal justice costs (Anderson and Schoen, 1985; Binder and Geis, 1984; Osgood, 1983). For example, in 1974, the Youth Section of the Dallas (Texas) Police Department established diversion to combat the 50 percent recidivism rates among juveniles (Williams, 1984). Between 1975 and 1982, the program serviced 19,745 youths, and the recidivism rate dropped to 21 percent (Williams, 1984).

In 1981, a juvenile diversion program was implemented in New Orleans, Louisiana, by the New Orleans District Attorney's Office. The program was designed to serve as an alternative to being petitioned and adjudicated as delinquent, and it was targeted at first-offender juvenile felons (Litton and Marye, 1983). The services provided to these diverted juveniles included intensive counseling, parent involvement, restitution to victims, and utilization of certain community services. While the project did not realize its original goals fully, 80 percent of the youths served did not recidivate within 1 year after their release from the program (Litton and Marye, 1983).

Critics of diversion claim that often, net widening occurs (Decker, 1985; Schneider, 1984b). For instance, a status offender service unit was operated in St. Louis, Missouri, in 1977. Between 1977 and 1981, net widening occurred as increasing numbers of juveniles were referred to juvenile court by police and other authorities (Decker, 1985). Given police officers' predominant values, it is unrealistic to expect them to support true diversion programs enthusiastically (Decker, 1985). Apparently, police officers want to retain their discretionary powers regarding status offenders and do not want a status offender service unit telling them how to handle juveniles in the field. One unfortunate consequence of the status offender program in St. Louis was the abuse of police discretion at the expense of the status offenders the program was originally designed to help. Police officers began arresting and detaining juveniles for relatively minor offenses, which would have drawn only verbal warnings and token wrist slaps prior to the establishment of the status offender service unit.

Intake screening results in one of three kinds of dispositions of juvenile cases. In the first instance, juveniles are released to their parents or referred to the appropriate community services for assistance. No further contact with the juvenile justice system takes place. In the second instance, juveniles are released into the custody of their parents prior to a possible court appearance at a later date. In the third instance, juveniles are detained in appropriate juvenile shelters, possibly even jail facilities until formal detention hearings can be held.

A **detention hearing** is a judicial or quasi-judicial proceeding held to determine whether or not it is appropriate to continue to hold a juvenile in a shelter facility (Black, 1979:404). Detention hearings are similar to adult preliminary hearings. The court determines whether there is a factual basis for the offenses alleged and probable cause. If there are insufficient grounds to hold juveniles, they are released, but if probable cause is established that an offense was committed and the particular juvenile committed the offense, the court will usually issue a detention order, whereby the juvenile is detained in a juvenile shelter or other similar facility until an adjudication hearing can be held.

The Juvenile Court

If the detention hearing results in the juvenile's detention in a juvenile facility or if juveniles are temporarily in the custody of their parents as a result of the intake screening, a delinquency petition is filed with the juvenile court by a juvenile officer for an adjudication hearing (Mahoney, 1985). An **adjudication hearing** is a formal proceeding involving a prosecutor and a defense attorney, where evidence is presented and the juvenile's guilt or innocence is determined by the juvenile judge. Essentially, adjudication is the point in the juvenile justice process where a juvenile is either found delinquent or not delinquent (Harris, 1986:112; Krisberg and Austin, 1978:102).

The three main types of cases that reach the adjudication stage are juvenile delinquency, status offenses (sometimes called dependency cases), and child neglect or abuse (Rubin, 1985). Juveniles answer the petition either admitting or denying that they are delinquent. The adjudication hearing resolves this issue. If the finding of the court is in favor of the juveniles, they are released from the juvenile justice system. However, if delinquency is established beyond a reasonable doubt, then a sentence is imposed (*In re Winship*, 1970).

Between the time a delinquency petition is filed and the adjudication hearing is held, as well as during the adjudication hearing, prosecutors may ask the court to waive the juvenile to the adult court. Waiver, or transfer, motions are made in a case where a juvenile has committed an especially severe offense or is within a certain age range. The purpose of a **waiver motion (transfer,** certification) is to transfer the jurisdiction of the juvenile case to criminal court, where the juvenile may sustain adult penalties. If a juvenile has committed murder, the juvenile court cannot impose the death penalty. However, if the juvenile is waived by motion to criminal court, the death penalty may be imposed upon a determination of the juvenile's guilt. (Some jurisdictions in the United States label such waiver proceedings also as bindover, or decline.)

There are three types of waivers: (1) the legislative waiver, (2) the prosecutorial waiver, and (3) the judicial waiver. The **legislative waiver,** or excluded offense provision, compels the juvenile court to remand certain youths to criminal courts because of the specific offenses committed (such as murder) or age considerations. The **prosecutorial waiver** vests prosecutors with the authority to choose whether to

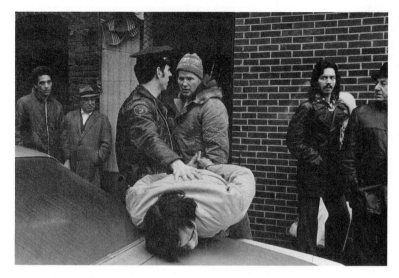

When juveniles are arrested for serious offenses, such as cocaine possession and resale, robbery, murder, and rape, they may be waived, or transferred, to the jurisdiction of the adult court, where they may suffer adult penalties. Any juvenile is entitled to a hearing before being waived to the adult court for processing.

proceed by criminal court or juvenile court processes with juveniles above a specified age (Rubin, 1985:31). The prosecutorial waiver is available only for specified offenses. The **judicial waiver** involves the same decision associated with a prosecutorial waiver, except that the juvenile judge exercises the discretion rather than the prosecutor (Rubin, 1985:32).

In 1985, a defendant's youth prohibited the imposition of the death penalty for a capital crime in eight states (Just, 1985). In thirteen other states, juries had to consider a defendant's youth as a mitigating factor in determining whether or not the death penalty should be imposed if the law violation warranted it (Just, 1985).

By 1982, 14,029 legal executions had occurred in the United States. Of these, 287 were executions of juveniles under age 18 (Streib, 1983). Currently, there is considerable disagreement over whether juveniles should be subjected to capital punishment (Wilson, 1983; Just, 1985). In 1987, the United States Supreme Court agreed to decide whether children as young as age 10 can be sentenced to death. A key case relating to this issue involved William Wayne Thompson, 19, of Oklahoma, a convicted murderer who claimed that imposing the death penalty against minors is cruel and unusual punishment. Thompson was 15 when the slaying occurred and 16 when brought to trial (UPI, 1987). The Supreme Court overturned Thompson's death sentence by a vote of 5 to 3 (Justice Kennedy did not participate) (*Thompson v. Oklahoma,* 1988). In 1989, the U.S. Supreme Court upheld the constitutionality of the death penalty for two youths, Heath Wilkins, of Missouri, and Kevin Stanford, of Kentucky. They were 16 and 17, respectively, when they committed murder. Thus, the U.S. Supreme Court has declared that the Eighth and Fourteenth Amendments prohibit the execution of youths under age 16 at the time their offense was committed.

For many years, juvenile court judges have had extensive powers in granting motions to remand or waive juveniles to criminal court jurisdiction (Osbun and Rode, 1984). However, in the 1970s, many states passed legislation limiting a juvenile court judge's discretion in this matter. In many jurisdictions, state statutes require that juveniles fitting particular criteria be automatically waived to criminal courts (Sagatun, McCollum, and Edwards, 1985).

The 1980 Minnesota legislature established a classification scheme that defined a class of juveniles as unfit for juvenile court treatment (Osbun and Rode, 1984). This scheme identified juveniles on the basis of age (16 and over), the alleged offense and its seriousness, and the record of prior felony offenses (Osbun and Rode, 1984). In 1978, New York enacted a juvenile offender law that provides for automatic criminal court jurisdiction over certain juveniles who have committed serious offenses (Singer, 1985). Together with a number of other states, Illinois enacted similar legislation in 1982 (August, 1981; Reed, 1983; Sagatun, McCollum, and Edwards, 1985).

In New Jersey, juvenile cases waived to the jurisdiction of the criminal courts generally involve violent crimes (New Jersey Division of Criminal Justice, 1985). However, there is evidence that in some jurisdictions, neither the juveniles who are remanded to criminal courts nor their alleged offenses are particularly violent, dangerous, or significant risks to public safety (Bortner, 1986). In a study of 214 juveniles waived to criminal courts in a large western metropolitan county, for instance, the rate of remanding juveniles to criminal courts tripled between 1979 and 1981. However, the rate of delinquency referrals, including major felonies, remained stable during the same period (Bortner, 1986). In this situation, organizational and political factors were primarily responsible for waiver motions. By remanding certain juveniles to criminal courts, juvenile court judges were able to protect their own interests and extend their jurisdiction over the vast majority of juveniles in the county by diverting criticisms of case handling away from their own courts.

There are at least twelve dispositional alternatives available to a juvenile court judge in an adjudication hearing. First, based upon a careful consideration of evidence presented, the judge can dismiss the case outright. The remaining eleven alternatives involve nominal, conditional, or custodial penalties. These are:

1. A verbal warning.
2. A stern reprimand.
3. An order to provide restitution to victims.
4. An order to pay a fine.
5. An order to perform a certain amount of community service.
6. An order to submit to the supervision of some type of community agency on a probationary basis.
7. A sentence and a suspension of it, providing for a term of probation.
8. An order for the placement of the juvenile in a foster home.
9. An order for the placement of the juvenile in a residential center.
10. An order to participate under supervision at a camp ranch or special school.
11. An order to be confined for a specified period in a secure facility.

Juvenile Corrections

The final stage of the juvenile justice system includes several corrections alternatives, ranging from probation to secure confinement. A nominal disposition of a juvenile's case, especially a first offender, will be a warning or reprimand. Going through the process of adjudication and appearing before a judge are sometimes sufficient to frighten a juvenile from committing further offenses.

Conditional dispositions include restitution, fines, community service, and supervised probation. The purpose of imposing either restitution or a fine on the adjudicated delinquent is to hold the juvenile accountable for the wrong committed (Bumsted, 1985; Griffith, 1983). In some jurisdictions, restitution is the preferred method of punishing juvenile offenders, as opposed to some form of secure confinement (Seljan, 1983).

Restitution programs in Clayton County (suburban Atlanta), Georgia, and Dane County, Wisconsin, have reduced recidivism rates among serious juvenile offenders (Schneider and Schneider, 1984; Schneider and Schneider, 1985; Seljan, 1983). In the Georgia study, for example, 258 juvenile offenders were required to make restitution to their victims, either through community service or monetary payments (Schneider and Schneider, 1985). Generally, these youths had significantly lower recidivism rates than did juveniles who received more traditional juvenile court dispositions, such as counseling or secure confinement. Restitution programs of any kind are difficult to implement, however (Schneider, 1985). Some of the problems include determining adequate compensation for emotional as well as financial losses to victims, supervising the restitution programs, and monitoring the juvenile's behavior during the restitution period.

Restitution programs are not without critics. Are the positive results achieved by various restitution programs, such as those in Georgia and Wisconsin, influenced significantly by the inclusion of large numbers of youths considered to be low risks for recidivism? Are only the best risk cases (that is, those normally not considered for incarceration or severe sanctions anyway) targeted for participation in these restitution programs? Another question is whether such programs are merely additional punitive provisions associated with a probationary status. Ohio's experiments with restitution for serious offenders suggest deliberate application to both high- and low-risk offenders, however. Almost all studies show that where restitution programs have been implemented, the programs have helped to reduce recidivism among delinquent youths.

Another conditional alternative is community supervision or probation, where the juvenile is expected to conform to a set of fairly specific behavioral requirements and report regularly to probation officials (Lundman, 1986; Thomson and McAnany, 1984). One interesting probation program is the Sierra II Wilderness Adventure Program, which was begun in 1975 in Virginia Beach, Virginia (Callahan, 1985). Between 1975 and 1985, over 500 youths participated. Results have been favorable, with an 84 percent decrease in delinquent activity, a significant increase in self-esteem and school attendance, and a substantial decline in negative remarks by teachers about the program participants (Callahan, 1985). These youths meet twice a month, attend weekend outings once a month, and participate in a 12-day primitive expedition in the summer months. The program is designed to handle small groups (no more than eleven juveniles per group) and give personalized attention from program officials.

Custodial dispositions imposed at the discretion of a juvenile court judge may include nonsecure and secure confinement. Nonsecure confinement might include assignment of a juvenile to a foster home or group home if there is evidence of child neglect or abuse (Brooks, 1985; Meier, 1985). Evidence presented at the adjudication stage usually establishes the nature of the juvenile's home environment, and the presiding judge, together with other juvenile officials, can select the most appropriate alternative under the existing circumstances.

In 1950, Congress enacted the **Youth Corrections Act,** which expanded significantly the number of sentencing options available to federal district judges (Andreycak, 1983). At that time, judges could impose either probation or indeterminate sentences of up to 6 years for any offender age 22 or under at the time of conviction or adjudication. This was regardless of the length of sentence an adult could receive for committing the same crime. This act was originally intended to provide a number of alternatives to incarceration, which seemed to have little, if any, effect on recidivism among juvenile offenders. The act was repealed in 1984, largely because of the fact that during the intervening years, it did not produce the desired rehabilitative results (Kane, 1985). Most jurisdictions continue to use indeterminate sentencing of juvenile offenders for probation or incarceration (Frost, Fisher, and Coates, 1985). Thus, juvenile court judges have maintained a high degree of flexibility in their general sentencing practices over the last few decades.

Among the nonsecure sentencing alternatives are community-based projects and neighborhood correctional programs that stress services and supervised, but limited, control of the juvenile offenders (Miller and Ohlin, 1985; Pabon, 1985; Sykes, 1982). For instance, a boys' center residential program was created in North County, California, in 1960 as an alternative to secure confinement (Blomberg, 1984). Originally intended as a major juvenile sentencing reform, the center appeared to effectively reduce the number of recidivists among program participants in subsequent years of operation.

Another community-based nonsecure custodial program was the Pine Hills Experiment (also known as the **Provo Experiment**), which was conducted in Provo, Utah, in the 1960s (Empey and Erickson, 1972). Pine Hills was a large home converted into a juvenile treatment facility by local social scientists. Juvenile court judges diverted youths randomly to Pine Hills and placed them under the limited supervision of researchers. These youths would otherwise have been sent to the Utah State Industrial School, a secure confinement facility fashioned after a prison or penitentiary. In the Provo Experiment, juveniles could continue to live at home and go to school, but they were required to report to Pine Hills every day and participate in community cleanup projects and other activities on weekends. Their treatment at Pine Hills consisted of group therapy and self-disclosure sessions, where they attempted to determine the true reasons for their delinquent conduct. The authorities maintained indirect, yet total, control over the youths, because if the juveniles failed to abide by the conditions of the Pine Hills facility they would be immediately removed to the state industrial school. During the years that the Provo Experiment operated, recidivism rates were reduced drastically, and several hundred juveniles appeared "cured" based on the data gathered in intensive follow-ups (Empey and Erickson, 1972; Pabon, 1985).

The most extreme sentence a juvenile court judge can impose by statute is incarceration in a local or state juvenile secure facility for either a determinate or indeterminate period. Many judges regard this alternative as the last resort, and it is usually reserved for the most serious offenders or chronic recidivists. In recent years, some jurisdictions have reported major shifts in juvenile sentencing philosophy from traditional rehabilitative thinking to a just-deserts model (Schneider, 1984c). A 1978 reform in Washington state's juvenile justice system clearly reflects this shift (Schneider, 1984c). Referrals of juveniles to the court by police were increasingly likely to result in incarceration for adjudicated youths over the next several years. However, this major philosophical shift in sentencing has had little impact on recidivism rates. In such states as Utah and North Dakota, there are industrial schools for particularly unruly and delinquent youths (Ehrenkrantz Group, 1985). These schools are secure detention facilities offering a variety of services, including counseling and development of a number of skills. Most states have some form of juvenile detention facility or secure confinement, even if it places juveniles in adult jails for specified periods (Krisberg et al., 1985; Oklahoma Coalition for the Promotion of Alternatives to Jailing Juveniles, 1985).

The California Youth Authority includes secure confinement facilities for juveniles (California Department of the Youth Authority, 1985). As is the case with many adult prisons, there is considerable overcrowding of many of the Youth Authority institutions in California. In response to overcrowding, the Youth Authority has devised the short-term, Planned Re-Entry Program (PREP) for incarcerated juvenile offenders. This program emphasizes counseling, casework, life skills development, and community reentry over a 4- or 5-month treatment period. Two California program sites are the Karl Holton and Ventura schools (California Department of the Youth Authority, 1985). Juveniles who are soon to be paroled are assigned to PREP as a means of facilitating parole adjustment. In this respect, PREP functions much like a halfway house for adult offenders, but with more stringent restrictions.

Interestingly, there was a 24 percent recidivism rate among PREP parolees within the first year of their release between 1979 and 1983, compared with a 28 percent recidivism rate among parolees not assigned to PREP. In spite of this small difference in recidivism rates, Youth Authority officials have been generally satisfied with the cost effectiveness of the program and its results for affecting parole outcomes compared with other methods or approaches. Youth services similar to those provided in California are currently in operation in other jurisdictions, including Ohio (Wiebush, Hamparian, and Davis, 1985).

■ THE LEGAL RIGHTS OF JUVENILES

Historically, juveniles have been subjected to the independent decisions and discretionary whims of juvenile court judges, referees, intake officers, chancellors, and a host of other authorities. The state has traditionally functioned under the *parens patriae* doctrine for looking after the interests of its minors. For decades, the idea of applying constitutional laws to juveniles was unthinkable to many juvenile judges and other officers. No concerted effort to investigate a juvenile's rights under the Constitution took place in the United States until the mid-1960s. At the beginning of this century, efforts to implement a juvenile justice system and establish juvenile courts were sporadic, and only selected jurisdictions, such as Illinois, New York, and Massachusetts, engaged in significant efforts to develop mechanisms for dealing with juvenile offenses in a formal, consistent fashion.

Juvenile delinquency was not recognized as a national social problem until well into the 1950s, although some persons, including J. Edgar Hoover, had attempted to alert the United States about its seriousness as early as 1943 (Gilbert, 1986). An analysis of the cultural history of the United States reveals that the public discovered delinquency during the 2 decades following the end of World War II (Gilbert, 1986). In the 1950s and 1960s, films such as *Rebel Without a Cause, Blackboard Jungle,* and *Twelve Angry Men* portrayed America's youth as violent, gang-affiliated, immoral, and intent on disrupting society's value system. Stereotypical notions of juveniles were fostered, in part, by the post-World War II period where both parents worked at jobs outside the home and teenagers had little or no adult supervision (Gilbert, 1986).

Between 1912 and 1940, the United States Children's Bureau operated to formulate delinquency policy (Rosenthal, 1983). During these years, many interested persons, including a number of child welfare reformers, enthusiastically supported the development and operation of the juvenile court as the most appropriate prevention and treatment structure for delinquents (Rosenthal, 1983). However, during the 1930s, a general disenchantment with juvenile court effectiveness occurred. This was accompanied by the increased use of psychological treatment methods associated with some of our current juvenile rehabilitation programs (Rosenthal, 1983). According to some writers, we are now in the midst of an era of juvenile justice reform (Krisberg et al., 1985).

Not surprisingly, the period 1960–1970 established three important United States Supreme Court precedents regarding the rights of juveniles under the Constitution of the United States. Sometimes referred to as the big three cases of the juvenile justice system, these include (1) *Kent v. United States* (1966), (2) *In re Gault* (1967), and (3) *In re Winship* (1970). *In re* means in the matter of or in the affair of and is applied to

The deinstitutionalization of status offenses in some states has lessened the discretionary powers of police in dealing with loitering youths, truants, and runaways. In past years, loitering could have resulted in an adjudication of delinquency.

cases where there is no adversarial party. Applied to juveniles, this expression is frequently used in law suits where a juvenile's rights are at issue.

Kent v. United States (1966)

In this case, Kent was a 16-year-old male resident of the District of Columbia. He was arrested and charged with robbery, rape, and burglary. Acting on its own authority in Kent's case, the juvenile court waived the matter to a criminal court, and Kent was tried as an adult. It is significant that if he had been tried as a juvenile, the maximum penalty he would have faced was 5 years' incarceration in a juvenile secure facility between his sixteenth and twenty-first birthdays. In being tried for these same offenses as an adult, Kent faced the maximum sentence of the death penalty if convicted. Although the District of Columbia statutes provided for a waiver hearing in juvenile remand motions, there was no hearing in Kent's case. Kent was ultimately convicted.

Kent appealed the juvenile court's decision to waive him to the jurisdiction of a criminal court, and the United States Supreme Court heard his case. The Supreme Court concluded that Kent had been deprived of his rights to due process under the United States Constitution and was not treated fairly. He was entitled to a waiver hearing under the law and did not receive one. The United States Supreme Court reversed Kent's conviction and took the liberty on this occasion of being openly critical of the juvenile court process generally. It said:

> While there can be no doubt of the original laudable purpose of juvenile courts, studies and critiques in recent years raise serious questions as to whether actual performance measures well enough against theoretical purpose to make tolerable the immunity of the process from the reach of Constitutional guarantees applicable to adults. . . . There is evidence, in fact, that there may be grounds for concern that the child *receives the worst of both worlds; that he gets neither the protections accorded to adults nor the solicitous care and regenerative treatment postulated for children.* [Emphasis mine]

The *Kent* case is significant, in part, because it represents a successful challenge of juvenile court discretion. Clearly, statutes in effect governed the conduct of the court concerning a waiver hearing, but the court acted in a cavalier and indifferent fashion and ignored the statute. Although the Supreme Court decision pertained strictly to the right of juveniles to a waiver hearing, it provided the groundwork for subsequent decisions.

In re Gault (1967)

Gerald Gault was a 15-year-old residing in Gila County, Arizona. One day, he and another boy allegedly made an obscene telephone call to a woman, Mrs. Cook, in his neighborhood. Mrs. Cook made a complaint to the police, who then arrested Gault. An investigation of Gault's juvenile record disclosed that he was currently serving a 6-month probationary sentence for stealing someone's wallet. Gault was immediately removed to a children's home in the county and detained. His parents were not immediately notified of his apprehension or confinement. A day later, they were advised that a police officer had filed a petition with the juvenile court alleging Gault's delinquency.

The day following Gault's arrest and detention, Gault, his mother, and the arresting officer appeared before a judge, where Gault was interrogated about the alleged

CRIME BEAT

The Supreme Court agreed Monday to decide whether children as young as 10 can be sentenced to death.

The justices will hear arguments next term in an appeal by William Wayne Thompson, 19, of Oklahoma, a convicted murderer who says imposing the death penalty against minors is cruel and unusual punishment.

Thompson was 15 when the slaying occurred and 16 when brought to trial.

Twenty-seven of 37 states with the death penalty allow executions of people under 18, legal authorities said. Indiana specifically permits execution of children as young as 10 and about a dozen other states have no age limit but consider it a factor in sentencing.

Under Tennessee law, juveniles cannot be sentenced to death.

During the past five years, six states have adopted a minimum age of 18 for executions.

At least 271 juveniles, some as young as 10, have been sentenced to death throughout the history of the United States.

Since the Supreme Court reinstated the death penalty in 1976, no juveniles have been executed, but, due to extended appeals that can take years, there have been three executions of adults who were under 18 when a murder was committed.

In other action Monday, the justices:

□ Agreed to decide the constitutionality of a Virginia law that bars bookstores from displaying best-sellers, health books and other material that might be harmful to children.
□ Agreed to decide if U.S. law bars school districts from immediately removing violent handicapped children from the classroom.

Author's note: In 1989, the United States Supreme Court upheld the constitutionality of the death penalty for those age 16 or 17 at the time they committed capital crimes, such as murder. However, the court ruled in *Thompson v. Oklahoma* (1988) that the death penalty could not be applied in cases where juveniles were under age 16 when they committed capital offenses.

Source: Reprinted with permission from United Press International, "Court to Rule on Death Penalty for Juveniles," *The Knoxville News-Sentinel* (February 24, 1987), p. A2.

---

obscene telephone call. Mrs. Cook was not present at this time. Gault was sent back to the detention facility after this court encounter and released a few days later. When Gault was released, his mother received a letter from the court advising that a hearing on Gault's delinquency would be held in a few days. The hearing eventually was held, again with Mrs. Cook absent. No transcript of the proceedings was made, and the investigating juvenile officer testified that Gault had made an admission to him about making the obscene telephone call. At no time was Gault advised of his rights or told that he could remain silent. When the proceedings ended, Gault was judged by the court as a juvenile delinquent and sentenced to the Arizona State Industrial School until he reached age 21. This meant that he would have to serve 5–6 years in secure confinement. Had an adult been convicted of making an obscene telephone call, he or she would have received a maximum $50 fine and no more than 2 months in jail.

Mrs. Gault hired an attorney, who petitioned the Arizona Supreme Court to overturn the decision of the juvenile court. The Arizona Supreme Court upheld the juvenile court's decision. The case eventually came before the United States Supreme Court. Specifically, Gault's appeal alleged that his basic due process rights had been violated, that he did not have a timely notice of charges against him, that he was not informed of his right to counsel, that he did not have the opportunity to confront and cross-examine his accuser (Mrs. Cook), that he had a right to a transcript of the proceedings and was denied such a transcript, and that he was not advised of his right against self-incrimination or his right to an appellate review.

The United States Supreme Court reversed the Arizona decision in Gault's case and set forth specific constitutional rights for all juveniles. Essentially, the Supreme Court declared that the Fourteenth Amendment due process provision extends to juveniles as well as to adults. It held that all juveniles have the right to adequate written notice of charges against them, the right to representation by counsel, the privilege against self-incrimination, and an opportunity to confront witnesses, particularly when charged with acts that would be criminal and involve possible incarceration if committed by adults. While the Supreme Court decision in Gault's case pertained to the adjudicatory hearing, or trial phase of the juvenile justice process, an extension of the court's decision has been made applicable to other phases of the juvenile justice process as well, such as the arrest stage and detention hearing. This case became the most significant decision affecting a juvenile's constitutional rights.

In re Winship (1970)

Winship was a 12-year-old boy who was found guilty of larceny under a New York Family Court Act. In Winship's case, the court relied upon the preponderance of the evidence against him rather than the standard of beyond a reasonable doubt, which otherwise would be applicable in a criminal case. Until Winship's case was heard by the United States Supreme Court, three standards of proof had been acceptable in various state and local juvenile courts. These were (1) proof of delinquency beyond a reasonable doubt, (2) delinquent by clear and convincing evidence, and (3) delinquent established by a preponderance of the evidence. The United States Supreme Court heard Winship's appeal and reversed the New York court on the grounds that the beyond a reasonable doubt standard had not been employed in deciding Winship's delinquency. It further declared:

> When one assesses the consequences of an erroneous factual determination in a juvenile delinquency proceeding in which a youth is accused of a crime, I think it must be concluded that, while the consequences are not identical to those in a criminal case, the differences will not support a distinction in the standard of proof. First, and of paramount importance, a factual error here, as in a criminal case, exposes the accused to a complete loss of his personal liberty through a self-imposed confinement away from his home, family, and friends. And, second, a delinquency determination, to some extent at least, stigmatizes a youth in that it is by definition bottomed on a finding that the accused committed a crime.

Other Precedent-Setting Juvenile Cases

Several other United States Supreme Court cases have been crucial in affecting a juvenile's constitutional rights over the years. A year after *In re Winship* (1970) was decided, the Supreme Court heard the case of *McKeiver v. Pennsylvania* (1971). McKeiver was a juvenile who appealed to the Supreme Court, alleging that he was denied the right to a trial by jury. In McKeiver's case, the Supreme Court declared that he did not have an absolute right to a trial by jury. Justice Blackmun observed that the mandatory jury trial might "remake the juvenile proceeding into a formal adversary proceeding, thus ending the aim for an intimate, informal protective proceeding" intended by juvenile courts (Vorenberg, 1981:118). The *McKeiver* case did not absolutely eliminate the possibility that a juvenile could be tried by a jury. Some jurisdictions currently make available jury trials to juveniles charged with particularly serious offenses. In other words, the juvenile's right to a trial by jury is purely discretionary among state and local authorities.

In the case of *Breed v. Jones* (1975), Breed was a juvenile who was adjudicated as delinquent in an adjudicatory proceeding in a California juvenile court. Later, he was remanded to a criminal court, the California Superior Court, and tried as an adult for the same offenses alleged in his earlier adjudicatory hearing. He was convicted and sentenced. The United States Supreme Court heard Breed's case and concluded that he had been placed in double jeopardy as the result of the adjudicatory hearing and the conviction for the same offense in criminal court. His Fifth Amendment rights had been violated and his conviction was overturned.

In 1984, the United States Supreme Court heard the case of *Schall v. Martin* (1984). This case questioned the right of New York juvenile officials to detain an accused prior to trial, in violation of the due process clause of the Fourteenth Amendment (Nathan, 1984). The court held that in this matter, pretrial detention is not in violation of the right to due process under the law. However, in order to justify a juvenile's detention, the state must demonstrate a serious risk of further crimes before the return date. Within the context of fundamental fairness, the New York statute authorizing pretrial detention for certain juveniles protected both the juvenile and society.

One particularly sensitive area of concern to juveniles is the Fourth Amendment right against unreasonable search and seizure while in school. In the past, school officials in various jurisdictions have acted haphazardly in conducting warrantless searches of school lockers, desks, and other storage places that students use while in school. In 1985, the search and seizure actions of school officials were challenged in the case of *New Jersey v. T.L.O.* (1985). While the Supreme Court upheld a student's right against unreasonable search and seizure, it held that a student's rights are diminished while in school under the school-student relationship (Dunaway, 1985). It held that school officials, as agents of the state, are authorized to conduct reasonable searches without warrant, provided that a reasonable suspicion exists that a crime has been committed or that illegal contraband is being secreted by a particular student. Blanket locker searches are violative of the Fourth Amendment right against unreasonable searches and seizures, however.

How well do juveniles understand their rights under the law if they are subject to arrest by law enforcement officers? Several studies have examined this question in some detail, and the results are somewhat disappointing. For example, Lawrence (1984) studied a small sample of forty-five juveniles who had appeared before the juvenile court of a major metropolitan area in the southwestern United States. Through questionnaires and interviews with the juveniles, attorneys, and juvenile probation officers, Lawrence discovered that probation officers themselves are often the major source of legal information available to juveniles. Generally, the juveniles interviewed tended to have a very poor understanding of their legal rights. More than a fourth did not remember or understand the police Miranda warning. This raises some serious questions about a juvenile's capacity to make intelligent and informed decisions about waivers of rights and consent to police interrogation (Lawrence, 1984).

If juveniles are arrested and are asked to waive their rights and submit to police interrogation, under what circumstances is it valid to accept the juveniles' waiver of rights (for example, to an attorney and to refuse to answer questions)? Custodial interrogations involve a number of important rights for adults. Should these same rights be extended to juveniles? In *Fare v. Michael C.* (1979), the United States Supreme Court has provided a totality of circumstances test of the validity of juvenile waivers of constitutional rights. In this case, a juvenile disclosed some incriminating information about an offense in the absence of parental guidance or consent (Shaffner, 1985). The United States Supreme Court ruled that considering the totality of circumstances surrounding the juvenile's waiver of his constitutional rights, his disclosures were admissible in court later. In short, considering all circumstances, he knowingly gave up his right to remain silent and to obtain an attorney before questioning. Currently, appellate courts use the totality of circumstances test in determining the permissible-ness of juveniles' admissions and confessions.

In 1982, a California case was heard concerning whether a parent can be separated from a juvenile suspect prior to a confession (Gonzalez, 1982). *In re Myron* (1982) concerned a juvenile who was arrested and was read his rights by police with his mother present. Myron said that he understood his rights and would speak to the officers. At that point, he seemed uneasy with his mother in the room, and the officers asked her to leave. After she left, Myron made a full confession of his crime to police. Later, Myron appealed on the grounds that the separation from his mother made the confession inadmissible in court. A higher California court rejected his appeal. The court held in his case that "the purpose of a parent's presence, when requested, is to assist the juvenile in understanding his or her rights and in making a decision to waive those rights" (Gonzalez, 1982). Once that decision had been made, the parent's presence is no longer necessary to the protection of the juvenile's rights.

In recent years, the American Bar Association (ABA) has established a Juvenile Justice Standards Project (Green, 1984). This project has resulted in an ABA recommendation that the rights of minors be protected by legislative action in each state by narrowly defining juvenile court jurisdiction. There appears to be a trend toward granting greater autonomy to juveniles in legal matters (Green, 1984). Courts have increasingly requested guidance concerning the maturity and capacity of juveniles in their right to choose parents, to act as witnesses, and to choose medical interventions (Green, 1984; Ream, 1985).

■ SELECTED PROBLEMS IN JUVENILE JUSTICE

Some of the major issues confronting the juvenile justice system have already been discussed. A continuing issue is whether to deinstitutionalize and separate status offenders from the jurisdiction of the juvenile court. Another issue is whether to divert juvenile offenders to community projects and services as alternatives to adjudication and secure confinement. For each of these issues, there are proponents and opponents. Court officials and judges are often reluctant to relinquish control over status offenders (Schneider, 1984a). By the same token, some researchers argue that status offenders are in a class different from juveniles who commit misdemeanors and felonies and that as a result, status offenders should be distinguished from juvenile delinquents (Bortner, Sunderland, and Winn, 1985; Rankin and Wells, 1985).

Diversion is viewed as too lenient on juvenile offenders and not necessarily living up to its rehabilitative potential (Polk, 1984). Some critics say that a certain amount of net widening occurs (Decker, 1985). The just-deserts proponents favor making juvenile offenders go through the rigors of the juvenile justice system to make them more accountable to the persons they victimize. Those in favor of diversion argue that by avoiding formal contact with the juvenile justice system, juveniles who commit minor or status offenses are less likely to be labeled as delinquent or to develop delinquent self-definitions (Anderson and Schoen, 1985; Binder and Geis, 1984; Osgood, 1983).

A third issue is the waiving of a juvenile to the jurisdiction of a criminal court. The primary reason for transferring a juvenile's case to criminal court is that the juvenile is not amenable to treatment in the juvenile justice system (Sagatun, McCollum, and Edwards, 1985). In a criminal court, a juvenile offender is subject to more severe penalties for particularly serious offenses committed, but not everyone is in favor of motions to transfer juveniles from juvenile court jurisdiction for a variety of reasons, including both financial and social (Bortner, 1986; Reed, 1983).

Additional concerns of juvenile officials and other persons interested in the juvenile justice system are (1) female delinquency, (2) juvenile violence and violent offenders, (3) juvenile drug use, (4) the state of juvenile corrections, (5) juvenile rehabilitation, and (6) delinquency prevention. This list is not exhaustive, but it includes some of the more important areas of interest to researchers.

Female Delinquency

Interest in female delinquency has risen sharply in recent years among justice professionals (Ageton, 1983; Bowker and Klein, 1983; Campbell, 1984). Some persons say this is because of growing numbers of female delinquents or greater involvement of females in delinquent activities. The women's movement supposedly has generated several significant changes in both the quality and quantity of female juvenile offenses (Curran, 1984). The alleged escalations of female delinquency are also linked with allegations that juvenile delinquency is increasing generally. By citing statistical compilations of delinquency rates in various jurisdictions, the Office of Juvenile Justice and Delinquency Prevention has justified a national crackdown on juvenile delinquency. For example, the Maryland Department of Corrections established an SOS (See Our Side) juvenile "aversion" program to curb the rising tide of crime among juveniles (Mitchell and Williams, 1986). In Prince George's County, Maryland, juvenile delinquency purportedly rose 26 percent between 1981 and 1983, and alarmists reacted by formulating SOS.

However, on a national scale, little evidence supports these assertions. During the period 1974–1986, the proportion of juvenile delinquency has not increased; instead, it has remained fairly constant (Stapleton, 1987), and only a fourth of all juvenile delinquency is attributable to females (Curran, 1984). Some say the rising number of female delinquents is pure fiction (Curran, 1984). The influence of political policy changes and the election of so-called law-and-order district attorneys in various jurisdictions influence juvenile arrest statistics and trends.

In Philadelphia, Pennsylvania, three political-legal periods have been identified between 1960 and 1980. In the period 1960–1967, a paternalistic philosophy prevailed, during which female delinquents were harshly treated by juvenile courts for their own good. In the period 1968–1976, a due process orientation existed, which emphasized the legal rights of juveniles stimulated by the case of *In re Gault* (1967). Finally, a third period, 1977–1980, was characterized as a "law and order" phase, during which the juvenile court adjusted to the new conservatism of the 1970s (Curran, 1984). Thus, growing female delinquency is more a function of legal and political shifts than growing numbers of females committing delinquent acts.

Other evidence that female delinquency is not increasing in an analysis of data from the National Youth Survey, which involved nearly 2,400 adolescents and disclosed that the incidence of serious female delinquency appears to decline with age. Furthermore, females ages 15–17 in 1980 were significantly less involved in delinquency than were their peers in 1976 (Ageton, 1983). The typical female juvenile offenses include primarily (1) property crimes, such as shoplifting; (2) sex offenses, such as prostitution; and (3) various status violations, including runaway behavior and truancy (Stewart and Zaenglein, 1984). Violent offenses, such as homicide and aggravated assault, among female juveniles are relatively rare (Russell, 1985; Sampson, 1985; Weisberg, 1984, 1985).

Juvenile Violence and Violent Offenders

The National Crime Survey and *Uniform Crime Reports* have indicated that violent juvenile crime increased between 1950 and 1975. Between 1960 and 1975, for example, juvenile arrests rose about 300 percent, more than twice the adult rate (Strasburg, 1984). Although juveniles constituted only 20 percent of the nation's population in 1975, they accounted for 43 percent of all arrests for all index offenses. Since 1975, however, the rate of juvenile crime has either remained steady or has decreased in various index categories (Strasburg, 1984).

In 1985, juveniles accounted for 17 percent of all violent crime arrests and for 34 percent of all property crime arrests. This represents a significant downward trend compared with 1975 figures (U.S. Department of Justice, 1986). A growing crime among juveniles, however, is arson. In 1985, 41 percent of all arson arrests involved persons under age 18 and 26 percent of all arson arrests involved persons under age 15. Interestingly, the frequency of arson arrests for juveniles peaks at age 15 and declines rapidly for subsequent years. Some mental health research reveals that young arsonists either don't know the seriousness of their actions or seek to cause damage, injury, or even death (Karchmer, 1984).

Perhaps the incidence of juvenile violence that peaked in 1975 partially accounts for the increased frequency of remand or waiver motions by prosecutors to pass violent juvenile offenders along to criminal courts, where they can be punished more severely. These actions are usually based on the theory that if these juveniles are not punished severely, they will progress to more violent crimes or repeat their previous violent behaviors (Lab, 1984; Rudman et al., 1986), but studies of juvenile violence reveal that often, these youths do not repeat their violent offenses. Usually, these offenses have been triggered by family incidents, abuse of drugs or alcohol, or psychological disorders

CRIME BEAT

Officials hope to have a program going in nine months to curb repeat juvenile criminals.

About 40 officials of city, county and state agencies spent this week working on a plan to implement the Serious Habitual Offender Comprehensive Action Program (SHOCAP). Friday, they presented a timetable that calls for the program to operate by May 31, 1987.

Knoxville Police Lt. Phillip Keith said police analyzed data and found a small number of juveniles in Knoxville account for a large amount of the crime.

Studying the criminal records of 977 juveniles, they found that 60 had been arrested five times or more, 33 had been arrested five times within the past 12 months—twice for a felony. Of the 33, 22 also had at least one charge of a violent crime.

Representative Maria Peroulas, who attended the seminar Friday, said she was shocked at the extent of juvenile crime and would propose legislation that would allow the criminal record of a serious habitual offender to follow that person after the age of 18 into adult courts.

Most think it will take about two years to see the SHOCAP program in full sway. It is intended to identify serious habitual juvenile offenders and coordinate the agencies that deal with them in taking action. Officials with the Knoxville Police Department, Knox County Sheriff's Department, Knox County Schools, Department of Human Services, Department of Corrections, Knox County Juvenile Court and the Knox County Attorney General's office are involved in the program.

Once these juveniles are tagged, they are to be singled out for special treatment. Prosecutors will ask for stiffer penalties when they come before juvenile court. Those not incarcerated would be placed under the strict supervision.

"I think the program is a good idea, but people must realize it is not going to solve juvenile crime. These kids are going to be back in the community eventually," said Jim Keebler, Knox County Juvenile Court director.

Juvenile Court Judge Carey Garrett said he believes the program is still a good idea, though, because it should reduce crime and give citizens some extra protection.

Keebler and Judge Garrett believe the court will probably be picked as responsible for keeping records on the SHOCAP offenders. The federal government has allocated no funds for the program other than those to pay for the weeklong training seminar. The Juvenile Court officials believe that extra personnel may need to be hired or extra computer equipment bought to handle the record-keeping.

Criteria for defining the juveniles will have to be set. Knoxville police officer Ken Fralick said authorities will have to be extremely careful about deciding a youth is a serious repeat offender.

"We're putting a label on a kid. We'd better have our ducks in a row before we do it," he said.

Fralick said he didn't think officials would have great difficulty making cases against most of the juveniles they will target.

"We're not talking about kids that have had a little trouble with the law two or even three times. We are talking about dangerous criminals who have robbed, burglarized, even raped or killed," he said.

Once juveniles tagged as serious habitual offenders come before the law, judges would be asked by SHOCAP agencies to hand down lengthier sentences.

Garrett said he thinks this is a good idea, but he believes it would be even more effective if there were a regional correctional center where they could be sent.

"They need to be close enough so their families can be involved in the rehabilitation program. It doesn't do much good to try to rehabilitate a kid if you put him or her back into an environment that might be part of the problem," Garrett said.

Juveniles not considered dangerous enough to need incarceration would be placed under strict probation programs. Garrett said this would probably be done through a program at the Helen Ross McNabb Center where a counselor would work with a small number of juveniles, checking on them throughout the day.

Keith said the long-term aim of the program is the revitalization of downtown Knoxville, by making some of its neighborhoods more livable.

"This program is one part of the Crime Prevention Program for Knoxville. We want to get back control of some neighborhoods so people will want to move into the inner city," Keith said.

Source: Reprinted with permission from Ed Marcum, "Repeat Offenders: Program Planned to Identify Juveniles Often Involved in Crime," *The Knoxville News-Sentinel* (August 29, 1987), p. B6.

CRIME BEAT

Greeneville, Tennessee. Today's session of Ginger Turnmire's trial on charges she killed her parents will begin with the 15-year-old taking the witness stand, according to her attorney.

Kidwell King Jr. said the identity of the "Charles Manson type" man whom King alleges is the real murderer will be revealed.

King's defense of the girl has revolved around a man who appeared "from nowhere" at the Turnmire home in search of drugs. King said this man murdered J. R. and Velma Turnmire and coerced their daughter into admitting the slayings.

The prosecution presented witnesses who testified that Ginger admitted to friends and to authorities that she shot her parents.

State prosecutors rested their case Tuesday after Greene County Criminal Court Judge James E. Beckner refused to allow the testimony of a ballistics expert.

Prosecutors had called Dr. A. M. "Buster" Brown, from Walters State Community College, to reconstruct where the murder weapon was fired and the sequence of events involved in the slaying of the Turnmires.

King objected to the witness, saying prosecutors waited too long to do the ballistics test. He said it would be impossible to accurately re-create the murder scene since the bed, which Brown was using as a reference point, had been dismantled. After a lengthy discussion outside the jury's presence, Beckner agreed with King.

Tuesday's testimony revolved around events which occurred after the shooting of the Turnmires. Several teenagers, who reportedly saw Ginger at Tweed's Arcade after the shooting, testified she came to the arcade seeking help.

"She offered me $500 and 300 Valiums to help her," said Fred Hawkins. "Ginger told me she shot her parents. Then she told me how she did it. Her mother was in the bedroom when she shot her. Then Ginger said when her father came into the hallway to see what happened she shot him too," he said.

Kimberly Jo Showman, a girlfriend who Ginger reportedly called that night, recounted the same basic story about the shooting. "Ginger called me and told me what happened . . . she said her mother looked up at her once after she had been shot and said 'I love you Ginger,' " the girl said.

The prosecution entered the song "Scene of the Crime" by the rock group Ratt into evidence Tuesday. Prosecutors said the song and its lyrics related to Ginger's allegedly being told that J. W. Turnmire was not her natural father.

The song deals with infidelity and involves a man catching his girlfriend in bed with another man. The lyrics say "I got me a weapon . . . got me a gun . . . I think you've been caught at the scene of the crime . . . you've been lying to me, and that's a felony."

Investigators said the tape was on the family stereo when they arrived to investigate the slayings. In a statement to police, Ginger said the lyrics of the song were running through her head all day the day her parents were killed.

The woman Ginger alleges told her that J. W. Turnmire was not her father testified Tuesday that she did not remember the conversation. Susie Tipton, a cousin, testified she was "drunk" on the night the alleged conversation took place. She said she could not remember anything related to that evening.

Bill Solomon, chief detective for the Greene County Sheriff's Department, testified about devil worship rumors that spread around the county after the Turnmire shootings. Solomon said after the shootings occurred he attended a class on the subject in Florida. "I learned most of the talk surrounding this kind of activity is actually related to drug use." He suggested that devil worship was used to cover up drug activities.

Before Tuesday's recess the defense presented one witness—Wilma Hunt, Velma Turnmire's sister. She testified that Ginger had never spoken harshly or threatened her parents in her presence.

Source: Reprinted with permission from P. D. Little, "Teen Accused of Killing Parents to Take Stand," *The Knoxville News-Sentinel* (January 28, 1987), p. A8.

that can be dealt with therapeutically (Geller and Ford-Somma, 1984; Mathias, DeMuro, and Allinson, 1984). Delinquent gang violence is also prevalent in various cities throughout the United States (Maxson, Gordon, and Klein, 1986; Spergel, 1986).

A Wisconsin study conducted in 1980 showed, for example, that of 265 cases of juvenile offenders investigated, the number of chronically violent juveniles was quite small (Youth Policy and Law Center, 1984). Only 3 percent of these juveniles had been arrested more than two or three times for violent acts, and the probability of committing new violent crimes did not increase with the number of arrests. Although juvenile courts have been widely criticized in recent years for their supposedly lenient handling of violent juvenile offenders, juvenile judges at the 1984 meeting of the National Council of Juvenile and Family Court Judges recommended overwhelmingly to emphasize rehabilitation as the primary goal of the juvenile court (National Council of Juvenile and Family Court Judges, 1984).

Simply remanding or waiving a serious juvenile offender to a criminal court does not automatically result in incarceration and severe punishment, however. For example, in 1980, Oregon juvenile courts remanded ninety-nine juveniles to criminal courts for processing (Heuser, 1985). These cases involved felonies, such as homicide, rape, robbery, burglary, larceny, motor vehicle theft, and arson. Of the juvenile cases remanded, sixty-eight juveniles were convicted, but only thirty-seven of these were incarcerated (Heuser, 1985). In addition, predictions of further juvenile violence based upon previously demonstrated violent behavior have been frequently criticized (Fisher, 1984). Experimental treatments and therapeutic intervention techniques have had mixed results. It is likely that clinical and legal issues pertaining to the prediction of juvenile violence will continue to be hotly debated in future years, unless a more effective solution to curbing juvenile violence can be discovered (Keith, 1984).

Juvenile Drug Use

About a fourth of all liquor law violations in 1985 were by persons under age 18. About 12 percent of all drug arrests in 1985 involved juveniles as well (U.S. Department of Justice, 1986). Drug arrest figures for 1976 involved only 3 percent who were juveniles, but national figures also reveal that in 1980, for example, over 40 percent of all illicit drug users were also serious delinquent offenders (Elliott and Huizinga, 1984). Drinking and illicit drug use are frequently associated with both minor and major juvenile offenses (Kandel, Simcha-Fagan, Davies, 1986; White, Johnson, and Garrison, 1985). In 1984, the Practitioner's Conference on Juvenile Offenders with Serious Drug, Alcohol, and Mental Health Problems was held in Washington, D.C. Promising strategies for dealing with juvenile alcohol and drug abusers included (1) intensive individualized treatment of serious delinquents with serious mental disorders in secure confinement, (2) implementation of case management programs to integrate community resources into a comprehensive system, and (3) community- and school-based intervention programs (Juvenile Justice Resource Center, 1985). Diversion, prevention and educational programs in schools, and selective prosecution of more violent juvenile offenders have also been recommended on a national scale (Arthur D. Little, 1984).

CRIME BEAT

Though rising only slightly since 1980, suicides among 15- to 19-year-olds have tripled in the last quarter-century. At greatest risk are adolescents who have experienced bitter custody battles, violent homes or a recent death in the family.

Warning Signs

☐ Preoccupation with pain, death or suicide
☐ Giving away prized possessions
☐ Loss of interest in schoolwork or favorite activities, such as participation in athletics
☐ Erratic sleeping patterns and appetite loss
☐ Use of drugs or alcohol
☐ Sudden personality change
☐ Frequent irritability or unexplained crying
☐ Impulsive or reckless behavior

Source: From NEWSWEEK March 23, 1987 and © 1987 Newsweek, Inc. All rights reserved.

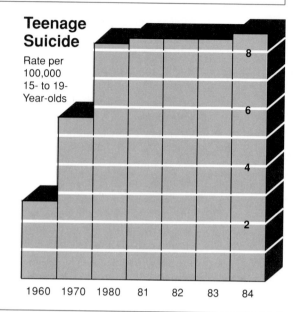

Teenage Suicide

Rate per 100,000 15- to 19-Year-olds

1960 1970 1980 81 82 83 84

Juvenile Corrections

In some jurisdictions, a juvenile's perceived severity of punishment appears to be inversely related to subsequent delinquency (Paternoster and Iovanni, 1986). Incarceration or secure confinement is the most severe form of punishment to be inflicted upon juvenile offenders. Fines, restitution, and various rehabilitative strategies not involving incarceration certainly affect one's propensity to commit further delinquent activities, but incarceration is threatening to anyone, especially juvenile offenders. Like adult corrections, juvenile corrections involves an array of programs and alternatives, ranging from diversion and supervised probation to secure confinement. One problem that many jurisdictions in the United States face is where to confine juvenile offenders. Until recent years, a majority of jurisdictions confined juvenile offenders in adult jails or other adult facilities. In many instances, no attempt was made to separate adult and youthful offenders. Currently, most jurisdictions have separate juvenile facilities, although many of these facilities are grossly inadequate for juvenile offender rehabilitation (Ehrenkrantz Group, 1985; Kansas Juvenile Jail Removal Impact Study Committee, 1984; Virginia Assembly, 1984).

Overcrowding characterizes many juvenile detention centers and secure confinement facilities (Kane, 1985; Krisberg et al., 1985). Approximately 500,000 juveniles enter one form of detention or another every year (Loveless, 1987). Responses to overcrowding are increased use of probation or parole. Another controversial strategy is the privatization of juvenile corrections facilities (Field, 1987). Juvenile facility contracting has occurred in several jurisdictions, involving private organizations such as the Correction Corporation of America (Field, 1987). Such private enterprises have eased juvenile secure confinement overcrowding to some degree.

Juvenile Rehabilitation

Finding the right rehabilitative program for juveniles is a juvenile justice problem closely associated with other corrections issues. Many experimental programs have been tested over the years, but most have not achieved their original, optimistic goals. Primary and secondary school law-related curriculum projects were undertaken between 1979 and 1983 in California, Michigan, and North Carolina. The goals included instructing the students on law-related topics, personal responsibilities and the rights of others, and constitutional rights and guarantees. However, the teachers in these programs did not have the technical knowledge or expertise to present the topics effectively. The lesson objectives were vague, teachers were complacent in their relations with the students, and no outside legal consultants were used to bolster the program effectiveness. The programs failed to positively affect the juvenile participants (Social Science Education Consortium, 1983).

Some consideration has been given to wilderness experience programs involving adult and juvenile outdoor experiences for curbing recidivism among delinquents (Clagett, 1987; Winterdyk and Griffiths, 1984), but a general lack of coordination between the program planners, coordinators, and staff has frequently led to disappointing results. Over fifty different kinds of programs provide specialized services, including reentry planning (for incarcerated juvenile offenders), academic or vocational education for violent offenders, mental health counseling, and education for drug and alcohol abusers (Arthur D. Little, Inc., 1984). Some researchers argue that the most promising intervention strategies for dealing with chronic juvenile offenders include the following features: (1) opportunities for each youth to overcome adversity and experience success; (2) facilitation of bonds of affection and mutual respect between juveniles and their guardians or parents; (3) frequent, timely, and accurate feedback for

The upsurge of delinquent gangs in the late 1940s and 1950s was an important issue in most communities. Juvenile gangs would control vast turfs (territories) and rumble (fight with other gangs) for political control. J. Edgar Hoover, Director of the FBI, took a personal interest in preventing delinquency during this period. He believed that controlling delinquency would eventually lessen the incidence of adult crime.

both positive and negative behavior; (4) a reduction or elimination of negative role models and peer support for negative attitudes or behavior; (5) requirements that juveniles recognize and understand the thought processes that rationalize negative behavior; (6) opportunities for juveniles to discuss family matters and early experiences in a relaxed, nonjudgmental atmosphere; and (7) adaptation of the sequence and amount of exposure to the program components to the needs and capabilities of each participating youth (Greenwood and Zimring, 1985).

Often, the policies intended to confine securely these juveniles for greater periods of time are troublesome because they don't decrease recidivism. Furthermore, graduates of traditional training schools in various states continue to commit high percentages of crimes (Greenwood and Zimring, 1985). Finally, much criminal behavior among juveniles is traceable to inadequate schools and other community resources.

Delinquency Prevention

The first community-based delinquency prevention program in the United States was the Chicago Area Project, which was implemented by Clifford Shaw in 1934. The project was originally targeted to serve juveniles with high delinquency potential: lower-class, inner-city youths and slum or ghetto dwellers, where rates of truancy were high and crime among juveniles flourished (Shaw, 1929; Shaw and McKay, 1972). The Chicago Area Project provided a variety of services to inner-city youths, including several juvenile recreational centers, supervisory staff to work with these youngsters, and other programs, but Shaw's focus upon such a limited sector of society drew criticism from much of the social scientific community. The primary criticism he received was a failure to recognize that delinquency was prevalent in other socioeconomic strata and suburban areas and that these areas were deserving of attention as well. In spite of this criticism, Shaw's work has been regarded as effective in the long-term arresting of delinquency in selected urban areas (Schlossman et al., 1984).

Believed to be the most effective deterrent to delinquency is the threat of incarceration, but incarcerating delinquent offenders is an ineffective deterrent to further delinquency when the recidivism rates of parolees are reviewed. Experiments with shocking juveniles in various ways about the seriousness of their offenses often backfire. For instance, the Honolulu (Hawaii) Police Department created a truancy detail in 1981–1982. This detail was assigned the task of seeking out truants, taking them into custody, and returning them to school (Ikeda, Chesney-Lind, and Kameoka, 1985). Being picked up by police for truancy would ordinarily be a shocking experience for a young truant, but in the Honolulu case, most of the students' grades failed to improve after being picked up for truancy. The antitruancy program had absolutely no effect on official delinquency behaviors among the apprehended status offenders. In fact, truancy *increased* for these truants after their exposure to the program (Ikeda, Chesney-Lind, and Kameoka, 1985).

Popular delinquency prevention programs expose elementary and secondary school students to antidelinquency educational messages (California Office of Criminal Justice Planning, 1984; National School Boards Association, 1984). In certain instances, particularly troublesome juveniles have been identified by school authorities as prime candidates for juvenile delinquency. These students have been uprooted from their classes and subjected to certain educational experiences by local police, probation officers, and other authorities, but there are serious ethical questions about such practices. First, attempts to forecast delinquent youths have been largely unsuccessful. Furthermore, the labeling that such selective measures inspire (that is, "We think you are a predelinquent!") appears to be counterproductive (Williams and Williams, 1987).

The programs that seem to work best at preventing future delinquent activity involve diversion of juvenile offenders to supervised, community-based services. Currently, antidelinquency educational efforts reduce the vulnerability of juveniles to certain crimes. Such programs tend to stress personal safety, property protection, and responsible behavior (California Office of Criminal Justice Planning, 1984).

■ SUMMARY

The juvenile justice system parallels the criminal justice system in several respects. Juveniles are arrested and booked. Depending upon the seriousness of offense, they may be released to the custody of their parents or detained. Minor offenses are status offenses, in contrast with more serious delinquency violations, which are equivalent to felonies or misdemeanors.

The true amount of juvenile delinquency in the United States is unknown. Juveniles under age 18 are believed to account for about 31 percent of all index offenses reported by the *Uniform Crime Reports*. Self-reporting of delinquent acts not detected by police shows delinquency to be much higher than official figures suggest.

The juvenile justice system consists of prevention and diversion measures, the juvenile court, and juvenile corrections. An intake hearing is held prior to a formal adjudication of a juvenile's status as a delinquent. Some of the more serious juvenile offenders are detained for adjudication, while others are placed on bond and released to the custody of parents. For certain youths, a prosecutor may recommend or move to waive the juvenile to the jurisdiction of a criminal court. This is usually, though not always, reserved for the most serious or violent offenders. The juvenile court is a formal proceeding where a juvenile is adjudicated as either delinquent or nondelinquent. Adjudication as delinquent results in a number of correctional alternatives, ranging from a verbal warning, to community service, to formal secure confinement for a specified period.

Juveniles have rights as the result of several significant cases, including *In re Gault* (1967) and *Kent v. United States* (1966). These United States Supreme Court decisions gave juveniles rights equivalent to adults, including the right to counsel, the right to confront witnesses, and the right to due process.

The problems in juvenile justice include the issue of deinstitutionalization of status offenses; the issue of remanding juveniles to the jurisdiction of the criminal court; female juvenile offenders; juvenile drug use; juvenile violence; determining the effectiveness of various nonincarcerative alternatives, detention and secure confinement, and diversion programs; and delinquency prevention.

KEY TERMS

adjudication hearing

deinstitutionalization of status offenses (DSO)

delinquent child

detention hearing

infants

intake screening

judicial waiver

juvenile delinquency

juveniles

legislative waiver

net widening

parens patriae

prosecutorial waiver

Provo Experiment

self-report survey

status offenses

transfer

waiver motion

Youth Corrections Act

QUESTIONS FOR REVIEW

1. Who are juveniles? Is there a consistent definition of a juvenile in all jurisdictions? What are some exceptions?

2. Define *juvenile delinquency*. Differentiate between status offenses and delinquency.

3. What is deinstitutionalization of status offenses? Is everyone in favor of the deinstitutionalization of status offenses? Why or why not? What are some of the arguments favoring deinstitutionalization of status offenses? What are some arguments opposing it?

4. How much juvenile delinquency is in the United States? What is the amount of delinquency as measured by the 1985 arrest figures for the *Uniform Crime Reports?*

5. What is a self-report survey? What is its purpose? How does it compare with official delinquency reports?

6. What are the three major components of the juvenile justice system? Describe each briefly and the functions it serves.

7. What is the doctrine of *parens patriae?* What was this origin of this doctrine?

8. What is an intake screening? What is its purpose? What are three alternatives that may occur as the result of an intake screening?

9. What is meant by adjudication? What does an adjudication hearing accomplish?

10. What is a detention hearing? Under what circumstances is it used?

11. What is the purpose of a remand order or a waiver motion? What is the punitive aim of a waiver motion?

12. What was the Provo Experiment? What were some of its objectives? Was the experiment successful?

13. Identify three major United States Supreme Court cases dealing with the legal rights of juveniles. In each of these cases, identify the major issue(s) involved.

14. What was the landmark case involving the legal rights of juveniles? Why is it considered the landmark case?

15. What is the incidence of female delinquency in relation to male delinquency? What offenses typify female delinquency?

16. Are delinquent acts and alcohol or drug abuse related? What evidence exists to support such a relationship?

17. What are two problems associated with juvenile corrections, especially the secure confinement of juveniles?

18. What programs appear to be most effective at rehabilitating delinquents?

19. Does incarceration cure delinquency? What are three alternatives to incarceration?

20. What was the Chicago Area Project? What population was its target? Was it successful?

21. Describe educational programs designed to prevent delinquency. Describe briefly a shock experiment to deter juveniles from being truant.

22. What ethical problem is associated with attempting to identify an adolescent as a predelinquent?

SUGGESTED READINGS

Burchard, John D., and Sara N. Burchard (Eds.) (1987). *Prevention of delinquent behavior.* Beverly Hills, CA: Sage.

Kaplan, Howard B. (1984). *Patterns of juvenile delinquency.* Beverly Hills, CA: Sage.

Rubin, H. Ted (1985). *Behind the black robes: Juvenile court judges and the court.* Beverly Hills, CA: Sage.

Streib, Victor L. (1987). *Death penalty for juveniles.* Bloomington, IN: Indiana Univ. Press.

Weisheit, Ralph A., and Robert G. Culbertson (1985). *Juvenile delinquency: A justice perspective.* Prospect Heights, IL: Waveland Press.

Comparative Perspectives on Criminal Justice

■ INTRODUCTION

This chapter describes several criminal justice systems throughout the world and compares and contrasts these systems with the United States criminal justice system. Certain acts labeled as criminal by American authorities may not be labeled as criminal in other countries. By the same token, certain acts committed in other countries may not be regarded as criminal by the United States criminal justice system. In the Soviet Union, for instance, a person who remains unemployed longer than 4 months faces prosecution and a possible jail term for a crime known as parasitism (Zeldes, 1981:xii). By comparison, an unemployed person in the United States draws unemployment benefits, including substantial monetary supplements for up to 6½ months—even for longer periods under certain circumstances. A petty thief in the United States may receive probation, whereas a thief in another country may be sentenced to and serve a term of 10 years or longer. In selected jurisdictions throughout the world, a thief may suffer the loss of a hand or even death.

All countries have a crime problem. Some countries tend to have more of a crime problem than others, and the types of classifications of crimes vary from one country to the next. By the same token, each country deals with its criminal element differently, and the nature and severity of penalties imposed for various law violations fluctuate considerably. Studies of the criminal justice systems of other countries fall within the rubric of **comparative criminal justice.**

Comparative analyses of the criminal justice systems of other countries reveal significant departures from the United States criminal justice system (Abraham, 1983; Beirne, 1983; Holyst, 1979). Considerable variations in definitions of crime are found in each country. Cultural variations in the seriousness and severity of punishment are found for similar offenses among countries.

Persons interested in comparative criminal justice examine the functions of law enforcement officers and agencies of other countries, court procedures, sentencing patterns, and corrections alternatives. Citizens of other countries have different rights than do United States citizens. The burden of proof is not always on the prosecution in a criminal case. In some countries, a citizen charged with an offense may have to prove his or her innocence to the satisfaction of the court. Jury trials are not universal either, and some justice systems dispense with trials altogether.

This chapter looks at three countries for comparison. These are the Soviet Union, Canada, and Great Britain. The Soviet Union was selected because it is a totalitarian state; it has a justice system alien to the justice systems of most English-speaking countries. It offers an interesting contrast to how offenders in the United States are processed. Canada was selected because it is a metropolitan state that has consistently exhibited a strong research interest in police and the courts. It has a multilingual population, including both French- and English-speaking subjects, and it shares a number of crime problems with the United States. In addition, Canada has undertaken substantial reform of its criminal justice system (Canada Law Reform Commission, 1985). Finally, Great Britain was chosen because the United States criminal justice system has been influenced significantly by British customs and values. However, Britain and the United States have taken different paths in their justice systems. A comparison of two justice systems stemming from a common source illustrates each country's unique reaction to similar crime problems.

This chapter also looks at international law. International terrorism, intercontinental drug trafficking, and frequent disputes over natural resources have stimulated the introduction of legal machinery designed to bring the criminal justice systems and law enforcement agencies of various countries together in a cooperative enterprise toward eventual establishment of world laws.

■ THE CRIMINAL JUSTICE SYSTEM OF THE SOVIET UNION

At the end of World War II, most countries involved published statistical information concerning the numbers of civilians killed, wounded, or missing; numbers of military personnel killed, wounded, or missing; the millions, perhaps billions, of dollars allocated to the war effort; and a host of other war facts. The Soviet Union, however, released no figures for Soviet troops killed, wounded, or missing. War facts concerning Soviet

Soviet citizens have an abiding respect for the law. Certainty of punishment and citizen participation in the punishment of offenders deters persons from committing serious crimes. Little information is made available to the public about crime in the Soviet Union.

losses were based primarily on crude estimates from war correspondents, military leaders from various countries, and tourist observations.

During the post-World War II years, the Soviet Union created an iron curtain of censorship concerning even the most trivial facts about the Soviet Union and its satellite states. Some experts claim the Soviet Union suffers from an inferiority complex—even a paranoia—relating to virtually every facet of its social, economic, and political life (Zeldes, 1981:vii). Soviet censorship pervades al' itizens' lives. The ordinary citizen cannot have access to a photocopying or mimeograph machine, and he or she is forbidden to enter a radio or television station (Zeldes, 1981:vii). Because of such censorship, little official information exists concerning crime, crime rates, and criminals in the Soviet Union. State-owned and -operated newspapers, radio stations, and television agencies screen all information for the citizenry. The government advises people what it wants them to hear. No negative news about the Soviet Union is published by either of the two state newspapers, *Pravda* (meaning truth) and *Izvestia* (meaning news). Soviet citizens remark, "There is no truth in *Pravda* and no news in *Izvestia*" (Zeldes, 1981:viii), and there are even laws prohibiting such criticisms.

Crime in the Soviet Union

There is crime in the Soviet Union, but in many respects, it is unlike crime as the United States defines it. For example, bank robbery in the Soviet Union is almost nonexistent. If a person were suddenly to acquire a large amount of money, he or she would immediately become suspect in the eyes of the community residents. Soviet officials would be notified and would investigate. Privileges, not money, are highly prized and sought after by most Soviet citizens (Zeldes, 1981:xii). Almost half of all Soviet crimes are economic crimes (Zeldes, 1981:xii). Anti-Soviet agitation and propaganda are forbidden by the criminal code, and mocking governmental leaders can draw 10 years at hard labor (Zeldes, 1981:xii). Economic crimes might involve exchanging rubles for hard currency or speculating in hard currency for scarce consumer goods.

It has been estimated that two crimes occur in the Soviet Union every 3 seconds (Zeldes, 1981:59). Shtromas (1977) suggests that any report of criminal activity in the Soviet Union, regardless of the source, should be considered suspect. Some of the reasons for these inaccuracies are the same as those for the *Uniform Crime Reports* in the United States: poor communication, inconsistent crime reporting methods from one jurisdiction to the next, and laxity on the part of regional officials. Reasons peculiar to the Soviet Union include the unwillingness of local officials to report high crime levels for fear of incurring the wrath of their superiors and the distance of different regions from the central data center (Shtromas, 1977; Zeldes, 1981:59). Another reason many crimes are unrecorded is either that the authorities do not learn of them or they want to claim credit with their superiors for being successful in their fight against crime (Chalidze, 1977:201–202). In such cases, authorities often do not prosecute offenders, even though they have conclusive evidence and specific suspects. In addition, several different agencies are involved in collecting and recording crime figures. Zeldes (1981:60) observes:

> The so-called accounting along the lines of criminal investigation records crimes that become known to the police. The Procurator has his own system for the registration of criminal affairs.

Judicial statistics are kept by various courts. Statistical data on convicts is collected and kept by the Ministry of Internal Affairs. As a result of this, the total data for each of the above-mentioned systems of accounting differs essentially from one to the other.

The best crime statistics are those kept by the Ministry of Justice concerning convicts (Zeldes, 1981:60–61). Soviet criminologists cite these sources when referring to crime trends. The worst statistics are those dealing with criminal investigations. The best estimates of the number of prisoners in Russian prisons today is between 2.5 and 3 million, although the Ministry of Justice figures place the prison population at 1 million. There are over 3,000 Soviet prisons, correctional-labor camps, and colonies, purportedly holding approximately 5 million prisoners (Shifrin, 1978). Only the Soviets know the precise numbers for sure, and they do not easily disclose such information. The Soviet equivalent to the index offenses of the *Uniform Crime Reports,* by category of offense, is shown in Table 17.1.

Hooliganism is a catchall crime category, which may include prostitution, drunk and disorderly behavior, alcohol and drug abuse, and loitering. Hooliganism is generally defined as "intentional acts which seriously disturb public order and show clear disrespect for society" (Chalidze, 1977:78–79). Hooliganism can include the relatively harmless offense of daubing tar on the gate of a house inhabited by a new bride of doubtful reputation (Chalidze, 1977:83).

In 1977, there were 250,000 convictions for theft of socialist property; 200,000 convictions for hooliganism; 120,000 convictions for crimes against the person, such as murder and rape; 150,000 convictions for crimes against private property; and 50,000 convictions for vehicular theft (Chalidze, 1977:201). The scarcity of automobile ownership in the Soviet Union severely restricts vehicular theft opportunities, and persons who steal cars are usually apprehended and punished. In the United States, there were 115,621 motor vehicle thefts by comparison. According to Soviet authorities, 90 percent of all crimes committed in the Soviet Union are solved, but Russia does not disclose how much time lapses between the commission of a crime and the arrest of a suspect (Chalidze, 1977:201).

TABLE 17.1 Crime in the Soviet Union by Category of Offense (Circa 1967)

Crime	Percent
Theft of state and public property	17.0
Hooliganism	24.0
Crimes against citizens' personal property	16.0
Crimes against person	17.0
Economic crimes	5.0
Official crimes	4.0
Vehicular crimes	5.0
Crimes against the system of justice	1.5
Crimes against the system of administration	4.0
Other crimes	6.5
Total	100.0

Source: S. S. Ostroumov, *Sovetskaia Sudebnaia Statistika* (Moscow: Isdatel'stvo Moskovskogo Universiteta, 1970), p. 248.

Compared with the United States, the Soviet Union does not have a significant drug problem. Nevertheless, poppy fields are sources of several thousand pounds of narcotic drug base that is located and disposed of annually by the Soviet police.

The Soviet Court System

The Soviet government has adopted several measures to consolidate law and order in the country (Ferracuti and Wolfgang, 1983:411). Between 1971 and 1975, the Soviets undertook a social development program during the so-called ninth 5-year plan (Ferracuti and Wolfgang, 1983:412). According to the best Soviet estimates, crime in recent years has declined appreciably. Accounting for this decrease in the crime rate are (1) the continued rise in worker prosperity in terms of real income and social consumption funds, (2) improvements in basic and professional education, (3) improvements in public health care, (4) implementation of a broad system of time- and labor-saving measures, (5) more free time and improvements in popular cultural services, (6) advancing economies in underdeveloped regions, and (7) limited growth of large cities and greater growth of medium-sized and smaller cities (Ferracuti and Wolfgang, 1983:413).

Depending upon the seriousness of the offense committed, the Soviet Union has a number of procedural alternatives available to defendants. Petty violations may be handled by a local chief of police, who can impose a fine on the offender without a formal trial. The police chief may also elect to hand over the defendant to a court or representatives of the public (Connor, 1972:194). Local militia may impose fines for public drunkenness or disorderly conduct (Connor, 1972:194). These agencies derive authority from the Ministries of Internal Affairs. Private citizens take an active role in judicial activities. Informal court arrangements include the comrades' courts and the Volunteer Auxillary Police (Chalidze, 1977:212). **Comrades' courts** are established in factories, organizations, collective farms, and apartment blocks. They have jurisdiction over small property crimes, labor violations, antisocial behavior, petty hooliganism, petty speculation, petty theft, petty embezzlement of state property, minor assaults, and a host of other minor offenses (Connor, 1972:195). The penalties are most often fines, condemnations, and reprimands. They may also include restitution orders, disciplinary action from management at the offender's workplace, and recommending eviction from one's housing (Connor, 1972:195). Squads of people's volunteers, **druzhiny,** are also called upon to dispense justice to wrongdoers (Ferracuti and Wolfgang, 1983:415). Particularly in the 1950s and mid-1960s, people's volunteers enforced antiparasite laws, which prohibited persons from not working for long periods (Connor, 1972:194). These squads operated in sizable numbers during the 1960s in various factories and in conjunction with police agencies. Antiparasite laws were for persons who were otherwise able-bodied but avoided useful labor (Connor, 1972:196).

Soviet courts employ an accusatory or inquisatorial process rather than an adversarial one. For more serious offenders, however, formal courts incorporate an adversary system similar to that of the United States courts. Prosecutors present cases against defendants, and Soviet defense attorneys do their best to free their clients from criminal penalties. In United States courts, a presumption of innocence is afforded the defendant. In Soviet courts, however, there is no such presumption. Soviet courts are fact-finding enterprises, and there is currently a debate among Soviet criminologists, judges, and criminal justice professionals concerning the presumption-of-innocence issue (Fletcher, 1984).

The Soviet Criminal Code contains a wide range of punishments, including (1) deprivation of freedom, (2) exile, (3) banishment, (4) corrective works without deprivation of freedom, (5) deprivation of the right to occupy certain offices or engage in certain activities, (6) fines, (7) dismissal from office, (8) imposition of the duty to make amends for harm caused, (9) social censure, (10) confiscation of property, and (11) deprivation of military or special rank and privileges (Connor, 1972:199). Soviet courts impose the death penalty regularly for a variety of offenses. It is estimated that the death penalty is implemented on the average for at least five persons per day or 1,750 persons a year (Zeldes, 1981:xiii). In fact, currently, the USSR leads the world in absolute numbers of executions (Zeldes, 1981:xiii).

Soviet Corrections

Soviet corrections emphasize crime prevention and stress the rehabilitative model. Criminal punishment is designed to curb recidivism and prevent persons from committing new crimes (Zeldes, 1981:105). About 1 percent of all criminal sentences involve imprisonment for terms of 10 or more years. The average confinement in prison is 3.4 years (Chalidze, 1977:200–201). Like many other nations, the Soviet Union stresses both punishment and rehabilitation or readjustment to society as correctional goals (Connor, 1972:263). Soviet courts have probation and parole options available in sentencing convicted offenders. In 1970, the Presidium of the Supreme Soviet established certain probation guidelines relevant to first offenders. In cases where an offender has committed a single offense involving labor discipline or disrupting the social order, he or she is obliged to adhere to strict measures of a disciplinary or administrative nature, such as reporting regularly to the equivalent of a probation officer (Ferracuti and Wolfgang, 1983:417). Persistent offenders fulfill the remainder of their sentences in prison.

Soviet correctional institutions educate offenders and train them to perform productive work (Johnson, 1983:626). Soviet prisoners are always involved in productive work activity, whether it be manual labor or academic endeavors. The most certain fact about Soviet justice is the certainty of punishment. Soviet citizens are fully aware of the Soviet Criminal Code and the penalties for violating it. Offenders are imprisoned for fixed periods and are expected to be productive while incarcerated. Prison overcrowding is ignored by Soviet officials, because imprisonment is punishment. Interestingly, Soviet criminal law is a significant deterrent to recidivism (Ferracuti and Wolfgang, 1983:416). Exile and the relocation of Soviet offenders to undesirable settlements literally removes offenders from their present surroundings and guarantees to citizens that these persons will commit no future crimes in their localities.

Dangerous criminals and persons with high recidivism potential are eventually placed on parole under intensive police supervision. Police supervision obligates parolees to remain at their residences during certain hours and to limit their travel severely, but Soviet officials are confronted with many of the same problems of United States probation and parole officers, where parolees and probationers engage in a wide variety of violations of the conditions of their probation or parole (Connor, 1972:228–229). One corrections alternative involves corrective works. **Corrective works** involve productive labor in corrective labor colonies. Corrective labor colonies require the performance of specialized productive tasks, including mass production, professional-technical and general educational instruction, internal order, mass cultural tasks, and sanitary maintenance (Connor, 1972:210–211). Working in corrective labor colonies instills offenders with a spirit of collectivism and supposedly fosters feelings of interest and involvement in the welfare of others (Connor, 1972:212). Some of the corrective labor colonies report recidivism rates as low as 4 percent. Soviet figures place the general recidivism rate among criminals at 9 percent (Solomon, 1978).

■ THE CRIMINAL JUSTICE SYSTEM OF CANADA

Canadian criminal law has its basis in the Constitution Act of 1867. Crime in Canada is any act done in violation of duties an individual owes to the community, for which act the law has provided that the offender shall be punished. Similar to the United States, Canada has undergone a number of revisions of its criminal code during the past 100 years. This act infused the Canadian Parliament with legislative authority extending to all criminal law.

Canada consists of a number of provinces, such as Quebec, Manitoba, and Ontario. Each of the provinces has a provincial legislature, which makes laws and gives provincial courts jurisdiction over most criminal matters. Until 1893, there was considerable variation from one province to the next relating to various criminal laws and the severity of penalties for violations of such laws. The Criminal Code of Canada was created in 1893, and it defined for the first time a set of offenses common to all provinces. These include offenses against public order, firearms and other offensive weapons violations, sexual offenses, offenses against public morals and disorderly conduct, invasion of privacy, offenses concerning disorderly houses, gaming and betting, offenses against the person and reputation, offenses against rights of property, fraudulent transactions, willful and forbidden acts in respect of certain property, and offenses relating to currency such as counterfeiting.

In 1971, the Law Reform Commission Act provided for innovations in the development of new approaches to and new concepts of the law. Basically, the Law Reform Commission was designed to keep pace with changing Canadian society and to make appropriate reform recommendations when the situation warranted such legislative intervention (Canada Law Reform Commission, 1985).

Crime in Canada

Canadian crime is reported in much the same fashion as United States crime is reported in the *Uniform Crime Reports*. Table 17.2 shows criminal offenses for different crime categories for the years 1977–1982. During the 6-year period shown in Table 17.2, there was a general decrease in homicides, or a 5.2 percent reduction between 1977 and 1982. Among the various violent crimes reported, robbery, especially armed robbery, has increased dramatically over these years by almost 40 percent. A number of criminal justice professionals have given considerable attention to the problem of armed robbery in Canada in recent years (Baril and Morissette, 1985; Bellot, 1985; Elie and Kapetanaki-Barake, 1985; Elie and Normandeau, 1984; Gagnon and Leblanc, 1985; Poirier, 1985). Sexual offenses have increased substantially, including rape with a 34 percent increase.

Property crimes reported during this same period reflect the greatest increase in theft involving property valued over $200. A 159 percent increase in theft over $200 was observed between 1977 and 1982. Possession of stolen goods (receiving stolen property) has risen by 40 percent, and breaking and entering (burglary) has escalated by almost 37 percent. The least amount of variation has been observed for motor vehicle theft, with only a 3 percent increase during the 6-year period. Property crimes considered as an aggregate have increased 38 percent for the period 1977–1982, while violent offenses have risen by 24 percent for the same time frame. Drug offenses, which involve violations of Canadian federal statutes, have decreased by 2 percent, while the total number of all federal statute violations has decreased by 14 percent. A portion of the general increase in crime can be attributable to the natural population growth of Canada, which was 6 percent between 1977 and 1982 (Solicitor General Canada, 1984).

The Canadian Police

There are three major police forces in Canada. These include the federal police, provincial police, and municipal police. The federal police are known as the **Royal Canadian Mounted Police (RCMP)**. In 1983, there were 19,577 RCMP to supervise the various provinces. Table 17.3 shows the total number of full-time police personnel by type of force for some of the provinces for the years 1978–1983. In 1983, there were 67,818 police officers including RCMP, auxiliary personnel, highway patrol officers, municipal police, and railways police. The numbers of law enforcement personnel steadily increased during the 1978–1983 period.

TABLE 17.2   Canadian Crime Trends, 1977–1982[1]

Type of Offense	1977	1978	1979	1980	1981	1982	Percent Change 1977–82
Violent offenses							
Homicide	707	658	631	593	647	670	-5.2
Attempted murder	684	742	754	792	900	943	17.9
Sexual offenses	10,932	11,598	12,333	12,787	13,313	13,864	26.8
Rape	1,886	2,014	2,291	2,315	2,559	2,528	34.0
Other sexual offenses	9,046	9,584	10,042	10,472	10,754	11,336	25.1
Assaults (not indecent)	103,931	106,301	112,911	117,111	121,076	125,912	21.1
Robbery	19,491	19,673	20,899	24,581	26,292	27,257	39.8
Violent offenses—total	135,745	138,972	147,528	155,864	162,228	168,646	24.2
Property offenses							
Breaking and entering	270,659	278,480	296,437	349,694	367,250	269,882	36.7
Theft—motor vehicle	84,252	83,130	91,445	93,928	96,229	86,997	3.2
Theft over $200	114,000	130,024	169,950	224,595	266,288	295,261	159.0
Theft under $200	486,821	497,336	516,184	539,490	561,827	570,556	17.2
Have stolen goods	18,433	19,715	20,977	24,657	25,599	25,830	40.1
Frauds	85,523	88,557	91,684	102,255	112,327	118,397	38.4
Property offenses—total	1,059,688	1,097,242	1,186,697	1,334,619	1,429,520	1,466,923	38.4
Other criminal code offenses	458,587	478,083	521,046	554,916	576,453	568,099	23.9
Total criminal code offenses	1,654,020	1,714,297	1,855,271	2,045,399	2,168,201	2,203,668	13.3
Federal statute offenses							
Drug offenses	65,938	60,747	64,923	74,196	75,104	64,636	-2.0
Other federal statutes	65,782	73,284	57,634	45,589	45,320	48,229	26.7
Total federal statutes	131,720	134,031	122,557	119,785	120,424	112,865	14.3
Total provincial statutes	379,588	398,324	438,204	452,812	481,232	434,351	14.4
Total municipal bylaws	61,237	59,313	69,598	74,163	80,202	87,956	43.6
Total offenses	2,226,565	2,305,965	2,485,630	2,692,159	2,850,059	2,838,840	27.4

[1]Based on uniform crime reporting.

Source: Reprinted from Canadian Centre for Justice Statistics, *Canada Yearbook* (Ottawa, Canada: Canadian Centre for Justice Statistics, 1984), p. 20.4.1.

TABLE 17.3 Full-time Police Personnel in Canada, 1978–1983[1]

Type of Force	1978	1979	1980	1981	1982	1983
Royal Canadian						
Mounted Police	18,330	18,288	18,978	19,696	20,035	19,577
Officers	13,991	14,021	13,879	14,417	14,178	14,159
Other[2]	4,339	4,267	5,099	5,279	5,857	5,418
Ontario Provincial						
Police	5,278	5,226	5,247	5,285	5,358	5,315
Officers	4,095	4,050	4,064	4,094	4,203	4,188
Other[2]	1,183	1,176	1,183	1,191	1,155	1,127
Quebec Police Force	5,418	5,461	5,582	5,544	5,470	5,391
Officers	4,403	4,445	4,585	4,571	4,518	4,450
Other[2]	1,015	1,016	997	973	952	941
Municipal Police						
(excl. RCMP and						
OPP contracts)	35,342	35,090	35,742	36,427	36,601	36,421
Officers	28,973	29,164	29,493	29,862	29,877	29,679
Other[2]	6,369	5,926	6,249	6,565	6,724	6,742
Canadian National						
Railways Police	456	456	451	446	422	394
Officers	431	431	427	422	402	376
Other[2]	25	25	24	24	20	18
Canadian Pacific						
Railways Police	425	424	423	399	404	402
Officers	327	322	334	311	312	307
Other[2]	98	102	89	88	92	95
Ports Canada						
Police	298	288	264	252	266	256
Officers	220	213	204	194	206	199
Other[2]	78	75	60	58	60	57
New Brunswick						
Highway Patrol[3]	..	..	..	30	33	62
Officers	..	..	..	26	29	55
Other[2]	..	..	..	4	4	7
Canada	65,547	65,233	66,687	68,079	68,589	67,818
Officers	52,440	52,646	52,986	53,897	53,725	53,413
Other[2]	13,107	12,587	13,701	14,182	14,864	14,405

[1]As at December 31 of each year.
[2]Includes civilians, cadets, and other full-time personnel.
[3]The collection of New Brunswick Highway Patrol staffing information began in the 1981 reporting year.
Source: Reprinted from Canadian Centre for Justice Statistics, *Canada Yearbook* (Ottawa, Canada: Canadian Centre for Justice Statistics, 1984), p. 20.4.3.

Originally called the Northwest Mounted Police, the Royal Canadian Mounted Police have jurisdiction in all Canadian provinces to enforce federal laws and apprehend criminal offenders.

The RCMP is a civil force maintained by the Canadian government. It was created in 1873 and originally labeled the Northwest Mounted Police. Currently, the RCMP derives its authority from the Royal Canadian Mounted Police Act of 1970. It is administered by a commissioner who has the authority to appoint officers in all provinces and territories. With the exception of Ontario and Quebec, the provinces have contracts with the RCMP to enforce criminal provincial laws. Actually, the RCMP have jurisdiction in each of these provinces and territories for all criminal offenses, federal statute violations, and ordinance offenses. The RCMP have traditionally decided what rules to enforce in various provinces, and also how to enforce them, who violated the rules, and what was to be done with violators. Some proposals have suggested the elimination of the RCMP, or at the very least, a considerable reduction in its authority within the provinces to give local authorities greater control over crime in their jurisdictions (Talbot and Jayewardene, 1984).

Ontario has provincial police. In 1983, the provincial police force of Ontario numbered 5,300 uniformed and civilian members. The Quebec Police Force consisted of 4,500 members in 1983, with about 1,000 civilian officers and personnel. Municipal police forces are common to almost all urban centers throughout Canada. The Canadian Pacific Railway Company and Ports Canada have separate police forces and ancillary personnel.

The police forces of Canada have some of the same kinds of problems confronting those in the United States. For instance, Canadian authorities are concerned about the exercise of police discretion and deadly force in apprehending suspects, as well as police corruption (Sewell, 1985). Canadian authorities conduct investigations relating to police morale and job satisfaction and manifest considerable interest in recruitment studies conducted by Canadian criminal justice professionals (Linden, 1983; McGinnis, 1985). Increasing turnover rates among the RCMP create increased training costs and suggest that drastic improvements in recruitment methods are necessary (Linden, 1983). There also has been recent emphasis on the recruitment of women in police officer roles (Linden, 1983). Finally, authorities have looked at police accountability to civilian authorities and the proper management and administration of police organization (Hann et al., 1985).

Canadian Criminal Courts

Canada has a supreme court, which was created in 1875. The court consists of a chief justice and eight other justices. This court is a general court of appeal for both criminal and civil cases. Beneath the supreme court are various courts of appeal. In each province there are superior, district, and county courts. Depending upon the type of court, judges are appointed by the federal government or by individual provincial officials. Each province has provincial, or territorial, courts, and each urban center has municipal, small claims, and traffic safety courts.

Adult criminal courts classify criminal offenses into three main categories: (1) **indictable offenses,** which include violations of the criminal code and offenses against federal statutes; (2) **summary conviction offenses** not expressly made indictable, such as violations of provincial statutes and municipal bylaws; and (3) **dual procedure offenses,** which allow the prosecutor to decide whether the prosecution is by summary conviction or by indictment. The major differences between summary conviction and indictable offenses are first, that indictable offenses are tried by a more complex and formal procedure, and second, the maximum penalty imposed for a summary conviction is a $500 fine, 6 months in prison, or both. Some indictable offenses permit the defendant to decide whether or not to be tried by a judge or jury. Serious offenses, such as armed robbery and murder, are usually tried by a jury before one of the higher, or superior, courts.

Canada also has a number of juvenile courts established by the Juvenile Delinquents Act. The Juvenile Delinquents Act originally defined a child as any boy or girl apparently or actually under 16 years or such other age as might be directed in any province. In Quebec and Manitoba, for example, the age provision was under 18, while in Newfoundland, the age provision was under 17.

In 1982, The Canadian Parliament passed the Young Offenders Act, which repealed the earlier Juvenile Delinquents Act. Interestingly, the act abolished the broadly defined offense of delinquency. Under some of the provisions of this act, a young person is defined as 12 years of age or older, but under 18 years. The uniform maximum age limit of 18 applied to all provinces as of April 1, 1985. Among the provisions of the Young Offenders Act, young people are responsible for their illegal actions. In return, young persons are guaranteed certain rights, which are the equivalent of those provided by *In re Gault* (1967). They have a right to be heard and to participate in various legal processes that lead to decisions that affect them and their freedoms.

Tables 17.4, 17.5, and 17.6 show the number of dispositions of various charges of delinquency and criminal code violations for young offenders for the years 1977–1982.

TABLE 17.4 Criminal Code and Other Federal Statute Charges Adjudicated in
Juvenile Courts[1], 1977–1982

Province or Territory	1977	1978	1979	1980	1981	1982
Newfoundland	1,391	1,690	2,295	2,553	3,057	2,424
Prince Edward Island	..	..	97	175	236	181
Nova Scotia	1,722	1,752	1,961	1,796	1,586	1,742
New Brunswick	1,169	1,245	1,645	1,703	1,552	1,536
Quebec	28,359	27,581	12,839	16,967	25,074	27,713
Ontario	23,050	21,834	22,044	22,154	23,922	22,885
Manitoba	10,792	10,367	9,869	10,274	12,312	11,574
Saskatchewan	1,681	1,875	1,567	2,167	2,794	2,440
Alberta	10,806	10,338	8,492	7,718	9,162	8,852
British Columbia	..	..	..	11,506	13,460	13,638
Yukon	215	212	157	145	251	212
Northwest Territories	..	..	..	460	542	486
Total	79,185	76,894	60,966	77,618	93,948	93,683

[1]Includes all federal statute charges adjudicated, regardless of court decision. A small percentage of charges
against adults (approximately 1% of the total in each year) are included.
Source: Canadian Centre for Justice Statistics, *Canada Yearbook* (Ottawa, Canada: Canadian Centre for
Justice Statistics, 1984), p. 20.3.

Table 17.4 shows that between 1977 and 1982 (with the exception of 1979), there was
an 18 percent increase in the number of juvenile charges involving violations of the
criminal code or federal statutes. Table 17.5 shows a distribution of specific charges
alleged for the same time frame. The two most frequent offenses alleged against
juveniles were breaking and entering and petty theft under $200. Table 17.6 shows the
number of persons with adjudicated charges for each of the provinces. Delinquency
adjudications fluctuated considerably during the 1977–1982 period.

Canadian Corrections

Canadian correctional facilities accommodate two types of offenders. Those sentenced
to terms in prison of 2 years or more, and those sentenced to prison terms of less than
2 years. Under the provisions of the Prison and Reformatories Act, each provincial
government has jurisdiction over and responsibility for the custody of convicts serving
sentences of less than 2 years. The federal government oversees the custody of
offenders serving prison terms of 2 or more years. There is no death penalty in Canada.

In 1982–1983, there were 27,000 convicts in custody in various provincial and federal
prisons. The federal inmate population in 1983 was about 10,000, while the provincial
inmate population was approximately 17,000. Table 17.7 reveals that Canada spent
about $1.1 billion on adult correction services for 1983, in the operation and
management of 235 correctional institutions and facilities. In 1983, there were 445
parole and probation officers operating in various Canadian provinces. Approximately
81,000 persons were either on probation or parole (Canadian Centre for Justice

TABLE 17.5   Number of Charges of Delinquency Adjudicated, by Type of Charge[1]

Type of Charge	1977[2]	1978[2]	1979[3]	1980	1981	1982
Criminal code offenses	74,897	72,032	57,497	72,961	89,376	89,349
Offensive weapons	694	755	802	919	1,341	1,456
Sexual offenses	374	406	433	473	502	495
Disorderly conduct	734	706	539	604	661	618
Murder	16	16	16	17	15	16
Attempted murder	12	21	37	21	20	32
Manslaughter	4	9	2	7	3	11
Assaults	1,813	1,884	1,784	2,186	2,368	2,589
Theft over $200	5,207	6,282	4,889	6,118	7,467	7,159
Theft under $200	13,501	15,045	12,093	13,217	16,159	16,471
Motor vehicle	1,609	1,448	1,263	1,452	1,543	1,322
Theft (amount unspecified)	4,989	1,754	779	1,212	1,845	2,494
Robbery	1,218	1,261	1,234	1,418	1,665	1,702
Break and enter	23,622	23,803	19,156	25,376	32,254	29,305
Possession of stolen goods	7,816	5,624	3,950	5,435	7,026	9,673
Forgery and similar crimes	974	1,147	960	1,365	1,352	1,539
Fraud	518	423	287	363	470	473
Mischief	6,676	6,112	5,233	6,641	7,476	6,959
Arson	430	343	330	437	369	389
Other criminal code offenses	4,690	4,993	3,710	5,700	6,840	6,646
Other federal statute offenses	4,288	4,862	3,469	4,657	4,572	4,334
Total	79,185	76,894	60,966	77,618	93,948	93,683

[1]Includes charges adjudicated which related to criminal code and federal statute offenses. Charges against adults adjudicated under the Juvenile Delinquents Act are included.
[2]The 1977 and 1978 totals exclude PEI, BC and NWT.
[3]The 1979 total excludes BC and NWT.
Source: Canadian Centre for Justice Statistics, *Canada Yearbook* (Ottawa, Canada: Canadian Centre for Justice Statistics, 1984), p. 20.7.

Statistics, 1984:20.7.4). There were about 11,000 corrections officers employed to supervise noncustodial parolees and probationers (Canadian Centre for Justice Statistics, 1984:20.7.5). Table 17.8 shows average offender caseloads for both custodial and noncustodial populations of offenders.

Table 17.9 discloses some of the characteristics of persons in custody and on probation. Within the provinces, for instance, the median custodial sentence length was about 1 month, compared with 42 months for federal correctional institutions. About 98 percent of all federal corrections inmates were male, while 94 percent of the provincial inmates were male. In contrast, 16 percent of the total number of persons on probation or parole were female, suggesting the possibility that Canadian courts are less severe in their sentencing practices for females than for males.

Community supervision is utilized to a great degree in monitoring parolees and probationers. Prosecutors and courts exert considerable effort to divert offenders to noncustodial alternatives. Specialized programs exist for certain offender categories,

TABLE 17.6 Number of Persons Having Charges Adjudicated, by Province and Court Decision[1]

Province or Territory	1978		1979		1980		1981		1982	
	Found Delinquent	Not Found Delinquent	Found Delinquent	Not Found Delinquent	Found Delinquent	Not Found Delinquent	Found Delinquent	Not Found Delinquent	Found Delinquent	Not Found Delinquent
Nfld.	1,165	74	1,433	98	1,845	147	1,856	130	1,551	111
PEI	..	..	49	6	87	5	110	14	70	17
NS	1,212	124	1,270	118	1,156	131	1,033	131	1,087	135
NB	848	39	1,042	106	1,041	78	790	115	816	88
Que.	15,303	1,624	4,750	674	4,546	871	6,264	986	7,733	1,199
Ont.	10,272	2,864	10,578	2,685	9,974	3,415	9,973	3,731	9,049	3,568
Man.[2]	2,921	1,205	2,666	1,111	4,504	2,344	9,567	2,777	8,339	2,278
Sask.	770	39	679	58	795	95	862	77	826	82
Alta.	5,697	605	4,283	411	3,766	372	4,447	372	4,053	321
BC	..	..	..	..	..	..	..	..	..	..
YT	99	7	67	12	73	10	84	9	76	20
NWT	..	..	..	..	221	15	286	20	209	19
Total	38,287	6,581	26,817	5,279	28,008	7,483	35,272	8,362	33,809	7,838
Persons having charges adjudicated	44,868		32,096		35,491		43,634		41,647	

[1]Includes persons having charges adjudicated which related to federal statute, provincial statute, and municipal bylaw offenses. Adults having charges adjudicated under the Juvenile Delinquents Act are included.

[2]No data for individuals facing charges under the Highway Traffic Act and Liquor Control Act in Manitoba for 1978 and 1979. The increase observed from 1980 to 1981 is attributable to improvements in reporting practices for these type of offenses.

Source: Canadian Centre for Justice Statistics, *Canada Yearbook* (Ottawa, Canada: Canadian Centre for Justice Statistics, 1984), p. 20.8.

TABLE 17.7 Expenditures, Facilities and Personnel for Provincial and Federal Corrections, Canada, Fiscal Year 1982–1983

Jurisdiction	Expenditure ($'000)	Number of Facilities		Person-Year Expended
		Custodial	Noncustodial	
Provincial corrections	516,011	174	387	13,343
Federal corrections	568,111	61	58	10,074
Canada, total	1,084,122	235	445	23,417

Source: Canadian Centre for Justice Statistics, *Canada Yearbook* (Ottawa, Canada: Canadian Centre for Justice Statistics, 1984), p. 20.1.

TABLE 17.8 Average Offender Caseload in Canadian Corrections[1], 1978–1979 to 1982–1983

Average Actual Caseload	Year	Provincial Corrections	Federal Corrections	Canada Total
Custodial[2]	1978–79	13,479	8,484	21,963
	1979–80	13,412	8,568	21,980
	1980–81	13,900	8,650	22,550
	1981–82	15,096	8,940	24,036
	1982–83	17,149	9,775	26,924
Non-custodial[3]	1978–79	54,639	7,099	61,738
	1979–80	60,799	6,486	67,285
	1980–81	64,744	6,043	70,787
	1981–82	67,764	6,541	74,305
	1982–83	74,215	6,697	80,912
Total	1978–79	68,118	15,583	83,701
	1979–80	74,211	15,054	89,265
	1980–81	78,644	14,693	93,337
	1981–82	82,860	15,481	98,341
	1982–83	91,364	16,472	107,836

[1]Includes the offender caseload handled by both the federal and provincial governments combined but excludes offenders in municipally operated corrections.

[2]Refers to actual count and therefore excludes inmates temporarily not in custody at the time of count. In 1982–83 approximately 2,500 provincial and 1,080 federal inmates fell into this category.

[3]Figures for the federal non-custodial population which include full parole, day parole and mandatory supervision represent year-end counts.

Source: Canadian Centre for Justice Statistics, *Canada Yearbook* (Ottawa, Canada: Canadian Centre for Justice Statistics, 1984), p. 20.7.4.

TABLE 17.9 Caseload Characteristics, Provincial and Federal Corrections, Canada, Fiscal Year 1982–1983

Jurisdiction	Sentenced Admissions				
	Total Number	Female %	Male %	Median Age	Median Sentence
Provincial corrections					
Custodial	131,291	6	94	25 yrs	26 days
Probation	66,008	16	84	21 yrs	11 months
Federal corrections[1]	4,080	2	98	28 yrs	42 months
Canadian adult population	18,440,200	51	49	37 yrs	

[1]Excludes releases to parole and mandatory supervision.

Source: Canadian Centre for Justice Statistics, *Canada Yearbook* (Ottawa, Canada: Canadian Centre for Justice Statistics, 1984), p. 20.7.5.

such as females and drunk-driving offenders, and volunteer workers often work in conjunction with regular probation officers and agencies to lighten caseloads. Canada has a National Parole Board, which oversees all federal and provincial inmates and has the authority to grant parole to any prisoner with accompanying conditions and provisions. In selected instances involving minor offenders who are incarcerated, sentences involve intermittent imprisonment, where not more than 90 days are served in prison (Dombeck and Chitra, 1984). When offenders are out of prison for the remainder of the sentence, they are under close supervision of parole officers and other officials. The imposition of short sentences under the intermittent sentencing alternative contributes to prison overcrowding in the various provinces, not unlike prison overcrowding in the United States.

Limited victim compensation programs were commenced in some of the provinces in the late 1960s, but by 1973, the federal justice system shared provincial expenses and the costs of criminal injury compensation programs. Usually, no compensation is paid to victims for property damage; payments are almost exclusively reserved for persons suffering from physical injuries. In 1982, for example, Canada reimbursed persons for injuries sustained as the result of criminal acts in the amount of $14.5 million (Canada Solicitor General, 1983).

Victim compensation programs are supplemented by restitution orders against particular convicts (Zapf and Cole, 1985). In the Yukon Territory, for example, 1,473 probation orders for convicted defendants in 1981–1982 were processed. They required restitution payments to victims in over 22 percent of the cases. Follow-up investigations revealed that offenders had made full restitution in about 61 percent of the cases, while another 4 percent were partially paid (Zapf and Cole, 1985). No charges were subsequently placed against the remainder of offenders for failing to provide restitution to victims. The restitution program was somewhat unsuccessful, largely because of the government's failure to enforce offender payments to victims (Zapf and Cole, 1985).

■ THE CRIMINAL JUSTICE SYSTEM OF GREAT BRITAIN

Until 1955, official records of crime and crime trends in Great Britain were rather sketchy, and they varied in quality from one locality to the next. In 1955, government officials began systematic record keeping of a variety of criminal offenses. Such record keeping was stimulated by the Criminal Justice Act of 1948, which infused the British Home Secretary with broad powers, including the discretion to conduct or support financially research into the "causes of delinquency and the treatment of offenders, and *matters connected herewith*" [Italics mine] (Johnson, 1983:80). Official figures pertaining to criminal offenses include both England and Wales, although some official international references are to the United Kingdom or simply to Britain or England. In 1955, a total of 438,085 known indictable crimes were reported. Between 1955 and 1970, the number of reported indictable crimes rose by over 300 percent, to 1,555,995.

Criminal acts prior to 1967 were usually differentiated into felony and misdemeanor classifications similar to those used by United States law enforcement agencies. The Criminal Law Act of 1967 replaced these terms with (1) summary offenses, (2) indictable offenses, and (3) hybrid offenses. **Summary offenses** include such violations as public drunkenness or disorderly conduct. Petty theft and solicitation are included as well. These are summarily heard and tried by magistrates (Stott, 1981:52). **Indictable offenses** are more serious crimes tried by a crown court. Indictable offenses include, but are not limited to, murder, rape, and robbery. However, regardless of the type of offense, all accused persons must first appear before a magistrate to determine the appropriate court action to be taken.

Hybrid offenses permit a defendant to elect to be heard by magistrates or to be tried by jury. An example of a hybrid offense is embezzlement, where a sentence of up to 14 years' imprisonment may be imposed by the court. Upon an indictment, a hybrid offense may be tried summarily at the discretion of the magistrate or by persuasion by the prosecutor. Penalties fixing two alternative maximum fines and terms of imprisonment may be imposed, depending upon whether the offender is tried summarily or on indictment (Walker, 1968:14). There is a rule pertaining to whether the offense is nonindictable, hybrid, or indictable but triable summarily. This rule specifies that if the offense is such that more than 3 months' imprisonment could be imposed, the alleged offender can claim to be tried on indictment. Such action requires a judicial review by a panel of examining magistrates (Walker, 1968:14).

Crime in Great Britain

Until 1980, much of the crime reported in Great Britain was manually recorded. The British Home Office decided in 1980 to overhaul the crime reporting system by installing a Home Office Large Major Enquiry System, or HOLMES (Barrington, 1985). This system makes it possible for rapid data retrieval and is considerably more efficient than the manual index cards formerly used. A central administrative center now compiles data for all major criminal investigations. The computerization of criminal records and intelligence information is creating significant changes in modern policing

CRIME BEAT

The police of Great Britain ordinarily do not carry firearms. The possession of handguns in Great Britain is tightly regulated, and those who commit crimes involving firearms are punished with lengthy prison terms. Yet, in August 1987, in a small English town, Hungerford, fifteen persons were killed and fourteen others were wounded when a man, Michael Ryan, armed himself with several handguns and assault rifles and went on a killing rampage. He used a Chinese-made AK-47 assault rifle similar to the one used by Patrick Purdy, the gunman who slaughtered five children and wounded a teacher and twenty-nine other pupils in Stockton, California, in January 1989.

Ryan, a 25-year-old, started by killing his mother. Then he went on a shooting spree throughout the town, where he killed fourteen others. Eventually, he turned one of his guns on himself and committed suicide. Police could offer no explanation for his actions, and Ryan apparently left no clues behind for why he committed these murders. The government of Margaret Thatcher was incensed by Ryan's act and called for harsher gun control. Despite the fact that police must issue permits in Great Britain even for shotgun ownership, Ryan had licenses for his weapons and belonged to several gun clubs.

How far should government go to ban the sale of firearms generally to the public? If firearms sales are permitted, what qualifications should purchasers have before being sold weapons?

---

activity. British police are gradually moving toward a broader exercise of discretionary policing (Pounder, 1983).

Crime in Great Britain has grown considerably between 1955 and 1983 (Bottomley and Coleman, 1984). One factor influencing crime trends is the lack of consistent investigative powers by police in apprehending and searching suspects and their vehicles or premises. An attempt to rectify this problem resulted in the passage of the Police and Criminal Evidence Act of 1984 (Bazell, 1985; Bevan and Lidstone, 1985; Her Majesty's Stationery Office, 1985; Alves and Shapland, 1985). It is both complex and controversial, although it is designed to define police discretion relative to statutory powers of stop and search; searching of premises and seizing property found on persons or premises; detention, treatment, and interrogation of suspects; and identification of persons by police (Jones, 1985).

Table 17.10 shows the distribution of officially recorded indictable offenses reported to police for 1985. The table reveals that murder and drug offenses are cleared by arrest more frequently. About 93 percent of all murders are solved, while 95 percent of all drug cases are successfully prosecuted. The offenses least likely to be solved are robbery and violent theft (24 percent), vehicular theft (26 percent), and aggravated theft (30 percent).

Since 1955, a considerable amount of criminological research has been undertaken. One explanation for this trend is that systematic crime statistics are now available to researchers for analysis (Johnson, 1983:83). Between 1951 and 1960, the government sponsored approximately twenty research projects by various British criminologists. By 1970, over fifty different research projects were in various stages of completion. By the mid-1970s, the government was allocating nearly $3 million per year for criminological research.

TABLE 17.10   Reported Indictable Offenses in Great Britain, 1985

Offense	Number of Cases Reported to Police	Cases Solved	Volume of Crime per 100,000 Pop.
Murder	678	93%	1.37
Sex Offenses	20,410	73	41.14
Rape	1,334	67	2.69
Serious Assault	108,980	75	219.69
Theft	2,541,429	35	5,123.15
Aggravated Theft	835,505	30	1,684.25
Robbery and Violent Theft	22,119	24	44.59
Breaking and Entering	813,386	30	1,639.67
Vehicular Theft	325,699	26	656.56
Other Thefts	1,380,225	40	2,782.33
Fraud	121,791	69	245.51
Drug Offenses	4,994	95	10.07
Total Offenses Included in National Crime Statistics	3,247,030	35	6,545.53
1985 Population of Great Britain & Wales: 49,606,800			

Source: International Crime Center, *International Crime Statistics, 1986* (Geneva, Switzerland: International Crime Center, 1986), p. 56.

Some persons take issue with officially reported crime estimates. *The British Crime Survey* began in 1981 as a means of securing from crime victims fairly accurate information about the amount of crime occurring in various jurisdictions (Chambers and Tombs, 1984). *The British Crime Survey* revealed in recent years that more crime occurs than is actually reported and reflected by official government estimates. Most of the discrepancies occur regarding crimes against the person, such as rapes and robberies. *The British Crime Survey* shows more of these offenses than are disclosed by official estimates from police reports (Mayhew and Smith, 1985). For most other offenses, however, the frequency of reporting is fairly similar (such as theft reports, fraud reports, and murders).

Prosecutions are a means of assessing the amount of crime and statute violations. Table 17.11 shows the total number of persons prosecuted for all offenses (including traffic violations) for the years 1977–1981. This table shows an increase in the number of prosecutions for various offenses. There is an increase in the prosecution rate of indictable offenses prosecuted over the 1977–1981 period. In 1977, there were 470,000 prosecutions for indictable offenses compared with 523,000 prosecutions for 1981. Caution should be exercised in interpreting such figures, however. Population growth is obviously an important factor in the increasing numbers of prosecutions, but independent evidence suggests a general rise in crime over these same years in proportion to

TABLE 17.11 Total Number of Prosecutions in Great Britain, 1977–1981

Year	Total No. Persons Prosecuted	Indictable Offenses
1977	2,093,000	470,000
1978	2,019,000	461,000
1979	2,049,000	460,000
1980	2,378,000	507,000
1981	2,294,000	523,000

Source: 1981 Criminal Statistics England and Wales Cmd. 8668, Table 6.1 at 118 (1982).

the existing population. Penalties that may be imposed for various offenses are shown in Table 17.12.

Criminological research conducted between 1955 and 1980 studied patterns of officially recorded crimes, the content and effectiveness of punishments and treatments, various crime prediction methods, the political administrations of penal institutions, and decision making within penal institutions (Johnson, 1983:86–87). Studies in the mid-1980s pertained to police stress and performance, police-community relations, crime prevention measures, plea bargaining, and mental illness (Craft and Craft, 1984; Roach and Thomaneck, 1985; Thackrah, 1985; Sabor, 1985).

The Criminal Court Structure of Great Britain

Under the Judicature Acts of 1873–1875, an organized system of criminal courts was established. All courts, regardless of their place in the judicial hierarchy, are bound to follow the precedents established by case law. In this respect, the British justice system follows the principle of *stare decisis,* which means simply that lower courts are bound to follow the previous decisions of higher courts in similar criminal matters. Figure 17.1 shows the criminal court structure of Great Britain.

Courts of the first instance are magistrates' courts and the crown court. The **magistrates' courts** handle about 85 percent of the indictable offenses (Hughes, 1984:568). Most often, these cases are resolved through guilty pleas entered by defendants and do not involve trial proceedings. Some of the incentives to plead guilty in a magistrate's court are (1) lesser penalties compared with other courts, (2) no plausible defense for the crimes alleged, (3) the avoidance of embarrassment of a public trial, and (4) lighter sentences imposed by magistrates (Hughes, 1984:569). Often, cases are disposed of without a trial through a pretrial settlement conference (Baldwin, 1985). Police often perform the role of prosecutor in magistrates' courts. For summary offenses, the police present the arrest information, previous background and prior offenses of the suspect, and the details of the crime. No attorneys are involved in these proceedings, and the cases are dispensed with summarily by the magistrate. Until fairly recently, there was no public defender or prosecutor present in magistrates' courts. The principal participants were the judge, the police, and the accused. In recent years, however, a duty solicitor has been appointed to be present in most magistrates' courts in order to provide rapid legal advice to defendants (Hughes, 1984:573).

TABLE 17.12   Selected Penalties for Various Offenses, Great Britain

Offense	Maximum Sentence
Offenses Against the Person Act 1861	
§ 16-Threats to kill	10 years imprisonment
§ 20-Inflicting bodily injury with or without a weapon	5 years imprisonment
§ 47-Assault occasioning bodily harm	5 years imprisonment
Theft Act 1968	
§ 7-Theft	10 years imprisonment
§ 12-Taking motor vehicle or other conveyance without authority	3 years imprisonment
§ 17-False accounting	7 years imprisonment
§ 22-Handling stolen goods	14 years imprisonment
Sexual Offenses Act 1956	
§ 6-Unlawful sexual intercourse with a girl under 16	2 years imprisonment
§ 13-Indecency between men if by a man 21 years or older with a man less than 21 years old:	5 years imprisonment
All other cases:	2 years imprisonment
Criminal Damage Act 1971	
§ 1(1) & (3)-Arson	Life imprisonment

Source: Report of the Interdepartmental Committee on the Distribution of Criminal Business Between the Crown Court and Magistrates' Courts, Cmd. No. 6323 at 149, app. E (1975) [commonly referred to as the *James Report*].

FIGURE 17.1   The Criminal Court Structure of Great Britain

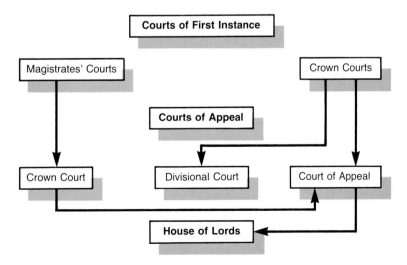

The other court of first instance is the crown court. Crown courts hear more serious offenses and may conduct trial proceedings. Crown courts are also appeals courts for decisions rendered against defendants by magistrates' courts. Crown courts consist of examining justices who hear the facts in the case presented by a prosecutor and determine whether or not the case should be tried by jury or summarily (Bottoms and McClean, 1976:2). Jury trials burgeoned in crown courts in the 1965–1975 period, so legislation has been passed to eliminate certain offenses from jury status. The Criminal Justice Act of 1976 made certain offenses purely summary violations, which must be dispensed with by magistrates (Hughes, 1984:587–588).

Trial proceedings in British courts are quite different from those in United States courts. The judge takes a strong role, vigorously interrogating defendants and witnesses, thus usurping much of the prosecutor's power (Hughes, 1984:588–589). Both the prosecution and defense counsels are restrained in their courtroom participation. Contemporary jury selection methods favor random jury panels that reflect a fairly representative cross-section of the British citizenry. Prior to 1972, jurors were selected from property records and had to be occupiers of dwellings with fixed minimum tax values. Women were almost entirely excluded from jury service as a result. The Criminal Justice Act of 1972 and the Juries Act of 1974 significantly modified these older practices, and now, defendants are tried by more representative juries. There is no such thing in England as a *voir dire* by either the prosecution or defense counsels. Thus, juror prejudices cannot be determined.

England and Wales have staffs of lawyers called solicitors, who are employed by police or local government (Hughes, 1984:541). Some national control is exercised from the office of the Director of Public Prosecutions, which theoretically has the power to take over any prosecution that has been instituted in England or Wales (Hughes, 1984:543). In actual practice, however, the director's office takes a limited role. In 1980, for example, the office of the Director of Public Prosecutions prosecuted only 1,671 cases out of the 507,000 indictable offenses prosecuted in Great Britain.

Defense counsels are available to all defendants upon request where serious crimes are alleged. The Legal Aid Act of 1974 provides for such legal assistance, and the expenses for such assistance are borne by the government, not the defendant. If defendants choose to use private counsel, this is their option. As an example of the infrequent use of such barristers, only 3 percent of the cases that went to trial in 1980 involved private counsel.

At the appellate level, there are three major appeals courts. The crown court functions as the appellate court for judgments rendered in magistrates' courts. Appeals from decisions rendered in crown courts are directed toward either the divisional court or the court of appeal, criminal division. The court of appeal consists of seventeen judges, although these judges usually sit in different divisions in panels of three judges each (Stott, 1981:13). Final appeals are directed to the House of Lords, which is the equivalent of the United States Supreme Court. The House of Lords is presided over by the lord chief justice, and lord justices are appointed by the prime minister. Qualifications include 15 years' experience as a barrister or judge.

In a British criminal court, the burden of proof prevails against a criminal defendant. The prosecutor must prove the facts beyond a reasonable doubt, and both the *actus reus* and a *mens rea* must be conclusively established. Like the Canadian justice system,

Great Britain's criminal courts attempt to provide appropriate punishments. In 1964, a criminal injuries compensation board was created to assist crime victims. In addition various criminal courts may require convicted defendants to provide some form of financial restitution.

Corrections in Great Britain

If a defendant pleads guilty to criminal charges or is found guilty by a magistrate or a jury, a number of sentencing options are available to judges. For lesser offenses, fines or imprisonment in local jails may be imposed, although incarceration is seldom used for minor offenses. Sometimes, if the offense is related to drug abuse, sexual misconduct, mental illness, or alcoholism, treatment includes therapy or hospitalization (Craft and Craft, 1984; Kingsley and Mari, 1983). It is possible for a court to defer sentencing for as long as 6 months after conviction in order to consider the offender's subsequent behavior (Jones, 1983). Based upon an assessment of the offender's conduct during the 6-month deferment period, the judge may impose a noncustodial sentence, such as probation, restitution, or community service (Jones, 1983; Vass, 1983).

For serious offenses, persons may be incarcerated in local jails or more formal British prison facilities. The death penalty has been abolished. The English penal system is divided into three major parts, including housing for juveniles, borstals (which may be either closed or open security facilities offering vocational or educational programs), and adult prisons for males and females. Women's prisons exist at Moor Court, Askham Grange, Drake Hall, and Cookham Wood (Mandaraka-Sheppard, 1986). Disparities exist regarding sentences imposed on various offenders, depending upon whether they enter not guilty pleas. For example, persons entering not guilty pleas who are subsequently found guilty receive some form of incarceration in 69 percent of the cases. By comparison, those entering guilty pleas to similar offenses are incarcerated only about 50 percent of the time. Those who enter late plea changes are incarcerated about 43 percent of the time (McConville and Baldwin, 1981:198).

A classification system segregates offenders into different penal facilities. Criteria used for classification include region of residence, availability of space, security risk, age, sex, and criminal sophistication (Ferracuti and Wolfgang, 1983:536). Great Britain instituted a parole system with the Criminal Justice Act of 1969. This act renders eligible for parole anyone who has been sentenced to more than 18 months of incarceration, and such persons become eligible after serving approximately one third of their original sentences (Ferracuti and Wolfgang, 1983:537–538). Local review committees and parole boards determine whether or not particular offenders receive early release. A significant factor affecting parole decisions is prisoner conduct while incarcerated.

An alternative to incarceration is community service. The sentencing court may impose community service orders upon a defendant and require the defendant to perform some form of public service for a designated time interval (Jardine, Moore, and Pease, 1983; Vass, 1983). This alternative sentencing is the equivalent of United States probation with certain conditions attached. In some cases, a mediation service operates as a probationary form. In South Yorkshire, for example, the South Yorkshire Probation Service was instituted in November 1983 to mediate between offenders and their victims. The probation may involve some form of restitution, and it has been especially constructive for offenses committed against local victims (Smith, Blagg, and Derricourt, 1985).

In 1974, Great Britain established the National Association for the Care and Resettlement of Offenders in the United Kingdom to function as a type of halfway house for ex-convicts or parolees (Glickman, 1983). The major purpose of the program, headquartered in Cambridge, was to provide formal education to ex-offenders. A number of hostels in various cities served fairly large numbers of ex-convicts. Recidivism rates were such, however, that the program was regarded unsuccessful. By 1980, the centers were converted into probationary agencies for housing probation officers and their staffs (Glickman, 1983).

■ INTERNATIONAL LAW AND TERRORISM

Each country in the world establishes laws for its citizenry. As we have seen, there is considerable variation from one country to the next in defining crime and the range of punishments for various offenses. The Soviet Union punishes persons who are out of work for more than 4 months. The United States "rewards" such persons with unemployment benefits for extended periods. The Soviet Union punishes political dissidents, sometimes by death. The United States gives considerable media attention to political dissidents, and their activities are often rewarded by the very government they criticize.

Currently, no world criminal justice system has specific laws applicable to the citizens of all countries. Some organizations of an international nature, however, have moved toward the development of international laws to govern their memberships. The United Nations, for example, was established in San Francisco, California, in 1945, shortly after the conclusion of World War II. Its objectives are to promote world peace and security, maintain treaty obligations, observe international law, and cooperate in the furtherance of social progress.

Not all countries throughout the world are members of the United Nations, and new nations are admitted to the United Nations only by a majority vote of the existing members. Conflicts between nations frequently arise over such matters as fishing rights in international waters because each country has a different definition of its territorial waters. North Korea, for instance, regards its territorial waters as extending 200 miles from its shoreline. The United States defines its territorial waters as 2 miles beyond its coastline. Thus, conflicts invariably arise.

Between 1945 and 1960, international laws principally addressed territorial disputes over natural resources and the like. World leaders displayed little interest in establishing international criminal laws and penalties. Since 1960, however, several trends have prompted the United Nations and other international organizations to gravitate toward a codification of criminal laws for all member nations.

International Crime

Significant improvements in world technology, including more efficient transportation systems, and large-scale international cartels have prompted greater cooperative efforts between nations. The rapid escalation of skyjacking by international terrorist organizations has stimulated public outrage and interest in more effective international security. International drug trafficking is increasingly affecting both adults and children of many nations. The popular film *The French Connection* depicted heroin smuggling between Marseilles, France, and New York City in the 1970s. This film was based upon a real heroin-smuggling incident of gigantic proportions. It promoted the cooperation of police departments in both France and the United States.

International cooperation was involved in the apprehension of one of Colombia's most powerful drug lords in early 1987. Carlos Lehder, 37, was the leader of the so-called Medellin cartel, a powerful crime cabal that is said to have supplied 80 percent of the world's cocaine. Originally indicted by a federal grand jury in 1981, Lehder slipped out of the country to head operations involving the smuggling of 15 tons of cocaine per month into the United States from Colombia. The government of Bogota, Colombia, together with the United States Drug Enforcement Administration, pooled all information relating to Lehder's movements and actions between 1981 and 1987. Lehder was arrested in a mansion about 20 miles outside the city of Medellin, Colombia, where a 20-man elite police unit moved in and arrested fifteen persons, including Lehder. The

In 1987, Carlos Lehder was arrested in a cooperative effort between the United States Drug Enforcement Administration and the government of Bogota, Colombia. Lehder was the reputed kingpin of a multimillion dollar cocaine supply empire. The billions of dollars that he made were based on cocaine trafficking of 15 tons per month to the United States and several European countries.

Colombian government permitted the immediate extradition of Lehder to Florida, where he faced trial on drug smuggling charges. Lehder was subsequently convicted in a Florida federal court in 1988 and sentenced to life imprisonment for his crimes.

Another case of international cooperation involved a Nazi war criminal, Klaus Barbie, who had been a captain of the SS Einsatzkommando at Lyons, France, between 1942 and 1944. He captured, tortured, and deported thousands of the French people to Nazi concentration camps for eventual extermination. Barbie escaped capture at war's end and escaped with friends to Bolivia in 1951, where he became a successful and wealthy businessman. He changed his name to Klaus Altmann and lived in relative obscurity until 1971, when he was tracked down by Paris lawyer and Nazi hunter, Serge Klarsfeld. At first, the Bolivian government did nothing to assist the French officials in having Barbie extradited to Lyons to face trial for assorted war crimes, but in the early 1980s, a new regime in La Paz, Bolivia, permitted Barbie's extradition. Known as the Butcher of Lyons, Klaus Barbie faced a Lyons, France, court in May 1987. Barbie was subsequently convicted and sentenced to virtual life imprisonment.

International Terrorism

One of the most significant criminal activities to draw attention in recent years has been international terrorism (Green, 1985). Terrorists are most often politically motivated individuals who cause public incidents and promote fear among populations as means of obtaining their desired results. Terrorism takes many forms. The taking of hostages is one common form (International Law Enforcement, 1985). Another version is bombing innocent establishments, killing and maiming dozens of innocent people. Skyjacking of international flights creates worldwide attention quickly (Moorehead, 1985).

In 1987, Klaus Barbie, characterized by his surviving victims as the Butcher of Lyons, was convicted of crimes against humanity. Barbie was the Gestapo chief of Lyons during World War II who allegedly deported at least 842 persons to extermination camps, where 373 were executed. Although Barbie's lawyer contends that Barbie was extradited from Bolivia to France illegally, Barbie was sentenced to life imprisonment (France has abolished the death penalty). Even after his sentence of life imprisonment, Barbie faced another trial for his alleged role in the torture death of Jean Moulin, a French wartime Resistance leader.

Terrorists regard themselves as freedom fighters, and certain countries, such as Libya and Iran, openly condone their actions against the people of other nations (Netanyahu, 1986). Experts who study terrorism and its causes regard terrorism as a type of warfare. The media are used, likely exploited, by terrorists to advertise their causes and objectives (Freedman and Alexander, 1983:180). Freedman and Alexander (1983:18) say, "The [terrorists] depend upon the mass media to disseminate their sociopolitical message and the terror-inspiring nature of their act. . . . [T]he perpetrator anticipates and relies on media coverage . . . to further his objective of producing a social impact that would not otherwise occur." The media are often regarded as aiders of terrorism, hindering antiterrorist activities and efforts (Green, 1985).

In recent years, nuclear terrorism has become imminent. Fissionable materials are increasingly available to diverse groups and individuals, and it is conceivable that with proper backing financially, any interested organization can eventually create a crude nuclear device with which to threaten a city or nation (Freedman and Alexander, 1983:230–231). It has been estimated that between 1990 and 2000, various developing nations will be able to produce between 3,000 and 100,000 nuclear explosives or bombs each year (Freedman and Alexander, 1983:232–233).

The threat of nuclear terrorism is quite real. In 1978, the ETA, a Basque separatist terrorist organization, bombed the partially constructed nuclear plant in Lemoniz, Spain, causing $8.1 million in damage. Two workers were killed and fourteen were injured. Some months later, the ETA opened fire at workers on the same nuclear site. Given the obvious danger of the spread of radioactive materials in event of a sizable explosion at a fully operational nuclear facility, there is adequate cause for global concern over the potential threat from various terrorist organizations (Freedman and Alexander, 1983:238–239).

CRIME BEAT

In September 1988, several FBI agents arrested 28-year-old Fawaz Younis, alleged terrorist and Lebanese hijacker of a Jordanian airplane at a Beirut airport in 1985. After an intensive investigation and an elaborate plan, FBI agents attracted Younis to a yacht off Cyprus, where he was taken into custody by federal agents. He was flown to an American aircraft carrier and from there to the United States to stand trial.

International terrorism has rapidly escalated in recent years. The governments of several nations, including the United States, have vowed to fight terrorism and consider it a world crime priority. The United States has defended its seizure of Younis because several hostages in the 1985 hijacking were United States citizens. Furthermore, videotapes taken of the 1985 hijacking clearly show that Younis was the hijacker who claimed in Arabic that he would deliver the corpses if his demands were not met by Beirut officials. Ultimately, all of the passengers were released unharmed. While Younis's defense attorneys chided the FBI and United States for their actions, claiming that Younis's actions were only remotely related to United States interests, then-Attorney General Edwin Meese claimed that the capture of Younis was an important step in the new United States policy of bringing terrorists to justice. The arrest of Younis represented the first to charge a person under a 1984 federal hostage-taking statute that gives officials jurisdiction over terrorist actions in other countries where United States citizens are involved.

CRIME BEAT

The world's first antiterrorist summit convened last week. Interior and justice ministers from nine industrial nations—France, West Germany, Italy, Britain, Belgium, Denmark, the United States, Japan and Canada—met under tight guard at the Interior Ministry in Paris to discuss collaboration in the war against terrorism. The meeting was a preparatory session for the Venice economic summit on June 8. But it also signaled a change in French policy.

For years France resisted discussion of terrorism at international meetings, fearing erosion of both its cherished national autonomy and its historic role as a haven for political exiles. But following his election last year, conservative Prime Minister Jacques Chirac encouraged police cooperation with Germany and Italy. A similar agreement with Spain is in the works.

The new cooperation is already bearing fruit. French Interior Minister Charles Pasqua revealed that last week the United States helped French police uncover a cache of explosives, detonators and weapons in a forest near Paris. The explosives were of the same kind used in Paris bombings last September that killed 11 people and wounded at least 150.

France may soon need all the help it can get. Last week a letter from the Committee of Solidarity With Arab and Middle Eastern Political Prisoners (CSPPA)—the group that claimed responsibility for most of the Paris bombings—vowed to make the coming summer "very hot" unless three terrorists serving life terms in French jails were released. French officials promptly deployed 1,800 extra policemen on the streets of Paris.

Source: From NEWSWEEK, June 8, 1987 and © 1987 Newsweek, Inc. All rights reserved.

There is considerable debate among nations as to how to deal with terrorists and their impossible demands (Cordes et al., 1984). Some police authorities contend that it is best to fight fire with fire and not give in to any terrorist demand, regardless of the possible loss of hostage lives (Netanyahu, 1986). Other law enforcement agencies favor negotiating with terrorists in efforts to avoid loss of life. Some writers have contended that for the terrorist, there should be no hiding place in the world; only courage and determination will stop terrorism (Netanyahu, 1986).

Profiles of terrorists are varied and extreme. Some researchers divide terrorists into two types: (1) anarchic-ideologues, who are bent on destroying society and (2) nationalist-secessionists, who want to isolate themselves and their countries from the rest of the world (Post, 1984). The process of becoming a terrorist has been described as gradual, but one that nonetheless creates powerful pressures to conform to terrorist values and ideals (Post, 1984).

Terrorism is a frequent topic of interest at annual meetings of the International Association of Chiefs of Police, who are law enforcement leaders from around the world that meet regularly and exchange information on how best to defeat terrorist activities (C. J. International, 1986:19). An international symposium on terrorism conducted in Chicago, Illinois, in August 1986, concluded, "[T]he threat of terrorism has never been greater" (C. J. International, 1986:20).

Interpol

One international organization designed to deal with international offenders including terrorists in **Interpol,** or the International Criminal Police Organization (Fooner, 1973).

The latest lethal weapons, Glock 17s, are plastic guns, which are capable of bypassing metal detectors at major airports. With weapons such as these available to terrorists, law enforcement officials and airline security personnel have more diffi-culty preventing hijackings of air-craft and the taking of hostages by extremist groups.

The idea for the creation of an international police organization is traced to Baron Pasquier, the prefect of Paris police in 1809. His organization initially was limited to local crime and became known as the Surete. Pasquier acquired the services of an ex-criminal, Francois Vidocq, as a means of using a thief to catch a thief (Fooner, 1973:6–7). After a falling out with the French Surete in 1840, Vidocq struck out on his own to develop a number of innovations in police work, including the use of mug shots, or drawings of faces of criminals for identification purposes. His activities led to the acquisition of a vast number of dossiers on various criminals. Ultimately, these dossiers became so numerous that armies of clerks were required to locate a single dossier from the hundreds of thousands on file (Fooner, 1973:8).

The idea of an international police organization was suspended for several decades. In 1923, the police commissioner of Vienna, Dr. Johann Schoeber, revived the idea (Fooner, 1973:13). The parallel development of the League of Nations assisted Dr. Schoeber's efforts to form an international organization, but World War II curtailed the development of Interpol. In 1945, Florent Louwage, inspector of the Belgian police, took the initiative to reestablish Interpol. An executive committee was formed after a general meeting of European police leaders in Brussels, Belgium, and Paris, France, was chosen as the site of the newly formed commission's headquarters. In 1956, the International Criminal Police Commission changed its name to International Criminal Police Organization (Fooner, 1973:26). The word *commission* was regarded as too temporary by some of the organization's members.

Interestingly enough, it was skyjacking by terrorist groups that drew Interpol into the international limelight. More recently, Interpol has achieved remarkable feats in combating international crime. Almost all major countries have established communi-cation network links with Interpol, and information exchanges frequently lead to the apprehension of criminals, such as the Carlos Lehders and the Klaus Barbies of the world.

■ SUMMARY

This chapter examines the criminal justice systems of the Soviet Union, Canada, and Great Britain. Each of these justice systems differs from that of the United States in its definition and handling of crime. Comparative analyses of the criminal justice systems of other countries identify not only cultural variations in crime patterns but also look at certain problems shared by these justice systems.

The criminal justice system of the Soviet Union is decentralized, and persons within the community and one's place of work are often involved in judging criminal actions and prescribing punishments. Education and vocational training are emphasized, and Soviet prisons are oriented toward obtaining productive work from offenders. Little information exists publicly about the intimate operations of the Soviet criminal justice system. A majority of the Soviet crimes are related to economic matters. People's courts dispense justice in the various cities and territories. Russian correctional institutions are rehabilitation centered.

Canadian crime is the violation of duties an individual owes to the community for which punishments are provided. The various Canadian provinces have their own laws, but the Canadian government enforces national statutes as well through its Royal Canadian Mounted Police force. Canadian corrections foster alternatives to incarceration as much as possible and use community-based supervision extensively for probationers and parolees.

Great Britain's criminal justice system is similar to that of Canada. In Great Britain, criminal offenses are classified according to summary offenses, indictable offenses, and hybrid offenses. Indictable offenses are most serious and are dealt with in special courts. Interrogating defendants and their witnesses, judges play a major role in conducting trials. Prosecutors and defense counsels play relatively minor and passive roles in trial proceedings.

A problem facing many nations is the growing rate of international crime. Terrorist activities, such as bombings, taking hostages, and skyjacking commercial airliners, have prompted several countries to cooperate in concert to combat such crimes. An international police agency, Interpol, headquartered in Paris, France, exists to combat international crime as well.

KEY TERMS

comparative criminal justice
comrades' courts
corrective works
druzhiny
dual procedure offenses

hooliganism
hybrid offenses
indictable offenses
Interpol

magistrates' courts
Royal Canadian Mounted
  Police (RCMP)
summary conviction offenses
summary offenses

QUESTIONS FOR REVIEW

1. What is meant by comparative criminal justice? What do persons investigate when they engage in comparative analysis of justice systems?

2. Why is it difficult to obtain information about crime trends and the amount of crime in the Soviet Union?

3. In the Soviet Union, what is meant by hooliganism? What scrts of crimes are placed in this category?
4. What explanations have been given for reports that crime in the USSR has decreased in recent years?
5. To what extent are private citizens involved in the Soviet criminal justice process?
6. What punishments are set forth in the Soviet Criminal Code?
7. What appears to be the correctional philosophy associated with Soviet correctional institutions?
8. How is crime defined in Canada?
9. Based upon official estimates, is crime in Canada generally increasing or decreasing?
10. Differentiate between indictable offenses, summary conviction offenses, and dual procedure offenses in Canadian law.
11. Describe briefly the various police forces in Canada.
12. What two types of offenders do Canadian correctional facilities accommodate?

13. What alternatives to incarceration are provided for Canadian criminals?
14. What is the significance of the Canadian victim compensation program?
15. How does Canada determine whether or not a person is a delinquent offender or an adult offender?
16. What are the three classifications of offenses in Great Britain? What courts usually deal with each classification you have listed?
17. Is crime in Great Britain increasing or decreasing according to official estimates? What differences in crime rates, if any, are revealed by *The 1981 British Crime Survey?*
18. Differentiate between the jurisdictions of the crown court and the magistrates' court.
19. What is terrorism? What are some terrorist activities? Identify two types of terrorists.
20. What are some of the international organizations that combat international crime and terrorism?

SUGGESTED READINGS

Abadinsky, Howard (1985). *Organized crime* (2nd ed.). Chicago: Nelson-Hall.

Cole, George F., Stanislaw J. Frankowski, and Marc G. Gertz (1987). *Major criminal justice systems* (2nd ed.). Beverly Hills, CA: Sage.

Inciardi, James A. (1981). *The drugs-crime connection.* Beverly Hills, CA: Sage.

Morris, Allison (1987). *Women, crime and criminal justice.* New York: Basil Blackwell.

Myren, Richard A. (1988). *Law and justice: An introduction.* Monterey, CA: Brooks/Cole.

Terrill, Richard J. (1984). *World criminal justice systems: A survey.* Cincinnati, OH: Anderson Publishing Co.

Crime Prevention

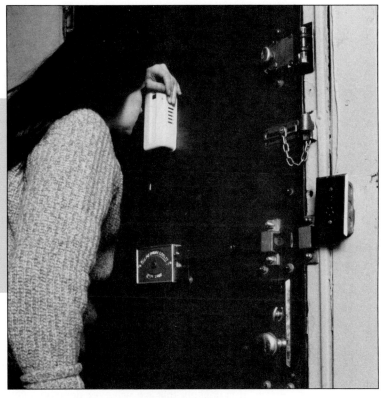

CHAPTER

18

■ INTRODUCTION

Samuel Walker (1985:5) says, "Can crime be prevented? No. Most current crime control proposals are nonsense. The best criminological minds of our time do not have anything practical to offer." This chapter examines the nature of crime control and the alternatives employed by public officials, law enforcement officers, and community residents to eliminate crime or at least control it. It looks at improvements in surveillance technology, including closed-circuit monitoring systems, and innovative crime detection methods. It explores more effective police training and more fruitful allocations of police officers. Finally, it reviews and assesses various efforts by community residents as crime fighting strategies.

A major concern of both criminologists and criminal justice professionals alike is crime prevention. **Crime prevention** is anticipation, recognition, and appraisal of crime risk and initiation of some action to remove or reduce it (National Crime Prevention Institute, 1986). Placing dead-bolt locks on doors in high-crime areas, jogging or walking through particular neighborhoods during daylight hours rather than at night, and establishing citizen's foot patrols to oversee certain residential areas are some of the many actions initiated to remove or reduce crime. Burglaries, assaults and muggings, and robberies are among the crimes believed to be reduced or prevented by taking such actions.

The Kansas City Preventive Patrol Experiment was designed to determine the precise impact of more police patrols in certain sectors of Kansas City. Some areas of the city were assigned three times the number of patrol cars normally assigned, while other sectors were not assigned any patrol cars (police responded only on a call-by-call basis). No differences in crime rates were reported in any sector, regardless of how heavily or lightly patrolled the sector happened to be.

Samuel Walker's (1985) gloomy comment regarding our current crime control policies is, unfortunately, all too accurate concerning our numerous efforts to prevent crime. It is unlikely that we will ever develop a set of crime prevention strategies that will put an end to burglary, rape, robbery, larceny, vehicular theft, aggravated assault, and all other crimes, but even Walker concedes that this does not mean that nothing can be done to control crime (Walker, 1985).

■ CRIMINAL VICTIMIZATION

Although any measure of crime trends is flawed by a number of conceptual and methodological problems, the National Crime Survey (NCS) is regarded as a fairly accurate barometer of criminal victimizations in the United States, especially when compared with the official estimates of crime provided by the *Uniform Crime Reports,* which is published by the FBI. One feature of the NCS that distinguishes it from more official estimates of crime is it obtains information about criminal victimizations from the crime victims themselves, regardless of whether they reported the crimes to the police (DeBerry and Timrots, 1986:1). Table 18.1 shows victimization levels in the United States between 1973 and 1987.

TABLE 18.1 Victimization Levels for Selected Crimes, 1973–1987

	Number of Victimizations (in 1,000s)			
	Total	Violent Crimes	Personal Theft	Household Crimes
1973	35,661	5,350	14,970	15,340
1974	38,411	5,510	15,889	17,012
1975	39,266	5,573	16,294	17,400
1976	39,318	5,599	16,519	17,199
1977	40,314	5,902	16,933	17,480
1978	40,412	5,941	17,050	17,421
1979	41,249	6,159	16,382	18,708
1980	40,252	6,130	15,300	18,821
1981	41,454	6,582	15,863	19,009
1982	39,756	6,459	15,553	17,744
1983	37,001	5,903	14,657	16,440
1984	35,544	6,021	13,789	15,733
1985	34,864	5,823	13,474	15,568
1986	34,118	5,515	13,235	15,368
1987	34,731	5,661	13,344	15,726
Percent change, 1981–87[a]	−16.2%[b]	−14.0%[b]	−15.9%[b]	−17.3%[b]

[a]Total victimizations peaked in 1981.
[b]The difference is statistically significant at the 95% confidence level.
Source: U.S. Department of Justice, "Criminal Victimization 1987," *Bureau of Justice Statistics Bulletin,* October 1988, p. 1.

Table 18.1 shows in 1987, there were 34.7 million victimizations for selected offenses. The crimes selected for these victimization reports include rape, robbery, assault, theft, burglary, household larceny, and motor vehicle theft. Interestingly, victimization peaked in 1981 at 41.5 million and then declined until 1986. Table 18.2 shows a contrast in the numbers of victimizations for selected crime categories for the years 1986 and 1987. In 1987, there were 5.6 million household burglaries and 969,000 motor vehicle thefts. That same year there were 1 million robberies and 4.5 million assaults.

In 1984, Congress enacted the **Victims of Crimes Act,** which formalized the collection of fines, penalties, and other assessments from those convicted of federal crimes. The act made available as much as $100 million for distribution to various states for victim compensation and victim services (Forst and Hernon, 1985:1).

Is a reduction in criminal victimizations attributable to better law enforcement? Are citizens responsive to the general need for greater community participation in crime prevention programs? Are criminals themselves responding favorably to alternative rehabilitative strategies and positively influencing recidivism rates? Is public apathy toward crime changing? At present, these and related questions cannot be answered

TABLE 18.2   Changes in Victimization Levels and Rates for Personal and Household Crimes, 1986–1987

	Number of Victimizations (1,000s)			Victimization Rates		
	1986	1987	Percent Change 1986–87	1986	1987	Percent Change 1986–87
All crimes	34,118	34,731	1.8%[a]	...	...	...
Personal crimes	18,751	19,005	1.4%	95.6	96.1	.5%
Crimes of violence	5,515	5,661	2.6	28.1	28.6	1.8
Completed	2,049	2,086	1.8	10.4	10.5	1.0
Attempted	3,466	3,575	3.1	17.7	18.1	2.3
Rape[c]	130	141	8.4	.7	.7	7.6
Robbery	1,009	1,030	2.1	5.1	5.2	1.3
Completed	622	678	9.1	3.2	3.4	8.2
With injury	234	276	17.8	1.2	1.4	16.9
Without injury	388	402	3.8	2.0	2.0	2.9
Attempted	387	352	−9.1	2.0	1.8	−9.8
With injury	117	97	−16.7	.6	.5	−17.3
Without injury	271	255	−5.8	1.4	1.3	−6.6
Assault	4,376	4,489	2.6	22.3	22.7	1.7
Aggravated	1,543	1,543	0	7.9	7.8	−.8
Completed with injury	562	481	−14.4[b]	2.9	2.4	−15.1[b]
Attempted assault with weapon	981	1,062	8.3	5.0	5.4	7.4
Simple	2,833	2,946	4.0	14.4	14.9	3.1
Completed with injury	820	862	5.1	4.2	4.4	4.3
Attempted assault without weapon	2,013	2,084	3.5	10.3	10.5	2.7
Crimes of theft	13,235	13,344	.8	67.5	67.5	0
Completed	12,402	12,510	.9	63.2	63.3	0
Attempted	833	834	.1	4.2	4.2	−.7
Personal larceny with contact	536	509	−5.1	2.7	2.6	−5.9
Purse snatching	163	185	13.3	.8	.9	12.4
Pocket picking	373	324	−13.2	1.9	1.6	−13.9

...Not applicable.

[a]The difference is statistically significant at the 95% confidence level.

[b]The difference is statistically significant at the 90% confidence level.

[c]There were 1.2 rapes per 1,000 women age 12 and older in 1986 and 1.3 in 1987.

TABLE 18.2
continued

	Number of Victimizations (1,000s)			Victimization Rates		
	1986	1987	Percent Change 1986–87	1986	1987	Percent Change 1986–87
Personal larceny without contact	12,699	12,835	1.1	64.7	64.9	.3
Completed	11,895	12,064	1.4	60.6	61.0	.6
Less than $50	5,516	5,317	−3.6	28.1	26.9	−4.4
$50 or more	5,731	6,163	7.5[a]	29.2	31.2	6.7[a]
Amount not available	648	584	−9.9	3.3	3.0	−10.7
Attempted	804	771	−4.1	4.1	3.9	−4.9
Household crimes	15,368	15,726	2.3%[b]	170.0	171.4	.8%
Completed	13,064	13,263	1.5	144.5	144.5	0
Attempted	2,304	2,463	6.9[b]	25.5	26.8	5.3
Household burglary	5,557	5,623	1.2	61.5	61.3	−.3
Completed	4,307	4,277	−.7	47.6	46.6	−2.2
Forcible entry	1,813	1,963	8.3	20.1	21.4	6.7
Unlawful entry without force	2,494	2,313	−7.3[b]	27.6	25.2	−8.6[a]
Attempted forcible entry	1,249	1,347	7.8	13.8	14.7	6.2
Household larceny	8,455	8,624	2.0	93.5	94.0	.5
Completed	7,869	8,018	1.9	87.1	87.4	.4
Less than $50	3,434	3,459	.7	38.0	37.7	−.8
$50 or more	3,884	4,080	5.1[b]	43.0	44.5	3.5
Amount not available	551	479	−13.2[b]	6.1	5.2	−14.5
Attempted	586	607	3.5	6.5	6.6	2.0
Motor vehicle theft	1,356	1,479	9.1	15.0	16.1	7.4
Completed	888	969	9.1	9.8	10.6	7.5
Attempted	468	510	8.9	5.2	5.6	7.3

Note: Detail may not add to total shown because of rounding. Percent change is based on unrounded figures. Victimization rates are calculated on the basis of the number of victimizations per 1,000 persons age 12 and older or per 1,000 households. The population age 12 and older grew from 196,160,200 in 1986 to 197,769,500 in 1987, an increase of 0.8%. The number of households grew from 90,394,700 to 91,764,000 between 1986 and 1987, an increase of 1.5%.

Source: U.S. Department of Justice, "Criminal Victimization 1987," *Bureau of Justice Statistics Bulletin,* October 1988, p. 2.

Some persons are cynical about police efforts to solve crimes and protect citizens. Various interest groups promote self-protection schemes, including purchasing firearms for self-defense and personal safety.

with certainty. Private citizens can take preventive measures to protect their property against burglary by engaging in target hardening, or making residences less susceptible to breaking and entering (Mayhew, 1984), and perhaps police can deter significant numbers of robberies by being highly visible in selected commercial areas, where banks and large businesses are located. Vehicular theft may be attacked by police officers through better training of officers in their initial investigation of theft reports and the establishment of antifencing programs and by private citizens through better property protection (Lee and Rikoski, 1984; Research and Forecasts, 1983; Weiner, Stephens, and Besachuk, 1983).

■ CRIME PREVENTION METHODS USED BY POLICE

Crime prevention has two primary meanings. For sociologists, crime prevention is a reduction in poverty, an elimination of city slum zones known for poor-quality housing and often labeled breeding grounds for crime. Another meaning is architectural change to make dwellings more secure against burglars, or target hardening. Crime prevention generally has been loosely applied to any effort aimed at controlling criminal behavior (National Crime Prevention Institute, 1986:2). Crime prevention may be either direct, where environmental opportunities for crime are reduced, or indirect, where measures such as job training, remedial education, police surveillance, imprisonment, probation, and parole are used (Jefferey, 1971:20). As used here, *crime prevention applies to all strategies designed to reduce criminal opportunity* (National Crime Prevention Institute, 1986:2).

Some authorities believe that police do not prevent crime or deter the commission of criminal acts (Walker, 1984; Clarke, 1983:233). Law enforcement officers are only occasionally in "the right place" when crime is committed. It is rare that police officers see a crime committed in their presence. Instead, police officers respond and investigate when crimes are reported. The solution of many cases is routine, resulting from leads provided by the victims themselves (Willman and Snortum, 1984). In a study of 5,336 crime reports in a large suburban police department, researchers monitored

Police respond to citizen complaints alleging crimes. However, the public does not always report crime. Technological improvements in crime detection and criminal apprehension have been made, but police cannot act in most instances where crimes are not reported.

3,243 hours of investigative activity. They found that most clearances by arrest of identified crime perpetrators were made before the cases were assigned to detectives (Willman and Snortum, 1984). Investigative activity is not exclusively reserved for detective personnel.

What crime control strategies can law enforcement agencies implement? Some of the options for police agencies include (1) greater visibility and surveillance, (2) modifications of patrol styles; (3) community policing, and (4) establishment of awareness programs.

Greater Visibility and Surveillance

Community residents and governmental leaders believe that increasing police visibility and surveillance will deter the occurrence of crime. Many of the programs promoted and supported by the now-defunct Law Enforcement Assistance Administration (LEAA) were based, in part, on the idea that greater expenditures of funds for law enforcement would result in reductions in crime levels from one city to the next. Unfortunately, during the tenure of the LEAA, crime rates remained unaffected.

The controversial Kansas City Preventive Patrol Experiment examined different deployments of police patrol units to various city sectors. Units in some sectors were tripled, and some sectors had all units withheld. In sectors without police patrol units, police nevertheless responded as rapidly as possible to crime reports from citizens. The results revealed no differences in crime rates in any sector (Kelling, Pate, Dieckman, and Brown, 1974).

High police visibility in one area often causes burglers and robbers to transfer their activities to other, less-threatening areas (Clarke, 1983). Placing police officers in subways may cause muggers to commit more muggings in back alleys. Increased efforts to reduce crime at night may shift crime more frequently to days (Clarke, 1983:227). Some observers say that police officers ought to return to a watchman style of police patrol instead of continue their present crime control orientation, but other critics, such as Walker (1985), argue that the crime control orientation of police patrolling has been greatly exaggerated, that police officers themselves have fostered such images, and that in reality, routine police work is primarily a matter of peacekeeping (Walker, 1985). According to Walker, the primary benefit of greater police visibility is the development of better police-community relations and a greater public sense of safety. Walker is probably correct in his assessment.

However, it may be a mistake to judge police solely on the basis of their ability to reduce crime (Wilson, 1983:74). After all, most police work involving crime occurs after crimes have been committed and reported. One of the original purposes of police was to maintain order in urban neighborhoods, and it might be important for us to view police in a broader perspective, one that assigns an important part in both crime control and the maintenance of orderly neighborhoods.

Modifications of Patrol Styles

Several experiments have looked at variations in police patrol styles (Meagher, 1985). In 1977, the San Diego, California, police experimented with one-officer and two-officer patrol cars and compared the relative effectiveness of their responses to crime scenes (Kessler, 1985). One-officer patrol cars were usually more responsive than were two-officer patrol cars, with an obvious saving of citizens' tax dollars.

In Flint, Michigan, an experiment used police foot patrols working in tandem with patrol car units (Payne and Trojanowicz, 1985). The benefits were improved relations between officers and citizens as well as improved officer moral. Police officers on foot patrol felt safer, more confident that community residents would help them if they got into trouble, that they were keeping up with problems in their patrol areas, and that they were improving police-community relations (Trojanowicz and Banas, 1985a; Trojanowicz and Banas, 1985b). Was crime in Flint, Michigan, prevented or controlled better as a result of the foot patrol program? The results were inconclusive.

Community Policing

Community policing is the permanent assignment of police officers to given sectors or neighborhoods in a community (Manning, 1984). Police officers are assigned a regular beat, where they can become closely acquainted with neighborhood residents and businesspersons. Obvious benefits resulting from community policing include instant recognition of unfamiliar faces and potential criminals and, of course, better police-community relations.

Tampa, Florida, has experimented with a variety of programs, including community policing (Smith and Taylor, 1985). Tampa established neighborhood police offices much like the ministations in Detroit, Michigan. During the first 6 months of operation, community policing appeared to reduce crime in the areas serviced by neighborhood stations compared with areas of Tampa not having such stations. One important implication of such an experiment was to increase a citizen's willingness to report crimes when they occurred as trust in and reliance upon the police officers increased.

Building interpersonal relations between community residents and police officers appears to increase the incidence of reporting crimes to police. Table 18.3 shows some of the most important reasons persons do not report crimes to police as determined from 1983 National Crime Survey figures. In 11 percent of the cases, citizens would not report crimes to police because they believed that the police wouldn't think it was important enough, wouldn't want to be bothered, or would be inefficient or insensitive (Harlow, 1985:9). Closely related was the idea that nothing could be done about it anyway. These cases involved stolen property that was either not identifiable or would be difficult to recover by police. One thing is certain, however. The police cannot act until a crime is reported. Property will not be recovered if it is not reported stolen. Any strategy to improve police-community relations and citizens' willingness to report crime to the police has some merit, but there is irony associated with the increased reporting of crime and better police work: Crime rates will appear to increase substantially, and such an apparent increase in crime may look to the community that the police are doing a worse, not a better, job in the long run.

Establishment of Awareness Programs

Particularly in theft crimes, police-sponsored citizen awareness programs assist police in their recovery and identification of stolen property. Awareness programs include **Operation Identification,** which involves the labeling of all valuable personal property on one's premises with an identifying number (Clarke and Hope, 1984). Many police departments furnish their community residents with devices for imprinting their social security numbers on valuable possessions, such as televisions and stereos. If these items are subsequently stolen and recovered, they can be traced more easily to the rightful owners. Also, such numbering of valuable property makes it less desirable to market, or fence, by the thieves (Clarke and Hope, 1984).

In Orlando, Florida, a Citizen Police Academy (CPA) gives private citizens a better understanding of police operations and enhances police effectiveness in the community (Ferguson, 1985). CPA consists of a 10-week course involving weekly 3-hour meetings. The course topics include almost every dimension of police work, including the functions of police patrols and undercover operations.

Operation Identification is a program sponsored by police and other agencies to help citizens identify their personal property as well as their children. Fingerprinting young children can help locate runaways, kidnap victims, and lost infants. Electronic devices can label valuables for future identification.

TABLE 18.3 Most Important Reason for Not Reporting to Police, 1983

Most Important Reason	All Crimes	Crimes of Violence				Crimes of Theft			Household Crimes					
		Total	Rob-bery	Aggra-vated Assault	Simple Assault	Total	Com-pleted	At-tempted	Total	Com-pleted	At-tempted	Bur-glary	House-hold Larceny	Motor Vehicle Theft
Total	100%	100%	100%	100%	100%	100%	100%	100%	100%	100%	100%	100%	100%	100%
Not serious														
Object recovered or offender unsuccessful	5	5	14	4	3	4	2	33	5	2	21	8	3	22
Did not think it important enough	30	22	15	20	26	30	30	24	32	34	22	21	38	13
Nothing could be done														
Didn't realize crime happened until later	7	1	--	--	--	7	7	5	8	9	8	11	7	9
Property hard to recover due to lack of identification number	4	--	--	--	--	5	5	--	5	6	--	3	7	--
Lack of proof, no way to find/identify offender	16	8	16	9	5	17	17	14	16	16	16	17	16	18

Reason													
Police wouldn't do anything / Police wouldn't think it was important enough—wouldn't want to be bothered	7	5	5	4	5	6	6	5	8	8	7	7	8	8
Police would be inefficient, insensitive	4	5	9	5	3	2	2	3	5	5	5	6	4	8
Reported to someone else	11	11	8	9	13	18	19	6	4	3	6	7	2	--
Private/personal matter or took care of it myself	9	28	13	33	30	4	4	3	8	8	4	8	7	10
Did not want to take time, too inconvenient	2	2	--	3	1	2	2	--	2	2	2	2	2	--
Afraid of reprisal by offender or his family or friends	1	4	5	4	4	0	0	--	1	1	--	1	0	--
Other	7	11	11	9	10	6	7	5	7	7	7	9	6	6

Note: Figures may not add to total because of rounding

--Too few cases to obtain statistically reliable data.

Source: Caroline Wolf Harlow, *Reporting Crimes to the Police* (Washington, DC: Bureau of Justice Statistics, 1985), p. 8.

In Texas, the Dallas Police Department conducts a similar program, holding monthly meetings between police officials and businesspersons, apartment owners, and other interested individuals concerning the latest crime prevention techniques and devices, security systems, and area crime information (Pierce, 1984). The New York City Police Department has assisted in the establishment of a Citizen's Crime Commission, which also emphasizes cooperation between the police and businesspersons for preventing crimes in commercial centers (New York Citizen's Crime Commission, 1985). In Atlanta, Georgia, the Bureau of Police Services' Partnership Against Crime Program encourages close cooperation between the citizens and the police in devising crime prevention strategies and identifying public safety problems (Napper, 1986).

In Alexandria, Virginia, police officers who work the evening shift in the Alexandria Police Operations Bureau visit new homeowners in their particular neighborhood sectors (Seiffert, 1984). They provide useful information concerning the neighborhood, city services, and particularly, the crime prevention responsibilities of the citizen. Included in their presentation is a free homeowner's packet of materials that includes emergency telephone numbers, tips on what to do if someone is breaking into the residence, and ways of making the residence less susceptible to burglars. Identification labels for valuables are also provided, as well as a checklist for listing serial numbers of portable appliances and equipment that are easily stolen and prime targets of theft.

The Detroit (Michigan) Police Department established an antifencing program between 1977 and 1981 (Weiner, Stephens, and Besachuk, 1983). Funded by a federal

CRIME BEAT

No wonder Florida residents are taking steps to arm themselves. Florida led all states in violent crimes in 1987, with 1,037 homicides, robberies, and aggravated assaults per 100,000 persons. A new law passed on October 1, 1987, made Florida one of the easiest states in which to acquire a handgun. Concealed weapon permits in Florida have escalated to an all-time high, as citizens protect themselves against an increasingly aggressive criminal element. In some Florida cities, such as Miami, citizens wearing handguns openly around their waists are reminiscent of scenes from the old West.

The controversy over handgun ownership has not abated. Almost every time a mass murder occurs, whether it be on a university campus, in a grade school, or in a McDonald's restaurant, the media highlight the weapon or weapons used and various interest groups lobby for tighter gun control laws. Specific weapons used in these assaults and massacres are targeted for prohibition, as if they were the causes of the assaults

initially. National Rifle Association representatives and those interested in preserving the freedom of gun ownership contend that people kill other people and that guns are only one of several killing instruments.

Regardless of one's position in the gun regulation controversy, several states, including Maryland, have taken serious steps to regulate who should own and carry weapons. The regulatory policy enacted by Maryland legislators is aimed at limiting access to Saturday night specials, or cheap handguns. The legislators have provided for stiff penalties and fines for any company manufacturing or distributing such weaponry. While this action will not prevent such weapons from falling into the wrong hands, it is a move toward greater handgun control.

Who should possess handguns? What restrictions should be placed on those intending to purchase firearms? What questions would you want to ask persons who purchase firearms? What sort of waiting period would you require, if any?

grant, this program involved a sting operation to purchase stolen goods from both fences and thieves. Out of 844 incidents with 395 subjects, there were 252 arrests during the experimental period and over $10 million in stolen property and $9 million in narcotics were recovered. Interestingly, the project did not deter burglars and thieves from criminal activity. Property crimes appeared to remain fairly stable during the antifencing program period, but community confidence in the police department was significantly enhanced (Weiner, Stephens, and Besachuk, 1983).

■ COMMUNITY CRIME PREVENTION

The **Victimization Risk Survey (VRS)** was conducted in 1984 as a supplement to the National Crime Survey (Whitaker, 1986). The survey was administered to 21,016 persons age 16 and over in 11,198 households randomly selected throughout the United States. According to the VRS, one third of the households reported one or more of the following crime prevention measures: (1) having a burglar alarm (7 percent), (2) participating in a neighborhood watch program (7 percent), or (3) engraving valuables with an identification number (25 percent) (Whitaker, 1986:1). Table 18.4 shows a distribution of various home crime prevention measures reported by the VRS by age, race, educational attainment, and other variables.

Table 18.4 shows that homeowners are much more likely than renters to employ one or more of the security strategies listed. Eight percent of the homeowners have security alarm systems compared with only 4 percent of the renters. This difference

Many neighborhoods have established neighborhood watches, which consist of volunteers who patrol their neighborhoods regularly. They report suspicious persons or circumstances to police, who investigate. Many citizens believe that police visibility deters burglars and other criminals.

TABLE 18.4 Home Crime Prevention Measures by Selected Demographic Characteristics

Demographic Characteristics[a]	Percent of Households That:			
	Have a Burglar Alarm	Joined a Neighborhood Watch Program	Engraved Valuables with an Identifying Number	Have Taken at Least One of These Measures
Total	7%	7%	25%	33%
Age				
16–19	—	6	36	41
20–24	4	4	30	34
25–34	5	7	29	35
35–49	8	10	29	38
50–64	8	9	23	32
65 and over	6	6	16	23
Race				
White	6	7	26	33
Black	8	10	23	33
Other	—	—	24	32
Ethnic origin				
Non-Hispanic	7	8	26	34
Hispanic	6	5	16	23
Educational attainment[b]				
Elementary school	5	4	12	18
High school	6	6	24	32
College	9	10	32	41
Family income[c]				
Less than $7,500	5	4	16	22
$7,500–9,999	5	5	20	26
$10,000–14,999	4	6	22	28

—Too few cases to obtain statistically reliable data.
[a]Individual characteristics are those of the household respondent.
[b]Educational attainment is the highest grade or year completed.
[c]Income is that of all family members during the 12 months prior to the interview.

may be a function of the fact that home security systems are expensive and often permanently attached to the dwelling. Renters would be less likely to install such expensive equipment. The same kind of difference between homeowners and renters extends to joining neighborhood watch programs. Persons most likely to have burglar alarm systems, engrave their valuables, and participate in neighborhood watch programs have more educational attainment and more family income than others. However, few differences were attributable to race or ethnic origin. Burglar alarms were possessed to the same degree for central city and suburban residents. Similar

TABLE 18.4 *continued*

Demographic Characteristics[a]	Percent of Households That:			
	Have a Burglar Alarm	Joined a Neighborhood Watch Program	Engraved Valuables with an Identifying Number	Have Taken at Least One of These Measures
$15,000–24,999	5	7	28	35
$25,000–29,999	7	9	31	40
$30,000–49,999	8	11	32	41
$50,000 or more	16	15	35	51
Tenure				
Owned	8	10	27	36
Rented	4	4	23	27
Number of persons in household				
1	7	5	19	26
2–3	7	8	27	35
4–5	7	10	29	38
6 or more	4	7	22	29
Number of units in structure				
1	7	9	27	36
2–3	5	5	21	27
4–9	5	3	22	27
10 or more	6	3	17	22
Mobile home	3	5	27	31
Location of residence[d]				
Metropolitan area	8	9	24	34
Central city				
Suburban area	8	8	28	36
Nonmetropolitan area	4	5	23	29

[d]A metropolitan area is a county or counties that contain a city or cities having at least 50,000 total population. A central city is the largest city of a metropolitan area. A suburban area is the portion outside the central city. Nonmetropolitan areas include rural areas and cities of fewer than 50,000.

Source: Reprinted from Catherine J. Whitaker, *Crime Prevention* (Washington, DC: National Institute of Justice, 1986), p. 2.

participation rates for neighborhood watch programs were observed for city and suburban residents. The engraving of valuables was similar for both groups as well.

About 95 percent of all American households need substantial improvement in security to achieve the minimum security standards suggested by local police agencies (Mayhew, 1984), but the evidence is sketchy concerning how effective security measures are in preventing crimes such as burglary, even in residences equipped with security systems. Target hardening, or making a residence less desirable as a target for burglary or theft by the use of various security measures, seems to be fairly effective

TABLE 18.5　Percent of Households Touched by Crime, by Selected Characteristics, 1987

Percent of Households Touched By:	Annual Family Income				Place of Residence[a]			Region			
	Low	Medium		High				North-east	Mid-west	South	West
	Under $7,500	$7,500–$14,999	$15,000–$24,999	$25,000 or More	Urban	Suburban	Rural				
Any NCS crime	23.9%	22.7%	24.0%	26.9%	28.6%	24.2%	18.5%	19.2%	24.7%	24.3%	29.4%
Violent crime	6.3	5.2	4.3	4.1	5.8	4.1	3.7	3.7	5.0	4.3	5.6
Rape	.2	.1	.1	.1	.1	.1	.1	.1	.1	.1	.1
Robbery	1.6	1.1	.8	.7	1.6	.7	.5	1.0	1.1	.8	1.0
Assault	4.8	4.3	3.4	3.5	4.3	3.4	3.3	2.7	4.0	3.5	4.7
Aggravated	1.8	1.6	1.3	1.2	1.8	1.1	1.3	.8	1.3	1.5	1.9
Simple	3.4	3.0	2.4	2.5	2.9	2.6	2.3	2.0	3.0	2.3	3.3
Total theft	14.9	14.9	17.4	20.1	19.2	17.7	13.0	12.6	17.3	17.1	21.7
Personal theft	8.6	8.8	10.8	14.0	11.9	12.0	8.0	8.1	10.9	10.5	13.4
Household theft	8.2	7.8	8.3	8.2	9.9	7.4	6.2	5.2	7.8	8.1	10.5
Burglary	7.3	5.6	4.7	4.8	6.3	4.7	4.3	3.6	5.1	5.8	5.8
Motor vehicle theft	1.0	1.3	1.5	1.8	2.2	1.5	.6	1.7	1.5	1.3	1.7
Serious violent crime[b]	3.5	2.7	2.2	2.0	3.5	1.8	1.8	1.9	2.3	2.3	2.9
Crimes of high concern[c]	9.8	7.9	6.9	7.0	9.4	6.8	5.6	5.5	7.4	7.7	8.7

Note: Detail does not add to total because of overlap in households touched by various crimes.

[a]These estimates are not comparable to estimates for place of residence prior to 1986 due to changes in geographic classification.

[b]Rape, robbery, or aggravated assault.

[c]A rape, robbery, or assault by a stranger, or a burglary.

Source: Michael R. Rand, *Households Touched by Crime, 1987* (Washington, DC: Bureau of Justice Statistics, 1988), p. 2.

for discouraging younger, less experienced offenders, such as teenagers. More professional criminals continually devise strategies to defeat almost any residential alarm system, and surveys tend to show that victims of burglars are no more poorly protected than nonvictims (Mayhew, 1984). (See Table 18.5.)

Various communities have formed voluntary citizen's neighborhood patrols that assist the neighborhood generally by providing a crime watch, reporting suspicious activities to police, observing and recording license numbers of suspicious automobiles, and visibly deterring persons from burglarizing homes (Neighborhood Crime Prevention Council, 1985). It has been estimated that as many as 6 million Americans currently participate in burglary prevention programs of one sort or another (Titus, 1984). In certain communities, citizen's patrol members receive training in first aid, what to do when witnessing a crime, making a citizen's arrest and the legal implications of doing so, and screening recruits for such patrols (Graves et al., 1985). However, not everyone is enthusiastic about the value of neighborhood patrols. At least one investigator has cautioned that neighborhood policing by citizen's patrols may inadvertently isolate certain neighborhoods from other sectors of the community (Einstadter, 1984).

Neighborhood watch groups have been established in many cities throughout the United States. One third of the city blocks in Detroit, Michigan, have been organized into neighborhood watch groups in recent years (Research and Forecasts, Inc., 1983). Sangamon County and Springfield, Illinois, have created 253 neighborhood watch groups and 330 community action groups to prevent burglaries (Research and Forecasts,

Street crime has become commonplace in New York City and other large urban areas. One means of combating crime is the establishment of citizens' protection groups, such as the Guardian Angels, who patrol subways and other high-crime areas in efforts to protect travelers and deter would-be muggers.

1983). The Kensington Joint Action Committee in Philadelphia, Pennsylvania, has mobilized a neighborhood watch group to combat the growing incidence of arson. In short, active involvement by community residents in securing their own possessions and property appears to be a key to successful reduction in the incidence of crime in the affected neighborhoods (Research and Forecasts, 1983).

One of the fastest growing and visible crime control programs operated at the community level is **Crime Stoppers** (Rosenbaum, Lurigio, and Lavrakas, 1986). According to James K. Stewart, Director of the National Institute of Justice in 1986, "[I]nformation is the lifeblood of a criminal investigation." The key to a successful investigation is accurate information about the crime committed, the witnesses, and the perpetrator(s). Crime Stoppers is a growing movement which appears to be taking a bite out of crime (Rosenbaum, Lurigio, and Lavrakas, 1986:1). Figure 18.1 shows the growth of the number of Crime Stoppers programs from 1980 to 1986.

Crime Stoppers was originated by a police officer, Greg MacAleese, in Albuquerque, New Mexico, in 1976. By 1978, he had established five programs in various cities. By 1986, Crime Stoppers programs had grown to an estimated 600 in the United States (Rosenbaum, Lurigio, and Lavrakas, 1986:2). The Crime Stoppers program is typically nonprofit. It consists of a board of directors from the community. These persons set policy, coordinate fund-raising, and formulate a system of rewards.

Figure 18.1 Number of Crime Stoppers Programs by Year

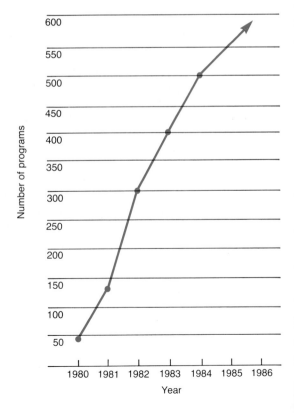

Source: Reprinted from Dennis P. Rosenbaum, Arthur J. Lurigio, and Paul J. Lavrakas, *Crime Stoppers: A National Evaluation* (Washington, DC: National Institute of Justice, 1986), p. 2.

Television and radio programs assist Crime Stoppers by presenting a crime of the week so that anyone with information about the crime can call the station and possibly receive a cash reward if the perpetrator is apprehended. Cash rewards average from $171 for reporting property crimes to $505 for solving the crime of the week.

The Crime Stoppers program was originally designed to assist police in solving certain dead-end felony cases (Rosenbaum, Lurigio, and Lavrakas, 1986:3). Preserving the confidentiality of callers, Crime Stoppers solicits information from community residents about crimes that have been committed. If reports lead to arrests, then rewards are paid. By the end of 1985, for example, Crime Stoppers International claimed solutions to 92,339 felonies and recovery of property and narcotics totaling $562.2 million, or an average of $6,089 per case. By the end of 1985, Crime Stoppers had paid out a total of $6.7 million in local rewards for information leading to felony arrests.

An evaluation of the effectiveness of Crime Stoppers tried to assess citizen participation, program organization, and general program success (Rosenbaum, Lurigio, and Lavrakas, 1986). While researchers regard Crime Stoppers' actions relating to recovery of property as significant, they are not inclined to see Crime Stoppers as a major crime prevention organization. Although numerous crimes have been cleared through Crime Stoppers information and action, they amount to only a small fraction of total serious crime in most communities (Rosenbaum, Lurigio, and Lavrakas, 1986:3).

Among the problems of Crime Stoppers cited by experts are certain legal issues relating to the potential for false arrest, defamation, invasion of privacy, and civil rights violations. It is difficult to establish true probable cause on the basis of an anonymous tip over the telephone. Another problem is whether or not the same kind of confidentiality exists between Crime Stoppers and an informant as exists between a lawyer and client (Rosenbaum, Lurigio, and Lavrakas, 1986:5). Should anonymity be preserved in the case of an arrest of an innocent person? Researchers suggest that among other things, Crime Stoppers should seek to teach proper interviewing techniques to its personnel so that informants yield sufficient information for criminal investigators to vigorously pursue a case. Crime Stoppers should also seek to employ the services of trained attorneys to advise about the appropriateness of certain investigative practices and procedures.

Besides neighborhood watches and patrols, Crime Stoppers, and Operation Identification, neighbors need to be more neighborly (Jacobs, 1961). Crime flourishes whenever neighbors do not know each other, when neighbors stay behind their doors and have no sense of identity with the neighborhoods in which they live (Clarke, 1983:234). Certain police efforts to meet with community residents and hold neighborhood meetings are regarded as positive steps toward reducing neighborhood anonymity.

▪ ALTERNATIVE CRIME PREVENTION STRATEGIES

Police and community residents attempt to prevent the occurrence of crime by visibility, watch programs, and defensive actions, such as target hardening and the installation of security systems. These actions are directed primarily toward burglars, arsonists, and

▪▪▪▪	**CRIME BEAT**

One of the most difficult crimes to prevent is arson. A skilled arsonist can plant a delayed-action device virtually anywhere and have it ignite at a predetermined time. Arson was suspected in the New Year's Eve fire at San Juan, Puerto Rico's, Dupont Plaza hotel, a twenty-two story luxury hotel on San Juan's Condado resort strip. The fire, believed to have been started in the hotel ballroom on the main floor, quickly spread throughout the hotel and upper floors. Because of the occasion, the hotel was packed with eight hundred guests. Although fire fighters and rescue teams saved nearly one hundred guests who fled to the rooftop and windows, nearly one hundred guests perished in the blaze. A hotel employee was eventually arrested for setting the fire that killed so many.

Should previously convicted arsonists be required to report regularly to probation or paroling authorities? What defensive measures can be taken against the possibility of arson in settings occupied by large numbers of people?

---

thieves, but some crimes are almost impossible to prevent. In 1986, a nighttime sniper cut down Alan Gorden in his Rhode Island home (Doherty, 1987). Within a few weeks, 42-year-old Rhode Island resident Anthony Amantea was shot in the neck by an outside sniper while watching television in his living room. Richard Galinis, another Rhode Islander, was grazed by rifle fire from an unknown sniper while trimming his Christmas tree. Local authorities suggested that Rhode Island residents keep their blinds and window shades closed, especially at night, in an effort to discourage the sniper from shooting at them. In spite of Rhode Island Governor Edward DiPrete's calling in the National Guard, state troopers, and the FBI to deal with this sniper menace, there have been no clues concerning the sniper's identity or whereabouts.

Previous chapters have explored other components of the criminal justice system pertaining to crime control. The area of corrections is designed, in part, to deter criminals from committing further crimes. Incarceration is regarded as both punishing as well as rehabilitative by groups with competing correctional philosophies. However, the ineffectiveness of incarceration is well documented. Recidivism rates are high among parolees and even probationers. Alternative sentencing programs, such as selective incapacitation, community service, felony probation, home confinement, and electronic surveillance, exhibit flaws and are only partially effective.

The judicial segment of the criminal justice system must make difficult choices in sentencing offenders for serious crimes. Jail and prison overcrowding and court-mandated prison population reductions undo whatever courts accomplish in the nature of sentencing severity. When offenders know that their prospects for long-term incarceration are remote, they have little incentive to obey the law. In any event, the severity of sentencing seems to have little effect, if any, on recidivism rates in most jurisdictions (Piliavin et al., 1986).

Emphasizing more effective juvenile delinquency rehabilitation programs and diverting first offenders to parental custody or probation has experienced limited success as well. On the record, Samuel Walker's (1985) nothing-works viewpoint is grounded in cold, hard facts that expose the ineffectiveness of the entire criminal justice system as an apparatus for preventing or seriously reducing crime, but even Walker himself is not

████ **CRIME BEAT**

Detecting drunk drivers before they harm others is difficult. Many drivers who are legally intoxicated seem to negotiate their vehicles well on the open highway, yet their reflexes and other responses are adversely affected by alcohol. Preventing drunk driving has become a national goal for many interested citizens, many of whom have lost close friends and relatives because of drunk drivers. Mothers Against Drunk Driving (MADD) is one organization devoted to ridding the highways of drunk drivers. One of its objectives is to create harsher penalties for those convicted of driving while intoxicated.

Legally, restaurants may become liable for the actions of their customers who consume too much alcohol. Bartenders and others, including hosts of private parties, make judgment calls when guests have too much to drink, but this type of monitoring is difficult. Bartenders may know how many drinks a customer has had in their bars, but they don't know how much the customer may have consumed elsewhere earlier.

Automobile manufacturers and others have suggested several safeguards. For example, Guardian Interlock Systems of Denver, Colorado, has devised a system aimed at persons convicted of driving while intoxicated. Their automobiles are equipped with breathalyzer devices. When a driver enters the automobile, he or she must breathe into the device. If the blood-alcohol level is acceptable, the automobile will start. If the reading is legal intoxication, the machine will prevent the car from starting. Of course, this does not rule out the possibility that a sober or less intoxicated passenger will breathe into the machine to beat the system, but it does represent a means of handling one of the nation's leading killers—drunk drivers.

Should all automobiles be required to have such devices to curtail possible drunk drivers from operating their vehicles?

completely discouraged. He says, "[W]e are not completely helpless in the face of our seemingly permanent high level of serious crime" (Walker, 1985:221). Walker concludes that, yes, we can do something about crime. We can strike back at crime indirectly by directly attacking economic opportunity (Walker, 1985:224).

In the case of rape, authorities provide useful information for avoiding areas and situations where rapes are most likely to occur, but the risk of rape continues to be quite high. One proposed method for dealing with known rapists is castration (Baker, 1984). However, surgical castration has been ruled cruel and unusual punishment under the Eighth Amendment and is therefore unconstitutional.

Even crime on an international scale is difficult to control. Drug Enforcement Administration officials claim, for example, that for every shipment of cocaine they intercept, one hundred shipments succeed in slipping through (Lawn, 1985). The Racketeer Influenced and Corrupt Organizations Act passed by Congress has only incidentally affected organized crime in the United States (Bentivoglio, 1985).

One of the potential problems in criminal justice research is the lack of long-range theory. Criminal justice research is sometimes regarded as lacking historical depth, having a narrowly utilitarian orientation, rarely grappling with important questions of power, and being primarily technical (Robinson, 1985). Instead, it ought to study how communal and societal structures influence formal and informal social control (Robinson, 1985). Organized crime, prostitution, credit card fraud, white-collar crime, drug abuse, child and spousal abuse, corporate deviance and espionage, television cable pirating, computer crime, drunk driving, pornography, mugging and other forms of assault, arson, counterfeiting of products as well as money, and shoplifting are among the many crimes targeted for investigation by both police and criminal justice professionals. For each of the crimes listed and for the greater number not listed, there are numerous alternative proposals for solution. It is unlikely that any of the offenses will be eliminated completely in the near future, but certain proposals show more promise than others for reducing the incidence of some of these crimes. New laws and improvements in computer technology are making it more difficult for persons to commit illegal electronic fund transfers at automatic teller windows at banks (Hawaii Criminal Justice Data Center, 1985).

In Japan, police have been using a device known as a passive sensor to detect alcohol in exhaled breath. The police officer waves a sensor, a type of wand, within the vehicle to detect alcohol. No blood tests are necessary, and the deterrence effect of such devices is significant (Voas and Layfield, 1983). The passive sensor is one detection instrument that might lead United States police to more rapid apprehensions of drunk driving suspects. It is predicted that a large-scale utilization of the passive sensor will eventually result in a reduction in the number of offending drivers and eventual reductions in drunk driving arrests (Voas and Layfield, 1983).

Again, the emphasis of most proposals for dealing with most types of crimes is upon control. While prevention itself is desirable, it is unlikely to occur.

■ SUMMARY

Crime prevention is the anticipation, recognition, and appraisal of crime risk and the initiation of some action to remove or reduce it. This chapter examined a number of crime prevention measures employed by police and the community to control and possibly prevent crime. Although some observers contend that almost nothing works to prevent crime from occurring, in recent years, criminal victimizations have decreased according to the National Crime Survey.

Police act to control crime by being highly visible, by modifying their patrol styles, by engaging in community policing, and by providing educational programs for community residents. Awareness programs, such as Operation Identification, assist homeowners and others in the identification and recovery of stolen property.

Community residents engage in target hardening by making their residences and businesses less vulnerable to burglars and thieves. Electronic alarm systems and identification of valuables are regarded as key crime prevention strategies. Neighborhood watch groups and Crime Stoppers also assist in controlling the amount of crime occurring in certain areas.

The police are regarded by many persons as keepers of the peace. They respond when crimes are reported; therefore, they emphasize strategies that improve police-community relations so that citizens will be more inclined to report offenses when they occur. No solution to the crime problem is insulated from criticism, and technological improvements and innovations will continue to be tested as means of dealing with and controlling certain criminal offenses.

KEY TERMS

community policing

crime prevention

Crime Stoppers

Operation Identification

Victimization Risk Survey
(VRS)

Victims of Crime Act

QUESTIONS FOR REVIEW

1. What is meant by crime prevention? Do we prevent crime or merely control it?
2. Was the Kansas City Prevention Patrol Experiment effective as a crime deterrent? What relationship was established between the visibility of police in certain areas of Kansas City and the rate of crime in those areas?
3. According to Table 18.2, has crime been increasing or decreasing? Which crimes appear to have changed the most between 1986 and 1987?
4. Does greater police visibility reduce crime? Was the LEAA successful in demonstrating that spending more money on crime meant a significant reduction of it?
5. Describe briefly the two modifications of police patrol styles observed in Tampa, Florida, and Newark, New Jersey.
6. What is meant by community policing? Does it appear to be effective in reducing crime? What appears to be its major benefit to police and the community?
7. What is Operation Identification? What function does it serve for community residents and police?
8. What are some of the most frequent reasons persons fail to report crimes to the police?
9. What are two community crime prevention or control strategies used in Springfield, Illinois, and Philadelphia, Pennsylvania?
10. What is the Crime Stoppers program? Briefly describe the Crime Stoppers program and some of its objectives?
11. Has Crime Stoppers been effective in detecting certain kinds of crimes?
12. What is a passive sensor? What is its purpose? Has it been used successfully in other countries?

SUGGESTED READINGS

Cramer, James Albert (Ed.) (1978). *Preventing crime.* Beverly Hills, CA: Sage.

Karmen, Andrew (1984). *Crime victims: An introduction to victimology.* Monterey, CA: Brooks/Cole.

Lab, Stephen P. (1988). *Crime prevention: Approaches, practices, and evaluations.* Cincinnati, OH: Pilgrimage Press.

O'Brien, Robert M. (1985). *Crime and victimization data.* Beverly Hills, CA: Sage.

Phillips, Llad, and Harold L. Votey, Jr. (1981). *The economics of crime control.* Beverly Hills, CA: Sage.

Rosenbaum, Dennis P. (Ed.) (1986). *Community crime prevention: Does it work?* Beverly Hills, CA: Sage.

BIBLIOGRAPHY

Abel, Ernest. 1987. *Homicide: A bibliography*. Westport, CT: Greenwood.

Abraham, Henry J. 1968. *The judicial process*. 2d ed. New York: Oxford Univ. Press.

———. 1983. *The judicial process: An introductory analysis of the courts of the United States, England, and France*. 4th ed. New York: Oxford Univ. Press.

Adamany, D., and P. DuBois. 1976. Electing state judges. *Wisconsin Law Review* 731:631–43.

Adams, Kenneth. 1983. The effect of evidentiary factors on charge reduction. *Journal of Criminal Justice* 11: 525–37.

Adamson, Christopher. 1984. Toward a Marxian penology: Captive criminal populations as economic threats and resources. *Social Problems* 31:435–58.

Advisory Commission on Intergovernmental Relations. 1971. *For a more perfect union: Court reform*. Washington, DC: U.S. Government Printing Office.

Ageton, Suzanne S. 1983. The dynamics of female delinquency, 1976–1980. *Criminology* 21:555–84.

Aikman, Alex B. 1986. Volunteer lawyer-judges bolster court resources. *NIJ Reports* 195:2–6.

Akers, Ronald L., et al. 1983. Are self-report studies of adolescent deviance valid? Biochemical measures, randomized response, and the bogus pipeline in smoking behavior. *Social Forces* 62:234–51.

Albanese, Jay. 1985. *Organized crime in America*. Cincinnati, OH: Anderson.

———. 1986. *Myths and realities of crime and justice*. 2d ed. Niagara Falls, NY: Apocalypse.

Alfini, James J. 1981. Mississippi judicial selection: Election, appointment, and bar anointment. In *Courts and judges*, ed. James A. Cramer. Beverly Hills, CA: Sage.

Alker, H. R., et al. 1976. Jury selection as biased social process: The cases of eastern Massachusetts. *Law and Society Review* 10:9–41.

Allen, Harry E., and Nancy J. Beran, eds. 1977. *Reform in corrections: Problems and issues.* New York: Praeger.

Allen, Harry E., Chris W. Eskridge, Edward J. Latessa, and Gennaro F. Vito. 1985. *Probation and parole in America.* New York: Macmillan.

Alpert, Geoffrey, P., and Patrick R. Anderson. 1986. The most deadly force: Police pursuits. *Justice Quarterly* 3:1–14.

Alpert, Geoffrey P., and Roger G. Dunham. 1988. *Policing urban America.* Prospects Heights, IL: Waveland.

Alschuler, Albert W. 1975. The prosecutor's role in plea bargaining. *University of Chicago Law Review* 36:50–59.

———. 1976. The trial judge's role in plea bargaining: Part I. *Columbia Law Review* 76:1059–1154.

———. 1979. Plea bargaining and its history. *Law and Society Review* 13:211–45.

Alves, E., and J. Shapland, eds. 1985. *Legislation for policing today: The police and criminal evidence act.* Leicester: British Psychological Society.

American Bar Association. 1967. ABA model state judicial article, 1962. In *The courts.* Washington, DC: U.S. Government Printing Office.

———. 1971. *Standards relating to prosecution function and the defense function.* New York: Institute for Judicial Administration.

———. 1973. *Standards relating to court organization.* Washington, DC: American Bar Association Commission on Standards of Judicial Administration.

———. 1975. *Standards relating to trial courts.* Washington, DC: American Bar Association Commission on Standards of Judicial Administration.

———. 1985. *A comprehensive perspective on civil and criminal RICO legislation and litigation.* Washington, DC: American Bar Association.

American Correctional Association. 1983. *The American prison: From the beginning . . . A pictorial history.* College Park, MD: American Correctional Association.

———. 1985. Facility design: Turning the page on a new generation. *Corrections Today* 47:4–177.

———. 1986. Probation and parole: Today's challenges: Future directions. *Corrections Today* 48:4–87.

American Judicature Society. 1977. *Courts of limited jurisdiction: A national survey.* Chicago: American Judicature Society.

———. 1983. *Report of the committee on qualification guidelines for judicial candidates.* Chicago: American Judicature Society.

American Law Institute. 1962. *Model penal code official draft.* Washington, DC: American Law Institute.

———. 1975. *A model code of pre-arraignment procedure.* Philadelphia: American Law Institute.

American Psychiatric Association. 1984. *Issues in forensic psychiatry.* Washington, DC: American Psychiatric Press.

Andersen, Brian David, and Kevon Andersen. 1984. *Prisoners of the deep.* San Francisco: Harper and Row.

Anderson, David P. 1985. Spreadsheet software: Making the microcomputer work for the court administrator. *Justice System Journal* 10:213–28.

Anderson, Dennis B., and Donald F. Schoen. 1985. Diversion programs: Effect of stigmatization on juvenile status offenders. *Juvenile Family Court Journal* 36: 13–25.

Anderson, J. A. 1984. On measuring productivity improvement. *Journal of Police Science and Administration* 12:373–78.

Anderson, Patrick, Charles R. Davoli, and Laura Moriarty. 1985. Private corrections: Feast or fiasco? *Prison Journal* 65:32–41.

Andreycak, Catherine B. 1983. Sentencing of youthful misdemeanants under the youth corrections act: Eliminating disparities. *Fordham Law Review* 51:1254–77.

Anechiarico, Frank. 1984. Suing the Philadelphia Police: The case for an institutional approach. *Law and Policy* 6:231–50.

Anson, Richard H. 1986. *An examination of an intensive probation program for alcohol offenders.* Albany, GA: Department of Criminal Justice, Albany State College.

Ares, Charles, A. Rankin, and A. Sturz. 1963. The Manhattan bail project: An interim report on the use of pretrial parole. *New York University Law Review* 38: 67–75.

Arthur D. Little, Inc. 1984. *Innovative juvenile law enforcement programs.* Washington, DC: Arthur D. Little.

———. 1984. *Programming for institutionalized youth.* Washington, DC: Arthur D. Little.

Ashman, A., and James J. Alfini. 1974. *The key to judicial merit selection: The nominating process.* Chicago: American Judicature Society.

Ashman, A., and J. Parness. 1974. The concept of a unified court system. *DePaul Law Review* 24:1–41.

Atlas, Randy. 1983. Crime site selection for assaults in four Florida prisons. *Prison Journal* 58:59–72.

Attorney General's Advisory Commission. 1973. *The police in the California community.* Sacramento, CA: State of California Attorney General's Advisory Commission on Community-Police Relations.

Auerbach, Barbara. 1982. New prison industries legislation: The private sector re-enters the field. *Prison Journal* 42:25–36.

August, Robin. 1981. A study of juveniles transferred for prosecution to the adult system. Miami: Office of the Dade-Miami Criminal Justice Council.

Austin, James. 1983. Assessing the new prison classification models. *Crime and Delinquency* 29:561–76.

Austin, James, and Barry Krisberg. 1982. The unmet promise of alternatives to incarceration. *Crime and Delinquency* 28:374–409.

Austin, James, Barry Krisberg, and Paul Litsky. 1984. *Evaluation of the field test of supervised pretrial release: Final report.* San Francisco: National Council on Crime and Delinquency.

Austin, James, and Paul Litsky. 1985. *Identifying absconders from parole and probation supervision: An evaluation of Nevada's risk screening instruments.* San Francisco: National Council on Crime and Delinquency.

Austin, James, Barry Krisberg, and Shirley Melnicoe. 1985. *Marin County jail alternatives study: Final report.* San Francisco: National Council on Crime and Delinquency.

Aylward, Jack. 1985. Psychological testing and police selection. *Journal of Police Science and Administration* 13:201–210.

Babcock, William G., ed. 1985. Corrections and privatization: An overview. *Prison Journal* 65:1–121.

Babin, M. 1985. Minimizing the effects of stress. *RCMP Gazette* 47:4–8.

Bailey, F. Lee, and Henry B. Rothblatt. 1982. *Handling juvenile delinquency cases.* Rochester, NY: Lawyer's Co-Operative Publishing Company.

Bailey, William C. 1983. Disaggregation in deterrence and death penalty research: The case of murder in Chicago. *Journal of Criminal Law and Criminology* 74:827–59.

————. 1984. Murder and capital punishment in the nation's capital. *Justice Quarterly* 1:211–33.

Bainor, Maria H. 1985. The constitutionality of the use of two-way closed circuit television to take testimony of child victims of sex crimes. *Fordham Law Review* 53:995–1018.

Baker, Ralph, and Fred A. Meyer, Jr. 1980. *The criminal justice game: Politics and players.* North Scituate, MA: Duxbury.

Baker, William L. 1984. Castration of the male sex offender: A legally impermissible alternative. *Loyola Law Review* 30:377–99.

Baldassare, Mark. 1986. The elderly and fear of crime. *Sociology and Social Research* 70:218–21.

Baldwin, John D. 1985a. Pre-trial settlement in the magistrates' courts. *Howard Journal of Criminal Justice* 24:108–117.

————. 1985b. Thrill and adventure seeking and the age distribution of crime: Comment on Hirschi and Gottfredson. *American Journal of Sociology* 90:1326–30.

Baldwin, John D., and Michael McConville. 1977. *Negotiated justice: Pressures to plead guilty.* London: Martin Robinson.

Bandura, Albert. 1977. *Social learning theory.* Englewood Cliffs, NJ: Prentice-Hall.

Banks, Jerry. 1984. *Validation of risk and needs assessment instruments: Final report.* Atlanta: Georgia Department of Offender Rehabilitation.

Barak-Glantz, Israel L. 1985. Toward a conceptual schema of prison management styles. *Prison Journal* 60:42–60.

Barber, Susanna R. 1985. Televised trials: Weighing advantages against disadvantages. *Justice System Journal* 10:279–91.

Barberis, Peter, and Arnold Skelton. 1985. Police attitudes and styles of control. *Police Studies* 8:198–213.

Baril, Micheline, and Anne Morissette. 1985. Du coté des victimes, une autre perspective sur le vol à main armée. *Criminologie,* 18:117–33.

Barker, Thomas. 1983. Rookie police officers' perceptions of police occupational deviance. *Police Studies* 6:30–38.

Barker, Thomas, and David L. Carter. 1986. *Police Deviance.* Cincinnati, OH: Pilgrimage.

Barker, Thomas, and Julian Roebuck. 1973. *An empirical typology of police corruption.* Springfield, IL: Charles C. Thomas.

Barnett, A. I., T. F. Rich, and R. C. Lawson. 1984. *Revealed preferences of the criminal justice system during a period of workload shedding.* Cambridge, MA: Public Systems Evaluation.

Barrington, R. C. 1985. The development of a computerized major crime investigation system. *Police Journal* 58:207–233.

Bartollas, Clemens, S. J. Miller, and S. Dinitz. 1976. *Juvenile victimization: The institutional paradox.* New York: Halsted.

Bartollas, Clemens, and Christopher M. Sieverdes. 1983. Coeducational training schools: Are they really a panacea for juvenile corrections? *Juvenile and Family Court Journal* 34:15–20.

Barton, William, and Josefina Figueira-McDonough. 1985. Attachments, gender, and delinquency. *Deviant Behavior* 6:119–44.

Bass, M. 1982. Stress: A woman officer's view. *Police Stress* 5:30–33.

Baunach, Phyllis Jo, Melissa Sickmund, and Betty Ford. 1986. *Jail inmates 1984.* Washington, DC: U.S. Department of Justice, Bureau of Justice Statistics.

Bayley, David H. 1984. Learning the skills of policing. *Law and Contemporary Problems* 47:35–60.

———. 1985. *Patterns of policing: A comparative international analysis.* New Brunswick, NJ: Rutgers Univ. Press.

Bazell, C. E. 1985. Police and Criminal Evidence Act 1984—Entry, search, and seizure. *Justice of the Peace* 149:724–26.

Beck, James L. 1979. An evaluation of federal community treatment centers. *Federal Probation* 43:36–40.

Beck, James L., and Peter B. Hoffman. 1985. Reliability in guideline application: Initial hearings—1982. *Federal Probation* 49:33–41.

Becker, Harold K., and Jack E. Whitehouse. 1980. *Police of America: A personal view, introduction, and commentary.* Springfield, IL: Charles C. Thomas.

Becker, Howard S. 1963. *Outsiders: Studies in the sociology of deviance.* New York: Free Press.

———. 1973. Labeling theory reconsidered. In *Outsiders: Studies in the sociology of deviance.* New York: Free Press.

Beckman, E. 1983. High speed chases: In pursuit of a balanced policy. *Police Chief* 50:34–57.

Bedau, Hugo A. 1982. *The death penalty in America.* New York: Oxford Univ. Press.

Beeley, Arthur. 1927. *The bail system in Chicago.* Chicago: Univ. of Chicago Press.

Beirne, Piers. 1983. Cultural relativism and comparative criminology. *Contemporary Crises* 7:371–91.

Bell, Bernard P. 1983. Closure of pretrial suppression hearings: Resolving the fair trial/free press conflict. *Fordham Law Review* 51:1297–1316.

Bell, Daniel. 1984. Plea bargaining: Contradiction or justice? In *Legal issues in criminal justice,* ed. Sloan Letman et al. Cincinnati, OH: Pilgrimage.

Bell, Duran, and Kevin Land. 1985. The intake dispositions of juvenile offenders. *Journal of Research on Crime and Delinquency* 22:309–328.

Bell, Raymond, et al. 1983. *The nature and prevalence of learning deficiencies among adult inmates.* Washington, DC: National Institute of Justice.

Bellot, Sylvie. 1985. Les auteurs de vols à main armée à Montreal: Une typologie empirique. *Criminologie* 18:35–45.

Bennett, Laurence A. 1970. The study of violence in California prisons: A review with policy implications. In *Prison Violence,* ed. A. K. Cohen, G. F. Cole, and R. C. Bailey. Lexington, MA: Heath.

Bennett, Richard R., and Sandra Baxter. 1985. Police and community participation in anti-crime programs. In *Police management today: Issues and case studies,* ed. J. J. Fyfe. Washington, DC: International City Management Association.

Bentivoglio, John T., et al. 1985. *State laws and procedures affecting drug trafficking control: A national view.* Washington, DC: National Governor's Association and National Criminal Justice Association.

Berkson, L. C., S. W. Hays, and S. J. Carbon. 1977. *Managing the state courts: Text and readings.* St. Paul, MN: West.

Berliner, Lucy, and Mary Kay Barbieri. 1984. The testimony of the child victim of sexual assault. *Journal of Social Issues* 40:125–37.

Berman, Leonard N. 1983. Meeting the goals of sentencing: The client specific plan. *New England Journal on Criminal and Civil Confinement* 9:331–42.

Bermant, G., and R. Coppock. 1973. Outcomes of six- and twelve-member jury trials: An analysis of 128 civil cases in the state of Washington. *Washington Law Review* 48:593–96.

Bernard, Thomas J. 1983. The development of federal parole guidelines. *Criminal Justice Review* 8:24–28.

Bernat, Frances P. 1984. Gender disparity in the setting of bail: Prostitution offenses in Buffalo, NY 1977–79. *Journal of Offender Counseling, Services, and Rehabilitation* 9:21–47.

Bernstein, Ilene N., William R. Kelly, and Patricia A. Doyle. 1977. Societal reaction to deviants: The case of criminal defendants. *American Sociological Review* 42:743–55.

Berry, Bonnie. 1985. Electronic jails: A new criminal justice concern. *Justice Quarterly* 2:1–22.

Beschner, George M., and Alfred S. Friedman. 1985. *Teen drug use.* Lexington, MA: Lexington.

Besner, H. F. 1985. Employee assistance programs: A valuable asset for police departments. *Police Chief* 52: 34–5.

Better Homes and Gardens. 1978. *A report on the American family,* p. 66, Des Moines, IA: Meredith.

Bevan, V., and K. Lidstone. 1985. *A guide to the Police and Criminal Evidence Act 1984.* London: Butterworths.

Binder, Arnold, and Gilbert Geis. 1984. Ad populum argumentation in criminology: Juvenile diversion as rhetoric. *Crime and Delinquency* 30:309–333.

Bittner, Egon. 1970. *The functions of the police in modern society: A review of background factors, current practices, and possible role models.* Chevy Chase, MD: National Institute of Mental Health.

———. 1975. *The functions of the police in modern society.* New York: Jason Aronson.

———. 1985. The capacity to use force as the core of the police role. In *Moral issues in police work,* ed. F. A. Elliston and M. Feldberg. Totowa, NJ: Rowman and Allanheld.

Black, Donald J., and Albert J. Reiss, Jr. 1970. Police control of juveniles. *American Sociological Review* 35: 63–77.

Black, Henry Campbell. 1979. *Black's law dictionary.* St. Paul, MN: West.

Blackmore, John, and Jane Welsh. 1983. Selective incapacitation: Sentencing according to risk. *Crime and Delinquency* 29:504–528.

Blasi, A. 1980. Bridging moral cognition and moral action: A critical review of the literature. *Psychological Bulletin* 88:1–45.

Bloch, Peter B., and David Specht. 1973. *Neighborhood team policing.* Washington, DC: U.S. Department of Justice.

Blomberg, Thomas G. 1984. *Juvenile court and community corrections.* Lanham, MD: Univ. Press of America.

Blomberg, Thomas G., Gordon P. Waldo, and Lisa C. Burcroff. 1987. Home confinement and electronic surveillance. In *Intermediate punishments,* ed. Belinda R. McCarthy. Monsey, NY: Criminal Justice Press.

Blumberg, A. 1967. *Criminal justice.* Chicago: Quadrangle.

Blumberg, M. 1985. Research on police use of deadly force: The state of the art. In *The ambivalent force,* ed.

A. Blumberg and E. Niderhoffer. New York: Holt, Rinehart, and Winston.

———. 1986. Issues and controversies with respect to the use of deadly force by the police. In *Police Deviance,* ed. T. Barker and D. Carter. Cincinnati, OH: Pilgrimage.

Blumstein, Alfred. 1983. Selective incapacitation as a means of crime control. *American Behavioral Scientist* 27:87–108.

Blumstein, Alfred, and Jacqueline Cohen. 1979. Estimation of individual crime rates from arrest records. *Journal of Criminal Law and Criminology* 70:585–90.

Blumstein, Alfred, and Joseph B. Kadane. 1983. An approach to the allocation of scarce imprisonment resources. *Crime and Delinquency* 29:546–60.

Boehm, L. 1962. The development of conscience. *Child Development* 33:575–90.

Bohm, Robert M. 1986. Crime, criminal and crime control policy myths. *Justice Quarterly* 3:193–214.

Boland, Barbara, and Elizabeth Brady. 1985. *The prosecution of felony arrests, 1980.* Washington, DC: U.S. Department of Justice.

Boland, Barbara, and Brian Forst. 1985. Prosecutors don't always aim to pleas. *Federal Probation* 49:10–15.

Bond, James E. 1981. *Plea bargaining and guilty pleas.* New York: Clark Boardman.

Bonham, Gene, et al. 1984. Predicting parole outcome via discriminant analysis. *Justice Quarterly* 1:329–41.

Bonham, Gene, Galan Janeksela, and John Bardo. 1986. Predicting parole decision in Kansas via discriminant analysis. *Journal of Criminal Justice* 14:123–33.

Bonora, B., and E. Krauss. 1979. *Jury work: Systematic techniques.* Washington, DC: National Jury Project.

Boostrom, R. L., and J. J. Henderson. 1984. Crime prevention models and police community relations. *Police Journal* 57:373–81.

Bortner, M. A. 1986. Traditional rhetoric, organizational realities: Remand of juveniles to adult court. *Crime and Delinquency* 32:53–73.

———. 1988. *Delinquency and Justice: An age of crisis.* New York: McGraw-Hill.

Bortner, M. A., Mary L. Sunderland, and Russ Winn. 1985. Race and the impact of juvenile deinstitutionalization. *Crime and Delinquency* 31:35–46.

Bottomley, A. Keith. 1984. Dilemmas of parole in a penal crisis. *Howard Journal of Criminal Justice* 23:24–40.

Bottomley, A. Keith, and Clive Coleman. 1984. Law and order: Crime problem, moral panic, or penal crisis? In

Law and order in British politics, ed. Philip Norton. Brookfield, VT: Gower.

Bottoms, A. E., and J. D. McClean. 1976. *Defendants in the criminal process.* London: Routledge and Kegan Paul.

Boudouris, James. 1983. *The recidivism of releasees from the Iowa State Penetentiary at Fort Madison.* Des Moines: Iowa Division of Adult Corrections.

————. 1985. *The revocation process in Iowa.* Des Moines: Iowa Department of Corrections, Bureau of Data, Research, and Planning.

Bowker, Lee H., and Malcolm W. Klein. 1983. The etiology of female juvenile delinquency and gang membership: A test of psychological and social structural explanations. *Adolescence* 18:739–52.

Bradel, Don. 1979. The mythology of law enforcement. In *Critical issues in criminal justice,* ed. R. G. Iacovetta and Dae H. Chang. Durham, NC: Carolina Academic Press.

Bradley, J. M. 1986. Training doesn't have to be expensive to be good. *FBI Law Enforcement Bulletin* 55: 11–14.

Brady, James. 1983. The justifiability of hollow-point bullets. *Criminal Justice Ethics* 2:9–18.

Braithwaite, John. 1981. The myth of social class and criminality reconsidered. *American Sociological Review* 46:36–58.

Brams, S. J., and M. D. Davis. 1978. Optimal jury selection: A game-theoretic model for the exercise of peremptory challenges. *Operations Research* 26:966–91.

Brantingham, Patricia L. 1985. Sentencing disparity: An analysis of judicial consistency. *Journal of Quantitative Criminology* 1:281–305.

Braswell, Michael C., Steven D. Dillingham, and Reid H. Montgomery. 1985. *Prison Violence in America.* Cincinnati, OH: Anderson.

Breed, Allen F. 1984. Don't throw the parole baby out with the justice bath water. *Federal Probation* 48:11–15.

Brennan, Dennis T. 1975. *The other police.* Cleveland, OH: Governmental Research Institute.

Brennan, Tim. 1985. *Offender classification and jail crowding: Examining the connection between poor classification and the problem of jail crowding.* Boulder, CO: HSI.

Brennan, W. J., Jr. 1971. *California unified trial court feasibility study.* San Francisco: Booz, Allen, and Hamilton.

Brereton, D., and J. D. Casper. 1981. Does it pay to plead guilty? Differential sentencing and the function of criminal courts. *Law and Society Review* 16:45–70.

Brill, A. A., and C. Winick. 1985. *Yearbook of substance use and abuse.* New York: Human Sciences.

Britt, David W., and Charles R. Tittle. 1975. Crime rates and police behavior: A test of two hypotheses. *Social Forces* 44:441–51.

Bronstein, Alvin J. 1985. Prisoners and their endangered rights. *Prison Journal* 65:3–17.

Brooks, L. 1985. Child abuse: The community as a treatment site. *New Designs for Youth Development* 6: 21–25.

Brown, Lee P. 1984. A police department and its values. *Police Chief* 51:24–25.

————. 1984. Strategies to reduce the fear of crime. *Police Chief* 51:45–46.

Brown, M. K. 1981. *Working the street: Police discretion and the dilemmas of reform.* New York: Russell Sage Foundation.

Brown, Marjorie E., et al. 1985. *Convictions and sentences for rape under staircase sentencing.* Boston: Office of Commissioner of Probation, Massachusetts Trial Court.

Brown, Marjorie E., and Donald Cochran. 1984. Executive summary of research findings from the *Massachusetts risk/need classification system, Report #5.* Boston: Office of the Commissioner of Probation.

Brown, Michael F. 1984. Use of deadly force by patrol officers: Training implications. *Journal of Police Science and Administration* 12:133–40.

Brown, S. E., and Ron E. Vogel. 1983. Police Professionalism. *Journal of Crime and Justice* 6:17–37.

Brown, Steven S., and Valerie A. Willison. 1985. *Restitution: A historical and legal review.* Albany: New York State Division of Criminal Justice Services.

Brzeczek, Richard J. 1985. Chief-mayor relations: The view from the chief's chair. In *Police Leadership in America: Crisis and opportunity,* ed. W. A. Geller. New York: Praeger.

Buckout, R., S. Weg, V. Reilly, and R. Frohboese. 1977. Jury verdicts: Comparison of 6- and 12- person juries and unanimous vs. majority decision rule in a murder trial. *Bulletin of the Psychonomic Society* 10:175–78.

Buddingh, Jan D. 1982. California's 'use a gun—go to prison' laws and their relationship to the determinate sentencing scheme. *Criminal Justice Journal* 5:297–324.

Bugliosi, Vincent, and Curt Gentry. 1974. *Helter skelter.* New York: Norton.

Buikema, Charles, Frank Horvath, and Minot Dodson. 1983. Security regulation: A state-by-state update. *Security Management* 28:39–48.

Bularik, Mary J. 1984. The Dedham Temporary Asylum for Discharged Female Prisoners, 1864–1909. *Historical Journal of Massachusetts* 12:28–35.

Bulkley, Josephine A. 1985. *Evidentiary and procedural trends in state legislation and other emerging issues in child sexual abuse cases.* Washington, DC: American Bar Association.

Bullock, H. 1961. Significance of the racial factor in the length of prison sentences. *Journal of Criminal Law, Criminology, and Police Science* 52:411–17.

Bumstead, Keith. 1985. Managing the complex components of juvenile restitution: An automated system helps to administer information. *State Court Journal* 9:6–17.

Burbeck, Elizabeth, and Adrian Furnham. 1985. Police officer selection: A critical review of the literature. *Journal of Police Science and Administration,* 13:58–69.

Bureau of Justice Statistics. 1985. *National crime survey summary.* Washington, DC: U.S. Government Printing Office.

———. 1986. *Prisoners in 1985.* Washington, DC: U.S. Department of Justice.

———. 1987. *Jail inmates 1987.* Washington, DC: U.S. Department of Justice.

Buren, R. M., and W. W. Stenzel. 1985. Indicators of effective patrol division work scheduling. *Police Chief* 52:34–38.

Burgess, Ann W. 1984. *Child pornography and sex rings.* Lexington, MA: Lexington.

Burke, R. J., and E. Deszca. 1986. Correlates of psychological burnout phases among police officers. *Human Relations* 39:487–502.

Burks, David N., and Dean DeHeer. 1986. Jail suicide prevention. *Corrections Today* 48:52–88.

Butler, T. 1985. Objectives and accountability in policing. *Policing,* 1:174–86.

Bynum, Timothy. 1977. An empirical exploration of the factors influencing release on recognizance. Ph.D. diss., Florida State University, Tallahassee.

C. J. International. 1986. International terrorism. *Criminal Justice International,* 2:1–20.

California Board of Prison Terms. 1984. *Sentencing practices under the determinate sentencing law.* Sacramento, CA: Youth and Adult Correctional Agency.

California Department of the Youth Authority. 1985. *Assessment of planned re-entry program.* Sacramento: California Department of the Youth Authority.

———. 1985. *Youth service bureaus: Report to the legislature.* Sacramento: California Department of the Youth Authority.

California Joint Committee for Revision of the Penal Code. 1984. *Prison overcrowding: Emergency measures and alternative forms of punishment.* Sacramento: California Joint Committee for Revision of the Penal Code.

California Legislative Analyst. 1985. *The impact of recent legislation on California's burglary rate and sentencing practices.* Sacramento: California Legislative Analyst.

California Office of Criminal Justice Planning. 1984. *Governor's youth crime prevention program: Training guide.* Sacramento: California Office of Criminal Justice Planning.

Callahan, Robert. 1985. Wilderness probation: A decade later. *Juvenile and Family Court Journal* 36:31–35.

Cameron, Joy. 1983. *Prisons and punishment in Scotland from the Middle Ages.* Edinburgh: Canongate.

Camp, Camille, and George Camp. 1985. Correctional privatization in perspective. *Prison Journal* 65:14–31.

Camp, Damon D. 1985. Mandated correctional training: A task analysis approach to curriculum design. *Criminal Justice Review* 10:32–39.

Campagna, Daniel S., and Donald L. Poffenberger. 1987. *The sexual trafficking in children: An investigation of the child sex trade.* Dover, MA: Auburn House.

Campbell, Anne. 1984. *The girls in the gang: A report from New York.* New York: Basil Blackwell.

Canada Law Reform Commission. 1985. *Post-seizure procedures.* Ottawa: Canada Law Reform Commission.

Canada Solicitor General. 1983. *Canadian urban victimization survey—Bulletin I.* Ottawa: Programs Branch/Research and Statistics Group.

Carbonell, Joyce Lunn. 1983. Inmate classification systems: A cross-tabulation of two methods. *Criminal Justice and Behavior* 10:285–92.

Carney, Louis P. 1979. *Introduction to correctional science.* 2d ed. New York: McGraw-Hill.

Carp, Robert A., and Ronald Stidham. 1985. *The federal courts.* Washington, DC: Congressional Quarterly.

Carpenter, Cheryl, et al. 1987. *Kids, drugs and crime.* Lexington, MA: Lexington.

Carroll, John M. 1987. *Computer security.* Stoneham, MA: Butterworth.

Carroll, Leo. 1974. *Hacks, blacks and cons: Race relations in a maximum security prison.* Lexington, MA: Lexington.

Carroll, Leo, and Mary Beth Doubet. 1983. U.S. social structure and imprisonment. *Criminology* 21:449–56.

Carroll, Leo, and Claire P. Cornell. 1985. Racial composition, sentencing reforms, and rates of incarceration, 1970–1980. *Justice Quarterly* 2:473–90.

Carter, David L. 1985. Hispanic perception of police performance: An empirical assessment. *Journal of Criminal Justice* 13:487–500.

————. 1986. A taxonomy of prejudice and discrimination by police officers. In *Police deviance*, ed. T. Barker and David L. Carter. Cincinnati, OH: Pilgrimage.

Cavanaugh, James L., and Orest E. Wasyaliw. 1985. Treating the not guilty by reason of insanity outpatient: A two-year study. *Bulletin of the American Academy of Psychiatry and Law,* 13:407–416.

Cavender, Gray. 1984. A critique of sanctioning reform. *Justice Quarterly* 1:1–16.

Cecil, Joe S. 1985. *Administration of justice in a large appellate court: The Ninth Circuit innovations project.* Washington, DC: Federal Judicial Center.

Chaiken, Marcia R., and Jan M. Chaiken. 1984. Offender types and public policy. *Crime and Delinquency* 30:195–226.

Chalidze, Valery. 1977. *Criminal Russia: Essays on crime in the Soviet Union.* New York: Random House.

Chambers, Gerry, and Jacqueline Tombs, eds. 1984. *The British Crime Survey: Scotland.* Edinburgh: Her Majesty's Stationery Office.

Champion, Dean J. 1981. The organization of trial judges. In *Courts and judges,* ed. James A. Cramer. Beverly Hills, CA: Sage.

————. 1987a. Felony offenders, plea bargaining, and probation. *The Justice Professional* 2:1–18.

————. 1987b. Guilty plea hearings and judicial supervision: Some differences between federal and state judges regarding Rule 11 and a defendant's right to due process. *American Journal of Criminal Justice* 11:62–81.

————. 1987c. The metamorphosis of the insanity defense in Tennessee criminal proceedings: Some judicial preferences. *Journal of Crime and Justice* 11:101–121.

————. 1988a. The severity of sentencing: Do federal judges really go easier on elderly offenders? In *Older offenders,* ed. Belinda R. McCarthy and Robert Langworthy. New York: Praeger.

————. 1988b. Private counsels and public defenders: A look at weak cases, prior records, and leniency in plea bargaining. *Journal of Criminal Justice* 17:253–63.

————. 1988c. Felony plea bargaining and probation: A growing judicial and prosecutorial dilemma. *Journal of Criminal Justice* 11:165–79.

————. 1989. *The U.S. Sentencing Guidelines: Some implications for criminal justice.* New York: Praeger.

Chaneles, Sol. 1983. Financing prison education in the United States. *Journal of Offender Counseling, Services, and Rehabilitation* 7:ix–xiv.

Chapman, Jane Roberts, et al. 1983. *Women employed in corrections.* Washington, DC: U.S. Government Printing Office.

Cheatwood, Derral. 1985. Capital punishment and corrections: Is there an impending crisis? *Crime and Delinquency* 31:461–79.

Christopher, D., Mark H. Ben-Aron, and Stephen J. Hucker. 1985. *Dangerousness: Probability and prediction, psychiatry and public policy.* Cambridge: Cambridge Univ. Press.

Church, Thomas W. 1979. Plea bargaining, concessions, and the courts: Analysis of a quasi experiment. *Law and Society Review* 13:509–525.

Cissell, James. 1983. *Federal criminal trials.* Charlottesville, VA: Michie.

Citizens Crime Commission of Connecticut, Inc. 1984. *Connecticut intensive supervision probation.* Hartford: Citizens Crime Commission of Connecticut.

Cizanckas, Victor, and Donald Hanna. 1977. *Modern police management and organization.* Englewood Cliffs, NJ: Prentice-Hall.

Czajlowski, Susan M. 1985. *Alternatives to incarceration: The community correctional center.* Washington, DC: U.S. Bureau of Prisons.

Clagett, Arthur. 1987. Hope Center for Youth Therapeutic Wilderness Camp: Programs for emotionally disturbed, problem teenagers and delinquents. Paper presented at Academy of Criminal Justice Science meetings, April, St. Louis, MO.

Clanon, T. L., and C. Jew. 1985. Predictions from assessments of violent offenders under stress. *Criminal Justice and Behavior,* 12:485–99.

Clarke, Ronald V. 1983. Situational crime prevention: Its theoretical basis and practical scope. *Crime and Justice* 4:225–56.

Clarke, Ronald V., and Tim Hope. 1984. *Coping with burglary.* Boston: Kluwer-Nijhoff.

Clarke, Ronald V., and J. Mike Hough, eds. 1980. *The effectiveness of policing.* Farnborough, UK: Gower.

Clarke, Stevens H., et al. 1983. *North Carolina's determinate sentencing legislation: An evaluation of the first year's experience.* Chapel Hill: Institute of Government, Univ. of North Carolina.

Clarke, Stevens H., and Larry Crum. 1985. *Returns to prison in North Carolina.* Chapel Hill: Institute of Government, Univ. of North Carolina at Chapel Hill.

Clarke, Stevens H., and Susan T. Kurtz. 1983. The importance of interim decisions to felony trial court dispositions. *Journal of Criminal Law and Criminology* 74:476–518.

Clarke, Stevens H., Christopher Ringwalt, and Andrea Cimimello. 1985. *Perspectives on juvenile status offenders: A report to the North Carolina Governor's Crime Commission.* Chapel Hill: Institute of Government, Univ. of North Carolina.

Clayton, Obie, Jr. 1983. Reconsideration of the effects of race in criminal sentencing. *Criminal Justice Review* 8:15–20.

Clayton, Obie, and Anne C. Baird. 1987. Dependency: A structural determinant of homicide involving the elderly. Paper presented at the American Society of Criminology meetings, November, Montreal.

Clear, Todd R., and Donald M. Barry. 1983. Some conceptual issues in incapacitating offenders. *Crime and Delinquency* 29:529–45.

Clear, Todd R., Suzanne Flynn, and Carol Shapiro. 1987. Intensive supervision in probation: A comparison of three projects. In *Intermediate punishments,* ed. Belinda R. McCarthy. Monsey, NY: Criminal Justice.

Clear, Todd R., and Kenneth W. Gallagher. 1985. Probation and parole supervision: A review of current classification practices. *Crime and Delinquency* 31:423–44.

Clear, Todd R., and Vincent O'Leary. 1983. *Controlling the offender in the community.* Lexington, MA: Lexington.

Clemente, Frank, and Michael B. Kleiman. 1976. Fear of crime among the aged. *The Gerontologist* 16:207–211.

Clemmer, D.C. 1940. *The prison community.* New York: Holt, Rinehart and Winston.

Coates, Robert B. 1985. *Victim meets offender: An evaluation of victim-offender reconciliation programs.* Valparaiso, IN: PACT Institute.

Coddon, R. E. 1985. *Tennessee v. Garner:* Comment. *Law Focus* 1:14–16.

Coffin, Frank M. 1980. *The ways of a judge: Reflections from the federal appellate bench.* Boston: Houghton Mifflin.

Cohen, Albert K. 1955. *Delinquent boys.* Glencoe, IL: Free Press.

Cohen, Howard. 1985a. A dilemma for discretion. In *Police ethics: Hard choices in law enforcement,* ed. W. C. Heffernan and T. Stroup. New York: John Jay.

———. 1985b. Authority: The limits of discretion. In *Moral issues in police work,* ed. F. A. Elliston and M. Feldberg. Totowa, NJ: Rowman and Allanheld.

Cole, George F. 1970. The decision to prosecute. *Law and Society Review* 4:313–43.

———. 1975. *The American system of criminal justice.* North Scituate, MA: Duxbury.

Cole, George F., Roger A. Hanson, and Jonathan E. Silbert. 1984. *Alternative dispute resolution mechanisms for prisoner grievances: A reference manual for averting litigation.* Washington, DC: National Institute of Corrections.

Coleman, Stephen F. 1988. *Street cops.* Salem, WI: Sheffield.

Colquhoun, P. 1806. *1796–1806 treatise on the police in the metropolis.* Republished by Patterson-Smith, Montclair, NJ, 1969.

Comment. 1968. Effect of *Mapp v. Ohio* on police search and seizure practices in narcotics cases. *Columbia Journal of Law and Social Problems* 4:94.

Conley, John A. 1982. Working in prisons: Personnel, politics, patronage. *Prison Journal* 42:68–84.

Connecticut Prison and Jail Overcrowding Commission. 1985. *Prison and jail overcrowding: A report to the governor and legislature.* Hartford: Office of Policy and Management.

Conner, G. 1986. Use of force continuum. *Law and Order* 34:18–60.

Connor, Walter D. 1972. *Deviance in Soviet society: Crime, delinquency, and alcoholism.* New York: Columbia Univ. Press.

Conrad, John P. 1984. Corrections and its constituencies. *Prison Journal* 64:47–55.

———. 1985a. The view from the witness chair. *Prison Journal* 65:18–25.

———. 1985b. *The dangerous and the endangered.* Lexington, MA: Lexington.

Conti, Samuel D., et al. 1985. *Hudson County (NJ) criminal justice project evaluation.* North Andover, MA: National Center for State Courts.

Cook, B. B. 1973. Sentencing behavior of federal judges: draft cases—1972. *University of Cincinnati Law Review* 42:597–633.

Cooper, Caroline S., Debra Kelley, and Sharon Larson. 1982. *Judicial and executive discretion in the sentencing process: Analysis of state felony code provisions.* Washington, DC: Washington College of Law, American Univ.

Copeland, A. R. 1986. Police shootings: The metropolitan Dade County experience from 1956 to 1982. *American Journal of Forensic Medicine and Pathology* 7:39–45.

Corbett, Ronald P., and A. L. Ellsworth Fersch. 1985. Home as prison: The use of house arrest. *Federal Probation* 49:13–17.

Cordes, B., et al. 1984. *Trends in international terrorism, 1982 and 1983.* Santa Monica, CA: Rand.

Cordrey, J., and G. K. Pence. 1972. An analysis of team policing in Dayton, Ohio. *Police Chief* 39:44–49.

Corrections Compendium. 1984. Correctional officers. *Corrections Compendium* 8:1, 4.

Cotton, Donald J., and Nicholas A. Groth. 1984. Sexual assault in correctional institutions: Prevention and intervention. In *Victims of sexual aggression,* ed. Irving R. Stuart and J. Greer. New York: Van Nostrand Reinhold.

Covey, H. C., and Mary Mande. 1985. Determinate sentencing in Colorado. *Justice Quarterly* 2:259–70.

Covey, H. C., and S. Menard. 1984. Community corrections diversion in Colorado. *Journal of Criminal Justice* 12:1–10.

Cox, William B., F. Lovell Bixby, and William T. Root, eds. 1933. *Handbook of American prisons and reformatories, vol. I.* New York: National Society of Penal Information.

Coyle, William J. 1987. *Libraries in prisons: A blending of institutions.* Westport, CT: Greenwood.

Coyne, R. 1975. Has court management changed since Vanderbilt?: Alternate models of court organization. *Judicature* 58:266–68.

Craft, Michael, and Ann Craft, eds. 1984. *Mentally abnormal offenders.* London: Bailliere Tindall.

Craig, Michael D. 1983. Improving jury deliberations: A reconsideration of lesser included offense instructions. *Journal of Law Reform* 16:561–84.

Cramer, James A. 1981. *Courts and judges.* Beverly Hills, CA: Sage.

Cullen, Francis T., et al. 1985. The impact of social supports on police stress. *Criminology* 23:503–522.

Cullen, Francis T., Gregory A. Clark, and John F. Wozniak. 1985. Explaining the get tough movement: Can the public be blamed? *Federal Probation* 49:16–24.

Cullen, Francis T., and Karen E. Gilbert. 1982. *Reaffirming rehabilitation.* Cincinnati, OH: Anderson.

Cullen, Francis T., and Lawrence F. Travis. 1984. Work as an avenue of prison reform. *New England Journal on Criminal and Civil Confinement* 10:45–64.

Cunniff, Mark A. 1985. *Felony sentencing in 18 local jurisdictions.* Washington, DC: U.S. Department of Justice, Bureau of Justice Statistics.

Cunningham, William, and Todd Taylor. 1984. *The growing role of private security.* Washington, DC: U.S. Government Printing Office.

———. 1985. Doing more with less: Private security options for decreasing police workload. *Police Chief* 52:62–63.

Curran, Daniel J. 1984. The myth of the 'new' female delinquent. *Crime and Delinquency* 30:386–99.

Currie, Elliott. 1985. *Confronting crime: An American challenge.* New York: Pantheon.

Curtis, Russell L., and Sam Schulman. 1984. Ex-offenders, family relations, and economic supports: The 'significant women' study of the TARP Project. *Crime and Delinquency* 30:507–528.

Czajkoski, Eugene H., and Laurin A. Wollan, Jr. 1986. Creative sentencing: A critical analysis. *Justice Quarterly* 3:215–29.

Czajkowski, Susan M., et al. 1985. Responses to the accreditation program: What correctional staff think about accreditation. *Federal Probation* 49:42–49.

Danto, B. L. 1978. Police suicide. *Police Stress* 1: 32–36, 40.

Dantzker, Mark L. 1986. Law enforcement, professionalism, and a college degree. *Justice Professional* 1:1–17.

Das, Dilip K. 1983. Conflict views on policing: An evaluation. *Journal of Police* 3:51–81.

———. 1984. Some issues in state-mandated human relations training. *Journal of Police Science and Administration* 12:412–24.

———. 1985. A review of progress toward state-mandated police human relations training. *Police Journal* 58:147–62.

———. 1987. Bureaucratization or professionalization: A perspective on police training. Paper presented at the American Society of Criminology meetings, November, Montreal.

Datesman, Susan K., and Mikel Aickin. 1985. Offense specialization and escalation among status offenders. *Journal of Criminal Law and Criminology* 75:1246–75.

Datesman, Susan K., and Frank R. Scarpitti. 1980. *Women, crime, and justice.* New York: Oxford Univ. Press.

David, James A. 1984. Perspectives of policewomen in Texas and Oklahoma. *Journal of Police Science and Administration* 12:395–403.

Davidson, Bill. 1968. The worst jail I've ever seen. *Saturday Evening Post*, July 13, 1968:17–22.

Davis, A. J. 1968. Sexual assaults in the Philadelphia prison system and sheriffs' vans. *Transaction* 6:8–16.

Davis, E. M. 1978. *Staff one: A perspective on effective police management.* Englewood Cliffs, NJ: Prentice-Hall.

Davis, J. A. 1984. Perspectives of policewomen in Texas and Oklahoma. *Journal of Police Science and Administration* 12:395–403.

Davis, J. H., et al. 1977. Victim consequences, sentence severity, and the decision processes in mock juries. *Organizational Behavior and Human Performance* 18:346–65.

Davis, Mark S. 1984. *Selected issues in adult probation: The officers and their work.* Columbus, OH: Governor's Office of Criminal Justice Services.

Davis, Robert C. 1983. Victim/witness noncooperation: A second look at a persistent phenomenon. *Journal of Criminal Justice* 11:287–99.

Davis, Samuel M., and Mortimer D. Schwartz. 1988. *Children's rights and the law.* Lexington, MA: Lexington.

Davis, William E. 1985. Language and the justice system: Problems and issues. *Justice System Journal* 10:353–64.

Dawkins, Russell L., and Marvin P. Dawkins. 1983. Alcohol use Among black, white, and Hispanic adolescent offenders. *Adolescence* 18:799–810.

Day, Steven C. 1978. Shooting the fleeing felon: State of the law. *Criminal Law Bulletin* 4:285–310.

DeBerry, Marshall, and Anita Timrots. 1986. *Criminal Victimization 1985.* Washington, DC: U.S. Department of Justice, Bureau of Justice Statistics.

Decker, Scott H. 1977. Official crime rates and victim surveys: An empirical comparison. *Journal of Criminal Justice* 5:47–54.

———, ed. 1984. *Juvenile justice policy: Analyzing trends and outcomes.* Beverly Hills, CA: Sage.

———. 1985. A systematic analysis of diversion: Net widening and beyond. *Journal of Criminal Justice* 13:207–216.

Decker, Scott H., and C. W. Kohfeld. 1984. A deterrence study of the death penalty in Illinois, 1933–1980. *Journal of Criminal Justice* 12:367–77.

———. 1985. Crime, crime rates, arrests, and arrest ratios: Implications for deterrence theory. *Criminology* 23:437–50.

DeFoor, J. Allison, ed. 1984. Special topic: Telecommunications in the courtroom. *University of Miami Law Review* 38:590–675.

DeGraw, Darrel, and Michelle Hunter. 1987. Victim-witness assistance evaluation. Paper presented at the Third World Victimology Congress, July, San Francisco.

del Carmen, Rolando. 1986. *Potential liabilities of probation and parole officers.* Cincinnati, OH: Anderson.

del Carmen, Rolando, and Harlee Field. 1985. *Model guidelines for probation revocation: A manual.* Washington, DC: National Institute of Corrections.

Delaware Executive Department. 1984. *Recidivism in Delaware: A study of rearrest after release from incarceration.* Dover: Delaware Executive Department, Statistical Analysis Center.

Denkowski, George C., and Kathryn M. Denkowski. 1985. The mentally retarded offender in the state prison system: Identification, prevalence, adjustment, and rehabilitation. *Criminal Justice and Behavior* 12:55–69.

DeWitt, Charles B. 1986a. *Florida sets example with use of concrete modules.* Washington, DC: U.S. Department of Justice, National Institute of Justice.

———. 1986b. *New construction methods for correctional facilities.* Washington, DC: U.S. Department of Justice, National Institute of Justice.

———. 1986c. *Ohio's new approach to prison and jail financing.* Washington, DC: U.S. Department of Justice, National Institute of Justice.

DiCharia, Albert, and John F. Galliher. 1984. Thirty years of deterrence research: Characteristics, causes, and consequences. *Contemporary Crises* 8:243–63.

Dietz, Christopher. 1985. Parole: Crucial to our criminal justice system. *Corrections Today* 47:30–32.

Diiulio, John. 1986. *Prisons, profits, and the public good: The privatization of corrections.* Huntsville, TX: Sam Houston State Univ.

Dillehay, Ronald C., and Michael T. Nietzel. 1985. Juror experience and jury verdicts. *Law and Human Behavior* 9:179–91.

DiPerna, Paula. 1984. *Juries on trial: Faces of American justice.* New York: Red Dembner.

Doan, R., and R. Shapiro. 1976. *State court administrators.* Chicago: American Judicature Society.

Dobash, Russell P. 1983. Labour and discipline in Scottish and English prisons: Moral correction, punishment, and useful toil. *Sociology* 17:1–27.

Doeren, Stephen E., and Mary J. Hageman. 1982. *Community corrections.* Cincinnati, OH: Anderson.

Doherty, Shawn. 1987. Stalking the nighttime sniper. *Newsweek,* January 26, 29.

Dombeck, Carl F., and Murray W. Chitra. 1984. The intermittent sentence in Canada: The law and its problems. *Canadian Journal of Criminology* 26:43–63.

Donahue, Michael E. 1983. *Halt . . . police! An analysis of the police use of deadly force in a large metropolitan city.* Ann Arbor, MI: University Microfilms International.

Donnelly, Patrick G., and Brian Forschner. 1984. Client success or failure in a halfway house. *Federal Probation* 48:38–44.

Dowell, David A., Cecilia Klein, and Cheryl Krichmar. 1985. Evaluation of a halfway house for women. *Journal of Criminal Justice* 13:217–26.

Doyle, James F. 1985. Police discretion, legality, and morality. In *Police Ethics: Hard choices in law enforcement,* ed. W. C. Heffernan and T. Stroup. New York: John Jay.

Draper, Thomas, ed. 1985. *Capital punishment.* New York: H. W. Wilson.

Drechsel, Robert E. 1985. Judicial selection and trial judge-journalist interaction in two states. *Justice System Journal* 10:6–18.

Dressler, David. 1962. *Practice and theory of probation and parole.* New York: Columbia Univ. Press.

Drummond, Douglas S. 1976. *Police culture.* Beverly Hills, CA: Sage.

DuBois, Philip L. 1983. The influence of selection system and region on the characteristics of a trial court bench: The case of California. *Justice System Journal* 8:59–87.

Ducker, W. Marc. 1984. Dispute resolution in prisons: An overview and assessment. *Rutgers Law Review* 36: 145–78.

Dudley, Patricia A. 1983. *Survey of Missouri's 1982 Detention practices.* Jefferson City: Missouri Juvenile Justice Association.

Dugdale, Richard. 1910. *The Jukes: A study in crime, pauperism, disease, and heredity.* New York: G. P. Putnam.

Duguid, Stephen. 1984. *Ameliorating savage man: Humanities in prison.* Vancouver, BC: Program for Correctional Education, Research and Training.

Dunaway, David M. 1985. *A legal analysis of the prevailing law of search and seizure in public elementary and secondary schools.* Ann Arbor, MI: University Microfilms International.

Duncan, Beverly. 1985. Legalization of marijuana and year of birth: Public opinion 1969–1980. In *Yearbook of substance use and abuse,* ed. A. A. Brill and C. Winick. NY: Human Sciences.

Dunn, R. S., and M. M. Dunn, eds. 1982. *The papers of William Penn:* Vol. 2, *1680–1684.* Philadelphia: Univ. of Pennsylvania Press.

Ebbesen, Ebbe B., and Vladimir J. Konecni. 1985. Criticisms of the Criminal Justice System: A Decision-Making Analysis. *Behavioral Sciences and the Law* 3:177–194.

Editor. 1984. Criminal sentencing in transition. *Judicature* 68:124–201.

———. 1984. Escapes. *Corrections Compendium* 9: 1–11.

———. 1984. Prison violence. *Corrections Compendium* 8:1–10.

Ehrenkrantz Group. 1984. *State of Maine, Department of Corrections—Legislation impact study.* New York: Ehrenkrantz Group.

———. 1985. *North Dakota juvenile correctional system analysis. Final report: Phase I.* New York: Ehrenkrantz Group.

Einstadter, W. J. 1984. Citizen patrols: Prevention or control? *Crime and Social Justice* 21:200–212.

Eisenberg, Michael. 1985. *Factors associated with recidivism.* Austin: Texas Board of Pardons and Paroles.

———. 1985. *Release outcome study: Early mandatory release.* Austin: Texas Board of Pardons and Paroles.

————. 1985. *Selective early release: Research-based criteria.* Austin: Texas Board of Pardons and Paroles.

Eisenstein, James, and Herbert Jacob. 1977. *Felony Justice.* Boston: Little, Brown.

Ekland-Olsen, Sheldon, Dennis M. Barrick, and Lawrence E. Cohen. 1983. Prison overcrowding and disciplinary problems: An analysis of the Texas prison system. *Journal of Applied Behavioral Science* 19:163–76.

Elias, Robert. 1986. *The politics of victimization: Victims, victimology, and human rights.* New York: Oxford Univ. Press.

Elie, Daniel, and Anne Kapetanaki-Barake. 1985. L'impact de la reaction policière sur l'évolution des vols avec violence. *Criminologie* 18:47–61.

Elie, Daniel, and Andre Normandeau. 1984. *Armed robbery in North America: Current trends.* Montreal: International Centre for Comparative Criminology, Univ. of Montreal.

Elliott, C. J. 1986. Police misconduct: Municipal liability under Section 1983. *Kentucky Law Journal* 74:651–66.

Elliott, Delbert, et al. 1983. *The prevalence and incidence of delinquent behavior: 1976–1980.* Boulder, CO: Behavioral Research Institute.

Elliott, Delbert, and David Huizinga. 1984. *The relationship between delinquent behavior and ADM problems.* Boulder, CO: Behavioral Research Institute.

Ellis, Lee. 1982. Genetics and criminal behavior. *Criminology* 20:59–66.

Elliston, Frederick A. 1985. Deadly force and capital punishment: A comparative appraisal. In *Police ethics: Hard choices in law enforcement,* ed. W. C. Heffernan and T. Stroup. New York: John Jay.

Elliston, Frederick A., and Michael Feldberg. 1985. *Moral issues in police work.* Totowa, NJ: Rowman and Allanheld.

Elvin, Jan. 1985. A civil liberties view of private prisons. *Prison Journal* 65:48–52.

Empey, Lamar T. 1978. *American delinquency: Its meaning and construction.* Homewood, IL: Dorsey.

Empey, LaMar T., and Maynard Erickson. 1972. *The Provo experiment: Evaluation of community control of delinquency.* Lexington, MA: Lexington.

Erez, Edna. 1984. Self-defined 'desert' and citizen's assessment of police. *Journal of Criminal Law and Criminology* 75:1276–99.

Erickson, Maynard, and LaMar T. Empey. 1963. Court records, undetected delinquency, and decision-making. *Journal of Criminal Law, Criminology, and Police Science,* 54:456–69.

Erickson, William H. 1983. Colorado's answer to the local rules problem. *Journal of Law Reform* 16:493–516.

Evans, Robin. 1982. *The fabrication of virtue: English prison architecture, 1750–1840.* New York: Cambridge Univ. Press.

Ewing, Charles P. 1987. *Battered women who kill.* Lexington, MA: Lexington.

Fabriacatore, Joseph M., and Jerry Dash. 1977. Suicide, divorce, and psychological health among police officers. *Essence* 1:225–29.

Fagan, M. M., and K. Ayers, Jr. 1985. Professors of the street: Police mentors. *FBI Law Enforcement Bulletin* 54:8–13.

Fallen, David L. 1986. Preliminary evaluations of Washington's sentencing guidelines. Paper presented at the American Society of Criminology meetings, October, Atlanta.

Faller, Kathleen C. 1988. *Child sexual abuse: An interdisciplinary manual for diagnosis, case management, and treatment.* Irvington, NY: Columbia Univ. Press.

Fannin, Leon F. 1984. Indian thugs as professional criminals. Paper presented at the annual meeting of the Eastern Sociological Society, April, Boston.

Farbstein, Jay, and Richard Goldman. 1983. *Housing pretrial inmates: The costs and benefits of single cells, multiple cells, and dormitories.* Sacramento, CA: Sacramento County Board of Corrections.

Farkas, Gerald M., and Robert H. Fosen. 1983. Responding to accreditation. *Corrections Today* 45:40–42.

Farr, Kathryn Ann. 1984. Administration and justice: Maintaining balance through an institutionalized plea negotiation process. *Criminology* 22:291–319.

Farrington, David P., and Roger Tarling. 1985. *Prediction in criminology.* Albany: State Univ. of New York Press.

Fattah, Ezzat A. 1985. The preventive mechanisms of the death penalty: A discussion. *Crimcare Journal* 1:109–137.

Federal Bureau of Investigation. 1981. *Uniform crime reports: Crime in the United States.* Washington, DC: U.S. Government Printing Office.

————. 1987. *Uniform crime reports.* Washington, DC: U.S. Government Printing Office.

Federal Offender. 1971. Plea bargaining and sentencing: Comment. *Federal Offender* 14:31–36.

Feeley, Malcolm M. 1979. *Court reform on trial: Why simple solutions fail. A Twentieth Century Fund report.* New York: Basic.

————. 1979. *The process is the punishment.* New York: Russell Sage Foundation.

————. 1983. *Court reform on trial: Why simple solutions fail.* 2d ed. New York: Basic.

Feinman, Clarice. 1985. *Women in the criminal justice system.* New York: Praeger.

Feldberg, Michael. 1985. Gratuities, corruption, and the democratic ethos of policing: The case of the free cup of coffee. In *Moral issues in police work,* ed. F. A. Elliston and M. Feldberg. Totowa, NJ: Rowman and Allanheld.

Fenton, Joseph. 1985. A private alternative to public prisons. *Prison Journal* 65:42–47.

Ferguson, R. E. 1985. The citizen policy academy. *FBI Law Enforcement Bulletin* 54:5–7.

Ferracuti, Franco, and Marvin E. Wolfgang. 1983. *Criminological diagnosis: An international perspective.* Vol. 2. Lexington, MA: D. C. Heath.

Ferri, Enrico. 1909. *Criminal sociology.* New York: Appleton.

Field, Harlee. 1987. Commercial juvenile corrections: Anatomy of a model. Paper presented at the Academy of Criminal Justice Sciences meetings, March, St. Louis, MO.

Fields, Charles B., Harlee Field, and Frank P. Williams. 1983. *Using and improving probation.* Huntsville, TX: Institute for Criminal Justice Policy Analysis.

Figueira-McDonough, Josefina. 1985. Gender differences in informal processing: A look at charge bargaining and sentence reduction in Washington, DC. *Journal of Research in Crime and Delinquency* 22:101–133.

Finkelhor, David. 1983. Removing the child—Prosecuting the offender in cases of sexual abuse. *Child Abuse and Neglect* 7:203–4.

————. 1984. How widespread is child sexual abuse? *Children Today* 13:18–20.

Finn, Peter. 1984. Judicial responses to prison overcrowding. *Judicature* 67:318–26.

————. 1984. Prison crowding: The responses of probation and parole. *Crime and Delinquency* 30:141–53.

————. 1985. Decriminalization of public drunkenness: Response of the health care system. *Journal of Studies on Alcohol* 46:7–23.

Finn, Peter, and B. Lee. 1985. Collaboration with victim-witness assistance programs: Payoffs and concerns for prosecutors. *Prosecutor* 18:27–36.

Fishbein, Paula, Donna Hamparian, and Joseph M. Davis. 1984. *Restitution programming for juvenile offenders: Its use for serious juvenile offenders in Ohio.* Cleveland, OH: Federation for Community Planning.

Fisher, R. B. 1984. Predicting adolescent violence. In *The aggressive adolescent: Clinical perspectives,* ed. C. R. Keith. New York: Free Press.

Fisher, Robert, Kathryn Golden, and Bruce Heininger. 1985. Issues in higher education for law enforcement officers: An Illinois study. *Journal of Criminal Justice* 13:329–38.

Fitzgerald, Robert, and Phoebe C. Ellsworth. 1984. Due process vs. crime control: Death qualification and jury attitudes. *Law and Human Behavior* 8:31–51.

Fitzharris, Timothy L. 1984. The federal role in probation reform. In *Probation and justice,* ed. P. D. McAnany, D. Thomson, and D. Fogel. Cambridge, MA: Oelgeschlager, Gunn, and Hain.

Flanagan, Timothy, and Susan Caulfield. 1984. Public opinion and prison policy: A review. *Prison Journal* 64:31–46.

Flango, Victor E., Robert T. Roper, and Mary E. Elsner. 1983. *The business of state trial courts.* Williamsburg, VA: National Center for State Courts.

Fletcher, George P. 1984. The ongoing Soviet debate about the presumption of innocence. *Criminal Justice Ethics* 3:69–75.

Florida Commission on Bail Bond Reform. 1984. *Final Report.* Tallahassee: Florida Commission on Bail Bond Reform.

Florida Law Review. 1970. Accepting the indigent defendant's waiver of counsel and plea of guilty. *Florida Law Review* 13:453–59.

Florida Probation and Parole Services. 1984. *Preliminary report on community control.* Tallahassee: Florida Department of Corrections.

Flowers, Ronald B. 1986. *Children and criminality: The child as victim and perpetrator.* Westport, CT: Greenwood.

————. 1987. *Women and criminality: The woman as victim, offender, and practitioner.* Westport, CT: Greenwood.

Fogel, David. 1978. *We are the living proof.* Cincinnati, OH: Anderson.

Fooner, Michael. 1973. *Interpol: The inside story of the international crime-fighting organization.* Chicago: Henry Regnery.

Forer, Lois G. 1984. *Money and justice: Who owns the courts?* New York: Norton.

Forrester, Ruth. 1984. Fostering and the adult offender. *Probation Journal* 31:48–50.

Forst, Brian E. 1983a. Capital punishment and deterrence: Conflicting evidence? *Journal of Criminal Law and Criminology* 74:927–42.

———. 1983b. Selective incapacitation: An idea whose time has come? *Federal Probation* 46:19–22.

Forst, Brian E., and Jolene C. Hernon. 1985. *The criminal justice response to victim harm.* Washington, DC: U.S. Department of Justice, National Institute of Justice.

Forst, Brian E., Judith Lucianovic, and Sara J. Cox. 1977. *What happens after arrest? A court perspective of police operations in the District of Columbia.* Washington, DC: Institute for Law and Social Research.

Foss, R. D. 1981. Structural effects in simulated jury decision making. *Journal of Personality and Social Psychology* 40:1055–62.

Fote, Dominic J. 1985. Child witnesses in sexual abuse proceedings: Their capabilities, special problems, and proposals for reform. *Pepperdine Law Review* 13:157–84.

Fowler, J. M. 1985. Police training . . . The macho teaching the macho to be macho: Time for a new perspective. *Journal of California Law Enforcement* 19:61–67.

Fowler, W. Gary. 1984. Judicial selection under Reagan and Carter: A comparison of their initial recommendation procedures. *Judicature* 67:265–83.

Fox, James G. 1984. Women's prison policy: Prisoner activism and the impact of the contemporary feminist movement: A case study. *Prison Journal* 64:15–36.

Fox, Richard G. 1971. The XYZ offender: A modern myth? *Journal of Criminal Law, Criminology, and Police Science* 62:59–73.

Franz, Verl, and David M. Jones. 1987. Perceptions of organization performance in suburban police departments: A critique of the military model. *Journal of Police Science and Administration* 15:153–61.

Frazer, Donald M. 1985. Politics and police leadership: The view from city hall. In *Police leadership in America: Crisis and opportunity,* ed. W. A. Geller. New York: Praeger.

Frazier, C. E., and E. W. Bock. 1982. Effects of court officials on sentence severity: Do judges make a difference? *Criminology* 20:257–72.

Frederick, Bruce C., Edward T. Guider, and Vincent D. Monti. 1984. *The effects of limiting discretion in sentencing.* New York: New York State Division of Criminal Justice Services.

Freedman, Estelle B. 181. *Their sisters' keepers: Women's prison reform in America, 1830–1930.* Ann Arbor, MI: Univ. of Michigan Press.

Freedman, Lawrence Z., and Yonah Alexander. 1983. *Perspectives on terrorism.* Wilmington, DE: Scholarly Resources.

Friedman, Lawrence. 1979. Plea bargaining in historical perspective. *Law and Society Review* 13:253–60.

Friedman, P. 1968. Suicide among police: A study of ninety-three suicides among New York policemen 1934–1940. In *Essays in self-destruction,* ed. E. Schneidrean. New York: Science House.

Friesen, E. C., E. C. Gallas, and N. M. Gallas. 1971. *Managing the courts.* Indianapolis, IN: Bobbs-Merrill.

Frost, Martin L., Bruce A. Fisher, and Robert B. Coates. 1985. Indeterminate and determinate sentencing of juvenile delinquents: A national survey of approaches. *Juvenile and Family Court Journal* 36:1–12.

Frost, Thomas M., and Magnus J. Seng. 1983. Police recruit training in urban departments: A look at instructors. *Journal of Police Science Administration* 11:296–302.

Funke, Gail S., et al. 1982. The future of correctional industries. *Prison Journal* 42:37–51.

Fyfe, James J. 1979. Administrative interventions on police shooting discretion. *Journal of Criminal Justice* 7:309–324.

———. 1983. Enforcement workshop: Fleeing felons and the Fourth Amendment. *Criminal Law Bulletin* 19:525–28.

———, ed. 1985. *Police Management Today: Issues and case studies.* Washington, DC: International City Management Association.

———. 1985. Reviewing citizens' complaints against the police. In *Police management today,* ed. J. Fyfe. Washington, DC: International City Management Association.

———. 1986. The Supreme Court's new rules for police use of deadly force. *Criminal Law Bulletin* 22:62–68.

Fyfe, James J., and Mark Blumberg. 1985. Response to Griswold: A more valid test of the justifiability of police actions. *American Journal of Police* 4:110–32.

Gable, Ralph Kirkland. 1986. Application of personal telemonitoring to current problems in corrections. *Journal of Criminal Justice* 14:167–76.

Gabor, Thomas, and Andre Normandeau. 1987. *Armed robbery: Cops, robbers, and victims.* Springfield, IL: Charles C. Thomas.

Gaes, Gerald G., and William J. McGuire. 1985. Prison violence: The contribution of crowding versus other determinants of prison assault rates. *Journal of Research on Crime and Delinquency* 22:41–65.

Gagnon, John H., and William Simon. 1973. The social meaning of prison homosexuality. *Federal Probation* 32:23–29.

Gagnon, Rosette, and Marc Leblanc. 1985. Les voleurs à main armée adultes devant les tribunaux: Etude du cheminement des plaintes. *Criminologie* 18:63–83.

Galaway, Burt, and Joe Hudson. 1981. *Perspectives on crime victims.* St. Louis, MO: Mosby.

Gallas, E. C. 1968. The profession of court management. *Judicature* 51:334–36.

Garofalo, James, and Richard D. Clark. 1985. The inmate subculture in jails. *Criminal Justice and Behavior* 12: 415–34.

Garofalo, Raffaele. 1914. *Criminology.* Trans. Robert Miller. Boston: Little, Brown.

Garrow, David J. 1981. *The FBI and Martin Luther King, Jr.* New York: Norton.

Garry, Eileen. 1984. *Options to prison crowding.* Washington, DC: National Criminal Justice Reference Service, U.S. National Institute of Justice.

Garwood, M. 1985. Two issues on the validity of personnel screening polygraph examinations. Paper presented at the 20th Annual Seminar of the American Polygraph Association, Reno, NV.

Gay, W. G., J. P. Woodward, H. T. Day, J. P. O'Neal, and C. J. Tucker. 1977. *Issues in team policing: A review of the literature.* Washington, DC: U.S. Government Printing Office.

Gazell, J. A. 1971. State trial courts: An odyssey into faltering bureaucracies. *San Diego Law Reiew* 8:275–332.

———. 1975. *State trial courts as bureaucracies: A study in judicial management.* New York: Dunellen.

Geary, David Patrick. 1975. *Community relations and the administration of justice.* New York: Wiley.

Geimer, William S. 1985. Death at any cost: A critique of the Supreme Court's recent retreat from its death penalty standards. *Florida State University Law Review* 12:737–80.

Gelb, Barbara. 1983. *Varnished brass: The decade after Serpico.* New York: Putnam.

Geller, Mark, and Lynn Ford-Somma. 1984. *Violent homes, violent children.* Trenton, NJ: Division of Juvenile Services, New Jersey Department of Corrections.

Geller, William A. 1985a. Officer restraint in the use of deadly force: The next frontier in police shooting research. *Journal of Police Science and Administration* 13:153–71.

———. 1985b. Shooting reduction techniques: Controlling the use of deadly force by and against police officers. *Police Chief* 52:56–58.

———, ed. 1985c. *Police leadership in America: Crisis and opportunity.* New York: Praeger.

Gelles, Richard J. 1976. Abused wives. *Journal of Marriage and the Family* 38:659–68.

Gelles, Richard J., and Jane B. Lancaster. 1987. *Child abuse and neglect: Biosocial dimensions.* Hawthorne, NY: Aldine de Gruyter.

Gelles, Richard J., and Murray A. Strauss. 1979. Violence in the American family. *Journal of Social Issues* 35:15–39.

Genevie, L., et al. 1983. *Trends in the effectiveness of correctional intervention.* Washington, DC: U.S. National Institute of Justice.

Georgia Department of Audits. 1985. *Performance audit: Department of Corrections Probation operations program, August, 1985.* Atlanta: Georgia Department of Audits.

Gerry, Martin H. 1985. *Monitoring the special education programs of correctional institutions: A guide for special education monitoring staff.* Washington, DC: National Association of State Directors of Special Education.

Gershman, Bennett L. 1985. The Burger court and prosecutorial misconduct. *Criminal Law Bulletin* 21:217–26.

Gertz, Marc G., and Albert C. Price. 1985. Variables influencing sentencing severity: Intercourt differences in Connecticut. *Journal of Criminal Justice* 13:131–39.

Gettinger, Stephen. 1984. *Assessing criminal justice needs.* Washington, DC: U.S. National Institute of Justice.

Gettys, V. S., and J. D. Elam. 1985. Validation demystified: Personnel selection techniques that work. *Police Chief* 52:41–43.

Ghali, Moheb, and Meda Chesney-Lind. 1986. Gender bias and the criminal justice system: An empirical investigation. *Sociology and Social Research* 70:164–71.

Gibbons, Don C. 1968. *Society, crime, and criminal careers.* Englewood Cliffs, NJ: Prentice-Hall.

Gibbs, John J. 1975. Jailing and stress. In *Men in crisis: Human breakdowns in prison,* ed. H. Toch. Chicago: Aldine.

Gibson, Dale, and Janet K. Baldwin, eds. 1985. *Law in a cynical society? Opinion and law in the 1980s.* Calgary, Canada: Carswell.

Gibson, H. 1973. Women's prisons: Laboratories for penal reform. *Wisconsin Law Review* 13:210–33.

Gibson, J. 1978. Race as a determinant of criminal sentences. *Law and Society Review* 12:455–78.

Gilbert, James. 1986. *A cycle of outrage: America's reaction to the juvenile delinquent in the 1950s.* New York: Oxford Univ. Press.

Giordano, Peggy, Stephen A. Cernkovich, and M. D. Pugh. 1986. Friendships and delinquency. *American Journal of Sociology* 91:1170–1202.

Glauser, Michael, and William Tullar. 1985. Citizen satisfaction with police officer/citizen interaction: Implications for the changing role of police organizations. *Journal of Applied Psychology* 70:514–27.

Glenn, Myra C. 1984. *Campaigns against corporal punishment: Prisoners, sailors, women, and children in antebellum America.* Albany: State Univ. of New York Press.

Glick, H. R., and K. N. Vines. 1973. *State court systems.* Englewood Cliffs, NJ: Prentice-Hall.

Glick, Ruth. 1978. *National study of women's correctional programs.* Washington, DC: National Institute of Law Enforcement and Criminal Justice.

Glickman, M. J. A. 1983. *From crime to rehabilitation.* Brookfield, VT: Gower.

Glueck, Sheldon, and Eleanor Glueck. 1956. *Physique and delinquency.* New York: Harper and Row.

Goddard, Henry. 1927. *The Kallikak family: A study in the heredity of feeblemindedness.* New York: Macmillan.

Goebel, Jr., Julius. 1971. *Antecedents and beginnings to 1801.* Vol. I of *The Oliver Wendell Holmes Devise history of the Supreme Court of the United States.* New York: Macmillan.

Goetting, Ann. 1985. Racism, sexism, and ageism in the prison community. *Federal Probation* 49:10–22.

Goetting, Ann, and R. M. Howsen. 1986. Correlates of prisoner misconduct. *Journal of Quantitative Criminology* 2:49–67.

Golbin, James J. 1983. *Intensive special supervision: The development of a promising probation strategy for serious offenders.* Suffolk County, NY: Suffolk County Department of Probation.

Goldberg, Arthur J. 1984. Managing the Supreme Court's workload. *Hastings Constitutional Law Quarterly* 11:353–57.

Goldberg, Paula. 1984. *Network of knowledge: Directory of criminal justice information sources.* Washington, DC: U.S. Department of Justice.

Goldkamp, John S. 1983. Judicial reform of bail practices: The Philadelphia experiment. *Court Management Journal* 14:16–20.

———. 1984. Bail: Discrimination and control. *Criminal Justice Abstracts* 16:103–127.

Goldkamp, John S., and Michael R. Gottfredson. 1984. *Judicial guidelines for bail: The Philadelphia experiment.* Washington, DC: U.S. Government Printing Office, National Institute of Justice.

———. 1985. *Policy guidelines for bail: An experiment in court reform.* Philadelphia: Temple Univ. Press.

Goldman, Sheldon. 1985. Reaganizing the judiciary: The first term appointments. *Judicature* 68:313–29.

Goldsmith, Jack, and Sharon S. Goldsmith, eds. 1976. *Crime and the elderly.* Lexington, MA: Lexington.

Goldstein, Herman. 1975. *Police corruption.* Washington, DC: Police Foundation.

———. 1977. *Policing a free society.* Cambridge, MA: Ballinger.

Gonzalez, Gil P. 1982. *In re Myron:* Juvenile confessions. *Criminal Justice Journal* 5:349–58.

Goodman, Gail S. 1984. Children's testimony in historical perspective. *Journal of Social Issues* 40:9–31.

Goodpaster, Gary. 1983. Judicial review of death sentences. *Journal of Criminal Law and Criminology* 74:786–826.

Goodroe, C. 1985. Federal training for state and local police. *Law and Order* 33:22–24.

Goodstein, Lynne, and John Hepburn. 1985. *Determinate sentencing and imprisonment: A failure of reform.* Cincinnati, OH: Anderson.

Goodstein, Lynne, John Kramer, and Laura Nuss. 1984. Defining determinacy: Components of the sentencing process ensuring equity and release certainty. *Justice Quarterly* 1:47–73.

Goolkasian, Gail A., Ronald W. Geddes, and William DeJong. 1985. *Coping with police stress.* Washington, DC: U.S. Department of Justice Office of Development, Testing, and Dissemination.

Gordon, Frank X. 1985. The judicial image: Is a facelift necessary? *Justice System Journal* 10:315–24.

Gorer, Geoffrey. 1955. Modification of national character: The role of the police in England. *Journal of Social Issues* 11:25–32.

Gottfredson, Michael R., and Don M. Gottfredson. 1987. *Decision making in criminal justice: Toward the rational exercise of discretion.* New York: Plenum.

———. 1988. *Decision making in criminal justice: Toward the rational exercise of discretion.* 2d ed. New York: Plenum.

Gottfredson, Stephen D. 1984. Institutional responses to prison overcrowding. *New York University Review of Law and Social Change* 12:259–73.

Gottfredson, Stephen D., and Don M. Gottfredson. 1985. Screening for risk among parolees: Policy, practice and method. In *Prediction in criminology*, ed. D. Farrington and R. Tarling. Albany: State Univ. of New York Press.

Gottfredson, Stephen D., and Sean D. McConville. 1987. *America's correctional crisis: Prison populations and public policy.* Westport, CT: Greenwood.

Gottlieb, Barbara. 1984. *The pretrial processing of 'dangerous' defendants: A comparative analysis of state laws.* Washington, DC: Toborg.

Gottlieb, Barbara, and Phillip Rosen. 1984. *Public danger as a factor in pretrial release: Summaries of state danger laws.* Washington, DC: Toborg.

Gotwalt, Deborah A. 1984. *Evaluation of Savannah transitional centers.* Atlanta: Georgia Department of Offender Rehabilitation.

Gove, W. R., M. Hughes, and M. Geerken. 1985. Are Uniform Crime Reports a valid indicator of index crimes? *Criminology* 23:451–501.

Graham, Michael H. 1985. *Witness intimidation: The law's response.* Westport, CT: Quorum.

Graves, G., et al. 1985. *Developing a street patrol: A guide for neighborhood crime prevention groups.* Boston: Neighborhood Crime Prevention Council, Justice Resource Institute.

Green, G. S. 1985. The representativeness of the Uniform Crime Reports: Ages of persons arrested. *Journal of Police Science and Administration* 13:46–52.

Green, Gion, and Robert J. Fisher. 1987. *Introduction to security.* Stoneham, MA: Butterworths.

Green, L. C. 1985. Terrorism and its responses. *Terrorism: An International Journal* 8:33–77.

Green, Maurice. 1984. Child advocacy: Rites and rights in juvenile justice. In *Advances in forensic psychology and psychiatry*, ed. Robert W. Rieber. Norwood, NJ: Ablex.

Greenberg, David. 1981. *Crime and capitalism.* Palo Alto, CA: Mayfield.

Greenberg, David F. 1975. The incapacitative effect of imprisonment: Some estimates. *Law and Society Review* 9:566–70.

———. 1985. Age, crime, and social explanation. *American Journal of Sociology* 91:1–21.

Greenberg, David F., Ronald C. Kessler, and Colin Loftin. 1983. The effect of police employment on crime. *Criminology* 21:375–94.

Greenberg, Martin Alan. 1984. *Auxillary police: The citizen's approach to public safety.* Westport, CT: Greenwood.

Greene, Edith. 1986. A jury researcher joins the jury. *Case and Comment* 91:28–38.

Greenfeld, Lawrence. 1985. *Examining recidivism.* Washington, DC: U.S. Department of Justice, Bureau of Justice Statistics.

———. 1986. *Capital punishment, 1985.* Washington, DC: U.S. Government Printing Office, Bureau of Justice Statistics.

———. 1986. *Probation and parole, 1984.* Washington, DC: U.S. Department of Justice, Bureau of Justice Statistics.

———. 1986. *Prisoners in 1985.* Washington, DC: U.S. Department of Justice, Bureau of Justice Statistics.

———. 1988. *Prisoners in 1987.* Washington, DC: U.S. Department of Justice.

Greenwood, Peter W. 1982. *Selective incapacitation.* Santa Monica, CA: Rand.

———. 1986. *Intervention strategies for chronic juvenile offenders.* Westport, CT: Greenwood.

Greenwood, Peter W., J. Chaiken, and Joan M. Petersilia. 1977. *The criminal investigation process.* Lexington, MA: D. C. Heath.

Greenwood, Peter W., and Franklin E. Zimring. 1985. *One more chance: The pursuit of promising intervention strategies for chronic juvenile offenders.* Santa Monica, CA: Rand.

Grieser, Robert C., Thomas McCrae Crawford, and Gail S. Funke. 1985. *The development of jail industries.* Washington, DC: National Institute of Corrections.

Grieser, Robert C., Neal Miller, and Gail S. Funke. 1983. *Guidelines for prison industries.* Washington, DC: U.S. National Institute of Corrections.

———. 1984. *Guidelines for prison industries.* Washington, DC: National Institute of Corrections.

Griffin, Kenyon N., and Michael J. Horan. 1983. Patterns of voting behavior in judicial retention elections for Supreme Court justices in Wyoming. *Judicature* 67:68–77.

Griffith, W. R. 1983. *Self-report instrument: A description and analysis of results in the national evaluation sites.* Eugene, OR: Institute of Policy Analysis.

———. 1983.*Victim survey: An overview and description of results in the six national evaluation sites.* Eugene, OR: Institute of Policy Analysis.

Griswold, David B. 1985. Controlling the police use of deadly force: Exploring the alternatives. *American Journal of Police* 4:93–109.

———. 1985. Florida's sentencing guidelines: Progression or regression? *Federal Probation* 49:25–32.

Gross, Sally. 1984. Women becoming cops: Developmental issues and solutions. *Police Chief* 51:32–35.

Gross, Samuel R., and Robert Mauro. 1984. Patterns of death: An analysis of racial disparities in capital sentencing and homicide victimization. *Stanford Law Review* 37:27–153.

Gruber, G. 1986. The police applicant test: A predictive validity study. *Journal of Police Science and Administration* 14:121–29.

Guy, Edward, et al. 1985. Mental health status of prisoners in an urban jail. *Criminal Justice and Behavior* 12:29–53.

Guyot, Dorothy. 1985. Building bridges between police and public. *FBI Law Enforcement Bulletin* 54:1–8.

Hagan, Frank E. 1986. *Introduction to criminology: Theories, methods, and criminal behavior.* Chicago: Nelson-Hall.

Hagan, J., and M. S. Zatz. 1985. The social organization of criminal justice processing: An event history analysis. *Social Science Research* 14:103–125.

Hahn, Paul H. 1984. *The juvenile offender and the law.* Cincinnati, OH: Anderson.

Hall, Jerome. 1947. *Theft, law, and society.* Indianapolis, IN: Bobbs- Merrill.

Hall, R. 1967. Court organization and administration. *Alabama Lawyer* 28:148–52.

Haller, Mark H. 1979. Plea bargaining: The nineteenth century context. *Law and Society Review* 13:273–79.

Hammrock, Edward R., and Anne Marie Santangelo. 1985. Sentencing disaster?: Will determinate sentencing do the job? *Corrections Today* 47:91–93.

Hanewicz, Wayne B. 1985. Discretion and order. In *Moral issues in police work,* ed. Frederick A. Elliston and Michael Feldberg. Totowa, NJ: Rowman and Allanheld.

Haney, Craig. 1984. On the selection of capital juries: The biasing effects of the death-qualification process. *Law and Human Behavior* 8:121–32.

Hann, Robert G., et al. 1985. Municipal police governance and accountability in Canada: An empirical study. *Canadian Police College Journal* 9:1–85.

Hannah, S. B. 1978. Competition in Michigan's judicial elections: Democratic ideals vs. judicial realities. *Wayne Law Review* 24:1267–71.

Hans, Valerie P., and Neil Vidmar. 1986. *Judging the jury.* New York: Plenum.

Hanson, Richard W., et al. 1983. Predicting inmate penitentiary adjustment: An assessment of four classificatory methods. *Criminal Justice and Behavior* 10:293–309.

Hanson, Roger A., ed. 1984. Prisoner litigation: Problems, processes, and solutions. *Justice System Journal* 9:252–350.

Harding, Christopher, et al. 1985. *Imprisonment in England and Wales: A concise history.* Dover, NH: Croom Helm.

Hargrave, G. E. 1985. Using the MMPI and CPI to screen law enforcement applicants: A study of reliability and validity of clinicians' decisions. *Journal of Police Science and Administration* 13:221–24.

Hargrave, G. E., and J. G. Berner. 1986. A 'psychological skills analysis' for California peace officers. *Police Chief* 53:34–36.

Harlow, Caroline Wolf. 1985. *Reporting crimes to the police.* Washington, DC: U.S. Department of Justice, Bureau of Justice Statistics.

Harrell, Adele Vogel. 1983. *Criminal sanctions and conformity with the law.* Ann Arbor, MI: University Microfilms International.

Harris, Diana K., and William E. Cole. 1980. *Sociology of aging.* Boston: Houghton Mifflin.

Harris, M. Kay. 1984a. Strategies, values and the emerging generation of alternatives to incarceration. *New York University Review of Law and Social Change* 12:141–70.

———. 1984b. Rethinking probation in the context of the justice model. In *Probation and justice,* ed. P. McAnany, D. Thomson, and D. Fogel. Cambridge, MA: Oelgeschlager, Gunn and Hain.

Harris, Patricia M. 1986. Is the juvenile justice system lenient? *Criminal Justice Abstracts* 18:104–18.

Harrison, J. 1985. Police complaints: Pitfalls for the unwary litigant. *New Law Journal* 135:1239–40.

Hart, Henry L., and Herbert Wechsler. 1973. The federal courts and the federal system. New York: Foundation.

Harvard Law Review Association. 1981. *A Uniform system of citation.* 13th ed. Cambridge, MA: Harvard Law Review Association.

Hastie, Reid, Steven D. Penrod, and Nancy Pennington. 1983. *Inside the jury.* Cambridge, MA: Harvard Univ. Press.

Hawaii Crime Commission. 1984. *Mandatory sentencing: A preliminary assessment.* Honolulu, HI: Hawaii Crime Commission.

Hawaii Criminal Justice Data Center. 1985. *Electronic fund transfer crime: An overview.* Honolulu, HI: Hawaii Criminal Justice Data Center.

Hawkins, Darnell F. 1984. State vs. county: Prison policy and conflicts of interest in North Carolina. In *Criminal justice history: An international annual.* Vol. 4. Westport, CT: Meckler.

Hawkins, Gordon. 1983. Prison labor and prison industries. In *Crime and justice: An annual review of research,* ed. M. Tonry and N. Morris. Chicago: Univ. of Chicago Press.

Heffernan, William C. 1985. The police and their rules of office: An ethical analysis. In *Police ethics: Hard choices in law enforcement,* ed. W. C. Heffernan and T. Stroup. New York: John Jay.

Heffernan, William C., and Timothy Stroup, eds. 1985. *Police ethics: Hard choices in law enforcement.* New York: John Jay.

Henderson, Dwight F. 1971. *Courts for a new nation.* Washington, DC: Public Affairs.

Henderson, Thomas A., et al. 1984. *The significance of judicial structure: The effect of unification on trial court operations.* Washington, DC: U.S. Government Printing Office.

Henderson, Thomas A., Randall Guynes, and Carl Baar. 1981. Organizational design for courts. In *Courts and judges,* ed. James A. Cramer. Beverly Hills, CA: Sage.

Her Majesty's Stationery Office. 1985. *Police and Criminal Evidence Act 1984.* London: Her Majesty's Stationery Office.

Hereford, W. 1966. Why not one court? *Florida Bar Journal* 40:1068–72.

Herman, Susan N. 1984. Institutional litigation in the post-Chapman world. *New York University Review of Law and Social Change* 12:299–321.

Hertig, C. A. 1985. Police officer recruitment and affirmative action policy. *FBI Law Enforcement Bulletin* 54:11–13.

Hester, Thomas. 1987. *Probation and parole, 1986.* Washington, DC: U.S. Department of Justice, Bureau of Justice Statistics.

———. 1988. *Probation and parole, 1987.* Washington, DC: U.S. Department of Justice, Bureau of Justice Statistics.

Heumann, Milton. 1975. A note on plea bargaining and case pressure. *Law and Society Review* 9:515–28.

———. 1978. *Plea bargaining: The experiences of prosecutors, judges, and defense attorneys.* Chicago: Univ. of Chicago Press.

Heumann, Milton, and C. Loftin. 1979. Mandatory sentencing and the abolition of plea bargaining: The Michigan felony firearms statute. *Law and Society Review* 13:393–431.

Heuser, James P. 1985. *Juveniles arrested for serious felony crimes in Oregon and "remanded" to adult criminal courts: A statistical study.* Salem: Oregon Department of Justice, Crime Analysis Center.

Hewitt, John D., Eric D. Poole, and Robert M. Regoli. 1984. Self-reported and observed rule-breaking in prison: A look at disciplinary response. *Justice Quarterly* 1:437–47.

Hickman, Kenneth Gary. 1983. *Measuring job performance success for female officers of the Los Angeles Police Department.* Ann Arbor, MI: University Microfilms International.

Hill, Gillian. 1985. Predicting recidivism using institutional measures. In *Prediction in criminology,* ed. David P. Farrington and Roger Tarling. Albany: State Univ. of New York Press.

Hill, Michael O. 1984. Permanent confiscation of prison contraband: The Fifth Amendment behind bars. *Yale Law Journal* 93:901–917.

Hillsman, Sally T. 1982. Pretrial diversion of youthful adults: A decade of reform and research. *Justice System Journal* 7:361–87.

Hillsman, Sally T., Joyce L. Sichel, and Barry Mahoney. 1984. *Fines in sentencing: A study of the use of the fine as a criminal sanction.* Washington, DC: National Institute of Justice, Vera Institute of Justice and Court Management.

Hippchen, Leonard. 1981. Some possible biochemical aspects of criminal behavior. *Journal of Behavioral Ecology* 2:1–6.

Hirschi, Travis. 1969. *Causes of delinquency.* Berkeley: Univ. of California Press.

Hirschi, Travis, and Michael Gottfredson. 1985. Age and crime, logic and scholarship: Comment on Greenberg. *American Journal of Sociology* 91:22–28.

Hirschi, Travis, and Michael J. Hindelang. 1977. Intelligence and delinquency: A revisionist review. *American Sociological Review* 42:571–87.

Hochstedler, Ellen, Robert M. Regoli, and Eric D. Poole. 1984. Changing the guard in American cities: A current empirical assessment of integration in 20 municipal police departments. *Criminal Justice Review* 9:8–14.

Hoffman, Peter B. 1983. Screening for risk: A revised salient factor score. *Journal of Criminal Justice* 11: 539–47.

Hoffman, Peter B., and Sheldon Adelberg. 1980. The salient factor score: A nontechnical overview. *Federal Probation* 44:44–52.

Hoffman, Peter B., and James L. Beck. 1985. Recidivism among released federal prisoners: Salient factor score and five-year follow-up. *Criminal Justice and Behavior* 12:501–7.

Hoffman, Peter B., and Barbara Stone-Meierhoefer. 1980. Reporting recidivism rates: The criterion and follow-up issues. *Journal of Criminal Justice* 8:53–60.

Holeman, Herbert, and B. J. Krepps-Hess. 1983. *Women correctional officers in the California Department of Corrections.* Sacramento: Research Unit, California Department of Corrections.

Holland, L. H. 1985. Police and the community: The Detroit ministation experience. *FBI Law Enforcement Bulletin* 54:1–6.

Holmes, Malcolm, and Howard C. Daudistel. 1984. Ethnicity and justice in the Southwest: The sentencing of Anglo, Black, and Mexican origin defendants. *Social Science Quarterly* 65:265–77.

Holt, Linda K. 1984. *Patterns of enrollment in adult education programs during incarceration.* Boston: Massachusetts Department of Corrections.

Holten, N. Gary, and Melvin E. Jones. 1982. *The system of criminal justice,* 2d ed. Boston: Little, Brown.

Holyst, Brunon. 1979. *Comparative criminology.* Lexington, MA: D. C. Heath.

Homans, George. 1950. *The human group.* New York: Harcourt, Brace, and World.

Homant, Robert J., and Daniel B. Kennedy. 1985. The effect of prior experience on expert witnesses' opinions. *Criminal Justice Review* 10:18–26.

Hooton, Ernest. 1939. *Crime and the man.* Westport, CT: Greenwood.

Hope, Tim. 1985. Building design and burglary. In *Coping with burglary,* ed. Ronald Clarke and Tim Hope. Boston: Kluwer- Nijhoff.

Hopper, Columbus B. 1985. The impact of litigation on Mississippi's prison system. *Prison Journal* 65:54–63.

Horowitz, Robert M., and Howard A. Davidson, eds. 1984. *Legal rights of children.* Colorado Springs, CO: Shepards/McGraw- Hill.

Houk, Julie M. 1984. Electronic monitoring of probationers: A step toward Big Brother? *Golden Gate University Law Review* 14:431–46.

Hucker, S. J., and M. H. Ben-Aron. 1984. Violent elderly offenders—A comparative study. In *Elderly criminals,* ed. W. Wilbanks and P. Kim. Lanham, MD: Univ. Press of America.

Hudnut, William H. 1985. The police and the polis: A mayor's perspective. In *Police leadership in America: Crisis and opportunity,* ed. William A. Geller. New York: Praeger.

Hudson, Paul S. 1980. A Bill of Rights for crime victims. *Victimology* 5:428–37.

Hudzik, John K. 1984. *Federal aid to criminal justice: Rhetoric, results, lessons.* Washington, DC: National Criminal Justice Association.

Hughes, Charles Evans. 1966. *The Supreme Court of the United States.* New York: Columbia Univ. Press.

Hughes, G. 1984. English criminal justice: Is it better than ours? *Arizona Law Review* 26:507–614.

Hughes, Robert. 1987. *The fatal shore.* New York: Knopf.

Humphries, Drew. 1984. Reconsidering the justice model. *Contemporary Crises* 8:167–73.

Hunt, R. G., and K. S. McCadden. 1985. A survey of work attitudes of police officers: Commitment and satisfaction. *Police Studies* 8:17–25.

Hunter, Susan M. 1985. Issues and challenges facing women's prisons in the 1980s. *Criminal Justice Abstracts* 17:129–35.

Hunzeker, Donna. 1985. Habitual offender statutes. *Corrections Compendium* 10:1–5.

Hunzeker, Donna, and Cindy Conger, eds. 1985. *Inmate lawsuits: A report on inmate lawsuits against state and federal correctional systems resulting in monetary damages and settlements.* Lincoln, NE: Contact Center.

Hyman, Harold M., and Catherine M. Tarrant. 1975. Aspects of American trial jury history. In *The jury system in America,* ed. Rita J. Simon. Beverly Hills, CA: Sage.

Hyman, J. M. 1979. Philosophical implications of plea bargaining: Some comments. *Law and Society Review* 13:565–66.

Iacovetta, R. G., and Dae H. Chang. 1979. *Critical issues in criminal justice.* Durham, NC: Carolina Academic Press.

Ikeda, Lisa, Meda Chesney-Lind, and Keith Kameoka. 1985. *The Honolulu anti-truancy program: An evaluation.* Manoa, HI: Youth Development Research Center.

Illinois Governor's Task Force on Prison Overcrowding. 1983. *Recommendations.* Springfield, IL: Governor's Task Force on Prison Overcrowding.

Immarigeon, Russ. 1985a. Private prisons, private programs, and their implications for reducing reliance on imprisonment in the United States. *Prison Journal* 65:60–74.

———. 1985b. *Probation at the crossroads: Innovative programs in Massachusetts.* Boston: Massachusetts Council for Public Justice.

Ingraham, Barton L. 1987. *The structure of criminal procedure: Laws and practice of France, Soviet Union, China, and the United States.* Westport, CT: Greenwood.

Ingram, Jefferson. 1986. The recent change in the federal insanity statute: A misplaced burden of proof? Paper presented at Academy of Criminal Justice Sciences, Orlando, FL.

International Association of Chiefs of Police. 1965. *Law enforcement code of ethics.* Training Key #15. College Park, MD: International Association of Chiefs of Police.

International Law Enforcement. 1984. Hostage release operations. *International Law Enforcement* 1:5–20.

Inwald, Robin. 1985. Administrative legal and ethical practices in the psychological testing of law enforcement officers. *Journal of Criminal Justice* 13:367–72.

Iowa Law Review. 1975. Note: The elimination of plea bargaining in Black Hawk County, a case study. *Iowa Law Review* 60:1063–75.

Iowa Legislative Fiscal Bureau. 1983. *Iowa Department of Social Sciences adult community based corrections.* Des Moines: Iowa Legislative Fiscal Bureau.

Iowa Office for Criminal Justice and Juvenile Justice Planning. 1983. *The impact of objective parole criteria on parole release rates and public protection.* Des Moines: Office for Criminal Justice and Juvenile Justice Planning.

Iowa Statistical Analysis Center. 1985. *Prison population, parole, and offender risk assessment in Iowa: An overview.* Des Moines: Office for Planning and Programming.

Irwin, John. 1970. *The felon.* Englewood Cliffs, NJ: Prentice-Hall.

———. 1985. *The jail: Managing the underclass in American society.* Berkeley: Univ. of California Press.

———. 1987. *The felon.* Berkeley: Univ. of California Press.

Irwin, John, and W. Holder. 1973. History of the prisoner's union. *The Outlaw: Journal of Prisoner's Union* 2:1–3.

Israel, Michael. 1983. Jack Henry Abbott, American prison writing, and the experience of punishment. *Criminal Justice and Behavior* 10:441–60.

Jacks, Irving. 1984. Positive interaction: Everyday principles of correctional rehabilitation. In *Psychological approaches to crime and its correction,* ed. I. Jacks and S. Cox. Chicago: Nelson-Hall.

Jackson, J. D. 1986. The insufficiency of identification evidence based on personal impression. *Criminal Law Review* 16:203–214.

Jacobs, J. 1974. Participant observation in prison. *Urban Life and Culture* 3:221–40.

———. 1977. *Stateville: The penitentiary in mass society.* Chicago: Univ. of Chicago Press.

Janus, Mark-David, Arlene McCormick, Ann W. Burgess, and Carol P. Hartman. 1987. *Adolescent Runaways: Causes and consequences.* Lexington, MA: Lexington.

Jardine, Edward, Grace Moore, and Ken Pease. 1983. Community service orders, employment, and the tariff. *Criminal Law Review* 13:17–20.

Jayewardene, C. H. S., and F. E. McWatt. 1984. The police and the female delinquent. *Canadian Police College Journal* 8:203–217.

Jeffrey C. Ray. 1978. Criminology as an interdisciplinary behavioral science. *Criminology* 16:161–62.

John Howard Association. 1984. *Release study.* Chicago: John Howard Association.

Johnson, Charles A., and Bradley C. Canon. 1984. *Judicial Policies: Implementation and impact.* Washington, DC: Congressional Quarterly.

Johnson, David R. 1981. *American law enforcement: A history.* St. Louis, MO: Forum.

Johnson, Dennis L., James G. Simmons, and Carl B. Gordon. 1983. Temporal consistency of the Meyer-Megargee Typology. *Criminal Justice and Behavior* 10:263–68.

Johnson, E. E. 1984. Problems in assessing police and fire fighter candidates. *Journal of Police Science Administration* 12:412–24.

Johnson, Edwin S. 1981. *Research methods in criminology and criminal justice.* Englewood Cliffs, NJ: Prentice-Hall.

Johnson, Elmer H. 1983. *International handbook of contemporary developments in criminology: Europe, Africa, the Middle East, and Asia.* Westport, CT: Greenwood.

———. 1987. *Handbook on crime and delinquency prevention.* Westport, CT: Greenwood.

Johnson, Judith, Keith McKeown, and Roberta James. 1984. *Removing the chronically mentally ill from jail: Case studies of collaboration between local criminal justice and mental health systems.* Washington, DC: National Coalition for Jail Reform.

Johnson, Leslie G. 1985. Punishment in an age of scarcity: A judicial perspective. *Court Review* 22:7–12.

Johnson, Marcia K., and Mary Ann Foley. 1984. Differentiating fact from fantasy: The reliability of children's memory. *Journal of Social Issues* 40:33–50.

Johnson, Paul H. 1984. Police-community relations: The management factor. *American Journal of Police* 3:185–204.

Johnson, Richard E. 1980. Social class and delinquent behavior: A new test. *Criminology* 18:86–93.

Johnson, Sheri Lynn. 1985. Black innocence and the white jury. *Michigan Law Review* 83:1611–1708.

Johnson, Thomas A., Gordon E. Misner, and Lee P. Brown. 1981. *The police and society: An environment for collaboration and confrontation.* Englewood Cliffs, NJ: Prentice-Hall.

Johnston, Michael. 1982. *Political corruption and public policy in America.* Monterey, CA: Brooks/Cole.

Jolin, Annette, and Don Gibbons. 1984. Policing the polilce: The Portland experience. *Journal of Police Science and Administration* 12:315–22.

Jolly, Robert W., and Edward Sagarin. 1984. The first eight after Furman: Who was executed with the return of the death penalty? *Crime and Delinquency* 30:610–23.

Jones, Michael. 1982. *A report on the Virginia work release program.* Alexandria: Virginia Department of Corrections.

Jones, S., and R. Joss. 1985. Do police officers survive their training? *Policing* 1:206–225.

Jones, Stephen. 1983. Deferment of sentence: An appraisal ten years on. *British Journal of Criminology* 23:381–93.

———. 1985. The Police and Criminal Evidence Act 1984. *Modern Law Review* 48:679–93.

Jurik, Nancy C. 1985. An officer and a lady: Organizational barriers to women working as correctional officers in men's prisons. *Social Problems* 32:375–88.

Jurik, Nancy C., and Michael C. Musheno. 1986. The internal crisis of corrections: Professionalization and the work environment. *Justice Quarterly* 3:457–80.

Just, Rona L. 1985. Executing youthful offenders: The unanswered question in *Eddings v. Oklahoma. Fordham Urban Law Journal* 13:471–510.

Juvenile Justice Resource Center. 1985. *Drug abuse, mental health and delinquency: Summary of proceedings of the Practitioner's Conference on Juvenile Offenders.* Washington, DC: U.S. Government Printing Office.

Kadane, Joseph B. 1984. After Hovey: A note on taking account of the automatic death penalty jurors. *Law and Human Behavior* 8:115–20.

Kadane, Joseph B., and D. Kairys. 1979. Fair numbers of peremptory challenges in jury trials. *Journal of the American Statistical Association* 74:747–53.

Kagan, Robert A., Bobby D. Infelise, and Robert R. Detlefsen. 1984. American state supreme court justices, 1900–1970. *American Bar Foundation Research Journal* 2:371–407.

Kaine, Tim. 1983. Capital punishment and the waiver of sentence review. *Harvard Civil Rights–Civil Liberties Review* 18:483–524.

Kakalik, James S., and Sorrel Wildhorn. 1972. *Private police in the United States: Findings and recommendations*. Santa Monica, CA: Rand.

———. 1977. *Private police: Security and danger*. New York: Crane Russak.

Kales, A. H. 1914. *Unpopular government in the United States*. Chicago: Univ. of Chicago Press.

Kalven, Jr., Harry, and Hans Ziesel. 1966. *The American jury*. Boston: Little, Brown.

Kaminskaya, Dina. 1982. *Final judgment: My life as a Soviet defense attorney*. New York: Simon and Schuster.

Kandel, Denise, Ora Simcha-Fagan, and Mark Davies. 1986. Risk factors for delinquency and illicit drug use from adolescence to young adulthood. *Journal of Drug Issues* 16:67–90.

Kane, Thomas R. 1985. *Research Review: Impact of the Youth Corrections Act*. Washington, DC: U.S. Federal Bureau of Prisons.

Kansas Juvenile Jail Removal Impact Study Committee. 1984. *Juveniles in jail in Kansas*. Topeka: Advisory Commission on Juvenile Offender Programs, Kansas Department of Social and Rehabilitation Services.

Kaplan, Howard, and Joseph Meyerowitz. 1969. Evaluation of a halfway house: Integrated community approach in the rehabilitation of narcotic addicts. *International Journal of Addictions* 4:65–69.

Kapsch, Stefan J., and Diane M. Luther. 1985. *Punishment and risk management as an Oregon sanctioning model*. Portland: Oregon Prison Overcrowding Project.

Karchmer, C. L. 1984. Young arsonists. *Society* 22:78–83.

Kassin, Saul M., and Ralph Juhnke. 1983. Juror experience and decision making. *Journal of Personality and Social Psychology* 44:1182–91.

Katz, Louis R. 1980. *The justice imperative*. Cincinnati, OH: Anderson.

Keating, J. Michael. 1984. *Public ends and private means: Accountability among private providers of public social services*. Pawtucket, RI: Institute for Conflict Management.

———. 1985. *Seeking profit in punishment: The private management of correctional institutions*. Washington, DC: American Federation of State, County, and Municipal Employees.

Keith, C. R. 1984. *The aggressive adolescent: Clinical perspectives*. New York: Free Press.

Kelling, George L., and Tony Pate. 1981. A study of foot patrol: The Newark experiment. Research Bulletin #11. London: House Office Research Unit.

Kelling, George L., Tony Pate, Duane Dieckman, and Charles E. Brown. 1974. *The Kansas City Preventive Patrol Experiment: A summary report*. Washington, DC: Police Foundation.

Kelling, George L., and James Q. Wilson. 1982. Broken windows: The police and neighborhood safety. *Atlantic Monthly* 249:29–38.

Kempf, K. L., and R. L. Austin. 1986. Older and more recent evidence on racial discrimination in sentencing. *Journal of Quantitative Criminology* 2:29–48.

Kempinen, Cynthia. 1983. Changes in the sentencing patterns of male and female defendants. *Prison Journal* 63:3–11.

Kennedy, Daniel B. 1984. A theory of suicide while in police custody. *Journal of Police Science and Administration* 12:191–200.

Kennedy, Ludovic. 1985. *The airman and the carpenter: The Lindbergh kidnapping and the framing of Richard Hauptmann*. New York: Viking Penguin.

Kenny, Camille. 1984. Federal criminal jurisdiction: A case against making federal cases. *Seton Hall Law Review* 14:574–98.

Kerle, Kenneth E. 1985. The American woman county jail officer. In *The changing roles of women in the criminal justice system*, ed. Imogene Moyer. Prospect Heights, IL: Waveland.

Kerr, N. L., et al. 1976. Guilt beyond a reasonable doubt: Effects of concept definition and assigned rule on the judgment of mock jurors. *Journal of Consulting and Social Psychology* 34:282–94.

Kessler, David A. 1985. One- or two-officer cars? A perspective from Kansas City. *Journal of Criminal Justice* 13:49–64.

Keve, Paul W. 1984. *The consequences of prohibiting the jailing of juveniles*. Richmond: Virginia Commonwealth Univ.

Kidd, Robert F., and Ellen F. Chayet. 1984. Why do victims fail to report?: The psychology of criminal victimization. *Journal of Social Issues* 40:39–50.

Kingsley, Sue, and George Mari. 1983. *Diverting drunks from the criminal justice system*. London: Home Office.

Kirby, Michael P. 1977. *The effectiveness of the point scale*. Washington, DC: Pretrial Services Resource Center.

Kitsuse, J. I. 1962. Societal reaction to deviant behavior: Problems of theory and method. *Social Problems* 9: 247–56.

Kizziah, Carol A. 1984. *The state of the jails in California: Report #1. Overcrowding in the jails.* Sacramento: California Board of Corrections.

Klein, John F. 1978. Inducements to plead guilty: Frontier justice revisited. In *Readings in criminology,* ed. Peter Wickman and P. Whitten. Lexington, MA: D. C. Heath.

Klemm, Margaret F. 1986. A look at case processing time in five cities. *Journal of Criminal Justice* 14:9–23.

Kline, Susan. 1987. *Jail inmates 1986.* Washington, DC: U.S. Department of Justice.

Klockars, Carl B. 1985. The Dirty Harry problem. In *Moral issues in police work,* ed. Frederick A. Elliston and Michael Feldberg. Totowa, NJ: Rowman and Allanheld.

Knapp, Whitman, et al. 1972. *Report of the Commission to Investigate Alleged Police Corruption.* New York: George Braziller.

Knapp Commission. 1973. *Knapp Commission report on police corruption.* New York: George Braziller.

Knee, S. L., and L. G. Heywood. 1984. *Differential police response to citizen-initiated calls for service: Executive summary part 2.* Garden Grove, CA: Garden Grove Police Department.

Knowles, Lyle, and Kenneth Hickman. 1984. Selecting a jury of peers: How close do we get? *Journal of Police Science and Administration* 12:207–212.

Koebel, Theodore C. 1983. The problem of bias in judicial evaluation surveys. *Judicature* 67:224–33.

Kohlberg, L. 1963. The development of children's orientations toward a moral order.I: Sequence in the development of human thought. *Vita Humana* 6:11–33.

———. 1981. *The philosophy of moral development.* New York: Harper and Row.

Koneazny, Peter M., and Karl D. Schwartz, eds. 1984. Colloquium: The prison overcrowding crisis. *New York University Review of Law and Social Change* 12:1–356.

Konecni, Vladimir J., and Ebbe B. Ebbesen. 1986. Courtroom testimony by psychologists on eyewitness identification issues: Critical notes and reflections. *Law and Human Behavior* 10:117–26.

Koppel, Herbert. 1984. *Sentencing practices in 13 states.* Washington, DC: U.S. Department of Justice, Bureau of Justice Statistics.

Kramer, John H., and Robin L. Lubitz. 1985. Pennsylvania's sentencing reform: The impact of commission-established guidelines. *Crime and Delinquency* 31:481–500.

Krisberg, Barry, et al. 1985. *Planning study for the Colorado Division of Youth Services.* San Francisco: National Council on Crime and Delinquency.

———. 1985. *The watershed of juvenile justice reform.* Minneapolis: Hubert H. Humphrey Institute of Public Affairs, Univ. of Minnesota.

Krisberg, Barry, and James Austin. 1978. *The children of Ishmael.* Palo Alto, CA: Mayfield.

Kroes, William H. 1976. *Society's victim—The policeman: An analysis of job stress in policing.* Springfield, IL: Charles C. Thomas.

Krohn, Marvin D., R. L. Akers, M. Radosevich, and L. Lanza-Kaduce. 1980. Social status and deviance. *Criminology* 18:303–18.

Krug, Robert E. 1961. An analysis of the F Scale: 1. Item factor analysis. *Journal of Social Psychology* 53:288–91.

Kruttschnitt, Candace. 1984. Sex and criminal court dispositions. *Journal of Research in Crime and Delinquency* 21:213–32.

———. 1985. Are businesses treated differently? A comparison of the individual victim and the corporate victim in the criminal courtroom. *Sociological Inquiry* 55:225–38.

Kruttschnitt, Candace, and Donald E. Green. 1984. The sex-sanctioning issue: Is it history? *American Sociological Review* 49:541–51.

Kunen, James S. 1983. *How can you defend those people? The making of a criminal lawyer.* New York: Random House.

Kuykendall, Jack L. 1985. Police managerial styles: A grid analysis. *American Journal of Police* 4:38–70.

Kuykendall, Jack L., and David E. Burns. 1983. The black police officer: An historical perspective. *Criminal Justice* 19:41–45.

Lab, Steven P. 1984. Patterns in juvenile misbehavior. *Crime and Delinquency* 30:293–308.

LaFree, Gary D. 1985. Adversarial and nonadversarial justice: A comparison of guilty pleas and trials. *Criminology* 23:289–312.

———. 1985. Official reactions to Hispanic defendants in the Southwest. *Journal of Research on Crime and Delinquency* 22:213–37.

Lamborn, Leroy L. 1979. Reparations for victims of crime: Developments and directions. *Victimology* 4: 229–35.

Lambuth, Lynn. 1984. An employee assistance program that works. *Police Chief* 51:36–38.

Lampert, Nick. 1984. Law and order in the USSR: The case of economic and official crime. *Soviet Studies* 36: 366–85.

Lane, R. 1967. *Policing the city—Boston, 1822–1885.* Cambridge: Harvard Univ. Press.

Langbein, John H. 1979. Understanding the short history of plea bargaining. *Law and Society Review* 13:261–72.

Langdon, Anthony J. 1983. *The New Jersey delay reduction program.* Denver, CO: Institute for Court Management.

Langworthy, Robert H. 1985. Wilson's theory of police behavior: A replication of the constraint theory. *Justice Quarterly* 2:89–98.

———. 1986. *The structure of police organizations.* Westport, CT: Greenwood.

Larson, Richard C. 1975. What happened to patrol operations in Kansas City? A review of the Kansas City Preventive Patrol Experiment. *Journal of Criminal Justice* 3:267–97.

Latessa, Edward J. 1983. *The fifth evaluation of the Lucas County Adult Probation Department's Incarceration Diversion Unit.* Cincinnati, OH: Univ. of Cincinnati Criminal Justice Program.

Latessa, Edward J., and Harry E. Allen. 1982. *Management issues in parole.* San Jose, CA: San Jose State University Foundation.

Latessa, Edward J., Lawrence F. Travis, and Harry E. Allen. 1983. Volunteers and paraprofessionals in parole: Current practices. *Journal of Offender Counseling Services and Rehabilitation* 8:91–106.

Lawn, J. C. 1985. The DEA's role in the prevention of drug trafficking and abuse. *Police Chief* 52:31–41.

Lawrence, Richard A. 1984. The role of legal counsel in juveniles' understanding of their rights. *Juvenile and Family Court Journal* 34:49–58.

———. 1985. Jail educational programs: Helping inmates cope with overcrowded conditions. *Journal of Correctional Education* 36:15–20.

Lay, Donald P., and Jill DeLaHunt. 1985. The Bail Reform Act of 1984: A discussion. *William Mitchell Law Review* 11:929–66.

LeClair, Daniel P. 1985. *The effect of community reintegration on rates of recidivism: A statistical overview of data for the years 1971 through 1982.* Boston: Massachusetts Department of Corrections.

Lee, Beverly N. W., and Giannina P. Rikoski. 1984. *Vehicle theft prevention strategies.* Washington, DC: U.S. Government Printing Office.

Lee, W. L. M. 1901. *A history of police in England.* London: Methuen.

Leeke, William D., and Heidi Mohn. 1986. Violent offenders: AIMS and unit management maintain control. *Corrections Today* 48:22–24.

Leger, Robert G., and Harvey Gray Barnes. 1986. Black attitudes in prison: A sociological analysis. *Journal of Criminal Justice* 14:105–122.

Lemert, Edwin. 1951. *Social Pathology.* New York: McGraw-Hill.

———. 1967. *Human deviance, social problems, and social control.* Englewood Cliffs, NJ: Prentice-Hall.

———. 1974. Beyond Mead: The societal reaction to deviance. *Social Problems* 21:458–68.

Lempert, R. O. 1975. Uncovering nondiscernible differences: Empirical research and the jury-size cases. *Michigan Law Review* 73:643–708.

Lester, David. 1987. *Correctional counseling.* Cincinnati, OH: Anderson.

Levinson, Marc R. 1983. Should licensing commissions put police on trial? *Police* 6:23–43.

Lewis, Donald E. 1986. The general deterrent effect of longer sentences. *British Journal of Criminology* 26: 47–62.

Library Information Specialists, Inc. 1983. *Alternative financing of jail construction.* Boulder, CO: Information Center, U.S. National Institute of Corrections.

———. 1984. *Resources for prison design.* Boulder, CO: Information Center, U.S. National Institute of Corrections.

Lieberman, Jethro K., ed. 1984. *The role of courts in American society.* St. Paul, MN: West.

Lilly, J. Robert, Richard A. Ball, and Jennifer Wright. 1987. Home incarceration with electronic monitoring in Kenton City, Kentucky: An evaluation. In *Intermediate punishments,* ed. B. McCarthy. Monsey, NY: Criminal Justice.

Linden, Rick. 1983. Women in policing: A study of lower mainland R.C.M.P. detachments. *Canadian Police College Journal* 7:217–19.

———. 1985. Attrition among male and female members of the RCMP. *Canadian Police College Journal* 9:86–97.

Lindner, Charles, and Margaret R. Savarese. 1984. The evolution of probation: University settlement and the beginning of statutory probation in New York City. *Federal Probation* 48:3–12.

Lipton, D., R. Martinson, and J. Wilks. 1975. *The effectiveness of correctional treatment: A survey of treatment evaluation studies.* Springfield, MA: Praeger.

Litton, Gilbert, and Linda Marye. 1983. *An evaluation of the juvenile diversion program in the Orleans Parish District Attorney's office: A preliminary impact evaluation.* New Orleans, LA: Mayor's Criminal Justice Council.

Littrell, W. B. 1979. *Bureaucratic justice: Police, prosecutors, and plea bargaining.* Beverly Hills, CA: Sage.

Lockwood, Daniel. 1980. *Prison sexual violence.* New York: Elsevier.

———. 1982. The contribution of sexual harassment to stress and coping in confinement. In *Coping with confinement*, ed. Nicolette Parisi. Beverly Hills, CA: Sage.

Loftus, Elizabeth F., and Graham M. Davies. 1984. Distortions in the memory of children. *Journal of Social Issues* 40:51–67.

Logan, Charles H., and Sharla P. Rausch. 1985. Punish and profit: The emergence of private enterprise prisons. *Justice Quarterly* 2:303–318.

———. 1985. Why deinstitutionalizing status offenders is pointless. *Crime and Delinquency* 31:501–517.

Logan, Dianne. 1986. Harris County Juvenile Probation Department: Growing services, shrinking budget. *Corrections Today* 48:22–26.

Lombroso, Cesare. 1981. Crime: Its causes and remedies. Boston: Little, Brown.

Londer, Randi. 1987. Can bad air make bad things happen? *Parade Magazine*, August 9, 6.

Louscher, P. Kent, Ray E. Hosford, and C. Scott Moss. 1983. Predicting dangerous behavior in a penitentiary using Megargee typology. *Criminal Justice and Behavior* 10:269–84.

Lovejoy, Frances. 1983. *What color are America's prisons? U.S. incarceration rates by state, by race, and by sex.* Washington, DC: National Moratorium on Prison Construction.

Loveless, Pauline. 1987. Juvenile detention needs attention. Paper presented at the annual Academy of Criminal Justice Science meetings, April, St. Louis, MO.

Lovell, David G. 1985. *Sentencing reform and the treatment of offenders.* Olympia, WA: Washington Council on Crime and Delinquency.

Lundman, Richard J. 1974. Routine police arrest practices: A commonweal perspective. *Social Problems* 22:127–41.

———. 1979. Origins of police misconduct. In *Critical issues in criminal justice*, ed. R. G. Iacovetta and Dae H. Chang. Durham, NC: Carolina Academic Press.

———. 1980. *Police behavior: A sociological perspective.* New York: Oxford Univ. Press.

———. 1984. *Prevention and control of juvenile delinquency.* New York: Oxford Univ. Press.

———. 1986. Beyond probation: Assessing the generalizability of the delinquency suppression effect measures reported by Murray and Cox. *Crime and Delinquency* 32:134–47.

Lundman, Richard J., Richard E. Sykes, and John P. Clark. 1978. Police control of juveniles: A replication. *Journal of Research on Crime and Delinquency* 15:74–91.

Lynch, Richard. 1976. Improving the treatment of victims: Some guides for action. In *Criminal justice and the victim,* ed. William McDonald. Beverly Hills, CA: Sage.

MacDonald, Donald, and Gerald Bala. 1983. *Follow-up study: Sample of Rochester work release participants.* Albany, NY: Division of Program Planning, Research, and Evaluation, New York Department of Correctional Services.

———. 1984. *Follow-up study: Sample of Fishkill work release participants.* Albany, NY: Division of Program Planning, Research, and Evaluation, New York Department of Correctional Services.

MacDonald, V. N., M. A. Martin, and A. J. Richarson. 1985. Physical and verbal excesses in policing. *Canadian Police College Journal* 9:295–341.

MacKenzie, Doris Layton, and Lynne Goodstein. 1985. Long-term incarceration impacts and characteristics of long-term offenders: An empirical analysis. *Criminal Justice and Behavior* 12:395–412.

Maeder, Thomas. 1984. *Crime and madness: The origins and evolution of the insanity defense.* New York: Harper and Row.

Mahoney, Anne Rankin. 1985. Time and process in juvenile court. *Justice System Journal* 10:37–55.

Mahoney, Barry, Larry L. Sipes, and Jeanne A. Ito. 1985. *Implementing delay reduction and delay prevention programs in urban trial courts.* Williamsburg, VA: National Center for State Courts.

Malinchak, Alan. 1980. *Crime and Gerontology.* Englewood Cliffs, NJ: Prentice-Hall.

Malloy, Thomas E., and G. Larry Mays. 1984. The police stress hypothesis: A critical evaluation. *Criminal Justice and Behavior* 11:197–224.

Maltz, Michael D. 1984. *Recidivism*. Orlando, FL: Academic.

Mandaraka-Sheppard, Alexandra. 1986. *The dynamics of aggression in women's prisons in England*. Brookfield, VT: Gower.

Mande, M., and H. C. Covey. 1982. Perceived criteria used by criminal justice and mental health professionals to predict dangerousness behavior of mentally ill persons. *Justice Quarterly* 1:343–456.

Manning, Peter K. 1977. *Police work*. Cambridge: MIT Press.

———. 1978. *Police work: The social organization of policing*. Cambridge: MIT Press.

———. 1984. Community policing. *American Journal of Police* 3:205–227.

Marcus, Paul, et al. 1983. Symposium: White collar crime. *University of Cincinnati Law Review* 52:378–463.

Marquart, James W. 1986. Doing research in prison. The strengths and weaknesses of full participation as a guard. *Justice Quarterly* 3:15–32.

Marquart, James W., and Julian B. Roebuck. 1986. Prison guards and snitches. In *Dilemmas of punishment: Readings in contemporary corrections*, ed. K. C. Haas and G. P. Alpert. Prospect Heights, IL: Waveland.

Marques, Janice K. 1984. *An innovative treatment program for sex offenders*. Sacramento: California Department of Mental Health.

———. 1985. *The sex offender treatment and evaluation project*. Sacramento: California Department of Mental Health.

Marshall, Tony F., et al. 1985. *Alternatives to criminal courts: The potential for non-judicial dispute settlement*. Brookfield, VT: Gower.

Martin, Susan E. 1983. Commutation of prison sentences. *Crime and Delinquency* 29:593–612.

Martinez, Pablo, and Antonio Fabelo. 1985. *Texas correctional system: Growth and policy alternatives*. Austin: Texas Criminal Justice Policy Council.

Marx, Gary T. 1985. Who really gets stung? Some issues raised by the new police undercover work. In *Moral issues in police work*, ed. F. A. Elliston and M. Feldberg. Totowa, NJ: Rowman and Allanheld.

Maryland Committee on Prison Overcrowding. 1984. *Report*. Towson, MD: Maryland Criminal Justice Coordinating Council, Committee on Prison Overcrowding.

Maslach, Christina, and Susan E. Jackson. 1979. Burned-out cops and their families. *Psychology Today* 12:59.

Mason, Pamela. 1984. Services for the mentally abnormal offender: An overview. In *Options for the mentally abnormal offender*, ed. T. Williams et al. Leicester: British Psychological Association.

Mastrofski, Stephen. 1979. The primary assignment area: Measuring an aspect of police patrol organization. Paper presented at the annual meeting of the Midwest Political Science Association, November, Chicago.

———. 1981. Policing the beat: The impact of organizational scale on patrol officer behavior in urban residential neighborhoods. *Journal of Criminal Justice* 9:343–58.

Mather, Lynn W. 1979a. *Plea bargaining or trial? The process of criminal case disposition*. Lexington, MA: Lexington.

———. 1979b. Comments on the history of plea bargaining. *Law and Society Review* 13:281–85.

Mathias, Robert A., Paul DeMuro, and Richard S. Allinson, eds. 1984. *Violent juvenile offenders: An anthology*. San Francisco: National Council on Crime and Delinquency.

Mathis, Edward J., and Charles E. Zech. 1985. The community demand for police officers, relative to the maximum base salary, citizen wants tend to be elastic. *Journal of Economics and Sociology* 44:401–410.

Mauer, Marc. 1985. *The lessons of Marion: The failure of a maximum security prison: A history and analysis, with voices of prisoners*. Philadelphia: American Friends Services Committee.

Mawby, R. I., and M. L. Gill. 1987. *Crime victims: Needs, services and the voluntary sector*. New York: Methuen.

Maxfield, M. G. 1979. *Discretion and the delivery of police services: Demand, client characteristics, and street-level bureaucrats in two cities*. Ph.D. diss., Northwestern University, Chicago.

Maxson, Cheryl L., Margaret A. Gordon, and Malcolm W. Klein. 1986. Differences between gang and nongang homicides. *Criminology* 23:209–222.

Mayhew, Pat. 1984. Target-hardening: How much of an answer? In *Coping with burglary*, ed. Ronald Clarke and Tim Hope. Boston: Kluwer-Nijhoff.

Mayhew, Pat, and Lorna J. F. Smith. 1985. Crime in England and Wales and Scotland: A British Crime Survey comparison. *British Journal of Criminology* 25:148–59.

Maynard, D. W. 1982. Defendant attributes in plea bargaining: Notes on the modeling of sentencing decisions. *Social Problems* 29:347–60.

Mays, G. Larry, and William A. Taggart. 1985. The impact of litigation on changing New Mexico prison conditions. *Prison Journal* 65:38–53.

McAnany, Patrick D., Doug Thomson, and David Fogel, eds. 1984. *Probation and justice: Reconsideration of a mission.* Cambridge, MA: Oelgeschlager, Gunn and Hain.

McCarthy, Belinda. 1985. An analysis of detention. *Juvenile and Family Court Journal* 36:49–50.

———. 1987. *Intermediate punishments: Intensive supervision, home confinement, and electronic surveillance.* Monsey, NY: Criminal Justice.

McCarthy, Belinda, and Robert Langworthy. 1988. *Older offenders: Perspectives in criminology and criminal justice.* New York: Praeger.

McCarthy, Belinda, and Charles A. Lindquist. 1985. Ambiguity and conflict in sentencing research: Partial resolution through crime-specific analysis. *Journal of Criminal Justice* 13:155–69.

———. 1985. Certainty of punishment and sentence mitigation in plea behavior. *Justice Quarterly* 2:363–83.

McCarthy, Francis B., and James G. Carr. 1980. *Juvenile law and its processes.* Indianapolis, IN: Bobbs-Merrill.

McChesney, K. 1986. Law enforcement recruiting: Strategies for the 1980s. *FBI Law Enforcement Bulletin* 55:11–18.

McClearn, Gerald E. 1969. Biological bases of social behavior with specific reference to violent behavior. In *Crimes of Violence,* Vol. 13, ed. D. J. Mulvihill et al. Washington, DC: U.S. Government Printing Office.

McCloskey, Michael, Howard Egeth, and Judith McKenna. 1986. The ethics of expert testimony. *Law and Human Behavior* 10:1–185.

McConahay, J., C. Mullin, and J. Frederick. 1977. The uses of social science in trials with political and racial overtones: The trial of Joan Little. *Law and Contemporary Problems* 41:205–229.

McConnell, E. 1968. The administration of a state court system. *Judicature* 51:253–56.

McConville, Michael, and John Baldwin. 1981. *Courts, prosecution, and conviction.* Oxford: Clarendon Press.

McCormick, Kenneth, Carol Garrison, and David Arbogast. 1983. Public and private law enforcement: The Ohio experience suggests a model for the future. *Journal of Security Administration* 6:45–52.

McCoy, Candace. 1984a. Affirmative action in police organizations: Checklists for supporting a compelling state interest. *Criminal Law Bulletin* 20:245–54.

———. 1984b. Lawsuits against police: What impact do they have? *Criminal Law Bulletin* 20:49–56.

———. 1984c. Determinate sentencing, plea bargaining bans, and hydraulic discretion in California. *Justice System Journal* 9:256–75.

McDonald, William F. 1985. *Plea bargaining: Critical issues and common practices.* Washington, DC: U.S. Department of Justice, National Institute of Justice.

McEleney, Barbara Lavin. 1985. *Correctional reform in New York: The Rockefeller years and beyond.* Lanham, MD: Univ. Press of America.

McGee, Thomas P. 1985. Preventing juvenile crime: What a judge can do. *Judges Journal* 24:20–22.

McGillis, Daniel, and Joan Mullin. 1977. *Neighborhood justice centers: An analysis of potential models.* Washington, DC: National Institute of Law Enforcement and Criminal Justice.

McGinnis, James. 1985. Career development in municipal policing: Part II. *Canadian Police College Journal* 9: 254–95.

McGowan, B.G. and K.L. Blumenthal. 1978. *Why punish the children? A study of children of women prisoners.* Hackensack, NJ: National Council on Crime and Delinquency.

McGriff, M. David. 1985. *A test of incapacitation theory on burglars.* Ann Arbor, MI: University Microfilms International.

McGuire, James, and Philip Priestley. 1985. *Offending behavior: Skills and stratagems for going straight.* New York, St. Martin's.

McIntyre, Lisa J. 1988. *The public defender: The practice of law in the shadows of repute.* Chicago: Univ. of Chicago Press.

McLaren, John A. 1986. A lawyer's guide to search warrants and the new federalism. *Criminal Law Bulletin* 22:5–17.

McLeod, Donald K. 1979. The police training dilemma. In *Critical issues in criminal justice,* ed. R. G. Iacovetta and Dae H. Chang. Durham, NC: Carolina Academic Press.

McNeese, Margaret, and Jean Hebeler. 1977. The abused child: A clinical approach to identification. *Clinical Symposia* 29:2–36.

McShane, Marilyn. 1985. *The effect of detainer on prison overcrowding.* Huntsville, TX: Criminal Justice Center, Sam Houston State Univ.

Mead, Margaret. 1935. *Sex and temperament in three primitive societies.* New York: Morrow.

Meador, Daniel J. 1983. An appellate court dilemma and a solution through subject matter organization. *Journal of Law Reform* 16:471–92.

———. 1983. Straightening out federal review of state criminal cases. *Ohio State Law Journal* 44:273–85.

Meadows, Robert J. 1985. Police training strategies and the role perceptions of police recruits. *Journal of Police Science and Administration* 13:195–200.

Meagher, M. Steven. 1983. *Examination of the variation in the police patrol function by agency size and agency type.* Ann Arbor, MI: University Microfilms International.

———. 1985. Police patrol styles: How pervasive is community variation? *Journal of Police Science and Administration* 13:36–45.

Medler, Jerry F. 1985. *Oregon community corrections, 1977–1984: An evaluation.* Salem: Oregon Department of Human Resources.

Mednick, S. A., and J. Volavka. 1980. Biology and crime. In *Crime and justice: An annual review of research,* ed. N. Morris and M. Tonry. Chicago: Univ. of Chicago Press.

Meeker, James W. 1984. Criminal appeals over the last 100 years: Are the odds of winning increasing? *Criminology* 22:551–71.

Meeker, James W., and Henry N. Pontell. 1985. Court caseloads, plea bargains, and criminal sanctions: The effects of Section 17 P.C. in California. *Criminology* 23:119–43.

Megargee, Edwin I., and Joyce L. Carbonell. 1985. Predicting prison adjustment with MMPI correctional scales. *Journal of Consulting and Clinical Psychology* 53:874–83.

Meier, John, ed. 1985. *Assault against children: Why it happens—How to stop it.* San Diego, CA: College-Hill.

Meisenhelder, Thomas. 1985. An essay on time and the phenomenology of imprisonment. *Deviant Behavior* 6:39–56.

Melone, A. P. 1977. Political realities and democratic ideals: Accession and competition in a state judicial system. *North Dakota Law Review* 54:187–92.

Menzies, Robert, Christopher Webster, and Diana Sepejak. 1985. Hitting the forensic sound barrier: Predictions of dangerousness in a pre-trial psychiatric clinic. In *Dangerousness probability and prediction.* Cambridge: Cambridge Press.

Merritt, Frank S. 1984. Restitution under the Victim and Witness Protection Act of 1982. *Criminal Law Bulletin* 20:44–48.

Merton, Robert K. 1938. Social structure and anomie. *American Sociological Review* 3:672–82.

———. 1957. *Social theory and social structure.* New York: Free Press.

Messinger, Sheldon L., et al. 1985. The foundations of parole in California. *Law and Society Review* 19:69–106.

Metropolitan Police Department. 1974. *The shadow of the past—The light of the future: 1974 annual report.* Washington, DC: Metropolitan Police Department, Planning and Development Division.

Michalowski, Raymond J. 1985. *Order, law, and crime: An introduction to criminology.* New York: Random House.

Miers, David R. 1981. Victim compensation as a labeling process. *Victimology* 5:3–16.

———. 1983. Compensation and conceptions of victims of crime. *Victimology* 8:204–212.

Milkman, R. H. 1985. *Employment services for ex-offenders field test: Summary report.* Washington, DC: National Institute of Justice.

Miller, Alden, and Lloyd Ohlin. 1985. *Delinquency and the community.* Beverly Hills, CA: Sage.

Miller, Arthur Selwyn. 1978. *The Supreme Court: Myth and reality.* Westport, CT: Greenwood.

Miller, D. 1985. The harassment of forensic psychiatrists outside of court. *Bulletin of the American Academy of Psychiatry and the Law* 13:337–44.

Miller, Dallas. 1984. *A survey of recidivism research in the United States and Canada.* Boston: Massachusetts Department of Corrections.

Miller, Debra T. 1984. *Profile of inmates in the Texas Department of Corrections 60 years of age and older as of May 31, 1984.* Huntsville: Texas Department of Corrections.

Miller, Gilbert B., Jr. 1983. Inmate grievance procedures certified. *Corrections Today* 45:76–77.

Miller, Herbert S., James A. Cramer, and William F. McDonald. 1978. *Plea bargaining in the United States: Phase I Report.* Washington, DC: U.S. Government Printing Office.

Miller, Jerome G. 1986. Sentencing: What lies between sentiment and ignorance? *Justice Quarterly* 3:231–39.

Miller, Larry S. 1985. Jury reform: An analysis of juror perceptions of the criminal court system. *Criminal Justice Review* 10:11–16.

Miller, W. B. 1976. *Violence by youth gangs and youth groups as a crime problem in major American cities.* Washington, DC: U.S. Government Printing Office.

Miller, Wilbur R. 1985. Cops and bobbies in the mid-nineteenth century. In *Policing Society: An occupational view,* ed. W. Clinton Terry. New York: Wiley.

Minnesota Board of Peace Officer Standards and Training. 1980. *Learning objectives for skills in law enforcement.* St. Paul: Minnesota Board of Peace Officer Standards and Training.

Minnesota Sentencing Guidelines Commission. 1984. *The impact of the Minnesota Sentencing Guidelines: Three-year evaluation.* St. Paul: Minnesota Sentencing Guidelines Commission.

Mitchell, John J., and Sharon A. Williams. 1986. SOS: Reducing juvenile recidivism. *Corrections Today* 48:70–71.

Monahan, John. 1984. The prediction of violent behavior: Toward a second generation of theory and policy. *American Journal of Psychiatry* 141:10–15.

Montagu, A. 1968. Chromosomes and crime. *Psychology Today* 2:43–49.

Moorehead, C. 1985. Terrorism in the air. *New Society* 72:471–72.

Moran, T. Kenneth, and Charles Lindner. 1985. Probation and the hi-technology revolution: Is a reconceptualization of the traditional officer role inevitable? *Criminal Justice Review* 10:25–32.

More, Harry W. 1985. *Critical issues in law enforcement.* Cincinnati, OH: Anderson.

Morrill, S. 1984. Tampa likes sector patrolling. *Law and order* 32:37–40.

Morris, Norval. 1984. On dangerousness in the judicial process. *Record of the Association of the Bar of the City of New York* 39:102–128.

Morris, Norval, and Marc Miller. 1985. Predictions of dangerousness. In *Crime and justice: An annual review of research,* ed. M. Tonry and N. Morris. Chicago: Univ. of Chicago Press.

Mrad, David F., Robert Kabacoff, and Paul Duckro. 1983. Validation of the Megargee typology in a halfway house setting. *Criminal Justice and Behavior* 10:252–62.

Muir, W. K., Jr. 1977. *Police: Street corner politicians.* Chicago: Univ. of Chicago Press.

Mullen, Joan. 1982. Corrections and the private sector. *Privatization Review* 1:10–19.

———. 1985. Prison overcrowding and the evaluation of public policy. *Annals* 47:31–46.

———. 1986. *Corrections and the private sector.* Washington, DC: U.S. Department of Justice, National Institute of Justice.

Murphy, Patrick V. 1985. The prospective chief's negotiation of authority with the mayor. In *Police leadership in America: Crisis and opportunity,* ed. W. A. Geller. New York: Praeger.

Murphy, Patrick V., and T. Plate. 1977. *Commissioner.* New York: Simon and Schuster.

Muth, William R., and Thom Gehring. 1986. The correctional education/prison reform link: 1913–1940 and conclusion. *Journal of Correctional Education* 37:14–17.

Myers, Martha A., and Susette M. Talarico. 1987. *The social contexts of sentencing.* Secaucus, NJ: Springer-Verlag.

Nacci, Peter, and Thomas R. Kane. 1983. Incidence of sex and sexual aggression in federal prisons. *Federal Probation* 47:31–36.

Nagao, D. H., and J. H. Davis. 1980. The effects of prior experience on mock juror case judgments. *Social Psychology Quarterly* 43:190–99.

Nagel, S. S. 1982. Discretion in the criminal justice system: Analyzing, channeling, reducing, and controlling it. *Emory Law Review* 31:603–633.

Nagel, Stuart, and Robert Geraci. 1983. Effects of reducing judicial sentencing discretion. *Criminology* 21:309–331.

Nagel, William G. 1984. Corrections and punishment. *Corrections Today* 46:32–62.

Napper, G. 1986. Partnerships against crime: Sharing problems and power. *Police Chief* 53:45–46.

Nardulli, Peter F. 1978. *The courtroom elite: An organizational perspective on criminal justice.* Cambridge, MA: Ballinger.

————. 1979. *The study of criminal courts: Political perspectives.* Cambridge, MA: Ballinger.

Nassi, Alberta J., and Stephen I. Abramowitz. 1976. From phrenology to psychosurgery and back again: Biological studies of criminality. *American Journal of Orthopsychiatry* 46:595–96.

Nathan, Winifred. 1984. Whose rights are they? The Supreme Court and the rights of juveniles. *Children and Youth Services Review* 6:329–44.

Nathanson, Stephen. 1985. Does it matter if the death penalty is arbitrarily administered? *Philosophy and Public Affairs* 14:149–64.

National Advisory Commission on Criminal Justice Standards and Goals. 1973. *Report of the National Advisory Commission on Criminal Justice Standards and Goals,* Washington, DC: U.S. Government Printing Office.

————. 1976. *Juvenile justice and delinquency prevention.* Washington, DC: U.S. Government Printing Office.

National Alliance of Business. 1983. *Employment and training of ex-offenders: A community program approach.* Washington, DC: National Alliance of Business.

National Center for State Courts. 1984. *Word processing in the courts.* Williamsburg, VA: National Center for State Courts.

National Center for State Courts, Western Regional Office. 1985. *Sentencing felons in New Mexico: A proposal for guidelines.* San Francisco: National Center for State Courts, Western Regional Office.

National Commission on Criminal Justice Standards and Goals. 1973. *Corrections task force report.* Washington, DC: National Commission on Criminal Justice Standards and Goals.

National Council of Juvenile and Family Court Judges. 1984. *The juvenile court and serious offenders: 38 recommendations.* Reno, NV: National Council of Juvenile and Family Court Judges.

National Council on Crime and Delinquency. 1983. Computerized cuffs come of age. *Criminal Justice Newsletter,* March 28.

National Crime Prevention Institute. 1986. *Understanding crime prevention.* Boston: Butterworths.

National Crime Survey. 1986. *The national crime survey.* Washington, DC: Bureau of Justice Statistics.

National Employment Listing Service. 1982. *The police employment guide—1982 edition.* Huntsville, TX: Criminal Justice Center, Sam Houston State Univ.

National Institute of Corrections. 1985. *Designs for contemporary correctional facilities.* Crofton, MD: Capitol.

National Institute of Justice. 1985. *Corrections and the private sector.* Washington, DC: U.S. Department of Justice, March, 1985.

————. 1985. *Felony court case-processing time.* Washington, DC: U.S. Department of Justice.

————. 1985. *Topical bibliography: Policewomen.* Washington, DC: U.S. Department of Justice.

National Minority Advisory Council on Criminal Justice. 1982. *The inequality of justice.* Washington, DC: U.S. Department of Justice.

National School Boards Association. 1984. *Toward better and safer schools: A school leader's guide to delinquency prevention.* Washington, DC: U.S. Department of Justice.

Neighborhood Crime Prevention Council. 1985. *Developing a street patrol: A guide for neighborhood crime prevention groups.* Boston: Neighborhood Crime Prevention Council.

Nelson, E. Kim, Lenora Segal, and Nora Harlow. 1984. *Probation under fiscal restraints.* Washington, DC: U.S. Government Printing Office.

Nelson, Z. P., and W. Smith. 1970. The law enforcement profession: An incident of high suicide. *Omega* 1:293–99.

Nesbary, Dale. 1985. *Recent trends in state corrections spending: Legislative finance paper #51.* Denver, CO: National Conference of State Legislatures.

Nesson, Charles. 1985. The evidence or the event? On judicial proof and the acceptability of verdicts. *Harvard Law Review* 98:1157–1392.

Netanyahu, Benjamin. 1986. *Terrorism: How the West can win.* New York, NY: Farrar, Straus and Giroux.

Nettler, Gwynn. 1974. Embezzlement without problems. *British Journal of Criminology* 14:70–77.

————. 1984. *Explaining crime.* New York: McGraw-Hill.

Neubauer, David W. 1974. *Criminal justice in Middle America.* Morristown, NJ: General Learning.

————. 1979. *America's courts and the criminal justice system.* North Scituate, MA: Duxbury.

Nevada Legislative Commission. 1984. *The function of parole in the criminal justice system.* Carson City: Nevada Legislative Commission.

New Jersey Division of Criminal Justice. 1985. *Juvenile waivers to adult court: A report to the New Jersey State Legislature.* Trenton: New Jersey Division of Criminal Justice.

New Jersey Governor's Management Improvement Plan. 1983. *Department of corrections: The correctional system, strategic issues, and alternatives.* Trenton: New Jersey Governor's Management Improvement Plan.

New York Citizen's Crime Commission. 1985. *Downtown safety, security and economic development.* New York: Downtown Research and Development Center.

New York Legislative Commission on Expenditure Review. 1984. *Program audit: State prison release programs.* Albany: New York Legislative Commission on Expenditure Review.

New York State. 1984. *The community dispute resolution centers program: A progress report.* New York: New York State Unified Court System.

New York State Defenders Association, Inc. 1985. *What prisons do to people.* Albany: New York State Defenders Association.

Newman, Donald J. 1966. *Conviction: The determination of guilt or innocence without trial.* Boston: Little, Brown.

Newman, Donald J., and Evelyn S. Newman. 1982. Senior citizen crime. *Justice Reporter* 2:5.

Newman, Evelyn S., Donald J. Newman, and Mindy L. Gewirtz. 1984. *Elderly criminals.* Cambridge, MA: Oelgeschlager, Gunn, and Hain.

Newsweek. 1984. A hidden epidemic. *Newsweek,* May 14, 31.

————. 1987. Wall Street's top cop. *Newsweek,* March 2, 48–50.

Niederhoffer, Arthur, and Alexander B. Smith. 1978. *The police family.* Lexington, MA: Lexington.

Nielsen, Dennis W. 1984. U.S. probation officers as jail monitors: A new responsibility on the horizon? *Federal Probation* 48:29–33.

Norland, Stephen, and Priscilla J. Mann. 1984. Being troublesome: Women on probation. *Criminal Justice and Behavior* 11:115–35.

Norton, Philip, ed. 1984. *Law and order in British politics.* Brookfield, VT: Gower.

Nova Institute. 1978. *Crime against the elderly: The role of the criminal justice system in New York City.* New York: Nova.

O'Brien, Barbara. 1986. *Stress: Its impact on the recruitment and retention of policewomen.* Washington, DC: U.S. Government Printing Office.

O'Leary, Vincent, and Joan Nuffield. 1972. *The organization of parole systems in the United States.* Hackensack, NJ: National Council on Crime and Delinquency.

O'Neill, Timothy P. 1984. The good, the bad, and the Burger court: Victim's rights and a new model of criminal review. *Journal of Criminal Law and Criminology* 75:363–87.

Office of Management and Budget. 1982. *Budget of the United States Government, fiscal year 1983.* Washington, DC: U.S. Government Printing Office.

Oklahoma Coalition for Alternatives to Jailing Juveniles. 1985. *Juveniles in jail: What is happening in Oklahoma?* Oklahoma City: Oklahoma Institute for Child Advocacy.

Oklahoma State Board of Corrections. 1984. *Recommendations for controlling prison population growth: A response to HB 1483.* Oklahoma City: Oklahoma Department of Corrections.

Oregon Crime Analysis Center. 1984. *Recidivism of releasees from Oregon corrections institutions.* Salem: Oregon Crime Analysis Center.

Orsagh, Thomas, and Mary Ellen Marsden. 1985. What works when: Rational-choice theory and offender rehabilitation. *Journal of Criminal Justice* 13:269–77.

Osborne, Yvonne H., and Neil B. Rappaport. 1985. Sentencing severity with mock jurors: Predictive validity of three variable categories. *Behavioral Sciences and the Law* 3:467–73.

Osbun, Lee Ann, and Peter A. Rode. 1984. Prosecuting juveniles as adults: The quest for 'objective' decisions. *Criminology* 22:187–202.

Osgood, D. Wayne. 1983. Offense history and juvenile diversion. *Evaluation Review* 7:793–806.

Pabon, Edward. 1985. A neighborhood correctional program for juvenile offenders. *Juvenile and Family Court Journal* 36:43–47.

Packer, Herbert. 1968. *The limits of the criminal sanction.* Stanford, CA: Stanford Univ. Press.

Padawer-Singer, A. M., A. N. Singer, and R. L. J. Singer. 1977. An experimental study of twelve vs. six member juries under unanimous vs. nonunanimous decisions. In *Psychology in the legal process,* ed. B. D. Sales. New York: Spectrum.

Padgett, John F. 1985. The emergent organization of plea bargaining. *American Journal of Sociology* 90:753–800.

Palmer, John W. 1985. *Constitutional Rights of Prisoners.* Cincinnati, OH: Anderson.

Park, Roger. 1976. The entrapment controversy. *Minnesota Law Review* 60:1231–35.

Parker, James T., ed. 1985. Adult basic education: Programs that work. *Journal of Correctional Education* 36:41–85.

Parks, R. B. 1979. *Assessing the influence of organization on performance: A study of police services in residential neighborhoods.* Ph.D. diss., Indiana University, Bloomington.

———. 1980. *Using sample surveys to compare police performance.* Bloomington, IN: Workshop in Political Theory and Policy Analysis.

Parnas, Raymond I., and Riley J. Atkins. 1978. Abolishing plea bargaining: A proposal. *Criminal Law Bulletin* 14:101–8.

Pasewark, R. A. 1981. Insanity plea: A review of the research literature. *Journal of Psychiatry and Law* 9:357–401.

Paternoster, Raymond. 1984. Prosecutorial discretion in requesting the death penalty: A case of victim-based racial discrimination. *Law and Society Review* 18:437–78.

Paternoster, Raymond, and Leeann Iovanni. 1986. The deterrent effect of perceived severity: A reexamination. *Social Forces* 64:751–77.

Patti, P. 1984. New concepts in use of force reporting. *Law and Order* 32:61–63.

Paulus, Paul, Verne C. Cox, and Gavin McCain. 1988. *Prison crowding: A psychological perspective.* Secaucus, NJ: Springer-Verlag.

Paulus, Paul, Garvin McCain, and Verne Cox. 1985. The effects of crowding in prisons and jails. In *Reaction to crime: The public, the police, courts, and prisons,* ed. D. Farrington and J. Gunn. New York: Wiley.

Payne, D. M., and R. C. Trojanowicz. 1985. *National Neighborhood Foot Patrol Center, Michigan State University.* Community Policing Series No. 6. East Lansing, MI: National Neighborhood Foot Patrol Center.

———. 1985. *Performance profiles of foot versus motor officers.* East Lansing, MI: National Neighborhood Foot Patrol Center.

Peak, Kenneth. 1983. Directors of correctional education programs: A demographic and attitudinal profile. *Journal of Correctional Education* 34:79–83.

———. 1985. Correctional research in theory and praxis: Political and operational hindrances. *Criminal Justice Review* 10:27–31.

Pearson, Frank S. 1985. New Jersey's intensive supervision program: A progress report. *Crime and Delinquency* 31:393–410.

Pellenberg-Fixen, Amy R. 1983. Plea bargaining: The New Hampshire ban. *New England Journal on Criminal and Civil Confinement* 9:387–405.

Pennsylvania Advisory Committee to the U.S. Commission on Civil Rights. 1983. *Doing time: A study of prison conditions at U.S. Penitentiary, Lewisburg, Pennsylvania.* Washington, DC: U.S. Government Printing Office.

Pennsylvania Commission on Criime and Delinquency. 1985. *A strategy to alleviate overcrowding in Pennsylvania's prisons and jails.* Harrisburg: Pennsylvania Commission on Crime and Delinquency, Prison and Jail Overcrowding Task Force.

Pepinsky, Harold E. 1979. *Crime control strategies: An introduction to the study of crime.* New York: Oxford Univ. Press.

———. 1980. *Crime control strategies: An introduction to the study of crime.* New York: Oxford Univ. Press.

Pepinsky, Harold E., and P. Jesilow. 1984. *Myths that cause crime.* College Park, MD: Seven Locks.

Persico, J. E., and George Sunderland. 1985. *Keeping out of crime's way: The practical guide for people over 50.* Glenview, IL: Scott, Foresman.

Petersilia, Joan. 1983. *Racial disparities in the criminal justice system.* Washington, DC: U.S. Department of Justice, National Institute of Corrections.

———. 1985. *Probation and felony offenders.* Washington, DC: U.S. Department of Justice, National Institute of Justice.

———. 1987. *Expanding options for criminal sentencing.* Santa Monica, CA: Rand.

Petersilia, Joan, Susan Turner, James Kahan, and Joyce Peterson. 1985. *Granting felons probation: Public risks and alternatives.* Santa Monica, CA: Rand.

Peterson, J., and M. Pogrebin. 1977. Team policing: A modern approach to decentralization of police decision-making. *Abstracts on Police Science* 5:1–13.

Peterson, Ruth D., and John Hagan. 1984. Changing conceptions of race: Towards an account of anomalous findings of sentencing research. *American Sociological Review* 49:56–70.

Petrone, S., and M. Reiser. 1985. A home visit program for stressed police officers. *Police Chief* 52:36–37.

Phillips, Barry. 1983. *Overcrowding in Massachusetts prisons: Sources and solutions.* Boston: Massachusetts Joint Legislative Committee on Human Services and Elderly Affairs.

Phillips, R. G., Jr. 1984. State and local law enforcement training needs. *FBI Law Enforcement Bulletin* 53:6–15.

Piaget, J. 1948. *The moral judgment of the child.* New York: Free Press.

Pierce, J. A. 1984. High density area community relations. *Law and Order* 32:29–30.

Pierce, Lois H. 1985. Selecting children for residential treatment. *Children and Youth Services Review* 7:299–308.

Piliavin, Irving, et al. 1986. Crime, deterrence, and rational choice. *American Sociological Review* 51:101–119.

Pillemer, Karl. 1987. Elder abuse: Definitional dilemmas. Paper presented at the American Society of Criminology meetings, November, Montreal.

Pinkele, Carl F., and William C. Louthan. 1985. *Discretion, justice and democracy: A public policy perspective.* Ames: Iowa State Univ. Press.

Pisciotta, Alexander W. 1983. Scientific reform: The 'new penology' at Elmira, 1876–1900. *Crime and Delinquency* 29:613–30.

Poggio, Eugene C., et al. 1985. *Blueprint for the future of the Uniform Crime Reporting program: Final report of UCR study.* Washington, DC: U.S. Government Printing Office.

Pogrebin, M. 1986. The changing role of women: Female police officers' occupational problems. *Police Journal* 59:127–33.

Poirier, Donate. 1985. Prevenir la vol à main armée. *Criminologie* 18:135–45.

Police Executive Research Forum. 1978. *Survey of police operational and administrative practices—1977.* Ed. M. T. Farmer. Washington, DC: Police Executive Research Forum.

———. 1983. *Police agency handling of citizen complaints: A model policy statement.* Washington, DC: Police Executive Research Forum.

Police Foundation. 1978. *Police practices: The general administration survey.* Ed. J. F. Heaphy. Washington, DC: Police Foundation.

Polk, Kenneth. 1984. Juvenile diversion: A look at the record. *Crime and delinquency* 30:648–59.

Pollac, Harriet, and Alexander B. Smith. 1983. White-collar v. street crime sentencing disparity: How judges see the problem. *Judicature* 67:174–82.

Pollock, Joycelyn M. 1986. *Sex and supervision: Guarding male and female inmates.* Westport, CT: Greenwood.

Pomery, Thomas W. 1982. *Pennsylvania's unified judicial system: An analysis with recommendations.* Harrisburg: Committee to Study Pennsylvania's Unified Judicial System.

Pope, D. W. 1985. Developments and problems in police-community relations. In *Contemporary policing,* ed. J. R. Thackrah. London: Sphere.

Post, J. M. 1984. Notes on psychodynamic theory of terrorist behavior. *Terrorism: An international journal* 7:241–56.

Potas, Ivan, ed. 1985. *Prosecutorial discretion.* Canberra, AUS: Australian Institute of Criminology.

Potas, Ivan, and Debra Rickwood. 1984. *Do juries understand? Concerning the ability of lay persons to understand and apply certain standard jury instructions for possible use in criminal courts.* Canberra, AUS: Australian Institute of Criminology.

Potas, Ivan, and John Walker. 1983. *Sentencing the federal drug offender: An experiment in computer-aided sentencing.* Canberra, AUS: Australian Institute of Criminology.

Potler, Cathy. 1985. *A neglected population: Women prisoners at Bayview.* New York: Correctional Association of New York.

Potts, L. W. 1983. Equal employment opportunity and female employment in police agencies. *Journal of Criminal Justice* 11:505–523.

Pound, R. 1940. Principles and outlines of a modern unified court organization. *Journal of the American Judicature Society* 11:81–82.

Pounder, Chris. 1983. Data protection and the police. *Journal of Law and Society* 10:109–118.

Poveda, Tony G. 1985. The effects of scandal on organizational deviance: The case of the FBI. *Justice Quarterly* 2:237–58.

Powers, Matthew T. 1983. Employment motivation for women in policing. *Police Chief* 50:60–63.

President's Commission on Law Enforcement. 1967. *President's Commission on Law Enforcement and the Administration of Justice.* Washington, DC: U.S. Government Printing Office.

———. 1967. *Task force report: The courts.* Washington, DC: U.S. Government Printing Office.

President's National Commission on Law Observance and Enforcement. 1931. *Report on criminal statistics.* Washington, DC: U.S. Government Printing Office.

Price, Albert C., et al. 1983. Judicial discretion and jail overcrowding. *Justice System Journal* 8:222–38.

Priestley, Philip. 1985. *Victorian prison lives: English prison biography, 1830–1914.* New York: Methuen.

Priestley, Philip, et al. 1984. *Social skills in prison and the community: Problem-solving offenders.* Boston: Routledge and Kegan Paul.

Pringle, P. 1955. *Hue and cry.* London: Museum Press.

Prior, L. E. 1985. Polygraph testing of Vermont state police officers. *Polygraph* 14:256–57.

Prison Reform Trust. 1984. *Beyond restraint: The use of body belts, special stripped and padded cells in Britain's prisons.* London: Prison Reform Trust.

Prottas, J. M. 1979. *People processing: The street-level bureaucrat in public service bureaucracies.* Lexington, MA: Lexington.

Provine, Doris Marie. 1986. *Judging credentials: Nonlawyer judges and the politics of professionalism.* Chicago: Univ. of Chicago Press.

Pruitt, Charles R., and James Q. Wilson. 1983. A longitudinal study of the effect of race on sentencing. *Law and Society Review* 17:613–35.

Pugh, George. 1985a. Situation tests and police selection. *Journal of Police Science and Administration* 13:30–35.

———. 1985b. The California psychological inventory and police selection. *Journal of Police Science and Administration* 13:172–77.

Punch, Maurice, ed. 1983. *Control in the police organization.* Cambridge: MIT Press.

Pynoos, Robert S., and Spencer Eth. 1984. The child as witness to homicide. *Journal of Social Issues* 40:87–108.

Quarles, Chester L. 1985. A validation study of a police managerial assessment center. *American Journal of Police* 4:71–91.

Quetelet, Adolph. 1839. *A treatise on man and the development of his faculties.* Gainesville, FL: Scholars, Facsimiles, and Reprints.

Rabasca, Michael H., and Lyle Milton Baltrusch. 1985. *Lifers in Delaware: Future costs and populations through 1994.* Dover: Delaware Statistical Analysis Center.

Rafky, D. 1975. Racial discrimination in urban police departments. *Crime and Delinquency* 21:233–42.

Rafter, Nicole H. 1983. Prisons for women, 1790–1980. In *Crime and justice: An annual review of research,* ed. M. Tonry and N. Morris. Chicago: Univ. of Chicago Press.

———. 1985. *Partial justice: Women in state prisons, 1800–1935.* Boston: Northeastern Univ. Press.

Ragona, Anthony J., and John Paul Ryan. 1983. Misdemeanor courts and the choice of sanctions: A comparative view. *Justice System Journal* 8:199–221.

Rankin, J. H., and L. E. Wells. 1985. From status to delinquent offenses: Escalation? *Journal of Criminal Justice* 13:171–80.

Rasicot, James. 1983. *Jury selection, body language, and the visual trial.* Minneapolis, MN: AB.

Rasmussen, Teri G. 1983. Recognizing a constitutional right of media access to evidentiary hearings in criminal trials. *Michigan Journal of Law Reform* 17:121–39.

Ream, B. D., ed. 1985. The child and the law: Special biographical issue. *Children's Legal Rights Journal* 6:1–70.

Reed, David. 1983. *Needed: Serious solutions for serious juvenile crime.* Chicago: Chicago Law Enforcement Study Group.

Reiman, Jeffrey H. 1985. Justice, civilization, and the death penalty: Answering van den Haag. *Philosophy and Public Affairs* 14:115–48.

Reiss, Jr., Albert J. 1971. *The police and the public.* New Haven, CT: Yale Univ. Press.

———. 1985. Shaping and serving the community: The role of the police chief executive. In *Police leadership in America,* ed. William A. Geller. New York: Praeger.

Reith, Charles. 1938. *The Police Idea.* London: Oxford Univ. Press.

———. 1943. *British police and the democratic ideal.* Oxford: Oxford Univ. Press.

———. 1952. *Blind eye of history.* Montclair, NJ: Patterson Smith.

———. 1956. *A new study of police history.* Edinburgh: Oliver and Boyd.

———. 1956. *A short history of the British police.* London: Oliver and Boyd.

Remington, Frank J. 1983. State prisoner access to postconviction relief: A lessening role for federal courts, an increasingly important role for state courts. *Ohio State Law Journal* 44:287–305.

Reppetto, Thomas A. 1984. Police anti-burglary strategies in the United States. In *Coping with burglary,* ed. R. Clarke and T. Hope. Boston: Kluwer-Nijhoff.

Research and Forecasts, Inc. 1983. *The Figgie Report Part 4: Reducing crime in America— Successful Community Efforts.* Willoughby, OH: Figgie International.

Rhode Island Governor's Commission. 1984. *Rhode Island's Overcrowded Prisons.* Providence: Rhode Island Governor's Commission.

Rhodes, W. M. 1978. *Plea bargaining: Who gains? Who loses?* Washington, DC: Institute for Law and Social Research.

————. 1979. Plea bargaining: Its effect on sentencing and convictions in the District of Columbia. *Journal of Criminal Law and Criminology* 70:360–75.

Rich, T. F., S. T. Davis, and R. C. Larson. 1984. *Revealed preference of the criminal justice system during a period of workload shedding: Coping with overcrowded prisons.* Cambridge, MA: Public Systems Evaluation.

Richardson, J. 1970. *The New York Police.* New York. Oxford Univ. Press.

Ricks, Truett A., Bill G. Tillett, and Clifford W. Van Meter. 1987. *Principles of security.* Cincinnati, OH: Anderson.

Riemer, Carolyn E. 1985. Television coverage of trials: Constitutional protection against absolute denial of access in the absence of compelling interest. *Villanova Law Review* 30:1267–1308.

Roach, John, and Jurgen Thomaneck, eds. 1985. *Police and public order in Europe.* London: Croom Helm.

Roberts, Albert R., and Gerald T. Powers. 1985. The privatization of corrections: Methodological issues and dilemmas involved in evaluative research. *Prison Journal* 65:95–107.

Robinson, Cyril. 1985. Criminal justice research: Two competing futures. *Crime and Social Justice* 23:101–128.

Rogers, Joseph W., and M. D. Buffalo. 1974. Fighting back: Nine modes of adaptation to a deviant label. *Social Problems* 22:101–118.

Romero, Joseph, and Linda M. Williams. 1983. Group psychotherapy and intensive probation supervision: A comparative study. *Federal Probation* 47:36–42.

Roper, Robert T., and Victor E. Flango. 1983. Trials before judges and juries. *Justice System Journal* 8:187–98.

Rosenbaum, Dennis P., Arthur J. Lurigio, and Paul J. Lavrakas. 1986. *Crime Stoppers: A national evaluation.*

Washington, DC: U.S. Department of Justice, National Institute of Justice.

Rosenthal, Marguerite G. 1983. *Social policy for delinquent children: Delinquency activities of the U.S. Children's Bureau, 1912–1940.* Ann Arbor, MI: University Microfilms International.

Rosentraub, Mark S., et al. 1986. *Citizen involvement in the production of personal safety: What citizens do and what police officers want them to do.* Arlington, TX: Institute of Urban Studies.

Rosett, Arthur, and Donald R. Cressey. 1976. *Justice by consent.* Philadelphia, PA: Lippincott.

Rossi, Peter H., Jon E. Simpson, and JoAnn L. Miller. 1985. Beyond crime seriousness: Fitting the punishment to the crime. *Journal of Quantitative Criminology* 1:59–90.

Rossum, Ralph. 1978. The entrapment defense and the teaching of political responsibility: The Supreme Court as republican school master. *American Journal of Criminal Law* 6:225–29.

Roth, A., J. B. Kadane, and M. H. DeGroot. 1977. Optimal peremptory challenges in trials by juries: A bilateral sequential process. *Operations Research* 25:901–919.

Rothman, David J. 1983. Sentencing reforms in historical perspective. *Crime and Delinquency* 29:631–47.

Roundtree, George A., Dan W. Edwards, and Jack B. Parker. 1984. A study of the personal characteristics of probationers as related to recidivism. *Journal of Offender Counseling, Services, and Rehabilitation* 8:53–61.

Rouse, J. J. 1985. The relationship between police presence and crime deterrence. *Police Journal* 58:118–31.

Rousey, Dennis C. 1984. Cops and guns: Police use of deadly force in nineteenth-century New Orleans. *American Journal of Legal History* 28:41–66.

Rowe, David C., and D. Wayne Osgood. 1984. Heredity and sociological theories of delinquency: A reconsideration. *American Sociological Review* 49:526–40.

Roy, Robert E., and J. S. Wormith. 1985. *The effects of incarceration. 1: Measuring criminal sentiments.* Ottawa: Ministry of the Solicitor General of Canada.

Ruark, Michael P. 1982. The Sentencing Reform Act of 1981: A critique of 'presumptive sentencing' in Washington. *Gonzaga Law Review* 17:583–608.

Ruback, R. Barry, and Timothy S. Carr. 1984. Crowding in a women's prison: Attitudinal and behavioral effects. *Journal of Applied Social Psychology* 14:57–68.

Rubin, H. Ted. 1984. *The courts.* 2d ed. New York: Random House.

———. 1985. *Behind the black robes: Juvenile court judges and the court.* Beverly Hills, CA: Sage.

———. 1985. *Juvenile justice: Policy, practice, and law.* New York: Random House.

Rubinstein, Jonathan. 1973. *City police.* New York: Farrar, Straus, and Giroux.

Rubinstein, Michael L., and Teresa J. White. 1980. Alaska's ban on plea bargaining. In *Plea bargaining,* ed. William F. MacDonald and James A. Cramer. Lexington, MA: Lexington.

Ruchelman, Leonard. 1973. *Who rules the police?* New York: New York Univ. Press.

Rudman, Gary, et al. 1986. Violent youth in adult court: Process and punishment. *Crime and Delinquency* 32: 75–96.

Russell, Donald H. 1985. Girls who kill. *International Journal of Offender Therapy and Comparative Criminology* 29:171–76.

Ryan, C. L., and K. S. Williams. 1986. Police discretion. *Public Law* 19:285–310.

Ryan, John P., and James Alfini. 1978. Trial judges' participation in plea bargaining: An empirical perspective. *Law and Society Review* 13:486–95.

Ryan, T. A. 1984. *State of the art analysis of adult female offenders and institutional programs.* Washington, DC: National Institute of Corrections.

Saari, D. 1976. Modern court management: Trends in court organization concepts—1976. *Justice System Journal* 2:19–33.

Sabor, Monika. 1985. Plea bargaining: A neglected issue? *Probation Journal* 32:139–43.

Sacks, Howard, and Charles Logan. 1980. *Parole: Crime prevention or crime postponement?* Storrs, CT: Univ. of Connecticut School of Law Press.

Sagatun, Inger, Loretta L. McCollum, and Leonard P. Edwards. 1985. The effect of transfers from juvenile to criminal court: A loglinear analysis. *Journal of Crime and Justice* 8:65–92.

Saks, M. J. 1977. *Jury verdicts.* Lexington, MA: Lexington.

———. 1978. Jury case: Benchmark for behavioral research. *APA Monitor* 9:4–8.

———. 1982. Innovation and change in the courtroom. In *The psychology of the courtroom,* ed. N. L. Kerr and R. M. Bray. New York: Academic.

Saltzburg, Stephen A., and Kenneth R. Redden. 1986. *Federal rules of evidence manual.* 4th ed. Charlottesville, VA: Michie.

Sampson, Robert J. 1985. Sex differences in self-reported delinquency and official records: A multiple group structural modeling approach. *Journal of Quantitative Criminology* 1:345–67.

Sandberg, David N. 1987. *Chronic acting-out students and child abuse.* Lexington, MA: Lexington.

Saney, Parviz. 1986. *Crime and culture in America: A comparative perspective.* Westport, CT: Greenwood.

Sapp, Allen D. 1984. *Administration responses to prison overcrowding: A survey of prison administrators.* Warrensburg, MO: Central Missouri State Univ.

———. 1986. Sexual misconduct and sexual harassment by police officers. In *Police deviance,* ed. Thomas Barker and David L. Carter. Cincinnati, OH: Pilgrimage.

Sarat, Austin. 1979. Doing the dirty business of coping with crime: The contemporary 'crisis' of American criminal courts. In *The study of criminal courts,* ed. P. Nardulli. Cambridge, MA: Ballinger.

Sarbin, Theodore R., and Jeffrey E. Miller. 1970. Demonism revisited: The XYY chromosomal anomaly. *Issues in Criminology* 5:195–207.

Satchell, Mitchell. 1980. The end of the line: Marion, Illinois. *Parade,* September 28, 6.

Scarfone, Anthony C. 1986. The mandatory death penalty for murder by lifers: Foregoing procedural safeguards on the illusory promise of deterrence. *Syracuse Law Review* 36:1303–1340.

Scharf, Peter, and Arnold Binder. 1983. *The badge and the bullet: Police use of deadly force.* New York: Praeger.

Scheff, Thomas C. 1966. *Being mentally ill.* Chicago: Aldine.

Schiffern, L. 1985. Justice for all: Why crime rates are falling for the third straight year. *Policy Review* 32:56–57.

Schlossman, Steven, et al. 1984. *Delinquency prevention in South Chicago: A fifty-year assessment of the Chicago area project.* Santa Monica, CA: Rand.

Schmidt, Annesley. 1985. Deaths in the line of duty. *NIJ Reports* 189:6–8.

Schmidt, Annesley, and Christine E. Curtis. 1987. Electronic monitors. In *Intermediate punishments,* ed. Belinda McCarthy. Monsey, NY: Criminal Justice.

Schneider, Anne. 1984a. Divesting status offenses from juvenile court jurisdiction. *Crime and Delinquency* 30:347–70.

———. 1984b. Deinstitutionalization of status offenders: The impact on recidivism and secure confinement. *Criminal Justice Abstracts* 16:410–32.

———. 1984c. Sentencing guidelines and recidivism rates of juvenile offenders. *Justice Quarterly* 1:107–124.

Schneider, Anne, and Peter R. Schneider. 1984. A comparison of programmatic and 'ad hoc' restitution in juvenile courts. *Justice Quarterly* 1:529–47.

———. 1985. The impact of restitution on recidivism of juvenile offenders: An experiment in Clayton County, Georgia. *Criminal Justice Review* 10:1–10.

Schoolbred, C. F. 1966. *The administration of criminal justice in England and Wales.* Oxford: Pergamon.

Schrag, Clarence. 1971. *Crime and Justice: American style.* Washington, DC: U.S. Government Printing Office.

Schreiber, F. B., and J. Sietzinger. 1985. The stress pressure cooker: A comprehensive model of stress management. *Police Chief* 52:45–49.

Schuiteman, J. G. 1985. Allocating state troopers: The Virginia experience. *Police Chief* 52:40–48.

Schulhofer, Stephen J. 1985. No job too small: Justice without bargaining in the lower criminal courts. *American Bar Foundation* 13:221–29.

Schumacher, Michael A. 1985. Implementation of a client classification and case management system: A practitioner's view. *Crime and Delinquency* 31:445–55.

Schur, Edwin M. 1965. *Crimes without victims.* Englewood Cliffs, NJ: Prentice-Hall.

Schwartz, A. I., and S. N. Clarren. 1977. *The Cincinnati team policing experiment: A summary report.* Washington, DC: Police Foundation.

———. 1978. *The Cincinnati team policing experiment: A technical report.* Washington, DC: Police Foundation.

Schweber, Claudine. 1984. Beauty marks and blemishes: The coed prison as a microcosm of integrated society. *Prison Journal* 64:3–14.

Schweitzer, James A. 1985. *Computer crime and business information: A practical guide for managers.* New York: Elsevier.

Schwitzgebel (now Gable), Ralph K., et al. 1964. A program of research in behavior electronics. *Behavioral Science* 9:233–38.

Scott, William R. 1986. College education requirements for police entry level and promotion: A case study. *Journal of Police and Criminal Psychology* 2:10–28.

Scull, Andrew. 1977. *Decarceration: Community treatment and the deviant: A radical view.* Englewood Cliffs, NJ: Prentice-Hall.

Security Management. 1984. Intrusion detection: The future unfolds. Editorial. *Security Management* 28:93–98.

Seiffert, J. M. 1984. Alexandria's citizen awareness program. *FBI Law Enforcement Bulletin* 53:16–20.

Seljan, B. J. 1983. *The community survey: An overview and description of results from the evaluation sites.* Eugene, OR: Institute of Policy Analysis.

Selye, Hans. 1974. *Stress without distress.* Philadelphia: Lippincott.

Sewell, John. 1985. *Police: Urban policing in Canada.* Toronto: James Lorimer.

Shaffner, Paula D. 1985. Around and around on Pennsylvania's juvenile justice confession carousel: This time the police get the brass ring. *Villanova Law Review* 30: 1235–66.

Shah, Saleem A., and Loren H. Roth. 1974. Biological and psychophysiological factors in criminality. In *Handbook of criminology,* ed. Daniel Glaser. Chicago: Rand McNally.

Shanahan, Michael G. 1985. Private enterprise and the public police: The professionalizing effects of a new partnership. In *Police leadership in America,* ed. W. A. Geller. New York: Praeger.

Shane-DuBow, Sandra, Alice P. Brown, and Eric Olsen. 1985. *Sentencing reform in the United States: History, content, and effect.* Washington, DC: U.S. Department of Justice.

Shavell, Steven. 1985. *The optimal use of nonmonetary sanctions as a deterrent.* Cambridge: Harvard Law School.

Shaw, Clifford R., et al. 1929. *Delinquency areas.* Chicago: Univ. of Chicago Press.

Shaw, Clifford R., and Henry D. McKay. 1929. *Juvenile delinquency and urban areas.* Chicago: Univ. of Chicago Press.

Shaw, R. A. 1986. Which hat should I wear? *Law and Order* 34:41–43.

Shearing, Clifford D., Philip C. Stenning, and Susan M. Addario. 1985. Police perceptions of private security. *Canadian Police College Journal* 9:127–54.

Sheldon, William H. 1949. *Varieties of delinquent youth.* New York: Harper and Row.

Shelley, Louise I. 1984. *Lawyers in Soviet work life.* New Brunswick, NJ: Rutgers Univ. Press.

Sherman, Lawrence W. 1974. *Police corruption: A sociological perspective.* Garden City, NY: Doubleday.

———. 1984. Experiments in police discretion: Scientific boom or dangerous knowledge? *Law and Contemporary Problems* 47:61–82.

———. 1985. Becoming bent: Moral careers of corrupt policemen. In *Moral issues in police work,* ed. Frederick A. Elliston and Michael Feldberg. Totowa, NJ: Rowman and Allanheld.

Sherman, Lawrence W., et al. 1973. *Team policing: Seven case studies.* Washington, DC: Police Foundation.

Sherman, Lawrence W., and Barry D. Glick. 1984. The quality of arrest statistics. *Police Foundation Reports* 2:1–8.

Sherman, N. W. 1977. Obstacles to implementing court reform. In *Managing the state courts: Text and readings,* ed. L. C. Berkson et al. St. Paul, MN: West.

Shernock, Stanley K. 1986. A profile of the citizen crime prevention activist. *Journal of Criminal Justice* 14: 211–28.

Sheskin, Arlene. 1981. Trial courts on trial: Examining dominant assumptions. In *Courts and judges,* ed. James A. Cramer. Beverly Hills, CA: Sage.

Shichor, David. 1984. National trends in arrest data concerning elderly offenders. In *Elderly criminals,* ed. E. S. Newman, D. J. Newman, and M. Gewirtz. Cambridge, MA: Oelgeschlager, Gunn, and Hain.

———. 1985. Male-female differences in elderly arrests: An exploratory analysis. *Justice Quarterly* 2:399–414.

Shifrin, A. 1978. How many concentration camps are there in the USSR? *Novoe Russkoe Slovo* #24656:3.

Shigley, Richard T. 1987. The emerging professional education model for police and the Minnesota experience. Paper presented at the Academy of Criminal Justice Science meetings, St. Louis, MO.

Shinnar, Shlomo, and Reuel Shinnar. 1975. The effects of the criminal justice system on the control of crime: A quantitative approach. *Law and Society Review* 9:581–611.

Shoemaker, Donald J. 1984. *Theories of delinquency: An examination of explanations of delinquent behavior.* New York: Oxford Univ. Press.

Shtromas, A. 1977. Crime, law, and penal practice in the USSR. *Possev,* 9:61–62.

Sigler, Robert T., and Bridgett McGraw. 1984. Adult probation and parole officers: Influence of their weapons, role perceptions and role conflict. *Criminal Justice Review* 9:28–32.

Silverstein, J. M. 1986. New roles for psychologists in police personnel selection. *Police Chief* 53:32–33.

Simon, Rita J. 1975. *The jury system in America.* Beverly Hills, CA: Sage

———. 1980. *The jury: Its role in American society.* Lexington, MA: D. C. Heath.

Simpson, Anthony. 1977. *The literature of police corruption.* New York: John Jay.

Sims, Brian, and Jack O'Connell. 1985. *Early release: Prison overcrowding and public policy implications.* Olympia, WA: Washington Office of Financial Management.

Singer, Richard G. 1984. Desert sentencing and prison overcrowding: Some doubts and tentative answers. *New York University Review of Law and Social Change* 12:85–110.

Singer, Simon I. 1985. *Relocating juvenile crime: The shift from juvenile to criminal justice.* Albany: Nelson A. Rockefeller Institute of Government, State Univ. of New York.

Skelton, Paul. 1984. *Comprehensive statewide study to determine current and future needs for correctional facilities.* Tallahassee: Florida Department of Corrections.

Skogan, Wesley G. 1981. *Issues in the measurement of victimization.* Washington, DC: U.S. Department of Justice, Bureau of Justice Statistics.

Skolnick, Jerome H. 1966. *Justice without trial: Law enforcement in democratic society.* New York: Wiley.

———. 1985. Deception by police. In *Moral issues in police work,* ed. Frederick A. Elliston and Michael Feldberg. Totowa, NJ: Rowman and Allanheld.

Skolnick, Jerome H., and Thomas C. Gray. 1975. *Police in America.* Boston: Little, Brown.

Smith, Alexander B., and Alexander Bassin. 1984. Research in a probation department: Twenty-two years later. *Federal Probation* 48:25–28.

Smith, Alexander B., and Harriet Pollack. 1975. *Some sins are not crimes.* New York: New Viewpoints.

Smith, Betsey, Ann Bristow, and Lila Austin. 1985. *Expectant mothers in the Massachusetts criminal justice system.* Boston: Women's Health and Learning Center, and Community Services for Women.

Smith, Brent L., and Edward H. Stevens. 1984. Sentence disparity and the judge-jury sentencing debate: An analysis of robbery sentences in six southern states. *Criminal Justice Review* 9:1–7.

Smith, David. 1983. The demise of transportation: Mid-Victorian penal policy. In *Criminal justice history, an international annual.* Vol. 3. Westport, CT: Meckler.

———. 1984. Police community involvement: A planned approach to effective crime prevention. In *Community policing: Proceedings, 2–3 August, 1984.* Canberra, AUS: Australian Institute of Criminology.

Smith, David, Harry Blagg, and Nick Derricourt. 1985. Does mediation work in practice? *Probation Journal* 32:135–38.

Smith, Michael E. 1984. Will the real alternatives please stand up? *New York University Review of Law and Social Change* 12:171–97.

Smith, R. L., and R. W. Taylor. 1985. A return to neighborhood policing: The Tampa, Florida experience. *Police Chief* 52:39–44.

Smith, Robert L. 1986. The quiet revolution revisited. *Crime and Delinquency* 32:97–133.

Smith, Robert R. 1984. Reported ex-offender employment in American adult corrections. *Journal of Offender Counseling Services and Rehabilitation* 8:5–12.

Smykla, John Ortiz. 1980. *Coed prison.* New York: Human Sciences.

Snellenburg, Sidney C. 1986. A normative alternative to the death penalty. Paper presented at a meeting of the Southern Association of Criminal Justice Educators, Atlanta.

Social Science Education Consortium. 1983. *Evaluation of law-related education programs.* Boulder, CO: Social Science Education Consortium, Center for Action Research.

Solicitor General Canada. 1984. *Selected trends in Canadian criminal justice.* Ottawa: Communication Division, Solicitor General Canada.

Solomon, Hassim M. 1976. *Community corrections.* Boston: Holbrook.

Solomon, Peter H. 1978. *Soviet criminologists and criminal policy.* New York: Columbia Univ. Press.

———. 1985. The Law Reform Commission of Canada's proposals for reforms of police powers: An assessment. *Criminal Law Quarterly* 27:321–51.

Solomon, Rayman L. 1984. The politics of appointment and the federal courts' role in regulating America: U.S. courts of appeals judgeships from T.R. to F.D.R. *American Bar Foundation Journal* 2:285–343.

Sorrentino, Frank M. 1985. *Ideological warfare: The FBI's path toward power.* Port Washington, NY: Associated Faculty.

Souryal, Sam S. 1985. *Police organization and administration.* Cincinnati, OH: Anderson.

South Carolina Sentencing Guidelines Commission. 1984. *South Carolina sentencing guidelines: A proposal for reform.* Columbia: South Carolina Sentencing Guidelines Commission.

Spergel, Irving A. 1986. The violent gang in Chicago: A local community approach. *Social Service Review* 60:94–131.

Spinetta, J. J., and D. Rigler. 1975. The child-abusing parent: A psychological view. *Psychological Bulletin* 77:296–304.

Spohn, Cassia, John Gruhl, and Susan Welch. 1981. The effect of race on sentencing. *Law and Society Review* 16:71–88.

Spohn, Cassia, Susan Welch, and John Gruhl. 1985. Women defendants in court: The interaction between sex and race in convicting and sentencing. *Social Science Quarterly* 66:178–85.

Stafford, Linda, and Pamela Hepke. 1984. *Where have all the children gone?* Louisville: Kentucky Youth Advocates.

Stanley, Stephen, and Mary Baginsky. 1984. *Alternatives to prison: An examination of non-custodial sentencing of offenders.* London: Peter Owen.

Stapleton, Vaughan. 1987. Manipulating juvenile crime rates. Paper presented at the annual Academy of Criminal Justice Science Meetings, St. Louis, MO.

Stasser, G., N. L. Kerr, and R. M. Bray. 1982. The social psychology of jury deliberations. In *The psychology of the courtroom,* ed. N. L. Kerr and R. M. Bray. New York: Academic.

Steelman, Diane. 1984. *Doing idle time: An investigation of inmate idleness in New York's prisons and recommendations for change.* New York: Correctional Association of New York.

———. 1985. *Toward a crime prevention strategy: Using savings from jail budget to support anti-crime programs.* New York: Correctional Association of New York.

Steinberg, Allen. 1984. From private prosecution to plea bargaining: Criminal prosecution, the district attorney, and American legal history. *Crime and Delinquency* 30:568–92.

Steinman, M., and C. W. Eskridge. 1985. The rhetoric of police professionalism. *Police Chief* 52:26–29.

Steppe, Cecil H. 1986. Public support: Probation's backbone. *Corrections Today* 48:12–16.

Stevens, James C., and David W. MacKenna. 1985. Criteria and procedures for selection of criminal investigators in the United States and West Germany. *Police Studies* 8:220–26.

Stewart, C. S., and M. Zaenglein-Senger. 1984. Female delinquency, family problems, and parental interactions. *Social Casework* 65:428–32.

Stienstra, D. 1985. *Joint trial calendars in the Western District of Missouri.* Washington, DC: Federal Judicial Center.

Stitt, B. Grant, and Gene G. James. 1985. Entrapment: An ethical analysis. In *Moral issues in police work,* ed. Frederick A. Elliston and Michael Feldberg. Totowa, NJ: Rowman and Allanheld.

Stitt, B. Grant, and Sheldon Siegel. 1986. The ethics of plea bargaining. Paper presented at the annual meeting of the Academy of Criminal Justice Sciences, Orlando, FL.

Stojkovic, Stan. 1986. Social bases of power and control mechanisms among correctional administrators in a prison organization. *Journal of Criminal Justice* 14:157–66.

Stolz, Barbara Ann. 1984. Interest groups and criminal law: The case of federal criminal code revision. *Crime and Delinquency* 30:91–106.

Stone, Alan A. 1985. The new legal standard of dangerousness: Fair in theory, unfair in practice. In *Dangerousness: Probability and prediction,* ed. C. Webster, M. H. Ben-Aron, and S. J. Hacker. Cambridge: Cambridge Univ. Press.

Stott, Vanessa. 1981. *English legal system.* London: Anderson Keenan.

Strafer, G. Richard. 1983. Volunteering for execution: Competency, voluntariness, and propriety of third party intervention. *Journal of Criminal Law and Criminology* 74:860–912.

Stratton, John G. 1978. Police stress: An overview. *Police Chief* 44:58–62.

———. 1984. *Police passages.* Manhattan Beach, CA: Glennon.

Straus, M. A., R. J. Gelles, and S. K. Steinmetz. 1980. *Behind closed doors: Violence in the American family.* New York: Anchor.

Streib, Victor L. 1983. Death penalty for children: The American experience with capital punishment for crimes committed while under age eighteen. *Oklahoma Law Review* 36:613–41.

———. 1987. *Death penalty for juveniles.* Bloomington: Indiana Univ. Press.

Stroup, Timothy. 1985. Affirmative action and the police. In *Police ethics: Hard choices in law enforcement,* ed. W. C. Heffernan and T. Stroup. New York: John Jay.

Suall, Irvin. 1987. Extremist groups seek recruits in prisons. *USA Today* 116:23–28.

Suggs, D., and B. D. Sales. 1978. Using communication cues to evaluate perspective jurors in the voir dire. *Arizona Law Review* 20:629–42.

Surette, R. 1985. Crimes, arrests, and elections: Predicting winners and losers. *Journal of Criminal Justice* 13:321–27.

Sutherland, Edwin. 1937. *The professional thief.* Chicago: Univ. of Chicago Press.

Sutherland, Edwin H. 1940. White-collar criminality. *American Sociological Review* 5:1–11.

———. 1973. *On analyzing crime.* Chicago: Univ. of Chicago Press.

Sutherland, Edwin H., and Donald R. Cressey. 1978. *Criminology.* 9th ed. Philadelphia: Lippincott.

Sykes, Gary W. 1985. The functional nature of police reform: The 'myth' of controlling the police. *Justice Quarterly* 2:51–65.

Sykes, Gresham. 1958. *The society of captives: A study of a maximum security prison.* Princeton, NJ: Princeton Univ. Press.

———. 1974. The rise of critical criminology. *Journal of Criminal Law and Criminology* 65:39–45.

Sykes, Thomas M. 1982. *Evaluation of the Community Corrections Pilot Project.* Seattle: Washington State Department of Social and Health Services.

Taggart, William A., and G. Larry Mays. 1984. Preparing to manage the courts: The educational backgrounds of court administrators. *Judicature* 67:284–91.

Talbot, C. K., and C. H. S. Jayewardene. 1984. Policing in Canada: A development perspective. *Canadian Police College Journal* 8:218–88.

Talley, R. A. 1986. A new methodology for evaluating the curricula relevancy of police academy training. *Journal of Police Science and administration* 14:112–20.

Talty, Richard B. 1985. *Intensive supervision program: Report to the advisory committee.* Trenton: New Jersey Administrative Office of the Courts.

Tannehill, R. L. 1985. A critical analysis of police management education and training. *American Journal of Police* 4:156–66.

Taylor, R. W. 1984. Historical developments and contemporary concepts in police community relations. *American Journal of Police* 3:145–67.

Teitelbaum, Lee E., Gale Sutton-Barbere, and Peder Johnson. 1983. Evaluating the prejudicial effect of evidence: Can judges identify the impact of improper evidence on juries? *Wisconsin Law Review* 5:1147–1201.

Terry, W. Clinton. 1981. Police stress: The empirical evidence. *Journal of Police Science and Administration* 9:61–75.

———. 1985. Police stress as a professional self-image. *Journal of Criminal Justice* 13:501–512.

Thackrah, J. R. 1985. *Contemporary policing: An examination of society in the 1980s.* London: Sphere.

Thio, Alex. 1975. A critical look at Merton's anomie theory. *Pacific Sociological Review* 18:83–97.

Thomas, James, et al. 1985. Rethinking prisoner litigation: Some preliminary distinctions between habeas corpus and civil rights. *Prison Journal* 65:83–106.

Thomas, Wayne. 1976. *Bail reform in America.* Berkeley: Univ. of California Press.

———. 1977. *National evaluation program, Phase 1 summary report: Pretrial release programs.* Washington, DC: Law Enforcement Assistance Administration.

Thomasic, Roman, and Malcolm M. Feeley. 1982. *Neighborhood justice: Assessment of an emerging idea.* New York: Longman.

Thompson, James R., et al. 1984. Symposium: prison crowding. *University of Illinois Law Review* 2:203–421.

Thompson, Joel A. 1986. The American jail: Problems, politics, prospects. *American Journal of Criminal Justice* 10:205–221.

Thomson, Doug, and Patrick D. McAnany. 1984. Punishment and responsibility in juvenile court. In *Probation and justice,* ed. P. D. McAnany, D. Thomson, and D. Fogel. Cambridge, MA: Oelgeschlager, Gunn, and Hain.

Thornberry, Terence P., and Margaret Farnworth. 1982. Social correlates of criminal involvement: Further evidence on the relationship between social status and criminal behavior. *American Sociological Review* 47:505–518.

Thornton, William E., Jr., Jennifer James, and William G. Doerner. 1982. *Delinquency and justice.* Glenview, IL: Scott, Foresman.

Thornton, William E., Lydia Voigt, and William G. Doerner. 1987. *Delinquency and justice.* 2d ed. New York: Random House.

Tiffany, Lawrence P., Yakov Avichai, and Geoffrey W. Peters. 1975. A statistical analysis of sentencing in federal courts: Defendants convicted after trial, 1967–68. *Journal of Legal Studies* 4:369–80.

Time. 1987. Assault with a deadly virus. *Time,* July 20, 63. (article by Richard Lacayo)

Tinker, John N., John Quiring, and Yvonne Pimentel. 1985. Ethnic bias in California courts: A case study of Chicano and Anglo felony defendants. *Sociological Inquiry* 55:83–96.

Titus, Richard M. 1984. Residential burglary and the community response. In *Coping with burglary,* ed. R. Clarke and T. Hope. Boston: Kluwer-Nijhoff.

Tobin, Patricia. 1983. *1982 yearly statistical report of the furlough program.* Boston: Massachusetts Department of Corrections.

Toborg, Mary A. 1981. *Pretrial release: A national evaluation of practices and outcomes.* Washington, DC: National Institute of Justice.

———. 1984. *Pretrial release assessment of danger and flight: Method makes a difference.* McLean, VA: Lazar Management Group.

Toch, Hans, and Kenneth Adams. 1986. Pathology and disruptiveness among prison inmates. *Journal of Research in Crime and Delinquency* 23:7–21.

Tomasevski, Katarina. 1986. *Children in adult prisons: An international perspective.* New York: St. Martin's.

Tompkins, D. C. 1973. *Court organization and administration: A bibliography.* Berkeley, CA: Institute of Governmental Studies.

Tonry, Michael, and Franklin Zimring. 1983. *Reform and punishment: Essays on criminal sentencing.* Chicago: Univ. of Chicago Press.

Torres, Donald A. 1985. *Handbook of federal police and investigative agencies*. Westport, CT: Greenwood.

———. 1987. *Handbook of state police, highway patrols, and investigative agencies*. Westport, CT: Greenwood.

Tracy, Paul E., Marvin E. Wolfgang, and Robert M. Figlio. 1985. *Delinquency in two birth cohorts: Executive summary*. Washington, DC: U.S. National Institute for Juvenile Justice and Delinquency Prevention.

Travis, Lawrence F. 1984. Intensive supervision in probation and parole. *Corrections Today* 46:34–40.

Travisono, Anthony P., et al. 1986. Special needs offenders: Handle with care. *Corrections Today* 48:4–80.

Troia, Nina. 1983. *An evaluation of the Milwaukee community corrections residential centers*. Madison: Division of Policy and Budget, Wisconsin Department of Health and Social Services.

Trojanowicz, Robert C., and Dennis W. Banas. 1985a. *Perceptions of safety: A comparison of foot patrol versus motor patrol officers*. East Lansing: National Neighborhood Foot Patrol Center, Michigan State University.

———. 1985b. *Job satisfaction: A comparison of foot patrol versus motor patrol officers*. East Lansing: National Neighborhood Foot Patrol Center, Michigan State University.

———. 1985c. *The impact of foot patrol on black and white perceptions of policing*. East Lansing: National Neighborhood Foot Patrol Center, Michigan State University.

Trojanowicz, Robert C., and H. A. Harden. 1985. *The status of contemporary community policing programs*. East Lansing: National Neighborhood Foot Patrol Center, Michigan State University.

Trojanowicz, Robert C., M. Steele, and S. Trojanowicz. 1986. *Community policing: A taxpayer's perspective*. East Lansing: National Neighborhood Foot Patrol Center, Michigan State University.

———. 1986. *National neighborhood foot patrol center*. Community Policing Series No. 7. East Lansing: National Neighborhood Foot Patrol Center, Michigan State University.

Turner, Billy M., et al. 1986. Race and peremptory challenge during voir dire: Do prosecution and defense agree? *Journal of Criminal Justice* 14:61–69.

Tyler, Tom R. 1984. The influence of citizen satisfaction with police behavior upon public support for increases in police authority. *Law and Policy* 6:329–38.

U.S. Bureau of Justice Statistics. 1983. *Setting prison terms*. Washington, DC: U.S. Department of Justice, U.S. Bureau of Justice Statistics.

———. 1985. *Felony sentencing in 18 jurisdictions*. Washington, DC: U.S. Department of Justice.

U.S. Code. 1968. *United States Code annotated*. St. Paul, MN: West.

———. 1985. *United States Code annotated*. St. Paul, MN: West.

———. 1986. *United States Code*. St. Paul, MN: West.

———. 1989. *United States Code annotated*. St. Paul, MN: West.

U.S. Code Annotated. 1987. *United States Code annotated*. St. Paul, MN: West.

U.S. Department of Health and Human Services. 1984. *National study on child neglect and abuse reporting*. Denver, CO: American Humane Association.

U.S. Department of Justice. 1981. *Expenditure and employment data for the criminal justice system*. Washington, DC: U.S. Government Printing Office.

———. 1983. *Capital punishment*. Washington, DC: U.S. Government Printing Office.

———. 1984. *Capital punishment 1984*. Washington, DC: Bureau of Justice Statistics.

———. 1986. *Crime and justice facts*. Washington, DC: U.S. Government Printing Office, Bureau of Justice Statistics.

———. 1986. *Uniform crime reports*. Washington, DC: U.S. Government Printing Office.

U.S. Dept. of Justice, Bureau of Justice Statistics. 1985. *Criminal victimization in the United States*. Washington, DC: U.S. Government Printing Office.

U.S. General Accounting Office. 1983. *Improved federal efforts needed to change juvenile detention practices*. Washington, DC: U.S. Government Printing Office.

———. 1985. *Organized crime figures and major drug traffickers: Parole decisions and sentences saved*. Washington, DC: U.S. Government Printing Office.

———. 1985. *UNICOR products: Federal prison industries can further ensure customer satisfaction*. Washington, DC: U.S. General Accounting Office.

U.S. Parole Commission. 1984. *United States Parole Commission: Rules and procedures*. Washington, DC: U.S. Department of Justice.

U.S. Senate Judiciary Committee. 1984. *Deinstitutionalization of juvenile nonoffenders: Hearing, June 21, 1983.* Washington, DC: U.S. Government Printing Office.

U.S. Sentencing Commission. 1987, October. *United States Sentencing Commission guidelines manual.* Washington, DC: U.S. Sentencing Commission.

Uhlman, T., and D. Walker. 1979. A plea is no bargain. *Social Science Quarterly* 60:218–34.

Uniform Crime Reports. 1987. *Crime in the United States.* Washington, DC: U.S. Government Printing Office.

University of Hawaii. 1984. *Recidivism of 1979 Adult probation, Third Circuit Court Hawaii.* Honolulu: Univ. of Hawaii, Manoa Youth Development and Research Center.

University of Pennsylvania Law Review. 1984. Constitutional alternatives to plea bargaining: A new wave. *University of Pennsylvania Law Review* 132:327–53.

Utz, Pamela J. 1978. *Settling the facts: Discretion and negotiation in criminal court.* Lexington, MA: Lexington.

———. 1979. Two models of prosecutorial professionalism. In *The prosecutor,* ed. William F. McDonald. Beverly Hills, CA: Sage.

Valenti, A. C., and L. L. Downing. 1975. Differential effects of jury size on verdicts following deliberation as a function of the apparent guilt of defendant. *Journal of Personality and Consulting Psychology* 32:655–63.

Van den Haag, Ernest, and John P. Conrad. 1983. *The death penalty: A debate.* New York: Plenum.

van Dijk, Jan J. M. 1985. *Compensation by the state or by the offender: The victim's perspective.* The Hague: Netherlands Ministry of Justice.

Van Dine, Stephen, et al. 1977. The incapacitation of the dangerous offender: A statistical experiment. *Journal of Research in Crime and Delinquency* 14:22–34.

Vanagunas, S., and J. F. Elliott. 1980. *Administration of police organizations.* Boston: Allyn and Bacon.

VanderZanden, James W. 1984. *Social psychology.* 3d ed. New York: Random House.

Vass, Anthony. 1983. A working sketch of a community service session. *Probation Journal* 30:148–52.

Vaughn, Joseph B. 1987. Planning for change: The use of electronic monitoring as a correctional alternative. In *Intermediate punishments,* ed. Belinda R. McCarthy. Monsey, NY: Criminal Justice.

Vera Institute of Justice. 1984. *The Community Police Officer Program: A pilot program in community oriented policing in the 72nd Precinct.* Interim Report. New York: Vera Institute of Justice.

Vicary, Judith R., and Roland Good. 1983. The effects of a self-esteem counseling group on male prisoners' self-concept. *Journal of Offender Counseling, Services and Rehabilitation* 7:107–117.

Violanti, John M., and James R. Marshall. 1983. The police stress process. *Journal of Police Science and Administration* 11:389–94.

Violanti, John M., J. R. Marshall, and B. Howe. 1985. Stress, coping, and alcohol use: The police connection. *Journal of Police Science and Administration* 13:106–110.

Virginia Assembly. 1984. *Report of the Joint Subcommittee Studying the Placement of Juveniles in Adult Jails.* Richmond: Virginia Assembly.

Virginia Department of Mental Health and Retardation. 1984. *Mentally ill in Virginia's jails: Final report of the Joint Task Force.* Richmond, VA: Department of Corrections.

Virginia Joint Legislative Audit and Review Commission. 1985. *The community diversion incentive program of the Virginia Department of Corrections.* Richmond: Virginia Joint Legislative Audit and Review Commission.

Voas, Robert B., and Wayne A. Layfield. 1983. Creating general deterrence: Can passive sensing of alcohol help? *Police Chief* 50:56–61.

von Hirsch, Andrew. 1983. Recent trends in American criminal sentencing theory. *Maryland Law Review* 42:6–36.

———. 1984. The ethics of selective incapacitation: Observations on the contemporary debate. *Crime and Delinquency* 30:175–94.

———. 1985. *Past or future crimes: Deservedness and dangerousness in the sentencing of criminals.* New Brunswick, NJ: Rutgers Univ. Press.

———. 1987. Hybrid principles in allocating sanctions: A response to Professor Robinson. *Northwestern University Law Review* 82:64–72.

Vorenberg, James. 1981. *Criminal law and procedure: Cases and materials.* 2d ed. St. Paul, MN: West.

Waddington, P. J. 1984. Community policing: A sceptical appraisal. In *Law and order and British politics,* ed. Phillip Norton. Brookfield, VT: Gower.

Waegel, William. 1984a. The use of lethal force by police: The effect of statutory change. *Crime and Delinquency* 30:121–140.

———. 1984b. How police justify the use of deadly force. *Social Problems* 32:144–55.

Wahler, Cindy, and Paul Gendreau. 1985. Assessing correctional officers. *Federal Probation* 49:70–74.

Wakefield, Penny. 1985. The sentencing process: Redefining objectives. In *State laws and procedures affecting drug trafficking control,* ed. J. Bentivoglio et al. Washington, DC: NCJA.

Walker, Donald B., and Peter C. Kratcoski. 1985. A cross cultural perspective on police values and police-community relations. *Criminal Justice Review* 10:17–24.

Walker, Nigel. 1968. *Crime and punishment in Britain.* Chicago: Aldine.

Walker, Nigel, and Mike Hough. 1988. *Public attitudes to sentencing: Surveys from five countries.* Brookfield, VT: Gower.

Walker, Samuel. 1977. *A critical history of police reform: The emergence of professionalism.* Lexington, MA: Lexington.

———. 1979. Professionalism at the crossroads: Police administration in the 1980s. In *Critical issues in criminal justice,* ed. R. G. Iacovetta & D. H. Chang. Boston: Houghton Mifflin.

———. 1983. Employment of black and Hispanic police officers. *Academy of Criminal Justice Sciences Today* 10:1–5.

———. 1984. Broken windows and fractured history: The use and misuse of history in recent police patrol analysis. *Justice Quarterly* 1:75–90.

———. 1985. Racial minority and female employment in policing: The implications of 'glacial' change. *Crime and Delinquency* 31:555–72.

———. 1985. *Sense and nonsense about crime: A policy guide.* Monterey, CA: Brooks/Cole.

Wallace, Paul A., Roy R. Roberg, and Harry E. Allen. 1985. Job burnout among narcotics investigators: An exploratory study. *Journal of Criminal Justice* 13:549–59.

Wallace, W. LeAnn, and Stevens H. Clarke. 1986. The Sentencing Alternatives Center in Greensboro, NC: An evaluation of its effects on prison sentences. Paper presented at the meeting of the American Society of Criminology, Atlanta.

Wallace, William L. 1980. Psychological job stress and the police officer. *Journal of Police Science and Administration* 8:139–44.

Wallerstedt, John F. 1984. *Returning to prison.* Washington, DC: Bureau of Justice Statistics.

Walsh, Anthony. 1985. Ideology and arithmetic: The hidden agenda of sentencing guidelines. *Journal of Crime and Justice* 8:41–63.

Ward, David A., and Allen F. Breed. 1985. *The United States Penitentiary, Marion, Illinois: Consultants report submitted to Committee on the Judiciary.* Washington, DC: U.S. Government Printing Office.

Warr, Mark, and Mark Stafford. 1984. Public goals of punishment and support for the death penalty. *Journal of Research in Crime and Delinquency* 21:95–111.

Washington Governor's Commission on Prison Overcrowding. 1983. *Report of the Governor's Emergency Commission on Prison Overcrowding.* Olympia, WA: Office of the Governor.

Washington Office of Financial Management. 1985. *Prison and inmate population forecast.* Olympia, WA: Washington State Office of Financial Management, Policy Analysis and Forecasting Division.

Watson, Nelson A., and James W. Sterling. 1969. *Police and their opinions.* Washington, DC: International Association of Chiefs of Police.

Watson, R. A., and R. Downing. 1969. *The politics of the bench and bar.* New York: Wiley.

Wayson, Billy L., Gail S. Funke, Sally F. Hamilton, and Peter Meyer. 1977. *Local jails: The new correctional dilemma.* Lexington, MA: Lexington.

Weatherburn, D. J. 1983. Sentencing for what? In *Issues in criminal justice administration,* ed. M. Findlay, S. Egger and J. Sutton. Sydney, AUS: Allen & Unwin.

Webb, Gary L. 1984. *The prison ordeal.* Fayetteville, GA: Coker.

Weibush, Richard, Donna Hamparian, and Joe M. Davis. 1985. *Juveniles in the Ohio Department of Youth Services institutions 1982–1984.* Cleveland: Ohio Serious Juvenile Offender Project.

Weisberg, D. Kelly. 1984. Children of the night: The adequacy of statutory treatment of juvenile prostitution. *American Journal of Criminal Law* 12:1–67.

———. 1985. *Children of the night: A study of adolescent prostitution.* Lexington, MA: Lexington.

Weisheit, Ralph, and Sue Mahan. 1988. *Women, crime, and criminal justice.* Cincinnati, OH: Anderson.

Welch, Susan, John Gruhl, and Cassia Spohn. 1984. Sentencing: The influence of alternative measures of prior record. *Criminology* 22:215–27.

Wellford, Charles. 1975. Labelling theory and criminology: An assessment. *Social Problems* 22:332–45.

Wells, Gary L., and Elizabeth F. Loftus. 1984. *Eyewitness testimony: Psychological perspectives.* Cambridge: Cambridge Univ. Press.

Wengerd, Al. 1984. *Life after prison.* Scottdale, PA: Herald.

Werner, Carol M., et al. 1985. The impact of case characteristics and prior jury experience on jury verdicts. *Journal of Applied Psychology* 15:409–427.

West, M. L. 1986. Sexual harassment complaints: A growing concern for police management. *Journal of California Law Enforcement* 20:55–58.

Westat, Inc. 1984. *Survey of facilities and programs for mentally retarded offenders: Advance report.* Rockville, MD: Center for Studies of Antisocial and Violent Behavior, National Institute of Mental Health.

Westerfield, Louis. 1984. A study of the Louisiana sentencing system and its relationship to prison overcrowding: Some realistic solutions. *Loyola Law Review* 30:5–86.

Wexler, J. G., and D. D. Logan. 1983. Sources of stress among women police officers. *Journal of Police Science and Administration* 11:46–53.

Wheatley, John. 1974. Plea bargaining: A case for its continuance. *Massachusetts Law Quarterly* 59:31–40.

Whitaker, Catherine J. 1986. *Crime prevention measures.* Washington, DC: U.S. Department of Justice, Bureau of Justice Statistics.

———. 1987. *Elderly victims.* Washington, DC: Bureau of Justice Statistics.

Whitaker, Gordon P. 1983. Police department size and the quality and cost of police services. In *The political science of criminal justice,* ed. S. Nagel et al. Springfield, IL: Charles C. Thomas.

———. 1984. *Understanding police agency performance.* Washington, DC: National Institute of Justice.

Whitcomb, Debra, Elizabeth R. Shapiro, and Lindsey D. Stellwagen, eds. 1985. *When the victim is a child: Issues for judges and prosecutors.* Washington, DC: U.S. National Institute of Justice.

White, Helene, Valerie Johnson, and Carole Garrison. 1985. The drug-crime nexus among adolescents and their peers. *Deviant Behavior* 6:183–204.

White, J. W. 1985. Factors of stress among police officers. *Criminal Justice and Behavior* 12:111–28.

Whitehead, John, and Charles Lindquist. 1985. Job stress and burnout among probation parole officers: Perceptions and causal factors. *International Journal of Offender Therapy and Comparative Criminology* 29:109–119.

———. 1986. Correctional officer job burnout: A path model. *Journal of Research in Crime and Delinquency* 23:23–42.

Wiatrowski, M. D. 1985. Issues in police performance evaluation. *Police Journal* 58:49–59.

Wickersham Commission. 1931. *Report on prosecution.* Washington, DC: National Commission on Law Observance and Enforcement.

Wickman, Peter, and P. Whitten, eds. 1978. *Readings in criminology.* Lexington, MA: D. C. Heath.

Wilbanks, William. 1985. Predicting failure on parole. In *Prediction in criminology,* ed. D. P. Farrington and R. Tarling. Albany: State Univ. of New York Press.

Wilbanks, William, and Paul K. H. Kim. 1984. *Elderly criminals.* Lanham, MD: Univ. Press of America.

Wilk, Ruth J., and Carolyn R. McCarthy. 1986. Intervention in child sexual abuse: A survey of attitudes. *Social Casework* 67:20–26.

Wilkenson, T., and J. Chattin-McNichols. 1985. The effectiveness of computer-assisted instruction for police officers. *Journal of Police Science and Administration* 13:230–35.

Wilkins, Leslie T. 1985. The politics of prediction? In *Prediction in criminology,* ed. David P. Farrington and Roger Tarling. Albany: State Univ. of New York Press.

Williams, Frank P., et al. 1982. *Assessing diversionary impact: An evaluation of the intensive supervision program of the Bexar County Adult Probation Department.* Huntsville, TX: Sam Houston State Univ.

Williams, J. Sherwood, et al. 1983. Situational use of police force: Public reactions. *American Journal of Police* 3:37–50.

Williams, Levi. 1984. A police diversion alternative for juvenile offenders. *Police Chief* 51:54–57.

Williams, Vergil L., and Velma A. Williams. 1987. Preschool prevention of juvenile crime: Issues and ethics.

Paper presented at the annual meeting of the Academy of Criminal Justice Sciences, April, St. Louis, MO.

Willison, David. 1984. The effects of counsel on the severity of criminal sentences: A statistical assessment. *Justice System Journal* 9:87–101.

Willman, Mark T., and John R. Snortum. 1984. Detective work: The criminal investigation process in a medium-sized police department. *Criminal Justice Review* 9: 33–39.

Willoughby, K. R., and W. R. Blount. 1985. The relationship between law enforcement officer height, aggression, and job performance. *Journal of Police Science and Administration* 13:225–29.

Willstadter, R. 1984. *Time served: Does it relate to patterns of criminal recidivism?* Final Report #1. Seattle, WA: Spectrum Analysis.

Wilson, Edward O. 1975. *Sociobiology: The new synthesis.* Cambridge, MA: Harvard Univ. Press.

Wilson, James Q. 1968. *Varieties of police behavior: The management of law and order in eight communities.* Cambridge: Harvard Univ. Press.

———. 1974. *Varieties of police behavior.* New York: Atheneum.

———. 1983. *Thinking about crime.* New York: Basic.

Wilson, James Q., and Richard J. Hernstein. 1985. *Crime and human nature.* New York: Simon and Schuster.

Wilson, M. J. 1983. *Restitution as an alternative to incarceration: An interrupted time series assessment of five federally funded restitution programs.* Eugene, OR: Institute for Political Analysis.

Wilson, O. W., and Roy McLaren. 1975. *Police administration.* New York: McGraw-Hill.

Wilson, William. 1983. Juvenile offenders and the electric chair: Cruel and unusual punishment or firm discipline for the hopelessly delinquent? *University of Florida Law Review* 35:344–371.

Winterdyk, M. A., and Curt Griffiths. 1984. Wilderness experience programs: Reforming delinquents or beating around the bush? *Juvenile and Family Court Journal* 35:35–44.

Winters, G. R. 1973. *Selected readings on judicial selection and tenure.* Chicago: American Judicature Society.

Wisconsin Department of Health and Social Services. 1982. *An evaluation of the Milwaukee community corrections residential centers.* Madison: Bureau of Evaluation, Division of Policy and Budget.

———. 1985. *Alternative to prison revocation study.* Madison: Wisconsin Department of Health and Social Services.

Witham, Donald C. 1985. *The American law enforcement chief executive: A management profile.* Washington, DC: Police Executive Research Forum.

Wolf, J. B. 1981. *Fear of fear: A survey of terrorist operations and controls in open societies.* New York: Plenum.

Wolfgang, M. E., et al. 1985. *The National Survey of Crime Severity.* Washington, DC: Bureau of Justice Statistics, U.S. Department of Justice.

Wolfgang, Marvin E. 1983. Delinquency in two birth cohorts. In *Prospective studies of crime and delinquency,* ed. Katherine Teilmann Van Dusen and Sarnoff A. Mednick. Boston: Kluwer-Nijhoff.

Wolfgang, Marvin E., Robert M. Figlio, and Thorsten Sellin. 1972. *Delinquency in a birth cohort.* Chicago: Univ. of Chicago Press.

Wood, Dorothy, Jean Verber, and Mary Reddin. 1985. *A study of the inmate population of the Milwaukee County Jail.* Milwaukee: Wisconsin Correctional Service and Benedict Center for Criminal Justice.

Wright, James D., and Peter H. Rossi. 1986. *Armed and considered dangerous: A survey of felons and their firearms.* Hawthorne, NY: Aldine de Gruyter.

Wright, Kevin N. 1985. Developing the prison environment inventory. *Journal of Research in Crime and Delinquency* 22:257–77.

———. 1986. *Improving correctional classification through a study of the placement of inmates in environmental settings.* Binghamton, NY: Center for Social Analysis.

Wright, Kevin N., Todd R. Clear, and Paul Dickson. 1984. Universal applicability of probation, risk-assessment instruments: A critique. *Criminology* 22:113–34.

Yablon, Marvin. 1986. Probability of exceeding a given prison population size. *Journal of Criminal Justice* 14:177–82.

Yarborough, Thelma B. 1985. Some inmate viewpoints on teaching and curriculum in community college programs. *Journal of Correctional Education* 36:92–93.

Yarborough, Tinsley E. 1984. The Alabama prison litigation. *Justice System Journal* 9:276–90.

Yaryura-Tobias, J. A., and F. Neziroglu. 1975. Violent behavior brain dysrhythmia and glucose dysfunction: A new syndrome. *Journal of Orthopsychiatry* 4:182–88.

Yochelson, Samuel, and Stanton E. Samenow. 1976. *The criminal personality.* Vols. 1 and 2. New York: Jason Aronson.

Youth Policy and Law Center, Inc. 1984. *Violent delinquents: A Wisconsin study.* Madison, WI: Youth Policy and Law Center, Inc.

Zamble, Edward, and Frank J. Porporino. 1988. *Coping, behavior, and adaptation in prison inmates.* Secaucus, NJ: Springer-Verlag.

Zapf, Michael Kim, and Bob Cole. 1985. Yukon restitution study. *Canadian Journal of Criminology* 27:477–90.

Zeisel, Hans. 1971. . . . And then there were none: The diminution of the federal jury. *University of Chicago Law Review* 38:710–24.

Zeisel, Hans, and S. S. Diamond. 1974. Convincing empirical evidence on the six-member jury. *University of Chicago Law Review* 41:281–95.

Zeldes, Ilya. 1981. *The problems of crime in the USSR.* Springfield, IL: Charles C. Thomas.

Zemans, Frances Kahn. 1979. Dispute processing: The medium and the message of criminal justice. In *The study of criminal courts: Political perspectives,* ed. Peter F. Nardulli. Cambridge, MA: Ballinger.

Zimmerman, Joseph F. 1981. *The government and politics of New York State.* New York: New York Univ. Press.

Zingraff, Matthew, and Randall Thomson. 1984. Differential sentencing of women and men in the USA. *International Journal of the Sociology of Law* 12:401–413.

Zwetchkenbaum-Segal, Rebecca. 1984a. *Case preparation aid follow-up study: Major findings.* Boston: Planning, Research, and Program Development Unit, Massachusetts Parole Board.

———. 1984b. *Re-parole study: Major findings.* Boston: Planning, Research and Program Development Unit, Massachusetts Parole Board.

GLOSSARY

Actions at law Court litigation where one party opposes another for a wrong allegedly committed, for the protection of a right, or for the prevention of a wrong

Actus reus Criminal or overt act

Adjudication hearing Formal proceeding involving a prosecuting attorney and a defense attorney where evidence is presented and the juvenile's guilt or innocence is determined by the juvenile judge

Aggravated assault An unlawful attack by one person on another for the purpose of inflicting severe or aggravated bodily injury

Aggravating circumstances Circumstances about crime that may intensify the severity of punishment, including bodily injury or death to victim, brutality of act

AIDS Acquired Immune Deficiency Syndrome, deadly virus often spread through sexual contact

Alibi Device used by suspects to prove they were not in the vicinity of a crime when it supposedly occurred

Alternative sentencing *See* Creative sentencing

American Correctional Association (ACA) An association established in 1870 to formulate a national correctional policy, design and implement standards for correctional services and methods for measuring compliance, and provide publications, training, and technical assistance to correctional institutions

Anomie theory Robert Merton's theory alleging persons generally acquire desires for culturally approved goals to strive to achieve, but they may adopt innovative, sometimes deviant, means to achieve these goals; anomie implies normlessness; innovators accept societal goals but reject institutionalized means to achieve them

Arraignment The official proceeding where defendants are informed of the formal charges against them and enter a plea

Arrest Taking a suspected law violator into custody

Arson Any willful or malicious burning or attempt to burn, with or without intent to defraud, a dwelling house, public building, motor vehicle or aircraft, and the personal property of another

Assault A verbal threat of harm

Assembly-line justice Term applied to overworked, inadequately staffed court which is unsympathetic and unfair to criminal defendants; excessive delay in court action

Auburn State Penitentiary A model penitentiary system that introduced the maximum, medium, and minimum security prison conditions found in penitentiaries today

Bail Surety provided by defendants or others to guarantee their subsequent appearance in court to face criminal charges; available to anyone entitled to bail; denied when suspects are considered dangerous or likely to flee (*see* Preventive detention)

Bail bond A written guarantee, often accompanied by money or other securities, that the person charged with an offense will remain within the court's jurisdiction to face trial at a time in the future

Bailiff Court officer who has charge of maintaining order in the court while it is in session; jury is placed in custody of baliff during a trial proceeding; sometimes the bailiff has custody of prisoners while they are in the courtroom; also known as messengers

Banishment Also referred to as transportation; physical removal of undesirables, criminals, political and religious dissidents to remote locations; practiced by England until 1800s; popular sites for banishment included American colonies and Australia

Battery The unlawful touching of another without justification or excuse

Beat Habitual patrol conducted by police officers

Behavioral approach Type of police discretion typified by a blend of sociology, psychology, and political science; a developmental scheme whereby police officers attempt to negotiate their way through each public encounter

Bench trial Trial where guilt or innocence of defendant is determined by the judge rather than a jury

Bifurcated trial Trial in capital cases where jury is asked to make two decisions; first decision is to determine guilt or innocence of defendant; if guilty, jury meets to decide punishment which may include the death penalty

Bobbies Term for British police; named after Sir Robert "Bobby" Peel, the British Home Secretary, in the 1820s

Body belt Restraining device worn by prisoners, with wrist restraints at the center of the abdomen

Bonding theory Theory of criminal behavior implying that criminality is the result of a loosening of bonds or attachments with society; builds on differential association theory; primarily designed to account for juvenile delinquency

Booking Process of making written report of arrest, including name and address of arrested persons, the alleged crimes, arresting officers, place and time of arrest, physical description of suspect, photograph (sometimes called "mug shots"), and fingerprints

Bounty hunter Person who earns living by apprehending defendants who jump bail and leave the jurisdiction where they have been arrested and are awaiting trial

Broken-windows approach Form of police patrol stressing better communication with citizens; foot patrols, team policing, and other "back to the people" programs are consistent with this patrol form

Bureau of Alcohol, Tobacco and Firearms (BATF) This bureau of the Treasury Department is responsible for law enforcement functions relating to liquor, tobacco, and firearms trafficking; arson; high explosives; and automatic weapons

Bureau of Justice Statistics (BJS) Established in 1979 to provide for and encourage the collection and analysis of statistical information concerning crime, juvenile delinquency, and the operation of the criminal justice system

Burglary Unlawful entry of a structure to commit a felony or theft

Burnout A disorder characterized by a loss of motivation and commitment related to task performance; burnout among police is measured by Maslach Burnout Inventory and other psychological devices that test degree of commitment to the job and the loss of motivation to be successful

Capital punishment Imposition of the death penalty for the most serious crimes; may be administered by electrocution, lethal injection, gas, hanging, or shooting

Caseload The number of cases a probation or parole officer is assigned according to a standard such as a week, month, or year

Central Intelligence Agency (CIA) Established under the CIA Act of 1949; participates in undercover and covert operations on an international scale

Certification *See* Waiver

Challenge *See* Peremptory challenge; Challenge for cause

Challenge for cause Action by prosecution or defense where certain jurors are excused for prospective jury duty because of obvious prejudices or other facts that would call their decision into question; each side has an unlimited number of challenges for cause

Charge reduction bargaining Where prosecutor downgrades the charges in return for a plea of guilty from the defendant (*see also* Plea bargaining)

Chicago Area Project Project commenced in 1934 by Clifford Shaw designed to establish recreational centers and counseling programs for high-risk youths; delinquency prevention program

Child abuse Any form of cruelty to physical, moral, or mental well-being, sexual abuse or exploitation, negligent treatment, or maltreatment of a child under the age of 18 by a person who is responsible for the child's welfare

Circuit courts One of the three tiers of courts created under the provisions of the Judiciary Act of 1789; each of the 13 circuits consists of three appellate judges who hear appeals from federal district courts within their circuits

Citizen's arrest Arrest of a criminal suspect by a private citizen unaffiliated with any law enforcement agency

Cognitive development theory Also called developmental theory; theory stressing stages of learning process, whereby persons acquire abilities to think and express themselves, respect the property and rights of others, and cultivate moral values

Common law Authority based on court decrees and judgments that recognize, affirm, and enforce certain usages and customs of the people; laws determined by judges in accordance with their rulings

Community control *See* Home incarceration

Community dispute resolution program A program used in New York State to resolve legal matters that would otherwise have to be heard in courts

Community policing The permanent assignment of police officers to a given sector or neighborhood in a community

Community-based corrections programs Locally operated services offering minimum-security, limited release, or work release alternatives to prisoners about to be paroled; may also serve probationers

Commutation To change or reduce the severity of a sentence, usually through administrative authority; death sentences may be commuted to life imprisonment, as an example

Comparative criminal justice Analyses of criminal justice systems of other countries, studying their similarities and differences

Complaint Written statement of essential facts constituting the offense alleged, made under oath before a magistrate or other qualified judicial officer

Comrades' court An informal Soviet court arrangement in which courts are established in factories, collective farms, etc., and have jurisdiction over small property crimes, labor violations, and other minor offenses

Concurrent jurisdiction A situation where alleged offenders may be prosecuted more than once for the same offense because federal, state, and local laws were violated simultaneously

Conflict criminology *See* Radical criminology

Conflict theory Also called Marxist theory; explains criminal conduct by focusing attention on the people who have the political power to define crime for the rest of society; divides the masses into the have-nots and the rich and powerful

Congregate system System introduced at Auburn State Penitentiary in New York where prisoners could work and eat together in common work and recreational areas; prisoners segregated at night

Conventional level of cognitive development As defined by Kohlberg, the second level in the development of a person's moral judgment, at which a child seeks approval of others and does his or her duty

Coordinate model Model developed by Alaska where neighboring male and female prisons share common facilities and programs

Corrections All of the agencies and personnel who deal with convicted offenders after court proceedings

Corrective works Productive labor in Soviet corrective-labor colonies

Corruption Behavior of public officials who accept money or the equivalent of money for doing something they are under a duty to do anyway or under a duty not to do, or to exercise a legitimate discretion for improper reasons

Court clerk Court officer who may file pleadings, motions, or judgment; issue process; and keep general records of court proceedings

Court of record Court where a written record is kept of court proceedings

Court reporter Court official who keeps a written word-for-word and/or tape-recorded record of court proceedings

Creative sentencing A broad class of punishments as alternatives to incarceration that are designed to fit particular crimes; may involve community service, restitution, fines, becoming involved in educational or vocational training programs, or becoming affiliated with other good works activity

Crime Violation of a criminal law, by a person held accountable by that law; consists of legality, *actus reus, mens rea,* consensus, harm, causation, and prescribed punishment

Crime clock Graph used in *Uniform Crime Reports* to show number of specific types of crime (e.g., robbery, murder, forcible rape) committed according to some time standard such as minutes or seconds; calculated by dividing number of crimes reported annually by number of minutes or seconds in a year

Crime prevention The anticipation, recognition, and appraisal of crime risk and the initiation of some action to remove or reduce it

Crime Stoppers Organization formed in 1976; goals are to provide law enforcement authorities with information about crime, who witnessed crime, and descriptions of the possible perpetrators

Crimes against property Nonviolent, or passive, crimes, where no physical harm is inflicted upon the crime victim (includes vehicular theft, burglary, and larceny); also called property crimes

Crimes against the person Violent crimes, including all crimes committed in the victim's presence (includes homicide, rape, robbery, and aggravated assault)

Crimes cleared by arrest Crimes included in *Uniform Crime Report* where an arrest has been made; possible offenders have been apprehended, sufficient evidence exists to connect them with the crime, and they have been taken into custody

Criminal bench trial A practice where the state promises to drop charges or reduce sentences if defendants waive the right to have a jury determine their guilt

Criminal information A written accusation made by a public prosecutor against a person for a criminal offense, without an indictment

Criminal justice Interdisciplinary field studying nature and operations of organizations providing justice services to society; consists of lawmaking bodies including state legislatures and Congress, local, state and federal agencies that try to enforce the law

Criminal justice system An interrelated set of lawmaking bodies, agencies, and organizations designed to control criminal behavior, to detect crime, and to apprehend, process, prosecute, punish, and/or rehabilitate criminal offenders

Criminal trial An adversarial proceeding within a particular jurisdiction, where a judicial examination and determination of issues can be made, and where a criminal defendant's guilt or innocence can be decided impartially by either a judge or jury

Criminology The study of crime; the science of crime and criminal behavior, including the forms of criminal behavior, the causes of crime, and the societal reaction to crime

Critical phase Phase of investigation by law enforcement officers where case moves from investigatory to accusatory against specific suspects

Cross examination Examination of one side's witnesses by the other side, either the prosecution or defense

Cruel and unusual punishment Issues include police brutality, prison overcrowding, indifference of prison officials, and capital punishment

Cultural transmission theory Theory emphasizing transmission of criminal behavior through socialization

Customs Service *See* United States Customs Service

Dangerousness Predicted risk of convicted offender or prison or jail inmate; likelihood of inflicting harm upon others

Deadly force Any force used by law enforcement officers or others, which may result in death or great bodily harm, to apprehend those suspected of or engaging in unlawful acts (*See* Fleeing felon rule)

Death-qualified jury Term applied to a jury that has been selected on the basis of their willingness to impose the death penalty in a capital case if the situation warrants such a decision; implies exclusion of persons from possible jury duty who could not vote for a death penalty even if defendant were guilty of capital crime

Debtor's prisons Prisons established in Middle Ages in England where debtors were imprisoned until they or their friends paid their debts

Deception, police *See* Entrapment

Decriminalization Legislative action whereby an act or omission, formerly criminal, is made noncriminal and without punitive sanctions; usually occurs through legislative action

Defendant The subject of a criminal proceeding

Defense attorney A licensed lawyer retained by a defendant or appointed by the court to defend a suspect who is unable to afford an attorney

Defense-of-life standard Standard by which law enforcement officers decide whether to use deadly force in effecting arrest of criminal suspects; involves discretion whether officer's life or the lives of others are in jeopardy as the result of suspect's actions

Deinstitutionalization of status offenses (DSO) Eliminating status offenses from the delinquency category and removing juveniles from or precluding their confinement in juvenile correction facilities

Delinquent child Infant of not more than a specified age who has violated criminal laws or engages in disobedient, indecent, or immoral conduct and is in need of treatment, rehabilitation, or supervision

Department of Justice The official legal arm of the United States government

Detention hearing A judicial or quasi-judicial proceeding held to determine whether it is appropriate to continue to hold or detain a juvenile in a shelter facility

Determinate sentencing Sentencing scheme where court sentences offender to incarceration for fixed period, and which must be served in full and without parole intervention, less any good time earned in prison

Deviance Conduct that departs from the accepted codes of society or a particular group

Differential association Edwin Sutherland's theory of deviance and criminality through associations with others who are deviant or criminal; theory includes dimensions of frequency, duration, priority, and intensity

Direct examination Questioning of witnesses by prosecution or defense attorney, where initial questioning is conducted by side calling witness

Discovery Procedure where prosecution shares information with defense attorney and defendant; specific types of information are made available to defendant before trial, including results of any tests conducted, psychiatric reports, transcripts or tape-recorded statements made by the defendant; also known as Brady materials after a specific court case

Discretion, police Relating to the police role, police discretion is the distribution of nonnegotiably coercive force employed in accordance with the dictates of an intuitive grasp of situational exigencies; police have authority to use force to enforce the law, if in the officer's opinion, the situation demands it (*see* Legal approach; Organizational approach; Behavioral approach)

Diversion *See* Pretrial diversion

Double-bunking Placing two or more inmates in a cell originally designed to accommodate one inmate

Driving under the influence (DUI) Operating a motor vehicle while under the influence of alcohol

Dropsy testimony Testimony given by police officers that the narcotics they found were dropped on the ground by defendants

Drug Enforcement Administration Agency established to investigate violations of all federal drug trafficking laws; regulates the legal manufacture of drugs and other controlled substances

Druzhiny Squads of people's volunteers used in the Soviet Union to dispense justice to wrong-doers; used particularly in the 1950s and 1960s

Dual procedure offenses Canadian category of criminal offenses which allow the prosecutor to decide whether the prosecution will be by summary conviction or by indictment

Due process Basic constitutional right to a fair trial, presumption of innocence until guilt is proven beyond a reasonable doubt, the opportunity to be heard, to be aware of a matter that is pending, to make an informed choice whether to acquiesce or contest, and to provide the reasons for such a choice before a judicial official

Duress Affirmative defense used by defendants to show lack of criminal intent, alleging force, psychological or physical, from others as stimulus for otherwise criminal conduct

Ectomorph Body type described by Sheldon; person is thin, sensitive, and delicate

Ego   Sigmund Freud's term describing the embodiment of society's standards, values, and conventional rules

Elderly criminal   Criminal age 65 and over; some researchers and jurisdictions define elderly differently; may include persons age 60 and over who are convicted of crimes

Electronic monitoring   The use of electronic devices that emit electronic signals; these devices, anklets or wristlets, are worn by offenders, probationers and parolees; the purpose of such monitoring is to monitor an offender's presence in a given environment where the offender is required to remain or to verify the offender's whereabouts

Elmira Reformatory   A reform-oriented prison established in Elmira, New York, in 1878; priority was given to prisoner educational development and vocational training

Employee assistance program   A program that offers diagnostic, referral, and treatment services for police officers suffering from job stress

Endomorph   Body type described by Sheldon; person is fat, soft, plump, and jolly

Entrapment   Activity by law enforcement officers that suggests, encourages, or aids others in the commission of crimes that would ordinarily not have occurred without officer intervention, encouragement, or assistance; defense used by defendants to show otherwise criminal act would not have occurred without police intervention, assistance, and/or encouragement

Exclusionary rule   Provides that evidence obtained in violation of a citizen's privileges must be excluded at a trial

Exclusive jurisdiction   A term that means that no other court can decide certain types of cases except the court having exclusive jurisdiction

Exigent circumstances   Circumstances surrounding arrest or search for and seizure of evidence where immediate action is warranted and justified

Expert witness   Sometimes called hired guns; witnesses who have expertise or special knowledge in a relevant field pertaining to the case at trial; a psychiatrist might be an expert witness in a case where the defense alleges insanity

Expungement   Deletion of one's arrest record from official sources; in most jurisdictions, juvenile delinquency records are expunged when one reaches the age of majority or adulthood

Eye witness   Witness who actually saw the crime committed

Federal Bureau of Investigation (FBI)   Established in 1908 through Department of Justice Appropriation Act; investigative agency that enforces all federal criminal laws; compiles information for *Uniform Crime Reports* annually

Federal Bureau of Prisons   Established in 1930; charged with providing suitable quarters for prisoners and safekeeping of all persons convicted of offenses against the United States; also contracts with local jails and state prisons for confinement of federal prisoners where there are insufficient federal facilities in the geographical area where the person has been convicted

Federal district courts   One of the three tiers of courts created by the Judiciary Act of 1789; each is presided over by a district judge

Federal Prison Industries (UNICOR)   Government-owned corporation that markets products to federal agencies and employs prisoners; *see* UNICOR

Felony   Crime punishable by incarceration in a state or federal prison for 1 year or longer

First offender   Person who has never been convicted of a criminal offense prior to the current conviction

Fleeing felon rule   Rule rendered unconstitutional by the United States Supreme Court in 1985 whereby law enforcement officers were permitted to use deadly force to apprehend felons attempting to escape apprehension

Foot patrol   Experimental police patrol method where police officers patrol neighborhoods on foot instead of in cruisers

Force continuum   Measure of the amount of force law enforcement officers apply in making arrests; subjective measure

Forcible rape   The carnal knowledge of persons forcibly and against their will; assaults or attempts to commit rape by force or threat of force

Fruits of the poisonous tree doctrine   United States Supreme Court decision in *Wong Sun v. United States* holding that evidence spawned or directly derived from an illegal search or an illegal interrogation is generally inadmissible against a defendant because of its original taint; if the tree is tainted, so is the fruit

Furlough   An unescorted or unsupervised leave granted to inmates for home visits, work, or educational activity

General jurisdiction Power of a court to hear a wide range of civil and criminal cases

Golf cart patrol Use of golf carts to patrol neighborhoods in Tampa, Florida, and several other cities; a "back-to-the-people" patrol style.

Grand jury Investigative bodies whose numbers vary among states; duties include determining probable cause regarding commission of a crime and returning formal charges against suspects (*see* True bill; No true bill)

Great Law of Pennsylvania William Penn's law to improve conditions in Pennsylvania's penal system; branding irons, gallows, stocks, and pillories were replaced with fines and a more humane standard of imprisonment

Habitual offender statutes Statutes vary among states; these statutes provide life imprisonment as a mandatory sentence for chronic offenders who have been convicted of three or more serious felonies within a specific time period

Halfway house House designed to assist pre-parolees in making a smooth adjustment to life outside of prison; many varieties of halfway houses throughout the United States; may be used to house probationers and others

Harmful errors Errors made by judges that may be prejudicial to a defendant's case; may lead to reversals of convictions against defendants and to new trials

Hawes-Cooper Act of 1929 Provided that all prison-made goods transported between states should be regulated by the commerce laws of the importing state

Heredity Theory that behaviors result from characteristics genetically transmitted; explains criminal behaviors according to inherited genes from parents or ancestors who were criminal or had criminal propensities

Home confinement *See* Home incarceration

Home incarceration Also house arrest, community control, or home confinement; the use of an offender's home as the primary place of incarceration in lieu of jail or prison

Hooliganism Term used by Soviets in defining a broad range of criminal conduct; included are disorderly conduct, alcohol or drug abuse, prostitution, and loitering

Hot pursuit Circumstance involving chase of suspects by law enforcement officers; often used to justify searches and seizures when suspect is eventually apprehended

House arrest *See* Home incarceration

Hybrid offense English term for offense involving discretionary authority of prosecutor whether to treat offense summarily or through indictment

Id The "I want" part of a person, formed in one's early years; Sigmund Freud's term to depict that part of personality concerned with individual gratification

Immigration and Naturalization Service (INS) Under the Department of Justice, regulates entries into the United States by persons from other nations; regulates applications for citizenship

Impeachment Attempt by prosecution or defense to question the credibility of each other's witnesses

Implicit plea bargaining Where defendant pleads guilty with the expectation of receiving a more lenient sentence (*see also* Plea bargaining)

Incident Specific criminal act involving one or more victims

Indeterminate sentencing Sentences of imprisonment by the court for either specified or unspecified durations, with the final release date determined by a parole board

Index offenses Specific felonies used by the Federal Bureau of Investigation in *Uniform Crime Reports* to chart crime trends; there are eight index offenses listed prior to 1988 (aggravated assault, larceny, burglary, motor vehicle theft, arson, robbery, forcible rape, and murder)

Indictable offenses Offenses in Canada or Great Britain that include violations of the criminal code or federal statutes

Indictment A charge or written accusation found and presented by a grand jury that a particular defendant probably committed a crime

Infant Legal term for juvenile

Information Sometimes called criminal information; written accusation made by a public prosecutor against a person for some criminal offense, without an indictment; usually restricted to minor crimes or misdemeanors

Initial appearance Formal proceeding during which the judge advises the defendant of the charges

Inmate code Code by which inmates live; exists separate from administratively established prison rules enforced by guards

Inmate grievance procedure Mandatory administrative grievance procedure in all state and federal prisons where inmates may bring grievances to attention of wardens and other supervisory personnel

Innovations Project A program suggested by the Federal Judicial Center to improve the processing of the backlog of cases awaiting argument; cases were presented without oral argument

Intake screening A critical phase where a determination is made by a juvenile probation officer or other official whether to release juveniles to their parent's custody, detain juveniles in formal detention facilities for a later court appearance, or release them to parents pending a later court appearance

Intensive supervision program Probation or parole program for offender; the officer-offender ratio is low, offenders receive frequent visits from their officer-supervisors, and continuous communication is maintained by the supervising agency or authority

Intermediate punishment Sanction imposed on offenders, where the sanctions range somewhere between incarceration and probation on a continuum of criminal penalties

Internal affairs division (IAD) Unit of police officers who investigate allegations of misconduct against other police officers

Internal Revenue Service (IRS) An agency of the Treasury Department whose main role is to monitor and collect federal income taxes; the Criminal Investigation Division investigates possible criminal violations of income tax laws

Interpol International Criminal Police Organization; international crimefighting organization headquartered in France

Intoxication Defense used by defendants to explain otherwise criminal conduct; does not overcome *actus reus*, but may be used as a mitigating circumstance to account for otherwise violent behavior; may be used to rebut presumption of premeditation

Jail City or county operated and financed facility to contain those offenders who are serving short sentences; jails also house more serious prisoners from state or federal prisons through contracts to alleviate overcrowding, pretrial detainees, witnesses, juveniles, vagrants, and others

Jailhouse lawyer Inmate in a prison or jail who becomes skilled in the law; inmate who learns about the law and assists other prisoners in filing suits against prison or jail administration

John Doe warrant Warrant issued when suspect's name is unknown, but an accurate description and location of suspect have been provided

Joint trial calendar system Method of case processing used by judges in certain jurisdictions; several judges share common court calendar; objective is to try all cases on calendar within a specified period; all judges share responsibility for clearing the calendar

Judicial adjuncts Lawyers and others who assist courts and judges on a temporary basis in minor offense cases; judicial adjuncts maintain law practice while performing these temporary duties

Judicial plea bargaining Where the judge offers a specific guilty plea sentence (*see also* Plea bargaining)

Judicial waiver Decision by juvenile judge to waive juvenile to jurisdiction of criminal court

Jump bail Act by defendant of leaving jurisdiction where trial is to be held; attempt by defendant to avoid prosecution on criminal charges

Jurisdiction Sphere of authority; the power of a court to hear and determine a particular type of case; also refers to territory within which court may exercise authority such as a city, county, state

Jury *See* Petit jury

Jury trial Trial where guilt or innocence of defendant is determined by jury instead of by the judge

Justice model Philosophy that emphasizes punishment as a primary objective of sentencing, fixed sentences, abolition of parole, and an abandonment of the rehabilitative ideal

Juvenile Person who has not achieved his eighteenth birthday or the age of majority; varies among jurisdictions

Juvenile delinquency The violation of criminal laws by juveniles; any illegal behavior or activity committed by persons who are within a particular age range and that subjects them to the jurisdiction of a juvenile court or its equivalent

Juvenile justice system The system through which juveniles are processed, sentenced, and corrected after arrests for juvenile delinquency

Kales Plan A plan for judicial selection which requires a nonpartisan group of lawyers, judges, and nonjudicial personnel to compile a list of the most qualified candidates on the basis of their records and expertise

Kansas City Preventive Patrol Experiment Experiment conducted in early 1970s in Kansas City;

experiment showed no relation between crime and the intensity of police patrolling in various city areas; controversial study

Labeling theory   Theory attributed to Edwin Lemert, whereby persons acquire self-definitions that are deviant or criminal; persons perceive themselves as deviant or criminal through labels applied to them by others; the more people are involved in the criminal justice system, the more they acquire self-definitions consistent with the criminal label

Larceny-theft   Unlawful taking, carrying, leading or riding away of property from the possession or constructive possession of another; includes shoplifting, pocket-picking, thefts from motor vehicles, and thefts of motor vehicle parts or accessories

Law   A body of rules of specific conduct, prescribed by existing, legitimate authority in a particular jurisdiction at a particular point in time

Law Enforcement Assistance Administration   Administration created by Congress in 1968 and terminated in late 1970s; agency designed to provide resources, leadership, and coordination to state and local law enforcement agencies to prevent and/or reduce adult crime and juvenile delinquency

Legal approach   Police discretion type characterized by codifications of discretion according to legal proscriptions; discretionary behavior is measured by amount of deviation from proscribed rules

Legislative waiver   Provision that compels juvenile court to remand certain youths to criminal courts because of specific offenses that have been committed or alleged

Libido   Sigmund Freud's term describing the sex drive, believed innate in everyone

Limited jurisdiction   Also known as special jurisdiction; court is restricted to handling certain types of cases such as probate matters or juvenile offenses

Litigant   Party involved in a lawsuit

Lockdowns   Complete removal of inmate privileges and permanent confinement in cells; usually follow prison riot or other serious prison disturbance

Magistrates' courts   Lower courts in Great Britain that try summary offenses

Mala in se   Crimes that are intrinsically evil or wrong, including murder, rape, and arson

Mala prohibita   Offenses defined by legislatures as crimes; many state and federal criminal statutes are *mala prohibita*

Mandatory sentencing   Sentencing where court is required to impose an incarcerative sentence of a specified length, without the option for probation, suspended sentence, or immediate parole eligibility

Marxist theory   *See* Radical criminology

Maximum-security   Designation given to prison where inmates are maintained in the highest degree of custody and supervision; inmates are ordinarily segregated from one another; restricted visitation privileges

Medium-security   Term applied to prisons where some direct supervision of inmates is maintained; prisoners are eligible for recreational activities; visitation privileges are more relaxed

Megargee Inmate Typology   Measure of inmate adjustment to prison life devised from items from the Minnesota Multiphasic Personality Inventory, a psychological personality assessment device; permits classification of prisoners into different risk levels

Mens rea   Intent to do harm; evil intent

Mesomorph   Body type described by Sheldon; person is strong, muscular, aggressive, and tough

Metropolitan Police of London   The first formal police department, established by Sir Robert Peel and the British Parliament in 1829 to maintain state security and protect citizens

Minimum-security   Term applied to prisons where inmates are permitted extensive freedoms and activities; little supervision by guards

Ministation   Small suburban police station, usually staffed by officers 24 hours a day; no provisions for detention of arrestees; assists in promoting better police-community relations

Miranda warning   Warning given to suspects by police officers advising suspects of their legal rights to counsel, to refuse to answer questions, to avoid self-incrimination, and other privileges

Misdemeanor   Crime punishable by a fine or imprisonment in a city or county jail for less than 1 year

Missouri plan   Method of selecting judges where merit system for appointments is used; believed to reduce political influence in the selection of judges

Mistake   Affirmative defense used by defendants to account for criminal conduct, where belief is that law violation was accidental or that knowledge of law was absent

Mitigating circumstances Circumstances about a crime that may lessen the severity of sentence imposed by the judge; cooperating with police to apprehend others involved, youthfulness or old age of defendant, mental instability, and having no prior record are considered mitigating circumstances

Model Penal Code (MPC) Code developed by the American Law Institute clarifying crimes and accompanying punishments; no jurisdictions are obligated to adhere to the Model Penal Code

Motion in limine *See* Pretrial motion

Motion to dismiss A pretrial motion designed to attack the prosecutor's evidence as insufficient or to signify the absence of a key prosecution witness upon which a conviction depends

Motor vehicle theft Theft or attempted theft of a motor vehicle, including automobiles, trucks, buses, motorcycles, motorscooters, and snowmobiles

Municipal liability theory Theory that says city is liable when its police officers or other agents act to cause unreasonable harm to citizens; theory of agency whereby city assumes responsibility for the actions of its employees, including the police

Murder and nonnegligent manslaughter The willful or nonnegligent killing of one human being by another

National Crime Information Center (NCIC) Center established by the FBI in 1967; central information source for stolen vehicles, accidents, stolen property, arrested persons, fingerprints, criminal offenses, and criminal offenders and their whereabouts

National Crime Survey (NCS) Published in cooperation with the United States Bureau of the Census, a random survey of 60,000 households, including 127,000 persons 12 years of age or older, and 50,000 businesses; measures crime committed against specific victims interviewed and not necessarily reported to law enforcement officers

National Institute of Justice (NIJ) An office of the Department of Justice devoted to research activities relating to the criminal justice system

Net widening Pulling into the juvenile system youths who would not have been involved before; term also applied to adult programs into which offenders are drawn who would otherwise be released from the criminal justice system

Nolo contendere Plea of no contest to charges; defendant does not contest facts, although issue may be taken with the legality or constitutionality of the law allegedly violated; treated as a guilty plea

Nonviolent offense Crime against property, nonviolent crime where no physical injury to victims is sustained; includes embezzlement, fraud, forgery, larceny, burglary, vehicular theft

No true bill Grand jury decision that insufficient evidence exists to establish probable cause that a crime was committed and a specific person committed it

Objective test Test for determining whether entrapment has occurred; test assumes suspects have criminal records and/or are disposed to particular type of crime; whatever means police wish to use to elicit behavior are acceptable

Operation Identification Program sponsored by local police and other agencies to assist citizens to identify their personal property; includes fingerprinting children for later identification if lost or kidnapped

Organizational approach Type of police discretion whereby police administrators create for officers a list of priorities and to clarify explicitly how police should handle encounters with citizens

Original jurisdiction The United States Supreme Court's right to recognize a case at its inception, hear the case, and try it without consultation with other courts or authorities

Overcharging Filing charges against a defendant more serious than the ones the prosecutor believes are justified by the evidence; charging more serious counts than those on which the prosecutor wants a conviction

Paraprofessional Person who works in a community agency or public organization; has some skills relating to corrections, but is not certified or has not completed any formal course of study culminating in a corrections certificate or degree

Parens patriae Doctrine where state has primary authority and responsibility for overseeing the welfare of juveniles

Parole The status of an offender conditionally released from a confinement facility prior to the expiration of the sentence, and placed under the supervision of a parole agency

Parole board Board of persons that determines whether those currently incarcerated in prisons should be granted parole, or early release short of serving their full sentences imposed at the time of sentencing

Parolee Inmates of prisons who have been released conditionally or unconditionally by a parole board short of serving full sentence; usually, parolees are under the supervision of a parole officer for a specified period and may have other conditions associated with their parole

Peremptory challenge Challenge of a juror by either prosecution or defense where no reason needs to be provided for excusing juror from jury duty; each side has a limited number of these types of challenges

Petit jury The trier of fact in a criminal case; the jury of one's peers called to hear the evidence and decide the defendant's guilt or innocence; varies in size among states

Phantom effect Belief of burglars and thieves that police may be patrolling a particular area; thus, burglars and thieves avoid area

Plain view doctrine Evidentiary doctrine whereby evidence may be introduced in a trial, where the evidence seized was in plain view or within the immediate visual range of officers; evidence may be used whether original search was lawful or unlawful

Plea Answer to charges by defendant; pleas vary among jurisdictions; not guilty, guilty, nolo contendere, not guilty by reason of insanity, and guilty but mentally ill are alternative pleas

Plea bargaining Also known as plea negotiating; a preconviction bargain or agreement between the state and the accused whereby the defendant exchanges a plea of guilty or nolo contendere for a reduction in charges, a promise of sentencing leniency, or some other concession from full, maximum implementation of the conviction and sentencing authority of the court; includes implicit plea bargaining, charge reduction bargaining, sentence recommendation bargaining, and judicial plea bargaining

Police Derived from the Greek word *polis,* meaning city, a term applied to the exercise of civil or collective authority

Police cautioning Verbal warning by law enforcement officer to person who may have committed or attempted to commit a crime; suspect is not arrested, but rather, cautioned

Police-community relations Philosophy of administering police services so that members of the community and police share decisions concerning police services

Positive school School of criminological thought emphasizing analysis of criminal behaviors through empirical indicators such as physical features compared with biochemical explanations (also known as Italian School)

Postconventional level of cognitive development As defined by Kohlberg, the third level in the development of a person's moral judgment; concerns individual rights and principles of conscience

Prebriefing conference program Method of streamlining case processing in court, where attorneys file appeals and discuss the structure and length of these appeals prior to their presentation before appellate courts

Preconventional level of cognitive development As defined by Kohlberg, the first level of development, at which a child obeys rules to avoid punishment and is motivated by the desire for reward

Preliminary examination *See* Preliminary hearing

Preliminary hearing Formal proceeding conducted by a magistrate or judicial official to determine whether a person charged with a crime should be held for trial

Presentence investigation reports Investigation of convicted offender by a probation officer; usually requested or ordered by the court; background information is obtained, including a victim impact statement; facts in the case are included; prior arrests, job and educational history of defendant are listed; used to influence sentence imposed by judge; also used by parole board in considering an inmate for early release

Presentment An accusation, initiated by the grand jury on its own authority, from their own knowledge or observation; it functions as an instruction for the preparation of an arrest warrant

Presumptive sentencing Statutory sentencing form that specifies normal sentences of particular lengths with limited judicial leeway to shorten or lengthen the term of the sentence

Pretrial diversion A procedure where criminal defendants are diverted to either a community-based agency for treatment or assigned to a counselor for social and/or psychiatric assistance

Pretrial motion Motion made by either defense or prosecution prior to trial; usually pertains to introduction or exclusion of specific evidence

Preventive detention Constitutionally approved method of detaining those charged with crimes, where the likelihood exists that they either pose a serious risk to others if released or will flee the jurisdiction to avoid prosecution

Preventive patrol Patrol scheme by police officers inspired by the belief that high police officer visibility will effectively deter crime

Primary deviations Minor violations of the law that are frequently overlooked by police (including streaking or swimming in a public pool after hours)

Prison State or federally operated facility to house long-term offenders; usually designed to house inmates serving incarcerative terms of one or more years; self-contained facilities; sometimes called total institutions

Private police Private security forces, including private detectives and investigators

Privatization of prison management Trend in prison and jail management and correctional operations where private interests are becoming increasingly involved in the management and operations of correctional institutions

Probable cause Reasonable suspicion or belief that a crime has been committed and a particular person committed it

Probation A sentence involving confinement, imposing conditions and retaining authority in the sentencing court to modify the conditions of sentence or to resentence the offender if the offender violates the conditions; such a sentence should not involve or require suspension of the imposition or execution of any other sentence

Probation officer Professional person who supervises probationers

Probationer Convicted offender sentenced to a non-incarcerative alternative including supervised release in the community, restitution, community service, fines, or other conditions

Procedural laws Laws that specify how statutes should be applied against those who violate the law; procedures whereby the substantive laws may be implemented

Professionalism As applied to police officers, signifies the attainment of five general objectives related to education and training

Property crime Crime against property; considered nonviolent or passive, such as theft or burglary

Prosecution Carrying forth of criminal proceedings against a person, culminating in a trial or other final disposition such as a plea of guilty in lieu of trial

Prosecutor A person who presents evidence against defendants and seeks convictions for crimes

Prosecutorial bluffing Attempt by prosecution to bluff defendant into believing case is much stronger than it really is; use of bluffing is to elicit guilty plea from defendant to avoid lengthy trial where proof of defendant's guilt may be difficult to establish

Prosecutorial waiver Authority of prosecutors in juvenile cases to have those cases transferred to the jurisdiction of criminal court

Protection of property A criminal defense used by defendants to explain criminal conduct while protecting one's property

Provo experiment Community-based custodial program established in Provo, Utah, in the 1960s; juveniles continued to live at home and go to school but were required to report to the facility daily for counseling and introspective experiences

Psychoanalytic theory Sigmund Freud's theory to explain the human personality and mental disorders through the interaction of four concepts: (1) the id, (2) the ego, (3) the superego, and (4) the libido

Public defender Attorneys appointed by the court to represent indigent defendants

Radical criminology Theory of criminal conduct stressing control of the poor by the wealthy and powerful; crime is defined by those in political and economic control so as to control lower socioeconomic classes or strata; vagrancy statutes are manifestations of control by wealthy over the poor

Randolph Plan Also called the Virginia Plan; established the concept of superior and inferior courts

Recidivism Has many definitions; most frequently used definitions include rearrests, reconvictions, and reincarcerations of previously convicted felons or misdemeanants

Recidivist Convicted offender who commits new offense and is convicted of the crime

Rehabilitation A correctional goal concerned with providing incarcerated offenders with vocational and educational skills to assist them in finding jobs when they are released from prison

Released on own recognizance (ROR) Temporary release from detention granted a defendant if his reputation in the community is such that it is unlikely he will flee from the jurisdiction

Reversible error Errors committed by judges during trial that may result in reversal of convictions against defendants

Risk assessment device Instrument that attempts to predict whether offenders will violate the terms of their parole or probation and recidivate and/or commit additional violent offenses

Robbery The taking or attempt to take anything of value from the care, custody, or control of a person or persons by force or threat of force or violence and/or by putting the victim in fear

Royal Canadian Mounted Police (RCMP) Canada's federal police force; has jurisdiction for criminal offenses, federal violations, and ordinance offenses in all Canadian provinces

Rules of criminal procedure Rules legislatively established whereby a criminal case is conducted; law enforcement officers, prosecutors, and judges use rules of criminal procedure in discretionary actions against suspects and defendants

Scale of patrol The scope of a police officer's routine geographical patrol

Screening Process in which the prosecutor evaluates the suitability of a particular offender for pretrial diversion

Search incident to an arrest Authority of arresting law enforcement officer to search immediate premises within control of arrestee; authority does not exist to search other areas not immediately within the control of the arrestee

Secondary deviations Law violations that have become incorporated into person's lifestyle or behavior pattern

Sector patrolling A patrol alternative in which police officers are assigned to sector commanders in city areas where police-citizen relationships are most vital because of economics, population, crime, and crowd behavior

Selective incapacitation Process of incarcerating certain offenders who are defined by various criteria as having a strong propensity to repeat serious crimes; belief that offenders who are recidivists or who have prior criminality should be incapacitated with relatively long prison sentences

Self-defense Affirmative defense where defendants explain otherwise criminal conduct by showing necessity to defend themselves against aggressive victims

Self-report survey Method whereby researchers ask adolescents or minors directly about various types of offenses they have committed, regardless of whether they have been arrested and/or charged with committing those offenses; also used for adults to determine amount of undetected crime

Sentence Penalty imposed upon a convicted person for a crime; may include incarceration, fine, or both, or some other alternative (*see also* Determinate sentencing; Indeterminate sentencing; Mandatory sentencing; Presumptive sentencing)

Sentence recommendation plea bargaining *See also* Plea bargaining; where the prosecutor proposes a sentence in exchange for a guilty plea

Sentencing disparity Inconsistency in sentencing of convicted offenders, where those committing similar crimes under similar circumstances are given widely disparate sentences by the same judge; usually based on gender, race, ethnic, or socioeconomic factors

Sentencing Reform Act of 1984 An effort to restate sentencing objectives and establish guidelines for judges in their leniency or harshness toward convicted defendants

Shakedown Intensive search conducted of inmate cells for the purpose of discovering weapons or contraband

Sheriff Chief executive officer of county; appoints jailers and other jail personnel; hires deputies to enforce county laws

Shock probation Sentencing offenders to prison or jail for a brief period, primarily to give them a taste or shock of prison or jail life, and then releasing them into the custody of a probation or parole officer through resentencing

Social control theory Also referred to as bonding theory; focuses upon the process aspects of becoming bonded, or attached, to the norms and values of society

Socialization Learning through contact with others; social learning

Social learning theory Theory applied to criminal behavior, stressing importance of learning through modeling others who are criminal

Sociobiology The scientific study of causal relations between genetic structure and social behavior

Solitary confinement Placement of prisoner in cell where no communication with others is permitted; originated in Walnut Street Jail in Philadelphia, Pennsylvania, in late 1700s

Son of Sam laws Laws prohibiting criminals from profiting from their crimes through sales and/or publications of their stories to or through the media

Speedy trial Term describing the period between the time an accused is formally charged with a crime and the date of the trial; also the Sixth Amendment right to speedy trial

Speedy Trial Act Act passed in 1974, amended 1984, to clarify rights of defendants, to ensure that alleged criminals are brought to justice promptly, and to give effect to a citizen's Sixth Amendment right to a speedy trial

Stare decisis Principle whereby lower courts issue rulings consistent with those of higher courts, where the same types of cases and facts are at issue; the principle of leaving undisturbed a settled point of law or particular precedent

State highway patrol Uniformed officers, known as state troopers, whose responsibilities include enforcing state motor vehicle laws on state roads and federal interstate highways

Status offense Violation of statutes or ordinances by minors which, if committed by adults, would not be considered either felonies or misdemeanors

Statutory law Enactments of a legislature; laws passed by legislatures

Stress The body's nonspecific response to any demand placed upon it; police stress refers to negative stress accompanied by an alarm reaction, resistance, and exhaustion

Stressors Factors that cause stress; stressors include boredom, constant threats to officer health and safety, responsibility for protecting the lives of others, and the fragmented nature of police work

Subject matter specialization Term applied when certain judges have exclusive jurisdiction over particular crimes

Subjective test Test for determining whether entrapment has occurred; test assumes that whatever record suspect may have is irrelevant; police conduct is reprehensible per se and should not be tolerated as a means of eliciting crime

Submission-without-argument program Program designed to streamline case processing; cases are presented without oral argument

Substantive laws Laws that govern behaviors that are required or prohibited; usually enacted by legislatures; such laws also specify punishments accompanying the violations

Summary conviction offenses Canadian category of criminal offenses that are not indictable, such as violation of provincial statutes and municipal bylaws

Summary offense Minor offense, equivalent to a misdemeanor, that may be decided by a local magistrate in lieu of trial

Summons Same form as a warrant, except it commands a defendant to appear before the magistrate at a particular time and place

Superego Sigmund Freud's term describing that part of personality concerned with moral values

Superior court Highest trial court with general jurisdiction; some states call it Circuit Court, District Court, Court of Common Pleas, and in New York, Supreme Court

Supreme Court One of the three tiers of courts established under the provisions of the Judiciary Act of 1789, consisting of a chief justice and eight associate justices; charged with interpreting federal legislation and balancing the interests between the state and the nation through the maintenance of the rights and duties of citizens

Target hardening Making residences or businesses less susceptible to breaking and entering through better security measures

Team policing The assignment of a small geographical area of a community to a team of 20 to 40 police officers who are commanded by a team leader

Terrorist Politically or socially motivated persons with diverse goals, who most often attempt to cause public incidents and promote fear among people through deadly acts, including blowing up airplanes or public buildings and assassinations

Texas model A popular model of state court organization

Theory Set of assumptions and propositions that attempts to explain and predict relationships between phenomena

Theory of opportunity A theory of criminal behavior that proposes that lower-class persons tend to achieve success by achieving objectives that are respected by other criminals

Tier system Method of establishing various floors for cells where prisoners of different types can be housed; started at Auburn State Penitentiary in 1816

Tort A civil wrong involving one's duty to another, a breach of that duty, and injuries arising from that breach

Traditional model Also called Texas model; model of state court organization

Transfer *See* Waiver motion

Transportation *See* Banishment

Treasury Department Department of the federal government that controls many agencies with law enforcement functions

Trial An adversarial proceeding within a particular jurisdiction, where a judicial examination and determination of issues can be made, and where a criminal defendant's guilt or innocence can be decided impartially by either a judge or jury (*See also* Bench trial; Jury trial)

True bill Grand jury decision that sufficient evidence exists that a crime has been committed and a specific suspect committed it; a charge of an alleged crime; an indictment

UNICOR Federal prison industry that manufactures goods for profit; workers are prisoners who are paid prevailing wage; considered a rehabilitative tool

Uniform Crime Reports (UCR) Annual publication by Federal Bureau of Investigation that describes crime from all reporting law enforcement agencies in the United States; new format in 1988 uses incident-based reporting instead of other reporting schemes used in past years

United States Customs Service Agency authorized to conduct searches and inspections of all ships, aircraft, and vehicles entering United States borders

United States Marshals Service (USMS) Established under the Judiciary Act of 1789, duties include serving subpoenas and summonses, arresting fugitive felons, and operation of the Witness Protection Program

United States Secret Service (USSS) A Department of Justice division charged with presidential security as well as having jurisdiction over counterfeiting activity, credit and debit card frauds

Unreasonable searches and seizures The Fourth Amendment imposes restrictions on law enforcement officials in searching homes and seizing personal possessions

Veniremen Also venire; persons who are potential jurors in a given jurisdiction

Victim compensation program Program designed to compensate victims of criminal acts

Victim impact statement Statement by victim appended to a presentence investigation report submitted by a probation officer

Victimization Basic measure of the occurrence of a crime; a specific criminal act affecting a specific victim

Victimization Risk Survey (VRS) A 1984 survey of home crime prevention measures

Victimless crime Crime committed where there are no apparent victims, or where victims are willing participants in the criminal activity; includes gambling and prostitution

Victimology The scientific study of victims; may include those affected by crime, including those who are injured or affected by accidents, discrimination, war, genocide, or political repression

Victim's Bill of Rights Rights established by New York State Compensation Board, outlining specific rights of crime victims; rights include victim notification of offender status and custody, case disposition, and incarceration-nonincarceration details

Victims of Crime Act A 1984 act that formalized the collection of fines, penalties, and other assessments from those convicted of federal crimes

Victim-witness assistance program Program intended to explain court procedures to witnesses and to notify them of court dates

Violent crime Crime characterized by extreme physical force, including murder or homicide, forcible rape or child sexual abuse, assault and battery by means of a dangerous weapon, robbery, and arson

Virginia Plan Plan deriving from England's royal court system, projecting superior and inferior courts; also called Randolph Plan

Voir dire Formal procedure where prosecutors and defense attorneys address jurors and inquire into their backgrounds and potential biases

Volunteer Any citizen who wishes to donate time to assist in the supervision, education, counseling, or training of probationers, parolees, or divertees

Waiver Also known as certification or transfer; made by motion, the waiver is the transfer of jurisdiction over a juvenile to a criminal court where the juvenile is subject to adult criminal penalties; includes judicial, prosecutorial, and legislative waivers

Waiver motion   A motion to transfer the jurisdiction of a juvenile case to a criminal court where the juvenile may sustain adult penalties

Walnut Street Jail   Created in Philadelphia in 1790; the first attempt to classify and segregate offenders according to the crimes they committed and the seriousness of their offenses

Warrant   A written order directing a suspect's arrest and issued by an official with the authority to issue the warrant; commands suspect to be arrested and brought before the nearest magistrate

Wickersham Reports   Reports published by National Commission on Law Observance and Enforcement, chaired by George W. Wickersham

Without undue delay   Standard used to determine whether suspect has been brought in a timely manner before a magistrate or other judicial authority after arrested; definition of undue delay varies among jurisdictions; circumstances of arrest, availability of judge, and time of arrest are factors that determine reasonableness of delay

Work release   Prisoners placed on work release are permitted to hold regular jobs during the daytime, but they must spend evenings at a community-based facility

Working personality of police officers   Term devised by Jerome Skolnick to describe police officers as having similar and distinctive cognitive tendencies and behavioral responses, including a particular life-style

***XYY* syndrome**   Theory of criminal behavior positing that criminals are born with an extra Y chromosome, characterized as the aggressive chromosome compared with the X chromosome

Youth Corrections Act   Expanded the number of sentencing options available to federal district judges

CASE INDEX

NAME INDEX

SUBJECT INDEX